W9-AED-002

ALONE WITH AMERICA

BOOKS BY RICHARD HOWARD

POETRY

Misgivings *1979*

Fellow Feelings *1976*

Two-Part Inventions *1974*

Findings *1971*

Untitled Subjects *1969*

The Damages *1967*

Quantities *1962*

CRITICISM

Alone with America *1969* *(Enlarged Edition, 1980)*

Preferences *1974*

RICHARD HOWARD

ALONE WITH AMERICA

Essays on the Art of Poetry

in the United States

Since 1950

ENLARGED EDITION

New York ATHENEUM *1980*

Some of the essays of the original edition appeared in some form or part in the following periodicals: *Tri-Quarterly* (A. R. Ammons, Carolyn Kizer, Denise Levertov, May Swenson); *Minnesota Review* (Robert Creeley, Allen Ginsberg); *Kenyon Review* (Edward Field); *Chelsea* (Gregory Corso); *Epoch* (John Logan, Gary Snyder); *Perspective* (Theodore Weiss, Donald Finkel); *Partisan Review* (James Dickey); *Poetry* (James Merrill, Daniel Hoffman, Howard Moss). Source of original publication of new material in the enlarged edition is given at the end of each of the supplementary essays.

Original edition copyright © 1965, 1966, 1967, 1968, 1969 by Richard Howard
This enlarged edition copyright © 1980 by Richard Howard
All rights reserved
Library of Congress catalog card number 79-64718
ISBN 0-689-11000-6 (clothbound); 0-689-70594-8 (paperback)
Published simultaneously in Canada by McClelland and Stewart Ltd
Manufactured by Halliday Lithograph Corporation,
West Hanover and Plympton, Massachusetts
Designed by Harry Ford
First Enlarged Edition

TO
EZRA POUND
AND TO
W. H. AUDEN

They looked in vain to history for an explanation of themselves; more and more it appeared that the meaning was not to be found in theology, even with the help of the covenantal dialectic. Thereupon these citizens found that they had no other place to search but within themselves—even though, at first sight, that repository appeared to be nothing but a sink of iniquity. Their errand having failed in the first sense of the term, an errand upon their Master's business, they were left with the second, an errand upon their own, a mission— and required to fill it with meaning by themselves and out of themselves. Having failed to rivet the eyes of the world upon their city on the hill, they were left alone with America.

Perry Miller *Errand into the Wilderness*

CONTENTS

PREFACE TO THE ENLARGED EDITION

THE criticism of criticism, as Irving Babbitt used to say, is a languid business, and even ten years after the publication of *Alone with America*, I am not prepared to determine the discrepancies and appositions between what I was trying to do and what it now appears I did: I cannot still remember the former and cannot yet discern the latter.

Others, of course, do not labor under my incomparable disadvantages, and I have had occasion to learn a good deal, in this decade, about my enterprise. If the book has even as much value as some have suggested, it would be temerarious to modify its design—to drop the essays on the three poets who have died, for example, or to add essays on the "new" poets who now appear to fulfill my qualifications. Certainly the perspectives of these essays *date*—that is perhaps their liveliest claim on our interest now, for without a history, what is any criticism? and I think it would be a falsification to alter the contours of the undertaking, though such modification might make me out to be more perceptive than I actually was. Yet perception is not the same thing as presbyopia, and I suspect the chief merit of these studies resides more probably in an immediate attention than in an ulterior deduction. Therefore I have left the book as it was, unplundered by hindsight.

But I have added to some of the texts. Not with the intention of rectifying, merely of extending the account. I recall, during the forties, how my stepfather, in the course of those Saturday afternoon Metropolitan Opera broadcasts, would step over to the piano and as the tiny French soprano reached her culminating F above the line, gravely and even righteously would sound the same key, just checking, as it were, that Lily Pons had got it right! My subscripts, though in some cases extensive, are offered with no such corrective intentions. I had chosen to write about a generation of poets "taken" very much *in medias res*, which "thing" is still very much going on; and in many of the cases, the subsequent developments are not only unforeseen but also infinitely attractive. Often I have been asked by editors to account for these developments, often my own fascination with them has obliged me to write further. So that in some instances —Ammons, Ashbery, Hollander, Merrill, Merwin, Wright—it is not that my tastes have changed but that the poets observably have, and it was my study to account for the metamorphosis. In other instances—Hecht, Moss, Rich, Strand—it was simply a pleasure to loiter a little over the provocations of a mastery already registered; that there are not extensions in still other cases implies no criticism (or lack of criticism) of those poets, whose high F may be still to come, but instead a kind of discretionary fatigue on the part of an author whose aims, and whose targets, were notably elsewhere. The new texts, then, are an indication of what *Alone with America* might be like if it were to be rewritten every five or six years, in which case it would have to be called, as John Ashbery once remarked, *Alone Again, Naturally;* but I prefer that initial solitude, somewhat infringed, suggestively it is to be hoped, by further perscrutations.

RH
1979

FOREWORD

"Such Tricks Hath Strong Imagination,
That If It Would but Apprehend Some Joy,
It Comprehends Some Bringer of That Joy."

IN THE forty-one studies which follow, an accounting is made of American poets who, with the publication of at least two volumes, have come into a characteristic and—as I see it—consequential identity since the time, say, of the Korean War. In the preceding period—between Pearl Harbor, say, and Hiroshima—six poets had "surfaced" to a critical assessment which has been, often enough, a matter indeed of surfaces, but which has nonetheless established them at least as types and at best as particulars in our literary landscape: Berryman, Bishop, Jarrell, Lowell, Roethke and Wilbur. (It is not a matter of generations, of chronology; it is a matter of critical conviction. These six poets have sustained a reading—I cite my own case as the one in point but by no means in isolation—which indicates an acceptance, a *yielding*. They remind us that we cannot be confident of ourselves unless we can consider if not actually consent to the surrender of ourselves, the giving of ourselves to another; for to give in the way I believe we have given ourselves to these six poets implies the knowledge that we have something to give. The work of these writers is *there* for us because it makes us know that *we* are there.) The poetry I wish to consider entertains a dialectical relation—acknowledged, disputed, *endured*—with the typical work of these six . . . masters as they now appear, yet for the most part this later poetry has not been described or, to retain my bookkeeping trope, *accounted for* very solicitously. First of all, therefore, my undertaking is a reconnaissance, in both senses of the word—an exploration of the ground, and a gratitude for what grows there.

The accounting, in this case or in these cases, is to myself. For if I intended to go on writing my own poetry, I discovered some years ago, there was a choice of coming to terms with the work of my contemporaries, my elders, my friends, or having no terms of my own to come to. I chose the first alternative with all the more alacrity not only because these poets are, simply, *what is there*, but because they have achieved, to my sense of it, great things for themselves, for us all. "If you cannot believe in the greatness of your own age and inheritance," Shaw wrote to Ellen Terry, "you will fall into confusion of mind and contrariety of spirit." This book is the rescuing anatomy of such a belief; the construction, piece by piece, of a *credendum*—articles of faith.

Though of course there are interferences, even contaminations, among the poets discussed, my discussions themselves are not made upon a premise of comparisons, of schools or associations. Of each poet the entire production—prose and verse, translation and criticism—is drawn on, is mined out to forge a free-standing *figure* which will suggest not only the monuments but the *career* encompassing them as moments of its course. I use the dubious verb "forge" because I am aware that there can be *other* figures than the ones I have erected, other constructions to be placed on the evidence, and because I am eager to echo a warning, Valéry's *caveat* never to confuse the man whom the poetry leads us to imagine with the real man who produced the poetry.

My initial interest, then, was to write essays whose subjects could not be collapsed into each other like so many lengths of a diminishing-lens; I wanted the poets, in my reading, to be irreducible. But even so, as the studies accumulated, there came upon me a conviction of a myth which might be central to this generation, an identifying fable so unshakeable in its implications that I thought, even, of calling the book *Hard Food for Midas*, after Bassanio's stern resolution: "gaudy gold, / hard food for Midas, I will none of thee!" It was the myth of Midas that sustained my hold upon the subject, the myth of a precious order longed for in delirium and chaos, attained in dread, and renounced in longing again. For though I would not blur so many poets into a single acceptation, yet if a myth is sufficiently open, affording occasions for change, for reversal, then it may serve to unify, in the speculating mind, what can never be uniform, may connect so many exploits for all their apparent divergence.

And the myth is such a gesture of accommodation: King Midas had a garden which a satyr visited to enjoy the water of its spring, and Midas, being curious to learn the wisdom of the satyr, mixed wine with the spring water; the satyr was thus made drunk and captured; in return for the king's kindness to his captive, Dionysus offered Midas anything he wished, and Midas asked that all he touched might become gold. Whereupon he found that the gift governed even his food, his women, his words . . . and he prayed to lose it. Upon the god's advice he bathed in the river Pactolus (which according to Ovid has ever since had golden sands) and gave up his power to the stream.

It is a story which begins and ends in water—in movement, in process. The first appeal is from ordinary experience to ecstasy, to intoxication, and that is an appeal these poets often acknowledge, though not so frequently as the second appeal from chaos to order, to an ideal presentment of permanence; yet this, too, is no more than an impulse endemic to all poetry—this craving that whatever passes through one's hands shall be immutable, immutably one's own. Rather, what seems to me especially proper to these poets in the myth is the last development, the longing to *lose* the gift of order, despoiling the self of all that had been, merely, *propriety*. These then are the children of Midas, who address themselves to the current, to the flux, to the process of experience rather than to its precepts. From Ammons to Wright, the course of the river Pactolus may be traced here, and in its gold sand, moreover, we shall see what has been given over, gainsaid in order to gain a universe not yet *manhandled*. As one of the poets of this generation implores—a poet who has not yet yielded the gift of the golden touch:

> *Before gold kills me as it kills all men,*
> *Dear Dionysus, give me back again*
> *Ten fingertips that leave the world alone.*

Another, entirely secondary, abjuration of gold is apparent, too: the poet in our Great Society cannot be greatly rewarded; is it not astonishing that so many men and women should have brought themselves to this pitch of utterance, to this attainment of idiom, when it is precisely their art, in America, which does not pay, which has nothing in it for them? Or perhaps only for them? There is of course an answer: they have been preceded—trained, *turned loose*—by a generation of great critics of poetry. And their debt to the Americans among them from Eliot and Ransom and Winters to Burke and Blackmur and Tate, to Frye and Wimsatt and Nemerov, is exceeded only by my own. As well as to these masters of criticism whom I have ransacked so gratefully for nomenclature, for category, for disposition, I am happy to set forth here my further thanks: to Sanford Friedman, who, having read all these essays as they were written, has sustained me through what must have seemed, over and over, a Sisyphean course; to Ben Raeburn and Coburn Britton of Horizon Press, who first induced me to undertake this book; and to Harry Ford, my editor, who has seen it through to the end.

ALONE WITH AMERICA

A. R. AMMONS

"The Spent Seer Consigns Order to the Vehicle of Change."

ALL OF A sudden, with an unheralded and largely unacknowl-
edged cumulus of books, a poet who accounts for himself with
laconic diversity as the holder of the B.S. degree from Wake Forest
College in North Carolina, as the principal of an elementary school in
that State at the age of 26, as an executive, thereafter and inconse-
quently, in the biological glass industry:

(how you buy a factory:
determine the lines of force
leading in and out, origins, destinations of lines
determine how
*   from the nexus of crossed and bundled lines*
*   the profit is*
obtained, the
forces realized, the cheap made dear,
and whether the incoming or outgoing forces are stronger)

and currently as an English teacher:

(I'm waiting to hear if
Cornell will give me
a job: I need
to work &
maybe I write
too much)

—suddenly, then, A. R. Ammons has exploded into the company of American poets which includes Whitman and Emerson and articulates the major impulse of the national expression: the paradox of poetry as process and yet impediment to process. More honestly than Whitman, acknowledging his doubts as the very source of his method ("teach me, father: behold one whose fears are the harnessed mares of his going!"), though without Whitman's dramatic surface, Ammons has traced out the abstractive tendency, the immaterialism that runs through all our *native strain*, in both acceptations of the phrase: to suffer or search out immersion in the stream of reality without surrendering all that is and makes one particularly oneself. The dialectic is rigorous in Ammons' version—the very senses which rehearse the nature of being for the self, the private instances of the sensuous world, must be surrendered to the experience of unity:

> *we can approach*
> *unity only by the loss*
> *of things*
> *a loss we're unwilling*
> *to take—*
> *since the gain of unity*
> *   would be a vision*
> *of something in the*
> *continuum of nothingness:*
> *we already have things:*
> *   why fool around?*

And how avoid the "humbling of reality to precept?" "Stake off no beginnings or ends, establish no walls," the poet urges, addressing that Unity: "I know if I find you I will have to leave the earth and go on out . . . farther than the loss of sight into the unseasonal, undifferentiated stark"—a region, a Death, to speak literally, where there is no poetry, no speech to one's kind, no correspondence perceived and maintained, but only the great soft whoosh of Being that has obsessed our literature from its classical figures, as Lawrence saw so clearly, down to Roethke, Wright Morris, Thornton Wilder.

In 1955, A. R. Ammons, a native and occasional resident of North Carolina, issued a wispy first book of poems * and then held his peace, or rather his pugnacity, for ten years. When he next broke the silence, with a triad of voluble and original books at the age of forty, the development from that initial and inconclusive—certainly unconcluded —effort, the achievement in the terms of means and meaning reached so far that it is difficult, now, to see *Ommateum* for what it is, rather

---

* A bibliography giving complete details of all books discussed will be found following the text.

than an omen, a symptom.

The title means *compound eye*, as in an insect, and to the magnifying vision of such "iridescence of complex eyes" Ammons returns in the posterior books:

> *I see how the bark cracks and winds like no other bark*
> *chasmal to my ant-soul running up and down . . .*

I suppose the thirty-some litanies in *Ommateum* are to be taken as so many various lenses, ways of looking at landscape, history and deity which together make up one of those strange bug-eyed views wherein the world is refracted into various but adjacent fragments. The book is dedicated to Josephine Miles, the distinguished poet and teacher Ammons had met during his studies (three semesters) at the University of California, and is prefaced by an arrogant, unsigned foreword which asserts that the poems "rather grow in the reader's mind than exhaust themselves in completed, external form." It is just such exhaustion, "the coercive charm of form" as Henry James called it, which the collection lacks, for all its nicely witnessed natural movements:

> *and the snake shed himself in ripples*
> *across a lake of sand*

or again, more wittily:

> *The next morning I was dead*
>   *excepting a few peripheral cells*
> *and the buzzards*
> *waiting for a savoring age to come*
> *sat over me in mournful conversations*
> *that sounded excellent to my eternal ear . . .*

and despite its many fine passages, aspirations to share yet shed a nature regarded, throughout, as a goal and equally as a prison, the pitch is insistently wordy and too shrill:

> *But the wind has sown loose dreams*
> *in my eyes*
>   *and telling unknown tongues*
> *drawn me out beyond the land's end*
>   *and rising in long*
>   *parabolas of bliss*
> *borne me safely*
> *from all those ungathered stones*

After many such vociferations, one wonders whose voice it is that utters these hymns to—and against—Earth. The sapless lines, terminated only by the criterion of conversational or rhetorical sense, cannot beat against a stiffening rhythmic constant, and we are reminded of Miss Moore's prescription, taking her words in whatever pejorative sense they may bear: "ecstasy affords the occasion, and *expediency determines the form.*" Whose, then, is the voice that chants these prayers to the unstringing of all harps? The only aid the young poet affords is the assumption in several poems of the identity of the prophet Ezra. In a later book too, "I Ezra" returns, "the dying portage of these deathless thoughts," and we recall that this prophet is generally regarded as responsible for the revision and editing of the earlier books of Scripture and the determination of the canon. The persona appears in Ammons' poems, I think, when he is desperate for an authoritative voice; the nature of his enterprise is so extreme, and the risks he is willing to take with hysterical form and unguarded statement (unguarded by image, as Coleridge said that "a whole Essay might be written on the Danger of *thinking* without Images") so parlous, that the need for such *authority* must be pretty constant:

> *I am Ezra*
> *as a word too much repeated*
> *falls out of being . . .*

Yet even in this first book, especially as we tend to read it with the later work in mind, as a propaedeutic function of that work, it is evident that Ammons has discovered his tremendous theme: putting off the flesh and taking on the universe. Despite a wavering form, an uncertain voice, Ammons means to take on the universe the way Hemingway used to speak of taking on Guy de Maupassant—the odds, it is implied, more than a little in favor of the challenger. Here in *Ommateum*, then, is the first enunciation of the theme, in the crude form of a romantic pantheism:

> *Leaving myself on the shore*
> *I went away*
> *and when a heavy wind caught me I said*
> * my body lies south*
> *given over to vultures and flies*
> *and wrung my hands*
> *so the wind went on . . .*
> *The flies were gone*
> *The vultures no longer searched*
> *the ends of my hingeless bones . . .*
> *Breathing the clean air*
> *I picked up a rib*
> * to draw figures in the sand . . .*

And more decisively, in one of the finest early pieces, with its many echoes of Pound's diction and of course the metric of Dr. Williams, properly assimilated to the poet's own requirements which are speed, ease, and the carol of the separate phrase:

> *Peeling off my being I plunged into*
> *the well*
> *The fingers of the water splashed*
> *   to grasp me up*
> *but finding only*
> *   a few shafts*
> *of light*
> *   too quick to grasp*
> *   became hysterical*
> *   jumped up and down*
> *   and wept copiously*
> *So I said I'm sorry dear well but*
> *went on deeper*
> *finding patched innertubes beer cans*
> *and black roothairs along the way*
> *but went on deeper*
> *till darkness snuffed the shafts of light*
> *   against the well's side*
> *   night kissing*
> *   the last bubbles from my lips.*

By the time, ten years later, of his second book, *Expressions of Sea Level*, Ammons had extended and enriched this theme to stunning effect—not only in versions of nature and the body, but in terms of poetics as well, enforcing the substitution of the negative All for the single possibility of being:

> *   go back:*
> *   how can I*
> *tell you what I have not said: you must look for it*
> *yourself: that*
> *side has weight, too, though words cannot bear it*
> *out: listen for the things I have left out:*
> *   I am*
> *   aware*
> *of them, as you must be, or you will miss*
> *the non-song*
> *in my singing.*

Here Ammons has found, or fetched out, besides a functioning arrangement of words on the page, the further device of the colon, which he henceforth wields in its widest application as almost his only mark of punctuation—a sign to indicate not only equivalence, but the node or point of passage on each side of which an existence hangs in the balance:

> *a tree, committed as a tree,*
> *cannot in a flood*
> * turn fish,*
> *sprout gills (leaves are*
> *a tree's gills) and fins:*
> * the molluscs*
> *dug out of mountain peaks*
> *are all dead . . .*

This observation, from a long poem called "Risks and Possibilities"— one of the penalties of his method, of course, is that Ammons requires length in order to indulge his effects, lacking that compression of substance which amounts to a "received form"—exhibits, too, a curious and rueful connivence with the universal doxology that to represent any one form of life is a limitation, a limitation that cannot be transcended beyond the mere consciousness of it. For only limited forms of life *matter*, and I intend the pun—are of *material consequence*. In one of his saddest poems, an astonishing meditation called "Guide," Ammons admits that it is not, really, worth "giving up everything to eternal being but direction," as the wind has done. With the humility of a man whose enormous ambitions have been chastened by a constatation of his restricted place in the world—and the chastening has been a religious experience, in the literal sense of religion: a linking, a binding, even a fettering—the poet returns to his body, his particular geography and even his rather bleak sociology. Stretching his long legs on late-afternoon walks down the Jersey coast, he has learned that "when I got past relevance the singing shores told me to turn back":

> *What light there*
> *no tongue turns to tell*
> *to willow and calling shore*
> *though willows weep and shores sing always*

In *Expressions of Sea Level* we are given a lot more to go on, and consequently go a lot farther, than the persona of Ezra and some rhapsodic landscapes of apocalypse. We are given, with great attention to vegetable detail and meteorological conditioning, the scenes of the poet's childhood in a North Carolina backwoods, the doctrine and rationale of his metaphysical aspirations:

> *the precise and*
> *necessary worked out of random, reproducible,*
> *the handiwork redeemed from chance . . .*

I will show you
the underlying that takes no image to itself,
cannot be shown or said,
but weaves in and out of moons and bladderweeds,
is all and
beyond destruction
because created fully in no
particular form . . .

and the resignation, the accommodation of himself to the tidal marshes of New Jersey as the site of the poet's individual drama. Here is a man obsessed by Pure Being who must put up with a human incarnation when he would prefer to embody only the wind, the *anima* of existence itself:

So it came time
for me to cede myself
and I chose
the wind
to be delivered to

The wind was glad
and said it needed all
the body
it could get
to show its motions with . . .

With the acknowledgment of these limitations has come an interest in other, equally limited, possibilities. One of Ammons' most interesting sidelines, a lagoon of his main drift, is a concern with archaic cultures whose aspect often reminds us, in its amalgam of the suggestive detail and the long loose line, in its own prose music, of Perse:

Returning silence unto silence
the Sumerian between the rivers lies.
His skull crushed and molded into rock
does not leak or peel.
The gold earring lies in the powder
of his silken perished lobe.
The incantations, sheep trades, and night-gatherings
with central leaping fires,
roar and glare still in the crow's foot
walking of his stylus on clay.

But not until a more recent book, *Corson's Inlet*, would this mode be brought into accord with the main burden of Ammons' song—the made thing of his impulse. Song may seem an odd word for a verse in which I have descried the music of prose, a verse which is as near as words can get us to our behavior, no more than a fairly cautious means of putting down phrases so that they will keep. Yet though the iambic cadence, and all it implies and demands by way of traditional lilt, has been jettisoned as utterly as Dr. Williams ever decreed, there *is* a song in Ammons' windy lines, a care for the motion of meaning in language which is the whole justice of prosody; consider this invocation to the wind, one more of many, and perhaps the loveliest:

> *When the tree of my bones*
> > *rises from the skin*
> *come and whirlwinding*
> *stroll my dust*
> > *around the plain*
> *so I can see*
> > *how the ocotillo does*
> *and how the saguaro-wren is*
> *and when you fall*
> > *with evening*
>
> *fall with me here*
> > *where we can watch*
> *the closing up of day*
> *and think how morning breaks*

There is another strand of discourse in *Expressions of Sea Level*, whose very title gives an idea of Ammons' use of a new vocabulary, one that Kenneth Burke would call "scientistic," I guess, to mean the dramatic use of an exact nomenclature, in Ammons' case a use quite properly managed:

> *An individual spider web*
> > *identifies a species:*
> *an order of instinct prevails*
> > *through all accidents of circumstance*
> > > *though possibility is*
> *high along the peripheries of*
> *spider*
> > *webs:*
> > *you can go all*
> > > *around the fringing attachments*
> > *and find*
> *disorder ripe,*
> *entropy rich, high levels of random,*
> > *numerous occasions of accident . . .*

this poem concludes:

> *if the web were perfectly pre-set*
> *the spider could*
> *never find*
> *a perfect place to set it in: and*
> *if the web were*
> *perfectly adaptable,*
> *if freedom and possibility were without limit,*
> *the web would*
> *lose its special identity . . .*

The dangers of this kind of thing, the dangers of which Coleridge spoke, were evident, of course, to the author of "River," whose mastery of natural imagery and vocalic music is exact and generous, as in this example of what Hopkins called "vowelling off":

> *I shall*
> *go down*
> *to the deep river, to the moonwaters*
> *where the silver*
> *willows are and the bay blossoms,*
>
> *to the songs*
> *of dark birds*
> *to the great wooded silence*
> *of flowing*
> *forever down the dark river*
>
> *silvered at the moon-singing of hidden birds.*

The repetition of the short *i* and the variants on the sound of "river" in "forever" and "silvered" in the last two lines—not to sound too much like the late Dr. Sitwell—indicate and insure a consciousness of effects that become the living twist of things we call idiom.

Insurance is what we shall mostly need in dealing with Ammons' next book. Mooning around the house and waiting for *Expressions of Sea Level* to come off the press in December of 1964, the poet produced, in a two month period, and with a determination to reach an end that became more than obsessive, became self-destructive, "a long thin poem" written on a huge roll of adding-machine tape run through the typewriter to its conclusion ("I am attracted to paper, visualize kitchen napkins scribbled with little masterpieces: so it was natural for me . . ."). The "serious novelty" of the enterprise is unquestionable, and there are many beautiful tropes in this long *Tape for the Turn of the Year*, chiefly in the form of pious assurances that the undertaking is or will be worthwhile:

> *let this song*
>   *make*
> *complex things salient,*
> *saliences clear, so*
>   *there can be some*
>   *understanding*

Enough to suggest that the text is not so much a poem as the ground of a poem, the dark backing of a mirror out of which all brightness may, as a condition, come. There are two moments of confrontation, when Ammons links his 200-page transcribed tape with the generality of his gift as a poet:

> *ecology is my word: tag*
>   *me with that: come*
>   *in there:*
>   *you will find yourself*
> *in a firmless country:*
>   *centers and peripheries*
>   *in motion,*
>   *organic*
>   *interrelations!*
>   *that's the door: ɔere's*
> *the key: come in,*
>   *celebrant,*
>   *to the one meaning*
> *that totals my meanings . . .*

The other moment of address follows closely:

> *my other word is*
>   provisional . . .
>   *you may guess*
> *the meanings from* ecology:
> *don't establish the*
>   *boundaries*
>   *first . . .*
>   *and then*
>   *pour*
>   *life into them, trimming*
> *off left-over edges,*
> *ending potential . . .*
>   *the center-arising*
>   *form*

adapts, tests the
  peripheries, draws in,
finds a new factor,
utilizes a new method,
gains a new foothold,
responds to inner and outer
  change . . .

This is the poet arguing himself onward. His book arrives, the Muse ("a woman in us who gives no rest") reassures him (if not us), and in acknowledgment he turns, a moment, to address us before returning to his vocation in the most luscious of his books so far, *Corson's Inlet:*

I've given you the
interstices: the
  space between . . .
  I've given you
  the dull days
when turning and turning
revealed nothing . . .
  I've given
you long
uninteresting walks
so you could experience vacancy: . . .
our journey is done:
thank you
for coming:
the sun's bright,
the wind rocks the
naked trees . . .

Published almost simultaneously with the indiscreet, revelatory *Tape, Corson's Inlet,* from the title poem with its sure grasp of site ("the 'field' of action with moving, incalculable center") to the fare-well to the reader, to poetry and to the spirit of place given at the end ("surrendered self among unwelcoming forms: stranger, hoist your burdens, get on down the road"), stands as the farthest and still the most representative reach into, upon, and against Being which the poet has yet made. It opens with a poem that nicely illustrates the perfected diction Ammons has now achieved, a rhythmical certainty which does not depend on syllable-counting or even accentual measure, but on the speed and retard of words as they move together in the mind, on the shape of the stanzas as they follow the intention of the discourse, and on the *rests* which not so much imitate as create the soft action of speech itself. There is a formality in these gentle lines which is new to American poetry, as we say that there is a draughtsmanship in the "drip-drawings" of Pollock which is new to American painting: each must be approached with a modulated set of expectations if we are to realize what the poet, the painter is about. Consider the close of this first poem, "Visit," in Ammons' fourth book, and compare its resonance—reserved but not evasive, convinced but not assertive—with the heartier music of a similar passage, too famous to quote, in Frost:

> *. . . or you can come by shore:*
>
> *choose the right: there the rocks*
> *cascade less frequently, the grade more gradual:*
> *treat yourself gently: the ascent thins both*
> *mind and blood and you must*
> *keep still a dense reserve*
>
> *of silence we can poise against*
> *conversation: there is little news:*
> *I found last month a root with shape and*
> *have heard a new sound among*
> *the insects: come.*

The device of the colon helps keep a dense reserve of silence to poise against the "conversation" here, and the reason for the visit—finding a root with shape and hearing a new sound—is a kind of compressed *ars poetica* of Ammons' enterprise, that understanding of natural process which will include the negative moment: "what destruction am I blessed by" the poet asks in "the moment's height," but his prosody asks the question in a firmer, more axiological *set*, the resources of imagism that are generally employed to accommodate a natural movement here made over to a powerful abstraction:

> *exhilaration*
> *sucking him up,*
>
> *shuddering and*
> *lifting*
>
> *him*
> *jaw and bone*
>
> *and he said*
> *what*
>
> *destruction am I*
> *blessed by?*

Then comes the book's title poem, like so many of Ammons' largest statements the account of "a walk over the dunes" which is also a natural history of the poem itself:

> *the walk liberating, I was released from forms,*
> *from the perpendiculars,*
> *straight lines, blocks, boxes, binds*
> *of thought*
> *into the hues, shadings, rises, flowing bends and blends*
> *of sight:*

the interrelations of *making* and of a beneficent destruction are here followed out ("I was released from forms"), the actions of sea and land serving as the just emblem of the mind's resources, so that the poet can discuss his undertaking precisely in the terms of his locus, and indeed acknowledges his inability to wield any terms *except* those afforded him by what Kenneth Burke calls the scene-agent ratio:

> *I allow myself eddies of meaning:*
> *yield to a direction of significance*
> *running*
> *like a stream through the geography of my work:*
> *you can find*
> *in my sayings*
> > *swerves of action*
> > *like the inlet's cutting edge:*
> > *there are dunes of motion,*
> *organizations of grass, white sandy paths of remembrance*
> *in the overall wandering of mirroring mind:*
>
> *but Overall is beyond me: is the sum of these events*
> *I cannot draw, the ledger I cannot keep, the accounting*
> *beyond the account . . .*

It is characteristic that so many of these poems—and in the previous book as in the one to come—take up their burden from the shore, the place where it is most clearly seen that "every living thing is in siege: the demand is life, to keep life"; whether he investigates the small white blacklegged egret, the fiddler crab, the black shoals of mussels, the reeds, grass, bayberry, yarrow, or "pulsations of order in the bellies of minnows," Ammons is concerned to enunciate a dialectic, "the working in and out, together and against, of millions of events," and *event* is precisely his word—

> *no finality of vision,*
> *I have perceived nothing completely,*
> *tomorrow a new walk is a new walk*

he insists: Ammons rehearses a marginal, a transitional experience, he is a littoralist of the imagination because the shore, the beach, or the coastal creek is not a *place* but an *event*, a transaction where land and water create and destroy each other, where life and death are exchanged, where shape and chaos are won and lost. It is here, examining "order tight with shape: blue tiny flowers on a leafless weed: carapace of crab: snail shell" that Ammons finds his rhythms, "fastening into order enlarging grasps of disorder," and as he makes his way down the dunes, rhythms are "reaching through seasons, motions weaving in and out!"

The rebellion against Being and into eternity is put down by the body itself on these expeditions the poet makes, safaris into mortality which convince him that "the eternal will not lie down on any temporal hill," and that he must "face piecemeal the sordid reacceptance of my world." It is not acceptance, but *re*acceptance which must be faced, the world which must be learned *again* as the poet, borrowing Shelley's beautiful image, "kindles his thoughts, blowing the coals of his day's bright conscious" in order "to make green religion in winter bones." In *Corson's Inlet* doctrine has been assimilated into "one song, an overreach from which all possibilities, like filaments, depend: killing, nesting, dying, sun or cloud, figure up and become song—simple, hard: removed." That is Ammons' definition of his aspiration—a long way from the breezy expostulations in *Ommateum*—and, I believe, of his achievement as well: his awareness and his imagination have coincided. Not that the poet has lost his initial impulse—for example, the close of the finest poem in that first volume, quoted earlier—"night kissing / the last bubbles from my lips"—finds itself enlarged and suited to the poet's wider utterance here, so that the poem called "Libation" in *Corson's Inlet* ends: "Now keep me virile and long at love: * let submission kiss off / the asking words from my lips." There is a loyalty to finite being, "losing the self to the victory of stones and trees, of bending sandpit lakes, crescent round groves of dwarf pine," Ammons says in the last poem of the book, "Gravelly Run," a central impulse that "extends the form, leads us on," and if there is also a freedom to explore an eccentric impulse, as in the brilliant poem "The Strait," it is a freedom granted because the divergent "filaments" have been braided back into the main strand, a rope of sand indeed. The poem concerns a worshipper at the pythoness' cave, questioning the ways of receiving the oracle, and ends with the kind of "simple, hard: removed" words which so often suggest, in this poet, the pre-Socratic impulse:

* Ammons has become increasingly explicit about the relations of sexuality and creative mind: "the mind cannot be rid *while it works* of remembered genitals" (my italics).

> *go*
> *to your fate:*
> *if you succeed, praise the*
> *god:*
> *if you fail,*
> *discover your flaw.*

Yet such terrors of self-knowledge are generally, by this climax of submissive response in the poet's work, abated by his more habitual reference to the design, the order, the form of the natural world: "for it is not so much to know the self," Ammons admits,

> *as to know it as it is known*
> *by galaxy and cedar cone,*
> *as if birth had never found it*
> *and death could never end it.*

In 1966 Ammons published his fifth book, in which again "events of sense alter old dunes of mind, release new channels of flow, free materials to new forms": *Northfield Poems* enacts Ammons' now familiar insurgence against finitude, and his resignation, once the impossibilities of both macrocosm and molecule are confessed, to the demands of form as *the vehicle of change:*

> *unlike wind*
> *that dies and*
> *never dies I said*
> *I must go on*
> *consigned to*
> *form that will not*
> *let me loose*
> *except to death*
> *till some syllable's rain*
> *anoints my tongue*
> *and makes it sing*
> *to strangers:*

"some syllable's rain" intimates this poet's trust in language, when any confidence in the body's identity, as in that of bog and bay, is lost; in all these "riding movements" the transformation finally relied on is the transformation of process into words; as Valéry said in the canonical utterance about such littoral metamorphoses, the poet comes to learn *le changement des rives en rumeur,* the change of shores to sound. For Ammons, there is a liberation as well as an acknowledgment of inadequacy about his failure to reduce himself to singleness or to swell to a "savage" chaos:

> *when I tried to think by what*
> *millions of grains of events*
>   *the tidal creek had altered course,*
>   *when I considered alone*
> *a record*
> *of the waves on the running blue creek,*
>   *I was released into a power beyond my easy failures:*

the power is the strength, the wit, the *balance* of mind which enables him to fall back on his verbal nature, acknowledging that "the dissolved reorganizes to resilience" in his language, that reflexive tool of his specific incarnation:

> *only the book of laws founded*
>   *against itself*
> *founded on freedom of each event to occur as itself*
> *lasts into the inevitable balance events will take.*

Ammons' poems are that book of laws founded against itself, perpetually questioning not only the finality, but the very finitude of the world, deploring in an almost Catharist way the "fact" that "coming into matter, spirit fallen trades eternity for temporal form," asserting that it is their part to consummate—by the "gist of 'concrete observations,' pliant to the drift"—the world's body which, as in "February Beach," is in constant modification:

> *creation may not be complete,*
> *the land may not have been*
> *given*
> *permanently,*
>   *something remains*
> *to be agreed on,*
> *a lofty burn of sound, a clamoring and*
>   *coming on . . .*

In this metaphysical breviary, the self is forever giving itself instructions about its own disembodied aspirations—"if you must leave the shores of mind," Ammons adjures his "Discoverer," reverting to his familiar accommodation of the Sea of Being in the salt marshes of Northfield,

> *if to gather darkness*
> *into light, evil into good,*
> *you must leave the shores of mind,*
> *remember us, return and rediscover us.*

The dissident Ezra, who reappears in one or another of these poems, is said to listen from terraces of mind "wind cannot reach or weedroots" —and at once we know this is not the Way: for Ammons, only what comes back into being by an eternal yet secular reversion—remembered, returned to, rediscovered—is viable:

> *The world is bright after rain*
> *for rain washes death out of the land and hides it far*
> *beneath the soil and it returns again cleansed with life*
> *and so all is a circle*
> *and nothing is separable . . .*

Indeed, the prophetic lurch to the edges of being—into that "scientific" area of "cytoplasm's grains and vacuoles" on the one hand, and the pulsing, shooting abstractions of "matter and energy" on the other —is repudiated in the final statement of *Northfield Poems*, though there are no final statements in this world of Ammons', of course, only articles of belief, only a mastered credulity:

> *energy's invisible*
> *swirls confused, surpassed*
> *me: from that edge*
> *I turned back,*
>
> *strict with limitation,*
> *to my world's*
> *bitter acorns*
> *and sweet branch water.*

Uplands: New Poems by A.R. AMMONS

What was it like, to bear witness to the articulation of a great career in American poetry, to account for volume as it succeeded volume, revision as it focused vision, until the trajectory was complete, the canon fulfilled? What did a critic *feel* in the presence of the new work (including "Acquainted with the Night") when in 1928 Frost's sixth book *West-Running Brook*, followed his *Selected Poems* at a five-year interval? We can look it up: a shift was remarked, was lamented, a shift to a more "philosophic" mode among the short poems which chiefly composed the book, the title poem now the sole "characteristic" regional dialogue once so distinctive in

Frost's work. "Slight" is used in three of the reviews to dismiss Frost's escape from his own previous selection. In other words the sliced-apple effect was evident: as soon as new work was exposed, it turned brown in the open air, and it was the *preceding* poems, mysteriously digested meanwhile, which were declared to exhibit the poet's true mastery, his authentic character, while the immediate achievement represented a wrong turning, a misapprehension, a falling off. If it is true, as Wordsworth said, that a poet must create the taste by which he is enjoyed, it is also true that he must continually dislodge himself if he is to create more than taste.

We can look up what the critics said of Frost's sixth book, or Stevens', or Auden's—indeed, it is a humbling exercise—but the retrospective, with regard to feeling, is always a category of bad faith, and we had better examine our own feelings *now*, for we are faced with just such an occasion, just such an opportunity. Here is Ammons' sixth book, two years after his *Selected Poems*, four years after his last new work. The situation, then, is parallel to Frost's in 1928: the poet reaches that stalled place in his career where it is necessary to inventory his resources, to take stock—what else is a Selected Poems?—of his possibilities, those behind him and those ahead. And then he must move, must find—invent—what there is in himself which will make further work identifiable yet not identical. It is the crisis of middle life which he must emblematically resolve: to acknowledge not only his future but his past, betraying neither:

> the problem is
> how
> to keep shape and flow

No wonder so many of these new poems are concerned with initiations, submissions to motion, giving way, getting started. But before Ammons wrests himself free, by so many "scoops scopes scrimps and scroungings," by the geological energies of "fill, siftings, winnowings, dregs, / cruds, chips," let me rehearse in a paragraph the mountainous achievements at his back, from which he is setting forth.

In 1955, Ammons' first book, *Ommateum*, discovered his tremendous theme: putting off the flesh and taking on the universe. For this poet, there is no windy abstraction in the notion, but a wonderful and rustling submission to the real, the incidental and the odd. Indeed, the poignance of momentary life in its combat with eternal design so haunted the poet that a decade later, in his magnificent second and third books, *Expressions of Sea Level* and *Corson's Inlet*, he had not yet come down on the side of transcendence, nor even taken off. Determined rather to suffer or search out immersion in the stream of reality without surrendering all that is and makes one particularly oneself, Ammons devised a notation of events as faithful to the wavering rhythm of metabolism as it might be to the larger fixities of celestial order:

> *for it is not so much to know the self*
> *as to know it as it is known*
> > *by galaxy and cedar cone,*
> *as if birth had never found it*
> *and death could never end it:*

that terminal colon is a characteristic of Ammons' verse—a sign to indicate not only equivalence but the node or point of passage on each side of which an existence hangs in the balance; and the balance is the movement of the verse itself, a constant experiment with the weight of language the line can bear, can meaningfully break beneath, so that the enjambment will *show* something more than completion or incompletion. Between these two books, Ammons published a kind of satyr play of selfhood, *Tape for the Turn of the Year*, "a long thin poem" written on a huge roll of adding-machine tape run though the typewriter to its conclusion, a poem about the specifications of identity by the very refusal to prune or clip. And these mediations led, or prodded, the poet to a further collection, *Northfield Poems*, in which the provisional is treasured as an earnest (though hardly a solemnizing) of survival: "no finality of vision, / I have perceived nothing completely, / tomorrow a new walk is a new walk." And then in 1968 Ammons chose from all these books (except for the indiscreet, revelatory *Tape*) a splendid series of *provisions*, stays against chaos as against finality, articles of belief, a mastered credulity, his *Selected Poems*. Insufficiently attended to, this book is a masterpiece of our period, the widest scope and the intensest focus American poetry has registered since Frost, since Stevens, since Roethke.

And now we have a new book, three dozen lyrical pieces, mostly no more than a page long, and two extended texts, the erotic experiment "Guitar Recitativos" and the superb dedication poem called "Summer Session" which closes "with trivia / I'll dispense dignity, a sense of office, / formality they [the poet's students] can define themselves against." A collection necessarily *slight* if measured against the massive accumulation of Ammons' past, yet if we recall the original sense of the word—*plain, simple*—then we can say, with Pope, "slight is the subject, but not so the praise," for in these sudden, attractive fits and starts the poet urges himself into a new economy, a bright particularity of diction entirely *gainful* to his panoply, a way of handling verse without giving up conversation:

> *arriving at ways*
> *water survives its motions.*

The way is enjambment, a wizardry in working with the right-hand margin, so that the line never relinquishes its energy until it can start up its successor. "Certain presuppositions are altered," Ammons announces talking about the look of "summit stones lying free and loose / out among the shrub trees" in the Alleghenies. We are no longer on the beach in these poems, but in the mountains, among masses, solids, fixities, and the problem is how to get moving again. It is the poet's situation, the poet's dilemma, to make the mountain come to Mohammed, and he has started the pebbles rolling:

> every
> exigency seems prepared for that might
> roll, bound, or give flight
> to stone: that is, the stones
> are prepared: they are round and ready.

Thus the book itself is an account—scrupulous in its details, its hesitations, its celebrations of minor incidents, lesser claims—of how a landscape or a man comes to realize motion, comes to be *on the way* rather than in it.

The Nation, 1971

Briefings: Poems Small and Easy by A.R. AMMONS

Hard upon *Uplands* appears *Briefings: Poems Small and Easy*. Small and easy! Ever since his deprecating "Foreword" to his first book and his embarrassed asides braided right into his adding-machine epyllion, it has been evident that Ammons is a great craftsman in his poems, but an erratic stage director or prompter from the wings. What he calls "small and easy" may not be anything of the kind, and need not be called anything at all. He is ever uneasy, this poet of what David Kalstone once identified as subversive bravado, as he walks his way into "song's improvident / center / lost in the green bush"; and like Ammons we shall be at a loss to say much that is to the point about his genre, about his poetics, though the affinities are there, the spectral precursors and the *a posteriori* spooks—Emerson, Dickinson, Whitman, then Pound, Williams, Stevens. It is not to the *point* that we are to speak, anyway, as Ammons keeps telling us—rather it is out of muddle and even mud that we get what matters; it is out of chaos that cosmos comes:

> between life and me obtrude
> no symbolic forms:
> grant me no mission . . .
> leave me this black rich country

uncertainty, labor, fear: do not
steal the rewards of my mortality.

We are, then, to be at a loss with Ammons, and happy to be there, for it is only when losses are permitted, invited even, that there are possibilities invoked. In the poem called, crucially, "Poetics", Ammons admits how he goes about making, precisely, by leaving off as much as by inventing, by finding:

> *I look for the forms*
> *things want to come as*
> *from what black wells of possibility,*
> *how a thing will unfold: . . .*
> *not so much looking for the shape*
> *as being available*
> *to any shape that may be*
> *summoning itself*
> *through me*
> *from the self not mine but ours.*

The search is for a poetic incarnation, but it is also an abandonment of the search, a hope of poetic disincarnation, a way of overcoming by literally *undergoing* the separate self. In this, Ammons' energies are dedicated concurrently with those of his fellow American poets. But it is only in Ammons that I find all three moments—the changing from, the changing, and the changing to—exalted equally. Only Ammons, I think, of all American poets today, has—when he is not diverted into his hip asides—the capacity to endow the moment of loss, the moment of metamorphosis and the moment of release with an equal light, "the blue obliteration of radiance".

Indeed the three moments are what Ammons calls, in his accounting for events, for outcomes, for irreversible exits and recurrences alike, ambiance, salience, radiance. These are his three favorite words for the phenomenon signified (there is a place), then for the phenomenon abandoned (the place can be left), then for the phenomenon sanctified (only loss reveals what the reward was to be). It is no accident, except insofar as everything in Ammons is literally an accident, a falling-to, a befalling, it is no accident that the greatest poem in this latest book is the last, and neither small nor easy, the cross-titled poem "The City Limits", which begins its 18-line single sentence "When you consider the radiance" and ends with the acknowledgment that each thing is merely what it is, and all that can be transcended is our desire for each thing to be more than what it is, so that for such a consideration of the losses of being, the very being of loss, "fear lit by the breadth of such calmly turns to praise." It is all there in Ammons—the fear and the light, the calm and the breadth, the turning and the praise, and that is why he is a great poet.

Partisan Review, 1972

Collected Poems 1951–1971 by A.R. AMMONS

I have published an account of each of Ammons' books as they appeared, following a first long essay on his work; I have taught, or been taught by, the poetry in seminars at two universities, where it became clear to my students as it became incontrovertible to me that for all our probable ignorance of the ruddy turnstone and its habits, here was a great poet, surely one of the largest to speak among us, today, of what we are and are not, speaking wherever we troubled to listen in a voice so reticent in all its authority, so gorgeous in all its immediacy, that we could scarcely miss the accents of its persuasion, overheard, underlying, central. My intention here, therefore, is not one of summing up what is in every sense a going concern; it is not yet appropriate to tabulate results, for the poet is still very much ahead of us, making his way by the light of what he calls *the noons of recurrence*. Rather I should like to record my sense, merely, of a stunned gratitude for the work as it masses thus provisionally, my response to a recent rereading of the territory covered so far, always with the understanding that as Ammons ruefully admits, "less than total is a bucketful of radiant toys."

It is difficult to speak of any quantity of Ammons' poems without employing spatial metaphors—he is the poet of walking, and his is the topography of what one pair of legs can stride over, studies in *enjambment* indeed—and I have not resisted the difficulty: in all its guises, Ammons' poetry is never disguised—it takes a spiral trajectory, so that wherever we take it, his art is complete *that far*. In fact, it is the nature of this book's unrelenting course ("I like the order that allows," is how Ammons puts it) to describe that arc between the impossible and the necessary which will be this poet's particular balance, his special poise: between metaphor (saying that something is something else) and identity (saying that something is what it is). This is an old argument in our poetry—the argument between Thoreau and Emerson, between nature and vision, between the natural and the visionary, and no one has more shrewdly *drawn the line* than Ammons by this showing of twenty years work. It is no accident that the word *coil* and the word *collection* writhe upward to the surface from the same root.

"The war of shape and loss" is Ammons's Homeric conflict, the beach his Troy, though in the later poems a backyard will do: any *place* is an event for this bordering imagination, and what comes as something of a surprise in the discovery of his solitude, his singleness (there are no friends in this poetry, no other people, in fact; most dialogue is with the wind, with mountains, and when Ammons turns away from "cytoplasm's grains" or from "energy's invisible swirls," what he turns *back* to is not any human bond:

> *I turned back*
> *strict with limitation,*
> *to my world's*
> *bitter acorns*
> *and sweet branch water.*)

—what comes as an astonishment, I was saying, with the poet's solitary contemplations is his sociability of *form*. Ammons is a great inventor of forms, and his poetry murmurs and glitters with the sensuality of his "boundaried vacancies." I think our expectation would be that a man of such lonely confrontations would have devised a sort of paradigm of utterance, an exemplary discourse by which to speak his piece, and would *by now* have settled down to "a perfect carriage / for resolved, continuous striving." Nothing of the kind. "Firm ground is not available ground," he observes, and risks his prosody in all the quicksands of variation. The characteristic somatic gesture in Ammons is that of testing his weight, seeing how much traffic any particular utterance can bear, from the favored mark of punctuation, the colon, to the endless open hexameters of "Hibernaculum":

> *a poem variable as a dying man, willing to try anything,*
> *or a living man, with the consistency of either direction:*
> *just what the mind offers to itself, bread or stone:*
>
> *in the swim and genesis of the underlying reality things*
> *assume metes and bounds, survive through the wear*
> *of free-being against flux, then break down to swim and*
>
> *genesis again: that's the main motion but several*
> *interturns have been concocted to confuse it: for example . . .*

and Ammons is off again. *Pages of examples*, his book might be called, and indeed it is exemplary, at a time of recipes and formulas, to find this supreme artificer inventing an unheard-of prosody each time he writes a poem. "Versification or diversification," he propounds, thereby suggesting that what has already been achieved is merely a chain—what Ammons cares about is the forging of new links, the finding of the next connection.

It is why so much of his poetry is given over—given away, as he likes to say—to erasure, destruction, loss, "the chant of vacancies, din of silences." Only when you have unmade something is there room for new making: "listen for the things I have left out." "Arrange me into disorder," Ammons implores his "Muse", and it is because his poetry hovers and shivers, in all its intonations (Ammons can be vatic, pop, sheepish, dogged, even kittenish, but the exactitude of his vocabulary makes his best poems geological, they are the *words of earth*), on the line, the arc, the curve between arrangement and chaos, that he is not merely a collected poet but a *collecting* one, that he keeps gathering within his circumference new reaches of the same substance, the same energy.

In the eight years since I began to read, and study, and love this man's poetry, I have had the opportunity to know the poet as well, and I presume it is appropriate to friendship that I "extend the form" of his collection, his coil, by adding to it a poem Ammons has not collected, but which he wrote after a visit I had made to his classes at Cornell, a poem which is a major provision—because provisional— for understanding the nature of his enterprise, the quality of his undertaking:

UNTELLING

Poetry is the word that has no other words,
the telling indistinguishable from the told:

it is all body (spirit) until it moves
and moving only is its declaring, divisible

neither into mind nor feeling, mind-felt,
form only if motion stays an instant into form,

otherwise form-motion, the body and the void
interpenetrating, an assuming, a perfect allowance:

how it moves away, returns, settles or
flashes by, how it works its worked space

into memory's body may tell tellings,
narratives, progressions beyond,

surrounding an instant's telling, though
only body-in-motion can place them there:

being is its afterlife whose life was becoming:
mind and other words confront, untell its dream.

It is sufficient excuse, this offering of an uncollected poem by A.R. Ammons, for my exultation over his collection: the poet who asks "what / destruction am I / blessed by?" is thereby a master maker of his period, and by the working together of his movement and his stillness, leaves us the monument we need; "and fear lit by the breadth of such calmly turns to praise."

Boundary 2 (Binghamton), 1973

JOHN ASHBERY

"You May Never Know How Much Is Pushed Back into the Night, Nor What May Return."

THIS POET has been bravely endorsed by his friends ("the illumi-
nation of life turned into language and language turned into
life"), brutally dismissed by his enemies ("garbage"), and acknowl-
edged with some bewilderment by his reviewers ("words often appear
in unexpectedly brilliant new combinations"). All agree broadly,
though, that Ashbery is *avant-garde* whatever else he may be, and it is
on that consensus I should like to loiter a little, before proceeding, with
the poet's help, to a ponderation of the achievements—or what I can
recognize as the achievements—in his chief volumes of verse.

The military figure commonly employed to describe the modern
artist in his experimental and initiating capacity is so natural to us—we
even use it pejoratively, to condemn what appears a timid reliance on
the conventional: a *rear-guard* artist is scarcely an artist at all, these
days—that it is something of an effort to disengage the notion of
opposition, of combat and conquest which is the activity we like to
associate with the artist as the antagonist of the bourgeoisie, from the
notion of *protection*, of scouting and reconnoitre which implies that
the vanguard is in advance precisely in order *to guard*. The point—I
shall concentrate here on the artist's custodial relation to his art, rather
than his hostility to the public—is not to abandon the main body of
your troops altogether, but to maintain certain exchanges, to insure
certain complicities which will make your own skirmishes up ahead of

some service to the more unwieldy forces in the rear—and perhaps the more unwieldy precisely because the more forceful.

In the saving, the conservative sense of the term, Ashbery is, sufficiently to compel our trust, an advance-guard poet. I hope to show how he has kept in touch with the tradition he outdistances, how he has remained ahead of something whose force and weight at his back he is fruitfully (if at times fearfully) aware of. That there are many occasions when, it seems to me, he has allowed his communication-lines with the regulars to be cut speaks neither for nor against him. It is a question of the terrain covered and of the engagements fought. The poet who wrote his master's essay on the novels of Henry Green and who invoked, presenting an *inédit by* Raymond Roussel in the French magazine *l'Arc,* that bewildering author's *particularités qui ajoutent à sa beauté strictement littéraire*—the poet who is also a playful scholiast of the hyperbaton is evidently well prepared to leave us in whatever lurch he finds ineluctable. We need not question his decision, or what seems to us his determination, so to leave us; let us merely remind him that a vanguard, as Roussel himself would certainly have known, is also a variety of hybrid peach valued not so much for its own fruit as for its grafting powers.

I spoke just now of enlisting Ashbery's help in our examination of his work. It is an assistance we have come to look for from those artists whose project is evidently going to make some demand upon our patience, or upon our capacity to be diverted. Lest we remain, like Napoleon, *inamusable,* many writers have provided a clue in the form of an imaginative schema or construct which heightens the work's inner resonance at the same time that it defines the *poetics* by which the contraption operates. For example, as early in his career as 1893, Gide noted the likelihood of such a device (and indeed its appeal, for him, extended to the method of Edouard's *Journal* within *The Counterfeiters* and to the *Journal of the Counterfeiters* published along with the novel):

> I like discovering in a work of art . . . transposed to the scale of the characters, the very subject of that work. Nothing illuminates it better, nothing establishes more surely the proportions of the whole. Thus in certain paintings by Memling or Quentin Metsys, a tiny dark convex mirror reflects the interior of the room where the scene painted occurs. Similarly, in Velasquez' *Meninas* (though in a different way). Finally, in *Hamlet's* play within the play, as in many other dramas. In *Wilhelm Meister,* the marionette scenes or the parties at the château. In *The Fall of the House of Usher,* the passage being read to Roderick, etc.

None of these examples is entirely fair. What would be much more so, what would say what I want . . . is the comparison with that method in heraldry which consists of putting a second blazon in the center of the first, *en abyme.*

In Ashbery's case, the blazon *en abyme* occurs at the start, rather than at the center, though in all this poet's larger pieces, there is an impulse to break out of the legalities of a compositional system and to address the reader directly ("But no doubt you have understood / it all now and I am a fool. It remains / for me to get better, and to understand you . . ."). If Ashbery's poems themselves are a *blazon of making,* which is after all what the word poem means, inside them we generally find that second blazon, the inclination to speak up without being mediated by the poem ("That something desperate was to be attempted was, however, quite plain"); the work criticizes its own text by accommodating in its texture an alternative patois. From the start, as I say, Ashbery has afforded us various admonitory nudges and eye-rollings: in the little play "Turandot," a kind of meiotic eclogue in three scenes and a sestina, the princess begins by calling for

> *Laughs and perfect excisions*
> *In which the matter biteth the manner,*

and when the hungry prince asks for her first question, she retorts

> *There are no questions.*
> *There are many answers . . .*

And if that is not quite enough to prepare us for a sestina, surely the only one in English, in which one of the teleutons is "radium," it suggests nonetheless, in a characteristically abrupt way, the embarrassment of riches we must confront. In 1953, the same year *Turandot and Other Poems* was published in a pamphlet by the Tibor de Nagy Gallery (all the poems were reprinted three years later in *Some Trees* except for a three-stanza piece called "White" and "Turandot" itself), this poet's one-act play *The Heroes* was produced off-Broadway (and later published in a collection which also included plays by Merrill and O'Hara). Ashbery's *dégagé* comedy about the heroes of the Trojan War, set in a Long Island house-party strongly reminiscent of the accommodations Henry Green affords *his* personnel, contains four speeches by Theseus, victor over the labyrinth and the minotaur, and one by Circe, sorceress and visionary, which become crucial to our understanding of his poetry—of what it will not do for us as well as of what it must. If we are bewildered by our first encounter with *Turandot and Other Poems,* if we are baffled not only by the imagery but by the syntax and the tonality of lines like these from "White":

Where is the tempest buttered? The giants
In their yachts have privately forgotten
by which hand slipped under the door
Its screaming face. I rode into
The scared dead town, parked the Plymouth—
No one in the central dark bar—
"Perhaps Pat is dead" but it buckled,
Came on, all puce zones alight
And in the death of muck and horror
Knelt one on the quiet trapeze of the sky.

—if we are defeated by such lines, which Ashbery has not chosen to carry over into the canon of his work and which I can therefore quote here without having to say more about them than that they suggest his disconcerting gift for placing a recognizeable, even a tantalizing "scene" (as here, from the movies: lines four through seven) among a cluster of irreconcileable propositions—and *disconcerting* must be our normative word here, for it identifies if it does not stigmatize this poet's powerful centrifugal, dissociative impulse—if such lines, then, bewilder, baffle, defeat and disconcert us, we will find our scandal rehearsed and in some senses relaxed and even redeemed by these speeches from *The Heroes*. Reading Theseus on the labyrinth, we are on the way to reading Ashbery on the art of poetry, a tiny dark convex mirror indeed:

. . . I took advantage of the fact that it was built like a maze. Whenever you do this, even if the problem is just one in algebra, everything becomes simple immediately. Because then you can sit back and get a picture of yourself doing whatever it is. If you do not grant its own peculiar nature to the problem, you can have no picture of yourself and consequently feel harassed and lonely. Without imagination nothing can be easy.

. . . I'd always supposed the world was full of fakes, but I was foolish enough to believe that it was made interesting by the varying degrees of skill with which they covered up their lack of integrity. It never occurred to me that the greatest fake of all [the minotaur] would make not the slightest effort to convince me of its reality . . . not a pretense! But there it was, a stupid unambitious piece of stage machinery! . . . There was nothing to do but give the thing a well-aimed kick and go home . . .

. . . There are large holes in the roof, so the visitor is free, if he wishes, to climb out on top and survey the ground plan of the whole edifice. In short, he is in the dubious position of a person who believes that dada is still alive . . . Now comes the strangest part of all: you have been in the maze several days and nights, and you are beginning to realize you have changed several times. Not just you, either, but your whole idea of the maze and the maze itself . . . The maze looks just the same as ever—it is more as if it were being looked at by a different person. But I was so happy there, for now at last I was seeing myself as I could only be—not as I might be seen by a person in the street: full of unfamiliarity and the resulting poetry. Before, I might have seemed beautiful to the passerby. I now seemed ten times more so to myself, for I saw that I meant nothing beyond the equivocal statement of my limbs and the space and time they happened to occupy . . . I realized I now possessed the only weapon by which the minotaur might be vanquished: the indifference of a true aesthete . . .

It is almost a catalogue of the modernist principles Ashbery has recited, a post-symbolist enchiridion: the poem as simultaneous structure, impersonal, autonomous, released from the charge of expression, of assertion; the poem as arbitrary construct, absurd, self-destroying, no longer aspiring to convince or even to hoax; the poem as an agent of transformation, equal in value to the poet himself and therefore capable of changing him; the poem as means of escape from identity, leading into a world of contemplation, indifference, bliss. Theseus' final statement of his situation, a *tirade* to Circe, brings us even closer to Ashbery's later poems:

. . . Let me tell you of an experience I had while I was on my way here. My train had stopped in the station directly opposite another. Through the glass I was able to watch a couple in the next train, a man and a woman who were having some sort of a conversation. For fifteen minutes I watched them. I had no idea what their relation was. I could form no idea of their conversation. They might have been speaking words of love, or planning a murder, or quarreling about their in-laws. Yet just from watching them talk, even though I could hear nothing, I feel I know those people better than anyone in the world . . .

The proposition of a reality that may be identifiable and even beautiful, though it outstrips understanding, is certainly what we shall need in exposing ourselves to Ashbery's first book, which was published by the Yale Series of Younger Poets in 1956 with a remarkably disaffected foreword by W. H. Auden. In the shade of *Some Trees*, I would cite the last of Ashbery's blazons, from the end of *The Heroes;* it is Circe's answer to Theseus' rather blithe assumption that it is enough to *recognize* reality whether one understands it or not. The old witch forces the triumphant hero to acknowledge how much harder it is going to be than he has been prepared to admit—and we stand admonished along with Theseus and Ashbery, *en abyme* in the face of *the poems:*

. . . So far this play has been easy. From now on it's going to be more difficult to follow. That's the way life is sometimes. Yea, a fine stifling mist springs up from the author's pure and moody mind. Confusion and hopelessness follow on the precise speech of spring. Just as, when the last line of this play is uttered, your memory will lift a torch to the dry twisted mass. Then it will not seem so much as if all this never happened, but as if parts continued to go on all the time in your head, rising up without warning whenever you start to do the simplest act.

A glance at the table of contents tells us, first of all, how thoroughly aware Ashbery is of his conventions—more than aware, elated to have them at hand: "Eclogue," "Canzone," "Sonnet," "Pantoum" and three sestinas dramatize this poet's fondness for the art's most intricate forms, and his facility with them. Other pieces are named for works of literature themselves—"Two Scenes," "Popular Songs," "The Instruction Manual," "Album Leaf," "Illustration," "A Long Novel," "A Pastoral"—suggesting that Ashbery has none of the advanced artist's habitual hostility to his own medium, for all his dissociative techniques and fragmenting designs. He has even taken Marvell's famous poem, or at least the title of it, and put himself into the photograph: "The Picture of Little J. A. in a Prospect of Flowers"—

> *. . . I cannot escape the picture*
> *Of my small self in that bank of flowers:*
> *My head among the blazing phlox*
> *Seemed a pale and gigantic fungus.*
> *I had a hard stare, accepting*
>
> *Everything, taking nothing,*
> *As though the rolled-up future might stink*
> *As loud as stood the sick moment*
> *The shutter clicked. Though I was wrong,*
> *Still, as the loveliest feelings*
>
> *Must soon find words, and these, yes,*
> *Displace them, so I am not wrong*
> *In calling this comic version of myself*
> *The true one. For as change is horror,*
> *Virtue is really stubbornness*
>
> *And only in the light of lost words*
> *Can we imagine our rewards.*

This is but the third section of a poem that runs through much of the diction of English poetry, and even its exaggerated symbolist postures ("the rolled-up future might stink / as loud as stood the sick moment / the shutter clicked") cannot decoy us from the discovery that this poet is obsessed by the most classical of poetic themes: the immortalization of experience by words. For a poet, even one who would leave Andrew Marvell behind him, "the loveliest feelings / must soon find words, and these, yes, / displace them . . . and only in the light of lost words / can we imagine our rewards." The placing of that "yes" betrays the argument Ashbery has had with himself on this subject, and also betokens the victory he has reached over his own love of incoherence (poems called "Errors" and "Chaos"). Most of the poems in the book aim, as one firing buckshot may be said to aim, at a single target: the elusive order of existence which the poet knows to be there, just beyond his reach.

> *From every corner comes a distinctive offering.*
> *The train comes bearing joy;*
> *For long we hadn't heard so much news, such noise . . .*
> *As laughing cadets say, "In the evening*
> *Everything has a schedule, if you can find out what it is."*

The notion that The Poem is already there, *in the world*, and must be collected somehow by the poet, is what keeps these pieces going. "Some Trees" itself puts the matter perfectly (though there is a second and probably a third way of reading that title—not only "Several Trees," but also "These Trees as opposed to Others," and even "Trees Indeed!" the way Churchill used to say "Some Chicken—Some Neck!")—

> *These are amazing: each*
> *Joining a neighbor, as though speech*
> *Were a still performance.*
> *Arranging by chance*
>
> *To meet as far this morning*
> *From the world as agreeing*
> *With it, you and I*
> *Are suddenly what the trees try*
>
> *To tell us we are:*
> *That their merely being there*
> *Means something; that soon*
> *We may touch, love, explain.*

By "logic of strange position" rather than by any emotional adequacy or correspondence, any psychological explanation, any moral recovery, this poet sweeps the world's body into his net. It is in this, surely, that Ashbery is truly advanced, even revolutionary—his notion that the world not only contains but *is* his poem, and that he cannot, in order to write it, draw the world into himself as has traditionally been attempted, but must rather extrude himself into the world, must *flee the center* in order to be on the verge at all points. As he had said, in *The Heroes,* "I saw that I meant nothing beyond the equivocal statement of my limbs and the space and time they happened to occupy," so he says in *Some Trees,* "What are lamps / when night is waiting?" and again,

> *The mythological poet, his face*
> *Fabulous and fastidious, accepts*
> *Beauty before it arrives . . . He is merely*
> *An ornament, a kind of lewd*
> *Cloud placed on the horizon.*
>
> *Close to the zoo, acquiescing*
> *To dust, candy, perverts; inserted in*
> *The panting forest, or openly*
> *Walking in the great and sullen square*
> *He has eloped with all music*
> *And does not care. For isn't there,*
> *He says, a final diversion, a greater*
> *Because it can be given, a gift*
> *Too simple even to be despised?*

Beyond the evident influence of Stevens ("We can only imagine a world in which a woman / walks and wears her hair and knows / all that she does not know. Yet we know / what her breasts are"), and the occasional note of Perse ("Lovely tribes have just moved to the north. / In the flickering evening the martins grow denser. / Rivers of wings surround us and vast tribulation"), the poems in *Some Trees* that most compel our trust in Ashbery's bond with what has already been made, his covenant with the convention, are two which owe most to Apollinaire: "The Instruction Manual" and "Illustration." These strike the note of "a gift too simple even to be despised"—one from inside: "The Instruction Manual," that deploys all of Ashbery's skill with direct statement, the narrative of an achieved identity confronting the given world; and one addressing the other: "Illustration," about a woman "who acts out," as Auden puts it, "her private mythology and denies the reality of anything outside herself." It is a comfort, in the presence of poems like "Grand Abacus"—the very title suggests the alien and alienating machinery, all those bright beads clicking back and forth on the wires, but not much being accounted for beyond a certain insanely "clever" calculation:

> *Perhaps this valley too leads into the head of long-ago days.*
> *What, if not its commercial and etiolated visage, could*
> *break through the meadow wires?*
> *It placed a chair in the meadow and then went far away.*
> *People come to visit in summer, they do not think about*
> *the head.*
> *Soldiers come down to see the head. The stick hides from them.*
> *The heavens say, "Here I am, boys and girls!"*
> *The stick tries to hide in the noise. The leaves, happy,*
> *drift over the dusty meadow.*
> *"I'd like to see it," someone said about the head, which*
> *has stopped pretending to be a town . . .*

—it is more than a comfort, it is a condition of our engagement to rehearse a poem as evidently entangled with consistency as "Illustration." The suicide about to leap from her cornice is presented to us as a "novice," though we do not at once know whether her novitiate is to life or death. The commandments of man and god against self-slaughter are reviewed in a pun:

> *. . . Angels*
>
> *Combined their prayers with those*
> *Of the police, begging her to come off it.*

The inducements of society (" 'I do not want a friend,' she said"), of adornment, pleasure and selfishness fail to persuade the woman against her resolution; only the blind man offering flowers approaches success,

> *For that the scene should be a ceremony*
>
> *Was what she wanted. "I desire*
> *Monuments," she said. "I want to move*
>
> *Figuratively, as waves caress*
> *The thoughtless shore. You people I know*
>
> *Will offer me every good thing*
> *I do not want. But please remember*
>
> *I died accepting them." With that, the wind*
> *Unpinned her bulky robes, and naked*

As a roc's egg, she drifted slowly downward
Out of the angels' tenderness and the minds of men.

There is an exactitude about this, and a wild imaginative choice of
analogy ("to move figuratively, as waves caress the thoughtless shore"
or "naked as a roc's egg") that conjugate to make something particu-
larly poignant. The private mythology, thirsty for ritual and "monu-
ments," pitted against the trivial life of the crowd watching, is seen as
an *illustration* in the old sense (the sense meaning *lustration* as well) in
which all objects and incidents are taken, by poetry, as a sanctification
of life. The *body* of any symbol, the Church says, is absurd, and
Ashbery's practice concurs. In the second part of this poem, which I
take it bears a reciprocal relation to the figure of the suicide, each part
being the "illustration" of the other, no such preposterous emblems are
devised (like "blue cornflakes in a white bowl" for the sea and its
curving beach); rather the poet immediately moralizes the fable:
"much that is beautiful must be discarded / so that we may resemble a
taller / impression of ourselves." And his final vision of the episode's
meaning is Ashbery at his most controlled, his most beautiful:

. . . *Moths climb in the flame,*
Alas, that wish only to be the flame:

They do not lessen our stature.
We twinkle under the weight

Of indiscretions. But how could we tell
That of the truth we know, she was

The somber vestment? For that night, rockets sighed
Elegantly over the city, and there was feasting:

There is so much in that moment!
So many attitudes toward that flame,

We might have soared from earth, watching her glide
Aloft in her peplum of bright leaves.

But she, of course, was only an effigy
Of indifference, a miracle

Not meant for us, as the leaves are not
Winter's because it is the end.

There is the same rueful adieu to experience in "The Instruction
Manual," or at least the same note of frustration sounded, as at the end

of "Illustration," but because the utterance is made in the poet's own persona there is a waggishness in the wistfulness—the comedian, as Ashbery would say, as the letter A—but lower-case. It is the Apollinaire attitude toward language if not the Apollonian one—the words set down with only so much care as to make them cope—that is most evident here, in this long exercise in projection:

> *I wish I did not have to write the instruction manual*
> *   on the uses of a new metal.*
> *I look down into the street and see people, each*
> *   walking with an inner peace,*
> *And envy them—they are so far away from me!*
> *Not one of them has to worry about getting out this*
> *   manual on schedule.*
> *And, as my way is, I begin to dream, resting my el-*
> *   bows on the desk and leaning out of the window a little*
> *Of dim Guadalajara! City of rose-colored flowers!*
> *City I wanted most to see, and most did not see, in*
> *   Mexico!*

There follows a long, exact travelogue, the phrasing so perfect and the feeling so painfully compressed in the objects selected for *émerveillement* that it almost seems as if Mr. James Fitzpatrick had had a possible genre going for himself after all; but then we reach the end, and realize how difficult this "simple" kind of writing must be to carry off, how disabused Ashbery's whimsy is, and how devastating his criticism of himself:

> *How limited, but how complete, has been*
> *   our experience of Guadalajara!*
> *We have seen young love, married love, and the*
> *   love of an aged mother for her son.*
> *We have heard the music, tasted the drinks, and*
> *   looked at colored houses.*
> *What more is there to do, except stay? And that*
> *   we cannot do.*
> *And as a last breeze freshens the top of the weathered*
> *   old tower, I turn my gaze*
> *Back to the instruction manual which has made me*
> *   dream of Guadalajara.*

None of Ashbery's other poems, even in this first book, exploit with such consecution, with such a progressive impulse, these characteristic modes of his; but their tonalities recur throughout the body of his work, no matter how spattered and pointillist the phrases ("murk plectrum" is probably the best—or worst—example), how discrepant the imagery. "The Instruction Manual" and "Illustration" afford us the framing possibilities: the hand-to-mouth music of a self locating its unavailable hopes wherever it can; and the aberrant mind, possessed of its own beautiful truth, disqualifying the accommodations of a cachectic world. I suspect that by now Ashbery is as sick of having these two poems lit upon by his admirers and even by his detractors as Eliot professed to be of having to recite "Prufrock"—in both cases, the poets would deplore the inroads of an early success upon their later style. But in Ashbery's instance, the later style is so extreme, so centrifugal, that it is well to be reminded of its wonderful and central antecedents before, as he says in his title poem,

> Our days put on such reticence
> These accents seem their own defense.

By the time *Some Trees* was published, Ashbery had moved to Paris where he was to live for a decade. It would be easy to suggest that his experiments in the loosening, explosion and relocation of the poem were a result, or at least a concomitant, of his isolation in a literary milieu where *anything* he might do would be incomprehensible—why not, therefore, do anything? Too easy, and also, I suspect, unjust to the odd strictness of the thirty poems of *The Tennis Court Oath*, published in 1962, six years after his first book. With work as demanding and as bewildering as this, there is always the tendency to cry havoc and let slip the cogs of boredom ("there is a terrible breath in the way of all this"). The compositional techniques of Roussel and of his own understanding of vanguard art * brought Ashbery, in this new collection—an extremely long and various one, by the way—to a pitch of distraction, of literal eccentricity, that leaves any consecutive or linear reading of his poems out of the question. In fact, it is only questions that are left. We must be guided in our response ("there are many answers") by the capital statement on poetics which Ashbery appended to his *curriculum vitae* after *The Tennis Court Oath* was published:·

> I feel I could express myself best in music. What I like about music is its ability of being convincing, of carrying an argument through successfully to the finish, though the terms of this argument remain unknown quantities. What remains is the structure, the architecture of the argument, scene or story. I would like to do this in poetry. I would also like to reproduce the power dreams

* Indeed, his exposure to it: in New York, the poet was on the staff of *Art News;* in Paris, he served as art editor of the *Paris Herald-Tribune* and is now an editor of *Art News.*

have of persuading you that a certain event has a meaning not logically connected with it, or that there is a hidden relation among disparate objects. But actually this is only a part of what I want to do, and I am not even sure I want to do it. I often change my mind about my poetry. I would prefer not to think I had any special aims in mind . . .

Remembering Theseus' image of the couple seen through the train window, whose words could not be made out, though the hero felt an intimacy "just from watching them talk," we know what to expect from these pieces, each of which generally contains its own monument and epitaph *en abyme*, my favorite being one that occurs in the four-page stream of images called "The New Realism":

> *Police formed a boundary to the works*
> *Where we played*
> A torn page with a passionate oasis.

Let me list (in the original sense of the word—to make a border or marginal accommodation) some of the passionate oases in these extraordinary poems—after all, it *is* extraordinary to set so many lines together with an evident concern for music, diction, "a more than usual order," and still remain subliminal in "message":

> *the year books*
> *authored the heart bees—*
> *beers over beads somewhat*
> *broken off from the rest . . .*

In the title poem, then, after the poet has declared "you come through but / are incomparable," he announces "there was no turning back but the end was in sight." In "America" he points to his Pierrot-preoccupations: "tears, hopeless adoration, passions / the fruit of carpentered night." In "Measles":

> *I write, trying to economize*
> *These lines, tingling. The very earth's*
> *A pension . . .*
> *You limit me to what I say.*
> *The sense of the words is*
> *With a backward motion, pinning me*
> *To the daylight mode of my declaration.*

In "The Lozenges" he declares: "We all have graves to travel from, vigorously exerting / the strongest possible influence on those about us." And in "A Last Word":

> *But these were not the best men*
> *But there were moments of the others*
> *Seen through indifference, only bare methods*
> *But we can remember them and so we are saved.*

Evidently there is little rhythmic enterprise in these poems, the images being for all purposes assorted one to a line in the cadences of a suburban speech-pattern ("I jest / was playing the piano of your halitosis"), and one supposes much less of an attraction to the closed, conventional forms than in the earlier book. In the first of the "Two Sonnets," for instance, there are only thirteen lines, and though the sonnet "feeling" is there, I suppose, it is difficult to see the force of it, so impatient is Ashbery with his own submission to the form:

> *The body's products become*
> *Fatal to it. Our spit*
> *Would kill us, but we*
> *Die of our heat.*
> *Though I say the things I wish to say*
> *They are needless, their own flame conceives it.*
> *So I am cheated of perfection.*

Here the poet is constantly tweaking his mind in the direction of his poetics ("though I say the things I wish to say they are needless"), and neglecting to pursue to their formal ends the emblems and figures which "the sonnet" ordinarily suggests, though the opening quoted here has all the *panache* of, say, Merrill Moore. There is still a sestina in this volume—a remarkable one called "Faust" which has more to do with Ashbery's earlier mode than with the cut-up-novel pieces like "Europe" that crowd this collection. What is new in "Faust" is a certain narrative glamor, an extension of phrasing that is to become one of Ashbery's surprising strengths, unclotting the preposterous imagery and committing the mind to a sustained experience:

> *If only the phantom would stop reappearing!*
> *Business, if you wanted to know, was punk at the opera.*
> *The heroine no longer appeared in* Faust.
> *The crowds strolled sadly away. The phantom*
> *Watched them from the roof, not guessing the hungers*
> *That must be stirred before disappointment can begin.*

"Thoughts of a Young Girl" and "To Redouté" are further—brief—respites in a host of disproportions—"these things," as Ashbery says in "The Shower," "these things that are the property of only the few." Mostly, *The Tennis Court Oath* is an exasperating book of improper fractions, lovable for its own love of earth:

> *. . . Confound it*
> *The arboretum is bursting with jasmine and lilac*
> *And all I can smell here is newsprint . . .*

or again,

> *Nothing can be harmed! Night and day are begin-*
> *ning again!*
> *So put away the book,*
> *The flowers you were keeping to give someone:*
> *Only the white, tremendous foam of the street*
> *has any importance,*
> *The new white flowers that are beginning to shoot*
> *up about now.*

and beyond construing, for all its evident and cunning construction.*
Valéry remarks somewhere that we call beautiful a work which makes
us aware, first, that it might not have existed (since its nonexistence
would have meant no vital loss), and secondly, that it could not have
been other than it is. In these middle poems of Ashbery's, I miss the tug
between the first proposition and the second, for there is too much
evidence in favor of the possibilities of nonexistence, not enough
credence given to inevitability. That Ashbery himself was aware of the
discrepancy accounts, I think, for all the self-carping *en abyme*, and
leads, happily, into the firmer, fuller achievements of his next volume,
which restores the tone of "The Instruction Manual"—diffident, tender
and, for all its irony, rapturous!—and the temper of "Illustration"—
penetrating, elegiac and, for all its wiliness, truthful.

In 1963, Ashbery interrupted the measured mystery of his expatria-
tion and, on the stage of the Living Theater in New York, gave a
reading of new poems to an audience as curious about what had
become of him as it was convinced of his accomplishment in the past.
In his absence, *The Compromise, or Queen of the Caribou,* a melo-
drama, had been performed at the Poets' Theater in Cambridge, and
To the Mill, a kind of Happening *avant la lettre* had been published in
Alfred Leslie's one-shot review *The Hasty Papers.* A glance at the end
of *To the Mill* will suggest, I think, the quality of the poet's own
performance, upon his first appearance in his native land for many
years:

* If you write a poem by taking the last line from every third chapter of each
green-bound book on your shelves, and rhyming the last word of each with the
first word of each fourth line, adding the name of a soft drink, an Aristotelian
category and an expletive from the comic strips to every other line, you will
have cunningly constructed a poem whose beauties are *strictement littéraire.*

(*The midwife empties a paper bag of dust over Tom & Katherine, who cough and sneeze.*)

KATHERINE: My sore throat.

(*The midwife disappears behind a rock. Cecilia exits left on the horse. Ernest exits to the left and reappears carrying a drum. The professor enters from the right, also carrying a drum.*)

ERNEST: My leg.

(*Bill exits to the left. Mary enters from the left and Cecilia, on the horse, from the right.*)

CURTAIN

For there was the poet, striding up and down the set of *The Brig*, behind strands of barbed wire (to protect him from us? us from him?), wreathed in clouds of smoke as he consumed one cigarette after the other and with remarkable skill and security read out the poems that already indicated how far he had come from the atomized shocks of *The Tennis Court Oath* ("The arctic honey blabbed over the report causing darkness"). In that last book, he had asked, of course:

> *Isn't Idaho the Wolverine state?*
> *Anyway Ohio is the flower state*
> *New York is the key state.*
> *Bandana is the population state.*
> *In the hay states of Pennsylvania and Arkansas*
> *I lay down and slept . . .*

thereby ringing a change beyond even Mr. Eliot's on "By the waters of Leman" and inventing a badly-needed "population state." This might have prepared us for "Into the Dusk-Charged Air"—a catalogue of 160 lines, each of which contains the name of a river and a characterizing landscape or location:

> *. . . Few ships navigate*
> *On the Housatonic, but quite a few can be seen*
> *On the Elbe. For centuries*
> *The Afton has flowed.*
> *If the Rio Negro*
> *Could abandon its song, and the Magdelena*
> *The jungle flowers, the Tagus*
> *Would still flow serenely, and the Ohio*
> *Abrade its slate banks . . .*

But there was no predicting the impulse of continuity, of rapt persistence which the other poems exalted to an altogether new pitch of identity; it was as if the poet had come to tell us "about the great drama that was being won":

> *To turn off the machinery*
> *And quietly move among the rustic landscape.*

That curious selfhood of Ashbery's which by fond abnegation found the poem in the world rather than in any centripetal operation or ordering of the sensibility, gathered and gleaned its ready-mades in what seemed, coming from the stage, a furthered capacity to *relate* in both the associative and the narrative senses of the word. And when, in 1966, Ashbery returned from Paris, his third book confirmed the sense one had at his reading three years before that here was perhaps the first poet in history in whose work anxiety (with all its shaping, climax-reaching concerns) had no place, a poet for whom the poem was poem *all through* and at any point, without emphases or repetitions (a maze, a labyrinth, rather than an obstacle-course). This, I think, is why we are rarely able to respond to this *oeuvre* in the way we do to the traditional modes anchored in what Northrop Frye calls the seasonal myths, for recurrence and the cyclical patterns of ritual simply do not apply to Ashbery's poetry in its characteristic extension here. Nothing in *Rivers and Mountains* "depends on everything's recurring till we answer from within" as Frost put it, "because," as Ashbery answers, "*all the true fragments are here.*" In the first poems in the book we find, *en abyme,* some more of those apologies for the poems themselves, but they are no longer militant or even apologetic, they are triumphant in accounting for the *over-all* texture of these anti-psychological poems: "continuance quickens the scrap which falls to us . . . a premise of so much that is to come, extracted, accepted gladly but within its narrow limits no knowledge yet, nothing which can be used." And again, most significantly: "*Each moment of utterance is the true one; likewise none are true.*" Existence is reported to be as ineffable as in the poems of *Some Trees,* but no longer beyond the poet's grasp because he is no longer grasping:

> *Here I am then, continuing but ever beginning*
> *My perennial voyage, into new memories, new hope and*
> *   flowers*
> *The way the coasts glide past you. I shall never*
> *   forget this moment*
> *Because it consists of purest ecstasy. I am happier*
> *   now than I ever dared believe*
> *Anyone could be. And we finger down the dog-eared*
> *   coasts . . .*
> *It is all passing! It is past! No, I am here,*

Bellow the coasts, and even the heavens roar their
assent
As we pick up a lemon-colored light horizontally
projected into the night, the night that heaven
Was kind enough to send, and I launch into the
happiest dreams,
Happier once again, because tomorrow is already here.

These *dasein*-dazzled lines are from *The Skaters*, a poem of some thirty pages and, with *Clepsydra*, Ashbery's largest statement, a telluric hymn (as the book's title and title poem indicate: "in the seclusion of a melody heard / as though through trees") to a confessed, a welcomed evanescence that somehow guarantees ecstasy. The poem is not about skaters, but takes the image of their action for its own:

. . . the intensity of minor acts
As skaters elaborate their distances,
Taking a separate line to its end. Returning to the mass,
they join each other
Blotted in an incredible mess of dark colors, and again
reappearing to take the theme
Some little distance, like fishing boats developing from the
land different parabolas,
Taking the exquisite theme far, into farness, to Land's End,
to the ends of the earth!
But the livery of the year, the changing air
Bring each to fulfillment . . .

And so Ashbery is off, inventorying "the human brain, with its tray of images" filled by his encounters with the world. Over and over, the object of the poem becomes its subject, its making its meaning; except for the late poems of Wallace Stevens, I know no more convincing meditation on the power the mind has to submit itself to forms, and by them be formed:

this poem
Which is in the form of falling snow:
That is, the individual flakes are not essential to the
importance of the whole . . .
Hence neither the importance of the individual flake,
Nor the importance of the whole impression of the storm,
if it has any, is what it is,
But the rhythm of the series of repeated jumps, from
abstract into positive and back to a slightly less
diluted abstract.

The long lines, loose though they are, keep a spring, a resilience, in part as a result of "the evidence of the visual," the surprising way Ashbery has of giving "the answer that is novelty / that guides these swift blades o'er the ice," and in part because we recognize the tone of voice as the innocent, astonished, ravished one we had heard in "The Instruction Manual"—only cleared of the old jerkiness, taking now more than bite-size morsels of the earthly meal and discovering "the declamatory nature of the distance travelled." In "Clepsydra," too, Ashbery offers a splendid pledge as much to his achievement as to his intention. The title means a water clock, of course, a contrivance to measure time by the graduated flow of a liquid through a small aperture ("each moment of utterance is the true one"), and in the terms of the poem itself "an invisible fountain that continually destroys and refreshes the previsions." As in "The Skaters," the poem becomes a meditation on its own being in the world:

> *. . . it was*
> *Like standing at the edge of a harbor early on a summer morning*
> *With the discreet shadows cast by the water all around*
> *And a feeling, again, of emptiness, but of richness in the way*
> *The whole thing is organized, on what a miraculous scale,*
> *Really what is meant by a human level, with the figures of giants*
> *Not too much bigger than the men who have come to petition them*
> *A moment that gave not only itself, but*
> *Also the means of keeping it, of not turning to dust*
> *Or gestures somewhere up ahead*
> *But of becoming complicated like the torrent*
> *In new dark passages, tears and laughter which*
> *Are a sign of life, of distant life in this case.*
> *And yet, as always happens, there would come a moment when*
> *Acts no longer sufficed and the calm*
> *Of this true progression hardened into shreds*
> *Of another kind of calm, returning to the conclusion, its premises*
> *Undertaken before any formal agreement had been reached, hence*
> *A writ that was the shadow of the colossal reason behind all this*
> *Like a second, rigid body behind the one you know is yours.*

Such poetry is no longer merely the realm, but the means of self-encounter; its method has been to pluck from the world the constituted terms of its being, but Ashbery has exalted his linguistic recognition-scene into something more than a product, a prey, a proof of being-in-the-world. He has made his discourse identical with his experience "in such a way as to form a channel," or again, as he says, "the delta of living into everything." In this way,

(*John Ashbery*)

. . . any direction taken was the right one,
Leading first to you, and through you to
Myself that is beyond you and which is the same thing as space
 . . . moving in the shadow of
Your single and twin existence, waking in intact
Appreciation of it, while morning is still and before the body
Is changed by the faces of evening.

The Double Dream of Spring by JOHN ASHBERY

Our servants, according to the symbolist anchorage in a society of masters—our servants will do our living for us. Our poets, we say now, with the same confidence, the same condescension—our poets, if only we submit to their poems, will do our criticism for us:

"You cannot take it all in, certain details are already hazy and the mind boggles . . . These things could be a lot clearer without hurting anybody. Tomorrow would alter the sense of what had already been learned . . . the moment of sinking in / is always past, yet always in question, on the surface / of the goggles of memory. . . . I am not so much at home with these memorabilia of vision as on a tour / of my remotest properties. There is so much to be said, and on the surface of it very little gets said . . . It is this blank carcass of whims and tentative afterthoughts / which is being delivered into your hand like a letter . . . Strange, isn't it, that the message makes some sense, if only a relative one in the larger context of message-receiving. A light wilderness of spoken words not / unkind for all their aimlessness . . . that sound like the wind / forgetting in the branches and meaning something / nobody can translate . . . But this new way, the way sentences suddenly spurt up like gas / or sting and jab, is it that we accepted each complication / as it came along, and are therefore happy with the result? / Or was it a condition of seeing / that we vouchsafed aid and comfort to the seasons / as each came begging? As though meaning could be cast aside someday / when it had been outgrown . . . our pyramiding memories, alert as dandelion fuzz, dart from one pretext to the next / seeking in occasions new sources of memories, for memory is a profit / until the day it spreads out all its accumulation, delta-like on the plain / for that day no good can come of remembering, and the anomalies cancel each other out. / But until then foreshortened memories will keep us going, alive, one to the other: a kind of activity that offers its own way of life. Perverse notations on an indisputable state of things / open out new passages of being among the correctness of familiar patterns . . . Thus your only world is an inside one / ironically fashioned out of external phenomena / having no rhyme or reason . . . As one figure supplants another and dies, / there is no remedy for this "packaging" which has supplanted the old sensations . . . Ideas were good only because they had to die, / leaving you alone and skinless, a drawing by Vesalius. For this is action, this not being sure, this careless preparing . . . making ready to forget, and always coming back / to the mooring of starting out . . ."

There are three notes at the end of Ashbery's fourth volume of poems (out of which I have stitched together the foregoing poetics of the "turmoil that is to be our route") which help a lot, as the poet says, "to get over the threshold of so much unmeaning, so much / Being, preparing us for its event, the active memorial." Yes, precisely, that is what Ashbery's poems are, an active memorial to themselves, writhing in dissolute, shimmering lines without emphases or repetitions around the column their own accumulation raises until "the convention gapes / prostrated before a monument disappearing into the dark." And if it is true that in reading poems which are habitually a gloss on their own singularity we need all the help we can get, it is also true that Ashbery wants us to enjoy our helplessness all the way: "these things are offered to your participation . . . Each hastens onward separately / in strange sensations of emptiness, anguish, romantic / outbursts, visions and wraiths. One meeting cancels another . . . becoming a medium in which it is possible to recognize oneself. Each new diversion adds its accurate touch to the ensemble, and so / a portrait is built up out of multiple corrections."

Keeping that constant cancellation in mind, then, consider Ashbery's three notes: 1) that the book's title comes from that of a painting by Giorgio di Chirico; 2) that the method of the poems is pursued "with the idea of avoiding customary word-patterns and associations"; and 3) that the title *Sortes Vergilianae* refers to the ancient practice of fortune-telling "by choosing a passage from Vergil's poetry at random."

Ashbery, executive editor of *Art News* who has written with venturesome finickiness about a great many painters, has suggested by several titles in this new book that the plastic arts are a starting-point, an inspiration: *Definition of Blue, Farm Implements and Rutabagas in a Landscape, Clouds*, and then the poem with Di Chirico's title, suffused as it is with the rural vernality characteristic of most of Ashbery's recent work. I think, too, that Di Chirico has been chosen as the psychopomp and intercessor of the book because his oneiric dissociations are the kind of thing Ashberry himself aspires to: "I would like to reproduce in poetry the power dreams have of persuading you that a certain event has a meaning not logically connected with it, or that there is a hidden relation among disparate objects," the poet has written about his program. Hence *The Double Dream of Spring*, double because it refers to an art of dreams and a dream of art. "In a dream touch bottom", the poet urges in the title poem—and indeed the bottom is so far down that the only way the poet can reach it is by rising to the surface: "I can tell you all about freedom that has turned into a painting."

Ashbery's second note about avoiding customary word patterns and associations is admonitory: only a man utterly oppressed by patterns and associations will seek at such cost to avoid them. As readers of *A Nest of Ninnies*, Ashbery's novel (written with the poet James Schuyler) remember, this poet's strategy is either to collapse helplessly into the customary, the commonplace, the cliché, or else to escape them by convulsive expeditions into "a desert of chance", warning us of "the incredible violence that is to be our route". If the world contains and even secretes Ashbery's poem ("It was the holiness of the day that fed our notions / and released them . . . a kind of fence-sitting / *raised to the level of an aesthetic ideal*"), then what the poet calls customary patterns and associations must not be allowed to distort, to atrophy or distend what is—merely, but also marvellously— there. A persistent derangement of expectation will permit the poem to collect itself from the world, to appear "slowly as from the center of some diamond / you begin to take in the world as it moves / in toward you." This new book, therefore has fewer poems than ever before which exploit or even explode the conventions of poetry, its hereditary intricacies—only one song, one sestina, while the poem "For John Clare" is in prose, and the "Variations, Calypso + Fugue" is, with derisive preposterousness, "on a Theme of Ella Wheeler Wilcox"! No, most of these poems carry on in a language without the tension of negativity, without irony, without the invoked anxiety of a closed form. The lines run on, or peter out, they do not shore up the poem's energy by any kind of rhythmic or musical constant: the poem is endlessly obliging but under no obligations. The longest poem in the book, insistently called "Fragment", is set up in what appear to be stanzas, but they are merely regular clusters, spaced off for the sake of convenience ("refreshment and ease to the statement"). Language in Ashbery's prodigious work is not wielded to convey the disciplinary, punitive passion which has been the art's contribution and resource in the past; it is intended rather—and manages—to convince by letting things alone: "a rhythm of standing still / keeps us in continual equilibrium . . . for each progress is negation, of movement and in particular of number." Recalling that verse is traditionally called "numbers", we can better understand the spell upon us of Ashbery's innumerable art, what he cherishes as "its articulate flatness, goal, barrier and climate."

Ashbery's third note, explaining the *Sortes Vergilianae*, affords the decisive expression: "choosing at random." The accent is on both processes equally, the operation of chance, the operation of choice. The poem is already there, and what Ashbery calls "the secret of the search" is that its given, its constituted existence in the world makes all choosing certain to succeed and therefore eliminates the necessity of choice. The objective of the poem is not subjective, it is the poem's subject, and the poem's "meaning" is in its making: "this banality which in the last analysis is our / most precious possession, because allowing us to / rise above ourselves."

By dilating the poet's notes I have tried to account for his necessities, and I have not hesitated to invoke the poems as their own exegesis. Indeed, the great innovation of Ashbery's poems is that they do not explain or symbolize or even refer to some experience the poet has had, something outside themselves in the world, something precedent. The poems are not about anything, they are something, they are their own creation, and it would be fair to say that the world is, instead, a comment on them, a criticism of them. For all his modesty and mildness, that is Ashbery's great symbolist assertion—that the world may exist to conclude in a book:

> *Sly breath of Eros,*
> *Anniversary on the woven city lament, that assures our arriving*
> *In hours, seconds, breath, watching our salary*
> *In the morning holocaust become one vast furnace, engaging all tears.*

Poetry, 1970

Three Poems by JOHN ASHBERY

In his previous collection, it was apparent—no, let us say it was apprehensible, that Ashbery's poems carried on in a language without the tension of negativity, without the invoked anxiety of a closed form. In short, or at length, the poems were moving toward—and some had already moved right in on—*prose*, an utterance unpoliced if not unpolicied (the policy turning out to be "to keep asking life the same question until the repeated question and the same silence become answer"), innovative or advanced, as everyone keeps saying about this writer, because the lines were not wielded to convey the disciplinary, punitive passion which has always been the art's contribution and conventional resource. Now in *Three Poems*, where discourse has "come to mean what it had been called on for," where "our narration seems to be trying to bury itself in the land-

scape," there are no lines at all, nor even clusters of enjambed state-
ments: there are prose *texts* (something woven, as a snare or *toil*),
"a kind of trilogy meant to be read in sequence," Ashbery says, con-
stituting "a glad mess" of the matte instances he had aspired to in
that last book as "articulate flatness, goal, barrier and climate,"
achieved now "far from the famous task, close to the meaningless but
real snippets that are today's doing."

The first text, "The New Spirit", about fifty pages long, is said
by the poet to record a spiritual awakening to earthly things; and
though very few earthly things are vouchsafed, the endeavor is
"to formulate oneself around this hollow, empty sphere . . . as
objects placed along the top of a wall," for in Ashbery's spiritual
exercises the aim is to be aimless, void, abluted, to get out of the way
of intention in order to enable "the emptiness that was the only
way you could express a thing." The second text, "The System",
about the same length, is said by Ashbery to be "a love story with
cosmological overtones," material handled, certainly fingered, by a
parody of dialectical homiletics. Love here consists of all the possi-
ble objections to it ("it prepares its own downfall while never quite
beginning"), and only comes to exist when it acknowledges "the
inner emptiness from which alone understanding can spring up."
The third text, "The Recital", is a much briefer embroidery on the
poet's relations to his victories in love and spiritual awakening which
are, of course, coincident with his losses ("I am quite ready to ad-
mit that I am alone"). But such résumés are merely pretexts—the texts
themselves, "provocative but baffling", weave a continuous meditation
upon a series of thematic oppositions—self against others or solitude,
presence in place and time against all the elsewheres of absence, art
against landscape—so many sermons upon Ashbery's real text: "the
major question that revolves around you, your being here."

Each poem or fiction (the words mean the same: a *made thing,*
what Ashbery calls "the created vacuum") begins with an aporia, a
confession of failure or incompetence, and then builds on that admis-
sion in a difficult welter of pronouns. "I", "you" and "he" are not
easily discriminated, though easily discredited—it is as if Aeschylus
had not yet summoned the second actor from the chorus to argue
against that first great voice, or as if the persons of the drama here,
"the debris of living", were indeed "proposed but never formu-
lated." However, once it is announced that "the system was break-
ing down," or that "the problem is that there is no new problem",
then the contraption can get started: "the note is struck, the develop-
ment of its resonances ready to snap into place. For the moment we
know nothing more than this." And by degrees, in a prose so un-
featured by nomination (the only allusions are to the Tarot deck,
Childe Roland, Don Quixote and Alice—all famous problems them-

selves), so unfettered to events ("things will do the rest . . . I re-
nounce my rights to ulterior commemoration"), that we are forever
in danger of wandering from its project, the poems rise to their odd
altitude, what Ashbery calls "an erect passivity," on their own
apotropaics, "no live projection beyond the fact of the words in
which they were written down."

And indeed Ashbery *wants* us to elude the notion of project—it is
only when he has warded off choice and emphasis that the poem has,
literally, the chance to assume its life—until then, "one senses only
separate instances and not the movement of the fall." Again, "noth-
ing is to be learned, only avoided"; *then* the text which started up
in self-erasure and which persisted in an articulation of emptiness,
can come to its end in fulfillment, its conclusion in Being, "a place
of ideal quiet" on which the world is merely a comment, a diacritical
marking. "All the facts are here, and it remains only to use them
in the right combination," Ashbery exults, for he knows that the
"right combination" must exclude any helping hand from *him*.
Such is the "cost that reality, as opposed to naturalness, exacts," he
muses, and it is an enormous cost, for it makes the poet's problem our
own: "Our apathy can always renew itself."

As long ago as *The Tennis Court Oath*, Ashbery had operated by
a prosody of intermittence and collage; here, for the same reason—to
make poems which are, rather than which are *about*, the world—he
invokes a poetics of continuity and encirclement ("I am to include
everything: the furniture of this room, everyday expressions, as well
as my rarest thoughts and dreams . . . the odd details resolved but
nesting in their quirkiness, free to come and go"), the enterprise now
being to get it all in rather than to leave it all out, as in the notorious
"cut-up" poems like "Europe" of over a decade ago. That is why
Three Poems must be in prose, the sole medium capable of cancelling
itself out, of using itself up: the texts must be capable of proceeding
without John Ashbery. How perfectly he knows this! "There comes
a time when what is to be revealed actually conceals itself in casting
off the mask of its identity." *Three Poems* marks that time.

Poetry, 1972

Self-Portrait in a Convex Mirror by John Ashbery

"I wrote in prose because my impulse was not to repeat myself,"
Ashbery told an interviewer about his last book, *Three Poems*. His
present one is again response to those elements of recuperation, of
recurrence and reversion which poetry—even such seamless poetry
as Ashbery's, which observes beginnings and ends by a prosody of

intermittence and collage rather than any such conventional markings as rhyme or repetition—is taken to incarnate, if not to incorporate. He has returned to returning—hence the self-portrait, hence the mirror, hence the convexity: "crooning the tunes, naming the name."

The subject of the self-portrait is the same new thing: if it is all there, the world, "this angle of impossible resolutions and irresolutions", then how do I get into it, how do I find a place in what is already *given,* and if I am already there, how can there be room for all that, "the many as noticed by the one"? The book is a series of meditations on this dilemma:

> And am I receiving
> This vision? Is it mine, or do I already owe it
> For other visions, unnoticed and unrecorded
> On the great relaxed curve of time . . .

long, radiant visions, cross-cut by the usual (usual for Ashbery: no one else could accustom us to "this painful freshness of each thing being exactly itself") opacities of diction and association which— "mutterings, splatterings"—one may like or loathe, depending . . . There is no choice, however, about the title poem and half a dozen others, which are, as everyone seems to be saying, among the finest things American poetry has to show, and certainly the finest things Ashbery has yet shown. "It's all bits and pieces, spangles, patches, really; nothing / stands alone," the poet has written since the book, and we must weave his observation back into the warp of what he calls "a complicated flirtation routine". When I speak of the wide-spread admiration for Ashbery's work, I do not mean to patronize him or his detractors; we are confronted with an utterance at times consistently firm, cool, inclusive, and resolute (and by "times" I mean pages and pages of verse—not since Wallace Stevens, indeed, has there been a voice in which "changes are merely / features of the whole"), and at times by verbal tantrums as preposterous as anything in the long lineage of self-indulgence; as the poet himself glosses the situation: "I tried each thing, only some were immortal and free." But in this book as in no other, the brooding seems to get out from under the allusive looniness that was always Ashbery's resource when the going got rough or smooth; *the ride,* as he says *continues,* and we are presented with "the major movement as a firm digression, a plain that slowly becomes a mountain." The poet, ruminating upon his relation to the past, especially upon the greatness of the past, and to the future, especially upon the grotesquerie of the future, is quite conscious of his idiopathy—as conscious as any of his critics:

> I know that I braid too much my own
> Snapped-off perceptions of things as they come to me.

They are private and always will be.
Where then are the private turns of event
Destined to boom later like golden chimes
Released over a city from a highest tower?
The quirky things that happen to me, and I tell you,
And you instantly know what I mean?

They are here, those private turns of event, and as Ashbery re-
marked to his interviewer, "in this kind of meditative verse the
things in a room and the events of everyday life can enter and be-
come almost fossilized in the poems." What keeps them from be-
coming entirely fossilized, what keeps the concrete from becoming
concretion and calculus, lethally lithic, immobile, is the sense of
before and after, the movement of time which washes through these
pages, these long-winded portages across "this wide, tepidly mean-
dering, civilized Lethe" which else would become "choked to the
point of silence."

"*The history of one who came too late*," Ashbery puts it in his
wonderful poem "As You Came from the Holy Land" (where Harold
Bloom was quick to seize upon it, exhibit A in the endless catalogue
of belatedness which for him constitutes poetry's knowledge of
itself); yet in the title poem, Ashbery puts it conversely: "*All we
know / is that we are a little early*": we are here, or there, and the
rendezvous has not been kept:

> . . . *everything is surface. The surface is what's there*
> *And nothing can exist except what's there* . . .

So speaks a man whom the world has failed, who is not yet fulfilled
by anything except his own existence, his abashed solipsism. The
point is not to decide, to determine whether one is early or late,
ahead of time or behind *the times* (the past of Parmagianino's por-
trait, which alas Viking Press has failed to reproduce just where and
when we need it, on the book jacket); the point is to discover there
is movement, change, and a linking-up, a being-in-league, however
bewildering, with all the rest. Again and again, in his room, or under
a tree, or looking at an old photograph (girls lounging around a
fighter bomber, 1942!), the poet has occasion to remind himself of
the recurrence—it is why he has returned to verse, why he has
reversed—of the reversion:

> *There is some connexion . . . among this. It connects up,*
> *Not to anything, but kind of like*
> *Closing the ranks so as to leave them open.*

For me the opacities, what used to register as accidents, are now
assimilated into the mastery, so that as John Hollander says, what

lingers on after their startlingness is their truth. The poet seems to me (it is what I mean by mastery) to have gained access to a part of his experience which was once merely a part of his imagination: he has made his experience and his imagination identical:

> *It is both the surface and the accidents*
> *Scarring the surface . . .*
> *These are parts of the same body.*

And this incorporation, this embodiment has required of his talents that he leave off prose; that he shed those aberrational nuttinesses which are so alluring that "to get to know them we must avoid them"; that he move in on his visions with all the instruments, the devices, the pharmacopoeia of, say, a Parmigianino; as Ashbery says, and never has he proved more accurate about himself, though the proof of the accuracy must *be* himself:

> *The great formal affair was beginning, orchestrated,*
> *Its colors concentrated in a glance, a ballade*
> *That takes in the whole world, now, but lightly,*
> *Still lightly, but with wide authority and tact.*

Poetry, 1976

Houseboat Days by JOHN ASHBERY

After the garland of prizes bestowed in docile succession upon *Self-Portrait in a Convex Mirror*, it is apparent that we have entered a new phase of Ashbery criticism, one we might call post-favorable. I doubt if it is more helpful (though I can see it is more highfalutin) to say, with John Brinnin, that Ashbery's "dazzling orchestrations of language open up whole areas of consciousness no other American poet has even begun to explore" than it was to say, with John Simon in the bad old days, that Ashbery's poems were "garbage". But it would appear that with this new book we are in the presence of a Figure who need not abide our question, "a living contemporary who should be beyond all critical dispute" (Harold Bloom). Here is the opening of a poem, "Bird's-Eye View of the Tool and Die Co.," which I promise is neither harder nor softer than many others in the book, though it begins with a nice reversal of Proust's first line:

> *For a long time I used to get up early.*
> *20-30 vision, hemorrhoids intact, he checks into the*
> *Enclosure of time familiarizing dreams*
> *For better or worse. The edges rub off,*
> *The slant gets lost. Whatever the villagers*

Are celebrating with less conviction is
The less you. Index of own organ-music playing,
Machinations over the architecture (too
Light to make much of a dent) against meditated
Gang-wars, ice cream, loss, palm terrain.

I should say that was beyond critical dispute, or should be, simply because it is largely inaccessible to critical procedure. Fortunately (for my enterprise) not all of Ashbery's work in his new book resists analysis or even interest so successfully. There is a great deal of poetry which is indeed beautiful and beguiling and benign in its transactions with our understanding; quite as characteristic as the teratoma I have just instanced is the *whole poem* "Blue Sonata", of which I quote the close, thereby giving equal time to the amazing clarity of this celebrated opacifier:

. . . It would be tragic to fit
Into the space created by our not having arrived yet,
To utter the speech that belongs there,
For progress occurs through re-inventing
These words from a dim recollection of them,
In violating that space in such a way as
To leave it intact. Yet we do after all
Belong here, and have moved a considerable
Distance; our passing is a facade.
But our understanding of it is justified.

Most of the poems in *Houseboat Days* which I can make out at all are like this bit, deliberations on the meaning of the present tense, its exactions and falsifications, its promises and rewards. "There are no other questions than these, / half-squashed in mud, emerging out of the moment / we all live, learning to like it"—Ashbery is often painfully clear as to what he would wring from his evasive experience ("what I am probably trying to do is to illustrate opacity and how it can suddeny descend over us . . . it's a kind of mimesis of how experience comes to me"), and the pain is there in the tone, now goofy and insolent, then again tender and self-deprecating, vulnerable but not without its gnomic assertions ("It is the nature of things to be seen only once"), various but not without a consistent grimace ("It's all bits and pieces, spangles, patches, really; nothing / stands alone").

The position from which these proceedings flow and flare is rather the converse of what I read in the *Self-Portrait*. Here there is a cool resolution about the dialectic of self and other; the poet seems more or less content (more or less sad) to be at grips with "this tangle of impossible resolutions and irresolutions", but only *for now.* The trouble, and his subject, is that the moment passes, that *now* becomes *then,* losing everything in the process. Whatever is easy-moving, free and pleasant tends to calcify or to rot, leaving dust and ash on the mind's plate: "The songs decorate our notion of the world / and mark its limits, like a frieze of soap-bubbles."

Whence a prosody, as I have called it, of intermittence and collage; no such conventional markings as rhyme or repetition—rather, *seamless verse,* jammed rather than enjambed, extended rather than intense; it must go on and on to keep the whole contraption from coming round again, and to work upon us its deepest effect, which is a kind of snake-charming. Quotation occasionally reveals the allure, but not the sense of endless possibilities, of merciless hopes:

> . . . . *To praise this, blame that,*
> *Leads one subtly away from the beginning, where*
> *We must stay, in motion. To flash light*
> *Into the house within, its many chambers,*
> *Its memories and associations, upon its inscribed*
> *And pictured walls, argues enough that life is various.*
> *Life is beautiful. He who reads that*
> *As in the window of some distant, speeding train*
> *Knows what he wants, and what will befall.*

The passage is from the title poem, which refers specifically, I believe, to living in the present, one's domicile upon an inconstant element, one's time at the mercy and the rigor of the stream: "The mind / is so hospitable, taking in everything / like boarders, and you don't see until / it's all over how little there was to learn / once the stench of knowledge has dissipated . . ." The misery in this poem, as in all the rest, is that of being deprived by the past and the future of the present; it is only now that the poet can see and seize the clutter as fertilizing, "not just the major events but the whole incredible / mass of everything happening simultaneously and pairing off, / channelling itself into history": experience is wrenched away—is no longer "his"—by the suspect neatness of memory, as by the sacrificial omissions of art, and so these poems are not to record a life, they are not memorials, any more than they are to decorate a tradition, they are not monuments. "What I am writing to say is, the timing, not / the contents, is what matters"—hence almost anything will turn up inside these "parts of the same body", and almost anyone—any pronoun—will become someone else. With a grim chuckle (he actually spells it out: "but perhaps, well, heh heh, temper the wind to the shorn lamb . . .") Ashbery twitches the text away from personality: "I don't think my poetry is inaccessible . . . I think it's about the privacy of everyone." And perhaps that is why they present such brutal clarifications: the privacy of everyone is a hard thing to acknowledge, especially when it is staring at you from the page, hysterically open to distraction, eager to grab the language of packaging and put it into the *perpetuum mobile* of poetry. The texts include everything, they leave out only the necessary transitions and gear-shifts which we call narrative and which have traditionally governed the decorum of our attention. In such a world, "things overheard in cafes assume an importance previously reserved for letters from the front"—and indeed, the front itself shifts to the back room, the view from the kitchen window, the voices overheard in the next bedroom. Of course no poem can keep pace with "eventuality," with the character and quality of existence as it becomes event —not even Ashbery's poem can satisfy him as to the scope and focus of "the present"—but the zany failures mount up as the only important enterprise, undertaking, overdrive:

> *And we made much of this sort of materiality*
> *That clogged the weight of starlight, made it seem*
> *Fibrous, yet there was a chance in this*
> *To see the present as it never had existed . . .*

The point or the patch is to be at the center of things, the beginning: better not prepare any received standard version of history or fable, "reread this / and the past slips through your fingers, wishing you were there." Better still, take the lesson of painting, which is always in the present, always on hand or it is nothing. So Ashbery's poems will be meditations on how to write his poems, where to begin in order always to be beginning, without that dying fall of classical recital, instead inscribed upon the evanescence of eternity: "a final flourish / that melts as it stays." Painting and music too will help—take the string quartet:

> *The different parts are always meddling with each other,*
> *Pestering each other, getting in each other's ways*
> *So as to withdraw skillfully at the end, leaving—what?*
> *A new kind of emptiness, maybe bathed in freshness,*
> *Maybe not. May be just a new kind of emptiness.*

That is the risk this poetry takes, of course: by jettisoning the traditional baggage of the art and assimilating instead the methods and "morality" of the other arts (though not architecture: Ashbery is against architecture the way his critics have learned to be against interpretation), the poet incurs the possibility of "maybe just a new kind of emptiness." But the risk is worth it to Ashbery, who has never dismissed the religious possibility of emptiness—affectlessness, abjection—as *the* condition of fulfillment. (Has he not written, in *Self-Portrait*, "there is some connexion . . . among this. It connects up, / not to anything, but kind of like /closing the ranks so as to leave them open", where he sounds kind of like a SOHO Simone Weil.) It is worth what I call the risk and what he would call the necessity of emptiness—boredom, confusion, irritation, even torment—to reach what he undoubtedly and diligently *does* reach, a world whose terms are refreshed to the point, to the pinnacle, where experience is without anxiety because it is *delivered*, in both senses of that word: presented and released. A world without anxiety, without repression, without the scandal and the labor of the negative. Or as Ashbery puts it:

> *Something*
> *Ought to be written about how this affects*
> *You when you write poetry:*
> *The extreme austerity of an almost empty mind*
> *Colliding with the lush, Rousseau-like foliage of its desire*
> *   to communicate*
> *Something between breaths, if only for the sake*
> *Of others and their desire to understand you and desert you*
> *For other centers of communication, so that understanding*
> *May begin, and in doing so be undone.*

New York Arts Journal, 1977

ROBERT BLY

"Like Those Before, We Move to the Death We Love."

ORN ON THE western plains of Minnesota, Robert Bly forty years later won the 1968 National Book Award, making in the curious words of its citation "a great leap . . . into a center of resemblances we had not recognized before" and of course mocking that corporate accolade by strong political disavowals which his very acceptance of such success in polite letters enabled him to emblazon. But I do not think Bly was belaureled (with whatever wreath of withered sassafras he might press upon his own brows in preference to Big City bays) for his poems of protest, his abuse of the Great Society and his abhorrence of the Small War ("Driving through Minnesota during the Hanoi Bombings," "Watching Television," "Listening to President Kennedy Lie about the Cuban Invasion"—the present participles in the titles suggest the journalistic immediacy, the lilt of the bulletin in these good intentions); any more than I think Bly has become a certain costive power in contemporary poetry just because of his intemperate, his downright ill-tempered assessments of contemporary poets, or just because of his tendentious magazine *The Sixties*, with its peppery offerings of parody, translation and critique. No, these things are distractions from the genuine achievement and even from the genuine aspiration as the body of Bly's work (a phrase employed advisedly) articulates them; we must not allow the foreground swagger, though expedient to the point of prize-winning and plausible to the point of praiseworthiness, to obscure by its mass and noisiness the real burden of this man's enterprise, latent in almost every poem and lovely beyond the measure of mere socializing energy—the burden, literally, of a body transfigured by the weight of its own death:

> *. . . The wind rises, the water is born,*
> *Spreading white tomb-clothes on a rocky shore,*
> *Drawing us up*
> *From the bed of the land.*
>
> *We did not come to remain whole.*
> *We came to lose our leaves like the trees,*
> *The trees that are broken*
> *And start again, drawing up from the great roots; . . .*
> *Men who live out*
> *A second life.*
>
> *That we should learn of poverty and rags . . .*
> *And swim in the sea,*
> *Not always walking on dry land,*
> *And, dancing, find in the trees a saviour,*
> *A home in dark grass,*
> *And nourishment in death.*

It is the characteristic Bly contract, a stipulation that in order to escape a living death, *i.e.*, a life which is no more than life in a dying body, the self must renounce its very principle of individuation, must invite death into the body not as a mere nothing at the end but as a positive force throughout, "a saviour, a home," dialectically unified with life; of course, when death and life unite in this inextricable trope, identity must be surrendered—that is what is meant when death is referred to as "the great leveller," not extinction but indistinction: going over to the majority, as the saying goes. And the terms of the contract afford the characteristic Bly music—lagging, irregular, profound, and casting about the image, the image alone, a kind of ontological glamor which leaves unattended so many other kinds of decorum, of propriety, of *keeping* which we may find, or hope to find, in poems; rhetorical splendor, rhyme, a rhythm constructed or at least contested by more than the drawing of breath, wit, elevation, even humor—none of these, but "a poetry in which the image comes forward and much more is said by suggestion . . . a poetry which disregards the conscious and the intellectual structure of the mind entirely and by the use of images, tries to bring forward another reality from *inward* experience." Robert Bly's own account of his undertaking suggests here how much he is willing to give up in order to gain what he must have even without much order, and how—by disregarding the usual congruity of the waking mind—he may even risk spoiling his finest things by an unregarded (or at least unguarded-against) intrusion of factitious material. I have twice used ellipses in the poem just quoted to indicate the omission of a line (not of a verse—Bly does not write verses, with all that the word implies of a return, a commitment to a constant; he writes *lines*, with all that the linear implies of a setting out, a movement in search of a form rather than *within* a form); in each case, the omitted line refers to the kind of specific situation which may have been the genesis of the poem, the grain of grit transcended by the pearl, but which is now irrelevant to the achieved form. In the second stanza, the elided line is "Like mad poets captured by the Moors," and in the third, "That we should taste the weed of Dillinger"—both allusions to the kind of external victimization it is Bly's special grace to refute and exceed by setting all of his poems under the sign—playful, reverent—of Jacob Boehme, who said (and Bly used the saying as the epigraph to his first book in 1962, *Silence in the Snowy Fields*) "we are all asleep in the outward man." Discarding the circumstantial husk, then, it is the inward man Bly is centrally concerned with, though it is not in fact a matter of giving up one thing for another, but rather of permitting reality and circumstance to penetrate each other. Boehme says, "As God plays with the time of this outward world, so also should the inward divine man play with the outward in the revealed wonders of God in this world," and Bly makes what he can of this when he says he "tries to bring forward another reality from inward experience"—that experience where, in an unprovable but not improbable sense, we are all awake. Some weight should be placed upon that "tries," for the "center of resemblances" the National Book Award citation referred to is one which Bly does not always himself recognize or relish or even regard, I believe—how could he? It is an unexplored region he is prospecting, a realm in which there is no such thing as work, sexual differentiation or individuality as we know it in our conscious lives. The "resemblances," then, are not to what we experience—the fall from eternity into time, the vain project of the part to become independent of the whole *—but to what we merely aspire to, what we long for. "I want to be a stream of water falling," Bly begins one of these ventures, though he is so tentative that he must still confuse the issue, which is one of the divine body, with the trappings of the body politic, and he calls his poem—for the most specious reasons—"John F. Kennedy":

I want to be a stream of water falling—
Water falling from high in the mountains, water
That dissolves everything,
And is never drunk, falling from ledge to ledge, from glass to glass . . .
I will carry the boulders with me to the valley.

* In "A Man Writes to a Part of Himself" Bly asks, and in his voice there is the despair of many dark nights: "Which of us two then is the worse off? / and how did this separation come about?"

Then ascending I will fall through space again: . . .
And when I ascend the third time, I will fall forever,
Missing the earth entirely.

In the same book—his second, *The Light Around the Body*, published in
1967 and whose title shows how urgently Boehme is again invoked for
the assurance, the ease of a doctrinal authority: "for according to the
outward man, we are in this world, and according to the inward man,
we are in the inward world . . . since then we are generated out of
both worlds, we speak in two languages, and we must be understood
also by two languages"—Bly rewrites the pseudo-Kennedy poem as
"The Hermit," evidently having realized its proper nature as a vision-
ary recital rather than a satirical lament, and by the final, obsessive
image, to which we shall return, of the open sea (in Minnesota!) the
poet reaches rather than merely reaches *for* that area of discourse
where all is transformed because all is reborn:

> *Darkness is falling through darkness,*
> *Falling from ledge*
> *To ledge.*
> *There is a man whose body is perfectly whole . . .*
> *Darkness is gathered in folds*
> *About his feet.*
> *He is no one. When we see*
> *Him, we grow calm,*
> *And sail on into the tunnels of joyful death.*

There was a fantasy of early Alexandrian philosophy which the
heretics of the Renaissance affected to revive and which achieves a
more genuine avatar in such poems as Bly's "Hermit"—the supposition
that the human race is an incarnation of those angels who, in the revolt
of Lucifer, were neither for Jehovah nor for His enemies. The very
beings a Dante scorns as unworthy alike of heaven and hell Bly accepts
in his own figure, inhabitants (or inhabitant: there is only one person
in this little apocalypse, as if all events were to occur inside a single
infinite body:

Inside the veins there are navies setting forth,
Tiny explosions at the water lines,
And seagulls weaving in the wind of the salty blood . . .

Now we wake, and rise from bed, and eat breakfast!—
Shouts rise from the harbor of the blood,
Mist, and masts rising, the knock of wooden tackle in the sunlight.
Now we sing, and do tiny dances on the kitchen floor.

Our whole body is like a harbor at dawn;
We know that our master has left us for the day.

"Our master" being the god that, in Groddeck's phrase, lives us while
we sleep, and it is to be noted that Bly casts, or casts off, his apocalyp-
tic metaphor in terms of a harbor scene, an embarkation, a setting out
to sea) of a middle world in which life takes no sides and settles no
great causes and indeed makes great refusals. There is in the very *façon*
of all these poems, in their repetitions and slacknesses, in their organic
fatigue that would send them into the ground for repose:

My body hung about me like an old grain elevator,
Useless, clogged, full of blackened wheat.
My body was sour, my life dishonest, and I fell asleep.

Now I want to go back among the dark roots;
I want to see nothing more than two feet high;
I want to go down and rest in the black earth of silence—

there is here a numbness or torpor, an inertia so new to art, which by
its traditional nature is the celebration of energy, of mastery, that
Robert Bly himself is not always certain of its accommodation in his
utterance; he suffers and thereby celebrates the inertia of a being who
would be saved, redeemed, not because he is he, but because he is here,
merely present with all the lethargy of a life which contains death—
and it is the requisite wonder of Bly's poetry that the physical qualities
of his language rehearse and enhance the containment, loyal to their
artlessness from the start, unwavering in their oscitance. It is his
uncertainty we hear, I think, when he says—as he sourly said in
1960—"our poetry, because of its clinging to things and to the surface
of life, has tended to become too barren"; or when he seizes upon the
sumptuous negations of a Neruda and renders them in his own embed-
ded accents, tendentiously *taking possession:*

. . . the extraordinary testimony I bring forward
with brutal efficiency and written down in the ashes,
is the form of oblivion that I prefer,
the name I give to the earth, the value of my dreams,
the endless abundance which I distribute
with my wintry eyes, every day this world goes on . . .

On these occasions he is making the gestures of a man possessed to the
point of self-suppression by his subject—not waving but drowning, as
it were. We must examine what his work betrays but does not parade,
what it reveals but does not translate—a sense of the center sufficiently
indicated, perhaps, if we say, merely, that all the poems, as we pick

them up one after the other, are seen to be *marinating:* they are all at sea.

I have referred to the "real burden" of Bly's poetry, and I have suggested that it coincides with Bly's real body—beyond or beneath the factitious encumbrance of his journalistic protest, though the outrage registered there, the objurgations rehearsed in these snake-dances, torchlight songs and rallying chants are anything but factitious: "We were the ones we intended to bomb!" he gasps, adding a darker outlook to Miss Moore's deep insight that there never was a war which was not inward, when he declares:

> *We long to abase ourselves*
>
> *We have carried around this cup of darkness*
> *We have longed to pour it over our heads*
>
> *We make war*
> *Like a man anointing himself*

—and beyond or above the factual record of those bleak, blatant midwestern landscapes, empty towns and choking farms, the history-less scenery of Wisconsin and Minnesota and Ohio whose reliance, for expression, on a set of declarative aspects ("one thing is also another thing") precludes drama or compression or humor; the real burden, then, of Bly's poetry, the corporal burden which distends language beyond the observation it can accommodate, until it sags into a statement it may no longer bear but merely deliver:

> *North of Columbus there is a sort of torpid joy:*
> *The slow and muddy river,*
> *The white barns leaning into the ground,*
> *Cottonwoods with their trunks painted white,*
> *And houses with small observatories on top,*
> *As if Ohio were the widow's coast, looking over*
> *The dangerous Atlantic.**
> *Now we drive north past the white cemeteries*
> *So rich in the morning air!*
> *All morning I have felt the sense of death;*
> *I am full of love, and love this torpid land.*
> *Some day I will go back, and inhabit again*
> *The sleepy ground where Harding was born.*

---

* Again, it is worth remarking Bly's discovery of the sea very close to the surface, wherever he is. Dry land is forever jeopardized, and validated, by the encroachment of that old catastrophe, the Flood: "the ground this house is on, / only free of the sea for five or six thousand years."

—the real burden of this poetry ("there is another darkness, / a darkness in the fences of the body") is one qualified throughout as *latent*, and we shall best come to terms with it, I believe—indeed, the terms we shall come to are what Boehme calls Adam's language, a sensual speech free from distortion and illusion, the language man will recover when he recovers paradise—if we dawdle somewhat over the sense of the word itself, in which the Sanskrit word for darkness transpires: when we say a significance is *latent* we mean that it lies, sunk as of its own weight, below the surface, in darkness, brought down by some oppression to that torpor, that inertia which need not show itself ("the clay is sending her gifts back to the center of the earth")—and we realize, with Skeat's help, that at least since the Greeks the word *latent* and the word *lethargy* have had the same root sense, have grown from the same dark ground. I have already deliberated a little on the phenomenology of lethargy in Robert Bly's poems, on the fact that he is the first laureate of "something inside us / like a ghost train in the Rockies / about to be buried in snow!" But now we can move in on a greater sense of this conjugation of the hidden and the heavy, the sense given when we remember that the concealed current, the buried river carrying all our experience out to sea is precisely the stream the Greeks called *Lethe:*

> *The black water swells up over the new hole.*
> *The grave moves forward from its ambush . . .*

And just as we must renounce, in order to be reborn to the divine body, all that we know, all that we remember, by immersion in that water of oblivion, we must also accept a kind of dying, a dying to ourselves; we must accept, Robert Bly murmurs, what is *lethal:*

> *There is a joyful night in which we lose*
> *Everything and drift*
> *Like a radish*
> *Rising and falling, and the ocean*
> *At last throws us into the ocean,*
> *And on the water we are sinking*
> *As if floating on darkness . . .*
> *Then the images appear:*
> *Images of death,*
> *Images of the body shaken in the grave,*
> *And the graves filled with seawater; . . .*
> *Then shall the talkative be silent,*
> *And the dumb shall speak.*

It remains merely (merely!)—relying on Boehme's Fifth Mystical Point that "Imagination is gentle and soft, and resembles water, but desire is harsh and dry, like a hunger that leads the nothing into something"—to trace this buried sea through the inland inertias of Robert Bly's poems, to collect, then, a little garland of kelp from the great plains. We start with the first poems in the first book, the "eleven poems of solitude," where the Ordeal by Water is of course the Trauma of Birth, and the longing to return to the womb is the longing for an introjected, incarnate ocean, as Ferenczi would call it:

> *We want to go back, to return to the sea,*
> *The sea of solitary corridors*
> *And halls of wild nights,*
> *Explosions of grief,*
> *Diving into the sea of death . . .*
> *What shall we find when we return?*
> *Friends changed, houses moved,*
> *Trees perhaps, with new leaves.*

And if the night is naturally construed as an oceanic envelopment, "an asylum of waters," the day too has its transfiguration-by-drowning to offer:

> *The new dawn sings of beaches*
> *Dazzling as sugar and clean as the clouds of Greece,*
> *Just as the exhausted dusk shall sing*
> *Of the waves on the western shore.*

Then, in the title poem of the ensuing section, "Awakening," we endure that process of penetration to sources, to centers and surds required by the epigraph to which I have alluded, Boehme's observation that "we are all asleep in the outward man"; from the long past into the long present we submit ourselves—

> *As the great wheel turns around, grinding*
> *The living in water.*
> *Washing, continual washing, in water now stained*
> *With blossoms and rotting logs,*
> *Cries, half-muffled, from beneath the earth, the living*
> *   awakened at last like the dead . . .*

—and our past life appears, Bly would say, as a wake behind us: "I am a ship, skirting a thousand harbors. The voyage goes on. The joy of sailing and the open sea!" In a poem of this group called "Unrest" the ship-figure is extended to piracy, of course, to a buccaneer's raid on the absolute: "This is the last dance, the wild tossing of Morgan's seas, / the division of spoils," and the gleeful destruction is echoed and enhanced to its ultimate sense in "Night":

I feel a joy, as if I had thought
Of a pirate ship ploughing through dark flowers.

Alive, we are like a sleek black water beetle,
Skating across still water in any direction
We choose, and soon to be swallowed
Suddenly from beneath.

The triumph of this central group in *Silence in the Snowy Fields*, however, is not one of Bly's countless committals of the body to darkness, depth and inertia, to that "silence on the roads" where "the dark weeds are waiting, as if under water"; it is, rather, a poem of wakefulness, of inspired consciousness, and the only poem in all his *oeuvre* not to be devised or derived "Driving through Ohio" or "Hunting Pheasants in a Cornfield," in that limitless chthonic expanse which so burdens the vertical self; the poem is called, exceptionally, "On the Ferry Across Chesapeake Bay," and because it is the one piece in the canon uttered in the actual presence of the real sea, of course it is that real sea which is put aside ("O deep green sea, it is not for you / this smoking body ploughs toward death"). The waking man, Bly discovers, cannot *bring forward* the images which will substantiate another reality; he must listen, rather, to Nietzsche's advice: "you must be a chaos, to give birth to a dancing star":

On the orchard of the sea, far out are whitecaps,
Water that answers questions no one has asked,
Silent speakers of the grave's rejoinders;
Having accomplished nothing, I am travelling somewhere else . . .
And the sea gives up its answer as it falls into itself.

The closing poems of the book return to the life and to the death-in-life of that Minnesota mariner so amazingly created out of midwestern elements: "I love to see boards lying on the ground in early spring—/ this is the wood one sees on the decks of ocean ships, / wood that carries us far from land . . . / this wood is like a man who has a simple life, / living through the spring and winter on the ship of his own desire . . ." There is nothing taut or wrought about the words, the phrases sink back into silence with all the morose languor of that marooned landscape; yet as Bly insists, in one of the last poems,

Strange muffled sounds come from the sea,
Sounds of muffled oarlocks,
And swampings in lonely bays,
Surf crashing on unchristened shores
And the wash of tiny snail shells in the wandering gravel.

Like Prospero, Bly *drowns* his book with a final image of renunciation: every hope of distinct and certainly of distinguished life is surrendered for the sake of "the true gift, beneath the pale lakes of Minnesota," the treasure beneath the black water:

> *The barn is full of corn, and moving toward us now,*
> *Like a hulk blown toward us in a storm at sea;*
> *All the sailors on deck have been blind for many years.*

"We float joyfully on the dark places," Bly exults in the first section of his second book, *The Light Around the Body*, and though the exultation is more than ever endangered by feedback from the public realm ("Romans Angry about the Inner World" as the title of one poem has it), the conviction persists that everywhere, at any time—even "Hearing Men Shout at Night on Macdougall Street"—

> *The street is a sea, and mud boils up*
> *When the anchor is lifted.*

The accent lies more heavily, in these later poems, on the death to be assimilated to a life little better than a dark probation: "I have already looked beneath the street / and there I saw the bitter waters going down ..." Indeed, in a poem crucially titled "The Fire of Despair Has Been Our Saviour" (no longer may we, "dancing, find in the trees a saviour"), there is none of that jolly submission to the destructive process which gave such a queer nimbus to Bly's discoveries, the sense that "our skin shall see far off, as it does under water," or that "our conversation stiffens the backbone of the sea"; here are rather "images of wasted life, / life lost, imagination mined, / the house fallen, / the gold sticks broken" and an emphasis on the loss rather than on the transfiguration:

> *This autumn, I*
> *Cannot find the road*
> *That way: the things that we must grasp,*
> *The signs, are gone, hidden by spring and fall, leaving*
> *A still sky here, a dusk there,*
> *A dry cornleaf in a field; where has the road gone? All*
> *Trace lost, like a ship sinking,*
> *Where what is left and what goes down both bring despair.*
> *Not finding a road, we are slowly pulled down.*

Yet Bly will not surrender his assurances, granted him by the morality of biology, by the lethargy of a body which must die, by that mortal process in which "the air of night changes to dark water, / the mountains alter and become the sea." The sea is inside him, and the release from selfhood Boehme recognized in Paul's astonishing aphorism:

"There can be no male and no female; for ye are all one man in Christ"
—and so "this grandson of fishes" as Bly calls himself in "Evolution
from the Fish" asserts—though in the unpriestly accents of oblivion,
the Lethean language of inertia—a sacramental stature:

> *This nephew of snails, six feet long, lies naked on a bed*
> *With a smiling woman, his head throws off light*
> *Under marble, he is moving toward his own life . . .*
> *Serpents rise from the ocean floor with spiral motions,*
> *A man goes inside a jewel, and sleeps. Do*
> *Not hold my hands down! Let me raise them!*
> *A fire is passing up through the soles of my feet!*

Nor is it the fire of despair only. "Moving inward at last," as Bly says,
"opening the surfs of the body," there is revealed a giant faith in the
dismembered flesh of this poetry, the substance of things hoped for and
—so far as words can heave them up to the surface of "the vast waters"
—the substance of things had:

> *I have risen to a body*
> *Not yet born,*
> *Existing like a light around the body,*
> *Through which the body moves like a sliding moon.*

EDGAR BOWERS

*"What Seems Won Paid
For as in Defeat."*

IN 1956, Edgar Bowers, a Southerner who had studied with Yvor Winters and served in Germany in the Second World War, surviving both disciplines to become a teacher at the University of California, published his first book when he was in his early thirties. Its twenty-six poems are charged with European experience, formal complacency and literary allusion; even so, the poet claims they are too much "tangled with the error and waste they would complete," and the very way he reaches through the "brain's entangled, mended mesh" to wisdom, "placing ten sounds together in one sound," is Bowers' characteristic gesture; a stoic intensity—the conscious nobility of exheredation that Conrad is always celebrating—is the pervading tone of his language, the temper of his rhythms, as if one were wading upstream through cold mineral-water:

> *I chose to live, who else had found no reason*
> *In vanity's contempt, by simple faith*
> *In what had been before me, and restored*
> *The name of duty to a shadow, spent*
> *Of meaning and obscure with rage and doubt*
> *Intense as cold. My son, who was the heir*
> *To every hope and trust, grew out of caring*
> *Into the form of loss as I had done,*
> *And then betrayed me who betrayed him first.*

This, surely, is artificial in the proper sense—something constructed rather than something generalized, and it is idiosyncratic that Bowers, out of such an unstarred passage in the book's longest poem, "The Prince," has plucked his stern title, *The Form of Loss,* here employed as a synonym for life itself. Little wonder that there should be no profusion of poems of such concentration, nothing included *for good measure* in work of such high specific density, each line "firm in erratic shade and dense with trial of who and what it is"; whether in a first book or at any point in a poet's career, drilling to this depth does not bring in a gusher:

> *My image of myself, apart, informed*
> *By many deaths, resists me, and I stay*
> *Almost as I have been, intact, aware,*
> *Alive, though proud and cautious, even afraid . . .*

What is more curious—a betrayal of the very self immured in all that pride and caution—is the fact that the work is prefaced, interlarded and dispatched with various protocols, epigrams, tail-pieces and dedications of self-diminishing admonition:

> *Mine be the life and failure. But do not look*
> *Too closely for the ghosts which claim my book.*

Bowers is not addressing himself or his reader, certainly, with reference to a maiden voyage, in extenuation or modesty; he is concerned with the entire life of the vessel, and such scholia and prospectuses have an initiatory rather than a defensive function. We are being told to watch our step, to notice the rind a mind must wear in order to survive without being victimized and in order to face, without shrinking, things as they happen on the surface. Prefaces and excusations and passages of reference to the person, as Bacon says, seem to proceed from modesty, yet are but bravery. They are like a fomentation, he goes on, to make the unguent enter—and surely in the ten years before his second little collection (*The Astronomers,* thirteen poems, the last in ten parts), Bowers' readers felt they had every justification to look for his ghosts just as closely as his marmoreal phrasing and chastened vocabulary would allow; had he not evidently looked himself:

> *Little book, you are the white flakes which fell*
> *In several quiet winters, from a sky*
> *Edging abandoned landscape, narrow and strange.*
> *You are the flakes, and all the rest was I,*
> *The sky, the landscape, and the freezing spell.*

Abandoned landscape, narrow and strange! Tell me by whom you are haunted and I will tell you who you are, runs the old surrealist recipe. And surely the ghosts laying claim to Bowers' books are more intimate, more native to his own structure than the militant angels standing guard over Dr. Winters' citadel of decorum, Castle Adamant on the Pacific, their flaming pens forbidding entrance to the flush and flux and flower of experience in favor of its form and formula. Surely what Bowers calls

> . . . *the mind's continual search*
> *To find the perfect note, emotional*
> *And mental, each the other one's reproach . . .*

was his own before it was eulogized by Doctor Winters or even inflected by Valéry and Stevens to a measure that is the stereotype of spiritual manners. Poems on "The Virgin Considered as a Picture"—

> *Yet what her pose conceals we might surmise*
> *And might pretend to gather from her eyes*
> *The final motion flesh gives up to art . . .*

on the Magi, close after Yeats—

> *Far to the east I see them in my mind*
> *Coming in every year to that one place.*
> *They carry in their hands what they must find,*
> *In their own faces bare what they shall face.*

as on Venice—

> *Eternal Venice sinking by degrees*
> *Into the very water that she lights . . .*

all suggest the cost of propriety, the agony of governance in this poet, who does not shrink even from such "literary" emblems of convention, and of conventional control, as centaurs—

> *Once I lived with my brothers, images*
> *Of what we know best and can best become . . .*
> *Now they are all gone. When I prance, the sound*
> *From dark caves where my hooves disturb the dead*
> *Orders no other promise . . .*

Andromache—

> *But memory disserves you where you go*
> *As in the manner of corrupted shades . . .*

and Mozart ("thy sweet and decorous rage"), to rehearse *his* rage for order. This poet is obsessed, is haunted by "chaos come again," and can exorcize it only by a terrible discipline, an acknowledged pain that is, indeed, the form of loss. Laid, conjured out of his verse, quite possibly scared off by so much poetic machinery, the apolaustic ghost, with all its attendant messiness, withdraws, leaving the poems in many cases flat, unsupported and insupportable. But when the wrestling match is on, not "fixed" but in force as we read, when the demon of disorder is beneath the heel of the seraph of constraint but still struggling there, then we get what Bowers calls "the order passion yields," an order necessarily compassing great disorder, the violence inside working out,

> *Until the brain, achieving what is lost,*
> *Assumes the living stone's integrity*
> *And fluid sameness, line by elusive line*
> *Of bitter, Phidian serenity.*

One of Bowers' most surprising gifts, and one that I think comes hard to him, harder even than his surrender of "the warm variety of risk," is his talent for characterization. It can be explained—insofar as any gift can be accounted for by our determination to get at the means as well as the meaning—by Bowers' relative freedom, once he has *embodied* his stratagem in a dramatic situation, to work it out. When he is speaking in his lyric void, neither as himself nor in impersonation, but as the dramatist of bodiless experience, we get a real breach with success:

> *If I can only be as I have been*
> *And yet through timeless time and spaceless space*
> *Vary by chance,*
> *You are the trust which my pretended pain*
> *And hope and purpose form here in the grace*
> *Of circumstance,*
> *The grace I cannot prove but would sustain.*

The poet is addressing death, but the poem is dead already, little but a clever shifting of counters with the appropriate rhymes attached. There is no pressure of the speaking voice against the situation in which it finds itself, and the reader must resist any mastery that seems as mastered as all this. An example of Bowers' inspired way with a *persona* occurs in the same collection as the stanza above, *The Astronomers*, and further reveals, given a passionate intensity which is not always the apanage of "the worst," how much of Dante can be got into the sestet of a sonnet, "In the Last Circle":

> *You are the irresponsible and damned,*
> *Alone in final cold athwart your prey.*
> *Your passion eats his brain. Compulsively,*
> *The crime which is your reason eats away*
> *Compassion, as they both have eaten you,*
> *Till what you are is merely what you do.*

In the earlier book, some of the highest achievements of this high art
are reached by an assumed identity—which after all is what metaphor
is. In a verse letter from "William Tyndale to John Frith," Tyndale's
most loyal disciple imprisoned in England and later burned at the stake,
the reformer urges his heretic follower not to recant:

> *Be certain of your fate. Though some, benign,*
> *Will urge by their sweet threats malicious love*
> *And counsel dangerous fear of violence,*
> *Theirs is illusion's goodness proving fair—*
> *Against your wisdom—worldly innocence*
> *And just persuasions' old hypocrisy.*
> *Making their choice, reflect what you become:*
> *Horror and misery bringing ruin where*
> *The saintly mind has treacherously gone numb;*
> *Despair in the deceit of your remorse*
> *As, doubly heretic, you waste your past*
> *Recanting, by all pitied, honorless,*
> *Until you choose more easy death at last . . .*

Here the person speaking is so exactly expressed by the voice we hear
the poem in, that there is no need for stage properties; the drama is all
in the situation, the character, and the passion generated by their
conflict. The supreme example, in *The Form of Loss*, of this histrionic
encounter of a self and a situation occurs in "The Prince," whose
"doubly heretic" subject is described by the Prince himself, a German
Junker whose son has just been shot; the poem gets under way with a
significant amount of framing apparatus—an ironic Latin quotation
(Virgil vowing to immortalize Nisus and Euryalis) and a dedication
"to the memory of George Emory Humphreys, Killed in France,
1924–1944." Like "Prufrock," which begins with a dedication to a
friend of the poet's who died in the Dardanelles in World War I, and
then a quotation from Dante, "The Prince" is a dramatic monologue of
impotence, the frozen will gulping after glory, and one which by
stricter means achieves as great a success. Only the nobility of Bowers'
speaker will keep this poem from being the representative achievement
of its generation:

> *I come to tell you that my son is dead.*
> *Americans have shot him as a spy.*
> *Our heritage has wasted what it shaped,*
> *And he the ruin's proof. I suffered once*
> *My self-destruction like a pleasure, gave*
> *Over to what I could not understand*
> *The one whom all my purpose was to save.*

Deceit was the desire to be deceived,
For, when I kissesd illusion's face, tears gushed
Warm under anguished eye-lids, and were dried
By new desire that chilled me like a wind—
As if it were defeat being alive
And hurt should yet restore me and be joy,
Joy without cause! . . .
You know despair's authority, the rite
And exaltation by which we are governed,
A state absurd with wrath that we are human,
Nothing, to which our nature would submit.
Such was the German state. Yet, like a fool,
I hated it, my image, and was glad
When he refused its service; now I know
That even his imprisonment was mine,
A gesture by the will to break the will . . .
By what persuasion he saw fit to change
Allegiance none need wonder. Let there be,
However, no mistake: those who deny
What they believe is true, desire shall mock
And crime's uncertain promise shall deceive.
Alas that he was not a German soldier
In his apostasy, but would put on
The parody of what caprice put off,
Enemy in disguise, the uniform
And speech of what the sceptic heart requires! . . .
I who remain perceive the dear, familiar
Unblemished face of possibility
Drenched by a waste profound with accident,
His childhood face concealed behind my face.
Where is the guile enough to comfort me?

In both these poems, the one on Tyndale and "The Prince," their
subject or their center—the will's reversal and search, in its opposite,
for what it lacks in itself—is marvellously mirrored in a device that is
crucial to Bowers' enterprise in general, and consistent with his proce-
dure on every level—theme, rhetoric and rhythm. The device finds its
supreme enactment in what I have called Bowers' ghost—his obsession
with what has to be conquered or surrendered or destroyed in order
that something else may prevail or triumph or merely survive. The
device or figure is called, by the classical rhetoricians, *enantiosis*, mean-
ing a trope which includes and expresses its own opposite; at its
exasperated pitch, it is called *enantiodromia*, meaning a turning-point
where a trope *becomes* its own opposite. The most famous "example"

in English poetry, I suppose, is in Shelley, at the end of *Prometheus Unbound:*

> *to hope till Hope creates*
> *From its own wreck the thing it contemplates.*

This reflexive, dialectical movement is the great character of Bowers' poetry, as so many lines of the fragments from "The Prince" which I have quoted show: "Our heritage has wasted what it shaped, / And he the ruin's proof." "As if it were defeat being alive / And hurt should yet restore me and be joy . . ." "A gesture by the will to break the will . . ." In a sense, *enantiosis* is poetry speaking as it must when it gets to a certain pitch of metaphorical concentration—the pitch Bowers aims at so accurately—a kind of poise where oppositions are seen to be creative, not merely in deadlock. Thus Bowers on Christ:

> *. . . To deck the chiseled cross above the hill*
> *Of Him whom life destroyed and death renewed.*

and in the same poem, "Palm Sunday," at its close:

> *"Yet still I strain to catch a sudden glint*
> *Reflected by the cross from lights that pass*
> *Precisely in their going on the road,*
> *Or from a star, or the empyreal mass*
> *That wheels the dome of night from pole to pole,*
> *Or from the frenzied pit of death itself,*
> *Or from the frame of time, where fire and ice*
> *Ignite and freeze together in the Will*
> *That makes and unmakes thee, O my sweet Christ!*

Less fashionably shriven, and less shrill, is the use Bowers makes of the figure in nature, as in his Valerian triumph "The Mountain Cemetery" —here "the bees renew the blossoms they destroy" and as the poet considers the crumbling tombs, he remarks, "The change that so renews itself is just. . ." for

> *Although the spring must come, it passes too*
> *To form the burden suffered for what comes.*

No wonder Mozart, the subject of two poems, is made the hero of all oppositions, the still point on which all music turns, "the most nearly perfect human pose," as Bowers' Haydn writes to the widowed Constanze. And in the line looping back with the sense that closes on itself to generate a new rhythm, the poet articulates his theme by its weight and movement in the mind:

The weight of cool, of imperceptible dust
That came from nothing and to nothing came*
Is light within the earth . . .

And finally, in his largest apprehension of the enantiotic vision, Bowers' very forms that struggle for permanence against "the darkness which I am" are an enactment of that eternity which is said to be in love with the productions of time; the poem of decorum gains its strength from the very chaos it has overcome. Such gain is the form of loss.

* Emphasis mine.

GREGORY CORSO

"Surely There'll Be Another Table . . ."

No POET likes to be clumsy. But I decided to heck with it, so long as it allows me to speak the truth. If the poet's mind is shapely then his poem will come out shapely." The poet's mind! Surely the last place one would expect to find shapeliness in the case of a poet who has announced, with characteristic, with indeed programmatic glee, "thought is all I know of death." But it is the mind under critical circumstances that Corso intends, the mind in its stretch toward transcendence, when he speaks of his poems as celebrating "an entranced moment in which the mind accelerates"—the speed and the magic are everything here, and the mind itself, "a subterranean lashed to a pinnacle," merely a machine to be driven wild:

> O for that madness again
> Where illusion spoke Truth's divine dialect!

Gregory Corso's decision,* then, to rely upon himself as both medium and message—"I discard my lyre of Orphic futility"—rather than upon an imposition of shapeliness within the conventions of written communication, may be due to his higher loyalty to the art, or to his lack of insight as an artist. In either case, the risk of that decision is our own as we consider, or perhaps a better action would be to *consent to* four

---

* Which he supports by this engaging contention, with its significant admission of fallibility: "I never felt badly about losing my early works because I felt myself to be inexhaustible—like I had a great big supply of this stuff called poetry. The only care I took, and maybe not even that so well, was not to lose the poet. As long as I had the poet I would have the poems." The little concessive clause here suggests that the poet himself is aware of the desperately marginal nature of his enterprise, its swelling omens of failure even in its apocalyptic finding: "Athene requests my unbecoming."

volumes of poems (though almost never of *verse* in any acceptation of
the word collected from the traditional disposition of language ordered
in some regular accord with its metrical possibilities) published be-
tween 1955, when the poet was 25 and had "learned, through Allen
Ginsberg, how to handle myself in an uninstitutional society, as I was
very much the institutional being . . . ," and 1962, when Corso already
promised, though he has as yet failed to produce, a fifth collection with
the rueful but viable title (for a man whom Jack Kerouac once called
Gregory the Herald): "There Is Yet Time to Run Back Through Life
and Expiate All That's Been Sadly Done."

A childhood of destitution and loss, an adolescence of vagrancy and
imprisonment account for Corso's image of himself as an "institutional
being," a youth with the imagination of confinement seeking to effect a
supreme escape ("where all beyond is true Byzantium") yet repeatedly
baffled by his disastrous circumstances, as he translated them in his first
book, *The Vestal Lady on Brattle*, where the poet's *daemon*, "my
vision-agent," is flouted by the surrogate of conformity, "the deserter":

> *I don't know the better things that people know*
> *All I know is the deserter condemned me to black—*
> *He said: Gregory, here's two boxes of night*
> *   one tube of moon*
> *And twenty capsules of starlight, go an' have a ball—*
> *He left and the creep took*
> *   all my Gerry Mulligan records with him.*

And though on the evidence of the enormous publicity Corso has
provoked ("They've reached the moon and I've reached Greece," he
proclaims, the two exploits evidently making an equivalent impact
upon the news agencies of the world and even beyond), the "handling"
Corso congratulates himself upon must seem more a matter of applause
than of restraint, of back- rather than wrist-slapping, still there is no
question that the orphanages of Manhattan, the cells of Clinton Prison,
and the crew quarters of a Norwegian freighter brought the frightened
kid—

> *Candy-colors fade*
> *long pants lead us elsewhere*
> *and a child's hands are getting hair*

—to a poetry of this world: "time a long long dog having chased its
orbited tail comes to grab my hand and leads me into conditional life,"
however freakishly delivered. Corso moralizes his situation in the note
to Donald Allen's anthology of *The New American Poetry*, announc-
ing with the sententiousness also typical of his associates Ginsberg and
Kerouac that "sometimes hell is a good place—if it proves that because

it exists so must heaven. And what was heaven? Poetry." To avoid the institutional, to transcend the System, then, is to deny the systematic. What is wanted is what Bacon called "a knowledge broken," arrived at by broken flesh, broken mind, broken speech—*parataxis* rather than method, exaggeration and grotesquerie rather than generality, excess rather than economy. The onset and origin of such knowledge is, to the poet, a natural mystery—"it comes," he says of his poetry, "a dark arriviste, from a dark river within"—and its presence at the moment of composition, or rather of transcription, for this poetry is a dictation from the Unknown, or as one of his symbolic titles has it, "Notes After Blacking Out," is a bewilderment, even an abnegation:

> *I renounce the present*
> *like a king blessing an epic . . .*
>
> *and I, as though tipping a pitcher of milk,*
> *pour secrecy upon the dying page;*

as for the future, the predictable continuation of such knowledge as poetry affords ("a poet is a spy . . . mankind's spy"), only the example of organic life, preferably in its least accessible forms ("impossible for me to betray even the simplest tree"), supplies the hope of an answer there. It is the kind of power which comes from below the intellect that reminds the poet of his own pulverized responsibilities, his own dashed hopes:

> *And so it's spring again   so what*
> *The leaves are leaves again   no tree forgot.*

Hence a poetry of fragments, of scatterings, even of droppings (one of Corso's regrets about "losing the horror of that 12-year-old Gregory" is the impoverishment of what was once a highly gratifying *Anal-erotik*); regenerative, seminal, fertilizing, but without sequence or lineal order. This is what Allen Ginsberg means, I think, when he says, in his introduction to Corso's second book *Gasoline* (1958), that "he wants a surface hilarious with ellipses" and underlines the organic analogy: "Corso's got the angelic power of making autonomous poems, like god making brooks." * Any process which spreads the self around after the fashion of nature is welcomed as constructive, even the mortal one, for in Corso's Commandments, "poetry is seeking the answer, joy is in knowing there is an answer, and death is knowing the answer." Hence

---

* The second part of this remark of Ginsberg's is distressing: to speak of "autonomous" poems is either a tautology or it is nonsense; but the comparison with (lower-case) god making brooks strikes a good note, and in its context in the introduction the description has the kind of generous rightness Ginsberg's comments characteristically achieve.

in the very properly titled third collection *The Happy Birthday of Death* (1960), one comes across the kind of necrophiliac nursery-rhyme whose tonality, a Gongoristic conjugation of the cute and the heroic, only this poet could get away with, though where he takes it *to* is less apparent than the claustration, the bondage, even, of life itself that he is abducting his consciousness *from:*

> *Let's all die*
> *Let's practice a little*
> *Let's play dead for a couple of hours*
> *Let's everybody weave elegant everlasting cerements*
>   *build fantastic tombs*
>   *carve lifelong coffins*
>   *and devise great ways to die let's!*

What we confront in all these insistent fooleries, each of which has the wonderful quality of assigning itself a new genre even as it hilariously judges itself—

> *I lean forward on a desk of science*
> *an astrologer dabbling in dragon prose*

—Corso will begin, and we think: that's it! dragon prose, and *dabbling* in it, that's just what he does, and then the poet continues with his high or highty-tighty mode which flings us into an ideal uncertainty:

> *knowing my words to be the acquainted prophecy of all men*

—what we must endure in Corso's work is a poetry which insists that its own process, its own fragmentary ritual—

> *No meaning to life can be found in this holy language*
> *nor beyond the lyrical fabricator's inescapable theme*
> *be found the loathed find—there is nothing to find*

—is *all that there is:* no meaning hinted, no symbolism proposed, no subjectivity revealed. For Gregory Corso the escape from inhibition is, merely, exhibition. In fact he does not write poems, he writes only poetry, and his refusal to select, to emphasize, to reject ("any door locked against a man is a sad business") is part of his general revulsion from the dialectic of our culture, in which the notion of weeds is automatically created by the notion of a garden, or as Corso's death-hymn "Bomb" puts it: "to die by cobra is not to die by bad pork." For Corso, like Freud, sees our civilization as one in which not only sexuality is repressed, but any form of transcendence; in the famous closing lines of "This Was My Meal" the bafflement of the orphaned corybant is celebrated, even as it is mourned, in overwhelming images of defeat:

I turned to father
and he ate my birthday
I drank my milk and saw trees outrun themselves
valleys outdo themselves
and no mountain stood a chance of not walking

Dessert came in the spindly hands of stepmother
I wanted to drop fire-engines from my mouth!
But in ran the moonlight and grabbed the prunes.

The great thing, for Corso, is *not to choose*, not to settle for the possible, but to take everything, to invent the new nourishment as well as to feed on the old. "Time takes me by the hand / born March 26, 1930 I am led 100 mph over the vast market of choice / what to choose? what to choose?" And with appropriate appetite and an inventiveness that is really hysterical, Corso answers in his last book, *Long Live Man* (1962):

Surely there'll be another table . . .
Wisconsin provisions
Insufficient when I have absolute dairy visions:
Corduroy eggs, owl cheese, pipe butter
Firing squad milk;
The farmer will never love me
Nor I, he . . .

The impulse to inventory as a form of invention is evident in all of Corso's shrinkings from choice, from singleness, from being "stuck here"; he offers an enormous list of alternative names for his third book of poems, what he calls "saleable titles," my favorites among which are

Fried Shoes
Remarkable
Cars are love
The Wet Sea
The Rumpled Backyard
Caesarean operation . . .

That last is another of his approximations to genre—all of Corso's poems are hasty productions, untimely ripped and never quite free of the shreds and shrieks of selfhood; in fact, he rejoices in a certain fakery, the suggestion that out of the anthology of Being he has never quite chosen, never really made his commitment to anything more than infinite potentiality: "Ah, this surfeit of charlatanry will never leave my organic pyx thank god . . ." He would not be "caught in a single fate," yet Gregory Corso's *poems* are thereby caught, for they cannot be complete or at least completed so long as their author must declare "all life is a rotary club," in the sense of a blunt instrument revolving endlessly, as well as a good-humored civic organization: "I still question if all life is a rotary club and if it's death to resign." And there are moments, beautiful ones, in Corso's production when the poet acknowledges the terrible waste in it all, the debauchery of talent and titanic hopes in his own method, or abnegation of method. Once "death has distributed its categorical blue," once

> *My body's quilt hath split*
> *and the porter sweeps*
> *what was once my meat,*

then the poems as he has dripped and dribbled and spattered them upon existence will have to create Gregory, and no longer Gregory them. Doubt, self-doubt is not a sentiment we expect to find very emphatically registered in Corso's *oeuvre*, but once "the horns are still and marriage drops its quiet shoe," there comes an occasion when the poet confronts what he has not so much made as failed to make of himself; it is a supreme occasion in the revels, and a moment of unsurpassable pathos:

> *Am I the person I did not want to be?*
> *That talks-to-himself person?*
> *That neighbors-make-fun-of person?*
> *Am I he who, on museum steps, sleeps on his side?*
> *Do I wear the cloth of a man who has failed?*
> *Am I the loony man?*
> *In the great serenade of things*
>   *am I the most cancelled passage?*

I think that if we were to seek one hostage to fortune out of Corso's work, one poem that is not merely a collage of high spirits, the "imitation of power" as Corso calls himself in a poem dedicated to Ginsberg, it is to be found smack in the middle of his output, which rises in a long slope to the crowning achievement "Marriage" in the third book, and then diminishes down to mutterings and defensiveness, as in the late "Paranoia in Crete":

> *Just sit here, knees up, amid amphora & aloe*
> *reading lusty potsherd, gobbling figs, needing no one—*
> *mine the true labyrinth, it is my soul, Theseus,*
>   *try a ball of string in that . . .*

The shape, then, is that of a fronton (Corso has been categorical about his architectural affinities in defining his charge: "I must *create* the room of my truth's desire; and then, and only then, may I enter and

dwell in peace and joy"), as the poet corroborates in this beautiful,
Cocteau-haunted distich:

> *The caryatid I am is Truth*
> *Lo! my pediment of Lie*

A glance, then, at this central poem in the pediment, a triumph of 112
lines, necessarily about the impossibility of choosing: "Should I get
married? Should I be good?" The poet runs through a number of
possible girls and what he would do to them, samples their favors and
families:

> *O how terrible it must be for a young man*
> *seated before a family and the family thinking*
> *We never saw him before! He wants our Mary Lou!*

Agonizing over the horrors of the wedding ("And I trembling what to
say say Pie Glue!"), Gregory finds himself protesting over the single-
ness of wedlock, Corso as some kind of wizard of promiscuity at
Niagara Falls:

> *Everybody knowing! I'd be almost inclined not to do anything!*
> *Stay up all night! Stare that hotel clerk in the eye!*
> *Screaming: I deny honeymoon! I deny honeymoon!*
> *running rampant into those almost climactic suites*
> *yelling Radio belly! Cat shovel!*
> *O I'd live in Niagara forever! in a dark cave beneath the Falls*
> *I'd sit there the Mad Honeymooner*
> *devising ways to break marriages, a scourge of bigamy*
> *a saint of divorce . . .*

Yet the prospect of withholding himself from the common fate is just
as painful for Corso as the doom of conformity, and the whole of his
poetic career is summed up in the terrors of the poem's final strophes:

> *Because what if I'm 60 years old and not married*
> *all alone in a furnished room with pee stains on my underwear*
> *and everybody else is married! All the universe married but me!*

And "Marriage" closes with the apocalyptic consolation of an ultimate
energy milked from the universe as the poet milks his own from
himself—it is the final mythological comfort of choosing nothing but
experience, or Everything:

> *Ah, yet well I know that were a woman possible as I am possible*
> *then marriage would be possible—*
> *Like SHE in her lonely alien gaud waiting her Egyptian lover*
> *So I wait—bereft of 2,000 years and the bath of life.*

●　●　●

I suspect that one reason for Corso's silence the last five years is his outrage upon discovering the irreversibility of somatic processes. If he refuses to choose a poetry that is more than "an assembly of great eye sounds," then his body will choose for him, as the later poems testify:

> *My beautiful hair is dead . . .*
> *How to stand thunderous on an English cliff*
> *a hectic Heathcliff?*
> *O my lovely stained-glass hair is dry　　dark　　invisible*
> *　　not there!*
> *Wigmaker! help me!*
> *I want a wig of winter's vast network!*
> *Samson bear with me! Just a moustache . . .*

The capacity to project himself alive and kicking and screaming into every and any possibility is being leached out of Gregory by living, or by *having lived:* "I am 32 years old and finally I look my age, if not more." The last poem in *Long Live Man* finally faces the possibility— and follows it with silence—that the very act of making, the poetic act, is a moral gesture because it involves choosing, the preference of one thing (life) over another (death):

> *I love poetry because it makes me love*
> *　　and presents me life.*
> *And of all the fires that die in me,*
> *there's one burns like the sun;*
> *it might not make day my personal life. . . .*
> *but it does tell me my soul has a shadow.*

It is easy to dismiss the truncated, violent work of Gregory Corso ("I cried," he says at the end, "for that which was no longer sovereign in me, stinking of dead dreams"), and indeed I have quoted in this essay all that I care to recall of his entire output, making my own anthology from the welter of alternatives. So much is a dither of self-promotion, illiteracy and native *strain* that to "care" in the common phrase as Corso himself cares for these productions—

> *Must I dry my inspiration in this sad concept?*
> *Delineate my entire stratagem?*
> *Must I settle into phantomness*
> *and not say I understand things better than God?*

—is to entertain one's prepossessions as a malady and a doom. But in all its vulgarities and distractions and boastings, there lie, disparate, yearning for union and the release of choosing, the elements of a giant art.

ROBERT CREELEY

"I Begin Where I Can, and End When I See the Whole Thing Returning."

W E MAY—and if we are poets we must, or risk bearing nothing else—learn to bear the indignities of success, as we have borne those of failure, in order to get on with the task:

> *The poem supreme, addressed to*
> *emptiness—this is the courage*
>
> *necessary. This is something*
> *quite different.*

The charge is a particularly American lesson (think of the "success" of Gertrude Stein, the "failure" of Melville)—one which requires, at least, a particular diligence of its American students, who are likely to find themselves hoisted up, with wisps of obloquy and neglect still clinging to the anfractuosities of a temperament not yet entirely sanded down by public relations, onto an eminence or, say, a plateau of publicity which surrounds their every utterance with—with platitude, precisely. We Americans are, or are made, leaders on a grand scale before we have left off skirmishing in the gang wars of our poetry, and it must be a strong as well as a good character which can resist all the platforms made available when a desk-top is the only relevant surface. To stick to one's last, as an American poet of achieved success, then, is to abide as well by one's first, is to

> *take oneself*
> *as measure,*

making the world
tacit description
of what's taken
from it

—to pursue one's initial impulse undeterred—and undiluted—by the imitations of oneself which one is urged to bestow upon a world thirsty for reasonable facsimiles, making "a pardonable wonder / of one's blunders."

Diligent, strong and good are surely the epithets which attach to Robert Creeley's aspiring character ("my method is not a / tenderness, but hope / defined"), for this poet shows, in his *poetry* at least, none of the distractions pressed upon him by the tendentious praise of *both* Leslie Fiedler and Hugh Kenner (poetry, what alliances are made in thy name!), by the *imprimatur* of William Carlos Williams and the impertinence of John Simon ("there are two things to be said about Creeley's poems: they are short; they are not short enough"), and most distracting of all, by the clamorous mimicry of his juniors:

The sound of waves killed speech
but there were gestures—

of my own . . .

Steering what he always accounts for as a highly tentative course ("I make a form of assumptions . . . or better, a jerking leap / toward impulse"), the contributor to *Wild Dog, Quagga* and *Fuck You: A Magazine of the Arts* acknowledges in return the "contribution" of the Guggenheim and Rockefeller Foundations to a career which, at just past forty and however uncertain of the Muse's patronage—

But the lady—
she, disdain-
ful, all
in white for

this occasion—cries
out petulantly, is
that all, is
that all

—has conferred upon him the status of a *chef d'école*. The school, though, is one of knocks and pratfalls, an academy of tumbling in which the "grace gained / from falling forward" specifically suggests Frost's account of his own poetics:

I have the habit of leaving my toys where people would be pretty sure to fall forward over them in the dark. Forward, you understand, *and* in the dark.

Indeed, it is astonishing that a poetry which questions so eagerly the very possibility of poetry, even as it queries the constitutive notion of the poet ("the mind's / vague structure, vague to me / because it is my own"), should have become so popular, or at least so influential; but we must remember that the scandal of the negative, the destructive energies of an enterprise of cancellation always light up the sky with an infernal glow. Frost's Myth of Daemonic Incoherence makes peace, Creeley says, with what is easy: there is every excuse for Creeley's war against poetry (for out of it, out of the experience of an impossible end, an intolerable return, comes what poetry is possible to him:

> *and there*
> *it was, a little*
>
> *faint thing*
> *hardly felt, a*
> *kind of small*
> *nothing*

—a poetry of the *given*, whose emphasis is on the feel of specific sites and moments as if they were totally detachable from the rest of life, not to be repeated, discriminated, or even named; the expression in literary form of certain enormous repudiations) but no excuse, unless they would share his *gran rifiuto*, for those who imitate him, even for those who "like" him.

Immensely out in the open now ("in private you are you," Creeley quotes Gertrude Stein aptly, "and in public you are in public and everybody knows that"), exploiting his forebears ("a quiet testament / a song / which one sings, if he sings it / with care"), explaining his followers ("the lines / talking, taking, always the beat from / the breath"), Creeley yet continues to explore his own function—or his failure to function—as a *poet* with a splendid unconcern for external relations, preferring to harbor his most freakish and obvious faults quite as if they were his most original and valuable impulses (and perhaps they are—in any case they are indistinguishable from his virtues in the ultimate effect of his work: thus Creeley quotes Valéry's definition of *lyric* as that mode of poetry in which the content and the form are realized simultaneously—neither one can precede the other as a possibility). So consistent, indeed, with themselves, so characteristic and even queer are Creeley's poems, all collected now in two volumes published—on a field argent, a very narrow rivulet of print between ample meadows of margin—in 1962 (*For Love*) and 1967 (*Words*), that they loom, or unravel, as much more like themselves than they are like any other poems, even poems by William Carlos Williams and Charles Olson. That is an extreme quality, the same quality which makes Gertrude Stein say that American literature is quite alone because in its choosing it has to be without any connection with that from which it is choosing; and in order to account for such extremity I shall have to ignore what is perhaps a certain drift in the course of the poems toward mediation ("now, as I begin to relax," Creeley says, incredibly, "as I grow . . . more at ease in my world, the line can become, as you say, more lyrical, *less afraid of concluding*"). After all, Creeley has chosen to remain alive in the world, which means there are occasions when he has recognized the necessity of relating or concluding or repeating an experience—"it is necessary," he says, "to suppose a continuity, though none comes readily to hand." Indeed, if there is in any conventional sense—remembering that a convention makes easy what would otherwise remain difficult—a *development* in the art of Robert Creeley, it is a development toward not away from extremity, toward the limit of experience which makes it possible to know what the experience is by learning what it is not, and away from the center where things are neighbored, accommodated, solaced by propinquity. What we get in Creeley, what he *wants* to get, or is compelled by his nature to give, is a "hammering at the final edge of contact" (his phrase, from a 1954 note on Williams). He is what Melville calls an *isolato*, not acknowledging the common continent of men, but rather the island of ego, the atoll of solipsism which life itself, as he says in the preface to his novel *The Island* (1963), forces us to leave:

> This island, in which the world will be at last a place circumscribed by visible horizons, is, finally, not real, however tangible it once seemed to me. I have found that time, even if it will not offer much more than a place to die in, nonetheless carries one on, away from this or any other island.

But in a novel, surely, the supposed continuity is more necessary than in poems—that is why Creeley writes poems, not because of some ulterior inclination of literary temperament: * poems are the one chance he has of focussing upon experience without a shift of view or voice ("I grew up on a farm. It gave me that sense of speech as a laconic, compressed way of saying something to someone. To say as little as possible as often as possible"), without, in every sense of the

---

* "I feel poems and prose equally are given me to write; I do not feel *I* create them, I have no patience or sympathy with writing which dictates its concerns as a *subject* proposed by 'choice.' 'Choice' for me is more accurately recognition. I want to live in the world—not 'use' it . . ."

word, *relating*. No connection and above all, no return. This notion of return (of recurrence and therefore of recollection, as Stevens has said that the poet is "he that of repetition is most master") is crucial to any art of verse, as the word *verse* itself indicates—Creeley writes not anti-poems, as has been said, but anti-verses. "The issue is the poem, a single event," Creeley insists, and by issue he means outcome, the specific and reified recognition of the momentary experience: "a poem is some *thing*, a structure possessed of its own organization in turn derived from the circumstances of its making." A poetry without recurrence, then, is a poetry without verse; a poetry without return or ending—

> things continue, but my sense is that I have, at best simply taken place with that fact. I see no progress in time or any other such situation . . . What I think to say is of no help to me—

is a poetry without rhyme or reason (*ratio*); for rhyme and reason do go together, since the aim of both is to bring things to an end in order that they may begin again; a poetry, as Yeats called it, of precision but no rhythms—there is not a single sentence anybody will ever murmur to himself. And that is just what Creeley is after, or rather, he is not *after* something but seeking to be *present* with it: a poetry that cannot be murmured, remembered, but rather encountered, confronted; as his mentor Charles Olson puts it:

> What really matters: that a thing, any thing, impinges on us by a more important fact, its self-existence, without reference to any other thing, in short, the very character of it which calls our attention to it, which wants us to know more about it, its particularity . . .

Experience, then, is for him a matter of separation, the substitution of incoherence for subject matter (hence the titles of Creeley's two books, which are concerned with precisely the subjects most often thought to involve connection, *love* and *language*, and which for Creeley afford a kind of ecstasy of isolation, each instance of the use of his body and of the use of words as discrete, singular, insistently unique:

> *now screaming*
> *it cannot be*
> *the same*)

—and the poem a strategy to avoid pattern (Creeley on Swinburne: "a tedium of accumulation and patterned manner"), to dissolve continuity and what used to be called the *keeping* of imagery; what is sought is the *losing*, an imagery out-of-keeping, an imagery kept out:

an egg of obdurate kind. The only possible reason of its existence is that it has, in itself, the fact of reality and the pressure. There in short is its form—no matter how random and broken that will seem.

This question of the broken form, of something made to be—or to appear—fragmentary, partial, incomplete is of great importance to Creeley's work; "the poems come from a context that was difficult to live in, and so I wanted the line used to register that kind of problem . . . now the truncated line, or the short, seemingly broken line . . . comes from the somewhat broken emotions involved." It is as though the contours of regular form must blur, dim and deceive us until we lose contact. Only the broken surface reveals the truth:

> *tear impression*
> *from impression*
> *making a fabric*
>
> *of pain.*

And the lines of cleavage will be irregular, the lunatic fringe of existence where we "live / on the edge, / looking." *Only disconnect*, Creeley urges; if I forget what *was*, I may be able to exist *now*:

> *. . . in the memory I fear*
> *the distortion. I do not feel*
> *what it was I was feeling. I am im-*
> *patient to begin again, open*
>
> *whatever door it was, find the weather*
> *is out there, grey, the rain then and*
> *now falling from the sky to the wet ground.*

It is the first time in the history of poetry that a man has written a poetry of forgetting:

> *There are ways beyond*
> *what I have here to work with*
> *what my head cannot push to any kind*
>
> *of conclusion*

—a poetry without any of the axiological signs and spells which serve to hold it in the mind; without images or rather with an imagery pulverized beyond the recognition of shared contours, an imagery hugged to the self, "played" close to the chest:

The

> *mind makes*
> *its own*
>
> *forms, looks*
> *into its terror*
>
> *so*
> *selfishly*
>
> *alone. Such*
> *a fact so simply*
>
> *managed there is*
> *no need for any*
>
> *one else.*

—a poetry without rhyme, or rather with a sonority parodied beyond belief, a music jeering at conventional accords:

> . . . rhyme, of course, is to me a balance not only of sounds, but a balance which implies agreement: that's why, I suppose, I stay away from rhymes . . . except for this kind of ironic throwback on what is being said.

—a poetry without any constants in its rhythmic behavior (for when the rhythm is variable, there is no *rhythmic* point in the run-on line: Creeley's enjambments are not a departure from something, but a coming *to* something, a dislocation "until the mind itself is broken, breaks back, *forcing the world to declare itself*"), though its rhythmic behavior is always the same in its very inconstancy, a kind of insistent unpredictability ("the slipshod, half-felt, heart's uneasiness in particular forms") which affords the single self its final locus, an ultimate accommodation of what Shelley said was "conscious, inseparable, one":

> *I wanted*
> *one place to be*
> *where I was*
> *always . . .*
>
> *Oh when regrets stop*
> *and the silence comes*
> *back to be*
> *a place still for us,*

> *our bodies will tell*
> *their own story, past*
> *all error*
> *come back to us.*

There are clusters here, a sense of energies focussed in "the virtues of an amulet / and quick surprise," but no way of telling that the set-up on the page must be one way rather than another, no way of discovering not only that the poem might not have been, but also that it could have been no other way than it is, the two discoveries *together* making what Valéry calls the Beautiful. Hence Creeley's method, a treatment rather than a technique, of destroying expectation, of *forgetting* in order to avoid ending, which would mean having to re-open the healed, scabbed-over trauma—instead, everything is kept raw and ruined here, giving or enforcing the impression both of debris:

> *some echoes,*
> *little pieces,*
> *falling, a dust*

and of contusion, the incurable wound:

> *My nature*
> *is a quagmire of unresolved*
> *confessions . . .*

> *We change, not multiplied but dispersed,*
> *sneaked out of childhood,*
> *the ritual of dismemberment.*

Yet though there can be no doubt about the dismemberment, preferred to any remembering, it is precisely the ritual which is in question, for Creeley's poetry is in opposition to all ceremony, all politeness, which is inevitably a long poem since it is full of recurrences. Here there is but "a drunken derision / of composition's accident" and a mockery of the mnemonic devices we employ to keep experience *in mind:*

> *The mind*
> *fast as it goes, loses*

> *pace, puts in place of it*
> *like rocks simple markers,*
> *for a way only to*
> *hopefully come back to*

> *where it cannot. All*
> *forgets. My mind sinks.*

> *I hold in both hands such weight*
> *it is my only description.*

We hang a jingling padlock on the mind, Pope said, and Creeley would release us from the bondage of that chime, not concerned like his moderate mentor Dr. Williams with the ideas in things (after all, when you say *no ideas but in things* you still assert the possibility of ideas), but with

> *the grit*
> *of things,*
> *a measure*
> *resistant . . .*
>
>   *no*
> *one ever*
> *quite the same.*

When the mind is unlocked, released from any servitude of repetition, when no experience is "quite the same," then we get a poetry without ending and without climax (for climax is what happens when things meet in a form and have an ending), a poetry without recurrence and without memory: a poetry of confession—"I write what I don't know" —of centripetal illumination, of paralyzed auto-fascination. Wordsworth's famous criticism of Goethe—that his poetry was not memorable enough—applies more aptly still to Creeley's fragments of a great confession, save that—and it is literally the *saving grace*—Creeley *wants* no poem remembered, wants each poem to enrich himself and us by what it reveals of his poverty, for in the entrancement of isolated experience the first obstacle to action is the absence of obstacles, of a resisting *norm* from which to vary:

> *. . . the interminable*
> *subject all but*
> *lost to my mind . . .*

The masters of linguistics tell us that there is no reason for the sentence, in its unconditioned state, to end—ever. There is every reason to suppose that we all, unwittingly, spend our lives within one and the same sentence, a single locution which is coterminous with our own bodies. This is what Robert Creeley means when he says that "words are common, and language knows more than one man can speak of"; it is his power (and, as well, his pathos) to have added his voice—sour, stumbling, secretive—to that enormous and obsessive murmur which sometimes rises from literature and which is perhaps its justification, the utterance of our becoming. "There is no more to live," Creeley says darkly in his preface to *For Love*, "than what there is, to live. I want the poem as close to this fact as I can bring it." He has brought his poems so close to that "no more" of his, to that irreducible absorption in what is *there*, that he speaks, or we hear him speak, out of an absolute gist of solitude—honorable certainly and enriching to us, as I have said, though I think too that it must be the greatest impoverishment to live in a world without recurrence, a world where nothing can happen more than once:

> *One is*
> *too lonely, one wants*
> *to stop there, at the edge of*
>
> *conception.*

JAMES DICKEY

"We Never Can Really Tell Whether Nature Condemns Us or Loves Us."

OF THE LATE Randall Jarrell, James Dickey once wrote, in his testy and cormorant collection of critical notes *The Suspect in Poetry:* "He gives you a foothold in a realm where literature itself is inessential, where your own world is more yours than you could ever have thought, or even felt, but is one you have always known." A close description of Dickey's own enterprise, and in its disputed tone (the essay on Jarrell is cast as a dialogue between the critic's warring allegiances to "form" and "life," each achievement "away" from literature being hotly and harshly opposed by the literary conscience, which is an impulse to get words down so they will not escape) a clue to this writer's ultimate yearning—that characteristic American tendency Emerson dramatized when he said "every new writer is only a new crater of an old volcano"—that yearning to transcend, by the flights and frauds of literature, literature itself, until the reader is separated from the writer by no more than his response to his own experience, and then united with that experience by a shared recognition of it.

The adventure of James Dickey's career, the pursuit of a poetry which must, in its transactions with love and death, self and circumstance, be as new as foam and as old as the rock (Emerson again), the heroic quest which is this poet's unending venture begins with an expression already complete, gorged on miracle and complacent as a sphere:

> *. . . a way out of dying*
> *Like a myth and a beast, conjoined.*

> *More kinship and majesty*
> *Could not be,*
> *And nothing could look away* . . .

in a first book of Orphic utterance, the meditative and metaphysical gnomons of *Into the Stone*, published in 1960. Here the poet has categorized, divided up and dealt out, like so many divining suits, his first two dozen poems into traditional categories: family, war, death and love. An imagery of sociability, of killing and of ecstasy is thus the vehicle for ruminations on life, death and resurrection, and so persuasive, so powerful is the plunge the poet takes into the deep well of his discourse that wisdom survives the interchangeability of the parts, vision sustains the replacement of elements, and language, quite simply, serves:

> *I sought how the spirit could fall*
> *Down this moss-feathered well:*
> *The motion by which my face*
> *Could descend through structureless grass,*
> *Dreaming of love, and pass*
> *Through solid earth, to rest*
> *On the unseen water's breast,*
> *Timelessly smiling, and free*
> *Of the world, of light, and of me.*

Free of the world in this wise, the self would put off time and matter and enter the universe of eternal being. But cannot, in safety, without the mediation of ritual, without the traditional politics of vision that hieratically arranges matter (and matters), that ministers and officiates in such negotiations with existence. The characteristic titles of Dickey's poems in this first assay of "animal music"—titles that suggest the archetypal events and symbols of the Grail legend: The Freeing of the Waters, The Fisher King, The Hidden Castle, The Bleeding Lance—"The Underground Stream," "The Vegetable King," "Into the Stone," "Walking on Water"—enforce the boundaries of this poet's world of primaries in experience. Here is a construct of water in lakes and wells ("best motions come from the river"), gold of metals and of the sun ("in this place where the sun is alone / the whole field stammers with gold"), stone of the earth and of the alien moon ("the night's one stone laid openly on the lost waves . . . a huge ruined stone in the sky"). Here nothing develops, grows or changes from its essence, yet everything can be transformed into anything else, the metal sun and stone moon, the winged tree and walking water woven into a net of correspondences thrown over life like a tarnhelm. And the energy that knots these elements together, that thrusts them against each other in har-

mony or thematic opposition, is a circular movement, a conjugation of
rituals: pieties of family, of kingship, of devotion to the divine Other, a
round-dance of service and mastery best expressed, in terms of action,
by the gerundive form. In the poetry of James Dickey, as he first
composes it, there is no end to action, one is always in the process of it:
"Awaiting the Swimmer," "Walking on Water," and most idiosyncrat-
ically, in the title of his second book, *Drowning with Others:*

> *God add one string to my lyre*
> *That the snow-flake and leaf-bud shall mingle*
> *As the sun within moonlight is shining:*
> *That the hillside be opened in heartbreak*
> *And the woman walk down, and be risen*
> *From the place where she changes, each season,*
> Her death at the center of waiting.

That is Dickey's Orpheus on his Eurydice, and the shape of it is
typical: the concluding stanza of five, heavily yet loosely anapaestic,
finished off with a refrain, a repeated and ever-varying comment
which refers the substance of the poem ("Orpheus Before Hades") to
something very old and very early underlying it. Here the last line has
been:

> . . . Whose leaf is the center of waiting . . .
> . . . And white is the center of waiting . . .
> . . . Where love is the center of waiting . . .
> . . . When flesh is the center of waiting . . .

and by the time we reach Eurydice's *"death at the center of waiting"*
we have a kind of morphology of the refrain as Dickey uses it, so that
as the poet himself does in another poem, we can put the refrain lines
together at the end of the poem and have yet another poem, a kind of
mythographic gloss on the experience presented, a marginalia which
accounts for and perhaps justifies the separate poem in this ritual
universe. The device is one taken over from Yeats; the rhetoric Val-
erian:

> *Like a new light I enter my life*
> *And hover, not yet consumed,*
> *With the trees in holy alliance,*
> *About to be offered up . . .*

and the tone, caught from Roethke and perhaps from such contempo-
rary French poets as Char and Supervielle, is achieved by the prepon-
derance of end-stopped lines, a succession of aphorisms that remind us
of the earliest wisdom-literatures and stun the mind thirsting for some
Becoming by their insistent fixities:

I take my deep heart from the air.
The road like a woman is singing.
It sings with what makes my heart beat
In the air, and the moon turn around.
The dead have their chance in my body.
The stars are drawn into their myths.
I bear nothing but moonlight upon me.
I am known; I know my love.

The entities combine but do not alter or elide. The dimensions of the gradual, of growth—of time, in fact—are absent or are only an element, never a dimension at all. The self has its absences in eternity, then *recurs* in time, bearing its burden, for others, of transgression and forgiveness:

Mother son and wife
Who live with me: I am in death
And waking. Give me the looks that recall me.
None knows why you have waited
In the cold, thin house for winter
To turn the inmost sunlight green

And blue and red with life,
But it must be so, since you have set
These flowers upon the table, and milk for him
Who, recurring in this body, bears you home
Magnificent pardon, and dread impending crime.

Yet even the crimes are not those of history, of *happening*, in which all of life's messy ontogeny is possible, but of myth and ritual, forgiven or punished by incantation, fixed into immutable categories of ascension and disgrace, dissolved ultimately into the natural round of violence and recurrence:

Like the dead about to be
Born, I watch for signs: by kings
Escaping, by shadows, by the gods of the body
Made, when wounded skillfully,
And out of their minds, descending
To the dead . . .

In this first book of Dickey's, then, there is an airless mastery, a sense of liturgical consummation, of life's chances being eliminated as we follow the self's necessary scheme, that is quite stifling: as in those adjectival tropics of Conrad's, nothing moves, every leaf attends the fatal moment when its life or its death is appointed. Accident is expunged, being made illustrious with fate:

Those waters see no more
Than air, than sun, than stone,
And stare it blind: in love, in love.

One of the rare accommodations of circumstance these poems afford
is, as we might expect, in a version of warfare. Himself a veteran of Air
Force service in both World War II and the Korean War, the violence
of war's demands makes an appeal, in every sense, to Dickey's under-
standing of honor, rank and vassalage, of the egalitarianism that is to be
found within royal bonds:

Each eye is equal in the mighty head
Of military gold.

In these experiences, though, there is an opportunity for the singular
event to appear, occurrence construed as the subject of narration
rather than of ritual, and in the poem aptly called "The Performance"
the tone moves toward prose, toward an incident remembered rather
than merely rehearsed as it is separated out from an Eternal Return:

The last time I saw Donald Armstrong
He was staggering oddly off into the sun,
Going down, of the Philippine Islands.
I let my shovel fall, and put that hand
Above my eyes, and moved some way to one side . . .

But that scene, too, is actually a visionary recital: the narrator imagines
his imprisoned, about-to-be-executed comrade in arms

Doing all his lean tricks to amaze them—
The back somersault, the kip-up—
And at last, the stand on his hands,
Perfect, with his feet together,
His head down, evenly breathing,
As the sun poured up from the sea

And the headsman broke down
In a blaze of tears, in that light
Of the thin, long human frame
Upside down in its own strange joy . . .

Even in the disjunct life, the captive fate, ritual prevails and the
language veers back into the cadences of incandescence, life is irra-
diated by formality and degree; the round-dance presides over action
as over suffering. Only then, once the "performance" was staged, could
Armstrong have risen:

In kingly, round-shouldered attendance,
And then knelt down in himself
Beside his hacked, glittering grave, having done
All things in this life that he could.

But to the degree that it accommodates a secular event, this poem is an exception in the liturgies of *Into the Stone*—the rest pursue their celebration in a world of Dying Gods, of which we know that Orpheus was a prime avatar: "My eyes," Dickey writes, speaking in that personation, "my eyes turn green with the silence . . . where love is the center of waiting." One wonders how a poet came by such an initiation—could the desecrated simulacrum of Southern courtesy have been still charismatic enough to help him on? What inherited convention of tribal response has furthered such intuitions of nature and duty? The only answer to such questions will be to discover how the poet gets *out* of the magic circle he has traced, how he escapes the hermetic music which already threatens to keep his mind from the movements of selfhood:

This is the time foresaid, when I must enter
The waking house, and return to a human love . . .
That time when I in the night

Of water lay, with sparkling animals of light
And distance made, with gods
Which move through Heaven only as the spheres
Are moved: by music, music.

Two years after *Into the Stone* appeared, Dickey published his second congregation of poems—three dozen of them this time, two very long, and the entire group constituting a movement toward the "productions of time" Blake said eternity was in love with—an impulse to break out of the archetypal spirals and into a linear history. There is still the aspiration, of course, to be free of the personal, what Shelley called "that burr of self that sticks to one so," to win free of contingency into an existence that would be an endless ring of ecstasy and regeneration; still that effort to discern

. . . how my light body
Falls through the still years of my life
On great other wings than its own.

For the bulk of *Drowning with Others*, then, James Dickey is still a poet of process rather than of particular presences, and of presences rather than persons, in his apprehension of nature as of selfhood. As its title suggests, the poem "Inside the River" is indentured to Heraclitus, the master of flux and pattern over fixity and identification; and if even more of this volume's notes are struck after Roethke than upon French models, the confidence in his eventual release and the mastery of his fluviose meters are all the closer to Dickey's consciousness of his burden ("the effect of the poem is really in the rapt continuation") for suggesting the pre-Socratic sage:

> *Crouch in the secret*
> *Released underground*
> *With the earth of the fields*
> *All around you, gone*
> *Into purposeful grains*
> *That stream like dust*
>
> *In a holy hallway.*
> *Weight more changed*
> *Than that of one*
> *Now being born,*
> *Let go the root.*
> *Move with the world*
> *As the deep dead move.*
> *Opposed to nothing.*
> *Release.   Enter the sea*
> *Like a winding wind.*
> *No.   Rise.   Draw breath.*
> *Sing.   See no one.*

Plumbing the water's depth, rising with flame, lying upon the earth, moving in air—the elements and the actions that must embrace them afford Dickey his *gestus*, but life itself urges a new drama, a modelling of experience which conflicts, at last, with the intuition of recurrence, an "accident" which counters ceremony and courtesy. In the book's longest poem, *Dover: Believing in Kings,* which is a kind of grand romantic fantasia on themes of inheritance and dispossession, there sounds the same grave, tender voice, the same chatoyancy of refrain and repetition, so that where the first stanza ends:

> . . . *In the sackcloth and breast-beating gray*
> The king wears newly, at evening.
> In a movement you cannot imagine
> Of air, the gulls fall, shaken

—the thirteenth concludes:

> . . . *it is I*
> The king wears newly, in lasting.

In a movement you cannot imagine
Of spells, the gulls fall, listening

—and the final apostrophe turns it again:

Who . . . goes up the cliffs to be crowned?
In a movement you cannot imagine
Of England, the king smiles, climbing: running.

It will be noted that there is the same dependence on the gerundive form, without subject or object, to imply perpetuation of the impulse itself. Yet in all this ritual action, the hieratic themes so rehearsed in nature that the world of water and stone, creature and plant, is an emblem of what runs to its source inside a man, there is a real event: the poet and his family, the wife and two sons to whom the book is dedicated, have driven "down the ramp from the boat," have "watched for channel swimmers / dim with grease, come, here, / to the ale of the shallows." There is a real woman in the poem, not a corn queen or Morgan le Fay, but "my wife," and the accidental motions of an individual life are allowed to resist, to oppose, to overcome finally the onset of myth and of a history that is static, Plutarchian:

I hove my father to my back
And climbed from his barrow, there.
Pride helped me pick a queen and get a son.
The heroic drink of the womb
Broke, then, into swanlike song.
One came with scepter, one with cup,
One goatlike back'd, and one with the head of a god . . .

Such a world of swords and gyves, parricide and piety in the archaic surround of the Dover cliffs, can be contemplated but it can also be left behind; the poet and his family get into the car and drive away, into their lives. Indeed most of the other poems in this book are vivid with the tension between the longed-for ritual and the lived reality, or the stress between an inherited ceremony and an unmediated response. The poet, in this latter case, walks outside his house, looking back at his family sitting on a screened porch:

All of them are sitting
Inside a lamp of coarse wire
And being in all directions
Shed upon darkness,
Their bodies softening to shadow . . .

But by the poem's end the ritual transfiguration, always at the ready in Dickey's sensibility, has operated upon them, and that same shadow becomes:

. . . the golden shadow
Where people are lying,
Emitted by their own house
So humanly that they become
More than human, and enter the place
Of small, blindly singing things,
Seeming to rejoice
Perpetually . . .

"So human that they become more than human"—that is one accommodation of the doxologizing vision. Another is the link between ritual and sport, especially when that sport is hunting, exploited in this book with a little more credit on the side of the quotidian, a little less assurance that selfhood must or even may be extinguished. Still, as in "Fog Envelops the Animals"—one of Dickey's most characteristic pieces and certainly one of the most original contemporary poems, as anything very old seems very original—the magical transcendence can function in a moment:

My arrows, keener than snowflakes,
Are with me whenever I touch them.
Above my head, the trees exchange their arms
In the purest fear upon earth.
Silence.   Whiteness.   Hunting.

Here the abrogation of identity delivers being over to the purely gerundive; not "I am silent in a white world in which I hunt," but "Silence.   Whiteness.   Hunting." From this focus upon action at the expense of agent, it is but a step to the universe of pure recurrence that is "The Heaven of Animals":

And those that are hunted
Know this as their life,
Their reward: to walk

Under such trees in full knowledge
Of what is in glory above them,
And to feel no fear,
But acceptance, compliance.
Fulfilling themselves without pain

At the cycle's center,
They tremble, they walk
Under the tree,
They fall, they are torn,
They rise, they walk again.

Animal recurrence identifies the world, too, of Dickey's other long poem in this book of commonplace prayer, "The Owl King," whose first section, "The Call," was printed as an independent poem or invocation in *Into the Stone;* the poet has enlarged its primal scene:

> . . . *in a ring in a meadow*
> *Round a child with a bird gravely dancing,*
> *I hear the king of the owls sing.*

and has thickened the progress of the naked ritual to an entire myth, as Cornford and Harrison discovered that the classical myths were developed to explain the primitive mysteries, to rationalize and thereby recover actions whose meanings were without an explanation. The narrative element in Dickey's art is furthered, too, in its propensity to enlarge liturgy into something more nearly approaching illumination ("all dark shall come to light"); observation of nature in the added sections "The Owl King" and "The Blind Child's Story" transform the rites of passage into a *Märchen:*

> *Each night, now, high on the oak,*
> *With his father calling like music,*
> *He sits with me here on the bough,*
> *His eyes inch by inch going forward*
> *Through stone dark, burning and picking*
> *The creatures out one by one,*
> *Each waiting alive in its own*
> *Peculiar light to be found:*
> *The mouse in its bundle of terror,*
> *The fox in the flame of its hair,*
> *And the snake in the form of all life.*

The longing, though, to be free of what is contingent, of the liable and limiting self lies inside this story nonetheless, its irreducible core and concept:

> *I understand*
> *The voice of my singing father.*
> *I shall be king of the wood.*
> *Our double throne shall grow*
> *Forever, until I see*
> *The self of every substance*
> *As it crouches, hidden and free.*

Until I see the self of every substance. To counter the thrust of such desperate visions, some saving sense of the appearances in James Dickey has summoned up William James' beautiful aphorism, and acted upon it: "The deeper features of reality are found only in perceptual experi-

ence." For a preponderant impulse in this second book is entrusted to
the limited, contingent, questioning experience of an individual iden-
tity laboring to transform its husk into its spirit. There is a quality of
sundered occasions, now, about the titles—still gerundive, but much
more specific, as in "Hunting Civil War Relics at Nimblewill Creek,"
or "To Landrum Guy, Beginning to Write at Sixty," or "A Dog
Sleeping on My Feet." There are portraits of temporal sites, like "The
Salt Marsh":

> *All you can see are the tall*
> *Stalks of sawgrass, not sawing,*
> *But each of them holding its tip*
> *Exactly where your hair*
> *Begins to grow from your forehead.*
> *Wherever you come to is*
> *The same as before . . .*

About such an accuracy, such an incursion upon what may be known,
there is an intensity and an inclusiveness which *earns* rather than
merely surrenders to the inescapable leap into spirit:

> *And nothing prevents your bending*
> *With them, helping their wave*
> *Upon wave upon wave upon wave*
> *By not opposing,*
> *By willing your supple inclusion*
> *Among fields without promise of harvest,*
> *In their marvelous spiritual walking*
> *Everywhere, anywhere.*

From the magical submersions of *Drowning with Others*, the de-
frocked poet rises or at least advances into a world without explicit
ceremony, conscious of his task and, dispossessed of his ministry, ready
to confront his heritage: he must invent his own.

In 1964 Dickey published another collection of poems, *Helmets*,
which confirmed him as the telluric maker Wallace Stevens had called
for in prophesying that the great poems of heaven and hell have been
written and the great poem of the earth remains to be written. Here,
more loosely cast in the emblems of battle and quest, are the same
gerundive preoccupations with process, though they are now content
with the poem as its own reward, rather than as a magical charm or
source of control over nature. The poet is no longer a necromancer, a
magus, but a man speaking to himself, for others, as in "Approaching
Prayer":

Hoping only that
The irrelevancies one thinks of
When trying to pray
Are the prayer
And that I have got by my own
Means to the hovering place
Where I can say . . .
Using images of earth . . .
That my stillness was violent enough . . .
That reason was dead enough
For something important to be:

That, if not heard,
It may have been somehow said.

One of the principal *images of earth* Dickey has always used is that of the helmet, which gives this new book its title: the word itself affords a clue to his major preoccupations, for it derives from two old verbs for protecting and concealing—protection, in Dickey's world, against the energies of earth, and concealment against those of the Unseen, crown and prison both. In his first book, Dickey had spoken of death as "the deadly king in a helmet glowing with spines"; had spoken of war as "the mighty head of military gold"; in *Drowning with Others*, the poem "Armor" discusses the use and despair of such things as helmets:

When this is the thing you put on
The world is pieced slowly together
In the power of the crab and the insect . . .

There is no way of being
More with the bound, shining dead,

. . . In the bright locust-shell of my strength
I have let the still sun
Down into the stare of the eyepiece
And raised its bird's beak to confront
What man is within to live with me
When I begin living forever.

But in this new book, such sacramental intuitions are discarded, and the helmet is no longer part of the archaic armor of the knight errant, but now one "I picked from the ground, not daring to take mine off"—simply a helmet filled with water, a tin hat from which, in the battle's lull, the soldier drinks—not Galahad sipping from the grail, but a tired G.I.:

> *I drank and finished*
> *Like tasting of Heaven,*
> *Which is simply of,*
> *At seventeen years,*
> *Not dying wherever you are.*

He realizes he has "inherited one of the dead" with the water accepted from the empty helmet, and imagines travelling to the home of its former tenant, in California where the poet once lived, and there he might

> *. . . walk with him into the wood*
> *Until we were lost,*
> *Then take off the helmet*
> *And tell him where I had stood,*
> *What poured, what spilled, what swallowed.*

> *And tell him I was the man.*

That impulse—to disarm and confront one's naked humanity—is what governs this entire book, its celebrations of life on earth and its imagined figures: "where my breath takes shape on the air / like a white helmet come from the lungs." The book begins with a group of poems corresponding, in their chthonic pieties, to earlier pieces: "The Dusk of Horses" is a pendent to "The Heaven of Animals" and a part of Dickey's Georgia bestiary or foxhound fables:

> *No beast ever lived who understood*
> *What happened among the sun's fields*
> *Or cared why the color of grass*
> *Fled over the hill while he stumbled,*
> *Led by the halter to sleep*
> *On his four taxed, worthy legs . . .*

just as "At Darien Bridge" refers back to the dream landscapes and heroic prowesses of "Near Darien" in the first book, *Into the Stone*. But where in the first poem concerned with this place the site is enchanted ground and everything seen or sensed is miracle, everything is *given:*

> *As I ride blindly home from the sun,*
> *Not wishing to know how she came there,*
> *Commanded by glorious powers:*
> *At night by the night's one stone*
> *Laid openly on the lost waves,*
> *By her eyes catching fire in the morning . . .*

in the new poem, even in its more particular title, we are afforded the circumstances, the details—that there is a bridge here built by chain-gangs laboring ankle-deep in the water, that as a child the poet had come here to watch them at work, that now the poet returns to the place and with the wedding band on his ring finger "recalling the chains of their feet" (for Dickey, marriage is a binding sacrament in every sense of the term, another limiting condition of selfhood), stands and looks out:

> . . . *over grasses*
> *At the bridge they built, long abandoned,*
>
> *Breaking down into water at last,*
> *And I long, like them, for freedom*
>
> *Or death, or to believe again*
> *That they worked on the ocean to give it*
>
> *The unchanging, hopeless look*
> *Out of which all miracles leap.*

The book is full of justice rendered to the visible world by a divining conscience ("Under the ice the trout rode, / trembling, in the mastered heart / of the creek, with what he could do") and echoes with a kind of morality collected from the instances of natural order, as in the luxuriant, leisurely triptych "On the Coosawattee," whose first section, *By Canoe through the Fir Forest*, concludes:

> *While the world fades, it is* becoming.
> *As the trees shut away all seeing,*
> *In my mouth I mix it with sunlight.*
> *Here, in the dark, it is* being.

The Wordsworth who fled the shape of the mountain when he had stolen a boat would have understood such sorting out of ethical conclusions from natural form and process. The second section, *Below Ellijay*, describes the corruption of the stream by a poultry-processing plant, through whose carnage the canoe advances:

> *Until we believed ourselves doomed*
> *And the planet corrupted forever . . .*
> *And could have been on the Styx*
> *In the blaze of noon, till we felt*
> *The quickening pulse of the rapids*
> *And entered upon it like men*
> *Who sense that the world can be cleansed . . .*
> *And plunged there like the unborn*

> *Who see earthly streams without taint*
> *Flow beneath them* . . .
> *As they dress in the blinding clothes*
> *Of nakedness for their fall.*

Here Dickey has succeeded, in his account of the characteristic spiritual journey or *ascensus,* in reconciling the starkest vocabulary of transcendence with the lush nature of the backwoods country. It is a moment of astonishing equilibrium in the poet's long quest, enriched in the final section, *The Inundation,* with a remembered rescue from the rapids by another Wordsworthian figure, "the strange woods boy" Lucas Gentry:

> *Who may have been the accepting spirit of the place*
> *Come to call us to higher ground,*
> *Bent to raise*
> *Us from the sleep of the yet-to-be-drowned,*
> *There, with the black dream of the dead canoe*
> *Over our faces.*

In thematic control, in sureness of their subject, these are poems so resolved that one would be at a loss—and quite happy to be there—to define the point where the poet's abiding struggle with himself might be located, were it not for the aura of incantation, of litany that Dickey still employs, even though he has steadily, painfully rid himself of the ritual imagination. Or rather, even though he has rejected the ritual as something given, and has instead cast it ahead of himself as something to be found, invented. By the end of *Helmets,* the litaneutical measure is disputed, the steady beat of the three- and four-foot lines, altered only by dactyl or spondee teleutons, and generally matching line length with sense unit, is breaking up. Moreover the long, regularly shaped stanzas give way to clusters of verse separated in arbitrary ways by blanks—as if the poet were reluctant to let the cadences coincide with the reader's breath, but must hurry him on when he would pause, slow him down just when he would gather momentum. What in the earlier books had sunk, with great virtuosity in diction, indeed with what Gide called a "diverse monotonie," into the ear to do its murmurous work is now offered in a less convinced form, or turned, as in "Cherrylog Road," to less reverent purposes. In this comic poem about meeting a forbidden sweetheart in an automobile graveyard, the dying fall is jacked up by a certain refusal to go along with the old ceremonies; even as the Balcony Scene is exchanged for the back seat of a "34 Ford without wheels," the poet is dissatisfied, for his newfound charge, with his old resonances, his mastered meters:

We left by separate doors
Into the changed, other bodies
Of cars, she down Cherrylog Road
And I to my motorcycle
Parked like the soul of the junkyard

Restored, a bicycle fleshed
With power, and tore off
Up Highway 106, continually
Drunk on the wind in my mouth,
Wringing the handlebar for speed,
Wild to be wreckage forever.

Or perhaps this is only the final virtuosity of such diction, and as Eliot said, its pathos, to be able to articulate only in the formalities of what one knows what one is trying to find out: "one has learnt to get the better of words for the thing one no longer has to say, or the way in which one is no longer disposed to say it." There is, either way, a shellac of complacency that is showing a crackle in itself, for all its luster, in many of these poems by

A middle-aged, softening man
Grinning and shaking his head
In amazement to last him forever.

Though Dickey will always retain, for strategic use, the rhythms he had early developed to be those in which he most naturally addresses himself, entrusts his consciousness to the language, it is evident that a formal metamorphosis must occur, after *Helmets*, to accommodate the other change, the transformation of ritual into romance, which Dickey has effected in his poetry:

. . . as though I myself
Were rising from stone

Held by a thread in midair,
Badly cut, local-looking, and totally uninspired,
Not a masterwork

Or even worth seeing at all
But the spirit of this place just the same,
Felt here as joy.

That metamorphosis has occurred in Dickey's next book, *Buckdancer's Choice*, of 1965, and occurred with such a rush of impulse that the reader of the earlier collections, having come to expect the somnambulist forms of Dickey's imagination of recurrence, will be jarred by the immediacy, the brutality of disjunct actions, performed once and, however celebrated, done away with. There are, of course, reminders—"Fox Blood" and "War Wound" are two—of the old incantatory pieties, the magical world where each Thing possesses the properties of Another, a world of available correspondences:

> *Touched with the moon's red silver,*
> *Back-hearing around*
> *The stream of his body the tongue of hounds*
> *Feather him. In his own animal sun*
> *Made of human moonlight*
> *He flies like a bolt running home . . .*

But for the most part, Dickey's universe, and the measures which accommodate and express his phenomenology of exchange, has ceased to be one of eternal return, of enchantment. Instead, once out of eternity, the poet confronts and laments (exults over) the outrage of individual death, of a linear movement within time—each event and each moment being unique, therefore lost. If the self can die, then others exist, survivors of what Newman, in another connection, called an aboriginal catastrophe. Obsession, madness, excess: the burden of *Buckdancer's Choice* is altogether new in this poet, and crowned, or ballasted, by a pervasive terror of extinction. That is the penalty of the historical imagination; its reward is the awareness of others, always incipient in this poet but never before, by the very system of his discourse, explicit. In two of the poems about graves in this book, it is notable that the poet speaks of that terror, and of that awareness. In "The Escape," Dickey envisions his own gravestone:

> *It is an open book*
> *Of cardboard and paper, a simulated Bible,*
> *All white, like a giant bride's,*
> *The only real pages the ones*
> *The book opens to . . .*

This is on a grave he has previously seen in a country cemetery in Alabama, where a young deer was standing among the tombstones, puzzling out the "not-quite-edible words of the book lying under / a panel of the surf":

> *I remember that, and sleep*
> *Easier, seeing the animal head*
> *Nuzzling the fragment of Scripture,*
> *Browsing, before the first blotting rain*
> *On the fragile book*
> *Of the new dead, on words I take care,*

> *Even in sleep, not to read,*
> *Hoping for Genesis.*

How different is that hope, and the tentative rhythm it assumes, from the old certainties of regeneration of *Into the Stone*! Paired with it, in the other determination of mortality "The Common Grave," is the realization that beyond the individual death

> *All creatures tumbled together*
> *Get back in their wildest arms*
> *No single thing but each other . . .*

and the final constatation is the last we might have expected from Dickey the poet of Being "revealed tremendously / in its fabulous, rigid, eternal / unlooked-for role," for it is an acknowledgment of greater possibilities than the One contains:

> *. . . An oak tree breaks*
> *Out and shoves for the moonlight,*
> *Bearing leaves which shall murmur for years,*
> *Dumbfoundedly, like mouths opened all at once*
> *At just the wrong time to be heard,*
>   *Others, others.*

Hoping for Genesis, believing in others (and no longer in kings)— these are the gerundive moments of Dickey's fulfilled consciousness. They are sustained by a compassion, in the shorter poems, unmatched by the old will-to-power and unwarranted by the old metric. There is more air around these words, more space between the lines. Even between the *words* in some of the poems, the blanks stretch, suggesting not only a pause in the reader's drone but a separateness in the writer's experience. The lines are either broken off short or very long, but nowhere, in the larger efforts, are there the assent-inducing rhythms of spiralling chant, the beautiful generalities of transfiguration. Here we get novelistic detail, as in "The Fiend," a poem explicitly about a voyeur:

Her stressed nipples rising like things about to crawl off her   as he gets
A hold on himself.   With that clasp she changes   senses something
Some breath through the fragile walls   some all-seeing eye

or deliberately parted fragments, the natural rhythms sundered:

> *. . . the tops of the sugar*
> *Cane soaring   the sawgrass walking:*
>   *I come past*

The stale pools left
Over from high tide   where the crab in the night sand
Is basting himself with his claws   moving ripples outward
Feasting on brightness
                    and above
A gull also crabs slowly,
Tacks, jibes   then turning the corner
Of wind, receives himself like a brother
As he glides upon his reflection . . .

Those last two lines remind us of the old incantations given over, and suggest what we may gain by keeping awake: an ability to confront the body's death as well as the spirit's life, without lulling the mind to sleep by hypnotic rhythms, occult correspondences.

Certainly a most remarkable poem in Dickey's later work is "The Firebombing," a very long poem in which, as I read it, the same movement outward upon a real world, magic discarded like Prospero's, books drowned and the natural man acknowledged—dolefully, awkwardly, but inevitably—is rehearsed in terms of the poet's own past and present circumstances. (A new irony is afforded by the epigraph from Gunther Eich: how perfect that it should be a contemporary German poet who remarks that "after the Catastrophe, each man will claim that he was innocent!") At the same time that he, he the poet James Dickey, no other man, in a waking dream carries out a napalm raid upon Japan, "sitting in a glass treasure-hole of blue light," he reviews his own suburban life twenty years later:

. . . in this half-paid-for pantry
Among the red lids that screw off
With an easy half-twist to the left
And the long drawers crammed with dim spoons. . . .

The poem is, surely, Dickey's most complete statement of the magical life in its appalling triumphs (military rank and power a part of the Old Order of kingship and vassalage) over against the slow conquests and defeats of an undistinguished reality. Here the pilot works an unimaginable and soundless destruction:

In a red costly blast
Flinging jelly over the walls

though he himself is "cool and enthralled in the cockpit,"

Turned blue by the power of beauty,
In a pale treasure-hole of soft light
Deep in æsthetic contemplation . . .

It is this detachment
The honored æsthetic evil,
The greatest sense of power in one's life
That must be shed.

And much of the poem's body, like the poet's, is dedicated to such shedding. The narrator, even as he executes the "anti-morale raid," lives his later life, worrying about being overweight, about his house "where the payments / for everything under the sun / pile peacefully up," and about his responsibility:

All this and I am still hungry,
Still twenty years overweight, still unable
To get down there or see
What really happened.

The failure or the refusal to imagine apocalypse, to accept the burden of the magical infliction of harm: that is the real subject of this poem. "Absolution? Sentence? No matter; / the thing itself is in that." Thus out of the conflict of the ritual imagination with the variety and complexity of life lived day by day, Dickey has made his most engrossing poem, one which challenges morality by magic, and chastens myth by life's daily texture.

The conflict operates on other levels too, as in "Slave Quarters," the other long poem that frames this book at its other end; here the same speaker visits a ruined plantation, "in the great place the great house is gone from," and romantically muses on the Master he would have been, his erotic disclosures paralleled by his supposed failure to acknowledge his illegitimate half-Negro scions. The burden is the same as in "The Firebombing": "How to take on the guilt"; and the shock of recognition which the present must sustain when confronted by the old dispensation, the magical immoralities of the past, is the same too. The poet stands in the ruined place by the tidal inlet where

The real moon begins to come
Apart on the water
And two hundred years are turned back
On with the headlights of a car,

and wonders what

It would be like   what it has been
What it is to look once a day
Into an only
Son's brown, waiting, wholly possessed
Amazing eyes, and not
Acknowledge, but own?

The old aristocratic duties are absorbed into the characteristic liberal doubts, the world in which "my body has a color not yet freed." History is a nightmare from which the self, struggling yet damned, may not escape. The wit of this poem and the broader humor of "The Firebombing" reveal a tension, an ironic balance Dickey has seldom shown, and it is as remarkable that he can encompass, in the first poem, a line like "my house / where the lawn mower rests on its laurels" or one like "another Bomb finds a home / and clings to it like a child" as that in "Slave Quarters" he can make the joke about the headlights already quoted, a joke effected by a line break. "Mangham," one of the middle poems of this book that points in diction back to the earlier style, wrests free of that ceremoniousness by its humor, its punning rueful account of an old geometry teacher's stroke; Mangham died explaining:

> . . . *what I never*
> *Could get to save my soul: those things that, once*
> *Established, cannot be changed by angels,*
> *Devils, lightning, ice or indifference:*
> *Identities! Identities!*

And even in one of the book's somberest pieces there is a gayety, a sense of relief which accompanies the daylight recognition of wreckage and despair. "Pursuit from Under" is a nightmare poem about a boy who imagines himself an arctic explorer on his southern farm, visualizing a killer whale striking up through the ice at shadows, even while the child's August weekends are passed barefoot on "the turf that will heave, / and the outraged breath of the dead, so long held, will form / unbreathably around the living." Like the old explorers, the boy—the boy he was—"had been given an image / of how the drowned dead pursue us." Here Dickey again asserts, as in the distance between the magical blue cockpit of the firebombing and the suburban etiolation of his everyday life, and as in the separation of the modern ruins from the ante-bellum rituals, what he knows to be the distinction between recurrence and reality; the dissension between an incantatory ageless order of transcendence with its themes of hierarchy, immutability and terror, and on the other, nearer side a prosaic, mortal accommodation of immanence with its themes of becoming, of change, waste and deperition. James Dickey has searched deep in himself and wide in the world for a criticism of eternity by history, of immortality by trapped lives, of sovereignty by freedom. He is the man who most deserves to say of himself, as he has said:

> . . . *the heart of my brain has spoken*
> *To me, like an unknown brother,*

> *Gently, of ends and beginnings,*
> *Gently, of sources and outcomes,*

so that what was once "impossible, brighter than sunlight" becomes

Something like three-dimensional dancing in the limbs   with age
Feeling more in two worlds than in one   in all worlds the growing
*   encounters.*

In 1967, Dickey gathered 15 of the two dozen poems from *Into the Stone*, 25 of the three dozen from *Drowning with Others*, 22 of the two dozen from *Helmets* and—the proportions are an indication, surely, of preference—all the poems from *Buckdancer's Choice* (which had won the National Book Award in 1965) into a single volume which also included 24 new poems, "growing encounters" indeed, some of them grown to a knowledge extended immensely beyond an encounter, the whole constituting 300 large, close-set pages of poetry, a decade's work, a lifetime's achievement, though the poet was at publication of *Poems: 1957–1967* only 44—a middle-age hugely concerned, however, to triumph over death, "that eternal process / most obsessively wrong with the world" and hungering for any means (reincarnation, apotheosis, witchcraft or that reversal of the signs which mystics and surrealists alike salute) to transcend the mortal body:

> *to be dead*
> *In one life is to enter*
> *Another   to break out   to rise above*

—somehow to live, convulsively, explosively, in a gigantic, legendary sense ("Lord, let me die   but not die / Out") which even the make-shift ardors of a shifting make ("Adultery") seem, momentarily, to afford:

> *. . . death is beaten by hazardous meetings that bridge*
> *A continent. One could never die here*
> *Never die   never die . . .*

The body of the new work is sensationally framed by two mythological set-pieces, "Sermon" and "Falling"—the former, one of those ecstatic southern *Märschen* hard upon the Io section of Faulkner's *Hamlet*, though with a characteristically Dickey flick of the lash:

> *get up   up in your socks and take*
> *The pain you were born for: that rose through her body straight*
> *Up from the earth like a plant, like the process that raised overhead*
> *The limbs of the uninjured willow . . .*

its subject a backwoods romance of abduction, murder and deësis (the
Paraclete figured by a motorcycle, of course), its speaker a "Woman
Preacher leaving the Baptist Church," and its style, as one might
expect, an inflammatory qualification of the poet's late prose disclo-
sures, perforated yet prolonged, which exist within the precincts of
poetry chiefly by an intensity of realization, an assertion wilder than
any mere music, any measure which might be brought to bear on the
segmented, limber phrases, the members:

> *. . . understand how a man casts finally*
> *Off everything that shields him from another   beholds his loins*
> *Shine with his children forever   burn with the very juice*
> *Of resurrection: such shining is how the spring creek comes*
> *Forth from its sunken rocks . . . ;*

and the latter, the closing poem, the most extreme of all Dickey's
gerundive studies, a gorgeous unpunctuated exultation of 250 lines in
which an airline stewardess, half Danaë, half Leda, falls three miles
from a plane into Kansas:

> *. . . All those who find her impressed*
> *In the soft loam   gone down   driven well into the image of her*
>   *body*
> *The furrows for miles flowing in upon her where she lies very deep*
> *In her mortal outline   in the earth as it is in cloud   can tell*
>   *nothing*
> *But that she is there   inexplicable   unquestionable   and re-*
>   *member*
> *That something broke in them as well   and began to live and die*
>   *more*
> *When they walked for no reason into their fields to where the whole*
>   *earth*
> *Caught her . . .*

There is, certainly, a loves-of-Jupiter aspect to all Dickey's late work,
an erotic mastery of metamorphosis by which he reconstitutes, in a
narrative utterly without ritual, the very mythology he has been at
such pains to disintegrate in his figures, his meters. Meanwhile the more
quietly handled poems between these two giant performances (*per-
formances* must be the word: the platform manner is not to be disso-
ciated, henceforth, from the galvanic achievements of this veteran
barnstormer who comes before his audiences "in renewed light, utterly
alone!") recapitulate every subject, every *subjection* of identity to the
chthonic energy, to that possession by the gods which Dickey has
owned up to throughout his work in order to own it; and if they are
poems still "possessing / music order   repose," they possess, as well,

that difference for which Dickey is now so often reproached by the very admirers of his old hieratic stance, his Heraclitean status; it is a mistake to reproach the poet for precisely what he has determined to do—his titanic choice is to recast the entire burden of utterance ("as though to be born   to awaken to what one is / were   to be carried"), transforming what has been recurrent and therefore change-less to what is, merely, real and released. Sublimity has become the substance of things hoped for, fable has become faith:

> *. . . The words of a love letter,*
> *Of a letter to a long-dead father,*
>
> *To an unborn son, to a woman*
> *Long another man's wife, to her children,*
> *To anyone out of reach, not born,*
> *Or dead, who lives again,*
> *Is born, is young, is the same;*
> *Anyone who can wait no longer*
>
> *Beneath the huge blackness of time*
> *Which lies concealing, concealing*
> *What must gleam forth in the end,*
> *Glimpsed, unchanging, and gone*
> *When memory stands without sleep*
> *And gets its strange spark from the world.*

The Eye-Beaters, Blood, Victory, Madness, Buckhead and Mercy by JAMES DICKEY

Those who come cold to this collection—a dozen extended texts playing fast and loose with a handful of intended emblems—will not, at first sight, be warmed. The look of these poems on the page is dis-concerting: forms are sundered, wrenched apart rather than wrought together; rhythms are an inference from the speaking voice rather than a condition of it; lines are spread or sprung between margin and gutter to produce luminous layered walls of print, a Rothko of lan-guage, often aerated by great white holes; or else the rifted phrases, cunningly enjambed, are centered, one over the other, to erect a column of symmetrical deformities, a kind of shaped prose. *Long lines in the air*, Dickey calls them, and like Blake's prophecies, their mere aspect intimidates—willed to the end, spacious enough to ac-

commodate death-defying leaps of revelation, spare enough to col-
lapse upon a single word.

As a poet of five incandescent volumes amassed within a decade
into a monument (*Poems 1957–1967*), as a critic whose appetite and
opinions range, indeed, *From Babel to Byzantium*, as a winner of the
National Book Award, as a Consultant in Poetry to the Library of
Congress, and pre-eminently as an athlete of the *personal appearance*
(what other kind? what less? as he would ask)—James Dickey has
seen to it that not many of us will approach his work cold. The very
persistence of such solicitude as his may have chilled some readers,
may have caused them to come, by now, cool to this ebullient career.
But whatever the temperature reading among Mr. Dickey's readers,
I should like to hover briefly over the situation of his poetry as it
was so handsomely packaged three years ago, before having a look
at recent manifestations, further developments.

Renewal, transcendence, ecstasy—he has sought these things in his
own person, and by any means, at all costs. At all costs to the art as
well as to the artist's life, Dickey seeks and speaks for a triumph over
death, a transformation within the merely mortal body, praying
somehow to live, convulsively, explosively, beyond the norms of
utterance. It cannot be socialized, this vision, it cannot even be
shared—it can only be given, given away, given over. Abjuring myth
and even narrative, foreswearing ritual and even recurrence, the poet
has recast the entire process of poetry as he himself has practiced
and proved it into an ecstasy without fixtures, an awakening without
constants, a sublimity without negation.

*Sleeping off the light / of the world . . . what could I do but
make the graveyards soar?* James Dickey now asks—though there is a
charged assertion in the "question" as the poet puts it, *like a king
starting out on a journey / away from all things that he knows.* This
new book is clamorous with unknowns, with quittances, with relega-
tions: *How the body works / how hard it works / is not every-
thing: everything is how / much glory in it. . . .* And though there
are recapitulations, too, inferences from the old imperial phenomen-
ology: *I thirsted like a prince / then like a king / then like an empire
like a world / on fire*—though there are echoes, contaminations of the
mineral litanies of moon and stone which had led to the wrong
ecstasy (wrong because unchanging, unrenewed): *On magic ground
/ of the dead new world . . . in the universal playground / of
stones . . . we walk, our glass heads shimmering with absolute
heat / and cold . . . We will take back the very stones / of Time,
and build it where we live*—though there are rueful and middle-aged
invocations to sport, punning imageries of physical prowess: *out over
water and back / to earth . . . that is all, but like all joy / on earth
and water, / in bones and in wings and in light / it is a gamble. It is*

play—there is in this latest, glancingly titled volume a gaining emphasis on release, on regeneration and renewal out of suffering and failure itself, out of the flagging and the painful and the hindered, which makes against any sustained performance, any consistency of practice in the art: *we are this world: we are / the only men. What hope is there at home / in the azure of breath, or here with the stone dead secret?*

From a fallen life, an aging body, a disgraceful age, Dickey craves not identity nor even delectation but *Deliverance*, as his new novel is called, and his impatience with the procedures of tradition (*tell me what I need to know about my time / in the world . . . light me a torch with what we have preserved / of lightning*), his fury with the delations of biography (*the mad weeping Keeper who can't keep / a God-damned thing who knows he can't keep everything / or anything alive: none of his rooms, his people, / his past, his youth, himself, / but cannot let them die*), explore the meaning of his search even as they no longer exploit but merely explode the means.

No poetry of our time is so determined upon exaltation, no poetry of our time is so exposed to debasement. The wonder of it, and the reward, is the success in submission (*so have you changed to this*), the assent which turns to ascent: *Companion, if we climb our mortal bodies/ high . . . we shall find ourselves / flying with the life / of the birds of death;* the assumption of mortality, darkness, torment (*pure triumph, pure acceptance*) which positively "enables" transfiguration: *the words written after the end / of every marriage manual, back / to the beginning, saying / Change; form again; flee.*

When it is said that a man has fallen, as I have said it of Dickey and as he so often says it of himself, though he says that he is falling, our latest Lucifer, *falling back / back to the body-raising fire . . . back from the dark side / of the mind*—when this world is called a fallen world, what is meant is that our soul, our aspirations, our hungers have collapsed into our present body, our present landscape, and that the instruments of our transcendence are at the same time the tools of undoing: *resurrection for a little while,* as Dickey laments and exults.

Visiting a home for blind children and inventing a fiction of archetypal reversion to have his reason, in the most exorbitant and inevitably the most intimate of all his title poems, "The Eye-Beaters," Dickey affords a clue if not a key to his extravagant, his excessive creations; what we merely see is not enough, yet the fictions—the poems—by which we might beguile our blindness are not the case (*Indeed I know it is not so / I am trying to make it / make something / make them make me / reinvent the vision of the race / knowing the blind must see / by magic or nothing*).

These contradictions between life as we know it to be and life as we make it up for ourselves (*I have put history out*), these terrible reversals of what is given and what is taken, generate for Dickey—he tells us straight out: *I pass beyond in secret / in perversity and the sheer / despair of invention*—a transcendental poetics of the fallen world, a phenomenology of light and darkness, rising and falling, burning, turning and submitting (to list his five favorite gerunds) which can accommodate any experience, even the most trivial, even the most degrading, or the most grandiose—such as being the Luce Publications laureate on the occasion of the moon-shot.

I. A. Richards once said that poems have been written on mountaintops during thunderstorms, but not good poems; nor is Dickey's "Apollo", addressed to us from the mind of an astronaut on the moon, a "good poem". But addressed to us from the mind of James Dickey it is a great poem, a hymn of recuperation, a reiteration in the original sense of the word, a going-over, from the merciless perfections of death to all the chronicles of diminution which star this book: "Diabetes", "The Cancer-Match", "Madness", "Venom", "Variations on Estrangement".

It is not the Pentagon-primed scapegoat who speaks thus, but the poet of natural consummation, traveling *back through the last dark / of the moon, past the dim ritual / random stones of oblivion, and through the blinding edge / of moonlight into the sun / beholding the blue planet steeped in its dream of reality, its calculated vision shaking with /the only love.* Consummation, the burning of the world and the fulfillment of a sacred marriage—that is the analogy of all Dickey's poetry: that is what he makes of the moon: *a final form / and color at last comes out / of you alone putting it all / together like nothing / here like the almighty / glory.*

In the unfallen world, which is to say in the risen world, the world where there is no contrast between a man's desire and his power, in what Blake calls Eden, there are two fundamental processes of the imagination, warfare and hunting. In the fallen world from which Dickey seeks deliverance, these processes are perverted into different kinds of murder; though as far back as "The Heaven of Animals" Dickey had articulated the intuition of a transfigured being: *at the cycle's center, / they fall, they are torn, / they rise, they walk again.*

My references to Blake, in characterizing the look of Dickey's new poems as well as their license, are merely a response to Dickey's own lead. In a glorious new poem of hunting, "The Lord in the Air", Dickey quotes Blake, who tells us to *make a friend and companion of these Images of wonder.* Dickey ends "The Eye-Beaters," moreover, with the line *bring me my spear.* And it is in Blake's spirit that Dickey celebrates his son's hunting in this poem, gloating when the boy blows a wood whistle that will lure the crows to *meet the Lord of their stolen voice in the air,* exulting that a man has the power *in a sound like warning, like marriage* . . . *to call out the black birds, but not for betrayal, or to call / up death or desire, but only to give give what was never.*

In the unfallen world to which these poems always allude, to which they sometimes approach, and which they even, at appalling moments, create; in the risen world, then, hunting and warfare become search and struggle, as Blake saw in his Titanic vision of Orc piercing into *the elemental Planets and the orbs of eccentric fire,* of the Creator God twisting the sinews of the Tyger's heart. That is the consummation of these texts which insist upon anguish and madness, which in their very presentment on the page rehearse mortality. It is James Dickey's achievement, a great achievement even for him, to see the risen world "through" the other one, through *an enormous green bright growing No / that frees forever.*

The cost to his poetry is tremendous, for it has cost him the poems themselves—there are not poems here, I mean to say, there is only—only!—poetry; the cost to himself he reckons up in a terrible litany of losses: *an everyday—a livable death at last.* What is gained is that giant utterance, the expression of a state wherein *the earth's whole history blazes / to become this light / for you are released to all others, / all places and times of all* . . . *dead, immortal, or coming.*

The Nation, 1970

ALAN DUGAN

"*Possessed of an Echo But Not a Fate*"

BETTER TO BEGIN—lest we never come to an end of it—with a little garland of invectives, a culling from the unweeded garden of Dugan's verses, which will display a note, a tonality never so resolutely sounded in our literature, or anyone's, since Thersites:

> *Three times dark, first in the mind,*
> *second in January, the pit of the year,*
> *and third in subways going up and down*
> *the hills and valleys underground,*
> *I go from indoors to indoors indoors,*
> *seeing the Hudson River three times a week*
> *from my analyst's penthouse window . . .*

> *The man-faced bat-winged worm*
> *looked up from his work*
> *on my love's corpse falling,*
> *his grin foul with his lights,*
> *and said, "So what?, Faller,*
> *I come in the works*
> *of your love's wounds, foaming.*
> *My sperm are his worms."*

> *. . . Every item has*
> *been cut out of its nature,*
> *wrapped disguised as something*
> *else, and sold clean by fractions.*

> *. . . I try*
> *to catch up on the action, eat*
> *a lunch for breakfast and pretend:*
> *What have I missed except life?*

> *The skin ripples over my body like moon-wooed water,*
> *rearing to escape me. Where would it find another*
> *animal as naked as this one it hates to cover?*

> *. . . the butchers*
> *have washed up and left*
> *after having killed and dressed*
> *the bodies of the lambs all night,*
> *and those who never have seen blood awake*
> *can drink it browned*
> *and call the past an unrepeatable mistake*
> *because this circus of their present is all gravy.*

And to conclude, in order that we may begin, here is the cynic coda from this poet's terrible Decalogue which ends his first book, "Wall, Cave, and Pillar Statements, After Asôka":

> *That is the end of the statements, but,*
> *in order to go on a way after the end*
> *so as to make up for having begun*
> *after the beginning, and thus to come around*
> *to it in order to include the whole thing,*
> *add: "In some places the poignant slogan,*
> *'Morality is a bad joke like everything else'*
> *may be written or not, granted that space*
> *exists for the vulgar remarks, the dates,*
> *initials and hearts of lovers, and all*
> *other graffiti of the prisoners of this world."*

It is to be seen that so inclusive a hatred *within* a man's poetry makes necessary and even entrancing a hatred *of* that poetry as well. Let us consider the case.

Flaunting his jealousy, his careful grudges in a cold and darkening world for his first forty years:

> *Oh I got up and went to work*
> *and worked and came back home*
> *and ate and talked and went to sleep.*
> *Then I got up and went to work*
> *and worked and came back home*
> *from work . . .*

a poet prepares—literally broods over, nurses, suckles in the sense that *parentage* and *preparation* share the one root—his message ("on Saturday / I could talk about the main thing!"), his admonition, his sentence passed upon a world which has returned the compliment:

> *But I am here poised*
> *within this eddy, sentenced to a shape*
> *and have to wrestle through a gust of violence*
> *before I sleep . . .*

or worse still, upon a world which has offered the insult in the first place, as a visit to any zoo demonstrates by analogy with a man's own way of staying *in shape, in place:*

> *The animals, hanging around in forms,*
> *are each resigned to be what each one is,*
> *imprisoned twice, in flesh first, then in irons . . .*
> *Caught in his double prison all the time,*
> *whatever he is, each goes on being what he is,*
> *although ridiculous in forced review,*
> *perseverant in not doing what he need not do.*

With the years, "walled away from wilderness / by absence in stone and iron," the pressure of an unregarded life—unregarded by others, of course: by the poet himself his existence is subject, and subjected, to a dissolving lens—builds up or at least rises, mounts, and the specific density of a poet's address, as recorded in all the cunning devices (epigrams, apostrophes, *essais*, idylls, elegies, songs, translations, monologues, prothalamia, portraits, letters, notes and tributes: *nostalgia for a language*, he calls it) by which he lets off what steam he can do without and still keep the engine idling, increases, encrusts—paronomasia as a sign of life, agnomination the very pulse of his recital. Then, when he is forty, as I say, the whole contraption—

> *This is hell,*
> *but I planned it, I sawed it,*
> *I nailed it, and I*
> *will live in it until it kills me . . .*

explodes, actually detonates ("to give out / all the temporary ornaments I can"), flinging into air with retributory violence the incandescent clots of utterance, splintered, flawed, broken off short to reveal the rainbows of possibility which inhere, otherwise hidden, in sharp edges, "jewels of indoor glass":

> *The broken glass on the stairs*
> *shines in the electric light . . .*
> *So the beauty goes, ground*

under heel but shining, it
is still sharp enough . . .
that I should try to praise
the pieces of harmony . . .

and incredibly garnering (justice being, after all, "an only natural human invention to begin with") every prize in sight and presumably out of reach: *Poems* by Alan Dugan, published in 1961 by the Yale Series of Younger Poets, was given both the National Book Award and the Pulitzer Prize for Poetry in 1962, and gained Dugan a Fellowship at the American Academy of Arts and Letters in Rome. "Encourage your essence!" the poet had some reason to adjure himself:

Be-
jewel your mallet and strike
for a world of growing joy.

And thereupon in short order—short, that is, for a man who had held his peace or been held back by it for those decades, and orderly for a poet who prefers to find his truth in fragments rather than in statues: "the stone thought of the stone figures is thus exposed"—*Poems 2* was published the following year, more inscriptions from some sort of Palatine Anthology of Victimization:

A flying pigeon hit me on a fall day
because an old clothes buyer's junk cart
had surprised it in the gutter: license 851. . . .
Death is a complete collector of antiques
who finds, takes, and bales each individual
of every species all the time for sale to god,
and I, too, now have been brushed by wings . . .

and in 1967, bringing the protest movement up to date, *Poems 3*, the series piling up, or digging down, into a single funneling crater of complaint, resentment, paranoia even, unvisited by further prizes and institutional embellishments against which so many of the poems expostulate or admonish in the first place, ducking the Orphic stance ("he was something of a prig, like Rilke, and as dangerous to women") and the formalities of the dais:

. . . I hear of Yeats's trick,
autocratic in the metal,
and of Picasso's normative dove,
gala with hopes, but what I eat
is this admonitory crow . . .

—and indeed unsampled, despite the instances of success, by the usual anthologies of the period, for Dugan is not to be enlisted in any battle of the books, will not side with a shaggy or a shorn poetry, a school or a wilderness—his is the opposing voice, disabused, gingerly for all its uncapitalized margins, and without trust:

> *. . . I have risen to the morning danger and feel proud,*
> *and after shaving off the night's disguises, after searching*
> *close to the bone for blood, and finding only a little,*
> *I shall walk out bravely into the daily accident.*

Of course one hears in the set of sentences, in the *inscription*like sureness of the long phrases, a hankering for the ancient graces, betokened or explicitly betrayed by a "Free Variation on a Translation from Greek," by "On Breeding, from Plutarch," by "On Lines 69–70, Book IV, of Virgil's *Aeneid*," by "On Alexander and Aristotle, on a Black-on-Red Greek Plate," but the Classical yens collapse quite as readily as the Union clichés into "my own incommensurate enemies, / the firms, establishment, and state," as in this beautiful simile from a poem both startlingly original and starkly characteristic, "The Natural Enemies of the Conch":*

> *Like Prince Hippolytus,*
> *when we behave too*
> *simply toward some law*
> *we have our image,*
> *father, from the sea:*
> *the sea-bull bellowing*
> *to foul our traces,*
> *dragging us to death*
> *behind disturbed machines.*

Here is to be found none of the gratitude toward life, the freedom from resentment which Nietzsche declared so characteristic of the ancient world,** but rather, as most of Dugan's titles suggest, the

---

* Life at the sea's edge affords Dugan a number of generally more lyric instances for his paranoid *sententiae*—the hermit crab in "Life Comparison" which "does what is appropriate within his means, within a case, and fails . . ." and the magnificent vision—perplexed by the cosmos but not past the accurate notation of events and weathers—of "Plague of Dead Sharks" which ends:

> *Who knows whether the sea heals or corrodes?:*
> *what the sun burns up of it, the moon puts back.*

Thales would not have disowned that, and were one to come upon such a fragment in the pre-Socratic collections, Dugan would have at last his true academy.
** "A man with spirit is unbearable if he does not also have at least two other things, gratitude and cleanliness." And again, "what is amazing about the religiosity of the ancient Greeks is the enormous abundance of gratitude it exudes: it is a very noble type of man that confronts nature and life in *this* way."—*Beyond Good and Evil.*

impulse of a cumulative umbrage, that shadow which lies across all experience: "Winter's Onset from an Alienated Point of View," "Fear of the Heights Reached," "A Sawyer's Rage Against Trees," "Not to Choose," "On Zero," "Two Hatreds of Action," "On Rape Unattempted," "Conspiracy of Two Against the World," "Winter: For an Untenable Situation" and so many more, consummated metonymically by "I Have Met the Enemy and I Am Theirs," in which the poet reports outright and at once that the very instruments of his art ("They praise the bloom. *I damn the means*") are his antagonists: "I have found my figures, love, and I am theirs." The figures—music, metaphors, "numbers" as poetry used to be called—are the enemy, they are encountered, and they envelop one. By their overcoming of oneself, one even wins prizes . . . their final victory.

For Alan Dugan initiates his career, and pursues it to an unresolved end, with a great discovery, as great as Paul Eluard's that "there *is* another world, but it is in this one"—the discovery that there *is* another language, a language appropriate to selfhood, to private experience, personal ecstasy and personal loss, but that it is in the public language; within the official received version, there is the shrinking secret which is life's, yet which must be recorded in the terms of the standard and the state—hence the perverse games, the playfulness, the wit, the evasive devices and contrivances intended to outwit language, to trick utterance into revealing the truth it shrouds. The frustration, the failure and the self-erosion follow on the logic of Dugan's situation ("Dugan's deathward, darling: you . . . need be only formally concerned"): the act of writing poetry is, precisely, an invocation of destruction, a luring of language to its wreck, and this tormented man's *exemplary* interest emerges from the record he leaves of an esthetic impoverishment and excruciation which we recognize as one source of our century's creative possibility. The dilemma is couched, as on a bed of nails, by Dugan's Midas, though he does not call himself that, who turns all things to pain:

> *My arms, though,*
> *were chains chained to my arms, so what I touched I struck.*

Unable to create a new language, or to confide in the old one, he contorts what is given. Indeed, his writhing incapacity to transcend the tradition (*traditio:* a passing on), however he populates it with the obscene or the bizarre or the gratuitous, determines Dugan's role in our poetry: Alan Dugan writes epigrams, inscriptions, even graffiti, spiels scrawled on the monuments, because he is trying to vindicate himself in language, and in language the conventions—what is agreed upon, shared—however overwrought, offer the only imaginative possibility.

He is a man *in extremis* (it does not matter whether the extremes are of ecstasy or of suffering—it is the *last rites,* in either case, which he would have) who writes to save himself, and he is too honest and desperate in his solitude for the consolation of some visionary transcendence of language. At the same time, his energy—the clenched, intense *resentment* of helplessness—immeasurably surpasses the limitations of the standard formulas, the common speech. So he does not exploit the formulas, the forms, he batters against them, as if they were his Bastille—the gruesome repetitions of incident in these poems, the ghastly paranoiac events and wisdoms which must be endured again and again are the scratchings and bangings of claustrophobia—and the poem is the lament against its own hardening:

> *well, fangs are promises*
> *to live on what is left,*
> *granted some leavings, and*
> *monsters are replies.*

Language itself is Dugan's prison: he is irrepressibly tempted by the demonism of breaking jail, of defenestrating the Word. And perhaps the one justifiable aspect of his hatred of everything outside himself is his hatred of language. Thus language or the resentment of it is the only aspect of his furious logorrheic longing for self-vindication which he cannot even begin to put into words. Dugan is transfixed by his will to rebellion—"always choose in favor of yourself" he keeps saying in an iconoclastic blaze:

The whole apparatus can be forgotten in the absence of individuals to whom to apply it, and the sensible man will have nothing to do with anything outside his inner, passional life except his position . . .

but despite the selfishness of a man living under a perpetual menace of petrification, Dugan cannot choose in favor of himself because he cannot *speak for himself*—to speak at all means to speak for others, and Dugan can only hear his own voice talking about others and his hatred of them. What is sweet and warm and transitive within, "the branching need / drumming in the red inside / the arteries or antlers of the heart," becomes no more than horns, non-conducting weapons, "the prides and hat-trees of the head / that climbed out of the brain / to show its matter: earth." These lines come from Dugan's finest poem, "The Branches of Water or Desire," which accounts, with a precision, power and wit equal to anything in contemporary poetry, for the impossibility of poetry, or for its inevitable distortion from what, in a man, had been a life-conveying system of blood or breathing, to a merely offensive apparatus for wounding, for inflicting pain:

the sounds and tines
must be some excess of the flesh
that wants beyond efficiency
in time, but cannot find
much permanence outside it: getting or not aside,
it must branch out in works
that cap itself, for some
imaginary reason out of mind.

Poems 4 by ALAN DUGAN

So many times, as I have had occasion to remark elsewhere, has Alan Dugan in his first three books cried wolf that one can scarcely expect him, here, to lie down with the lamb. Nor does he. No, the cry is raised again, the hue of dispirited accommodation and the cry of grievance, the impounded self banging against its imprisonments, striking "a hammer of images forged by deaths, the idea of death, and cash the savior."

Homo homini lupus, indeed, and though Dugan has impulses of relenting in the case of girls, whisky and fresh air (especially the case of whisky!), they are meager indeed compared to the generalized ferocity which tunes his instrument, which whets his whistle:

I felt an instantaneous tree of ice
invade my nervous system and connect
dreams' dreams to an historical reality.
Thus I expected subsequent atrocities
and woke for whisky and an armed life.

These new poems, mostly untitled, all brief—to the point of being bitten off hard, "a sculpture of neglect"—coming seven years after the old ones, are a little less sumptuous in their *ressentiment*, a little more withdrawn in their calculation, their stoniness, precisely. "This petrified obsession, perfect in tautology . . ." is pretty well content, or pretty ill, to inscribe itself, "strict as a meander," on the observed excruciation of it all, the terrible dialogue between public and private speech, the impossibility of the latter and the inadvisability of the former—hence the strange necessity, the compulsion to write these little poems:

The independent subway of the mind
must go beneath the crust and beds

> *of rivers, lovers, and the dead*
> *to hunt, as end, means, and cause,*
> *the star they say they're flying for . . .*

There are such glinting recalls, here and there, of Dugan's old and splendid figure, the phenomenology he has made so wonderfully his own in the first three books, the emblem of the branching artery-system doomed to become antlers, to harden into non-conducting weapons, as here in the "Portrait in the Form of an Extended Conceit," which begins "A coal mine is a hollow tree . . ." and as in that "instantaneous tree of ice" already cited. Here, though, there are few instances of the old recklessness, the old longing for civilities which the speaker cannot afford but—"what have I got to lose except securities?"—obtains anyway, anyhow, in a cloven-hoof-to-mouth music. There is mostly the reminder, the token, the wolf kept on the Capitol in memory of this authentic, this heroic grudgery among us, the life-sentences of a self which recognizes that paranoia is a means, though not the only means, of making the world beyond the wolf's cage *stand and deliver:*

> *Oh I look out for dangers other than myself,*
> *and rescue by and from the sounds and lights outside.*

North American Review, 1974

IRVING FELDMAN

"Who Will Call These Things His Own?"

T HE PRINCIPAL advantage of belonging to, and even—belatedly—
of being owned by, a rather traditionless country like America
is that the poet has to fall back on the Universe, or at least on the
university. Thus a *curriculum vitae* which appears, as Irving Feldman's
does, to be altogether a matter of studying and teaching, of listening in
one classroom and lecturing in another, can in fact disguise a heroic
conquest of identity, a private anabasis through Western Culture,
whose deities and dooms crowd the self with choices, or at least with
refusals, until at last one comes in sight of the sea (some vision of a life
governed by meaningful limits, measures, repetitions), exultantly
shouting "Tenure! Tenure!" but meaning, really, rebirth.

Of course falling back on the Universe, *and* on the university, is not
always or even often regarded as an advantage at all for a man's
poetry; poetry is so much a matter of local attachments, even when, as
in Irving Feldman's case, the poet feels attached to no localities—lan-
guage itself is a local attachment, and there are no poems written in the
universal languages. Yet the universal, and the abstract, and the imper-
sonal as they are accommodated in learning—in the university, in other
words—are precisely what the American Jewish poet, by this half of
the century, must come to terms with, must master in a life and a
country acknowledged to be dispossessed of the past.

Appropriately dedicated to his parents, Feldman's first book, an
investigation of the sources of power, a search for the attitude, the
posture of survival—

> *For me, the line I cannot cross.*
> *In exile, mourning I endure*
> *Every dying, every loss.*
>
> *My eye runs on! my heart clings.*
> *I wait upon the blackened shore,*
> *Remembering the time of kings.*

—was published in 1961 and called *Works and Days and Other Poems*. The title group is named, I suppose, after Hesiod's caustic maxims * intended to inculcate righteousness and efficiency, but in this instance memorializing, rather, the world of Henry Roth and Saul Bellow:

> *A liver lounging in a pot;*
> *Mama boiling the kitchen runes.*
> *Always I see her face a blot*
> *In the sacred oval of the spoons.*
>
> *Grey and sweet and shining eyes,*
> *Freckled arms that took with ardor*
> *The scalds and bundles of sacrifice*
> *—To fill again love's larder.*
>
> *She kneeled to dust the furniture,*
> *But rose with an abstracted eye.*
> *What was it she had seen there?*
> *In spite of all, people die . . .*
>
> *The radiator knocked like a ghost,*
> *Outside, the wind and bawling cats.*
> *My father nodded at his post,*
> *Messiah thundered fireside chats.*
>
> *That all proclaimed the quotidian,*
> *And should the day ache with glory,*
> *Prescribed a little medicine . . .*

The novelistic mishmash of housework endured and mortality anticipated, the infirmity which "saw Israel's shining tents / fold up like a doctor's bag" is the *medium*, the substantive level on which Irving Feldman seeks to repossess or repopulate his heritage by a series of dramatic and philosophical personations, emblems of the history he must invent, since nothing, evidently, is given to him outright:

* And then after Prufrock's "Works and days of hands / that lift and drop a question on your plate."

Here I am stupidly living in sackcloth and ash.
Why was I born just a year before the Crash?
Why'd my father lose his lots and his cash
And go jobless till a gentle lack of courage
Was inbred? Then why'd I grow in this image?
How can I be a hero if I'm not half a fake
Like my cousins Joe and Jake?
To be Chosen—that means having only one part.
But if I'm Elect, why all this fat around my heart?
Why was I born in Brooklyn with the lower middle-classes?
Is that a hero's place? Was Moses freckled! Samson wear glasses!
Why me? Haven't You had F.D.R. and Cecil de Mille?
(Pardon me, O Lord, if I question Your will,
But wouldn't Seymour or Sherman have done just as well?)
Why do you tell me to build when I want to destroy?

This instance of the poet as stand-up Jewish tragic (even Lennie Bruce would have had no difficulty finding the appropriate ethnic rhyme for "destroy") suggests how much Feldman has to overcome, how much chattering and whining, before he can confront himself. He is in the vexing situation of the artist who must move from the suburbs to the center of civilization, the center being always the most isolated place—and who must move by his own devices, under his own steam. Yet his devices are remarkable, and the steam he gets up is often powerful enough to whelm the poet's poverty of doctrine by his wealth of dramatic detail. Not only Moses and Samson (without glasses, though isolated: "where's the drunk idolatrous crowd?"), but Prometheus and Narcissus, Adam and Abraham, Theseus and of course the Wandering Jew clutch at his stupent imagination, force him to refashion the myths of heroism from an anti-heroic metal, contaminated by modern plumbing and even a college education: his Prometheus, "alone, and nailed through the heart into nature" suffers "of all things the worst: / to be a victim and have no torturer"; his Samson finds it "better to fall among the evil / than turn to stone standing alone"; his Wandering Jew demands of God:

> *Why for the pure task these tools of dirt?*
> *This abstracted heart, this fever, this world?*

Inevitably, gratefully, annihilation appears the proper path to heroic stature—or as one of Feldman's saints puts it, "Self-denial is the self's strongest wine."

Happiest in its dramatic voice, this copious first book—endorsed like a blank check by John Crowe Ransom, who "would not care to limit the extent of [Feldman's] triumph when I think about his promise as a poet," and by Lionel Trilling, who finds "the considerable size of the production in itself a virtue"; in other words, not positively detested by these cautious men—*Works and Days* affords the young poet many occasions to transcend his situation; he is possessed, evidently, by figures of religious authority—saint, prophet, god and martyr. With the authority of desperation, he speaks in their voices, offers his mewing handful of sacred and mythic negatives ("Although like Theseus I fought, / I have become what I have slain"), perverse, compulsive, haunted by a failure to have acted or even suffered heroically which is the endemic complaint of the American Jew of Feldman's generation; when a god (and it is, characteristically, "a god," not God, that the stage directions specify) speaks to his city "After the Judgment," we hear the poet condemning himself to his identity:

> . . . *The destiny you bear! to be as you are.*
>
> *To live was always to be judged, and what*
> *Was hardest: to be judged as right. For all things*
> *Are so, even you. And now you cannot*
> *Hide from the sunlight of your beings.*

Selfhood has its satyr-plays, of course. After so much sucking-up to the Sublime, there comes, gratifyingly for the poet's sanity, we must feel, a terrible Bronx cheer. Not always speaking about "Dying" in the noble character of Oedipus:

> *How will you know your chest from the night?*
> *—When the sphinx has come there asking*
> *Its inexorable question. How will you raise it up?*
> *How will you call? The night is here, asking*
> *'Where are you? You, where are you?'*
> *How will you inform the night?* . . .
> *How will you say, 'I am here. Here I am?'*
> *Breath is a question, breath the answer.*
> *But when your heart's hammerstrokes*
> *Stutter, I, I, I am,*
> *And your voice calls out, 'Where are you?'*
> *You!*
> *How will you know yourself from the night?*

nor about "Birth" in that of Theseus:

> . . . *if only*
> *We can praise the moment and what is given*
> *In it, even ourselves dying, then must*
> *We move by our heart's desire and all*
> *Its blest fatalities, and, living that*

Perfected hope, the sense of oneself moving,
Cannot misstep, if only we hallow
And will not violate . . .

Irving Feldman has a grotesque impersonation in his repertoire as well:
in his treatment of the Flood, one of his finest poems, it is only to be
expected that his speaker would be not Noah but one of his doomed
fellow-townsmen, outraged by the patriarch's greed for heroics:

One comes telling us Noah has built a boat
That through the flood he may ride about,
And filled it all with animals.
Just like the drunken fool, that slut-
Chaser, to think of no one else.

I feed my friends and kin; twenty nine thrived
In my home. But mad Noah harangues the air
Or goes muttering in his cuff
As though a god were up his sleeve.
Who is Noah to get saved? . . .

Out of its harness the mind wild as a horse
Roams the rooms and streets. There are some that say
Noah sits amid the rude beasts in his ark
And they feed one upon the other in the dark
And in the dark they mate. And some say worse . . .

Some here say a dove has come,
Sure, they think, the sign of a god.
And others say that Noah walks the street
Puffed with news. But bid him wait!
We are busy with our flood.

The wit and energy of the verse here, the vitality of the *contraption*, is
a product of a successful ventriloquism: when he speaks for himself,
Feldman is often slack, often slow to come to the point. Only at the
end of this first book, looking back at these funny stories and tragic
fables, the long series of poems in which solemnity is incurred like a
disease, and the grotesque furthered in a saving series of literally
gnomic verses where "The Gnome" speaks:

My Favorite Flower Is: the Red Rose.
My Favorite Occupation Is: Repose.
My Favorite Game: Articulation.
My Favorite Fear: Suffocation.
When I Grow Up I Want To Be: the Same,

> *Only endlessly and more fascinatingly more so!*
> *My Favorite Element Is: Earth.*
> *My Ultimate Aim*
> *Is (without further ado):*
> *Rebirth.*

—is Feldman able, wryly, reluctantly, deprecatingly ("I have eaten all my words, / and still I am not satisfied!") to speak out not as some Giant Form, not as some archetypal trope in that art of mistaken identities which is myth, but as his own man:

> Après le déluge, moi.
> *There it is, all the sad tale—*
> *A perfect post-diluvian male,*
> *And other humanist ta ran ta ra.*
> *For after all, it's only disgrace,*
> *At the very best, to outlive*
> *(Half-monadnock, half-sieve)*
> *The saddest thing in the life of the race.*

Irving Feldman's second book, *The Pripet Marshes and Other Poems*, published in 1965, leaves us in no doubt, from the first lines of the "Prologue," that the cue of that final poem in the first book had been taken, the self forced out of its camouflaging, buck-passing mythologies, the speaker identified:

> *I in the foreground, in the background I,*
> *And the stone in the center of all,*
> *I by the stone declaiming, I*
> *Writing here, I trundling in*
> *The moody mountain scene, the cardboard*
> *Couples, the dusty star, I turning*
> *From the page, my hand staying moonlit,*
> *My pen athwart the light, I dimming*
> *The moon with cloud . . . Thinking,*
> *Thinking . . . And, still by the stone, I*
> *Attent to my declamation, taking it down.*

The poet claims his responsibility, "pen athwart the light," to account for the world in his own person. Where in the first book the poet's vocation was explicitly mocked—"his Master File of Forms, Norms, and Storms"—and accommodated only *faute de mieux:*

> *It is to be doubted we live as well or die better.*

—Feldman can now summon his forces, enriched probably by the orders of the very figures he once mimicked and now assimilates to his own substance, "because I love dialectic and song," can bear to face "The Six Million":

> *Survivor, who are you?*
> *Ask the voices that disappeared,*
> *The faces broken and expunged.*
> *I am the one who was not there.*
> *Of such accidents I have made my death.*

We must not allow the heroism of this admission to pass unremarked —Feldman's survival as a poet is in it. There is, further, a wonderful courage in the long poem of this name, when Feldman accepts the burden laid upon him by his unparticipating history, an acceptance unmediated by myth or personation, a self-acceptance:

> *I heard the air (that was*
> *To be ashen) and the flesh*
> *(That was to be broken), I heard*
> *Cry out, Possess me! . . .*
>
> *Dear ones, what can I say?*
> *I must possess you no matter how,*
> *Father you, befriend you,*
> *And bring you to the lighthearted dance*
> *Beside the treasures and the springs,*
> *And be your brother and your son . . .*
> *Come in your widow's raiment of dust and ashes,*
> *Bereaved, newborn, gasping for*
> *The breath that was torn from you,*
> *That is returned to you . . .*
> *My heart is full, only the speech*
> *Of the ritual can express it.*
> *And after a little while,*
> *I will rouse you from your dawn sleep*
> *And accompany you in the streets.*

Much of the rest of this book—not all of it; no one element of a body of poetry can be as pre-emptive as it appears in discussion: if I detach certain notions which I call basic, it may turn out only that they are detachable—is devoted to an investigation of the ritual that alone can express a full heart, most brilliantly, I think, in a witty series of poems "after Picasso's Suite de 180 dessins" and in another such series "after Picasso's Portrait de Femme" (the solemnities of Goya and Michelangelo in the earlier book are exchanged for the contemporary's "spoor of anecdotes, vestigia, mask-droppings"; the myth of greatness and the myth of madness are dropped in favor of the artisan's "motley of loss"). In "vocations of hammer, stylus, string," Feldman now sees the possibility of "the small change of relation," as in the case of Picasso:

> *Quickly, this ease he translates*
> *to opportunities, discovers answers,*
> *Landfalls, clues to something hidden . . .*

And in a further poem, "Clown and Destiny," the problem of role-playing, of part-taking is worked out explicitly: Feldman addresses himself as a kind of comedian, trying masks, haunted by a tragic identity ("the dead one among the shifting figures") which cannot be beguiled by mere impersonations ("the renewals of your painted face"); in them he thereby discovers what he must oppose and so *becomes* the dead one:

> *Armored to battle what killing thing appears:*
> *Starlight or dog or turning ocean.*

Willing to speak as "the dead one," to assume the identities of the dead —"I am my dead brother (and I am you), / I survive . . ."—this poet turns and confronts his life with an astonishing nakedness of statement; his language is often, in the nature of his undertaking, abstract, his lines often have no metrical norm, despite the typographical appearance of initial capitals and rhymes, yet in them there is always what Hopkins called the rhythms of prose, that is, the native and natural rhythm of speech, the least forced, the most marked of all possible rhythms:

> *Many smile, but few are happy; my friends,*
> *Their lives hardening about them, are stern*
> *With misery, knowing too well their ends . . .*
>
> *Despair brutalizes. That is the law. (But*
> *Is there music in that?) My friends, feeling*
> *Their lives hardening, grow harder, less appealing;*
> *Almost the past condoning, almost a pleasure*
> *Finding there they cannot in their harder future,*
> *Though they know, as we say, the two go together.*
> *So wise men have said all things return.*
>
> *(Many smile, but few are happy; my friends,*
> *With misery, knowing too well their ends,*
> *Their lives hardening about them, are stern.)*

This is another kind of poetry than the personating voice, the dramatic monologues of *Works and Days*. There is a poetry that says one thing is another thing, which is the poetry of metaphor, of recognition; but there is also an ultimate poetry that says a thing is itself, which is the poetry of statement, of cognition. This poetry of cognition is what Irving Feldman has arrived at, has earned. In the title poem of his second book, a dream of persecution and death in which the oneiric elements, by the rhythm of the poet's voice, have penetrated so far into experience as to seem supremely *natural*, and in the final "Song" of that book, in which the nature addressed has become supremely *formal:*

So you are

Stone, stone or star,
Flower, seed,
Standing reed,
River going far

So you are

—in these acknowledgments there is a beautiful visionary exactitude; in such "speech of the ritual" we may hear the expression of a full heart, the longed-for rebirth. For it is only, Irving Feldman shows us—and how perfectly in those three syllables: "so you are"—it is only when we have identities that we can have transformations.

Magic Papers by IRVING FELDMAN

A decade ago, Irving Feldman's first book, *Works and Days*, articulated an identity in two ways: wry, brilliant, as a stand-up tragic; plangent, even solemn, as the puppet of enormous mythological personations (Oedipus, Moses, the Wandering Jew). In *The Pripet Marshes*, his second book, Feldman directed these voices upon the holocaust of contemporary history, sought relations between what survives and what is consumed. Under such pressure, the resonances fused, and Feldman forged an utterance which in his new book is unmistakable, though happily not invulnerable: that twist of the natural idiom we call a style.

The first thing to notice about these demanding, rewarding poems —generally long, generally low-pitched—is their sentences, that word itself a clue, for it meant, once, a discernment by the senses and the mind. Difficult as these poems are, if you listen simply to the modulated voice in which they are stated—even chanted, even sung—you are led through the toils of subject matter and out into understanding:

> *I detest the wryness of my voice,*
> *Its ulteriority, its suffering—*
> *What is not lived only*
> *Can suffer so. I wish to give birth to the deep,*
> *Deliver myself on this darkness, this devil.*

The accent is of wisdom. We are so used to cleverness, to knowingness, even to learning—and Feldman has helped us to be used to them —that the accent of wisdom, reticent, observant, matte, comes as a shock, a disquietude. Whether he is watching the fanatic girl who lives across the airshaft, or lovers on the Brighton Beach Local, whether he is moralizing his own childhood or his wife's nightmares, observing a girl dressing hornpout or partridges for a meal or merely —merely!—celebrating his unbelief, there is a gravity in Feldman's new poems that pinions the mind. It is not a gravity alien to wit, or even to fun, and it is wonderfully nimble in tracing a figure. Still, it is the gravity which is heavy with grief, for that is what gravity ultimately means: "Oh why is the soul sent on its errands / in the dark? with its list / of names, its fist of pennies, / its beating heart?" Feldman cannot answer, that is the entire burden of his book, but he goes on asking, interrogating the world, and his reward is to speak it: "eternity emerges at its growing point."

The New York Times Book Review, 1970

Lost Originals by Irving Feldman

Together, as the children say, is where it's at: the very word, which at its root means not only the *gate* through which we gather but the *good* which we gather for, exactly describes Feldman's achievement, his risk and his reward. Always till now in his work there has been a yoking together of what is felt—or known, or not even suspected—to be disjunct. Our shrewd Minos of poetry, R.W. Flint, has referred to Feldman driving pairs in tandem—Heine and Maimonides up front, Kafka and Blake behind. In speaking of the poet's earlier (three) books, I myself have referred to his "articulating an identity in two ways," and indeed if Flint and I have been right, the poet now drives right past us in that handsome equipage. If there has always been the tug between wit and wisdom, the war of survival against consumption or even against consummation in Feldman's two-chambered heart, what is fascinating here and now is the fused, annealed singularity of the voice, the energy of a diction which—out of so many refusals and losses—gets it all together: ". . . the missing world, / the hidden heart-attack were one."

The poet is released by his singular lack of duplicity into two kinds of energy inaccessible to him when he suffered the divisions of comment and criticism: he is enabled to wield, with stunning effect, a kind of polymorphous perversity of language, of words, of syllables: he can *play* more profitably than any other poet among us:

> *to hear*
> *love's lithe youngtongue's shaping son*
>
> *mouthoozemuse*
> *titwitwoostalk*
> *mamadrama*
> *stablebabelburble*
> *sleeperslupper*
> *bloomballoomboom*
> *sayseedsomescatterthing . . .*

and he can *mythologize* on his own, lost originals indeed, which have found the poet and forced him, as the original does, to the source. It is no accident that so many of the myths are of children—"The Jumping Children", "The Air Children", "The Marvel was Disaster"; indeed it is an intention that even the poems which are about the end—are "about" death, dissolution and destruction—return (where else could they go?) to the beginning, to what childhood may loom up as or illumine: "Dying, Morton saw a child who was / the child he'd been, who would become / the man he is . . ."

Finest, because fiercest, of these new myth-makings which so melt birth and becoming into bereavement is "My Olson Elegy." The insistent possessiveness of the very title suggests at once the kind of organized violence (and what else is poetry?) being done to a great tradition, acknowledged here as great and gradually operative in the enterprise of mourning: at the end, a means of releasing the elegist into his own powers, his own primacy. Astonishing in its decorum, a recuperation of baroque diction, it is, among other things, the source of his book's ominous title:

> *you plunge to the primitive deep*
> *where satire's puny dreadful monsters,*
> *its Follies and its Vices, cannot reach,*
> *and swim among their lost originals*
> *—free, forgotten, powerful, moving*
> *wholly in a universe of rhythm—*
> *and re-enter your own first Fool,*

inventing happiness out of nothing.
You are the legend death and the sea have seized
in order to become explicable.

Feldman's elegy asserts its incomparable modernity not by any sur-
render of magniloquence, not by a modish shrinking (or sinking)
from "superlative song", but by its reversal of conduct: whereas the
movement of "Lycidas", say, is from despair through a series of
insights to triumphant joy, that of "My Olson Elegy" is from *res-
sentiment* through a series of submissions to a dispersed, dispensing
illumination: death becomes an acceptance of earth (and water) so
enormous that what had appeared to be an immortal triumph of
poetry turns out merely another action of mortality, and that is the
true triumph—Adonis recycled. "The swimmer like the sea reaches
every shore."

Though I have admired, and indeed addressed myself to, each of
Feldman's books with the conscientiousness which fine work must
elicit from any fair reader, I admit that I should never have suspected
anything so incandescent to come from the author of those first three
collections. *Lost Originals* is not a collection, it is a triumph of
identity; it is, in pleasure and myth, one thing, "one with the world's
danger / that now is nothingness and now a tooth." He has made
himself a master, and what is most astonishing of all, Irving Feldman
is a master of joy.

Poetry, 1973

EDWARD FIELD

"His Body Comes Together Joyfully
from All Directions."

THEY RECOMMEND themselves from the very start, these two volumes of poems—the first, *Stand Up, Friend, with Me*, published in 1963 and the Lamont Poetry Selection of that year; the second, *Variety Photoplays*, published in 1967—by their extreme resistance to the habitual conventions of literature. Even the convention of experimentalism, to which acquiescence has become a second nature in most of our poets, fails to account for Field's poems which we may recognize, beyond the marshallings of polite letters, as spiels, recitals, routines; as embarrassments, confessions, rejected addresses, gropes—as anything, almost, but that loaded and irreversible transaction with language, policed always by the negative faculty (*irony*, modern criticism calls it, or *ambiguity*, or *tension*), which is the poem itself, at least since Mallarmé. Rejecting the common rules in the service of a common necessity—the vision of the transfigured body—Edward Field's work is free of the old customs and costumes, and docile only to a kind of meandering measure which owes nothing to the arbitraments of tradition. This author, then, has produced a canon of successful poems without meter, without rhyme, without music, without images, without any of the disciplines and strictures we think of as constituting that share—at best the lion's, and at the very least some jackal's scrap—of poetry required by *verse*. Field has remained perfectly indifferent to all that is usually demanded by those who believe poetry owes its merits to the felicities of a received form, to the responsibilities of an acknowledged constant element (and the acknowledgment, of course, is made largely by departing from such an element) in structure and diction, those for whom the poem exists only as a system whereby the incantatory asserts its privileges over the accidental.

Readers with such expectations—and they are more often than not on the side of the angels, though most *poets*, as Blake said of Milton, are of the devil's party without knowing it—will be inevitably disappointed by Edward Field's *oeuvre*. They will manifest their *parti pris* and their disdain by admiring these poems as anything but poems. They will grant them that strange compensation—the one we accord, in an analogous disquiet, to Virginia Woolf when we say that her novels are "really" poems—which consists in seeing a piece of splendid psychotherapy or sensational journalism in an unsuccessful poem.

Yet there is a reason for the apparent artlessness of these texts, there is even a formal necessity for their informality; and if we consider the radical nature of Field's undertaking, if we listen to what he is saying, in short, we shall discover the eminent dignity of his style, which in fact is not merely adequate to the demands of his enterprise but the only proper and even probable accommodation of his gift. In a case as ostensibly promiscuous as Field's, just as in the rigors of the fussiest sonneteer, we are restored to Stravinsky's beautiful truth: "We cannot observe the creative phenomenon independently of the form in which it is made manifest."

Its title is nowhere to be found in Edward Field's first book. The phrase comes in fact from a poem rather coquettishly omitted from that collection, but crucial enough to the poet's recondite design for him to have retained it as a general adjuration to himself:

> . . . *The nations send each other their favorite singers and dancers,*
> *the emissaries of love from one nation to another,*
> *the body of mankind whole, relaxed and growing.*
> Stand up, friend, with me.

The friend addressed is the poet's own penis, no less, that "little friend" which an esoteric tradition construes as a proportional image of the whole man. With this invocation to his own genital prowess and ecstasy, Field appropriately opens his discourse, which is to concern a world of consciousness *that does not negate any more*, a world of union with others and oneself based not on anxiety and aggression but on narcissism and erotic exuberance, "the body of mankind whole, relaxed and growing."

In such a world, inhabited, according to the Jewish adepts of the Cabala, by Adam's perfect body before the Fall—the criteria of an androgynous mode of being and of narcissistic self-expression pretty well repudiate the notion of art as the West has come to accept it, the notion of art as arduous taskmistress ("His true Penelope was Flaubert" and all that). It is Edward Field's pledge to "Love, the beloved republic," that he does not invoke the negative, the critical, in writing his poems. The language is set down with just enough solicitude to *set* —there is no expression that could not be replaced by some other, no locution irreversibly committed to its own rhythm and texture. What there is is a *vision*—to which the poet is so accountable that he relies on his entire identification with it to speak for him. His work, then, in Hegel's famous phrase, may be described as love playing with itself; but this idea sinks into triviality if, as Hegel also observed, the seriousness, the pain, the patience and the labor of the Negative are omitted. These things are not omitted by Edward Field's poetry—they simply have nothing to do with the *making*, the *façon* of that poetry. The Negative receives its due from Field, its needful reverence and utilization, rather, in an understanding of death—a response so deep that death is at last welcomed and rejoiced over as a part of life. Death is no longer separated from and opposed to existence, but seen as integral to a life that can be lived without repression, without sublimation, and therefore without history. In eternal delight, in endless play—

> *Making the movement of dancing and the noise of singing,*
> *Taking each others' bodies in our arms,*

—life and death are conjugated as they are by the animals, which as Rilke said see All where we see only the future, see "themselves in All and themselves healed forever." That is where Field begins, in the undifferentiated beatitude of creatures, and from animals and plants whose realm is eternity, not history, he takes his tropes, his emblems of that polymorphous-perverse world of eternal delight, without work, without art—an erotic sense of reality.

The first section of *Stand Up, Friend, with Me* is called "Greece," and though it includes a number of poems which pass themselves off as no more than clear-eyed, sharp-tongued mementos of a journey:

> *Naturally one doesn't always expect to see*
> *People wearing snakes for hair*
> *Or satyrs chasing youths*
> *Or charming gods turning into still more charming bulls,*
> *But such things do occur.*
> *One knows, for example, that men and goats*
> *Copulate with fertile success.*
> *Look now at this goat walking up the road*
> *Led by a young Greek with a definite goatish look:*

> *Goats and Greeks have lived together for so long*
> *That there are many similarities,*
> *Especially when they sing . . .*

though the poet indulges his reportage like any American fellowship holder, the chief burden of these natural songs is to collect a "doctrine of scattered occasions among the things wanting," as Bacon puts it; hints of a golden age from an archaic world. Typically, the poems "Donkeys" and "Goats" locate the desirable possibilities not in the present life of men, but in the eternal life-and-death of beasts:

> *Donkeys . . . are sensitive*
> *And cry continually under their burdens;*
> *Yes, they are animals of sensibility*
> *Even if they aren't intelligent enough*
> *To count money or discuss religion . . .*
>
> *I am sure that donkeys know what life should be*
> *But, alas, they do not own their bodies;*
> *And if they had their own way, I am sure*
> *That they would sit in a field of flowers*
> *Kissing each other, and maybe*
> *They would even invite us to join them.*
>
> *For they never let us forget that they know*
> *(As everyone knows who stays as sweet as children)*
> *That there is a far better way to spend time . . .*

Even the pagan culture is a failure when judged by the criterion of the animals; beyond even the most primitive intuitions of men, the donkeys and the pre-pubertal life of children are already designated as the sources of the insight Field has made his own. Even the modern Greek has his (capitalized) moment of participation, though, in the ecstatic process:

> *The gross butcher with small eyes and a stupid forehead*
> *Starts hosing away the pools of blood,*
> *And the expression on his face slowly changes*
> *From Eternal Destroyer to haggling merchant.*
>
> *. . . it would be ridiculous,*
> *Even though unskinned he looks like us,*
> *To mourn a goat.*
>
> *And besides there is nothing to mourn;*
> *Certainly not his death*

While he cooks in peace in various kitchens,
Nor his life when he leapt from rock to rock . . .

So let us be as joyful as he was,
Eating our goat stew,
Making the movement of dancing and the noise of singing,
Taking each others' bodies in our arms
And then filing simply off to bed.

Human felicity is here seen as only a partial approximation of the recurrent delights that are under the sign of Pan, the goat god. For human felicity is linear, moves into the "future," and can remember. Elsewhere in this group of poems, the implications of history are defined and decried—for Field, history is always connected with his own Jewishness, the failures of an apocalyptic mission—as a fall into time:

If one is a Jew who has a history
—Meaning simply to remember and be sad—
Then Ruth became a Jewess
When Naomi's kisses in her gentile blood
Turned the rumors garrulous in her veins . . .

and therefore as a fall out of genius "to the middling stature of the merely talented." Thus Field's Icarus, whose eyes had once "compelled the sun," ends up in the suburbs (" 'That nice Mr. Hicks' the neighbors called him") constructing small wings and trying to "fly / to the lighting fixture on the ceiling: / fails every time and hates himself for trying." Suitably, Field employs not only Greek and Biblical figures in this group of archaics, but even Aladdin to suggest—in the cadences of a disinherited Cavafy, a Cavafy who refuses to believe in the glories of vanished empire any more than he believes in the sordid present—the botched job men have made of their aspirations to restore the soul to the body:

There by the cemetery is the market
Where the junkmen spread their wares,
All the things we use, grow sick of, and throw away.
Go there, friend: For he who dares to pick the magic lamp
From row on row identically tarnished,
Knowing a dragon will issue from its wick,
And swing the monster by his jaggedy tail
Will have the power of a giant at his bidding.

Field's giant is the poem itself, the poem as multitudinous lover. Released by it into the world, into the profane City as well as into the sacred Past, collecting not only from myth but from fallen history, from the icons of a civilization without holy places, the vestiges of an undivided life, "the life of sensations rather than thoughts" Keats asked for, Edward Field addresses himself to his task:

> *over this paper I*
> *put hands to my desire*
> *that your waking eyes may see*
> *your thighs respond and open*
> *warm mouth and a thousand arms*
> *reach beloved poem for me.*

He ends this group with a "Prologue" to the fallen world which recalls that other great influence on his work, the Whitman whose claims on love and death are even more insistent than Cavafy's for being less ingenuous—the cataloguing Whitman whose invocation to "fish-shaped Paumanok" is deliberately echoed here as the lines funnel down to the self-asserting poet, crannied in the universe:

> *Look, friend, through the fog of gasses at this world*
> *With its skin of earth and rock, water and ice,*
> *With various creatures and rooted things;*
> *And up from the bulging waistline*
> *To this land of concrete towers,*
> *Its roads swarming like a hive cut open,*
> *Offshore to this island, long and fish shaped,*
> *Its mouth to a metropolis,*
> *And in its belly, this village,*
> *A gathering of families at a crossways,*
> *And in this house, upstairs and through the wide open door*
> *Of the front bedroom with a window on the world,*
> *Look, friend, at me.*

In the poems in the second section of his book, "A View of Jersey," Field moves in on the life of his transfigured body, intimated in the terms of a more—precisely—intimate mythology, interleaving the necropolis of his days against the condemned playground of his desires:

> *. . . I can see the ferry leave the shore*
> *With a load of commuters like refugees from a land*
> *Where faces have no face, and bodies only exist*
> *If you put your arms around them.*

In his most vatic accents, Field tells us he has chosen "The complete island for a vision not the desolate nation. / It is the holiest of mysteries"—and to that vision

My devotion shall be absolute
Like my faithfulness as a child
To Little Orphan Annie, Tom Mix,
And after dinner The Lone Ranger.

The love Field will lavish upon these luminous deities of his (of ours, certainly) is articulated here for the first time, and it is a theme which will be greatly amplified throughout his work; movies, radio programs, advertising—the media offer access to The Stars, those heavenly bodies whose promise never fails this poet, however remote their station and however oppressed his own circumstances:

I love you Chopin in spite of Merle Oberon
Although that was a pretty good movie where sweet Paul Muni
Still had two good eyes to see you were a genius.
I liked how he made you fight for Polish nationalism
That dead duck with two heads;
But of course really he was urging you
Not to turn over the Jews to the Germans
And your fingers flew like mad to save them,
But you couldn't save them since piano playing
Never saves anyone except the player if he's cute besides
(Like Van Cliburn walking through the Iron Curtain).
Anyway when my mother was a girl in Poland
It had become a nation already, a nation of Jewhaters
So it couldn't have been the result of your gorgeous music
Which clearly says, Love the Jews.

It is his adoration of the glamorous and gleaming divinities (they are, after all, the only versions around of the transfigured body, and if narcissism and androgynous exuberance are in order, the movie-star is not a bad surrogate) which sees Field through a great deal of dissatisfaction—with work, city living, cold weather, "a life of goose pimples and sweat," "mankind and his hungers." Indeed many of the poems in this section of the book are '30s-resonant invoices of protest and discontent, as in "Notes from a Slave Ship":

It is necessary to wait until the boss's eyes are on you
Then simply put your work aside,
Slip a fresh piece of paper in the typewriter,
And start to write a poem.

Let their eyes boggle at your impudence;
The time for a poem is the moment of assertion,
The moment when you say I exist—
Nobody can buy my time absolutely . . .

At the same time, there is a Chaplinesque modesty about his protest; gazing out at the harbor from his Wall Street prison, Field rejects as Penates the "enormous liners" ("What have I to do with ocean monsters?") and opts for the quotidian ferryboats "that cross from shore to shore." There is, for all his idolizing of the brave and the beautiful, a strong strain of the anti-heroic in his utopia:

> *I don't want Moses to walk on earth again*
> *And lead us, even to the promised land*
> *If there is one anywhere. I accept*
> *The size of man, the scope of his work, and his failure . . .*
>
> *Meanwhile evening has fallen . . . the great ship*
> *Has gone and I can look at the view again*
> *That I so depend on to free me from this office*
> *For trips to Hoboken and back like the ferryboat makes:*
> *The perfect space to read my heart in.*

But even in the worst of the City ("If you go there they have signs up 'POETS KEEP OUT'") and its "identical slums," Field is able to keep in mind his apocalyptic mission, "to reclaim this island and make it green again." One breath of spring invariably recalls him to his role as exemplary Narcissus, to his expansive erotic play:

> *If I were naked I think my body*
> *Would know where to go of its own accord;*
> *In the spring mist compounded with soot, barefoot,*
> *By the breeze on my skin and the feel of the stones*
> *I would go, not in a straight line of course,*
> *But this way and that, as human nature goes,*
> *Finding, if not the place, the way there.*

Yet there are distractions. Politics, for example, seems to offer all kinds of dramatic possibilities for the poet in search of an available Eden, and Field is ready to accept the challenge of Serious Subjects, however apprehensive he shows himself ("For I am going to write on World Issues / Which demands laughter where we most believe"). His apprehension is justified by the facts, for not only is he likely to make a fool of himself (however gladly) by the sort of sentimental campfire-Communism that must draw smiles, even now, in Peking, but he suggests that his enthusiasm for the Revolution has more to do with writing the new clean poem than with providing new clean housing-projects. Nor is this the first time that an artist has championed what seemed a likely historical process only to find himself flouted by the course of events. "My subject, Dear Muse, is Fidel Castro"—

Please, Sweet Seeker, don't discourage me from contradicting myself
But make everything sound like life, like people we like
And most of all give me strength not to lay aside this poem
Like so many others in the pile by my typewriter
But to write the whole thing from beginning to end
O Perfection, the way it wants to go.

But after several pages of fumbling—if furious—celebration, Field's distaste for the negative opens his eyes:

Then Castro is like a poet writing an ode
(Alas that poets should be rulers—
Revise that line, cut that stanza, lop off that phrase) . . .

What he did was kick out the bad men and good riddance Batista
What he is doing . . . Well, what he is trying to do is . . .
(Muse, why don't you help me with this,
Are you scared of socialist experiment?) . . .

The disillusionment sets in, and the incapacity to sustain the identification with a world of Forces and Factors beyond the sanction of individual will:

By the time you see this, Fidel, you might not even exist any more
My government is merciless and even now
The machine to destroy you is moving into action
The chances are you won't last long
Well so long pal it was nice knowing you
I can't go around with a broken heart all my life
After I got over the fall of the Spanish Republic
I guess I can get over anything
My job is just to survive . . .

So you're not perfect, poets don't look for perfect
It's your spirit we love and the glamor of your style
I hope someday the cameras of the world
Are turned on you and me in some spot like Harlem
And then you'll get a kiss that will make Khrushchev's be forgotten
A kiss of the poet, that will make you truly good
The way you meant to be.

Politics turns out to be no more than a breeding-culture for charismatic figures, tutelary deities who can recall the poet to his true role as King of the May, simpleton-prophet of the Earthly Paradise. Far more significant to Field than the public world he invariably recognizes as a cheat and a delusion is the family romance, the realm of sibling relations he can evoke so powerfully, and control by a mere act of memory. Of course the disappointments, capitalist bourgeois culture being what it is, are the same. Even as Fidel's fall from favor mirrors Field's:

> *Fidel, Fidel, Fidel . . .*
> *I am in love with the spotlight myself*
> *And would like the crowds to chant my name*
> *Which has the same letters as yours but rearranged*
> Where is my island Where my people
> What am I doing on this continent Where is my crown
> Where did everyone go that used to call me king
> And light up like votive candles when I smiled?
> (*I have given them all up for you sweet youth my muse*
> *Be truly mine.*)

so the baby sister, cherished as the poet's particular object-lesson in total erotics, deserts this generous narcissist:

But you grew up and went away and got married
As little girls grow up into women
Leaving us gasping and desperate and hurt.
And we recover and forget, or half-forget
Until sitting down to write a birthday poem we remember everything—
A little girl on her potty hunched seriously to the business
Or holding all of you at once in my arms, colt, calf, and pussy-cat:
All I mean is, I miss you my little sister.

What is missed, then, is a kind of communion in undifferentiated mutual play; it is no accident that the prelapsarian evocation of his sister locates the "little girl on her potty," for the Body, resurrected, will revel in all its functions, even those despised and censored by our crippling culture. Field ends his book, of course, with a poem to Eden, "The Garden," which opens with a cautious catalogue of "the plants on the window ledges" and swells magically to a vision of the Happy Omphalos:

> *The mango practically exploded it looked so pregnant*
> *Cherry, peach, apple and plum trees flourish*
>
> *The potato eyes threw up weird white shoots*
> *And the birdseed grew a good crop of ragweed*
>
> *We have formed a colony in a strange land*
> *Planting our seeds and making ourselves at home*

The laws are our own to make except those of growth
Which are God's and we obey His alone . . .

Thus Field keeps faith with the substance of things hoped for, his impulse being to help mankind toward that erasure of the traces of original sin which Baudelaire said was the true definition of progress. The poems in *Stand Up, Friend, with Me*—funny, tear-jerking, accurate and yet apocalyptic—achieve a miraculous balance between sentimentality and doctrine, between accident and law; they do so because Field has not yet been so damaged by life as to betray or merely decorate his vision (he was thirty-eight when the book was published); he sees clearly—"eating what's to eat and making love with what's available"—what he wants, for all its discrepancies from what he must put up with. His wit tinges his bliss with precisely the rusty flavor needed to keep the fruit of the tree from going mushy, on the one hand; yet his confidence in what he has seen, in his vision, keeps that same fruit from turning, cynically, into no more than an apple of Sodom on the other. By the end of this book, he is in a position to give free rein to his desire to express a kind of wisdom, compact of bitterness and confidence, of submission to the arbitrary and of aspiration to sense. In these poems, he seeks out formulations which seem to hesitate between paradox and the truth of the commonplace. Their simplicity is certainly the pinnacle of pride. We feel this poet has become his own oracle; the world in which he lives accepts only the presence of the character he has become: a prophet.

The Jews have invented, or at least promulgated, two great *personae* in the world's cast of characters: the prophet and the *shlemiehl*. They are, of course, the militant and the recessive avatars of the same figure, and just as every griping, victimized *kvetsh* is a soured Jeremiah, so in every seer is a transfigured *shlemiehl* who for once has had his own way. Field's second collection, *Variety Photoplays*, gives every indication that this poet has fallen back on the complaining, fault-finding side of the mask, one very much like Heine's; and if it were not for the very gentleness of his millennial predications we should probably be in for a good deal more harshness than we actually have to put up with in these long, prosy grumbles and bitchings. They enact a terrific sense of genre, these later poems: the adulation of the demigods which began in "Chopin" in the first book has now reached colossal—and carping—proportions. Not only is Field able to recount the peripities of, say, all the Frankenstein movies (including the Bride, the Son and the Return), but he manages to select just those saliences which serve his own purposes, as when he remarks of the returning monster:

Wasn't his flesh human flesh
even made from the bodies of criminals,
the worst the Baron could find?

But love is not necessarily implicit in human flesh:
Their hatred was now his hatred . . .

His idea—if his career now had an idea—
was to kill them all,
keep them in terror anyway,
let them feel hunted.
Then perhaps they would look at others
with a little pity and love.

Only a suffering people have any virtue.

This is a long, sad step from the donkeys kissing each other in the fields. It suggests the kind of reversal the poet has suffered, though it is just as evident that the change back into the pansexual prophet can be effected readily too. Not only movies (Field's range, though, is impressive here—from *all* the Joan Crawford films worked up into a single gigantic narrative through Simenon's *Touriste de Banane* to the revived vamp *à la* Louise Brooks: "Goodbye May Caspar. / We loved you / in the way we love— / faithlessly. Or are we, growing older, / ready to remember again / our great loves / of yesteryear / and go search for them / where we lost sight of them in those shabby places, / close to the brightest / lights / that cast the deepest / shadow"), but also comic strips ("Is Fritzy Nancy's aunt, or not?") and even the circus:

Oh no, he didn't die of cancer,
don't tell me that,
not Clyde Beatty who tamed lions and tigers . . .

it was Mr. Death who ate him up alive
as he does us all one way or another.
One day he introduces himself:
You Clyde, Me Death; let's go beautiful.
We are truly married to adventure . . .
I'd rather Clyde Beatty died in the ring . . .
but anyway, he's off now in the special heaven
with Frank Buck, Martin and Osa Johnson,
Hemingway, Tarzan, and Bomba,
where he belongs . . .

Field expends as much energy and talent seeing *through* these divinities of the popular iconography as he once did simply *seeing* them; the notion of roles obsesses him, and his narcissistic Eden is a good deal less heedlessly populated than before:

> *When last seen he was in a garden*
> *frisking with the creatures and the plants.*
> *He almost preferred the plants nowadays*
> *with their stillness that never exhausted you . . .*

> *He'll have to come out of that garden he so loves*
> *and step into the streets and join the throng*
> *hurrying down to the central marketplace*
> *where a throne and a gallows will be set up.*
> *He'll be chosen, as his fate demands,*
> *for one or the other, but never know which*
> *until the trapdoor falls or the crown descends.*

The vision of a world of infinite erotic possibilities, a world of pure play and endlessly available sex ("which means you are not allowed to say No, or choose"), jeopardizes, now, the notion of heroic pre-eminence ("Historians aren't writing our histories / so it is up to us to do it for ourselves") and cancels out politics along with monogamy in poem after poem spoken between clenched teeth; Eden appears to have shrunk with the passage of time:

> *Going out of my garden into the world of strangers*
> *I don't ask for a great god's help,*
> *I only ask a little one,*
> *say the god of stones . . .*

> *What choice have we got? None.*
> *Life has put me out of my garden. I go.*
> *Comfort me, stones.*
> *Leaves like lips, speak to me . . .*

Most important of all, the human body itself disappoints Field's notion of transfiguration—as Freud said, anatomy is fate, and no vision of a polymorphous-perverse paradise can withstand a thyroid deficiency:

> *To keep alive takes a larger army*
> *of servants and technicians every year,*
> *until by the time you are ninety*
> *you are a miracle of science . . .*

> *There are fewer and fewer hours in the day*
> *one can afford to stay awake . . .*

Withal, Field manages to hold onto his hopes, even if they less often assume the form of a revolutionary take-over which will transform all of Manhattan, say, into an "island paradise," so that you can "walk out of it into the nation pink and blue in the morning mist," and even if Field finds his exuberant analogies now chiefly with the life of plants and the other "lower" forms; he maintains, between the prophet's apocalypse and the *shlemiehl*'s complaint, a fine equilibrium in the best poems of this group, as in "Jellyfish Invasion":

> *. . . Some of the little creatures*
> *like to play kidneys and others*
> *are good for hearts*
> *okay everybody join hands*
> *and sing the national anthem*
>
> *there must have been a time*
> *when things were looser*
> *a time between gas and solid*
> *when things could shift about*
> *imagine seeing through people*
> *or whatever we were then*
> *and hugging vapor to vapor*
> *or jelly to jelly*
> *that was an inventive time*
> *this whole earth a big glob*
> *and everyone shifting sex like mad*
> *according to circumstance*
> *and trying out different shapes like hats*
> *lets get together and be dinosaurs gang*
> *we do it now*
> *but its like a tree trunk*
> *trying to take a walk*
> *better stay home*
> *there are some things decided on . . .*

Tempered, then, by a wry resignation to the facts ("Isn't it odd that there is no common word for foreskin?"), Edward Field suggests both the depths of our abasement and the heights of our aspiration in his final poem, "Grafitti"—the theme had been approached before, in the first book: "Blessings on all the kids who improve the signs in the subways"—in which a collector cuts out the whole wall, "an old wooden partition between the booths," leaving it just as it was "with its writings and pictures," a kind of palimpsest of our erotic yearnings toward the total bliss of life in the transfigured body, desecrated by the suppressions of a discontented civilization and yet exalted into a work of art:

and telephone numbers saying "call me"
and dates and times when free and where,
and descriptions of partners wanted
and acts or roles desired . . .
and instructive drawings of the sex organs in all positions
some half-washed out by the char, or painted over
but dug so deep or traced lovingly so often
they were still visible through the paint . . .

It is this Rosetta Stone of his lost world that stands as a suitable
monument to Field's own delightful achievement and despair:

He took that whole wall, the size of a school blackboard,
figured over as it was like an oriental temple,
the work of a people, a folk artifact,
the record of lifetimes of secret desires,
the forbidden and real history of man,
and leaving it just as it was, hung it up in his house.

Respecting tradition
he charged everyone a nickel to see it.

DONALD FINKEL

"There Is No Perfection Possible.
But There Is Tomorrow."

CHARACTERIZING the myths of Attis, Sallustius remarks—and it is
an observation I would extend to all myth, to the accommoda-
tion of life by myth—"this never happened, but it always is." The
problem of "happening," of occurring uniquely in time, is one that is
anathema to the absolute or obsessed mind, which insists upon recur-
rence, ritual, the regeneration of immediate experience our poet calls
"the ultimate phoenix." To such a mind,

> *Nothing is real that has happened*
> *Only once . . .*
> > *There*
> *Is something in certain events that*
> *Drives one to repetition.*

Yet we all believe ourselves, in the words of the Church, to be "unique
and irreplaceable," and the apparent conflict between our experience of
singularity and our culture's myths of recurrence underlies most of our
poetry; in a sense, the myth of history, linear rather than cyclical,
eventual rather than eternal, is the great modern myth, at variance with
the cycles and spirals of the traditional model. The poet, a man exposed
to "what happens" as much as any other, has customarily preferred the
cyclical convention (what else is the very form of poetry?), the myth
of return. Yet today, when he often feels its coils to be merely and
mostly a strangulation, his predicament is that he must work himself
into the very element most alien to his craft: *events*, single and mean-
ingless events which he knows to be "the garbage of his days." Retreat

from the periodic—the escape from myth into individuality, history and death—is the prime compulsion of Donald Finkel's poetry, and if I collect my evidence as to this poet's substantive purpose with some injustice to his achievement in *all* its articulations, it must be remembered that no feature of a body of poetry can loom so importantly as it appears in critical discourse; there is occasion for no more—but no less —than an essay in emphasis.

In 1959 Donald Finkel's first collection, *The Clothing's New Emperor and Other Poems*, was published. The first thing one notices is that the myths are there: Midas, Theseus, Bluebeard ("The room, once entered, held no mystery. The problem was to discover why one had entered in the first place."), Jacob, Odysseus, Orpheus, Dedalus, The Sirens, and the largest effort toward cyclical apprehension, "The Hunt of the Unicorn: A Tapestry in Five Acts." In this last series, Finkel·is explicit about his besetting difficulty: where to begin. He always mistrusts his own entrance into the poem, the event—for instance, he begins his version of "Le Jongleur de Notre Dame" with this nervous approximation: "It runs something like this"—for if reality is acquired solely through repetition or participation, there is a kind of damnation in *the first time:*

> *All starts are false: even Francis,*
> *Who bid the weavers add beginning*
> *And end to a fabulous enough encounter,*
> *Knew from his distance how all*
> *Eminence falls into a plane, no*
> *Rise, decline, only a continuous*
> *Between, tasting of both.*

Many of the poems in this book are about how to launch, how to initiate poems: "An Aesthetic of Imitation," "In the Beginning," "Beginnings," and "Poem as Seen from a Balcony," which opens:

> *Some days it is time to think about the poem*
> *That comes and goes in the mind.*

The figure here is of the mind-as-Juliet ambushed and beset by inaugurating possibilities ("Poems like Montagues prowl unseen in the night"), seeking a foyer of experiences from which one's actions can be radial rather than linear, not moving onward toward an end and a new beginning, but outward indefinitely. Hence many poems, here and in later collections, about bullfighting (Finkel lived in Mexico for a year), that primary instance of man in the center. Violence and sudden death, crucifixion and cruelty are seen both as the point whereby one breaks into the world of recurrence:

> *Knowing the ritual must be at all costs preserved,*
> *or man suffer the loss of his link with death,*
> *he bade the priest assume the place of the bull.*

> *As the bull leaned to the sword, he would lean to the horns,*
> *proffering the secrets of his groin and breast;*
> *he became the torero of three olés and an ay!*

> *And what was it for the mob . . .*
> *What was he worth, aloft, disdainful, withdrawn?*
> *Yet they left released, as if from actual chains,*
> *from the guilt which men call pity, from fear of death,*

> *in the exhausted bliss that follows the creative act . . .*

and as the punishment for failing to do so:

> *And, in any case, if after the recorte*
> *The bull has not been properly fixed, he*
> *is likely to find himself sitting bowel-deep*
> *On a pus-colored horn. Theseus. Olé.*

Violence and bloodshed obsess the other poems too, of course. The world of myth can afford to brutalize any encounter; nothing need be saved or spared, for all will come round again. The Unicorn series, which provides a learned and witty exergue to the famous tapestries, and thereby to the very history which their subject cancels out, manages to transcend the decorative not only by a tugging commitment to the Eternal Return, but by a voyeurism of carnage; Finkel really *looks:*

> *All of a joy the wrinkled sullen beast*
> *Turns up all fours, in a delicate frenzy.*
> *And so the hunters come, shedding their fear,*
> *And churn his guts to jelly with their spears.*

But the chief burden of all these poems, as the pivot of this series, is of course the sense of being possessed by eternity, once inside the myth. Such a possession is something of an embarrassment, at least for Finkel, who is as uneasy about getting *out* of the regenerative cycle as he was uncertain about getting into it; once the omphalos is located, man is indeed "preoccupied with his sinful belly-button":

> *In Dian's ring the one-horned stag is tied*
> *In navel-nuptial to virgin bride;*
> *While in the chamber chastely she turns her head,*
> *Seeing in woven dream the midnight wood,*

> *Where, self-begotten, the kinless unicorn*
> *Betrays himself to death to be reborn.*

Indeed, most of the poems in this first collection of Donald Finkel's reveal a truculent indenture to the myths of recurrence, a commitment to periodicity which is evidently a strain on the poet. Though the forms are closed, the rhymes are generally slant, and the jumpy lines consort awkwardly with sense units. Enjambment overcomes apothegm. There is a myth of form, in this poet's practice, quite as compelling as the old Greek fables, and quite as tyrannical. Finkel is seeking his freedom from the responsibility of forms as much as from the ritual of fictions. Crucial in this instance is "Hunting Song," a poem with certain obligations to Ransom's "Spiel of the Three Mountebanks," that forensic study of the varieties of religious experience in terms of totemic beasts—the lean hound, the patient elephant and the bleeding lamb. In Finkel's poem, a phenomenology of venery, the stanzas are similarly apportioned, each to its heraldic creature, in a diction of archaic rudeness; the "lolloping" fox:

> . . . *like death at the end of a string*
> *When he came to the hollow*
> *Log. He ran in one side*
> *And out the other. O*
> *He was sly.*

And in pursuit of this quarry, necessarily espousing the same turns of phrase, the "tumbling" hounds:

> *The sound of their breath was louder than death*
> *When they came to the hollow*
> *Log. They boiled at one end*
> *But a bitch found the scent. O*
> *They were mad.*

Then comes what we would expect to be the climax of this perverted ballad, with its dramatic variants askew, the "galloping" hunter:

> *His coat and his mouth were redder than death*
> *When he came to the hollow*
> *Log. He took in the rein*
> *And over he went. O*
> *He was fine.*

In each of these stanzas, as in the fragments of them quoted here, the traditional form has been flouted, used ironically as much in mockery of its conventional end-stopped periods as in exploitation of its "folk" tone and figures. It is at this point that Finkel transcends his device:

The log he just lay there, alone in
The clearing. No fox nor hound
Nor mounted man
Saw his black round eyes in their perfect disguise
(As the ends of a hollow
Log.) He watched death go through him,
Around him and over him. O
He was wise.

To avoid death, then, one must be already dead or "perfectly" disguised as death, the poem urges, and Finkel further orchestrates the mythology by the form itself: the stanza structure *is* the log around, over and through which the poem courses; it expresses the traditional wisdom (which is a cyclical avatar of death), while the Chase ("sly," "mad" and "fine") seethes on. Only the log—the form itself—is "wise," though it is the wisdom, we must not fail to note, of inertia, of submission.

There is a profound irony, an equilibrium or tension of allegiances here, as throughout *The Clothing's New Emperor*—indeed, for polemic reasons, the thrust of formal elements will never again in Finkel's work so evidently counter the impulses making for their cancellation. The very preservation of the form in "Hunting Song" can be cantilevered against the grim characterization of wisdom as a hollow log. There is, in this book, what I take to be a transitional poem, though, one in which the balance at last inclines against form in favor of experience (in favor, that is, of the fox, the hounds, the hunter), outweighing eternity and the superstition of ritual occurrences. This is the thematically complicated but formally loose apostrophe "Old Lady with Rosary on the Bus to Puebla." Here again, Finkel hesitates over the entrance into the poem:

Let me find my way to the beginning of this:
You count these beads so as to pray enough . . .
Or maybe it starts here: you count so as not
To pray too long . . .

Then, as the Bus sways through the perilous mountains (this poet is good at taking an observed decor and transforming it into a symbolic one; Journey, Mountains, Sorceress and Spell focus through the quotidian welter), Finkel watches the circle of beads slip through the old woman's fingers and fails still to find an initiation even in the mythic cruelty of Crucifixion:

Or is the beginning when you reach
The silver agony that by your thumb
Wings toward a fixity which hardly comes

But is gone again, and you begin
To jog him gently through another death,
While you plead amnesty under your breath?

Nothing is first, since you begin again;
When is enough if once, for you, and twice
Are one and the same?

And here, impatient perhaps with this symbolic violence, Finkel
twitches the poem away from the ignorant sibyl, ending (transfigur-
ing) once again by the emblem of the bullring, the ritual suffering
which the poet determines, finally, if not to escape or eschew, at least
to question:

O Chano, darling of the Plaza, how does it feel
When your number comes up, when you are turning
On the horn, as from the summit of an inverse hill
You look up a slope of sighs and death is a ring
Of eyes like beads flicking an endless string?

Yet if recurrence is jeopardized, interrogated, it is still observed, by the
rhymes, and by the very sequacity of Finkel's emblems. Henceforth,
this poet will jettison the very elements he has mastered, regarding
such losses as the guarantee of liberation.

In 1964 Donald Finkel published his second book of poems, *Simeon.*
Here the preoccupation with an absolute—eternity, recurrence, trans-
figuration—is dismissed, definitively mocked, or acknowledged to be
beyond the poet's grasp. The title poem consists of a group of sixteen
pieces (the fragmentary implication is appropriate) with some versified
footnotes—the whole affording a witty, deprecating account, mostly
by Simeon's brother "who had never learned to manage his life with
Simeon's chaste perfection," of what archetypal behavior appears to be
when seen from the perspective—the abyss—of "human clumsiness."
The notion of a ritual perfection is acknowledged, but dramatically
"placed" by wit, a rueful confession of failure and a suspicion of the
priestly "God." Simeon's brother is the secular self of Simeon, but
while the holy man sits up there on his pillar, where

He smelled not at all, resembled nothing, either
to pity or loathe, he offended no one. Really,
it was hard enough to remember he was once a man . . .

the bourgeois brother shuffles on through an all-too-human life, where
contingency prevails over any occasion:

It is from his hand we receive this little collection.
Or what remains. It is hard to believe he wrote
Nothing after this. As if Simeon's death
and his own all but coincided.

The hint is easily taken: Simeon and his brother, the handyman hagiographer, are but one man, the aspiration to an absolute shadowed by the aspirant to absolution, the faulty resentful ego, complaining:

His garbage
is not my garbage, his wound, remembered,
is clean as chiselled stone. His fetor rises
metaphysical as wind, his handkerchief
takes on the perfection of laundry: spit as he will,
it is no less perfect.
Can you wonder then why I need him?
why I hate him . . .

And the poems in which this spiritual schizophrenia is couched accommodate, by their abandonment of a closed or repetitive form, by their rejection of rhyme and the constants of a fixed rhythmical practice, Donald Finkel's commitment to a non-mythic process. The subtitle of the series, "The Death of God," suggests what is *bothering* the poet, who speaks in the person of the brother when he concludes:

Or have I the right to think, in the end, he doubted?
At the brink where man turns god, what darkness falls?
It is not revenge: that ignorance was his
humanity. It was the god I hated.

Haunted by an unrelenting cosmogony, the self abjures its absolute ambitions, the forms that would afford it a regeneration out of time and nature, preferring or at least settling for a destiny in lower case.

The other major effort in this determinative book of Finkel's is a cycle called "The Hero," seven poems each prefixed by a standard mythological label from Lord Raglan: "An Attempt is made to Kill him but he is Spirited Away and Reared by Foster-Parents in a Far Country" or "He Marries a Princess and Becomes a King. For a Time he Reigns Uneventfully." Yet under these ritual captions, the personal history unfolded is precisely the contradiction of eternity—accidental, singular, death-ridden, abject, the Happening of Finkel's "Hero" stands against the Being of the myth even more starkly than Simeon's cloddish brother opposed the saint on his pillar; for example, under the heading "The Hero's Mother is a Royal Virgin; His Father is a King," the suburban anamnesis encroaches on the fable:

Tuesday and Friday evenings at half-past five
regular as an alarm the doorbell rammed
my heart against my shoulder-blades. I opened,
suffered the scrape of that determined kiss;
and kissed him back. That was my end of it. Still,
lugging his coat into my mother's room,
I think I sensed his part was only the harsh
reflection of my own: to play at once
the stranger and the king in his own house.
Softly I laid that coat on my mother's bed
and turned and marched into the living room.

The contamination by life, the interference of a linear, contingent, overdetermined selfhood with the perfect world of the *Märchen* is articulated even more eloquently in "The Sleeping Kingdom," where the Hero, in his casual broken rhythms (the virtues of prose are always observed, though often transcended) describes the climax of his Quest:

For a while I walked the corridors when I came.
In every room they hung like tapestries,
as if time had snagged on the nail of four o'clock,
at day's dead center, banal afternoon:

neither the night begun nor the day ended . . .
And yet the dailiest gesture seemed to me,
simply by virtue of its hanging there,
translucent and inevitable and fine.

Even the dust stayed dancing in the sun
in formal patterns. I thought, And who am I
to blow like a wind behind such attitudes . . .

Later in the tower, watching those little breasts
lift toward me imperceptibly, and fall,
I felt desire sprout in the dark like a tuber.
But bending my mouth to that perfect mouth I wondered
from what it was I had meant to save this kingdom.

Other poems in this volume concern such storybook recurrences; "Sleeping Beauty" and "Rumpelstiltskin" and "Rapunzel" enact Finkel's discovery about negation: how much fact can be removed from myth and thereby allow him—the fallible Hero—to approach even closer to the fact:

. . . all that
about the twelfth fairy softening the curse

can be tossed aside . . . the twelve other fairies
for that matter can be tossed aside . . . even the king
and the court and the kingdom can be tossed aside . . .
What remains is the old lady . . . no even that
can be tossed aside . . . what remains
is the loud voice saying
even if there is nobody to hear: 'the Princess
shall prick herself with a distaff in her fifteenth year
and shall fall down dead' . . . there need in fact
not even be a princess . . .

By the end of this book, the poet wins through to the terrible, diminishing secularism of the bourgeois, preoccupied with death and violence, but approaching these matters in the voice of profane reason (as in "Bones," one of the finest poems in Finkel's entire canon and a triumph of the temporal order); there are still poems about matadors as about Midas, but even when Finkel writes about Oedipus now, he puts him in San Francisco, and gives him the sour diction of adolescence:

But mamma, that's something else; no peace with her.
You can't turn your back, she is everywhere, under
your feet, like the ground . . . every year
she gets harder and harder to push away. It isn't
enough, any more, that she rarely calls. She is there;
and there's no getting around it, I am a bastard.

That is the Oedipus of the complex, sick jokes and all, not the arrogant king. In form, rhythm, diction and indeed in inflection of the very myth, Finkel has discharged himself of the "always is" for the sake of "whatever happens." Hence the series of disturbing poems about the ailing body, unmediated by the myths of cyclical perfection: "The Hypochondriac," "Loss of Hearing," "Myopic," "Two Steps of a Lame Man"; and the wry, wistful pieces about family life ("the arrangement is essentially comic"): "Marriage," "To My Daughter at the end of her Second Year," "The Husband," "The Bachelor" and "The Father." In these domestic pieces, the poet defines his enterprise, the slangy, wisecracking discourse that seeks to avoid the lyric choice at any cost, lest it be wound up in the coils of regeneration once more:

the language of childhood looking for itself
under a mountain of masks and dolls—the poem.

Simeon is a book of over 100 pages, and there are many poems in it which make their raid on the absolute in ways not to be explored, or even catalogued, here. I cannot resist pointing out the irreverent version of "Simeon" itself, called "The Flagpole Sitter" which offers an alternative version of the saint's vision in its awful somatic drift:

I have begun to know the true weight of my body.
Slowly the fluid settles in my legs;
it seeps into my shoes, great blisters form,
my final illness. My rivers run into the air;
at the last, a dry leaf on a barren tree,
I shall release my hold, and be blown away . . .

Such is the end of a long comedy assimilating ironic commentary to the ecstatic elevation. Indeed, length, or at least exhaustiveness, becomes one of Finkel's necessities, since he must be chary of the compressions, the sorceries of ritual forms. I should like to emphasize, however, one point or impulse which Finkel handles with particular skill—the erotic. Naturally, this is the region of intent the myth-fugitive can best hide out in, wielding his messy, funny, time-obsessed jokes like so many rapiers. The insistence on *being true* which appeared in the very first poem of Finkel's first book: "Nothing can happen / Again and still be true"—the horror of the periodic and the insistence on the unique experience, even if it is a failure—are here rehearsed as fairly as the secular life will permit. The poem is called "Coming," and it is the second try (the first expostulated: "As if there were another place to go."):

Nothing can come up to it for making
one sure of his own existence. One is never
quite sure he has had a vision, felt an emotion,
written a poem, much less a perfect one.
But he can never doubt when he has come . . .

one can try and try till it is right,
the death, not only imminent, but chosen,
each day desired, each night enjoyed anew;
the birth, not only felt, but comprehended;
the poem, not only beautiful, but true.

By 1966 Finkel brought out another collection of his poems, *A Joyful Noise* (Psalms lxvi: "Make a Joyful Noise unto God, sing forth the honor of His name," etc.), whose very title has an acrid twist to it, when we recall that *Simeon* was about the death of God, profoundly skeptical of the role of the eternal in the quotidian, certainly dedicated to the elimination of the absolute from modern life. The problem of a secular delight is the burden of this new book, and once Finkel has ceased arguing with—emptying—the myths of recurrence, it is evident he is not always at ease with his life on earth: literally, the afflatus, the divine wind is out of his sails, and the vessel must proceed under its own steam: by will. As he says about the poet:

It's either off with the funny suit and join the party,
or back to the devil's feather and the holy stone,
muttering curses in Latin and mumbo jumbo.

Life without the divine can be a moribund business. Poems have names like "Heart Failure," "The Cure" and "Convalescence." Others are devoted entirely to the observation of the mortal—i.e., the urban—world, their loose lines and careful prose prodded into poetry by the very intensity of Finkel's compulsion to abjure myth. Hence, along with poems about tired florists and expropriated barbers, such poems of emblematic consequence as the brilliant "Chimp":

. . . He looks at me from under his rueful wrinkle;
I am less reassured.
I want to whisper: I am not with the others.
Essential man is alone, whether caged or free,
whether nose to tail with his mate in the bog of Desire,
or trailed by a half dozen wet-nosed consequences.

Through the hand-polished bars he hears it the way it comes out:
I am not your keeper.

and poems that wrestle with the cultural implications of our art, our absurdity objectified—take this from the long suite for Robert Rauschenberg:

I try to imagine the poem aspiring to the humility
of prose, the poem saintly enough to be content
to call attention to something beyond himself;
I contemplate the word holy enough
to hide his light under a trade mark; to say, Coca-Cola,
to himself, in a natural voice, over and over and over . . .

But it was a mistake to speak of the "prose" of Finkel's enterprise. Without the formal conventions which eased his first withdrawals from the archetypal world, and without the garrulous irony which made the work in *Simeon* so available, the thin pared poems of *A Joyful Noise* have made their separate peace with prosody, finding a propriety of their own, a responsive strictness that is, after all, only to be found in poetry. As mistrustful of charm as he is of charms, of entertainment as of incantation, Finkel's purpose is to establish the poem in a world without myth, on the surface: once we can set its absolute assumptions, its superstitions of "eternity" between parentheses, then objects in space, the feelings they generate, and the circulation of men among them are promoted to the rank of subjects. The poem becomes Finkel's direct experience of what surrounds him—imperfect, but continuing—without his being able to shield himself by a mythol-

ogy or a metaphysic in his combat with the damages of a lifetime, the
disgraces of a death. The poet becomes a man walking in his City with
no other horizon, as Roland Barthes has said, than the scene before him,
no other power than that of his own senses; and as Finkel says, in one
of his latest poems:

> *The poem makes truth a little more disturbing*
> *like a good bra, lifts it and holds it out*
> *in both hands . . .*
> *Devious or frank, in any case,*
> *the poem is calculated to arouse.*
> *Lean back and let its hands play freely on you:*
> *there comes a moment, lifted and aroused,*
> *when the two of you are equally beautiful.*

How to keep history from hardening into hagiography, how to
redeem mortal time from eternity, how to make the ecstatic into the
episodic *—the very titles of Donald Finkel's first three books of
poems (*The Clothing's New Emperor, Simeon, A Joyful Noise*)
rehearse this poet's effort against myth even as they reverse the
impulses of his art itself, impulses which move toward regener-
ation, toward—in a word—*verse*, a turning round. In his fourth
book, a single poem called *Answer Back*, published in 1968, Finkel
conversely collects, more responsibly than ever before, all the conse-
quences of his secular determination. Consider what he is after: the
achievement of an event, a single or, better, a singular happening which
may be rescued from recurrence, wrested from that ritual apprehen-
sion in which the individual is merely an instance, not an identity.
Evidently, in such an undertaking, the constants of verse, the proprie-
ties of diction must be jettisoned—"I am reluctant to dignify the tone
of this work . . ." Finkel warns at the outset. His language, chastened
from the hieratic stance, in the course of his preceding work, to a
supple, accurate instrument of response, a means of *answering back* to
the solicitations of a world which lies before him (where to choose?),
is free, invented, altogether confounded with (if not by) the energies
of "vice" or rebellion. In *Answer Back*, Finkel explores the ultimate
range of that language, from the silence in which takes place (happens)
the profound, telluric eroticism of the poet's masturbatory act:

> *In the glacier's belly*
> *I sing my brittle song,*
> *grind my wind-bitten face*

* Remembering that for the Greeks an episode was the part of a play *between*
the choric songs: if not the prose of life, at least its process.

> *between the mountain's thighs*
> *with the same grudging grace,*
> *work my magic without charms . . .*

to the convulsions of utterance which accompany his ecstasy, spasms, blasphemies, harangues, lectures, instructions ("condemned for life to the sound of my own voice / muttering over and over"); he can even —and this is his supreme freedom from the old disciplines, the old *keeping*—he can even delegate his discourse, so that in a very few pages of this poem, which includes but 38, he will cite, characteristically, from Jesus, Christopher Koch, Lenny Bruce, James Baldwin, the Missouri State Penitentiary, Jacob, Heraclitus and General S. L. A. Marshall. The lines will be broken, scattered, deliberately insecure:

> *I am the one now who stutters,*
> *begins and begins the word . . .*

for as we have seen in Finkel's earlier poems, inception is the trouble— *all starts*, he had said in his very first book, *are false*, and as he says in this last one,

> *How to begin what cannot be ended?*

Indeed, not only lines and rhythms, but the very organization of theme and structure must observe, must—it is the result of Finkel's theomachia: "my angel is mortal, for which, by the gods, / I believe in him the more"—derive from that random unity afforded by earth itself, by the disposition of significant soil. Hence titles of the poem's individual sections are taken from the names of cave passages in Mammoth Cave National Park, the subjects scooped out of what Tennyson called "Kentucky's chambers of eternal gloom." And initiations will be hand-to-mouth:

> *One goes where one can; the strategy of retreat.*
> *To the hills, down the hatch, to beginnings,*
> *a season in the corridors of the skull,*
> *under the skin of things.*

As the quotation suggests, Finkel makes short work of moving through the bowels of the earth and discovering he is in his own. Shovelsful from *Ideal Marriage* anatomizing the pubic arch, from Admiral Byrd admiring the pulsating arch of the aurora borealis, and from the official handbook to the National Park describing Wow Shaft indicate that *Answer Back* is nothing less than a somatic epyllion, or epic in miniature, conjugating the whole of nature, of erotic possibility and of political error into the content of an endless and everlasting human body.

Who knows how
the Old Ones entered?
We go in at the hole
that presents itself—

and for all his jokes and doubts ("an awkward song, may be, I have put together" sighs the poet in the words of the Eskimo Pluvkaq), Finkel has done just what he intended; has created a Book of Apocalypse without ritual, myth or recurrence, relying merely on his senses, his memory, his mortality: "bits of charcoal, charcoal smudges on the walls, occasional torch-ties, prints of naked human feet."

The Garbage Wars by DONALD FINKEL

Published two years ago, Finkel's fourth book, *Answer Back*, built the launching-pad for the explosive, or at least exploded, poems in *The Garbage Wars*. Episodic in its ecstasy, insistently abrupt and goofy, *Answer Back* composed a kind of somatic fugue, casual and indeed occasional, full of jokes and doubts, abjuring ritual (even those rituals of convention which poetry so heavily invests in: stanza, punctuation, rhyme, normative rhythm), snubbing recurrence and myth, relying merely on Finkel's own senses, his tastes and revulsions, his memory, his mortality.

This fifth book represents the consolidation of that stance, cheerfully acknowledging indebtedness to just about everything—the Old Testament and Roget's Thesaurus, Heraclitus and Stokely Carmichael—for the poet insists he is a part of whatever he has read. But all these "other voices" are dissolved into the poet's own which is raised, or rather plunged, in a song of destruction celebrating the surrender of selfhood, the descent ("falling from my incandescent bones") into that furnace where identity itself is shucked off and Eros released and realized. These poems are a devout submission to primary experience, and that is why so many are characterized by downward and backward movements, dropping, sinking, "the act of falling".

Like our culture and like our body, our spirit is in danger of being choked by its own waste products, its own perceptions. What we have known, Finkel fears, will blur over or blind us to what we might know. Hence "The Garbage Wars", a poem about the struggle—often by means of the inertia of subsidence ("I ride downstream")—to get through the crust to what is alive, to the place where Being has not yet hardened into Ego.

Consistently Finkel urges himself to let go, to drop; "open your deepest passages to the flame," he says, and surely the masterpiece in this collection is "Water Music", a collage-retelling of the story of Arion and the dolphin, for Arion is the proper emblem for trusting oneself to the destructive element, for discovering that at the very point of death there is a desperation in us which endures and prevails.

It is not what meets the eye that matters here, but what meets the ear: Finkel's convulsive, splintered utterances in which punctuation is replaced by blanks, are the harangues of a man likely to be saved from drowning, if at all, by letting himself loose. If the poems look jagged on the page, their cadence—for Finkel is a master of phrasing, "breathing all I have in and out"—is a true one, music not only of water but of earth and air and fire, elemental music.

The New York Times Book Review, 1970

Adequate Earth by DONALD FINKEL

In his fifth book of poems, published three years ago, Donald Finkel dramatized, by the double sense the word "refuse" has assumed for us, the problem and finally the probability that like our culture and our bodies, our spirit too can be choked by its own waste products, its own perceptions. What we have known, Finkel fears, will blur over or blind us to what we might know. Hence his *Garbage Wars*, poems about the struggle to get through the crust to what is alive. Now, and again—for in his third book too, the somatic epyllion *Answer Back*, the exploration of the earth's bowels revealed that the poet was in his own—Finkel overtakes the profound telluric eroticism of the maker's masturbatory act:

> *In the glacier's belly*
> *I sing my brittle song,*
> *work my magic without charms . . .*

A season in the ice-hell, where there are no perceptions because there is nothing to perceive, and a sorcery without charms because there is no toleration for anything beyond the mortal: here, in another of his collage narratives whose eponymous heroine begins as the Sleeping Beauty ("this ice-blue virgin waked to the frowsy / chores of generation") and ends or at least winds up forty-four pages later as Penelope ("Earth herself . . . shuttles as ever / through the desultory seasons / nor believes any longer / in the coming of her lord, if she ever did"), Finkel performs an act of the imagination by another of his enormous repudiations, jettisons, *refusals*, even, to write his own poem. There is no "own" if we are to survive in the Antarctic which is the site and solvent of his endeavor this time round, there is only collaboration and community in loss and subtraction ("nor can any man see the hand / of the man he holds . . . we die back / to diatoms for the common weal"). Hence the wonderful tear-sheets from Donne and Smart, from Frost and Snow (who else?), from Porchia and Warhol and from all the explorers of the dead plateau, the tray of mortality. Among all these, threaded among them with immense skill and glee, there is plenty of Finkel, often muffled up in his disguise of the "gospels of the Emperor penguins", a crypto-myth of the origin and goal of life—human and penguinal, in any case unlikely—as legendary unit, experienced fragmentation, glimpsed apocalypse:

> *the little stones*
> *will draw themselves together*
> *they will lift up their plumes to the sun*
> *they will fly again*
> *till then the People sing:*
> *Be glad for a stone*
> *be glad for feet be glad*
> *for a place to go round.*

That is adequate earth—a place to go round; we are broken here that we may be brought together, and it is enough to have——to *be*—very little indeed, as the disasters of Antarctic life are instanced to remind us. One reads through Finkel's brilliant structure without a moment's doubt of its gelid wisdom, for so astutely collected are the details, so fresh the phrases, and so clear, interval by icy interval, the lineaments of this forever ungratified desire, that the whole grim contraption hangs together, it makes one dangling poem, despite its ruinous systole and diastole of life, mere experience (whose root is *peril*), whether polar or personal:

> *For every step to the Pole there is one*
> *step back, each step more perilous*
> *than the last, unravelling what*
> *we wound before . . .*

Garbage and glacier intersect to pulverize this fine poem into existence: they are the limits of how we choke ourselves off and are choked from without. The point is—and the place—to *be without.* In both senses.

A Mote in Heaven's Eye by DONALD FINKEL

Donald Finkel has returned from the mock-grandiose world of his collage epyllions to a gracile fifth book of occasional, certainly casual poems: the effort here, increasingly, is to cast off—"divest thyself . . . then empty thyself" runs the commandment the poet takes, both from without and within. Such repudiations, as that word itself reminds, have something to do with shame, with sex, and with the reversals of habitual good manners. Finkel is a gentle but decisive Lord of Misrule among us, "stalking the timid constellations" and committed only to a program of noncommittal subversion, humbling the memory, that deceiver, and getting down to those abject ecstasies where "life" seethes in obscene interstices."

It is why he is apt to write a poem about the rebellion of our furniture or our pets, or eulogies of the instruments of our weakness, cane and wheelchair, which of course in Finkel's transvaluation become the likelihood of grace, flight, and mastery. "I give earth back nothing but her names"—it is all the poet has to give (or needs to give: poetry is naming the sacred places and events), and this poet prefers, of course, to destroy the suburban instances of such nomination (the typewriter named for the god of thieves, the insolence of media, "the clamor of motors / the laughter of saws"), to enhance *forgetting:*

> . . . *the poets have memories*
> *so frail*
> *they remember neither*
> *the nightmare nor the night before*
> *wake without history*
> *forebears*
> *crying*
> ma ma
> *a lamb on a stone*
>
> *each day*
> *they construct anew*
> *not merely their own*
> *truncated lives*
> *but the language of the tribe*

The image of sacrifice and the incantatory, unpunctuated dimeter show the way: there is in all Finkel's enterprise a theogony. "Hymns of discord" he may call them, but his poems—for all their mean wit and meandering horseplay—are so many little flowers, Franciscan canticles to the elements and elemental beings we were *given* to when we wakened on "adequate earth" (Finkel's genesis-poem is "Happy

Birthday", a portable cosmogony from which his title comes: man is the mote in heaven's eye, his personnel is Adam and the Lame Angel, Lilith and Cain, and his properties are the heterogeneous dreck of city life, to be washed out, melted down, given away). Scrawny and sidelong, the poems are yet the genuine religious article, and if it is Finkel's trivial triumph to have abjured solemnity and pomp, it is nonetheless his true one to afford the rudiments of worship in this corrosive missal; indeed it contains at least one devotion which the monk of Assisi (Mexico is Finkel's La Verna, where he received the stigmata of compassion as far back as his first book, in 1959) would have recognized and might have written. I quote it all, for this "Flying Song" is the psaltery of Finkel's twist of doings and undoings, and a masterpiece:

> *Smoke on the wind*
> *I travel light*
> *my way is flight*
> *my cries are music*
> *a bowl of earth*
> *a burning coal*
> *and at my feet*
> *the blessed weeds*
> *the earth's sweet trash*
> *are all I need*
>
> *a bowl for my hearth*
> *the fire my friend*
> *I fly when I can*
> *and damn the cost*
> *I think what I am*
> *I know what I'll be*
> *sweet trash sweet trash*
> *in the roadside dust*

The Yale Review, 1976

ALLEN GINSBERG

"O Brothers of the Laurel,
Is the World Real?
Is the Laurel a Joke or
a Crown of Thorns?"

N OT LONG AGO, at one of our recurrent poetry conferences which
suggest with all the force of an Euclidean proof—just look at
those celluloid identification badges, typed with each poet's name and
(of course) his university—that we are, even in our most notoriously
dissident callings, a nation not of joiners merely, but of *members;* at
one of those chapter meetings, then, in the endless volume of our
self-concern, I listened to an address by a celebrated poet, an elderly
professor it was, who had risen to the Collected Poems level and who,
before arriving at our conference somewhere in the midwest, had
reached for the wrong speech among (I imagine) several on his desk,
thereupon regaling his fellows with a description of the bare-breasted
beauties of Nigeria intended surely for the National Geographic So-
ciety. A married man, the father of daughters, it came rather as a shock
to hear him extol the rare privilege of moving among a race of women
proudly nude, and precisely then (though his own performance was
not scheduled until much later on the program) Allen Ginsberg . . .
performed! He got up from the ring of chairs where the ulterior
speakers were waiting for their turns to read their own poems, to speak
their own thoughts, to do their own thing, and advancing solemnly—
bearded, intent, unmistakeable—toward the old eulogist of noble sav-
agery, he stepped up onto the dais and without a word, without a

smile, without a single deprecating gesture, Allen Ginsberg took off all
his clothes.

> *To stand before you speechless and intelligent and*
> *shaking with shame, rejected yet confessing out the soul*
> *to conform to the rhythm of thought . . .*

The lines from *Howl* afford the right exergue for this experience,
and suggest too something of the extremity of the poet's situation: it is
Ginsberg's *presence*—quick-witted, slow-moving, imperturbably amia-
ble—which allows his *prophecy* its full function. As he says in one of
those countless places where the voice acknowledges itself to be void
even as it is unavoidable:

> *I am the defense early warning radar system*
> *History will make this poem prophetic and its awful silliness*
> *a hideous spiritual music.*

By prophecy, of course, he does not mean prediction, but truth-telling:
"What prophecy actually is is not that you know that the bomb will
fall in 1942. It's that you know and feel something which somebody
knows and feels in a hundred years." The prophet, then, is a man
personally accessible to anyone, and at any time, because he is—has
taken care to be—a person:

> *I'm trying to come to the point.*
> *I refuse to give up my obsession.*
> *America stop pushing I know what I'm doing . . .*
> *My mind is made up there's going to be trouble . . .*
> *America how can I write a holy litany in your silly mood? . . .*
> *It occurs to me that I am America . . .*

The prophetic voice, then, makes what Ginsberg calls "a complete
statement of Person," and to raise that voice is, simply, to acknowledge
the person as a sacramental reality. "The only poetic tradition," Gins-
berg declared in his *Paris Review* interview, "is the voice out of the
burning bush." And twenty years before, in the *Columbia Review*, he
was saying much the same thing: "My thought, though skeptic, still is
sacrament." There is a consent, as I hear it, in all Ginsberg's poems, in
the silliest scraps, the gravest platitudes:

> *Visions! omens! hallucinations! miracles! ecstasies gone*
> *down the American river! Dreams! adorations! illuminations!*
> *the whole boatload of sensitive bullshit! Breakthroughs!*
> *flips and crucifixions! highs!*

not only to expose (as in the episode I described at the beginning) but
to *exhaust* the person, to submit the body to the soul like Danaë to

Zeus, regardless of consequences, expecting the worst. "I am flesh and blood, but my mind is the focus of much lightning," Ginsberg says in "Psalm 1" from the collection of early poems *The Empty Mirror*, and the apposition of the two things, fitful body and focussed thunderbolt, afford an explosive entry into the prophetic arena. This poet, indeed, has ransacked the Biblical texts, Smart, Blake, Shelley, Whitman * for a generalized vatic *gestus*, an all-purpose ministry to the Gentiles whose chief outward sign he has determined upon as the *list*, in its original sense of a limit or rim, containing all possibilities and thereby constituting the place of combat or, as it used to be called, the *lists* where the tournament is fought. The poem is the place where occasions are exhausted, where opportunities are *used up*. He puts this situation, *the fate of prophecy as self-consumption*, more darkly or at least more discountably in a wisp ** of "Laughing Gas," one of a recent series of reports from the Artificial Paradise, communiqués which include "Aether," *** "Mescaline," "Lysergic Acid" (coming down from such highs "to recreate the syntax and measure of poor human prose," Ginsberg exclaims in a burst of startled self-discovery: "We're what's *left over* from perfection!"—perfection, we are to assume, representing some process working itself out on the far, the inaccessible side of prophecy), bulletins which follow Baudelaire and Cocteau and Michaux—the great *addicts* who remind us that the term denotes no more (or less) than a partisan of a personal form of speech, *a diction*—into the sediments of disintoxication, these poems being, as William Burroughs has said (to Ginsberg), scarcely anything but *withdrawal symptoms*, the grueling extrication of self from surround; here Ginsberg views the visionary hope with a certain alienated reserve, declaring in "Laughing Gas," as I was going to say—but no, not declaring, perhaps *dismissing* is what he is doing when the lines blurt it out:

> *any prophecy might have been right*
> *it's all a great Exception*

---

* The use to which Whitman has been put is exemplary. Here is how Ginsberg saw the native seer in 1955: "What thoughts I have of you tonight, *Walt Whitman . . . dreaming of your enumerations*. Ah, dear father, graybeard, lonely old courage-teacher, what America did you have when Charon quit poling his ferry and you got out on a smoking bank and stood watching the boat disappear on the black waters of Lethe?"

** which is his form; Ginsberg as a poet is, one might say, *the will of the wisp*, or as he *has* said, in the early "Marijuana Notation," "such fugitive feelings / have always been / my metier."

*** Ginsberg delights in old spellings, archaic forms which he employs, as Sherwood Anderson used to, to impart a certain scriptural accent to his writing: on the one hand "loony tunes, aethereal zigzag Poesy, nude minutes" and on the other "hymns, psalms, Kaddish"—and between the hands, "ashcan rantings / from park to pad to bar to Bellevue to museum to the Brooklyn Bridge / wondering where to go, and went . . ."

The prophecy must be funded, then, must be confirmed as exceptional, *made good* in all its literal exorbitance ("I dream nightly of an embarcation, / captains, captains / what jazz beyond jazz / in future blue saloons? what love in the cafes of God?") and in all its virtually scapegoat exposure ("yes, yes, that's what / I wanted, / I always wanted / to return / to the body where I was born") by the poet's person, by his body in fact, or let us say by his body in person. "I think," Ginsberg told the *Paris Review* interviewer, "if I were lying in bed dying, with my body pained, I would just give up, I mean, you know, because I don't think I could *exist* outside my body."

What! After so many "lofty incantations which in the yellow morning were stanzas of gibberish," after so many failures to "escape / the feeling of being closed in / and the sordidness of self," after inheriting a solitude in which "I could dismiss Allen with grim / pleasure," does it not come to us as something more than a shock, does it not come to him, even, as something of a chagrin that the "ancient heavenly connection" rests or wriggles in nothing but an identifiable body, an ego concerned, merely, to call itself its own? Then the effort, the aspiration was not to transcribe, "in the warm light of this poem's radio, the lost jazz of all Saturdays" apart from, ahead of the *corpus vile!* The need was not, then—by drugs, by art, by sex, "a few Traditions, / metrical, mystical, manly"—to transcend the flesh all this while, but rather to keep faith with it, "looking for evidences of humanity or secret thought or just actual truthfulness," to get us to read "a postcard from eternity sent by human hand."

In 1965, with the grave, sweet explicitness ("to manifest and work it out in a way that's materially communicable to people without scaring them or me") which has so little to do with the scapegoat Ginsberg when he is scared and therefore scary, exposing rather than revealing himself, the poet set down, with the patient care of a man who has understood himself, possessed of the courage to be literal in the context of a style aspiring to the sublime, no less than the reasons why he is alive:

> The problem I had found myself in was that it had seemed to me that the best thing to do was to drop dead. To go into death, go into the non-human, go into the cosmic; that God was death and if I wanted to attain God I had to die. So that what I was put up to was to break out of my body if I wanted to attain complete consciousness. Then on the train in Japan—when I realized that to attain the depth of consciousness I was seeking I had to cut myself off from the Blake vision * and renounce it in order to

* An experience of his identity with "Supreme Reality" vouchsafed by a reading, years ago, of Blake's poems, in which Blake's voice, "like the voice of the Ancient of Days," addressed him.

attain it; otherwise I'd be hung up on the *memory of an experi-
ence,* which is not the actual awareness of *now;* in order to get
back to contact with what was going on around me, or direct
vision of the moment, I'd have to give up this continual churning
thought process of yearning back to a visionary state—after the
train in Japan, I was completely in my body and had no more
mysterious obligations. And nothing more to fulfill, except to be
willing to die when I am dying, whenever that be. And be willing
to live as a human in this form now.

If we hear doubts, as we do from our parents' generation or from that
part of their generation in ourselves (James Dicky: "If a measure of
craft were to be exercised? What then? It is hardly fair to hope that
Ginsberg will ever come to agree with himself that this is necessary,
but should he do so I for one will buy and read what he writes"),
about the sources of Ginsberg's authority or even of his authenticity, I
think this accounting I have quoted at some length will convert our
doubts to the kind of devotion this poet wishes to inspire in us, a
devotion instinct with the sagacity of the Nemean priesthood: "I am
King of the May, that I may be expelled from my Kingdom with
Honor, as of old." Not only is Ginsberg capable of a great spiritual
revelation, but in his very wavering here between what in the poetry is
merely visionary and what is vital, he affords us a warrant of the poet's
relevance to himself: after all, a man's irresolution as to the necessity or
even the nature of his theme may reveal an exuberance rather than a
deficiency of interest in "subject matter."

> The worst I fear, considering the shallowness of Opinion, is that
> the poetry and prose may be taken too familiarly and be given the
> same shallow treatment, this time sympathetic, as, until recently,
> they were given shallow unsympathy. That would be the very
> woe of fame. The problem has been to communicate the very
> spark of life, and not some opinion about that spark of life.

The very woe of Ginsberg's fame, indeed, is that he has been cele-
brated as a poet when it has been necessary for him to divest himself of
the mantle, to drown his book and break his staff. As he says in
"Mescaline," *what can I do to heaven by pounding on a
Typewriter? / I'm going away from the poem.*
Ginsberg is not concerned with the poem as art. He is after "the
poem *discovered* in the mind and in the process of writing it out on the
page as notes, transcriptions." We recall the interviewer who found
that when Ginsberg read his poems to an audience in England "the
performance was as much a *discovery* for him as for them." And we do
more than recall, we *recover* in Jackson Pollock's famous statement a
particularly relevant shrinking from the respite of accomplishment:

When I am *in* my painting, I'm not aware of what I'm doing. It is only after . . . that I see what I have been about. I have no fears about making changes, destroying the image, etc., because the painting has a life of its own. I try to let it come through. It is only when I lose contact with the painting that the result is a mess. Otherwise there is pure harmony, an easy give and take, and the painting comes out well.

When Allen Ginsberg says "the mind must be trained, i.e., freed—to deal with itself as it actually is and not to impose on itself an arbitrarily preconceived pattern," we are in the same universe of risk which Pollock besieged and bequeathed. The writings of Allen Ginsberg— journals, scratchings, "scribbled secret notebooks and wild typewritten pages . . . impossible syntax of apocalypse, my own crude night imaginings, my own crude soul notes taken down in moments of isolation, dreams, piercings of nocturnal thought and primitive illuminations"— *are* the physical reality of the poet and the activity of expressing it, united to the spiritual reality of the poet in a figure which has (or can endure) no need for the mediation of metaphor or the myth of form. It is Action Poetry:

> *After all, what else is there to say?*
> *wait for a moment when*
>   *the poem itself*
> *is my way of speaking out, not*
> *declaiming or celebrating, yet,*
>   *but telling the truth.*

That is why Ginsberg dates all his pieces, "time's remnants and qualities for me to use—my words / piled up, my texts, my manuscripts, my loves." They are not to stand apart or aside from him, they are not to cohere *without him*. And when, in the *fragmenta monumenti* he gives in *Empty Mirror*—a clutch of the early work (before 1952) in which William Carlos Williams pertinently, for once, discerned "a new sort of line, measured by the passage of time without accent . . . it must be prose, but prose among whose words the terror of their truth has been discovered"—when Ginsberg records here the failure of his "vision," he does so in the accents of ecstasy, in the realization that a man is great or may be great who takes defeat as an opportunity * and victory as an ordeal:

---

* "His ability to survive, travel and go on writing astonishes me . . . he has gone through defeat as if it were an ordinary experience, a trivial experience."— Thus William Carlos Williams, in the introduction to *Howl* (1956), failing to realize that for this poet it is, beyond, a life-giving experience.

It was to have a structure, it
was going to tell a story;
it was to be a mass of images
moving on a page, with
a hollow voice at the center;
it was to have told of Time
and Eternity; to have begun
in the rainfall's hood and moon,
and ended under the street light
of the world's bare physical
appearance; begun among vultures
in the mountains of Mexico,
travelled through all America
and ended in garbage on River Street . . .

But it will not have a structure, it will not tell a story: it will be improvised ("transcription of organ music") and discovered ("my feeling is for a big long clanky statement, it's my *movement*") and, like English politics, it will be without design, therefore always ready when the day—and the dejection, the disrepute, the dysentery thereof—comes. It will not suffer from those provisions and calculations which, in the mere artist, become prejudices:

Conventional form is too symmetrical, geometrical, numbered and fixed—unlike to my own mind which has no beginning and end, nor fixed measures of thought other than its own cornerless mystery.

And though there *are* poems, discrete made things, in the "occurrence" of Ginsberg's *oeuvre*, the last collections—*T.V.Baby Poems* (1967) and *Airplane Dreams* and *Planet News* (1968)—make it clear that the impulse is rather to accrete one enormous notation, "not exactly poems, nor not poems: journal notations put together conveniently, a mental turn-on" which, indeed, will soon appear as the complete poems of Allen Ginsberg, binding blur and brutality together in the one great movement:

I have the secret, I carry
subversive salami in
my ragged briefcase
Garlic, Poverty, a will to Heaven
a strange dream in my meat.

The characteristic Ginsberg product nowadays, when he is to be found at any point in the world, is the transit poem ("Over Kansas," "Return to the States," "Wichita Vortex Sutra") in which "new sentences

spring forth out of the scene to describe spontaneous forms of time";
the poet has discovered that a temporary shift in space is "God's only
way of building the rickety structure of Time" and that is all there is
to it: the rest is raw talent, self-delusion and incantation.

The clue, certainly, to the ultimate Change which Ginsberg expects,
the transformation which will strike all his annotated prophecies, the
metamorphosis which will turn his dated fragments on—turn them into
poetry, I mean—the clue is given in his various dedications:

> to the Pure Imaginary Poet Gregory Corso (*Reality Sandwiches,*
> 1963)
> to Jack Kerouac, new Buddha of American prose; William Bur-
> roughs, author of *Naked Lunch,* an endless novel which will
> drive everybody mad; Neal Cassady, author of an autobiography
> which enlightened Buddha: *All these books are published in*
> *Heaven.*　　　　　　　　　　　　　　　　(*Howl,* 1956)
> to Peter Orlovsky in Paradise　　　　　　　(*Kaddish,* 1961)
> to Neal Cassady again Spirit to Spirit　　(*Planet News,* 1968)

Prophetic books, then, in that they will attain the existence they seek
only after the poet leaves off. Until then he is, like Gregory, an
imaginary poet, and his works, like Neal's and Jack's, are published in
Heaven, and he is in Paradise. When he dies, they will appear on earth.
"Die," Ginsberg says on the title page of *Kaddish,* "Die if thou wouldst
be with that which thou dost seek." It is the greatest hazard any poet
has dared to run in the history of literature, and if I would not judge it
any more than I would judge the naked poet standing before me on the
platform, "speechless, intelligent and shaking with shame," I know at
least that the enterprise inspires me with that sacred fear, that shudder
which is humanity's best part, as Goethe once said. "Sometimes I feel in
command when I'm writing, when I'm in the heat of some truthful
tears, yes," Allen Ginsberg has said, and when asked whether by
"command" he meant a sense of the whole poem rather than parts, he
replied, quite rightly by his lights, or by his darkness, "No—a sense of
being self-prophetic master of the universe."

PAUL GOODMAN

"The Form of Life,
the Art of Dissidence."

FOR THIRTY YEARS, Paul Goodman had been writing poems which appeared, according to his acknowledgments page, in many magazines as well as in a number of pamphlets under his own imprint, until in 1962, at the pinnacle of Goodman's celebrity as America's "in" polygraph, his time notoriously spent "haranguing scholars to rebel like men," *The Lordly Hudson, Collected Poems of Paul Goodman,* was published; a volume of 250 pages. The author of *Art & Social Nature,* we may expect, will continue to write poems—"to me," as he says, "it is panic to be speechless"—but his audience nowadays and his ambitions as a social polemicist will henceforth make it impossible for the poems he writes to bear the particular hermeneutic relation to the rest of his writing they have hitherto sustained:

> *. . . the provided lamp*
> *for Entry and Pavane.*

No longer can Goodman's verse accommodate the impulse which is the leading edge of his enterprise as a writer—"a man alive and a man of letters"—it can only follow and comment upon the enormously public and contentious transactions Goodman engages in with the world:

> *force flows from me with effortless ease,*
> *my hunch hits home, my whimsy works,*
> *my rebel bluff says a relevant speech,*
> *what I meant in malice my neighbor needs,*
> *and grateful foreigners offer me gifts . . .*

The more fortunate we, this being the case, to possess these "collected" poems whose symbolic and inclusive nature Goodman himself acknowledges when he says of them: "the best thing in them is their attitude, the proof that a man can still experience his life in this way. I have not tried much for individual beautiful poems—though I think I have occasionally hit one by luck—but I am more satisfied with the whole than with the parts." Their very existence, then, "proving" something, they represent, these poems taken as a whole, an important thrust of Goodman's total effort, an achievement refractory to assessment for two reasons: not only do we resist a reading of a man's poems as if they were one poem, the parts and pieces being no more than inflections of his cause rather than individual victories over the Silence, but further we resist regarding a man's poems as merely another weapon in his armory—modernism has made the poet's office such an hieratic one that it is something of a heresy to consider the writing of poems as no more than a normative function. Though there are some —usually elderly—men of letters around who manage, rustily enough, to express themselves in verse (Edmund Wilson and Kenneth Burke come to mind, the most venerable polyhistors of our intellectual estate), the phenomenon of an author ready and willing to take on our schools, our politics, our sexual nature and our delinquent youth, and *just* as likely to do so in poems, is something of an outrage. Not surprisingly, *The Lordly Hudson*—in which Goodman's perennial burden, man in the world he has made for himself, is explored, lamented and praised—has been largely unacknowledged *as poetry;* not so fortunate as Lawrence, with whom he shares, of course, an Old Testament moralizing and a thoroughly contemporary rebelliousness, and not so powerfully endowed, which may explain the unluckiness, Goodman has simply never *surfaced* as a poet. Indeed his fiction as well —his tremendous four-part novel *The Empire City*, his many volumes of stories, fables and plays—has become accessible, in the simplest bibliographical sense, only in the wake of his explicit denunciations and proposals, his criticisms of the way we live now and the way we might be living—what he calls "the choreography of society and solitude." The culture has received Goodman rather as Wagner received Meyerbeer—"a Jew banker to whom it occurred to write operas"—a Jewish rhetorician to whom it occurred to write poems. For one characteristic of our culture is a mistrust of the imagination as a practical instrument; we dismiss as utopian the insights which do not reach us by an interlocking directorate of committees, agencies, foundations and the sixteen-year chain-gang of our educational system. The kind of separation of powers that once obliged Walter Scott to divide himself between the knighted poet who wrote "Marmion" and the nameless author whose "Waverly Novels" revolutionized the sensibility of Eu-

rope—this scission has, in its exacerbated contemporary avatar, forced
Goodman to abandon the imaginative and embodied expression of his
vision and to speak—so desperate has the situation become—the lan-
guage of the marketplace, deserting the tripod, so to speak, for the
tribune.

This obligation to speak out, to become a public man, as he suffers
and sustains the role, is one of the principal subjects of Goodman's
verse, and a chief emblem for him of an endemic American failure of
nerve:

> *Such thoughts are horrible for me,*
> *the facts of my forty-third birthday,*
> *for I am not a lonesome man, I need*
> *a sociable occasion, and applause;*
> *otherwise I despond, my aim holds **true***
> *but I lose fire-power.*
> > *Oh, my God,*
> *for the one life and city that I have!*
> *I have fallen out of love with New York City,*
> *her blocks are merely boring till it hurts,*
> *big because at a loss for an idea*
> *the overgrown moron, and she has no sky,*
> *and she has locked Lordly my river out*
> *and faces in across a narrow alley.*
> *Violent men and women in her bars*
> *have an affrighted lust or none*
> *and the adolescents I was eager for*
> *to venture what I couldn't or didn't dare,*
> *just hang around, it breaks your heart*
> *how they have neither wonder nor ambition.*
> *I'll get no epic subject here nor friends*
> *nor even pleasure, why do I persist . . .*
> *Go elsewhere!*
> > *But I have no other tongue,*
> *not as a poet or a lover speaks*
> *simple in detail, as he paid attention,*
> *and this is what I paid attention to*
> *that never loved me and I no longer love.*
> *My hairs are graying. I have failed, I guess.*

America's inability to accommodate and profit by the whole of Paul
Goodman is, for Goodman, properly a sign and symptom of her
inability to deal with *any* experience in a spontaneous and inclusive
way (though it should be said, in America's defense, that to accommo-
date the whole of Paul Goodman is a considerable undertaking, one

that might make any republic fractious). Goodman's emphasis on a reading of his *Collected Poems* as a whole, as a *Leaves of Grass*-type experience, rather than as a series or even as a scattering of beautiful realizations, lucky hits and near misses, is part of the same impulse toward convergence, unity, completion, connections within the self. Though, as in the lines I have just quoted, he terminates with a rueful aporia more often than not, there is a possibility of fulfillment, a potential identity gained in harmony with what Thoreau called "the expectation of the land" which we may best trace out according to this poet's disposition of his poems in formal groups—short poems, longer poems, stories, sonnets, ballades, love poems, sentences and prayers.

In the Short Poems, the most disparate impulses find an articulation, of course, but there is I think a focus in the constatation of a natural surround, often rendered with a bow to precursors ("manner of Wordsworth"), or to the other artists and arts that have made reality accessible (Giacometti, Lipchitz, Mozart, Giovanni Gabrieli—

> He dared (what brass!) to bring the sea inside—
> St. Mark's was wide enough to harbor her.
> The Duke dismissed his ring into the water
> and took the Adriatic home his bride.)

and to the family occasions that prove such forays into nature disturbing or memorable:

> and through the water where we stand
> we see white pebbles in the sand
> and green pickerel about our feet
> nosing if this be likely meat.

Once he establishes himself somewhere, anywhere, the dialectic of Goodman's vision makes him acknowledge—reluctantly, painfully, but with a certain salubrity in sparing himself nothing—that within nature, his encounters with human beings are alienated, as in this instance of a cyclist:

> I'd speak with him, except his only lust
> is in his speedy ease. Now everywhere
> by moments and through rips, through the brilliant
> curtain of July I spy the Way
> whereon we deviate but do not err.

If nature is a success and the encounter with men leads inevitably to failure, then confrontation *inside* the self is inevitable. How to resolve

the terms? "My past is a wound I will not close," Goodman shrieks like
his Philoctetes, as he watches himself grow older:

> *So I have twenty years*
> *monomaniac*
> *withered, my face is lined*
> *today before the equinox*
> *no different tomorrow.*
> *Austere is the praise*
> *that I am able to sing*
> *in verses out of my life*
> *as burgeons the spring.*

The answer to such despair, as he muses over a birthday cake ("when
the candles on the icing are one two too many to blow out"), is an
apocalypse:

> *and isn't it time, isn't it time*
> *when the fires are too many*
> *to eat the fire and not the cake*
> *and drip the fires from my teeth*
> *as once I had my hot hot youth.*

The Longer Poems of his second group permit Goodman to dramatize
these gestures in a cathartic sense and to invoke the history he needs in
order to close his wounds. The visionary and Blakean music of the first
pieces, the kind of poems that begin with an anti-physis:

> *I walked in tears down Dyckman Street*
> *my present and past were at my side*
> *the future ahead by a couple of feet*
> *and we advanced with equal stride . . .*

is softened here by a more generous and more relaxed sense of the art,
of its possibilities for conciliation, and by a more confirmed self-con-
sciousness. Goodman can dismiss these emblematic figures and more
profitably invoke the formal gloaming of a Poussin:

> *The air is blue, that sun is gone*
> *and the inverted sky is white in the pool*
> *where the dirty shepherds and the tired women*
> *are bathing solemnly. The water is cool.*
> *A single happy cry—but from a fool*
> *or sage I do not know—rings in the air alone.*

As if lured by this music, the possibility of an alliterative self-accept-
ance draws near:

> . . . *My character endures,*
> *my destiny will not be accidental,*
> *and common reason must prevail at last*
> *but when? when? when shall I awake*
> *to a morning quick and can what I want?*
> *Long I labored to make me Goodman,*
> *did it in despite of pleasure and prudence* . . .
> *only a luck of my own I lack,*
> *only a task to wake up toward.*
> *O Opportunity! do come my way*
> *in such a guise, glancing one, that I*
> *may know you, for long study has estranged*
> *me from the common uses, but appear*
> *in a likely shape, sexy, operable,*
> *and whether I will or no imperious.*

The long poems on "The Death of Leon Trotsky, 1940" and "The Character of Washington" suggest the range and richness of Goodman's mind when duration and learning constitute dimensions of his verse. Yet the iron has entered his soul, and in the "Sentences for *Growing Up Absurd*" he offers the uneasy legacy he will leave, so many times in these poems, to the young:

> *In this unpleasing plight*
> *I have composed a book*
> *to show how youth is thwarted*
> *by the world we made.*
> *May they who read be stung*
> *by wrath I never felt*
> *for me but for these kids.*
> *Creator spirit come.*

And Goodman prints last in this section, as an envoi to his own efforts, a terrible poem "The Emblem," of which these are the first and last stanzas, the bitter measure of his success and failure:

> *If a life must be lost, let it be the rescuer's*
> *for that has a meaning, it is our Emblem.*
> *Therefore since all must be lost, be a rescuer* . . .
>
> *Warriors as they drown in death shout "Victory!"*
> *but a lifeguard when he rescues someone, curses.*

The stories Goodman tells are often made out of hints from the Bible, fleshed, as in the finest one, "The Well of Bethlehem," by a kind of rhetorical piety that keeps the verse moving with an *energeia* of actual speech. As Goodman remarks in his brisk and comprehensive manual *The Structure of Literature*, "what is directly conveyed is simply 'meaningfulness' that may or may not be given content by historical, psychological or religious considerations'; the hints are caught up into a diction that embraces the poet's own life, returning as though for ballast to the history that occasioned them:

> *What shall I do with this water?*
> *embarrassed that I have it in my hands*
> *and I am hot with shame.*
> *Lack and loss may be consoled, success*
> *only God can console.*
> *So King David*
> *poured out the water on the ground to God.*

Or Goodman will take clues from the newspapers, from anecdotes in the lives of the great, and out of the telling, always in his own terms, wrench a kind of desperate satisfaction:

> *I saw again the horrifying scene*
> *when Goethe burst in tears and Beethoven*
> *leapt up and shook him and cried out, 'Admit!*
> *admit! admit! admit that it means something!'*

Yet often the force of these moments, particularly when the stories do not have the authority of legend or the resonance of history but are casual, "found objects," is dissipated by their very duration, the time it takes to recount them in, and I find that Goodman's series of Sonnets, which are often stories in little, the form remarkably mastered by a technical ease not always apparent in the Short Poems, compress all his qualities and themes into their happiest body. The self-exhortation, the American *mythus*, and the intimate voice speaking through a formal convention (Goodman's most frequent breaches with success occur when he refuses a verse discipline and *speaks out;* he is not often possessed enough of means to sing *a capella*, as it were) produce, as in "For Henry Hudson" the type of his achievement, and it deserves to stand as a representative one:

> *I like to think because my Captain proved*
> *there was no Passage, mind and body lost*
> *in ice and darkness,* therefore *all the rest*
> *directed south their prows and richly braved*
> *the possible with pineapples and rust-*
> *colored wives. I envy. Yet I must*
> *continue as my great Captain believed:*
> There is a shorter Passage! . . .

Is that not Wallace Stevens, who "richly braved the possible with pineapples and rust-colored wives"? By his stubborn, forlorn pursuit of the "shorter passage," Goodman joins the Great American Deviators, and even the image of the great Captain suggests the Whitman he most spectacularly resembles, "forsaking all others." The section culminates in what might be called a series of Protest Sonnets, typical of the intercourse Goodman sustains with the young, concerning his efforts and failures in their behalf:

> *Foster excellence. If I do not*
> *who will do it? The vulgarity*
> *of my country makes the spirit faint, what we*
> *have misdone to our history and what*
> *to our landscape. The tasteless food we eat,*
> *our music, how we waste day after day*
> *child, woman, and man, have stunned me to dismay*
> *like an ox bludgeoned, swaying on his feet*
>
> *—John, rescue me by becoming! I have well*
> *deserved of this republic, though it has*
> *rewarded me with long oblivion . . .*

As if tired of all these efforts, Goodman follows the Sonnets by a series of Ballades, poems in which he more consciously "tries for individual beautiful poems," I would guess. Most extraordinary among them is a nightmarish glance at his career, "The Ballade of Dates," in which the backward life flashes by:

> *The fall of '44 down-slope,*
> *'40 I was in full career,*
> *by '35 I gave me rope*
> *to say what no one wished to hear*
> *and hang myself. Oh! earlier*
> *in '26 I saw from what beneath*
> *the water-lily snakes into a star*
> *and began to be convinced by death.*

That Shakespearean glimpse into the mud that is the matrix of form, from which the white flowers sprout, was given when Paul Goodman was fifteen, and of course informs with its sexual prepossessions the Love Poems that follow in the collection—hopeless, often abject, but always willing to be delighted by the Meaningful Stranger. The sexual heterodoxy in these spontaneous songs might have abashed any other social reformer, so often exposed on the platform to the rigors of an intimate inspection, but Goodman urges his case upon his frequently

reluctant lovers with all the glad and unchided abandon of a free man
—in what he calls the "manner of Sappho":

> *. . . uncurst*
> *by acts, therefore yet free*
> *to hear and grant, grant it me . . .*

and in what I would call the manner of the School of New York:

> *Because I love you, walking with you*
> *Seventh Avenue is blurry.*
> *You must have stolen my eyeglasses*
> *I am in a panic of surprise*
> *like the President of France assassinated*
> *fumbling for his glasses on his lap*
> *blood spreading on the heart of his shirtfront,*
> *the poor old man who ought to have retired*
> *during the revolutionary situation.*

There are Cavafy poems, Anacreontics, and Negro-dialect lyrics of
phallic regret, all signalized, I think, by a singular acknowledgment of
the Other's being and pleasure, a rare quality in love poems, as well as
by a pity and contempt for the ageing self:

> *When Urgent my prick*
> *and Squirmy my*
> *white body want you*
> *and Heat the wild*
> *pal of my youth*
> *who badly scorched me*
> *again like a ghost*
> *dancing blazes,*
> *my heart has stopped*
> *for you don't share*
> *my lust, yet you*
> *abide my need*
> *bitterly spent,*
> *loyal friend.*

Like Gide and in fact like Goethe, those self-praising and veteran
lovers outside the bourgeois fold, indeed beyond the bourgeois pale,
Paul Goodman has, for all his sexual ravages among the unresponding,
done far more to enlarge the family, the domestic circle, than to violate
and pinion it:

> *So, very cheerfully*
> *my fatherly*
> *harness assume I*

for this young fellow
whose eyes often
flash gratitude.

We may suspect that the gratitude is for the existence of the harness. And indeed, in the book's final section, Sentences and Prayers, the one in which the poet grapples closest with his fate, it is the role of service to the young which Goodman insists will save him (as Gide assumed it would save *him*—Goethe had no such confidence), ruefully marking the failures of his own lot even as he goes about attempting to remake that of others:

Fatherless I was, nobody offered
me to the muses, I imposed on them.
I had no father to rebel against
and I have lived by making trouble.

But for all his acknowledged and flaunted inadequacies, Goodman recognizes his triumphs in the City, as he must—

At last I know—for friends have said—
my shameless public ways have made
me scorned and fail and lonely in
this teeming city. Lord, between

us, I would not do otherwise
for Thy name's sake among these
Babylonians, although I long
for the people of whom I am one.

Even this rapid conspectus of Goodman's book suggests, surely, that he is, more than any American poet alive, the true heir and disciple of the Good Grey Poet, mining the verge of the inclusive experience; and if he does not have Whitman's genius for suggesting that he is a Cosmos in himself, relying of necessity on the received forms to stiffen his talent, he is apter to catch his own posture, even his own imposture, in a reflexive and restorative irony. The other, public irony is that Paul Goodman's poetry has been obscured—cancelled, as a Sacred Book— by its situation in his canon—if he had written only poems, he would I think have held the place in American poetry today that sexuality, say, has in our assessment of human possibilities—central, flawed, affording occasions for joy and fulfillment.

A hundred years ago, the desperate, prophetic note we hear in Goodman's voice, though without his humor and without his delight in the very nature man can disfigure, was first sounded in Western literature:

> We find it painful to be men—real men of flesh and blood, with *our own private bodies;* we're ashamed of it, and we long to turn ourselves into something hypothetical called the average man. We're stillborn, and for a long time we've been brought into the world by parents who are dead themselves; and we like it better. We're developing a taste for it, so to speak. Soon we'll invent a way to be begotten by ideas altogether. But that's enough, I've had enough of writing these *Notes from Underground* . . .

The passage from Dostoyevsky suggests Goodman's entire effort—in his poems where, as he says, he "sips his food from the meadow-flowers of reality"—to be a man with his own private body, reconciled to having been brought into the world by living parents, a father and a mother, and eager, in the heroic Oedipal tradition, to perform the tasks of actuality. "My world," he says, and more immediately of course in his poems than anywhere else he could say it,

> *My world my only one, whom I must love*
> *if I so hard persist and pursue*
> *to become a happy man with you*
> *just you, with only you, my obsession,*
> *and I cannot imagine*
> *another possibility than to make*
> *such idle passes at my only world.*

ANTHONY HECHT

"What Do We Know of Lasting Since the Fall?"

I N 1954, when Anthony Hecht was thirty, a year older than Louis Simpson and a year younger than Richard Wilbur (to adduce the most relevant practitioners of an art all three regard as "a craft particular to Man"); when he had already received and recovered from the first Writing Fellowship ever awarded to the American Academy in Rome; and when, most important of all if most improbable, he could assert that in nature—in the flow of water, the flight of birds, the flesh of women—as in an art of "double sonnets," "seascapes with figures" and "divisions on a ground" (all titles of poems inflected to the modes of literature, painting and music), *"the sum . . . was something planned"*; then, not a moment too soon, as the awful presence of words like "velure," "gree," "chatoyant" and "reticle" admonish, though not too late for the poet himself to declare that "the garden must allow for the recalcitrant," Hecht published his first book.

There was enough of what he calls "inflorescence of antique design" in *A Summoning of Stones* to make any poet, particularly so fastidious a maker as Hecht, hold his peace, hold it tight, and the thirty neoclassical poems of this astonishingly consistent first book remained—or rather, endured: "a grace won . . . from all losses"—the writer's *only* book until thirteen years later, when he brought out *The Hard Hours*, twenty-seven extended pieces which for all their local refinement and all their over-all extravagance, clearly the work of the same cunning hand, are of a very different stamp from the inceptive enterprise, those "whole notes of admiration and romance" which Hecht so strictly characterized by an epigraph to the entire book from Santayana: "to call the stones themselves to their ideal places, and enchant the very substance and skeleton of the world."

Whereas the later poems are more often than not the kind of work that is conventionally called narrative or dramatic, that celebrates or deplores the engrossment of existence by duration—in any case, not lyrics but personal meditations on succession, essays in chronology—the guarded forms of *A Summoning of Stones* (and it is precisely from *time* that their form guards them, from the mutability enforced by the sense of linear progression rather than exorcised by the force of cyclical recurrence) are, as Santayana's phrase implies, the celebration of an order, the naming of things once and for all in a delighted ceremonial of adequacy ('adequacy of apellation to object) acknowledged, even when the things named are wounded or depraved.

Naming is, of course, the primal poetic act, the first *making* which man undertook; and when Adam first assigned to the animals and plants of the Garden their designations, he was writing the first poems. Naming is that activity which was man's duty and recreation (indistinguishably) in an unfallen state, his characteristic and permanent action in a site without the erosions of mortal geography, his prophecy and history (simultaneously) in a time before time began. When I said, just now, that Anthony Hecht's earlier poems were neoclassical, I did not mean, of course, that they betrayed an unawareness, for all their decorum and indeed for all their decor—chiefly gardens—of our fallen, ragged state. For his first book is obsessed by an imagery of decline from some original standard of possibility, by the knowledge that if we are to return at all to the God-given Unity we fell from, it must be by some process (and thereby utilizing the temporal) of impurity—from the many, One:

> *Mourn not to see the Apple fall,*
> *For we are fallen, and may call*
> *Love into being only by*
> *The Shifts of Multiplicity.*

Those capitalized nouns are a characteristic note in Hecht's early work, a reverence, as the old word for a curtsey was *reverence*, to precisely the neoclassical certitudes, even when they were certitudes of a post-lapsarian world ("a style can teach us how / to know the world in little where the weed / has license . . .")

Of course we mistrust, nowadays, the neoclassical image of art ("how nature first declared for the baroque," as Hecht puts it, "in her design of water currents")—we mistrust what declares itself above the untidy for what it has foisted upon us: a language of ornament only, a vocabulary of embellishment that expresses no more than a failure to explore or create the world, offering instead that conventional failure

—or failed convention—a judgment on messiness, a regression (to a kind of precocious toilet-training which in art is fatal), a reiterated self-indulgence. "Doing things your own way," as Ivy Compton-Burnett put it recently, "is not really doing them." Hecht, too, is aware of the dangers of the mode he promotes, and in his first book ("making numbers human / by sheer extravagance") is forever crying out for "the liberal effect," for "disorder at the heart of everything"; though he has the imagination of Eden, he revels in his impotence, as a fallen creature, to correct the natural order, or natural disorder:

> *And all my thought, though diligent and tidy,*
> *Could not yet disestablish such a green*
> *Outburst.*

Indeed he ends one of his many garden poems with the intuition of wildness as the one thing that can redeem us; turning to his girl, the poet urges her to moralize, with him, the landscape (the gardens of the Villa d'Este, no less!) and in it see the emblem of their condition and union:

> *. . . Recall these words, let them be read*
> *Between us, let them signify that here*
> *Are more than formulas, that age sees no more clearly*
> *For its poor eyesight, and philosophy grows surly,*
> *That falling water and the blood's career*
> *Lead down the garden path to bed*
> *And win us both to May.*

The compression of Hecht's wit is characteristic here—it is down the path to bed that we are led, down *this garden*'s path, in fact, and what leads us to bed is not only the blood's career but the design imposed on the falling element by man's devices. A marriage has been arranged . . . And for all this poet's lip-service (and service of hand and brain as well) to the savage, the unmediated, the chaotic, Hecht knows and owns up to what he most securely owns, "that in me wherewith I most advance," a rhetoric of decorum which perpetually fences out the woods, cultivates its garden. The vision of death in a rotting monkey's corpse is enough, in Hecht's Parnassian anthology-piece "Alceste in the Wilderness," to send his Misanthrope back to the very society of degrees and distinctions against which he had so violently railed; mortality refers the poet, like Alceste, to manners, and the sight of the coming mortal decay (with all Hecht's witty prefiguration of Darwin —"nothing could disguise / how terribly the thing looked like Philinte") compels a reversion to society as, in every sense, "a going concern":

Before the bees have diagrammed their comb
Within the skull, before summer has cracked
The back of Daphnis, naked, polychrome,
Versailles shall see the tempered exile home,
Peruked and stately for the final act.

If we cannot reside in Eden, Hecht suggests, we are at least, as "tempered exiles," able to inhabit Versailles where we may face our "final act" in some bewigged state, and that vision of propriety, of courtliness, is enough to engage his loyalties in these poems inhabiting "a world of wigs":

The place is neither Paradise nor Hell,
But of their divers attributes a blend:
It is man's brief and natural estate.

Thus the "liberal effect" he calls for is, after all, one that "caprice and cunning spawn"; thus the "disorder at the heart of everything" he would acknowledge is, still, "controlled disorder":

While overhead the stars resolve
Every extravagance.

These days, our emblem of literature, of authorship at its most valuable, is not the *finished* work, varnished and out of the author's hands, but the career—the long curve of convention, experiment and repossession of means ("in the old human bondage to the facts / of day-to-day existence"). What we want is not accomplishment (which always threatens to turn into mere "accomplishments"—watercolors, some Scarlatti sonatas perfectly played, a little "art sewing"), but exploration, a venture into the possibilities of unexposed technique, a development of feeling beyond the resources of mere judgment. And we tend to discredit what I should call the neoclassical notion of an artist's producing no more than *what he has set out to make*, progressing from the arbitrary toward a previously defined necessity, from a certain disorder toward a certain order. Further and deeper—for it is here that Hecht most concerns us—we have learned to distrust a presentment of order and necessity (even when such a presentment is critically, is dialectically concerned with the chaotic and the arbitrary) which does not seem to have to *struggle* against a constant sense of despair and disorder resisting the thing which is coming into being.

It is to allay this mistrust of ours, to correct such discredit, that I think Anthony Hecht chose Santayana to intercede for him at the start of his first book. He recognized thereby that his was a poetry of essences, of moments recovered, of instances rescued from the flux of phenomena and granted a value precisely insofar as they resisted change, as they withstood a world in which everything is added, everything taken away, everything *transformed*. Thus it is to Santayana that he turns as to a tutelary genius, to the Santayana who said— and of Proust!—so fittingly:

An essence is simply the recognizeable character of any object or feeling, all of it that can actually be possessed in sensation or recovered in memory, or transcribed in art, or conveyed to another mind. All that was intrinsically real in past time is accordingly recoverable . . . Such essences are set over against existence everywhere and at all times, and it remains for existence, if it will, to embody their forms or to give attention to them, so that they may become evident to living spirits. And a living spirit finds great joy in conceiving them, not because they are all bēautiful or true, but because in conceiving them it is liberated from the pressure of ulterior things, energizes perfectly, and simply conceives.

Under this sign we have the poems of *A Summoning of Stones*, then, imparting joy not because they are all beautiful or true but because they liberate us from the pressure of ulterior things; their careful stanzas, their exuberant topiary assuring us that "the logic of the heart delights / in its first figure," insisting that "the nunnery of art" sustains "a searching discipline [that] can keep the eye still clear, as though in spite of Hell," and restoring some sense, as in "Hallowe'en," of the ritual holidays, vestiges of the Old Religion, the awful rites which, though they declared that "Blood is required, and it shall fall," at the same time initiated us into the posture of acceptance wherein we could acknowledge "the place of pain in the universe," could "learn, where pain was lost, how to recover pain":

> *Tonight our streets are filled*
> *With beardless pirates and their high-heeled wives*
> *Who own no maps of treasure and have killed*
> *Nobody with their aimless wooden knives;*
> *They cry us charity for their cups of tin.*
>   *Tonight their plea is styled*
> *With signs of poison and the threat of crones,*
> *While from behind a soap-scrawled windowpane,*
> *A pumpkin with a candle for a brain*
>   *Flashes its hacked-out grin*
> *At Jolly Roger, ensign of the child*
> *Who stalks the street, superfluous of bones.*
>
>   *One time the children came*
> Souling *with little songs for all the dead,*
> *Soliciting in Mystery's full name*

Apples and cakes and pies, for it was said
A hermit raised a trapdoor and was shown
  Where purgatory burned,
Whistled and hurt; he heard the demons yell
Against the monks of Cluny for their prayers
That lifted cripples up the spiraled stairs
  And singing made it known:
To do grace to the dead, lest they returned,
Apples were prayers and giving was a spell.

This is certainly to recover what was intrinsically real (even intrinsi-
cally recognizeable—as in "aimless knives" and the figure of the child
under the pirate ensign, stalking the street "superfluous of bones") in
past time, to recover not only the witty and visible presentment of the
moment, with remarkable fidelity to the virtues of reportage in the first
stanza, but to enact and dramatize, by form and language and tone,
what it meant in the second. The labor of fitting together the syllables
into a verse that will charm the mind in both senses (consider here
merely the discreet echo of "souling" in "soliciting") is so delightedly
accomplished, so firmly administered in the choice and what one must
call the chastity of the language, that we are indeed certain, by the end,
that such giving *is* a spell. The reclamation of significance from what is
little more than a date and a game is a typical Hecht project, of course,
and the rather terrifying essence—"grace to the dead, lest they re-
turned"—comes both as a surprise in such an instance and as an
inevitable release: like all the poems in *A Summoning of Stones* the
events of life, as well as the damages of a lifetime, are illuminated by a
primal vision which asserts, beyond growth as beyond decay, beyond
accident as beyond purpose, that there is a significant ordering in
experience, fall from it as we must; asserts is the wrong word, though
—it is not an assertion but a *recognition scene* which is provided for us
in these poems, and the shapes of the stanzas, the shoring up of energy
by the rhythms of particularity, the "neoclassical" transcendence of
the merely serious ("I say these things / not without difficulty. Death
is always here, / and birth, and sickness; also the accident / of Fate
bringing together four warm legs . . .") close together in a single
impulse, a radiance dependent upon, even as it rises from, the essential
conviction that Being *takes shape, takes place,* and that such places and
shapes can be—even accurately—*named;* as Anthony Hecht says
among the last lines of the last poems in this first book:

Now in these poems—*the well-balanced cat,*
This one of pliant clouds, this weeping skull,
The saint reeling with godliness—I hear
A voice behind these words, behind the green

Proliferation of the sparrow's home,
Behind the air. The speaker goes unseen.
Yet I would know him, if the heart were known.
Close with this world; incorporate this voice.

The emphasis is mine, but the Italy, the Eden of these poems(and of course it will not be to everyone's taste that the Gardens of the Villa d'Este are made into the Garden itself) are Anthony Hecht's—"cause for the lark, the animal spirit / to rise, aerated, but not beyond our reach."

Though the poems in Hecht's second collection, *The Hard Hours*, had almost all been published—with a certain complacency, in fact; with the assurance of furthering a distinguished, if discontinuous, career—in the best places where poetry may be published before it gets into the comparative security of a book; and though Hecht, in the thirteen years since the appearance of his first volume, had given many readings of the new work, renditions in which his enterprise had been remarkably furthered by his splendid gifts as a performer (so impressive are Hecht's powers as a "reader" of his own poems that I am not sure that his new tack—or nail, or spike: in any case, a fastening—has not been sharpened in order to accommodate his delivery, his *acting*, his mummery rather than his making); though it is expected, in our rather smug acceptance of the poet's trajectory in preference to his specific tribute of actual poems *written*, that any poet will "develop" into something not altogether articulated in his earliest statement, however consummate, as in Hecht's case, that initial claim may be; there is still a considerable jolt for the reader who left off, or expected to carry on, with a sense of Anthony Hecht as a namer of things, a poet of presence rather than of process, a celebrant of rites in which the act of praise takes precedence over the recording function.* The new, long, often confessional poems in *The Hard Hours* do not afford passages that may be exhibited as characteristic behavior; here the fringe benefits and local profits are ploughed back into the business, for these are poems of narrative, of event; accounts of happenings and interpretations of history (personal, ancient, mythical, journalistic), and their existence in the temporal dimension, with their concomitant acceptance of decay and change, commits them—as the very title suggests—to a different discipline: they are of the Devil's party.

For poetry is concerned with the perpetual asseveration of being; it is language intended not merely to be understood but remembered; as Hecht himself puts it in his rousing, reactionary essay "On the Methods and Ambitions of Poetry" (published in the *Hudson Review*, of

---

* The Recording Angel, as I shall suggest below, is always a Fallen One: to account for duration is to be damned.

which he has lately become an editor), poetry "in the end recovers for us the inexhaustible plenitude of the world"; it is, rather, prose which accounts for process, which accommodates, as Hegel puts it, "all the seriousness, the suffering, and the labor of the Negative." Indeed, prose is the language which denies itself, which cancels out its being so that the mind retains of it only the effect, the *action*. While poetry, as Hecht himself says, "serves to arrest action rather than promote it." That is why prose is the Satanic genre always, sacrificing presence as it does to process, to change, movement, decay and growth, but never, in its truest form, asserting Being over and beyond all Becoming. In Anthony Hecht's new book, the hours are hard precisely because they are *hours*, no longer stones summoned to their ideal places, but a dimension in which the world, no longer enchanted as by the spell of angels, may run to rot and ruin:

> *For human life is composed*
> *In reasonably equal parts*
> *Of triumph and chagrin,*
> *And the parts are so hotly fused*
> *As to seem a single thing.*
> *This is true as well*
> *Of wisdom and ignorance*
> *And of happiness and pain:*
> Nothing is purely itself
> But is linked . . .

it does not matter with what—the point of these intensely suffering poems is that they are no longer a spell but a spiel, "a speaking voice delivering itself on a ceremonious occasion," yet seeing beyond that occasion into the waste of ordinary time in which life occurs, for all our ceremonies. *Penser, c'est dire non*, Alain once remarked, and I would extend the dictum to the accommodation of any process: *to narrate is to say no*, and these are poems of narration. Hecht has dropped his beautiful vocabularies of stasis, for he is a fallen angel, is Lucifer now, and his favorite tone is a dark, despairing urbanity ("Message from the City," "Third Avenue in Sunlight," even "The Dover Bitch" have replaced the emblematic gardens):

> *Yesterday was nice.*
> *I took my boys to the park.*
> *We played Ogre on the grass.*
> *I am, of course, the Ogre,*
> *and invariably get killed.*
> *Merciless and barefooted,*
> *they sneak up from behind*
> *and they let me have it . . .*

These are shards of argument, of protest, outrage and terrible pain ("The Hill," "The Room" and "Consider the Lilies of the Field," all long dramatic monologues, are among the most agonizing poems to have appeared in America: only a poet of Hecht's truly burnished gifts could have managed to make them feasible and even, at times, funny); what is beautiful about these poems, or rather what is beautiful about the prose in these poems, for prose is the form to which argument is responsible—is their *doubt*, or at least their certainty that the meaning of experience is not evident of itself and available and merely to be celebrated. These poems smell of brimstone, of the Spirit that Denies, for they assert the scandal of the negative, of the narrative and the dubious, of all that does not appear to be true *of itself:*

> *What the intelligence*
> *Works out in pure delight*
> *The body must learn in pain,*

Hecht now insists, and makes his second Fate, "Clotho, or the Present," speak for him:

> *. . . only those*
> *Born with a Comic sense*
> *Can learn to content themselves.*
> *While heroes die to maintain*
> *Some part of existence clean*
> *And incontaminate . . .*

Of course there are still plenty of emblematic animals and weathers in these poems, but they are no longer emblems of pure being, but rather —as in "Birdwatchers of America," with its epigraph of a journal-entry by Baudelaire which specifically refers to time as the containing vessel—references, here both weather and bird, to an ongoing life which admits of no ecstatic or angelic form, but only of an endless, echoing fall into void:

> *But in our part of the country a false dusk*
> *   Lingers for hours; it steams*
> *From the soaked hay, wades in the cloudy woods,*
> *   Engendering other dreams.*
> *Formless and soft beyond the fence it broods*
> *Or rises as a faint and rotten musk*
> *   Out of a broken stalk.*
> *There are some things of which we seldom talk;*
>
> *For instance, the woman next door, whom we hear at night,*
> *   Claims that when she was small*
> *She found a man stone dead near the cedar trees*

After the first snowfall.
The air was clear. He seemed in ultimate peace
Except that he had no eyes. Rigid and bright
 Upon the forehead, furred
With a light frost, crouched an outrageous bird.

Of course it is evident that the careful control of stanzas and rhymes keeps Hecht well within the neat purlieus of verse; his virtuosity allows him to be as prosaic as he likes, or hates, to be: I am not saying that Hecht has ceased to be a poet because he has been expelled from Paradise, but that he has, *as* a poet, engaged in an altogether different Holy War, one in which the enemy is brought into being by the poem itself, instead of being left outside the shape and place of the poem, as in the landscape of Eden. The poet who can permit himself this version of "the speaking voice":

All this happened about ten years ago,
And it hasn't troubled me since, but at last, today,
I remember that hill; it lies just to the left
Of the road north of Poughkeepsie; and as a boy
I stood before it for hours in wintertime . . .

is no longer in any position "to maintain / some part of existence / clean and incontaminate"; he has found a way—and of course his old apprenticeship to, his old mastery of, the lyric impulse serves him wonderfully *on* that way—to include in his understanding our detestations, our heresies, our hates; it is a way that makes him more interesting (as the Devil is always more interesting than anything), and as far as I can see, more competent to deal with the world we live in; it is, though—and so to the credit and dismay of his poetry and our world it must be acknowledged—a *via negativa*.

Millions of Strange Shadows by ANTHONY HECHT

Lyric is an ablation of time. Celebrating an ecstasy, lamentation or joy, or merely—our modern instance—a predication of being, it is *all one:* lyric, then, confirms the moment, sustains a "now" which is invested with significance as long as the lyric structure endures, releasing us from the pressure of ulterior things. Anthony Hecht, who commenced his very rich, compressed career in 1954 with *A Summoning of Stones*, gave us there an anthology of essences, moments recovered, instances rescued from the flux of phenomena and granted a value precisely insofar as they resisted change, as they withstood a world in which everything is by addition or subtraction altered, everything is *transformed*. The attitude to language in that first book is profoundly conservative; indeed it is not an attitude or posture, but a conviction or dogma, whose sign is the retention of a vocabulary considered by some as archaic or—worse—*précieux*; but this was to misunderstand the poet's enterprise, by whose lights no word could suffer a diminution, no diction be darkened by disuse. In that first book, and in that fancied nomenclature, the events of life are illuminated by an ecstatic vision which asserts, beyond growth as beyond decay, beyond accident as beyond purpose, that there is a significant ordering within experience itself, fall from it as we must.

Thirteen years later, Hecht republished half the poems from his first book with the new poems in his second, *The Hard Hours;* this recuperation along with this reconnaissance suggests that the poet was by no means through with lyric, was not ready, or even willing, to give up a poetry which, in his words, "recovers for us the inexhaustible plenitude of the world." But the poems which fulfill the huge talent do so with a difference; the hours are hard precisely because they are *hours*, no longer stones summoned to their ideal places but a dimension in which the world, no longer enchanted as by the spell of angels, may run to rot and ruin. Lyric in the later work is foregone, replaced by monologue and rumination, argument, protest, outrage and terrible pain; the poems accommodate prose, now, the way they accommodate time—and for that very reason, though by accommodate I do not wish to suggest an obliging posture: time is still the enemy, but contended against, no longer *transcended;* and prose is still the dismaying form, but borrowed from, no longer *rejected*. The poet is engaged in an altogether different Holy War, one in which the foe is brought into being by the poem itself, instead of being left outside the poem's shape and diction. The poet who permits himself this version of the "speaking voice":

> *All this happened about ten years ago,*
> *And it hasn't troubled me since, but at last, today,*
> *I remember that hill; it lies just to the left*
> *Of the road north of Poughkeepsie; and as a boy*
> *I stood before it for hours in wintertime . . .*

is no longer concerned, is no longer *enchanted*, by lyric. Instead, the poems of *The Hard Hours* are chiefly exorcisms and wakenings, negations. And the poems of Hecht's new book, ten years later, pursue their course, a spiral course, "forever aslant in their moment and the mind's eye." Even when they proceed through the lovely topiary stanzas which make Hecht find in Herbert one of his masters—

> *Who could have known this better than St. George,*
> *The Poet, in whose work these things are woven*
>   *Or wrought as at a forge*
> *Of disappointed hopes, of triumphs won*
>   *Through strains of sound and soul*
> *In that small country church at Bemerton?*

—one feels that the lines are, in our phrase, going through the motions, and that the rapt circularities of lyric are not what enthrall him now. The verse is extended rather as upon a bed of nails, often invoking the structures and the strictures which asserted his immense gift, which still assert and even asseverate it, but to a tormented end, pierced everywhere by a sense that we are sons of yesterday, not of the morning. In Hecht's poems a man is pushed to his fortune by the hundreds of days he has buried, eager ghosts. And as Meredith says of those days, if you have not the habit of taking counsel with them, you are but an instrument in their hands.

Therefore the central issue of this densely qualified, masterfully varied new volume will be to consult with the past, to compact with time, in order to resolve upon an issue, an escape even: the poet seeks to keep from being an instrument, to become rather an *auctor*, even if it is merely by being an actor.

Most striking of all his instigations is the constant figure the poems form, a kind of triple structure in which the past is set forth, anatomized in all its alienated confusions, whereupon comes a vision (call it the vision of lyric: "some part of existence clean and incontaminate") which entirely transfigures speaker and words, returning us to the lost ecstasy, and then fading, vanishing, ending, until the world is restored, blunt and obtrusive, but with an addition to its freight—the poet knows he has had his vision, *and it has changed him.* He is no longer an instrument, a victim, and though he must give up what it was that the poem exists to record if not recuperate, it has made his life worth something, and worth sharing. That is the process, indeed the processional, of most of the poems in *Millions of Strange Shadows* (whose title, from the Sonnets, is braided back into the business: looking at a photograph of his wife as a girl, the poet has his vision, his release from the ulterior, and is moved by this eternal evanescence to ask Shakespeare's question, so properly put to the image "washed away in acides"). The poems stand, in all their magnificence, to permit the vision. In a note of this brevity I shall quote only one (magnificent) instance. The poet scrutinizes the nostalgias and finds himself, a child obsessed by all the tyrannical personnel of his family life, at the window, watching:

> *The streets became more luminous, the world*
> *Glinted and shone with an uncanny freshness.*

The brickwork of the house across the street
(A grim, run-down Victorian chateau)
Became distinct and legible; the air,
Full of excited imminence, stood still.
The streetcar tracks gleamed like the path of snails.
And all of this made me superbly happy,
But most of all a yellow Checker Cab
Parked at the corner. Something in the light
Was making this the yellowest thing on earth.
It was as if Adam, having completed
Naming the animals, had started in
On colors, and had found his primary pigment
Here, in a taxi cab, on Eighty-ninth Street
It was the absolute, parental yellow.
Trash littered the gutter, the chipped paint
Of the lamppost still was chipped, but everything
Seemed meant to be as it was, seemed so designed,
As if the world had just then been created,
Not as a garden, but a rather soiled,
Loud, urban intersection, by God's will.

What a transformation of style this registers! this and a dozen analogous passages in Hecht's new book, though of course there have been preparations, intimations, as in the much-admired poem "A Hill" from the previous one, whose close I quoted a moment ago. Hecht's is the only case I know, in our impoverished modernism— well, no, I would add Merrill and the selected Ashbery—where we can eat our cake and have it too, if by cake I am allowed to mean the visionary space in which life is seen to be good for being no more than itself, devoured, spent, even excrementally lost, and yet present—presented—once again to the mind's eye, and hand, and speaking lips. This happens because of pains taken, because of what I have called, glibly, a transformation of style; surely what I must mean is a change of heart, something that happens to the whole man, so that he no longer sees his life as a contest of losing wills in and against time, but as a possibility of ecstatic possession *because of time.* Rival claims such as those of past and present, decay and birth, movement and paralysis, even life and death, are seen not to be reconciled, but no longer to be rivals. It is a supreme achievement of character, not of style, though of course where else are we to look for style? Hecht tells us:

At the beginning of course there was a sense of loss,
Not of one's own life, but of what seemed
The easy, desirable lives one might have led.
Fame or wealth are hard to achieve,

And goodness even harder;
But the cost of all of them is a familiar deformity
Such as everyone suffers from . . .
What you learn has nothing whatever to do with joy,
Nor with sadness, either. You are mostly silent,
You come to a gentle indifference about being thought
Either a fool or someone with valuable secrets.
It may be that the ultimate wisdom
Lies in saying nothing.
I think I may already have said too much.

Poetry, 1977

DARYL HINE

"Between Dream and Doing,
Meaning Lurks."

A CANADIAN, specifically a British Columbian by background and birth some thirty years ago, Daryl Hine found in that Boreal accommodation, where "the invisible and unspoken reinforced every site and sentiment," a native market or at least a native medium for his nimble verses, his *numbers* as they used to be called when poetry was understood to be made up of measurable and hence of metrical quantities, by the time he was fifteen; in as many more years, within the narrow, neat-edged interstices—the buttonholes of a life richly embroidered with university degrees in Classics and Comparative Literature, with that old-fashioned kind of travel, neither derelict nor de luxe, known as *wayfaring* in France, Italy, Scotland, England and Poland, with translating (Euripides, Ronsard, Buchanan), with editing (in 1968, Hine assumed the mantle—the blanket?—of that venerable invalid *Poetry*) and with teaching, Daryl Hine nevertheless, indeed all the more knowingly, managed to produce a novel (*The Prince of Darkness & Co.*), a travel book (*Polish Subtitles*), and in 1965, after his first three collections of poetry, at the high noon of a career which for most poets would be in its small hours still, a fourth book of poems succeeded if it did not entirely supersede the others, *The Wooden Horse;* in 1968 Hine's fifth book of poems, *Minutes*—

> *The Time machine at last has broken down . . .*
> *There are so many minutes in our lives*
> *And not one second hand in which to live . . .**

* The pathos of an unusable past, Hine's great subject, is here rendered in Hine's characteristic style—depending upon a double reading of "second hand" as substantive and as modifier. What Hine says of poetry is true of himself: "where faith was feeling, wit prevailed."

—no longer followed but led his work into its resolution, a beautiful truce "between seem and be," though the lysis comes, actually, in the preceding volume, poems in which the jeopardized balance between the appearance and the motive of things, between the observed world and the world of will, is more strictly kept, or at least more stubbornly cared for, than in the high-gloss work which preceded it, though the response to experience, under the shellac, is the same: "reality survives / only as long as it can fool or charm"; whereupon the poet glosses in every sense his adage:

> *There at least we shall not come to harm;*
> *Therein we and our desires belong,*
> *Where lusts like bees perish as they sting.*

Hine's poetry is always a struggle with narcissism, whose outcome or issue (but never whose solution) may be either love or death; *intricate, mean and crystalline*, as he once called the city of Paris, the battlefield of these "fierce warres that moralize the song" is an acknowledgment of convention so rapt that we may wonder where the freedom is. Yet it would be a lapse to read this poet without realizing—upon reflection, as Hine would say, in these fervent surfaces—that the convention is not working against the freedom, against the emotion, but has *released* the emotion—it would be a lapse of sympathy with the poet's actual enterprise, for if we are at a loss in all these bonds and baffles, we must be simply happy there until we see what being out of them would mean. When Coleridge said that in poetry you have more than the usual emotion and more than usual order he surely meant—and this is Hine's case, even his casuistry—that the order was necessary to accommodate the emotions. Given, then, these hard conditions for reality's survival, that it must fool or charm—others? oneself? the *gift* does not specify—Hine's earlier books fail to meet them. Or meet them too easily (invulnerability is the true failure). Particularly in that teratoid toybox of virtuosity *The Devil's Picture-Book* (1960), the deception and the enchantment are too readily imposed on the shapes of natural life to gain much credit for the survival, and the leap of likeness we are told poetry shares with and derives from magic here takes its spring— "like charred tinsel overturned in marred snow"—from a ground that is all fuller's earth. We are not aware, in Daryl Hine's first poems, of the nagging presence of anything so extraneous or so impure as "the real world"—the poet never appeals to it as a means of settling or solving the difficulties of art; for him, the poem is always the statement of itself, a piece of language with which no more can be done and which, if it fails in its own terms, cannot be ransomed or relieved by "forgetting forms, confusing here and there / the word, the touch, the language and the look . . ."

Such a determination to write, always, *poems* rather than versified thoughts, philosophical rhapsodies, poetical equivalents for something else that came before and perhaps compelled the poem into being in the poet's mind, accounts, I think, both for the evident limitations of these poems (sometimes they do afford

> *not the green tree but the urinal,*
> *instead of magic, glandular hocus-pocus—*

but that is the defect of their quality, not their quality), and for a certain kind of acceptance they have gained, even a certain kind of success. Though I am concerned with what Coleridge, again, called the profession of literature rather than the trade of authorship, I cannot forbear emphasizing Hine's victorious precocity, his special status as a *Wunderkind*, for it is the sort that prepares, rather than pre-empts, a vocation:

> *a verbal gate and adjectival tower*
> *glutted with papers fallen from the air,*
> *telling of politics and sex and war,*
> *where we read our names among casualties*
> *as those that had laid aside wealth and power*
> *and fallen in vain as spiders fall to flies.*

Nor am I alone in realizing that something extraordinary was, from the first, under way, if only that. In 1954, Northrop Frye reviewed Hine's first collection, *Five Poems*, as a "remarkable volume," and what he remarked in it was the prospective impulse of the poet's young gifts: "The sense of a powerful gathering of forces is stronger than any other reaction." This is not altogether praise, of course, but its emphasis on the promise of Hine's work is accurate and characteristic of the critic who once said "all value-judgments that inhibit one's sympathies with anything outside a given tradition are dismally uncritical." In 1957, when Hine published a more inclusive book, *The Carnal and the Crane*, Professor Frye was still looking forward: "I doubt if any Canadian poet has potentially greater talents than Mr. Hine, and few in recent years have struck out more vivid and haunting lines, lines that can become part of one's permanent reading. He has a grotesque wit . . . and we may look forward to a poetry of released powers." We know now the work that was to follow, we know just how those powers were to be released, but we must not allow what we know to hamper our attention. That early book deserves more than the dismissive label *juvenilia*, even when we recall that its author was twenty—and we are given cause so to recall. There is a reason why Northrop Frye discerns "haunting lines" rather than the larger wholes—"the sort of alchemy that transfigures peril"—to be hoped for in the greatest potential talent among Canadian poets. The vestal dedication to artifice, to law and to decorum—

> *Rhetoric alone, without a glass,*
> *from private virtue fashions fas, nefas—*

makes an accommodation of the large spirit, of variety and complexity rather than of complication in experience, nearly impossible for this young poet—his successes will be local, without connections, correspondences or opposite numbers, so that he must say, with Holofernes, the pedant in *Love's Labors Lost:*

> This is a gift that I have, simple, simple; a foolish extravagant spirit, full of forms, figures, shapes, objects, ideas, apprehensions, motions, revolutions; these are begot in the ventricle of memory and delivered upon a mellowing of occasion. But the gift is good in those in whom it is acute, and I am thankful for it.

And so am I, for the formal exuberance of these "literary" pieces—a lesson, satires, eulogies, an epithalamium, an apology, a farewell: all the *topoi* of the apprentice. Classical, devotional and erotic ("one saw, even at that distance, / himself reflected in the victim's surface"), the poems of this book and the next all exhibit and indulge a wit "overgone," tremendously elaborated—grotesque, as Frye calls it—in order to discharge energy at all costs: "as if language," Hine was to say later on, "were a substitute / for love!" Often, of course, the cost is too great for the poise so far achieved, and there creeps a curious earnestness into the puns that reminds us how much better it is for a poet at the start to be foppish than earnest. Here are both manners, the deadly and the dandiacal, successive stanzas in the same poem, concerned with the prospect of the sleeping lover:

> *Above my sunken vanity your shapes*
> *as if they had digested time had tiered*
> *its chance to wake upon the sleeping head.*
> *Two seldom seem to say, Do we embrace,*
> *Shall we change the shallow air between us*
> *to water crowned and solid, base of ships.*
>
> *Ptolemy it was who wrote*
> *the map of the narrow world upon your throat,*
> *and Diaz who turned the cape*
> *of your body as it lies in sleep;*
> *Balboa in the bed's red ideogram*
> *sees you lie pacific in your dream.*

How gratifying to see Hine returning to the same theme, one made so standard a *topos* for Narcissus by Cocteau, in his newest book a decade later with an entirely possessed measure now, and a much deeper command of the image:

> *I admire but do not wish to enter,*
> *Like any wanderer beside*
> *Moonlit water in midwinter*
> *Who as a simulacrum for the tide*
> *Casting a pebble into the calm centre*
> *Watches the circles spread from side to side.*
> *I wait for you and morning at your side.*

The Carnal and the Crane continues with what the poet rather archly calls "fabulary satires," with some typically sharp words addressed to an unidentified lady I take to be Marianne Moore:

> *Be, at the end of your famous garden,*
> *admonished, who hated all illusion,*
> *to see your errant guest a skeleton,*
> *the poppy and the hollyhock worm-eaten . . .*

For Hine is hard on his elders. The novel he wrote about Robert Graves often cuts much too close to biography to be satire, and the whine of harpies' wings drowns out the laughs; yet in this bitchy book I find a proper diagnosis of Hine's own early difficulties, when he speaks of the novels written by the Laura Riding figure: "All the characters spoke what may be described as pure syntax; there was no meaning in what they said, only order." Meaning defeated by order— this is exactly the quality of Hine's more ambitious poems in *The Carnal and the Crane* and even in *The Devil's Picture-Book*, where "in the hospital of the particular thing, eternal principles sicken and expire." In the Masque "The Return from Unlikeness" in the earlier book, the dialogues among the three kings and Herod, between the shepherds Alexis and Corydon, and the speeches by Mary, Joseph and Gabriel are not pursued with any consecution of spirit, any development of theme, but for the sake of a dazzling surface, a rhetoric of marquetry:

> *Where is the damned man's praise of god,*
> *the only symphony among the dead?*
> *There must be more than the body's*
> *images of absent ladies,*
> *something for lack of language we call bright:*
> *at the centre of the universe a terrible joy*
> *whose love is sometimes very much like hate;*

Here the brilliancy and fervor of the diction, and the real danger of being easily intelligible, generate those impressive lines Professor Frye responded to, but the "beauties" rarely unite with the poems in which they appear, and get little authority from them. Two fine exceptions, I think, in this book are the five-sonnet sequence "At Pompey's Statua" and the Virgilian imitation "Avernus"—Hine's Roman affinities are evidently with the Rome of the Emperors, not the Republic. The first is a refraction of imperial themes convincing for its very basis in an extant "literature"; invention, Dryden said, is a finding of the thought, and if Daryl Hine has found his in Shakespeare's Roman plays, it is *miglior trovato* for that acquiescence:

> *Now that the act is done, the murderers,*
> *quick to absolve themselves, forget the way*
> *to walk among the painful souvenirs*
> *of simple action on a sunny day.*
> *Cassius broods; dear Brutus is away*
> *confronting crime with learning elsewhere, and*
> *all the minor figures in the play*
> *dream of a scholar's severed head and hand.*
>
> *The only virtues are imaginary:*
> *gone is the wisdom of conspiracy,*
> *gone are all the hero's attributes,*
> *save beauty; here, instead, are all the doubts*
> *that touched us as we sat before the fire*
> *at night, and watched the cities falling there.*

In "Avernus," a kind of impious Aeneas speaks, at the end, to the suicide Dido he has abandoned to her fate by pursuing his own:

> *It was just as if, returned*
> *from the island the inept call beautiful*
> *across the perilous equinoctial sound,*
> *I met the mourners still upon the shore:*
> *although I heard their tale without belief*
> *I knew that there was no escape from knowing*
> *whose love's defection underlay their grief.*
> *Some forms of speech are indissoluble,*
> *some axioms of language need no proof.*
> *I mourned as I rode back along the river,*
> *and not the precious lights that others mourn,*
> *but my own irremediable return.*
> *The wilderness on either side of me*
> *was bleak as paper, hard as words unborn,*

and no one sang there, for I was alone—
only my breathing, your trochaic name,
my exhalation, you upon the air:
that name that would have titled all my poems,
that shape that might have overcome my fear.

Love, for this poetical Aeneas, is realized not as loss but as elegy: the nimbly varied, knowing iambics, and the dandy's self-conscious specification of "your trochaic name . . . that would have titled all my poems" is the kind of spirited playfulness which keeps Hine, at his best, from going soft or solemn, from mistaking the profound for the accurate, the important for the true. "These, immaturity, were your miracles," he declared years later, "you followed language careless where it went / to final, all but metrical collapse / fetching the reader back from last to first / impressions at the regular rate of verse." But at this point in his career, seeking "worlds within words," Hine's achievements are wound upon an armature of indebtedness to the past, even if it is a past that cannot be recuperated—as he says of some buildings in Warsaw, described in *Polish Subtitles*, they are "like ghosts in a time not the time of the place"; nor will this poet ever dissociate his expressive impulse from the wrecked monuments and even from the bric-a-brac of culture—all his books are full of whatnots, ouija boards, urns and armorial bearings—but he will be able ("and no one sang there, for I was alone") to speak more securely in his own person about such emblems of love maimed, illusions lost and understanding gained at the price of trust, hope and ease . . .

Such disenchantments are the bravery of *The Devil's Picture-Book*, which for all its laughter up so many sleeves is a terribly grim affair:

Language of logic and nature of grace
Are mortal. Only vacua endure.
Each moment of its own disease
Shall perish and shall breathe this air no more.

Arid because airless, the *locus amoenus* in Hine's cold pastoral is recognized, rather helplessly, as no more than a deceptive torture-chamber of the heart—as the poet remarks so many years later, "disorder could not enter / our too formal gardens, moribund and private." The only signs of mending here are to be found in the fact or the phenomenon that the disjunct images from the earlier book, the startling figures like:

. . . the quiet Laplands of my breath
where my organs, when they do not freeze,
sing, occasionally handsome, in the trees . . .

and the dazzling lines, dozens to a customer but rarely more than one
to a poem in the earlier books, lines of preposterous mastery like:

> *. . . the twigs as if diseased with burgeoning . . .*
> *. . . the songbird's vision and the blindman's doubt . . .*

are now bound together into intricately molded poems, sestinas, villa-
nelles whose local astonishments and explosions are subject to a more
generalized and indeed exhaustive elaboration, a working-out which is
a workout. If not always to whole poems, there is an adjustment to the
stanza at least, an escape from the concentration camp of the single
image, the single line (in the entire sense of concentration and the
entire sense of camp). Hine is thereby able to develop at some length,
indeed by the very means of length, what Lovejoy has called a *meta-*
physical pathos, explicating, indeed over-determining his sense until we
no longer quite follow what he means, but rather hear the significance
in the sound, the signals:

> *In singleness there is no heart or soul*
> *And solitude is scarcely possible.*
> *The one-sailed ship, tossed on a divided sea*
> *As lightly as cork is tossed, as blindly as*
> *The partners toss on their oceanic bed*
> *And rise and fall, is wrecked and lost away.*
> *In singleness there is no heart or soul;*
> *Thus he sees wrong who sees in halves a whole,*
>   *Who searches heaven but for one,*
>   *And not a double of the sun,*
> *Forgets that, being light as cork, the day*
> *Can rise or fall, is wrecked and lost away.*

The control is enlarged then, not only so that a figure can be sustained,
mirrored in an acknowledgment of the observed world, doing what
Conrad called "the highest kind of justice to the visible," as in:

> *Venice raised like Venus from the sea,*
> *As mortal and as mythical as she*
> *(The sea divulges and the sea devours),*
> *Poses in her emblems and her powers,*
> *With beauty's price and her futility,*
>   *On the water—*

but so that the lawgiving impulse of Hine's strict forms serves the turn
(and what else is *verse* but the *serving of a turn?*) of his even stricter
mind:

> *No, not, and never—all the negatives*
> *Time like a censor to the senses gives.*

Likeness dies
In nature's eyes,
And everywhere it is by art one lives.

Virgil Burnett, who illustrated *Polish Subtitles* and *Heroics*, a privately-printed volume of Daryl Hine's poems now included in *The Wooden Horse*, further supplied a drawing for the latter book which adumbrates, which even defines, the situation of this poet with beautiful immediacy: the completed, composite head of the Trojan Horse (if Hine names his book for this terrible deception, we must not ignore his purpose, the smuggling of nature into art by letting art into nature) is stuck up on an enormous scaffolding, and facing it, his back to us, is a naked man, one hand raised to the blind, lifelike and death-dealing insigne which towers above him; his gesture is one of recognition and farewell. So the poems in this book. Perfectly formed responses to the dilemmas of civilization, the formal content, indeed, of discontent— amphisbaenic rhymes, as in "An English Elegy," merely dramatizing the double nature of Hine's ripened art which functions "*with* the accuracy of a report and the force of a *myth*"—these "heroics" are no longer described from the outside but espoused, shown up to be desperation as well as bravado, as in the final occasion of Sir Walter Raleigh:

The days grow shorter with the darkening year.
An adventurer's life is but a barren stalk.
The History of the World ends with the Prisoner's Walk
Though far and wide it seemed, and various and queer.
At the fall of the afternoon you brought me here,
To show me the axe, the headsman and the block.
Though you torture the dumb with silence you cannot make them talk.
Only the dead have nothing left to fear.

And as in the apostrophe to Pascal:

> *God pardon the polemicist*
> *Whose style, art or language must*
> *richly show how poor the just*
> *in what no sinner can resist.*
>
> *For the stars are far away*
> *and one that died a million years*
> *ago tonight as bright appears*
> *as one that burned out yesterday.*

Moreover, the increased willingness this poet shows to speak for himself ("for me," Hine says in his travel book, "there are two sorts of journey, away from or towards, normally someone. And usually with someone, too, of course; though seldom with the same person"; the thematics of such voyaging will be supported in his later books with an intimacy inaccessible to the terrorist of language Hine had once been) is yet another avatar of the heroic stance: in the finest of these poems, "Plain Fare," whose ingenious title is a triple pun on both words with regard to a bus-trip across the continent, the poet who has been reading *Villette* on the way to a "lost love" himself, glances retrospectively at his journey:

> *It is day, and the lights and roadside structures have vanished.*
> *The novel is finished and the reasons no longer exist*
> *For my visit. From heaven*
> *Out of sight an audible jet*
> *Covers in a mere hour or so*
> *The way that I could not afford to go.*

Like his Tristan and his Don Juan, like his Patroclus putting on the armor of Achilles, Daryl Hine, speaking in his own person, that ultimate mask, acknowledges the inadequacy of the weapons by which men storm the City—the horse is a wooden one, man is naked, and by such rituals of restraint as the poet commands, it is his nakedness which is finally, sadly, acknowledged to be his selfhood's guardian, not his armor . . . Hence the humility of these later "riddling hymnals," the rueful adjustment to a world unglorified, probably, by the divine:

> *. . . I think we all had the impression*
> *That something would come to us on the water,*
> *Music or a message or a god.*
> *Yes, and this held all of our attention,*
> *What was to come, whom, we must wait and see . . .*

The relaxation and the reticence of tone, so different from the crisp assertions of the previous books, the dissolve of convictions into mild conventions—partly an influence sustained from James Merrill, to whom the book is dedicated as an earlier, glassier one had been set under the sign of that expert Canadian artificer Jay Macpherson, and partly the result of a mellowing diction which can afford to follow the rhythms of behavior rather than those of law—characterizes most of *The Wooden Horse*, which is to say that it is in closer contact with the disorder of life than the earlier, the younger decorum of wit allowed. The defense, as Dr. Fenichel says of human personality, is invaded by the impulse; and the attempt to overcome by magic the order of time without going through it is here renounced. The world, in Hine's first poems, came to a stop but also lit up. Now it is no longer incandescent, but it moves—

in your hand
You held a new kind of machine, its moving parts . . .
Turned, and you took pleasure in their turning;
And these, you said, are the minutes that I am reading.

These poems, and those in the next book overwhelmingly titled
Minutes for so many reasons, "transformed or in the act of change,"
give pleasure by what they have permitted their author to gain; by
what they have enabled him, like Bluebeard's Wife in his telling of the
tale, to see:

. . . greater good than any she had seen:
A window upon the sacred text
Of natural things, whose number had not been
Created or conceived, nor did they mean
Other than what they were, splendid and strange.
One leaf is like another, and between
Them all the worlds of difference range;
The world is not destroyed and does not cease to change.

Ezra Pound once advised Yeats, when he was old and ill and felt him-
self incapable of work, to write plays for the sake of the songs they
would necessarily give rise to, the poems released by moments of dra-
matic realization. There is such a moment which jeopardizes if it does
not justify all the rest of Hine's verse-play *The Death of Seneca*, written
in the same years as *Moments*, in which the ancient Roman sage, waiting
for the order to commit suicide from his former pupil Nero, confronts
Saint Paul, a thin dark fanatic who looks like Trotsky and sounds
strangely like Hine's early poems. That is, Paul argues for an eternity
of illumination, and Seneca—dying of endurance—for a *temporal order*
moving in every sense, consonant with mortality and therefore content
with the earth. The scene is the final and furthest accommodation of
Hine's Roman impulse, his Stoic interest, and offers the right commen-
tary on his fifth book, whose very title articulates an absorption in time
("in our faces the minutes wait to strike and yawn") crucial now to this
poet's position, his life which admits all kinds of debility—boredom,
disease, fatigue:

Illness is idiosyncratic: healthier to ignore
The fact in favour of the metaphor . . .

to a duration that had been, literally, unendurable:

. . . Is it the end
Of a premeditated voyage
Or is it the beginning? . . .
I do not know who knows,

Save that one by one
The tenses are exploited,
Time itself is made
Slave to a different employment
As by a godlike labour
That could not be put off:
The soothing of the present
Painfully altered
To a picture of the past
Where any one may see
As in a rear-view mirror
What he imagines best
About that other world.

In these poems—emblem poems, travel poems, love poems, all clouded by the drift of dramatic intimacy, blurred from the old crystalline structures to something "glaucoptic," to use one of Hine's hard words —the narcissism is assumed by the form and therefore released from, precipitated out of the personality which addresses us, addresses itself:

It is as if in all of our embraces
The universe was made personal.

Poems like "The Copper Beech," in which "a syllable gives comfort / dependent on the time and place and person," or like "The Nap," at whose close "everything / vanishes backwards, love and suffering," have abandoned the stagey heroics of Hine's old order; indeed when the glamorous past is leafed-through now, it is with a shrug of condescension, as in "Lady Sara Bunbury Sacrificing to the Graces" or "Natasha's Letter Scene," though we must not ourselves condescend to the pleasures of these performances, pleasure being, always, in this poet, a pseudonym of love, "at least here and now." And the abandonment has occurred because Hine is concerned, here and now, to mythologize his own life, his own experience with a directness that must leave perfection out of the account, with a dependence on duration that can have nothing to do with the divine; as he says at the end of "Untitled," in which "the attribution of guilt is universal," in which the verse itself, for the first time in any Hine poem, consents *until* the end to *extend itself* into a kind of prose, an ongoing utterance ready to cancel itself out for the sake of *what* it utters, and only then recovers the form:

The birth and banquet of love look equally far away
and insignificant from here; the resurrection is also
inconceivable. Only the ignominious and painful

*moment of death has any meaning now, a meaning
without a future or a past.*

*The background is conventional, a wall too high to
see over, too smooth to climb, draped here and there
with a red linen cloth, its folds still visible.*

Beyond the wall there is a gold leaf sky.

*Remember that everything is possible,
The picture, the poem and ourselves,
The blood that we see shed, the tears that we
Shed, the wall, and the anonymous cross.*

DANIEL HOFFMAN

"A Testament of Change,
Melting into Song"

H E THINKS," Marianne Moore has said, with that gnomic thoughtfulness of her own which is so suggestive and so abrupt, from the tripod as it were—"he thinks and what he thinks has substance." Indeed it is the substantial—the sensuous, the dense, the indeterminate and literally understanding *stuff* of the world—which as Miss Moore just manages to observe is the making and the saving of this poet from the genteel limbo of versified intellection, that "nimbly dull" demesne of American Victoriana which Hoffman himself, "grown unhandy with real things / from much manipulation of abstractions," so grimly surveys in his study of Stephen Crane's poetry. The nature of this substance it must be our endeavor to qualify a little, winnowing a lot and lending, perhaps, more than giving ourselves outright to a poetry of what Richard Eberhart has characterized as one of "strong restraints." The point will be to discern what is being restrained, and why strength is requisite for the enterprise. There is, for Daniel Hoffman, at bottom—and indeed for him as for most of us the bottom is a long way down, not a place we can bring ourselves to look at very distinctly, very steadily—there is a terrible burden of brutality and fierce participation in an old unreasoning order of nature, an old service of life taken in its ritual sense ("somewhere, / a consecrated shore"), wherein the dignity and preservation of the self count for nothing at all. In this realm, entrances and exits are everything, the transit negligible, except as it might leave a clutter of clues, on the cavern walls for instance. Thus Hoffman's account, in a late poem, of the venture, the task, the frequent failure (though in these archaic instances, what can success be but the account of failure, the accent of futility?):

> . . . *he thrust a way*
> *Into a chamber none had known before*
> *Save who drew in colors deep as blood*
> *The great creatures on that sacred dome*
> *—Horned Huntsman, and the Woman, Moon—*
> *It was then he found the doorway*
> *To another country. Darkness*
> *There is brighter than familiar noon.*
> *The light that lights that land's like lightning.*
> *Its sudden crackle rends the skies.*
>
> *He tries*
> *To tell a prospect of that country,*
> *His words as much like lightning as the mutter*
> *Of seared cloud*
> *When the bolt's dazzle has come, and gone.*

The abyss—it is the archetypal world we glimpse in some of Golding's novels, in the work of Robert Graves of which Hoffman has said that "the ecstasy of religious possession is perilously attained . . . independently of history, of society, of everything in life save itself" —is overlaid, is draped in Hoffman's general practice with a moralized glamor of will, a civility which "the rhythm does not contradict," to quote Miss Moore again. That is the trouble, or the untroubled mask clapped upon much of Hoffman's work; unquestionably the product of a civilized mind ("it's gaiety that sustains us"), as his reviewers so often point out, we long to put it to the question, we hanker with some bloodthirstiness for the rhythm to contradict all this urbanity, or if it is to be the rhythm that is urbane, then we want a wilderness in what the rhythm carries, against which it may be pitted, matched or at least challenged. Daniel Hoffman's victories, I am certain, are gained precisely in those poems—they are not many, but enough: such quality is the touchstone of achievement, not of magnitude—in which the rhythm contradicts and criticizes, gainsays and thereby enforces the substance of the life "observed."

When Philip Booth, for example, says that Hoffman's mind is a "familiar of abstractions," he is suggesting one thrust of its energies, one thrust which counters another thrust, that primal concern with a world of rituals and dreams, a preoccupation with the unexplained, inexplicable, merely *given* realities of blood, myth and history; it is in the duel of these assertions, their insufferable twist together (for a twist is precisely the conflict of *two*, as in our word *twice*), that we get the discriminating act of perception called style. The rest of the time, when the sense-making apparatus, the mind that is a familiar of abstractions for which facts require or in any case receive no meanings —when the *civility* triumphs too easily, failing to engage the chaos around or below it, we get not authority but strictures, and dismiss the poet, as others have too indolently done, with the first weapon or shield that comes to hand, the easy label "academic," not in itself much of a pejorative except when applied to an enemy, in the conviction that the hysteria of institutions is more dreadful than that of individuals. Let us consider, then, this exemplary and well-behaved career, its bets hedged or at least its wagers buttressed by a number of industrious scholarly works, and the twisted, the double-tongued poems, from four volumes published over fifteen years, which ransom it from docility. About the rest, for or against those of Hoffman's—or Anyman's—poems which are not conspicuous in their engagement of the wild and the tame together, their power to create, in this poet's sense of it, "from both deprivation and delight," we must say with the terrible charity of Yeats' great phrase, *"wind shrieked, and where are they?"*

Daniel Hoffman's first book, *An Armada of Thirty Whales*, was chosen by Auden as the Yale Series of Younger Poets volume for 1954, when the poet was thirty. Angular, quirky, full of flinty strains and tenacities, its music "resounding on an inward anvil"—in other words, pounded out privately—the book displays or disposes of a number of handsome acknowledgments to the Masters; to Stevens in a title like "An Antelope of Cantaloupe," in stage properties like

> *Off Chichicastenango*
> *I saw a green flamingo flying* . . . ,

and in a theme like that of "Auricle's Oracle," with its explicit comment on—or exposure of—the vocabulary and hence the vocation of "Le Monocle de Mon Oncle":

> *Yet passion at its most intense*
> *Consumes the minuscule* . . . ;

to Hopkins, not the poet of devout and doctrinal submission, of course, but the Hopkins of hindered faith searching out its alliterative cause in the particulars of inscape:

> *. . . We walked beneath the birchgroves on the shore*
>
> *and watched the empty light on leaftips pour*
> *and out of nowhere whirled the nebulae,*
>
> *gadding gilded, all green energy, toward death* . . . ;

to Yeats as a matter of course (the course of fitting words together with that violent courtesy which holds abstraction and raw experience in the one understanding, purified):

> *May human hatred unto those*
> *Who take the armless bitch to bed . . .*
> *Invoke such violence on their heads*
> *That in an instantaneous change*
> *From animal flesh to maggot-food*
> *Their brains may momentarily seethe*
> *With knowledge of evil . . .*

But in each case, these salutes are tendered by the poet already secure in a position inside a citadel of idiosyncrasy: the poems of Daniel Hoffman, in his first book, enjoy an access of individual being, whatever influences they preen themselves upon, which results from a pronounced form, uttered and therefore audible. In his brilliant little preface, Auden is so beguiled by the problems of a modern nature poetry—"the preservation and renewal of natural piety toward every kind of created excellence"—which he sees to be one of Hoffman's overriding concerns, that he does not much attend the technical accomplishments they ride over; perhaps the mere appearance of the book in the Series under his editorship is the imprimatur of *that* kind of sanction. And Auden is right, of course—there is a poetry of "direct observation and description" which Hoffman over and over exemplifies, though it is important to discover that he does so, always, in connection with a ritual or cyclical image of birth, growth, death and regeneration, as here in "That the Pear Delights Me Now," tracing the tree's progress through the months, past the "roystering honeymakers, wholly unaware of the dust their bristles brought," past the fruit and the birds that "follow, thirsting," past the "maggots [that] rapaciously and noiseless fatten on fermented juices," to conclude in this epiphany of the ecliptic:

> *That the pear delighted me*
> *is wholly incidental,*
>
> *for the flower was for the fruit,*
> *the fruit is for the seed.*

The same seasonal round is observed, in Hoffman's next book, in "The Beech Tree," and in his newest one, in "The Tall Maple," but what makes the success of such tree-pieces is not their piety of observed detail, but their worship of Eternal Return: they are prayers in a divine service.

And serving *them*, as I noted, is a surprising range of formal devices, whose grace and savor will be preserved and enhanced in the poet's subsequent books, both in assurance of assonance, as:

> *Other wings across the harbor*
> *flash like swords and dive for garbage* . . .

(where the corrupt rhyme wonderfully correlates the noble cliché of flashing swords with the scavenging action), and the control of sense, the discipline of mere significance by more than its cause, by meters and repetitions:

> *What did the caterpillars do*
> *last time the Phoenix died?*
>   *They beat their breasts with a hundred fists*
> *till one of them espied*
> *the egg the ashes incubate.*
> *Then, sure that wings would flame again,*
> *they broke their bread on a mulberry leaf*
> *and out of himself each wove the sheath*
> *from which he'll burst on flaming wings*
>   *after the peace of a season's sleep,*
>   *after the peace of a season's sleep.*

These skills, the inflection of imagery by sound and the ordonnance of meaning by a pattern of rhythmical expectations, belong to a considerable armory: the manipulation of words in component rhythms, contrast, transition and suspense, the delay of ornament, the anticipation of the exactly situated dramatic trope, the development of image and observation to an inevitable end—the list of machines Blackmur said will make a poem cohere, move, and shine apart. Most frequently, Hoffman accommodates his devices in a "loose couplet, stopped between the lines and sometimes employing internal rhymes in lieu of end rhymes," as Auden reports (this is all he has to say of Hoffman's *verse*). Such a couplet, far as it is from the Augustan version, yet invokes rhyme as a characteristic tensor of the form, and carries the ear down the page through the poet's outrageous (which means, literally, his ultimate) argument—in this instance concerning clams and their analogy to human beings in ritual:

> *Lie ten-hours-buried in sand*
>
> *and the swirl of salt and the wet*
> *seems an Age before suffering began.*
>
> *All shrinks in the rage of the sun*
> *save the courage of clams and their faith:*

sacrificing the water they breathe
seems to urge the tall moon from her orbit;

she tugs ocean, cubit by cubit
over killdeer's kingdom

and ends parched freedom . . .

The argument, the analogy, is enlarged, or at least enlarged upon, in other poems in this book:

> *. . . Tempestuously*
> *the porpoise leaps, leaps, spreads his frantic fin*
> *but snoutward underwater rippling falls—*
> *on the rockledge I feel my own back arching.*

Or again, and here the metonymy is so enormous that the entire world of observed events is seen to transpire within the observer's body:

> *Over the wharves at Provincetown*
> *the gulls within our arteries soaring . . .*

And finally, describing his unborn daughter growing to her humanity, gestating inside his wife:

> *Who goes where we go? Who lives under*
> *That anonymous mound? Our image*
> *Through flickering centuries grows fuller*
>
> *Past the pickerel, cygnet, hare,*
> *Swims through sludge & stream & air*
> *And wears the womb as atmosphere . . .*

Auden admonishes that the danger of relying on such analogues for your subject, containers for the thing contained, is that you will become whimsical, decorative in using as an emblem ("pickerel, cygnet, hare" for the foetal stages) what you have no personal experience of as an animal. Whimsical and decorative Hoffman may be, then, though what he is decorating has the stench of mortality already "high" about it; significantly, his control of the diction lures us from any jeopardizing of *his* experience with whales, say—it is our own, *in the poem*, managed by sound and movement, which wins out in the title piece that, as Auden warns, uses natural objects as natural symbols:

> *But they who won't swim and can't stand*
>
> *lie mired in mud and in sand,*
> *and the sea and the wind and the worms*

> *will contest the last will of the Sperms.*

That last line gives a sense, surely, of the taking wit whereby this poet can engross our response: every word is used in a double or twisted sense, and by the clinching rhyme the reader's mind, so entrapped (like Mars) in a net of recognitions, identifications and substitutions, capitulates to its own pleasure.

Counting on such surrender will be Hoffman's danger, of course. In his second book there are too many poems which forget or forego the second of two complementary propositions: that order is imposed on chaos and that chaos is the substance of order. Consequently Hoffman exhibits an even more eccentric delight than in *An Armada of Thirty Whales*—under the sign, now, or the signature of John Crowe Ransom —in an archaic and an arcane vocabulary, a mounting sense of the willful, the arbitrary, though I am reluctant to condemn an impulse with so many meaty links to poems behind and ahead of the poet. The perplexity, then, about the miscellany of "poems and blessings" starting off Hoffman's second book, published five years after his first, is a nomenclature which not so much reveals as reviles the poetical: "chaunt," "burgeoning" (five times), "avast," "benison," "targe," "pinion and fin," "behest," "time's demesne," "aquiver," "garbed," "unmeet," "effable" and "couth" . . . It is not until the second part of this book, from which it takes its modest title *A Little Geste*, that we arrive at Hoffman's justification and perhaps his masterpiece. After reading the "Little Geste" itself, we can retrace the true perspective, the line of quickening wit, the series of poems in both these books which engage the most of life and refresh the terms of bewilderment, of wilderness: always it is the poems in which a ritual, cyclical, traditional version of service, in the hierological sense, is re-enacted. Here "child, magician, poet / by incantation rule." Typical of this group at its best is "Exploration" (the word, of course, means a crying-out upon events), whose speaker identifies himself in the riddling way we expect of the mythological hero, though he is clearly the well-read poet too:

> *I am who the trail took,*
> *nose of whom I followed,*
> *woodwit I confined in*
> *through thorned-and-briared hallows . . .*

Following his "right, trusted hand" until he is lost, the speaker wanders, errant in more than the one sense:

> *. . . Found*
> *I the maze I wander in*

> *where my right, trusted hand*
> *leads round and round a certain copse,*
> *a sudden mound of stone,*
> *an anthill humming in the rocks*
> *an expectant tune?*

Already the ritual sacrifice is readied, and we are prepared for the awful end of what might have been, under another dispensation—indeed, one that dispensed, precisely, with the sacred recurrences, with *kairos,* for the sake of mere duration, for *chronos*—just another walk in the woods:

> *. . . The firs*
> *lash me with angry tines,*
> *shred my clothes. A windwhipped will*
> *uncompassed, lacking fur or fang,*
> *strange to these parts, yet whom the anthill*
> *anticipating, sang.*

There are several such versions of a terrifying, a reducing yet somehow redeeming nature in the initiatory section of this book, none so powerful, I think, as "Safari" with its Genet-like account of a little boy (the persona shifts from a generalized "you" to the poet's authentic memory) obsessed with hunting snakes and bringing home in a "writhing bag that dangles / from the forked stick's horns"—home, where his mother makes him flush them down the toilet drain; thereat the boy, "rigid, goggling," imagines

> *. . . serpents hugely striding*
> *in the diamonded darkness agleam*
> *and thrashing the still black waters*
> *till they foam and rise like cream.*

Nature's terror and the rituals which serve to make her awful cycle accessible to the social are, in a larger structure, the *cause,* the proposal or the project of Hoffman's finest work thus far, a 20-page, 8-part poem that gives the book its title. A geste, of course, is a narrative, usually in assonant verse, about a real or a legendary hero. Much of Hoffman's story is in such verse, framed by various songs, chants, lays, ballads and carols. Here the curious old vocabulary works *for* our special wonder, and in the dreadful and dramatic rehearsal of Robin Hood not as the "democratic thief" to which he has shrunk "through fame's and history's reward," but as a version of the devoured cult-hero, a transubstantiated Osiris—indeed a pre-Christian fertility-god, dying at the height of his powers, whose data can be researched in Frazer if not in Miss Weston—Hoffman has put all his talents to their perfect and perfecting use. The array of archaic forms sustains the fable brilliantly: there is a terrible reality in the story. One recalls, even in the Howard Pyle versions of the legends foisted off on our modern childhood, the oddness of Robin Hood's downfall, bled to death by the pious prioress. Hoffman has taken this clue out of Robert Graves' hands and reconstructed the whole legend into an astonishingly condensed poem, of the type characterized by Northrop Frye as an ironic encyclopaedic form, "visions of a cycle of experience, often presided over by a female figure with lunar and *femme fatale* affiliations." Here, for example, is Friar Tuck to Maid Marian, Hoffman's White Goddess:

> *Stumbling through brambles, toward this cart I came*
> *Lured past bracken by sound of human mirth,*
> *And found you, Lady, and the meal, the game,*
>
> *And found the staff I walk with rise in flame*
> *And leaves burst from this long-dead oaken wood*
> *And I knelt, knowing now his Name, your Name*
> *O Maid and Mother, and laid my flowering rod*
> *Beside you, next the stag, the sack, and came*
> *With you, and Will, and Much, to Robin Hood.*

There is no idyllic echo to the poem's ultimate action, pretty though this first quote sounds and preposterous as it is to think of Tennyson, whose last idyll was "told, when the man was no more than a voice / in the white winter of his age, to those / with whom he dwelt, new faces, other minds," as merely decorative or dutiful—for there is in Hoffman's little geste the sanction of an ultimate horror: "That greenbriar bursts through a compost grave." The Merry Men are taken, Robin and Marian are destroyed, the mystery cult scattered:

> *But children, chanting Eeny Mo,*
> *Dimly remember us,*
> *Although the Eucharistic dough*
> *And unfermented juice*
> *Affirm a taste for crackermeal;*
> *Transubstantiated blood*
> *Runs thin. Indifferent seasons wheel*
> *Till man again will die as god*
> *And virtue hath the sun.*

This—the cheerful, imperfect octosyllabics mocking the very solemnity they commemorate, in dilution as it were, but in the insistent rhymes and the final dignity of the last two lines, with something of the old hieratic resonance—this is the resolution to a terrible question, asked on the murder of the interceding Robin:

The goatgod, his mad Maenads fade,
The green world turns to stone,
No sacrifices made,
Sacred trees hewn down.
What virtue hath the sun?

If "A Little Geste" enacts the passionate conflict between a primitive and instinctual life and the claims of civil order, it does so with a security of posture which Hoffman's work has not often elsewhere attained. I suppose this central triumph is in part due to the fact that he was working not only with information but with ideas—as Coleridge said one of his contemporaries had "no native passion because he was not a thinker." When Hoffman, in this brilliant, stirring poem, shows that the Church, by its insistence on being right against the claims of any rival order, became one of the heresies, one of the great heresies of the human mind, then "his thoughts are feelings and his feelings forms," as he remarks of one of the figures in his own book. Yet "to be a fabler in an age of fact / demands a stubborn stomach," as such writing as this must prove:

Little John turns, turns, turns, turns on the rack
Waiting. Four cropped stallions chomp the branches, waiting
At the great crossroads to the world's far corners.
His limbs each bound to each one's back they
spur them—his joints spurt—
For the renegade friar such clerks devise
Ingenuities more rare. My eyes
Burn, burn on the unforgiving scene . . .

Tremendous as the help has been that was given by "Captain Carpenter," the inflection is Hoffman's own, more savage, less genteel than the accommodation of Ransom's cult hero. Rarely, in his next collection published three years later, was Hoffman to reach, or even reach for, this kind of awful immediacy. But in it he added another strand to his braid, or brand to his strain, in a group of dream poems whose loosened diction and shifting imagery bring a further version of ritual, the nightmare repetition, into *The City of Satisfactions*. It is wonderful that this poet's resources of feeling are always stirred to intensest life by the fictive, the hieratic:

He had awaited me,
The jackal-headed.

He from Alexandria
In the days of the Dynasts,

I from Philadelphia
In a time of indecisions . . .

and that his imagination of forms is fired most by the ritual, the
legendary, the profoundly *impersonal*, while in most of his poems
dealing with the private life untouched or untampered with by a
cyclical resonance, we get the intended, willed *effect*, rather than an
achieved art. But it is a wonderment we suffer gratefully, its rewards
being so much weightier than its omissions; when we read, in this third
book, which gives so much the sense of a striving toward a containing
term, an emblem of the poet's situation which might tellingly embody
—might tell—this poet's insights: moral or psychological or religious;
when we read, in *The City of Satisfactions:*

> *While I turned in a warm cocoon*
> *Man and Rome fell.*
> *Furrows scarred the valleys.*
> *Haggle, blow and toil*
> *Echoed at the stony gates,*
> *Yet discipleship to the seasons*
> *Made gay the festival.*
>
> *All that long labor made me*
> *Who split my earthling skin*
> *In a fallen wind, a dusty sky.*
> *What patrimony I come by*
> *Lies, an empty sack,*
> *Shrivelled fables at my back.*
> *This is a new birth I begin.*

—when we read, with delighted astonishment for the accessible music
of the thing, the truth of entrances and exits, of births and deaths
rehearsed by a technical profundity equal to the fable of a total human
inheritance, when we read such lyrics as "A New Birth," then, we
know that as Hoffman says of Melville in his "academic" anthology of
American Poetry and Poetics, "the imagery projects catastrophe across
the spaces of heaven in the constellations, thence into mythology and
back through time to the present. This is how Ariel renders the real."

In Hoffman's fourth book of poems, published in 1968 five years
after the last, it is clear that accurate observation of the natural world,
as in his first book, and the consecration such observation bestows, as in
his second (under the sign of Wordsworth's great line: "I, at this
time, / saw blessings spread around me like a sea"), will no longer

suffice the poet's giant need. *Striking the Stones*—the very title is from a desperate, flinty lyric ("striking the stones to make them sing") which affords the poet mastery only upon his submission to the struggle, and to the failure of the struggle:

> *Then inward darkness burns away,*
> *Shards of silence frame the essential psalm—*

extends into everyday experience the catastrophe glimpsed in the dream songs of his third book, *City of Satisfactions*. Limping across those industrial landscapes "whose archetypes / have not yet been dreamed," or even, as once so promisingly, venturing into the natural realm, Hoffman now finds himself bound by mortality and circumstance to terrible limitations, as in "Moving among the Creatures":

> *I trip on vines, stumble in potholes*
> *And long for something of myself that's in them,*
> *In the gulls' windy coursing, in the frogs'*
> *Brief cadenza, even in the slug's*
> *Gift to leave*
> *A gleaming track, spun*
> *From his own*
> *Slippery gut.*

As the shifting movement and abrupt cadences of the verse suggest, Hoffman is no longer so certain as in the earlier books of his participation in the action which brings cosmos out of chaos; rather, his expectation is reversed—it is no longer the creatures which are *in him*, as in "A New Birth" quoted above, but a longing for something of himself which is *in them*, a longing to be contained by the world, a longing denied. For the *Mitwelt*, the usual world that accompanies and contains and accommodates us, the with-world as Heidegger calls it, is mistrusted and, merely, missed in this book, which is given over, rather, to a phenomenology of entrances and exits, always implicit in Hoffman's poetry but never before so insistent upon their sole significance, so determined to cancel out the territory athwart . . . In *Striking the Stones* there is birth and there is death, and the life that lies or lurks between is a bad dream:

> *Enmeshed in these traces*
> *Strain toward the doorway*
> *To the next room*
> *Entering doorways*
> *Exchanging rooms.*

Abandoning the noble artifice of his verse, the *turns* and temperament of civility, the poet here consigns himself ("to find the dooryard / to

234   (*Daniel Hoffman*)

that place") to a precarious priestly perspective which is a long, hard
way from the secular securities of the early work, though it is the *via
negativa* we must have been prepared for by the best in Hoffman's
work till now:

> *Was it we who stumbled*
> *Unawares across a border*
> *Into a bleaker diocese?*

asks the poet in the last poem in his latest book, inflected like most of
the others to a phenomenology of light and darkness, "one compre-
hending light / across our chaos and the night"; and he answers, with
the terrible resignation of the spiritual initiate who knows not only
that "poems / emerge in black weather," but that love instinctually
goes about its business, opening "for a dozen minutes, maybe
more, / the almost unendurable / delight before / the closing once
again / of its blazing door"—answers with that astounding renuncia-
tion of *personality* which is beyond ambition as it is beyond any but
the surest technique ("drawn inward by nets of song"):

> *No matter now*
> *Who crossed whom, these colder*
> *Wizened days that crowd us*
>
> *And you and I*
> *Thrusting impatient through their shorter*
> *Gaps of lessened light*
>
> *Move forward*
> *Toward another border*
> *—It must be there*
>
> *Awaiting us,*
> *That apostolic territory*
> *To which we go.*

In these bleak poems, yearning toward a "blazing door" but thrust
back, over and over again, into "the light of this / evacuated day,"
Hoffman aspires to find those "slits in the familiar / through which we
peer, / glimpsing then, / or here, the only / changelessness we'll
know." In these poems, I mean to say, by a doctrine of first and last
things first, of entrances and exits ("all doorways / leaned toward
possibility"), Hoffman turns from that "City of Satisfactions" which
has failed so utterly, and reaching outward,

> *Creates that past and future between which his way*
> *Unwinds with the fated freedom of a rhyme.*

Broken Laws by DANIEL HOFFMAN

This poet has already ventured so deep into his discovery of himself, into being discovered by his subject, that crowing or complaining about the "superiority" of later or earlier work would be an impertinence; pertinent is the notation of development, instancing where he's at, as we say, in a trajectory which already covers not only ground but grace. Hoffman, a university professor, a card-carrying intellectual, is nonetheless a student of chaos reluctant to bureaucratize the mess, preferring the pursuit of Order to the mere imposition of Power.

He sets his fifth book of poems—"the busy schedule of our fading / dreams bequeath / the broken laws / almost deciphered on / this air we breathe"—under a sentence from Aristotle urging us to discuss what kind of a thing actuality is. Judging by the beautifully rhymed quotation from which Hoffman's title comes, actuality is largely a matter of failures: fading dreams, broken laws not quite deciphered. As earlier in the nervous, aspiring poet's work, there is the craving to discern actuality and there is the perpetual, rather glorious frustration.

Hoffman permits himself two certainties. There is birth, there is death; the life that lies or lurks between them merely lies or lurks: "The world / outside ourselves." He himself is forever yearning toward "a blazing door" but then thrust back into "the light of this evacuated day." Again and again he accounts—proudly, precisely—for inadequacies: "we awaken / knowing that where we've been has led us onto the edge . . . and at our backs / memories . . . do not advance." As the broken lines, the fluttering rhythms indicate, Hoffman's poetry has become a lovely dubiety, no longer trusting itself to the neat forms, the clipped prearrangements of his earlier volumes. His is a doctrine of first and last things first, of exits and entrances, and the rest is "dominion of the dew."

For all his current skittishness about the proprieties, indeed about the very properties of verse-making, Hoffman repeatedly mounts to an ecstatic rhetoric, beating against "these fragments, these / wounds, self-serving anthems / and ridiculous longings" which are the modesty of an unassuming prosody. He aspires to find those slits in the familiar through which we peer, glimpsing then "an exhilaration of eternity / desiring nothing," and it is the urgency of his search which sets him to apostrophize the stars, in the accents of a Vaughan, a Traherne, as "piercing the sooty kettle of the sky / so that original light / pours through."

The New York Times Book Review, 1970

The Center of Attention by DANIEL HOFFMAN

On the dust-jacket of his sixth book of verse, praise from a formalist master, a Zen master, and from a senior master of American letters would seem to settle Daniel Hoffman's hash into the kind of gruel which has something in it for everyone, but perhaps not much left over for the poet himself. But no, it is just what is left over that enables Hoffman to be the poet he is—the leftovers of general and institutional approval are in fact the inception of his idiopathy, his self-disease. Consider the case, and the encasement: about one third of these hard, harsh poems, most scarcely a page long, are circumstantial evidence, topical glimpses, John Hollander calls them, of the physical and mental violence with which we have become overgrown. They are prevalently composed in drastically neat clutches, rhyme is distributed among the lines with a kind of systematic unpredictability, reminding us that it is one of the greatest impoverishments to live in a world where nothing happens twice; as Gary Snyder says, "formal but snaky":

> . . . *what desire*
> *Sentenced the soul*
> *To that dark cellar where all life became*
> *So foul*
> *With the pitch of rage,*
> *Rage, rage, rage to set aflame*
> *Father's house—what can assuage*
> *That fire or that misfire?*

And the other two thirds are gnomic, glyptic, emblematic pieces, spare but unsparing, and in them, as Robert Penn Warren says, Hoffman has found his moment, the kind of subject that brings his forces to focus. Readers of Hoffman's recent study of Poe will know what to expect: a responsible accounting, a remorseless ingenuity, a twingeing awareness, too, that one's privacies, however berated and chastized, are the source even so of one's publicity, even of one's publications.

In the pieces about The Way We Live Now, Hoffman's consciousness of contraption, of a pattern which governs—

> *such a piece of work*
> *That the stars in their circuits are driven through space*
> *By an analogue of its plan*

—is hypertrophic, for since it is conscious it knows it is governed, and rebels; the poems writhe through their remarkably kept stanzas, rarely ending a line on beat or a sentence with that dying fall which coincides with the last line of a stanza. Rather, everything is *kept up*, suspended in a skeptical inquiry into "a world lost in common." The gnomics seem to me better than the occasionals here—they participate better in Hoffman's great gift, a gritty intimacy with origins and elements, as in the characteristic "Shell."

> *I would have left the me that was then*
> *Clinging to a crack in the bark of the tree,*
>
> *Stiffened in the wind, the light translucent,*
> *A brittle shell that had the shape of me;*
>
> *And down the back a split through which had burst*
> *A new creature, from mean appearance free,*
>
> *Swaying now where the topmost boughs of the tree sway*
> *At the center of the sound that's at the center of the day.*

The poet's notion, he says—and here he gives us a lot to go on in the very opposition whereon he beds, couches, and upholsters his venture—is of "a healing art in which the wholeness of form offers bulwarks against the corrosive chaos of the world, and the intellect is not banished from the presence of numinous objects and passionate occasions." I know it sounds like being in favor of virtue, but regard the confrontation, the discernible sense that centers *can* hold only by being pressed in upon from countering directions. There is always an opposition, as I used to say about Hoffman's early work that there was always a tug between entrances and exits. Now that tug has become a tear, a rending between "the creature comfort . . . and surcease from being a creature." That is what Daniel Hoffman has left for himself in these poems, after we have plucked out their particular beauties, even their defects (vehemence, preaching, the presumption not only that the Good is known, but that he, Hoffman, knows it): the poet is left the battle, the collision, the convulsive process, if I may use that oxymoron, between order and cessation, between extinction and law. This is a poetry which punishes itself into shape—into shapeliness; when Hoffman speaks of the wholeness of form and the presence of the intellect, is he not talking about the instruments which enable him to get deeper in—into life, into trouble, into dissolution? He writes "the sentence of our sufferings" in what he calls *sponsored images;* he writes poems which will enable him to oppose mere bulwarks by corrosion, to counter decorum by perversity. It is only when he meets what I suppose is as good a nickname as any for poetry, when he meets his *opposite number* that Hoffman can unite with it and the oppositions fall; then he can reach that fiery center he wants to choose, if he does not always choose it:

> *Come, let's go together*
> *Into the burning*
> *House with its gaping door.*
> *The windows are all alight*
> *With the color of my deeds,*
> *My omissions.*
> *It's our life that's burning.*
> *Is it ever too late to thrust*
> *Ourselves into the ruins,*
> *Into the tempering flame?*

Poetry, 1975

JOHN HOLLANDER

"*Between the Deed and the Dream Is the Life Remembered.*"

W HEN Goethe announced to Eckermann, or to us, more likely, over Eckermann's sedulous head, that all his works were to be construed as the *fragments of a great confession*, he bequeathed, of course, along with so much else that was questionable, a method as well as an insight: even the marmoreal Sage of Weimar, then, could be investigated, as we have subsequently investigated everybody—sick and well, whole-hearted and half-witted—under the Sign of the Fragmentary. Even the most Olympian of men, who could manage to rise above no less an event than the French Revolution (and to sink below the Court routines of a minor principality), acknowledged that he had something to confess, something so tremendous (*Das Schaudern ist der Menschheit bestes Teil*), indeed, that it could be delivered to us only in bits and pieces, to be reconstructed by some ulterior archeologist of the psyche out of the shards and shreds plucked from his otherwise shining or at least shellacked masterpieces. And ever since—just consider the critical practice of a Sainte-Beuve, an Edmund Wilson!—we have mistrusted *works*, "monuments of unageing intellect," regarding the finished (especially the varnished) as a suspect or trivial façade, the truth, as Henry James once said, being in high fermentation on the other side. It is our claim to have eschewed the Parnassian for the personal, to have abandoned the Parian, as it were, for the paranoid, and even the most generalized—or at least, generalizing—of American poets, the one who so often liked to sound like "the Peter Pan of the N.A.M.," is treasured by most lovers of poetry now as a man of jeopardized roots, rotting branches and blasted flowers. Robert Frost, the poet of loneliness and obsession? Indeed, and what else, we retort, affords all that assurance about poetry as a successful game of baseball? What else but the Night Side of things ransoms the Apollonian toy, keeps the decasyllabic maker from being a regular faker? We tolerate such a man's contraptions only because—licensed by Goethe himself, as I say—we know that they conceal something, something which the structural properties of works will not express, any more than their surface placidities. The soul lies buried in the ink that writes, John Clare said in a famous fragment of his own, and we are all, since then, turned grave robbers and vandals, eager to disclose the smelly cave under the Doric pediment, to disinter, still smoking, the pythoness' lair beneath the neat pillars, even if we have to push them down to get to it.

Hieratically disposed, but with a characteristic invitation for that very reason to pillage, to *profanation*, the works of John Hollander, monuments indeed, shapely at times to the point of a glassy impenetrability, stand before us in an alluring perspective worthy of Poussin for its rhythmic passage of saliences and recessions, its fair *attitudes;* and though I intend to violate these marbles as relentlessly as Lord Elgin looted his, for it seems to me that Hollander is precisely the poet of an obsessive, overpoweringly confessional necessity, I think it is only justice to pause first and marvel a little at their presence among us as *completions.* In effect, it is because his exigencies are so painfully inward that this poet has been obliged to take a stand against his own hurt, lest he go flying off in all directions, fragmented indeed, the slivers as jagged as any connoisseur of chaos could require. Such surface complacencies—one of Hollander's critics once referred to him rather angrily as an armored tank, betraying what I think is our mistrust of a poet's express preparation to enter the engagement iron-clad; we seem to want the wounds on the outside, where everyone can see them—bewilder us only if we fail to realize that surfaces are not only intimate, but are insolent with depths. Hollander himself will help us on—for early enough in his career to be prophetic, he had this to say about the poet of the past he most resembles, writing in an introduction to the Laurel selection from the poems of Ben Jonson in 1961: "Considering that they are the work of a literary genius, these poems have had a curious critical fate . . . our own age acknowledges their importance and success and at the same time retains a fundamentally unsympathetic view toward them, seldom praising without apologizing." Which nicely puts the response of our critics toward an *oeuvre* that insists on a certain impregnability. Furthermore, as a scholar and critic of almost desperate appetite, so much so that it is not his *learning* we shrink from but his *knowingness,* Hollander presents a formidable obstacle to an age when, for the first time, the audience for poetry and the educated public do not at all coincide. Here again, Hollander on Jonson accounts, rather, for the orientation of this kind of writing: "Learning, for him, is not so much a play of light upon, or elevation of, the self, or a metamorphosis in the inner life, but rather an accumulation of treasure which cannot help but overflow." In applying this accommodation of the old lore, of the wisdom of the ages to Hollander, it is prudent to note that if the accumulated treasure cannot help but overflow, the bulk of it is kept for himself, an inside matter as we shall see, requiring, if we are to be initiated into the real mysteries, a certain abject posture on the part of the novice-reader. A final definition from the Jonson introduction admirably "places," then, in its minatory context this expansive yet centripetal canon; what Hollander has created, in a gleaming, grandiose trajectory of poems, is, with my italics, "a monument of literature that *seeks* to engage life, but on its own terms."

Before we proceed to a scrutiny of those terms, to a sampling of the engagement which proceeds with such confidence in the adequacy of art to experience, of verse to vision, it is just as well to break rather unceremoniously into these holy places, these shrines so unctuously *wrought* that our age chides them for an insufficient show of raggedness (it is a necessary irony that John Hollander and Allen Ginsberg were friends at college and have turned up so romantically in each other's work), simply to say what it is that is bothering Hollander into poetry in the first instance, or the last analysis: a contradiction between remembering and forgetting, a conflict between lying and letting go, between knowing and ignoring, waking and sleeping—between, in its largest accommodation, life and death which affords only *in the poem* a moment of release, a momentary transcendence of antagonisms in "a brilliant performance whose only lesson is its own worth." *

Believing, then, in the poem, relying in an almost unparalleled way on the art of poetry as a redeeming possibility, Hollander sacrifices nearly everything to that art, and it requires a considerable excursion into his work, on the reader's part, before the rewards of such an oblation are clearly discernible. From the poem, the thing made, Hol-

---

* The last words of Hollander's doctoral dissertation, an inquiry into "ideas of music in English poetry (1500–1700)." There is, refreshingly, an almost carnal liaison between this poet's scholarship and this professor's poetry: the notion that the sky is untuned, that "heavenly music . . . is rendered trivial, and the singing spheres silent" by music itself, by "practical music," is the generating impulse, transposed certainly to a private idiom, of Hollander's art. "The humming of human time is loud / and crowded with single, unbearable voices, that, hour by hour, / blend into timeless buzzing."

lander seeks an escape from remembering, or an end to it, a cure for forgetting, or a tranquilizer, and though the poem—certainly from his second book onward—abides his question, permitting him to stand like an Oedipus before an endless avenue of sphinxes, only twice in his entire career, I think, is his obsession abreacted, his desperation answered by the very instruments to which he has entrusted his questions. The powers of memory and oblivion are too strong—though they are not so easily lined up with life and death as their ordinary positive or negative charge would suggest. In fact, let us consider the uses of forgetting before we decide with Proust that remembering is where salvation lies. Salvation, after all, *lies*, and that is Hollander's torment, his theme and, in its secular acknowledgment of a sacred severance, his release.

There is a famous story, the most beautiful of Borges' fictions, I think, about a boy who is unable to forget—"he remembered the shapes of the clouds in the south at dawn on the 30th of April of 1882, and he could compare them in his recollection with the marbled grain in the design of a leather-bound book which he had seen only once, and with the lines in the spray which an oar raised in the Rio Negro . . ." This capacity is, of course, lethal, for we all live, Borges makes it clear, by leaving behind. "In this overly replete world, there were nothing but details, almost contiguous details. What this boy once meditated would not be erased." In this crowded inferno of memory, thought is impossible, meaning itself denied by being. If everything is "instantaneously and almost intolerably exact," then there is no possibility of relation, of movement and change. Consider Lucky in *Waiting for Godot*, who cannot forget anything he has ever known and must therefore suspend his mind altogether except for those hellish moments when his master makes him perform—that is the emblem of a world without oblivion, a world impossible for the poet who would make sense out of the report of his senses, would "only connect." Memory, moreover, is not only murderous when it is inordinate, as we see in Borges, in Beckett—it is mendacious in its normal form; and this is where Hollander suffers most from its abuses, discovering and dramatizing in his own biography the post-Freudian truth that what is remembered is not at all the same thing as what occurred. The mind creates its past, not recalls it, and the only escape, the only issue from these endless, crowding productions of memory is a kind of death— the death administered by language, the infliction of meaning upon being. (Thus it is memory that insists upon a death, forgetting that offers the gift of life.) No doubt, a poet's language kills no one. Yet when Hollander speaks, in his climactic vision of himself, of "that tall fat man," death, a real death is announced and already present in his language; his language means that this person, who is here, now, can be detached from himself, withdrawn from his existence and presence and suddenly plunged into a nothingness of existence and presence; his language signifies, essentially, the possibility of such destruction; it is, at every moment, a determined allusion to such an event. Of course Hollander's language kills no one. But if that tall fat man were not actually capable of dying, if he were not at each moment of his remembered life threatened with death, a death linked and united to himself by a bond of essence, Hollander could not achieve that ideal negation which is his poem, that postponed murder which is his language. It is therefore quite exact to say of this poet's speech: death speaks in and through him. Death, the death dealt by an adequate language, is for Hollander, in the poem, a rescue from the hypertrophy of memory, an escape from the fallacious past, from what Tolkien calls the burden of deathlessness, that kind of immortality or rather endless serial living which is (in fairy tales like Hollander's *The Quest of the Gole*) the deepest desire, the Great Escape.

Hollander's accommodation of this thanatomachia, his way of *embodying* the war to the death with oblivion and recall, is a dialectics of the seasons. It is the most conventional, yet the most radical of the available tropes, the widest yet the most familiar of poetical themes: the response to the cyclical, and the transcendence of the cyclical. His own emphasis on winter cannot surprise us, once we have realized that what is death to nature is life to the poet who would engage it *on his own terms*. The terms are hiemal ones—though we cannot speak of any season without implying them all and without implying something which leaves "all time, all seasons, and their change" behind. In the introduction to an anthology of "poems for young people" which he and Harold Bloom selected, Hollander speaks of his preferences this way:

> Of all the seasons, the Winter is richest in poetry. It is as though men sought to fill the gap left in nature, and to redeem the season by human passion. Poems of snowstorm are followed here by songs of separation and night, visions of winter birds, the crow and the raven, and many tales of haunting and unsought presences . . . Nature goes in cycles, but the human seasons finally need an expression that leaves cycles behind. So this book's end explores the world that is beyond Winter, and yet does so by speaking of nothing more than what we are.

It might be—it must be—of his own *oeuvre* that he is talking, this poet of "unsought presences" who like Browning's Pope in *The Ring and the Book* confronts us "with winter in my soul beyond the world's." Conjugating death and oblivion with winter and "what we are," Hollander clambers up to that position where significance can be meted out to the life which—in summer, say, and simply remembering (i.e., *making up*)—can be merely lived, endured, suffered. Fruit of the odd wedding of seventeenth-century diction to the speech-rhythms of New York ("this hospital"), it is a phenomenology of perception peculiarly his own that this poet has worked out: perception of time, of mutability, of the variable self. "A contemporary poet," he says in his essay on *The Music of Poetry*, "cannot help but invoke, even by explicit denial, one of what we should . . . call the dialects of the language of English poetry in his own speech." Not by denial but by intimacy, for Hollander the dialects are all available, and almost all invoked, from Spenser to William Carlos Williams, as we shall discover; what remains constant, determining, obsessive, is an inward war, the battle between fixity and failure, memory and possibility, death and change. It is time, now, we visited the arenas.

In 1958, Hollander's first book of poems, *A Crackling of Thorns*—the title is from Ecclesiastes, and provided with a commentary from the Midrash; thereby the poet manages to combine the prophet's severity ("as the crackling of thorns under a pot, so is the laughter of a fool") with the mediator's urbanity ("when thorns are kindled, their sound travels far, as though to say, 'We too are wood' "), arriving at a characteristic complexity of effect, devastating and funny, from which the tinge of an heroic pedantry (a chastising of the lesser tribes, really, for being without the law) is not absent—was published in the Yale Series of Younger Poets and prompted W. H. Auden in his introduction to remark about this poetic world that in it obstacles to knowledge are eliminated: "in a poem there are no strangers, and there is no time but the present—nothing can grow, die, or change." The variety and complexity of Hollander's poetic world, the element of physical diversity, both given and calculated, is to be discovered rather in the chatoyancy of the discourse, the fantastic proliferation of verse forms, imitations and virtuosities, echoes, parodies, allusions and correspondences. There is a compulsive single-heartedness about the consistency of that world itself, though, an undifferentiated fixity which begins where we might expect, at the very beginning, in the first line of the first poem: "*Winter, in a white rage of urgency . . .*" The poems are divided into groups: seventeen (all but one of them songs) "for actors," by which Hollander means, I take it, performers, role-takers, part-players as well as agents, doers, heroes; then ten (highly formalized recitals) "for tellers of tales," in the sense both of narrators and, of course, of liars—for the truth lasts only as long as the poet's utterance, is coterminous with the poem; and lastly a dozen (meditations and genre-pieces) "for certain others," among them the best things in the book, quite explicitly occurring within the poet's unmediated consciousness and the more relaxed for having a less circumscribed attribu-

tion or provenance, though the poet's vigilance—they are, these beauti-
fully phrased utterances, only for *certain* others—never relaxes out of a
narrow grace.

The initial poem, evidently composed later than all the other songs
in this first group, is one of those synoptic pieces in which, without
much of a *plot* but depending upon and revelling in a highly organized
verbal surface, the poet confides not so much to a subject as to a
substance (the language itself, taken in all its self-serving history) his
confidence in his own powers. Though the actor, the hero of "Icarus
Before Knossos"—an exuberant poem of a dozen 12-line stanzas, organ-
ized each into a verse paragraph so that the first and sixth lines rhyme,
the second and seventh, and so on, permitting a certain ruminative (*i.e.*,
prose) effect within a fugacious music—is apparently the Athenian son
of Daedalus on his way to "painted Crete" where, in a processing of
Auden's famous scene,

> . . . *at the brink of the bay, a ploughman turns*
> *His implement into the hill* . . . *all unaware*
> *Of my arrival and deliverance* . . .

he is also a kind of Goliard ("I journeyed from the North, and stopped
to sit / in this ringed city, in the South of Something") quite sure of his
medieval inheritance:

> *Thus reasoning and having thoroughly read*
> *Various journals of my own few seasons,*
> *I turned to that golden annal of the heart:*
> *The Very Rich Hours, the old illuminations*
> *Of love's most famous scenery, and marked*
> *How, through the very Hiems and the Vers,*
> *The prospect held its properties, and bred*
> *Simple disguises* . . .

The bookish bent of this wandering scholar who has read not only the
Duc de Berry's *Très Riches Heures* but Aristotle and a number of
treatises on music is apparent in his most confessional musings: "bright
distractions / bound in the book of all my own heart's work, / a pas-
sage too continuous to be parsed." That last phrase is the crux of
Icarus' problem, the sense of life refractory to order because of its own
"continuity." Only winter, "the fixed precision of cold and snow,"
permits an assessment, a parsing, yet winter

> . . . *dries up so much motion that the course*
> *Of measurement is shriveled to a trace* . . .

What Icarus wants, in his musical jargon, is a calendar which will, still
governed, account for "all the fluid processes / which comprehend

embellishment and changing." Some encompassing absolute is desider-
ated, beyond the seasons themselves ("We cannot accept our winter
propositions"), and beyond the Gothic (read, Scholastic) towers,

> . . . *where you*, maudit sois tu, *carilloneur,*
> *Rang changes out on the bronzed fruit, comprised*
> *Of seasonal intervals, till the bells in bunches*
> *Dropped, crying* Autumn, autumn! *to the winds.*
> *Those syllables rang our death* . . .

This wingless Icarus cannot find such an absolute in all his conjugations
of towers and trees—"the branch, or the eternal stone to come?"—and
turns south, where as Hollander and the player-Greek himself are
perfectly prepared to admit, that "unaware" ploughman will soon see
"the myth delivered at his feet":

> . . . *As though, tomorrow, full over the green ocean,*
> *He might behold it, falling from the air* . . .

That "agreeable emblem" of a death beyond "the bent / and rusted
relics of those seasonal changes / which fouled its triumph of redemp-
tion" is, of course, the Grand Design which Icarus is pursuing beyond
"fashions of careless and phenomenal change." This poem, rich as
Keats in its storybook imagery and in its careful tracing out of whole
congeries of idiom, the nomenclatures of horology ("the sun's own
seasonal miscellany / proclaims on every page our death's directions"),
is a remarkable pronouncement of the poet's intentions not only
toward language but toward his way of treating life. Perhaps they are
the same thing: from the first, we can be sure that, in the phrase of one
of Hollander's first masters, "words alone are certain good," and that if
there is any hope of attaining that *certain good,* beyond wit and
weather alike, this poet will make the attempt; if the effort is hopeless,
then words will commemorate the ecstasy, at least, of his failure.

Yeats, then, Stevens, Auden, Pound—and to a lesser degree
Ransom, Hardy, Empson: the masters and the monitors of the modern
style are laid under audible contribution in the poems which follow
"Icarus"—in the poems "after Knossos," so to speak; what signally
differentiates Hollander's apprenticeship to these writers from the
initiation ceremonies of any gifted young poet discovering his themes
of inheritance and dispossession by writing variations on those of other
men is a different kind of mastery: the mastery of the form and diction
of seventeenth-century English verse. No other poet of his generation,
I think, has found out the secret so perfectly of fitting words together
in the music that created the English lyric from Campion to Marvell;
from the beginning, Hollander's practice is more than practicing, more
than the recreation of an epigone—it is the freedom of a man who by

submitting in all good faith to the responsibilities of an achieved form (experience entrusted to an expressive convention: his true Daedalus was Dryden, etc.) relies on the poem's moment to bear him beyond its teeming surface to some high place. And if it seems, in this first book, merely high and dry that the poem sometimes leaves Hollander, stranding at least his reader above that line where the convention is still expressive, such is the risk of history; on the other hand, the authority and charm of these songs are history's rewards, the forgiveness after such knowledge. They open with two personations from the Bible, Orpah and Susanna, and both poems wield their refrains with the dramatic "placing" the poet must have learned from the songs of Shakespeare's plays; the lyric becomes what Nietzsche describes as a poem of experience—a poem which originates in song and passes temporarily through drama in order to articulate the song and refer us back to the song for meaning. Noteworthy in "Orpah Returns to Her People," in especial, is the winter refrain, the Boreal movement that offers a converse progress to Icarus' journey southward:

> *I'll return to our northern river, sourly*
> *Rained and snowed upon.*
> *Though their grain flourish, I must go*
> *Riverward, to cold and snow.*

The same dialectic is traced in "Susanna's Song" between sunlight and shadow, dark earth and bright water, black oaks and white skin. Here the kind of facile music which from Peele to Stevens has accompanied this subject:

> *Under trees a glade is shady*
> *And no place to bathe a lady . . .*

is turned to a sinister presage of the kind of mortality which obsesses this poet, the death beyond the body's change:

> *There are old men in mastic trees,*
> *Arms in oaks, and hands in the grass;*
> *Their shadows will reach above my knees*
> *And play with the light on me, unless*
> *The clouds go dark and drift too near*
> *And sun and shadows disappear.*
> *But they will stay while I undress*
> *Not far from where the ground is shady,*
> *The right place to bathe a lady.*

The following pair of songs for a Restoration play exhibit the kind of linear inevitability this form demands, but Hollander shows, under

such duress—the strict form, the required intelligibility—just the allu-
sive, metaphysical wit he has bred himself up on:

> *And so in every age we find*
> *Each Jack, destroying every Joan,*
> *Divides and conquers womankind*
> *In vengeance for his missing bone . . .*

The vocabulary of the act of Kind and the line of wit have always
come easily to Hollander, as the evidence of these earliest poems.
convinces us ("although each sweet's a little tart"), and we must not be
distracted from his immortal longings by the readiness of his erotic
imagery: the Elizabethans called it dying. Even in the group of five
bluestocking "Songs for Glaucon," with their quotations from the
Palatine Anthology, their allusions to Book VI of *The Republic,* to the
desolations of Bion and Theocritus ("like the sun, my pipe is
gone / with all the tunes done thereupon") and to the Greek geome-
ters ("who knew that circles broke / direction in a line"), Hollander
celebrates ("Glaucon Returns to School") the winter's capture of
measurement, the possibility of *certain good* indeed:

> *Sapped for the whole summer*
> *Of winter's chill, whose loss we sing*
> *Now that we have escaped the spring . . .*

And aspires, like the Stevens whose home state he alludes to in "Glau-
con and the Moon," to transcend a phenomenology of female encircle-
ment:

> *Now hard Connecticut will rock*
> *My dark departing train*
> *Past steel Bridgeport, wrapped in smoke,*
> *And the moon will wane.*
> *My mind is a moon; below, the track*
> *Runs by where some girl has lain.*
>
> *She was curved; the flat disc, round:*
> *My road is a line along the ground.*

Another pair of songs, equally dependent on Cowley and Browning,
on the Metaphysical's exploitation of a vocabulary of metaphor and on
the Victorian's romance of historical situation, articulate even more
showily Hollander's obsession with measurement:

> *Such serious merchants as myself have paid*
> *Higher costs for loving*
> *Than love's worth the having.*

> *Nothing done or changed or spent*
> *But must be served with increment;*
> *Thus custom and my care shall wed in trade.*
> ("The Shopkeeper's Madrigal")

and with the winter knowledge which must cancel love, even as it affords an exactitude of love's instance:

> *Wider than winter*
> *Lying over the river*
> *Or the frosty sky through the window*
> *That stretches forever*
> *Around the white pennants*
> *Above the battlements . . .*
> *Whiter than all I remember*
> *Was the bed in my Lady's chamber . . .*
> ("Carmen Ancillae")

The cycle of songs for "actors" closes with five ingenious pieces— "Fragments of a Picaresque Romance" Hollander calls them, and we are reminded of his evident taste for such Euphuistic narratives as Nashe's *Unfortunate Traveller*, with its elaborate rhetorical concern for the medium itself, at the expense of any ongoing impulse—about a young buck named, quaintly, Dick Dongworth whose courtship of his cousin Roseblush is cut short by her death:

> *Say that she was never brave*
> *But only greedy for the grave;*
> *Say Dongworth's rusty armor*
> *Served only to alarm her.*
> *Then write this of me:*
> *"Were she alive and free,*
> *   With lips like wine,*
> *John Thomas, my English cousin,*
> *Could pluck her like a raisin."*
> *   Waly O for Roseblush*
> *That she was never mine.*

But for all the attractiveness of their hearty male narcissism, the Dongworth poems are too clogged with *language behaving* to enforce our attention: the very obsessions which impelled Hollander into his extraordinary style seem to have relented, and we discover him to be, merely, stylish. For me, this is true of a number of the poems that follow, in the section "for tellers of tales"—the "Canzona: A Parting on Shipboard," the intolerably fluent Shakespearean pastiche "Upon the PHOENIX and the GANDER," the "Paysage Moralisé" which closes with an allusion so covert (as Hollander himself remarks in his essay "The Metrical Emblem") that only a line division seems to provide appropriate syntactic ambiguity:

> *Even in Arcady*
> *Ego needs must spoil*
> *Such a beautiful friendship!*

and another *souvenir de voyage*, "Late August on the Lido" whose terminal Jacques-jape has become the decade's canonical high-style pun:

> *Europe, Europe is over, but they lie here still,*
> *While the wind, increasing,*
> *Sands teeth, sands eyes, sands taste, sands everything . . .*

as well as a nasty cat-poem that might raise penis-envy in any reader, "Enter Machiavel, Waving His Tail." Happily, the others here work in Hollander's true vein, a strife between the cycle and "an expression beyond the cyclical," a continuing and fruitful friction between what is dismissed from the mind and what is recalled to it, as in "A Word Remembered," which begins: "All the young poets are writing about the seasons," and describes, with a kind of baffled urbanity, a scene in which a pregnant girl forgets something:

> *Then, mentioning some event of the past April,*
> *She had recourse to name the general season,*
> *But stopped suddenly, as if she had forgotten*
> *A street address she had written down somewhere:*
> *"It happened last—what is it comes before summer?"*
> *And we sat there, not quite believing that this had happened,*
> *Until she finally seemed to have remembered:*
> *"Oh. Yes. Spring." I mention this*
> *Only because we cannot remember now*
> *Who, or what, we felt was being outraged.*

The playing off of the pregnant girl, almost a victim of the cyclical, against her unaccountable dismissal of precisely the season of burgeoning, echoed in the narrator's uncertainty ("we cannot remember now") as to precisely the violence done, turns the casual run of the lines (Hollander once printed this piece as a prose-poem: it was a happy choice, I think, to rehabilitate these rhythms as verse) into a central situation. In a long poem on the divorce of old friends, Hollander builds up from an indictment ("What we lack are rituals adequate to things like this") to an illumination of our lonely civil status:

And since
Weeping's a thing we can no longer manage,
We must needs leave you to the Law's directive:
"You have unmade your bed, now lie about it."
Quickly now: which of you will keep the Lares,
Which the Penates? *And opening the door*
We turn like guilty children, mutter something,
And hide in the twilit street.
                          Along the river
The sky is purpling and signs flash out
And on, to beckon the darkness: THE TIME IS NOW . . .
(What time, what time?) Who stops to look in time
Ever, ever? We can do nothing again
For both of you together. And if I burn
An epithalamium six years old to prove
That what we learn is in some way a function
Of what we forget, I know that I should never
Mention it to anyone . . .

The unmarshalled iambics, the touch of Eliot's clerkly use of commercial slang, and the public-speaking of this poetry ("what we learn is in some way a function of what we forget"—a crucial Hollander conclusion, typical in its humility, or at least in its sense of being humbled by experience) must not disguise from us the astonishing aptness Hollander has for seizing on the resonant detail, the right figures in reality which will fit together to make some of the finest urban landscapes since Baudelaire (from whom Eliot learned the same address, the same responsiveness). This poem, "For Both of You, the Divorce Being Final," ends with a vision of the Fallen City prophetic of Hollander's later work and indicative, in its melting together of the personal and the public, the historical and the confidential, of a new, extroverted stage in this poet's accommodation of his mortality, his reproduction of the world outside by means of the world inside, which Goethe declared to be the beginning and end of all literary activity, a reproduction by which everything is grasped, related, recreated, shaped and reconstructed in a personal and original form:

                          . . . *When men*
Do in the sunny Plaza what they did
Only in dusky corners before, the sunset
Comes as no benison, the assuring license
Of the June night goes unobserved. The lights
Across the river are brighter than the stars;
The water is black and motionless; whatever

Has happened to all of us, it is too late
For something else ever to happen now.

The dozen poems in the third part of *A Crackling of Thorns*
confirm the modes that are this poet's strength: a reflective verse
paragraph, in which Hollander's often highly speculative philosophical
and scientific interests * are conjugated with his delight in literary
convention and imitation; and an elaborately wrought metaphysical
lyric, urging its often novelistic burden ("By the Sea"—the obverse of
Hollander's City Pieces are his seascapes; there will be many to come)
through the most sculptural verse forms—sestinas, villanelles, sonnets,
rondelays. There comes, again and again, that deliberative disquietude
about winter:

> *Our own fear is that the truth about the snow*
> *Can only be stated in terms of its expanse,*
> *That all that's real is the idea of extension;*
> *Then loves and attachments thaw, and turn to drenching*
> *White fields of Hope with wet, gray Anything*
> *No matter though we wander or keep to the footpath . . .*

and that discontent with the moment beyond measurement, when "we
are confronted / with our own dream entire, with the side / of the
image we never see: the sundial in darkness." But it is easy to be
distracted by all Hollander's gifts from what is centrally *given*. The
reader who is irritated by quotations from Locke and Quine, by
allusions to B. F. Skinner and by questions of epistemology slyly
wrested (or merely swiped) from Wittgenstein or Ayer:

> *. . . To understand*
> *Exactly what it means to shiver, when*
> *We have grown used to the chilly air, is, then*
> *Perhaps to know that our knowledge of what is true*
> *Of the world casts doubt on what we have thought we knew*
> *About ourselves, or at least on how it was*
> *We came to know it. And when other men*
> *With other minds stare at our hands, it is*
> *Because theirs tremble too . . .*

---

* Hollander has in fact compiled an anthology for young people of poems
about science, *The Stone and the Shell*, and with Ammons stands alone, probably,
among American poets since the Bomb in not regarding the scientific mind and
its achievements as necessarily the Muses' enemy. "We vainly hope / that certain
predictions can never be made, / that the mind can never spin the Golden Rope /
by which we feel bound, determined, and betrayed . . ." he remarks of us all in
"Science and Human Behavior," but it is evident that Hollander himself has
transcended this wistful stage of demonism and is perfectly prepared to confront
what can be known, even if it is everything.

will probably find it no easier to take the Horatian puns and the
coquetry of a camp backlash within the very impulse toward Grand
Style which speeds up the spin of Hollander's current coin; here, for
example, is a representative stretch of the first sea-piece in the Later
Manner, where Hollander speaks in his own person and almost without
a subject, or at least an object, the language and the form merely
entrusted (encrusted?) with the charge of his own reminiscence, his
own neglect:

> *Even this strange new beach becomes, beclouded*
> *By unforgetting eyes, one of the Good*
> *Old Places. And the roaring of the sand's edge,*
>> *Tunditur unda,*
>> *Thundering under*
> *High, loud breakers blasting the uneven*
> *Tides of silence, alternating with windy*
> *Pianissimi that whimper through the cold,*
>> *Sighing to cadence,*
>> *Is quickly cuddled*
>
> *By pampering recollection, in whose embrace*
> *All the wild music is drowned in the Old Song*
> *With the embarrassing title that is lodged*
>> *Deep in our hearing.*
>> *All its heaving,*
> *Precious, banal progressions work toward damping*
> *Everything that purports to be musical.*
> *The stodgiest tune will have its aftermath*
>> *(When once forgotten,*
>> *Or, like the gods of*
>
> *A place one has been banished from, remembered*
> *In all despite of better judgment) always*
> *Remaining . . .*

The relation, here in this almost Jamesian sentence that has been
processed by a lot of classical meters, between a failing selfhood and a
flourishing seascape, between an identity forgotten in a surround re-
membered, is, I think, dramatized to its maximum intellectual content
within a personal desperation, an intermittence of the heart just short
of frantic. It takes all the resources of Hollander's agility to keep these
"heaving, banal, precious, progressions" from "damping every-
thing that purports to be musical"—and from the very elaboration of
the phrases within their varying cadence we collect the anguish of this
mind at war with its own inconsistency, desperate to win through to a

fabled singleness of being yet aware that such a victory is the death of
all the things identity is valued for. It is the victory of the monumental
over the partial, and something of a Pyrrhic one. The final poem in this
first book, and probably the finest, certainly the fullest, "The Great
Bear," offers a cosmic declension of Hollander's repeated emblem of
himself as this vulnerable, appealing, dangerous mammal against the
black ground of his conscious forgetting; framing the book with a
terminal mortality ode in stanzas structured like those of the opening
"Icarus Before Knossos," this is a long revisionary rumination, full of
preposterous puns ("to bring another's eye to bear in such a fashion"),
citations ("the world is everything that happens to be true") and
allusions (". . . to require / something very like a constellation . . ."),
but its enamored grasp of the actual situation presented—children
standing on a hilltop trying to make out the contour of the Great Bear
in the stars ("frosty, irregular polygons of our own devising")—and its
effortless entanglement of a literary dialect with outrageous colloquial
trouvailles bring the poet—not, really, the poem—out into a touching
simplicity: never straying from his obsession with nothingness, that
Great Dark Bear beyond measurement as beyond forgetting, Hollander
manages simply—simply! when all the means of a technical prowess
probably without equal in American verse today have been mobilized
for the effort—to tell the truth:

> . . . *just because it might be there; because*
> *Some Ancients really traced it out, a broken*
> *And complicated line, webbing bright stars*
> *And fainter ones together; because a bear*
> *Habitually appeared—then even by day*
> *It is for us a thing that should be there.*
> *We should not want to train ourselves to see it.*
> *The world is everything that happens to*
> *Be true. The stars at night seem to suggest*
> *The shapes of what might be. If it were best,*
> *Even, to have it there (such a great bear!*
> *All hung with stars!), there still would be no bear.*

It is a hard truth to tell, but once this matter of a universe without
central myth or meaning, save as our aberrant minds can save them, is
settled for Hollander, he can get on with his *vocation*, his public role
and responsibility, as we shall now reconnoitre it.

I have rehearsed a lot of the notes this poet sounds in his initial
performance because he will, in the course of the subsequent ones,
seemingly renounce so many of them, cutting back the shoots and
suckers of his virtuosity and thereby reinforcing his insight, or at least
his obsessive strain which must serve him, often, in place of insight.

The almost manic dexterity is still there, of course, but it is there to serve the poet's obsessions, not to evade them: the verse is now, in Donne's phrase, the strict map of Hollander's despair. No longer shall we feel, in the books which follow, that we are lounging our way through a phenomenal couturier's showing, watching the languid mannequins parade down the ramp, each in yet another perfectly stitched period "creation"; for now we discover—by the end of *A Crackling of Thorns* we are already convinced—that it is one and the same person we so envied and admired in all those beautiful and borrowed clothes, an identity caught in a cunning trap: unable to believe in remembering ("the private mumming that harms beyond despair") or to bear forgetting ("marooned in strains and chords of habit"); indeed, a person *able to function* only because of a constant uncertainty as to his duration *as* that person, an uncertainty which he must course the real world, "the changing world outside," to extend—for to resolve it would mean the end of poetry. *I am transformed*, this poet cries, *therefore I am.*

In 1962 Hollander published his second book, *Movie-Going and Other Poems*, which again divides its contents into *roles* to accommodate the poet's several voices, his severed visions of a world in which the City and the Self, Nature and History, mortality and literature can lie down together, recognized, at least, if not reconciled as lion to lamb. The title poem is one of the most engaging Hollander has ever written, and by its throwaway gags, suffusing nostalgia, and structural pertinence "Movie-Going" even risks swamping some of his profounder things in the endless *entertainment* of the perfect anthology-piece. I suppose the poem lures us into its long, loose snares by the suggestion that even what we do to divert ourselves *matters* to "the state of the city," which is the rubric for the entire first group of poems. What we do inside those dream palaces, Hollander explains,

> *is after all, to keep the gleam*
> *Alive of something rather serious, to keep*
> *Faith, perhaps, with the City.*

What we do there, and what is done *to us:* the old problems of memory and belief, recurrence and eventuality, are taken up again in the poet's prescriptive analysis. Understanding media, Hollander insists, will help us learn

> *. . . beyond a trace of doubt*
> *How fragile are imagined scenes; the dimming-out*
> *Of all the brightness of the clear and highly lit*
> *Interior of the hero's cockpit, when the stock shot*
> *Of ancient dive-bombers peeling off cuts in, reshapes*

Our sense of what is, finally, plausible; the grays
Of living rooms, the blacks of cars whose window glass
At night allows the strips of fake Times Square to pass
Jerkily by on the last ride; even the patch
Of sudden white, and inverted letters dashing
Up during the projectionist's daydream, dying
Quickly—these are the colors of our inner life.

The slant rhymes and capacious hexameters perfectly convey the poem through its disabused dismissal of the stars ("having shined means having died") and its preference for the great Characters, "loved for their being, not for their burning"; blue movies are invoked to remind us that "even the natural act is phrased / in the terms and shapes of particular times and places"; and as the supermarkets and television aerials muscle in on the "pearls of two-and-a-half miles of Broadway!" the poet, with an injunction to Memory as strict as Milton's, urges us not to forget the "old places, for everyone's home has been a battle-field," to bear in mind how once their splendor—"caught in the toils of our lives' withering"—stretched across this country's "blasted distances and deserts," always holding out the hope of "something different from Everything Here, Now"; it is with an undying fall and a quadruple rhyme that Hollander ends his devotions to

the local Bijou, truest gem, the most bright
Because the most believed in, staving off the night
Perhaps, for a while longer with its flickering light.
These fade. All fade. Let us honor them with our own fading sight.

Continuing the social studies that had already found their sour tonality in his first book, Hollander's urban scenes turn, with the New Yorker's thwarted longing for a "home place," on the loved, lost city, and as in "A Lion Named Passion" accuse the Polis with all the "hollow dole" of the disappointed suitor:

Against the sky
Only these ruins show at dawn, like masts,
Useless in ships becalmed, but hung with dry
Corpses or like unheeded fruit that blasts
High in trees, wasted. Menacing, wild of eye,
The city, having missed its spring, now feasts,
Nastily, on itself. Jackals attend
The offal. And new cities raven and distend.

But the true visionary note is not encompassed here, cannot be until —in his third book of poems—Hollander risks putting himself into the picture along with the toppling towers. "The eye, more than the heart,

composes rusty ironies" in these brilliant poems, and we must first bear
with the other groups in *Movie-Going*—all the poems in "Sea-Pieces,"
in "Notebook" and in "Old Men and Others"—must solve the allusive
conundrums and sift through the art-historical fantasias on themes of
mutability and erotic myth, before we may rejoin Hollander in his
ultimate role, after so many walk-ons, so many *extras*, as empowered
psychopomp. We must first stick with him as no more than an ac-
credited artisan, responsible to the life he observes, exults in and
deplores, as it washes around him: hence *two* poems in answer to
Gregory Corso's challenge that "no square poet would ever begin a
poem with 'Fried Shoes,'" a sonnet "to the lady portrayed by Mar-
garet Dumont," an alliterative riddle, a schoolboy souvenir in the
metrics of William Carlos Williams, and even a pair of *shaped poems*
(bottle and hourglass—Hollander has since produced a series of these
emblem-pieces which will probably baffle the very readers he has set
out to amuse: they seem, these self-dramatizing shapes, to be a kind of
mad frivolity in an age when poetry is too much of a luxury to fool
around with, and they require a submission to Valéry's hard saying
that *content is only impure form* which most of us are reluctant to
make); beyond these observances, two of the central poems in *Movie-
Going* exhibit Hollander's response to learning as "an accumulation of
treasure which cannot help but overflow" yet deserve a harder look
through the flying spray, for they move him from the position of a
man "whose whole vocation," as Wordsworth says, "was endless imita-
tion" to that of the triumphant professional who has met all the
challenges and finds still within himself a generosity to persevere
further: "open it," Hollander says, "and a world is made manifest." He
is speaking of the Van Eyck altarpiece, and of all painting, in "The
Altarpiece Finished," dedicated to the artist Philip Guston, but he is
also accounting for his own art, "a most peculiar enclosure, through
the window of which lies the world." Here again is that idiosyncratic
reading of Winter in the North, of an oncoming darkness which will
defeat all mere alternation of day and night:

The light may go, too; and the light was always what seemed to
    matter
most, here in the North: a gray pond with five tiny figures gliding
over it; a street with a pair of burghers discussing something
underneath the Sign of the Ram's Head—to see these things in the
    thin, bright
glaze of daylight through the opened window was forever to be
reminded that winter's glare would finally shiver into the fine
thousand shards of warming, brilliant summer, that the endless,
    dark night,
immanent and imminent both, had, after all, not come just yet.

The implicit but unquestionable utterance of any art ("I cannot see how in time it will be possible to look at it without making all kinds of mistakes") is extended from the Altarpiece, down the museum corridors, to "new silences" such as Klee's *Twittering Machine* and Fragonard's *The Swing* and finally, "at ends of galleries like some famous accident," to Guston's own *Beggars' Joys*, "the only serious pink and white picture that there is." All these works of art are presented—in broken stanzas, as if we were walking from one *docent*'s gallery lecture to another, muddling the "old badges of meaning taken from the old books" with the terrible modern orthodoxy that if "it took so long to do, its cold completion was a sorry lot"—as expressions of a final transcending silence, beyond interpretation, beyond, even, expression itself, defeating time by a loving surrender to it, while we . . .

> *But what is time? something paintings take to finish, or to rot, or*
> *to become the way things look in. Time devours. I know about it.*
> *My name was Hubert Van Eyck and I may not have existed but*
> *now I am the food of worms. Stand quietly before what Jan and*
> *I have done; you can see it on the sixth of May. It will eat you.*

The other "overflowing" poem in the body of this book is "Aristotle to Phyllis," like so many of Hollander's works in "middle flight" dedicated to a distinguished person, on this occasion the philosopher Rogers Albritton; the connection is appropriate, for the poem concerns the medieval legend of Aristotle's submission to the girl sometimes called Campaspe, and the abasement of the mind by the power of Amor; in the poem itself, Hollander has, with an astonishing synoptic relevance, combined all the celebrated emblems by which the *clerc* is humiliated into acceptance of the flesh by the erotic powers beyond his will or wits: not only the actual story ("the speaker in this poem," he remarks in an introductory gloss, "is a composite of the medieval cleric and the lascivious humanist of the sixteenth-century pictures") but echoes of other poetic attitudes in which the will is downed by the sensibility: Mallarmé and Wordsworth. For instance, when Hollander's Aristotle ("old Staggerer," as he calls the Stagirite) begins:

> *This chair I trusted, lass, and I looted the leaves*
> *Of my own sense and of clerks' learning . . .*

we needn't listen too hard to hear: "*La chair est triste, hélas, et j'ai lu tous les livres.*" These echoes persist: "I sit at my desk, half in death, and staring down at / a wide papyrus, silenced, blanched and deafened / to pleas for eloquence" ("*ma lampe sur le vide papier que la blancheur défend . . .*") and, to any reader of "*Brise Marine*," resound even more scandalously: "faint sea-breezes . . . bruise marine depths, somersault / into a flood of sick sea-longing . . ." In fact, all anachronistically, Mallarmé himself appears: "One whose greatest voyages involved the vessel / from which he dipped pale ink of an exotic nature," and if we set those last six words over *"lève l'ancre pour une exotique nature"* we shall see how well Hollander has followed Lewis Carroll's punning advice to take care of the sounds and let the sense take care of itself. Aside from such cross-cultural jokes as "Only in middle age / did *meden agan* amount to anything," there is the final ignominy of sensual riot, when the copulation is not only accepted but cried out for "at the brink of the moment, mad, mad, for its coming":

> *Let's get on with it,*
> *The game in which the master turns the silly*
> *Ass, straining for breath, arousing the outraged gales of*
> *What should have been a season of calm weather.*

"What should have been . . ." Of course Wordsworth ends the "Immortality Ode":

> *Hence in a season of calm weather*
> *Though inland far we be,*
> *Our souls have sight of that immortal sea*
> *Which brought us hither . . .*

and into his "fussy, fretted cento that I have assembled from the poets" Hollander's philosopher embroiders the erotic exuberance of that visionary gleam ("see the Children sport upon the shore"), though of course the sexual weather has turned, now, to "outraged gales." Certainly the poem is too good to be true, or too clever to be good, and I confess a preference, in the same group, for the more intimate revelations of "Digging It Out" over these "reports of distant life." In the latter poem, Hollander confronts his own mortality in the process of shoveling his car out of a snowdrift:

> *. . . All along the street cars are*
> *Swallowed up in the sarcophagous*
> *Mounds, and digging out had better start*
> *Now, before the impulse to work dies,*
> *Frozen into neither terror nor*
> *Indifference, but a cold longing*
> *For sleep . . .*

Winter again allows the poet to dramatize his death-clogged situation in his most characteristic inward mode; the very movements that insure life remind Hollander of what all existence is moving *toward:*

> *. . . If my heart*
> *Attack itself here in the whitened*
> *Street, would there be bugles and the sound*

> *Of hoofbeats thumping on a hard-packed*
> *Shiny road of snow? Or is that great*
> *Onset of silences itself a*
> *Great white silence?*

And as he falls back to his task, we hear a new, premonitory ingenuousness—the prelude to his ultimate honesty in *Visions from the Ramble—in the verse,* its curious marriage of high style and low blood pressure, its absolute rhythmic certainty wedded to an almost maidenly reticence ("I seem to know") about discovering—or disclosing—the body's crude truths:

> *Down along*
> *The street a rustle of no leaves comes*
> *From somewhere. And as I realize*
> *What rest is, pause, and start in on a*
> *New corner, I seem to know that there*
> *Is no such thing as overtaxing,*
> *That digging snow is a rhythm, like*
> *Breathing, loving and waiting for night*
> *To end or, much the same, to begin.*

One might compose an almost Flemish bouquet with all the other flowers in *Movie-Going,* but the really enormous contribution to Hollander's special eminence here is not to be found in any incidental blossoming ("as if by the hammerings of repetition alone, one sort of myth might be pounded into another"), but in the long set-piece, the enormously "professional" and very Marvellian poem, "Upon Apthorp House" (in ninety 8-line octosyllabic stanzas, it comprises the history of the master's residence of Adams House at Harvard—where Hollander was a Junior Fellow—including portraits of Henry James, Henry Adams, T. S. Eliot, Whitehead, and even the self-exiled poet, at the end). Though he begins, deprecatingly enough, in that "university wit" manner

> *Whose modes of diction give assent*
> *To stuffing empty compliment*
> *With feelings of the complex kind*
> *For which this verse was first designed . . .*

for all his fun and games with Dryden ("whiter than any winters are / or, in time's greener series, far / more shaded than a house can be") and his frolic on the grave of Henry James ("a presence . . . rests / beneath that name that's followed by / 'OM,' like a huge, Vedantic sigh"), for all his kidding of the medium ("true perspective only shows / through the elastic lines of prose"), and for all his com-

fortable nestling into thematic clichés ("each season which succeeds
the last / recedes, like feelings in one's past, / into a darkness"), Hol-
lander does penetrate, in this tremendous *exercise*, to some of his
innermost truths so far, and defines not only his own relation to the
past his poetry enshrines, but to the past he himself has lived through
and fears dying from:

> *In cities that blot out the sun*
> *Moral imagination*
> *Is needed to discern the past*
> *Hidden among the wearied, gassed*
> *And mottled multitudes of lives,*
> *Cut up by steel and concrete knives . . .*

For all of its obligations toward the university as the Great Good
Place, its rich invocations of the learned shades of Cambridge, this is a
poem of farewell to a certain version of patronage; the poet *turns on*
his own college days, in both senses of the verb:

> *Goodbye, Old Tunes! Old modes and feet*
> *Were fine for singing in the street*
> *When all New York was now, and when*
> *Imagined history was then;*
> *When styles one had to find could be*
> *The ultimate morality,*
> *I worked progressions on the lute.*
> *Now I must learn to play the mute.*

And in the surrender of both classical and modern mentors, of both
Shakespeare and Auden ("onelie begetters, please go pack, / old
W. H., get off my back!"), determines to forge a style of his own, even
if it means the treason of one more clerk:

> *All the games I've tried to play*
> *Like ladders, to be thrown away*
> *Once the snug tree-house has been gained,*
> *Seem moments now to be explained*
> *And, in the understanding, die,*
> *Blending, like woodsmoke in the sky,*
> *Into the mind with which I make*
> *The world around me come awake.*

It is one of the most deliberate promises a poet can offer, and as we
shall see in his next major work, Hollander keeps it, though in doing so
his preference for the monument over the fragment is to be severely
punished. Here he faces his own city, as so many of his previous poems
have prepared him to, the New York where "nighttown is all abroad

by day; / where flowery *bodegas* thrive . . . There are no Apthorp
Houses here." Instead of learned puns and classical meters, Hollander
readies himself—and is in part readied by the very things he declares
himself about to jettison—to become the archeologist of a very differ-
ent kind of excavation:

> *. . . some forgotten year*
> *I have been troubling to restore*
> *From scraps; a summer by the shore*
> *(But one of many); two dead aunts;*
> *A party where I wet my pants;*
> *A fall and an acquired scar—*

A fall and an acquired scar is what the poet finds himself left with,
beginning with, returning from "the Eastern Charles, the Western
Past" to his own despoiled Manhattan, glimpsing himself as he was
before he ever went into exile:

> *. . . I was learning how to spell*
> *The signatures that time impressed*
> *Upon my visions. When I'd guessed*
> *That I should have to leave it soon,*
> *On a green sward, one night in June,*
> *I sat and hummed and rubbed my brow.*
> *What I saw then confronts me now:*
>
> *That thin black river, running by*
> *Mirrors, like some impending sky,*
> *The red and white lights of the cars*
> *That stream along below the stars;*
> *Hung in that dark and fluid void*
> *Each seems a man-made asteroid*
> *Or artificial satellite,*
> *O, vision of tomorrow night!*

We shall in a moment consider that vision, which articulates an even
grander confrontation with the poet's first self than these neat verses
afford. Already, though, the instrument is in the poet's hand, a direct
kind of poetry, almost without images, not dependent on figures of
speech—*eine Poesie ohne Tropen*, Goethe called it—because it is en-
tirely a trope, a figure, not committed to a line of wit any more than to
a lake of sentiment, but a poetry of statement. "What my style must
answer to / is really neither here nor there"—neither in Cambridge nor
in New York, Hollander means—"but in the thick, engulfing air." By
the end of *Movie-Going*, Hollander has transcended his own accepta-
tion of the poet's role as professional bard, responding to the challenge

of culture with a kind of preposterous virtuosity which in its excess almost appears to exclude an audience. He has done everything—everything a *maker* can be asked to do: he has translated and adapted from the Swedish, the French, the Greek, the Latin, the Hebrew, the Russian (knowing none of these languages *à fond:* Hollander is interested in Language, a very different thing); he has written not only shaped poems, poems that take up the challenge of a poet of alien style, but even a book of children's verses, each about a kind of owl ("the foul owl," "the howl owl," even "the towel owl"); he has written the lyrics for an (unproduced) Broadway musical; he has written a monodrama for the composer Milton Babbitt about that emblematic creature Philomela ("What is this humming? / I am becoming / my own song . . ."); he has written dozens of double-dactyls;* in other words —in all the words available—he has written precisely the responses to those gauntlets no one has ever picked up before, even solving in one poem the old phonemic problem of "light housekeeping" and "lighthouse keeping"—and now he is prepared, he announces his preparation as deliberately as Wordsworth, having made his poetry the instrument of truth, as I say, rather than merely the vehicle for it ("so that Imagination may / start learning how to live by day"), to make something no culture can ask of a maker but which he must respond to as his own demand: he must make himself.

The vision Hollander summoned at the end of *Movie-Going and Other Poems* was extended, explored, *realized* three years later, in 1965, when he published his finest work, his entire confrontation with himself and his ultimate acknowledgment—hence his acceptance—of the circumstances which have brought him to where he is, "the unmistakable city / safe for the heart": *Visions from the Ramble,* fourteen linked poems and a "proem" centering around the heart of Central Park, from some parts of which none of the surrounding city is visible. In "Manhattan, this hospital," the poet and his girl, his muse, "sit on the grass along the river," looking at much the same landscape apostrophized at the end of "On Apthorp House." The girl pulls off a band-aid from the poet's shoulder, and the Muse is invoked in the first of many homely equivalents for the grand stage properties Hollander

* *Viz.,* Higgledy-piggledy
    Herod Antipater
    After the dance had the
    Lunch table set.

    "Balletomania?"
    "Bah! I just wanted a
    Nice dish of *tête de pro-*
    Phète vinaigrette."

has left behind ("she stands and breathes behind me"), though certainly their felt presence is one of the organizing principles of this series, their "high trajectory lifting it / above the Common," as Hollander says of the firecrackers on Eliot Square:

> "Tear, Muse, this blinding bandage
> From the heart's eye that your hand
> And mouth alone have opened!"
> *She laughs, and, leaning over,*
> *Rips off the strip of whiteness,*
> *Kisses the place, and sighs . . .*
> *With hope now, I unfasten*
> *What has been bound and clasped*
> *And rip away a last*
> *Unfilled first page, a white*
> *Liar in its silence.*

The first wound explored in this anamnesis is childhood; a series of beautifully structured, richly textured memories fade into each other: "Waiting," "Fireworks," "The Ninth of July." The quick emblems of a season at the shore, the "pivotal green turf of unwinding summer" are overshadowed by the intrusions of history:

> *overhead*
> *All that long summer the Von Hindenburg seemed to be hanging*
> *Above the beaches: we Jews pointed into the glaring*
> *Sunlight, up at the long, gray beswastikaed bobbin*
> *While Europe unravelled behind it . . .*
> *I stood still and heard the Fourths of July echo contingently*
> *In the fading, brighter part of the early summer sky,*
> *Waiting for life to explode in the next golden moment,*
> *Waiting for cadence of waiting itself to come to light,*
> *Cracking and bursting, and flaring up into significance.*

The moralized ode to "Fireworks" which follows works the poet up to a triple expostulation of his forces, the incandescence of mind, body, and nature which are seen to explode in significant waste—the poem, the orgasm, the lightning:

> *For half of life*
> *Nights came so that I might burn*
> *Like a Roman candle, high inside*
> *The blacknesses of summer.*
> *Then there were fireworks. Flesh*
> *Learns of its half*
> *Of death from the mind's flashbulb white*

Coming into being, seeing
Something that must come of all this burning,
All this becoming something other than darkness.

On "The Ninth of July," "midway between the fourth of July and the fourteenth, / suspended somewhere in summer between the ceremonies / remembered from childhood and the historical conflagrations / imagined in sad, learned youth—somewhere," Hollander promises, "there always hangs / the American moment." In these poems, he explores it in the development of his own sexual powers, his own creative madness. He evades it in a trip to Europe, rediscovers its necessity and runs "to book the next flight back." And in the fifth poem, "Humming," he invokes, among the seventeen-year locusts, his own seventeenth year; as in *The Untuning of the Sky*, Hollander dissects the "timeless buzzing," the music of the turning spheres which we cannot hear because it never stops:

Even the maddened humming, wordless, always wordless,
We do ourselves, that is never an act of speech, like denying,
Blaming or pledging or lying, nor the raising of voice to heights
That singing is: this is the business of being. To have heard
These undying cicadas, immortal while yet they live, is to burn
For a time in the moment itself.

The sixth poem, "The Ninth of Ab," is in part a lamentation for the lost temple, in part a thanksgiving hymn for the body's elision of its own suffering in darkness and sleep: "when memories merely blur / a sweated lens for a moment, night is enough of a blessing / and enough of a fulfillment." Hollander is inspired, in these poems of the summer that find their summary, certainly, in the seventh of the series, "How to Remember the Summer"—Hollander is inspired as much by the lapses, gaps and blanks as by "what is remembered." Thus the message of the winter, "Freeze. Judge. Disconnect," is worked circumstantially into the healing myth of summer:

. . . winter
Always comprising two years
While summer hummed at the warm
Heart of one year only,
Enduring. Lasting. Connecting.
What winter broke, it mended.
What spring began, it ended.
What fall forgot, it knew.

The next three poems, "Losing Something," "Cornucopia" and "Sunday Evenings" are autumnal, back-to-school, and often despairing. The alternation of the long, prosy lines with tightly organized lyrics keeps the entire group from running down, and I know no more accurate presentment of the *ennui de dimanche* since Laforgue, though Hollander has inflected his *acedie* to the demands of such a different city, a different river:

> *At five-thirty or so on Sunday, when the big enlightening myths*
> *Have sunk beyond the river and we are alone in the dark . . .*
> *On Sunday afternoons, one can have followed the blackening*
> *Water of the river from eyes along the Drive*
> *And then climbed up a concrete hill to one's own walls*
> *And quietly opened a vein.*

Not suicide, though, but the poet's own vein, the Muses' Helicon is what is broached in the eleventh poem, partly an episodic account of selling blood ("five dollars a pint at St. Luke's") with Allen Ginsberg, partly a meditation on *the true cadence;* so that by playing off the newsy incidental manner:

> *Turnings; errors; wanderings; while Allen chattered on:*
> I mean someday to cry out against the cities; but first
> I must find the true cadence.

against the tone of symbolic, almost Dantesque confession, the tone of experience that has been searched for its farthest resonance:

> *I have bled since*
> *To many cadences, if not to the constant tune*
> *Of the heart's yielding and now I know . . .*

Hollander gets the advantages of both colloquial and high-style that he has been reaching for from the start, the energies of both novel and epic pouring into the hexameters,

> *Into a stream, whether thicker or thinner than blood, and I know*
> *That opening up at all is harder than meeting a measure:*
> *With night coming on like a death, a ruby of blood is a treasure.*

The twelfth piece, "West End Blues," is a broken fantasia on the themes of Hollander's own academic festival: portraits of the poet's friends, loves, and enemies are painfully located in Catullus' *salax taberna*, and through echoes of Keats ("half in death with easeful love"), the cavalier poets, Racine, and "a bouncy avatar of *Bye, Bye Blackbird,*" the vision is thickened, the atmosphere heightened to the crisis of the thirteenth poem, a winter journey into the "mind's landscapes . . . even barer / of the possibility of any images than his bleared / eye is barred to delights. Appearances have dimmed . . ." It is the dark night of revulsion, the crisis of the series which brings Hollander to final terms with himself in the fourteenth poem, "From the Ramble," his one truly visionary work, requiring the entire city, its downfall and phenomenal hopes to serve as the decor of his own *recognition scene*. Hunting down the emblematic place in the Ramble where he had, since childhood, remembered encounters with three pools, something between a Spenserian vision of the Graces and a Wordsworthian prelude to the forfeits of a lifetime, Hollander, in this very long poem of inclusive theme, apostrophizes his city's towers, "pinnacles springing"

> *Skyward—then penetrating the great blue open room*
> *Where all the sunsets burn; downward they disappear*
> *In unseen chambers of bedrock; outward, already ruins*
> *Of a wild, recent time, evoking all their fearful*
> *Doubles in Moscow; branchless stumps ringing a clearing*
> *In irony's forest. But inward, they glow in the dying sun*
> *To cauterize the minds that make them matter and give*
> *Them meaning: all the sad, ugly towers, mortared with mud,*
>   *Moribund, crumbling to dust.*
>
> *Even at dawn, even at fairer moments than these,*
> *Glimpses out at the boundaries of all this ruined garden*
> *Reveal a city to be achieved, the towers unreal,*
> *The glittering windows unapproachable, the far*
> *Finials and fretwork lifted almost to the stars*
> *Beyond even their own vulgarity, beyond*
> *The gestures of aspiration that left them scattered, sparkling*
> *At all the irrational hours, hung high, but yet unpromised*
>   *There where only the eye can follow.*

The poet makes his way through the park, wondering about his meeting, once again, with "those lost ponds," worrying whether he has a right to demand their presence, "deserved not by laboring / merely, but by a readiness of the heart to accept such fine / gifts of phenomena" and encounters the proof of that readiness: at the climax of the poem, in the last five stanzas, the poet invokes the time, as a boy, when he "pushed through a hedge of broken / privet and fell headlong against the concrete and oaken bench":

> . . . *where a tall fat man I now guess was thirty-five*
> *Or thereabouts, was stretched, brooding, with his whole*
> *Length extended along the bench, his head supported*
>   *Not with his palm, along the jaw,*
>
> *But on his wrist and the back of his hand—his fingertips*
> *Continuing past his chin; and he lay on his left side*
> *And watched me as I rubbed my scraped brow with my mitten.*
> *And from where I stood, I read on his face the kind of smile,*

Awkward, a little strained, that one can often find
In mirrors; and as the wind blew dead leaves on the path
Tangling his long, untidy hair, I turned, and behind me
He lay there motionless. I felt him bless me. I ran
  Away from the vision behind my back.

What did he see, that lying man? A boy, running
Down along an airless path between scrubby trees?
Three silent children playing in a ring, then? Something
Utterly different rising behind his eyesight weeks
Later and then forever? For whatever he had received,
Oh let him have been thankful, even as I am now:
It is a garden we fall from; a city, somehow, we feel
That we have been promised . . .

Even as the child is blessed by the man he is to become, Hollander
accepts, and thereby blesses, the child he was, and in a final explosion
of thematic relevance, ends his poem and his book with a loving song
of praise, praise to an end beyond the seasonal and yet enclosing the
seasons, above the human city and yet containing city, garden, and
"three small pools":

  . . . graces dance on a bare
Hilltop, a cycle of months spin around on a frail
Wheel of language and touch. O see this light! As a blaze
Of cloud above the western towers gleams for an instant
Up there! Firing the sky, higher than it should be able
To reach, a single firework launched from the unseen river
  Rises and dies, as we kiss and listen.

Visions from the Ramble is a major effort in American poetry to
recover for the art some of the energy and inclusiveness we now tend
to associate with fiction. As it seems to me, all of Hollander's previous
work prepared him for this enterprise, and he has here, by a rare
willingness—call it *need*—to risk *himself* in the undertaking, succeeded
in fusing all that he knows with all that he knows he has forgotten,
until we can merely say of him (but if we fail to say it, our reading of
his *oeuvre* is no more than the vain coincidence of a shadow and a
transparence: commentary is survival) what *he* has said, and we have
already quoted, about his choice of poems for children: "so this book's
end explores the world that is beyond Winter, and yet does so by
speaking of nothing more than what we are."

In 1966 was published *The Quest of the Gole*, a legend for children
told partly in the alliterative verse, riddles, and head-line songs that are

the delight of Hollander's virtuosity, and partly in a mortaring prose that holds together the fragmentary poems, purportedly rescued from "many ancient writings." Like Ruskin's *King of the Golden River* and other nineteenth-century set-pieces (a lot of Browning and William Morris has been used to stiffen the Tolkien pudding), Hollander's moral fable of self-renunciation and spiritual ultimogeniture lies well within the circle of his "adult" preoccupations. When his prologue ends:

> *Then I translated the tale they told:*
> *It was one of winter, a story of winds,*
> *Of fearful freezing, but looking forward*
> *Toward sun and the splendidness of summer*
> *And the golden greatness of the Gole . . .*

we recognize at once the poet of splendid cyclical obsessions; and when, in the story's climax and conclusion, Hollander suffuses his prose with a recognition scene beyond the common metamorphosis of such fairy-tales:

> Moad felt a strange kind of dizziness, as he realized what it was that was so remarkable about this common picture of the earth striving to meet something impossibly high above it. It was his way of seeing it: Moad knew that he was not looking *out* at this scene, and it would have been nonsense to think of his looking *in* at it. But just as he could, almost shuddering, imagine himself, cold and alone on those far, windy heights, so could he feel himself somehow expanding, so that the whole world of hills he now saw was somehow in his own heart . . . The vision of the mountains was eternal and unchanging, and yet Moad felt himself to be connected with it as he had never been with anything else he had ever looked at. As the roaring and sighing of his own cry of astonishment, and, now, of joy came to him, Moad saw that he beheld a picture of fulfillment; of the end of all quests that do not merely lead to new ones; of what would always lie beyond wanting and doing and getting; but of what was more clearly and certainly *there* than anything outside of himself that Moad had ever known.

—when, as I say, we hear this music, when we see this change that has been wrought by a submission to ignorance, we *connect* Moad's quest of the Gole with Hollander's own search for himself, and we know— reading uphill until we gain a view of the entire region—that there has been a finding. If Hollander has transformed himself, it is by his work that he has done so, until he can say, as the earth itself says to his Moad:

What you see now, for only an instant, you can never remember. But seeing it will change you, and even more, it will change your world.

and as he says to himself, peering into his ruined past, making a poem of the world that emerges from shadows:

Doing and then having done is having ruled and commanded
A world, a self, a poem, a heartbeat in the moonlight.
To imagine a language means to imagine a form of life.

The Night Mirror by JOHN HOLLANDER

In 1969, when John Hollander published *Types of Shape*, a collection of twenty-five emblems whose texts supply their own pictures (shapes of type, then, or as the poet polemically puts it in one of them, "no ideas but in forms"), he probably distracted his readers and viewers as much by providing (next slide, please) a respectable lineage for *Swan and Shadow*, say, or *The Figure in the Carpet* in the Alexandrian Greeks or George Herbert or Apollinaire, as by displaying the imperturbable *sprezzatura* of his typing. And what he distracted us *from*, I think, by the apparent gadgetry on the one side and the archaic governance on the other, is the entire congruence and continuity of these figured—even calculated—creations with the noble work which had preceded them, *Visions from the Ramble* (1965) and especially with his new book *The Night Mirror*, published in the fall of 1971. The very premonitory titles of so many of the iconographs—"A possible fake," "Playing an obsolete instrument", "Crise de coeur", "Vanished mansard", "Work problem", "Blots", "Broken column", "Last quarter"—declare the mortality, the evanescence and the wreckage of even these splendid things, their fallings from us, their vanishings, "the eclipse of old moonlights by the darkness of origin." The emblem book constitutes a handsome muscle—hinge, holding action, decorous hurdle—between the two valves, the secreting ovals which have perfected pain into pearl: the major poetry of John Hollander.

Such poetry is the way language behaves—not only acts but acts out—when subjected or even objected to certain extreme circumstances, chief among which, "where mean and mode unite", will be the negative. Hollander's grand celebration will be of failure, obscuration, nightfall, the world darkened by his own shadow, "a long memorial turbulence." The idiosyncratic title is "Power failure", just as the typical first line is "Not having disembarked" or again "Not from the unmapped valleys of darkness, nor": methods of summoning up the doom which in the poem subsides, allayed by its own domination. As I have elsewhere remarked of the glorious *Visions*, it is by fusing all that he knows with all that he knows he has forgotten; and as I would say of the glamorous *Types*, it is by letting his language "pour into forms it molds itself", that this poet articulates the conflict and concert of naming and making ("What I say is what I am mistaken for," Hollander gloats, almost, with a characteristic emphasis on misprision as victory); so I can see that this latest book, with all its mastery of natural objects (the music volute, the Alaskan brown bear, the slice of sequoia) and its mystery of mechanical or made ones (the spinning phonograph record, the golem, the night mirror itself), reflects, as its divided title insists, a phenomenology of dark/light, repetition/accident, memory/loss, affirmation/dissolution. Thus the form of Hollander's poetry (and "forms stand for their maker", as he told us in *Types of Shape*), the behavior of his language, will be *not this but THIS*, a negative assertion clearing the ground (or digging a grave) for what may yet stand, a decreating mode which will permit reality *to have transpired:* "I too was earth once / still I yielded up forms possible in me." Further, not only is something always cancelled out, occluded in these undertakings for the sake of something else, something other, so that "the unpromising blob of language may reassume its visionary form," but the very event or impulse which was made way for is known to become undone, and such knowledge is a cause for rejoicing, "the sound of an hour passing is that of another coming."

The title poem is a powerful tributary to the self-tracking stream or strain which is so urgent in this poet that he has had to ease it by what is probably the most resilient, vigorous and indeed overpowering syntactical administration in our modern poetry and indeed, I am tempted to say, since Milton, for that is the tonality so often caught here, "the shadow sunk beneath the broken mirror" if not the wat'ry floor. In "The Night Mirror," then, we have the little boy going to sleep, preferring the horrors of his mind over those of reality in a delicate dialectic of light, reflection, darkness and dreaming:

> . . . *The silver corona of moonlight*
> *That gloried his glimpsed head was enough*
> *To send him back into silences (choosing*
> *Fear in those chasms below), to reject*
> *Freedom of wakeful seeing, believing*
> *And feeling, for peace and the bondage to horrors*

> *Welling up only from deep within*
> *That dark planet head* . . .

The sentence proceeds, riverine, melodramatic, high, and its burden is that what might be seen in the mirror—the *night* mirror, as later in the book the *dark* museum and the *darkening* yard—is somehow worse than what the night itself gives up, yet even that,

> *his grandmother,*
> *Say, with a blood-red face, rising*
> *From her Windsor chair in the warm lamplight,*
> *To tell him something*

is inadmissible, and the subject sinks

> *beyond*
> *The rim of the night mirror's range, huge*
> *And cold, on the pillow's dark side.*

Nothing is trusted, everything is known to betray, and it is only by submission, by submersion in the deceiving element (darkness = time = memory = death) that Hollander achieves his curious cautious triumph, that of having mythologized his own losses into gain; he puts it so in a later poem, for *The Night Mirror* is not merely a book, it is a glyph of self-disclosure, glosses on a text of identity-as-debilitation:

> *We're water that remembers,*
> *Our surfaces reflecting*
> *Our deeps submerged in a dream,*
> *Veined with currents that falter,*
> *Moments that chill and quicken* . . .

It is why sentences here are so *hard*——they are death sentences. Hollander will not let his lines go until they have turned and, grammatically, blessed him. The sentence must be saturated, filling all its primary sites (the subject, the verb, the object) with expansions, interpolations, subordinate clauses, determinants; of course this saturation is utopian, for, structurally speaking, there is no reason to end a sentence—*something more* can always be added, never the truly conclusive addition. Only to the Muse will Hollander say "I gave. I recall." And those four words with their terrible pun, those two absolute sentences, are the program; but the realization, but *the performance*, in long circumstantial accounts of a city childhood, a travelled maturity, "whose end . . . I trudge toward, my shadow and I / annihilating each other as we approach / with a clap of sound-lessness . . ." must be elaborated, worked out indeed, so that all the resources of making may fulfill the negative ("crackling of no flame,

crunching / of no particular paper") by reflection of return, by the
mirror of verse, of revision, recuperation, *getting back*, as may be
said of all this intelligent, beautiful work:

> *They return*
> *Bright rightings of our sinisters,*
> *The mirrors.*

Poetry, 1972

Tales Told of the Fathers by JOHN HOLLANDER

Certainly since (and including) *The Night Mirror*, his last book,
published in 1971, every poem by John Hollander must be read *n*
times; any poem by John Hollander may be read *n* times. The two
sentences are the obligation of his mode—

> *visions of what in a Fallen*
> *City's highest rise wisely acknowledge their own*
> *Partial failure . . .*

and its reward. No poet comparably accoutered among us (but is
there such? who is so inventive, so learned, so funny, so cunning, so
severe?) demands so much, even as he gives so much; nor has any
poet so loaded every rift with more than one had thought the poor
fissure could hold: if one were to pluck, pettishly, at the hem of
Hollander's mantle, it would be to ask if there were really so many
rifts at all, thus to be filled, thus to be crammed—if the poet had not
purposely *made* the rifts, driven wedges between the given and the
taken—

> *searched*
> *The half-grayish folds*
> *Of the sheets for some*
> *Tokens of this loss . . .*

For it is always the lost, the absent, the negative which is Hollander's
reflection and fulfillment. "What had I fallen to?" is the question
which opens his book, and in the exploration of that foundering,
what makes the poem is of course what is *not:*

> *no light by which I might read*
> *The field, much less as I have always done*
> *Make it out through the Book of the Fair Field,*
> *Or some such book. There was surely no light . . .*

Thereupon follows a veritable anthology of impossibilities—cosmogonic fables, kabbalistic speculations, mementos of concatenation and rupture: most characteristic as well as accessible is perhaps "Cohen on the Telephone" and its after-image or resonance "Eine Kleine Nachtmusik" which celebrate

> . . . *the nothing that breath is,*
> *The word of hushed designatum*
> *Insisted endlessly upon* . . .

and most imposing, the long series called "The Head of the Bed," a study of the interaction of erotic dream and erratic life which for its theatrical mastery of surface and weltering mystery of depth is equaled only by some of the late introspections of Martha Graham; it is his masterpiece, and must be read not acquisitively but submissively, for here Hollander advances farther, deeper, more inextricably into the mighty language which will mythologize his losses into gain than elsewhere in the book, save perhaps at the end, in "The Shades", another major entertainment of flesh and spirit as they rehearse their dialogue through all the senses the word "shade" can have: blind, spectacles, shadow, "the masquerade of degree," death-in-life, until the cloudy self is restored, identity revived:

> *The body's pale nightmare of mind, faded;*
> *The mind's drop of frightened sweat at mere thought*
> *Of body, unglistening, chilled and dried.*

The book ends, after its "hoards of form hidden" in unrhyming words and burning leaves, in philosophers' examples and poets' elegies, in statue and fountain, have been exposed, the crammed rift emptied on the page, filling the mind with the most authoritative language anyone has ever wielded to account for "no shadow that we can see" or again, "mindfulls from outside the mills of light"— the book ends with "Kranich and Bach", crane and stream constituting the figure of (what else?) "a brand of piano no longer made", and here, very gently, very easily, Hollander, who has, as he lately told an interviewer, "an insane desire to eternalize", does just that, he walks into the circular, resonant realm (not even *The Night Mirror* is darker, nor gleams more desperately with its "increase over nothing, to the greater / glory of nothing") where what flows and what sings are seen together, no longer made but eternally making, followed into a silence,

> *As I will follow my father into his.*
> *Dark under the closed lid, Kranich and Bach wait,*
> *Silence standing up one-leggedly in song.*

It does little service to Hollander, at a moment when we like our poetry to do its work quickly and readily, like a good tax-accountant, it is no recommendation, I fear, to breathe thus heavily about the bush of his "difficulty"; yet I am so moved and amazed by the eternalized mortality of these emblems and echoes, "regions of erased shapes in the air", that it seems even sillier to suggest to the running reader that here he will get on expeditiously with his pursuit. Hollander is the laureate of questionable life, and thorny and dark his laurel genuinely is. It must be circled, as Keats says, without any irritable reaching after fact and reason (though there are facts in plenty here, and reasons to be heard out); the poems must be performed in the mind, allowed their silence and breath there, for "inside, the bright images and hard-edged, in the warmth, the radiance" will transform the briar hedge into a burning bush: as Keats goes on to say, with a great poet the sense of Beauty—and for Keats, was not beauty truth?—overcomes every other consideration, or rather obliterates all consideration.

The Yale Review, 1976

RICHARD HUGO

"Why Track Down Unity When the Diffuse Is So Exacting?"

To ATTACH the label *regional* to enterprises of more ambition and moment than publicity campaigns is to qualify a man's poetry, for example, as anything but central. And it is the omphalos we are after, a hub where things are initiated, from which they work outward. We want to find the characteristic site in the man, not the man in the characteristic site. For landscape, weather, the scene a man makes, always consist—are perceived only by means of—the most rigidly stylized conventions, and what a region finally suggests to a poet is not new content (the container for the thing contained) but new possibilities in the treatment of convention. In itself, the regional is merely a suburban literary world, whereas what we want from the poet is a prospect of the capital. The poet of a place, a *region*, must be king of it, as the word itself implies, remembering how kings in Shakespeare, say, are addressed as the epitome and living spirit of their countries: "What says France to these hard words?" So that what we lack in most (weakly) regional poetry is the notion—essential to any philosophy of metaphor—of dynamics, the concept of an energy that will link the incandescent "spots of time" with the man there to tell them. The middling regional poet seems to conceive of his site and its particulars as an organism apart, that is, as a Whole which bears a certain fixed relation to another Whole which is himself. But as a contemplative man, such a poet does not yet connect with this notion of organism or entity what must be its necessary complement: life itself, the incessant movement binding outer weather to inner, connecting space with events, history with theory. But to record such a dialectic is precisely the victory and visionary justification of the poetry of Richard Hugo. Instead of the usual analogical knowledge of the regional writer, resting on the concordance, the provisional "fit" of two given but static natures, Hugo recovers that rhythmic, dynamic, dialectical signification such knowledge possessed, we are told, for the thinkers of the Renaissance; in his characteristic transactions with the Northwest expanse, "this land too flat for secrets" that stands behind Mark Tobey and Theodore Roethke and the later Malcolm Lowry, the analogy moves not only from an ambient nature to the self, but from the life of the self to the evolution of nature:

> *I will cultivate the trout, teach their fins*
> *to wave in water like the legs of girls*
> *tormented black in pools. I will swim*
> *a week to be a witness to the spawning,*
> *be a trout, eat the eggs of salmon—*
> *anything to live until the trout and rain*
> *are running in the river in my ear.*
>
> *The river Sky is running in my hair,*
> *I am floating past the troutless pools*
> *learning water is the easy way to go.*
> *I will reach the sea before December*
> *when the Sky is turning gray and wild*
> *and rolling heavy from the east to say*
> *late autumn was an Oriental child.*

Modestly, Richard Hugo (whose ultimate project is not a modest one at all; like the great poet whose name he bears, alas, Hugo is determined to descend, awakened, the other side of the night) begins with a hard look at the dying creatures about him, enlarging his scope to their decaying surround, until the widening lens includes his own condition:

> *West of here the only west is failure,*
> *candlefish in sun, the heron's flight*
> *from symbol into common air.*

His first book, *A Run of Jacks*, published in 1961, proceeds from the very first poem as if the proper study of mankind was fish: kings and jacks which are salmon; cutthroats, rainbows and steelheads which are trout, sunfish, perch; the ling and orca which are the hake and the killer whale—"I have stared at steelhead teeth to know him," Hugo says, studying the red markings on the trout's side that are "like apples in a fog," finding "drama in the annual run of kings," exploring the land and the water and the sky, "that blue that kisses man forever out of form," all the Indian-named country around Seattle where he was raised and whose rivers the sea-run salmon mount to spawn. The poet would submit, like the trout, to the demands of such an environment, the better to survive in it:

> *Quick and yet he moves like silt.*
> *I envy dreams that see his curving*
> *Silver in the weeds . . .*

acknowledging at once that the observed natural movement becomes the metaphor of the unconscious mind; moreover, it is the conscious mind that watches the terrorizing bass, for example, to gain its emblems of aggression:

> *On his sides are recreated reeds,*
> *shadows of a log or pad,*
> *parts of an ambush pattern:*
> *his green-black fusion*
> *with the well-adjusted lily bed . . .*

> *Where shade extends*
> *panic is prerequisite to size.*

Hugo apostrophizes the birds which like himself are hunting "the eel and terror here"; in "Lone Cheer from the Stands for a Bitter Crane" he urges his rasorial rival, also his representative, onward to the heroic stance he covets:

> *No sun spotlights you. Salt*
> *does not applaud. There is no stage.*
> *Yet the edge*
> *of day is bruised by your abrasive flight . . .*

And of the many poems addressed to gulls, one about the "beachthief" dropping clams on rocks to break them open while the poet, too, is looting the beach for lunch or decor is perhaps the closest comradeship Hugo acknowledges with a fellow-inhabitant of this rotting wilderness:

> *These to him were crucial:*
> *aim and height, hard target, his corkscrew fall*
> *to where the take lay broken for his meal.*

> *No sound of water fought my social*
> *claim: a dipping wing when he, black*
> *felon, aimless dropped his felony on rock.*

The gull dipping its wing to another pillager, the falling clam, the watching poet on a rocky beach: these are characteristic figures in Hugo's first poems—hard, even harsh in their slant rhymes and their broken movement, checked abruptly, charged with a negligent wit (as in the "crucial aim" vs. the "aimless felon" above) and a sullen, cross-grained submission to the world where "laws like moon and slant prevailed." Even the few human beings seen—conjured up, rather—are cruelly immersed in a seethe of littoral transformations:

> *That girl along the stream, blonde*
> *and sleek with speckles on her back—*
> *would she sizzle if we threw her*
> *in the pool, or grow a gill*
> *and swim and reappear in fall,*
> *a Dolly Varden at the spawning grounds?*

And the landscape does not encourage man's presence here at all: the posts and piles of fallen piers testify to an industry exhausted; a "Schoolgirl at Seola" cannot reconstruct from rotting stumps what was once a pier used by smugglers of liquor from China; "why should she believe the road / she came on was not always road . . . if you spoke to her of contraband / she would only think you strange." An habitual prospector of cemeteries, the poet stalks knowingly around "The Graves at Mukilteo" where "markers spall and the mayor regrets / the dead can be this derelict." This is a fallen country, not a noble savagery, having passed, as American landscapes are said to do, from primitivism to decadence without the interval of civilization; its residues are generally recorded in a painter's imagery:

> *. . . fog that fakes the ocean's*
> *outer rim will smear your canvas, turn*
> *your art as savage as the Indian*
> *who bums you for a muscatel in Forks.*

The poet wonders what he, or anyone concerned with consciousness, is doing here. It is his uncertainty that constitutes the burden of his quest —or rather, a quest for his burden. What brings the artist?

> *. . . Not the poverty*
> *alone, but other ways of being,*
> *using basic heat: wood brought in*
> *by the same sea that is blaring*
> *wealthy ships to a freshly painted port.*

It is the same account which Malcolm Lowry gives of the same region, and one suffused with the same love of an infernal nature; the brutal rhythms, the brief commands of Hugo's reports are never so complacent as the swoon Lowry's logorrhea allows, but the vision is remarkably close, even to the emphasis on very simple words, almost none over two syllables:

> It was by now late in November, and we were still lingering on; the sparkling morning frosts, the blue and gold noons and evening fogs of October had turned suddenly into dark or stormy sunrises, with sullen clouds driving through the mountains before the north wind. The beach here, in a no man's land between the barge company and the Indian reserve, was very flat and low, not sandy but covered with a deep slimy ooze and growths of seaweed: when the tide was low the boat was grounded about a hundred feet from the waterfall on the shore, and you had to wrestle the barrel back from the creek over the ooze and through shallow water, sinking in the muck. Of course we got much of our wood from the beach, both for making repairs round the place and for firewood. It was on the beach we found one day the ladder . . .

Here is Hugo's pared-down analogue, the driftwood being already accounted for in the last quotation:

> *These are strange shores. No sand.*
> *No oysters. No slant to the earth*
> *yet the water ends.*
> *It is shore only because there is water*
> *and land.*
>
> *We can see the tragic forming*
> *hurricane and victim;*
> *and a man comes like a cat*
> *to wait by the colorless forest,*
> *his blue hands stuttering welcome. . . .*

The human world in *A Run of Jacks* (even the runs, of course, are depleted; "mills go on polluting, and the river, hot with sewage, steams") is dispossessed. In the crucial poem of this first book, "Duwamish," the urban environment, even in ripe summer, is diseased:

> *. . . this river's*
> *curves are slow and sick. Water knocks*
> *at mills and concrete plants, and crud*
> *compounds the gray. On the out-tide,*
> *water, half salt water from the sea,*
> *rambles by a barrel of molded nails,*
> *gray lumber piles, moss on ovens*
> *in the brickyard no one owns.*

Human nature too has been bled out, despoiled; the Indians, like the immigrants, corrupted to indifference: "Because the name is Indian, Indians ignore the river as it cruises past the tavern." Language sticks in the poet's throat as he constructs a *paysage moralisé* out of his ruin:

> *On the short days, looking for a word,*
> *. . . knowing this poverty*
> *is not a lack of money but of friends,*
> *I come here to be cold . . .*
>
> *But cold is a word. There is no word along*
> *this river I can understand or say . . .*
> *. . . All words are Indian.*
> *Love is Indian for water, and madness*
> *means, to Redmen, I am going home.*

Life has foundered here. Not only the graves, the "chapel further west than most," the statue of a saint "derelict in wind"—

> *the ocean protestant with tide*
> *and elegance abandoned in the foam*
> *four hundred years of idols with no blood—*

—but the displaced Greeks and Slavs, unemployed lumberjacks boozing it up in the slack taverns, the wrecks of commercial greed and spiritual hunger:

> *Their disease was motto and the gold beyond—*
> *ours what fifty years have done to dying.*
> *Today we come for nothing*
> *but we read the sea and wait.*

Characteristic is the poem "1614 Boren," which is the street address of an abandoned rooming-house. Here the poet pokes among the debris "for fun," wondering about the stranded selves whose sedimentation he considers coolly, as though he were an archeologist of some violently extinguished race:

> *Why could room 5 cook and 7 not?*
> *These dirty rooms were dirty even then,*
> *the toilets ancient when installed,*
> *and light was always weak and flat*
> *like now, or stark from a bare bulb.*
> *And the boarders when they spoke of this*
> *used "place" and "house," the one with photos*
> *of Alaska on his walls said "edifice."*
> *This home could be a joke on the horizon—*
> *bad proportions and the color of disease.*

And in "Neighbor," the poet admits his envy of the shabby ecstasy endured by the drunk "who lives across the street from us." This man is dead, but suggests a release beyond extinction which is more than the poet, committed to consciousness, can afford:

> *I plan my frown, certain he'll be carried out*
> *bleeding from the corners of his grin.*

From a single animal to the habitat of that animal, from the ransacked landscape to the riotous, littered city, Richard Hugo has traced in the short, cruel, matter-of-fact poems that crowd his first book a *descensus* into the blank of living. Not once has he failed to suggest, in these alienated pieces, that the war going on outside him, the decline and fall of reality, is not also transpiring within him. ("They always fight dirty in dreams.") There is no observation of a desolate river flat:

> *The crude dike*
> *slag and mud bending out of sight,*
> *left gray the only color for the sky,*
> *wind the only weather, neo-Holland*
> *printed with no laughter on the map . . .*

no notation of the failed faith of a deserted woman:

> *She believes that God is in the trees,*
> *perched like a bird, waiting for the crumbs*
> *she scatters on*
> *the snow for definite robins . . .*

no record of life, however bleak:

> *. . . Only smoke*
> *from two shacks and a scratchy radio*
> *prevent abandonment from falling*
> *on this lateral bare area like fog . . .*

—that is not aimed first at the poet himself. The scarred landscape, the flouted existences are not only projections of an ego trying to break free of its bonds, but actually projectiles, weapons against time, against the "snakey thought that art is always failure." Such ugliness of scene, even such insistence on clogged and clattering movements in order to report a surface that is grim, are not merely sensational devices: in fact, the hideous and the broken-down are eventually, inevitably, recuperated, transformed by the way they are *located*—with a firmness, a security of self-surrender—within. When a poet works this way, outward from a center and inward toward it as Hugo does, never carrying the warfare to others before he has waged it uncivilly against himself, he can transcend any mere site, ransom any material, even matter itself.

Thus it is his own being, even his own person which Richard Hugo puts in question when he interrogates the waters, the "stale sea" that runs through his own veins and guts as in the polluted rivers of Seattle; in verse that courses with a new fluidity, a gush of watery syllables to gain the rebirth fish try for as they fling themselves upstream, Hugo seeks out an initiation and a source as much as an apocalypse, some final cleansing:

> *With the Stilli thus defeated and the sea*
> *turned slough by close Camano, how can water die*
> *with drama, in a final rich cascade,*
> *a suicide, a victim of terrain, a martyr?*
> *Or need it die? Can't the stale sea tunnel,*
> *climb and start the stream again*
> *somewhere in the mountains where the clinks*
> *of trickle on the stones remind the fry*
> *ending is where rain and blackmouth runs begin?*
> *Now the blackmouth run. The Stilli quivers*
> *where it never moved before. Willows*
> *change to windmills in the spiteless eye.*
> *Listen. Fins are cracking like the wings*
> *of quick birds trailing rivers through the sky.*

In 1965 Hugo published his second book, *Death of the Kapowsin Tavern*, which starts off in character with some further cheerless views of the Northwest waterways: Duwamish, Skagit, Hoh. But the lens-aperture is wider now, the exposure longer, and it is easier for the poet to take in more territory at a glance. The poems are longer, and between the first group of studies in riparian decline—

> *My vision started at this river mouth,*
> *on a slack tide . . .*
> 　　　　　*Sight can be polluted*
> *like a river . . .*
> *To know is to be alien to rivers.*

and the final series, "Limited Access" with its further scrutiny of disinherited lives, wrecked, deceiving, self-deceptive:

> *A novel fakes a start in every bar,*
> *gives way to gin and talk. The talk gives way*
> *to memories of elk, and elk were never here.*
> *Freighters never give this town a second look.*
> *The dead are buried as an afterthought*
> *and when the tide comes glittering with smelt*
> *the grebes have gone to look for meaty ports.*

—between the landscape and its tenants, Hugo has thrust a long poem, ingeniously managed so that it never escapes him into mere research or data, about a bombing mission during World War II, his first composition to leave the Territory behind him (though it was written only three years after the war). The advantage of carrying your country around inside you is evident here, for Hugo is able to articulate his purposes, the fear of mortality even as one deals it out—a kind of emblem of life as the search for death—by the very figures and associations he no longer need employ in a specific sense:

Nothing is heard in the north,
and the northern temperatures grow cold with the height.
There is the stark crack of voice
taking oxygen checks and the sharp static answers.
You are beyond birds, a season called summer.
There are places away from the world where the air is always winter.

And again, the mission accomplished, survived rather, as the plane returns from the raid over Linz, the corresponding image is invoked over the Adriatic:

Summer is heard in the south,
and the southern temperatures grow warm as you drop.
The speed is easier, the brain
warmed by the sound of insult,
and you defend yourself by making fun
of others' fear, of your own prayers.
You come into birds, a sun that is warmer.
There is land away from the sky where the sound is always summer.

These are merely two moments of repose, or at least of equilibrium, in a long and intricate narrative, but they show how much Hugo has gained, and gainsaid, by his regionalism. The conventions of a place have given him a vocabulary in which to accommodate his action in whatever place it occurs, have given him a means of dealing importantly with the privations and privileges of a life:

> *If you think about it for a long time*
> *the mind, like engines, will sing*
> *you to the home of men . . .*

> *If you think of it you know soil*
> *is its own loveliness and you want to be on it . . .*

("his soil," as Wallace Stevens had put it in another mode, "is man's intelligence": this recognition Hugo comes to directly, without the ironic revision which Stevens, or his Crispin, imposes on his impulse to intellectualize the scenery). The body of this book, as it were, is the fleshing-out of a vision of impoverishment, the recovery or reclamation of an eroded manhood, poems correspondent to those in *A Run of Jacks;* as in "Duwamish No. 2," where the poet's return to his region is an acknowledgment of his difficulties with his feelings—"North is easy. North is never love," he says:

> *When the world hurts, I come back alone*
> *along the river, certain the salt*
> *of vague eyes makes me ready for the sea.*
> *And the river says: You're not unique—*
> *learn now there is one direction only—*
> *north, and, though terror to believe,*
> *quickly found by river and never love.*

In these extensions, the poet seems able to stand more. The sights are just as bleak, and the sites, but they are afforded, by their very duration, a kind of compositional strength which is what we mean, I suppose, by inevitability. In the poems about the tavern's death ("nothing dies as slowly as a scene"), as in those about more graveyards ("the weather hates our poses / but the sun deranges men with laughter"), there is the same cool investigation of meager careers and malign countrysides:

> *Where land is flat, words are far apart.*
> *Each word is seen coming from far off,*
> *a calm storm, almost familiar, across*
> *the plain. The word floats by, alive.*

But something has relented in, or been released into, the poet's fierce account of these fish and birds that are hunted and hunters both, of these markets and cemeteries that are at once source and summation of choice, of these whores and derelicts that are past either hunting or choosing, weathered beyond the operations of any selectivity into the other, stony sense of being a *quarry*, chosen, marked out by life only because there is nothing left in them to die. The regional strain in Hugo's apprehension of his subjects has grown so consistent with experience as to seem supremely general, universal, which is merely to say that by the end of his second book he has made his world exist.

And because it exists, it can afford to *invoke*, to call in upon itself and even to *object to*, to throw itself *against* what is not itself, another world. By 1969 Richard Hugo had completed his third and even his fourth book of poems. As we must expect, it is the Northwest poems which conduct Hugo's trial by landscape, his arraignment by weather,

to a further pitch of excruciation: the menace of place is acknowledged
to correspond to destructive energies in the self; as he says in the idio-
syncratic "Taneum Creek," in which the decor promises the destruction
of the very consciousness recognizing it as decor, "I am keen to harm."
The only recourse is withdrawal, a poem of five lines which begins "I
don't come here." Or as he says in the characteristically titled "Point No
Point," the claims of the negative produce a dialectical necessity in the
poet, "a need to respond to defeat . . . is heritage":

> *I know a flat and friendless north.*
> *A poem can end there, or a man . . .*

"Stagnant to a Scene of First Defeat" is the merciless title of one of
these poems, which all espouse the longing for change—not for victory
so much as for a wider arena in which the defeat can be staged. The
rivers all tug seaward, the energies drain from the landscape as from a
depleted life; Hugo is quite clear about what happens to the world if
he does not follow "Duwamish, On the Out Tide":

> *I remain. The sun perfects itself*
> *into a moon. Upstream, a headless bear*
> *prays he'll wake one yellow morning*
> *screaming: I am almost clean.*

The petition is for movement, break-up that will bring release: "The
river / full of peeling tugs, drives for the mouth, / a lovely bay . . ."
"My dream," Hugo says in another of these symptomatic accounts
of "our horizon always near and dark," "my dream is of a receptive
east." And the impulse carries him across the country to New York,
past another graveyard (this one in Queens "the morning after a
reading at the YMHA Poetry Center") and down another river to
another sea:

> *. . . Downriver with a clean view*
> *of New York, we see a city hung*
> *from sky, in ways a perfect day.*
> *We leave our land where all doors open out,*
> *Miss Liberty corroded with our green.*

And over that sea to another country. Turning from the familiar—in-
deed, the familial—desolations of the Pacific Northwest which he has
constituted as the grounds for his divorce from himself:

> *In my land only the ignored endure,*
> *the wolverine, nameless streams the State*
> *forgot to dam, ravines*
> *with don't dump signs where citizens*

of ghost towns dump their kissed debris,
sorry for the trash their eyes
will never own . . .

Hugo easily or at least eagerly sees himself in the country of his wartime service, "Italy a land / where all doors open in." Not that it is a place where he will seek to send down roots, or to succeed; success is never Hugo's interest so much as the Stoic effort. In fact, he will peregrinate to Puglia, "where the bomb group was"—manifestly Italy's least successful terrain. After forty years in "a country where we never fail, grow old or die, but simply move unnoticed to the next cold town," the poet readily grasps—and grasps, I think, is the right verb here, something between a gasp and a clutch—the meaning of these bare rocks and barely fertile fields. It is not a meaning comprehended so much as aspired to, and it begins with a disadvantage (of course it does, one is tempted to add: it is the unenviable, the unvisited, even the uninviting which this poet must invest with his own deprivations, his private war): as his ship enters the Palermo harbor, Hugo watches the emotional Sicilian emigrants, home again, and in the face of their ready tears apostrophizes himself:

You can't weep like them, can't pound the rail
with love for this or any land.
You never understood a cloudy north
so how these tears or that syllabic sun?
This rock that came at you for hours
came at others twenty years ago
in dread. You pass the bay
where they invaded, saying it was wrong . . .
                    Learn the names
of streets or give them names to fight.
You have five hours here. If here before
with hate, you walk a street called war
and beg a man who was a beggar then:
now I have no gun, show me how to cry.

Twenty years from the war that dropped him here and half-way round the world from the wild Washington that already draws him home, the displaced poet speculates on the military necessity during a picnic in the Saracen ruins "shaped like a ship," the rubbish of another war, remnants of another invader:

Remember forts at home, thick logs and flints
and photos of the men? Here the pines are thin . . .
Let's take our orange peels home. Those glints
are gulls or rough spots on the sea,

> *and men who can't be photoed must have turned*
> *toward the mountain and the gleaming town,*
> *memorizing nouns and starting up the stone.*

In the diction of these poems of a remembered war, as in the enacted comparison of the classical scenery ("The Bridge of Sighs," "Castel Sant' Angelo") and the cultural sedimentation ("Galileo's Chair," "Bruegel in the Doria") with the uninhabited wreckage, the wreaked havoc of the Pacific Northwest, there is an even clarity about the thing seen:

> *. . . The sky*
> *is yellow, moving right and back*
> *away from fight toward the dark*
> *behind Vesuvius, the private war of sky*
> *always far away from what you are . . .*

and a new completion of rhythms—not easy Frostbitten decasyllabics, but an overcoming of resistance, so that we feel the language of this, Hugo's third book, *Where All Doors Open In*, not running but pressing against the obstacles, on either side, of silence and screaming—an equal weight of tone in the thing said, which could be discovered only in odd lines in *A Run of Jacks:*

> *There is the river, split and yellow*
> *and this far down affected by the tide . . .*

and only in odd poems in *The Death of the Kapowsin Tavern:* "Duwamish Head," "The Anacortes-Sydney Run," "The Squatter on Company Land." In the new Italian poems, of course, the old preoccupations persist (the graveyard where Keats is buried, though "all signs point to Shelley and to Goethe's son") or are prophesied (as in the lament for a wartime comrade "on the Adriatic floor" like the lady "in Kicking Horse Reservoir": both out of reach), but they are joined with a fresh generosity, a distinctness of impulse that is related to, even derived from the poverty of the places: "April in Cerignola," "Spinnazola: Quella Cantina Là," local emanations yet free to be the poet's own. Each poem adds its incisive particulars to the general Stoic wreck, but the conclusive piece, a pendant to "Docking at Naples" and a kind of antiphonal rejoinder to "Sailing to Byzantium" is the last Italian exposure, "Sailing from Naples," a fantasia on all the themes of ignorance and ruin Hugo has been able to afford in his months in "South Italy, remote and stone." With its cautious celebration of human endurance among walls "older than decay," its wary lament for what is ignored:

I was rigid loving what was worn,
land no one would farm, the brown
those buildings had become from threat,
a reek peculiar to defeat.
I was home in ruin . . .

it releases Hugo home "where gulls reappear . . . one by one, white for life, gray for what must be, and unlock the bay . . ." Thus the Italian interval is shown to be a kind of developing-tank for what has been Hugo's all along, and in the latest poems of repatriation he conjugates his themes into their final obsessive twist:

What endures is what we have neglected.

These are reassessments of the Indian graves, the ghost-town binges, the abandoned ranches ("the world discards the world") and the impossible girls—they are also reimmersions in the element that holds not only the lady in the reservoir ("four months of ice will keep you firm") but the poet in his skin:

To live
stay put. The blackfoot, any river
has a million years to lend, and weather's
always wild to look at down the Hellgate—
solid gray forever trailing off white rain.
Our drinks are full of sun. These ageing eagles
climb the river on their own.

Hugo is demonstrably free now to talk about these things without pitying or priding himself upon them or upon his engagement among them—he can speak without giving himself away, and the language he has achieved is one that has worked loose from a local (or provincial) commitment only by being so determined to get down rather than away from what is *there:*

. . . You walk these streets
laid out by the insane, past hotels
that didn't last, bars that did, the tortured try
of local drivers to accelerate their lives . . .

Stevens once said that the poet operates in the flux between the thing as idea and the idea as thing. It is because of his responsibility to the thing as idea, if we understand "thing" as a place, a weather, a man moving through them and keeping his eyes open, that Richard Hugo can render his special justice (which is mercy) to the idea as thing, if we understand "idea" as the recovery of meaning from a world of refusals.

Here is a poet concerned not to console or even sanctify, but merely
—merely!—to make privation credible and therefore rich:

> *Children do not wave as we drive out.*
> *Like these graves ours may go unmarked.*
> *Can we be satisfied when dead*
> *with daffodils for stones? These Indians—*
> *whatever they once loved or used for God—*
> *the hill—the river—the bay burned by the moon—*
> *they knew that when you die you lose your name.*

Good Luck in Cracked Italian by RICHARD HUGO

The Italian interval—wartime service and the return, twenty years
later, to not only the tourist trappings (Keats's grave, Galileo's chair,
Tiberius's cliff) but to horrid Puglia, "a country where we never
fail, / grow old or die, but simply move unnoticed / to the next
cold town"—is shown, in this crisp, level book, to be a kind of de-
veloping-tank for what has been Richard Hugo's negative all along,
enabling him to conjugate his themes into their final, obsessive twist:
"what endures is what we have neglected".

Turning from the desolations of the Pacific Northwest which his
first two books had constituted as the grounds for his divorce from
himself, the poet easily or at least eagerly sees himself back in the
country of his wartime service. Not that he will seek to send down
roots here, or to succeed: success is never Hugo's concern. His con-
cern is the unenviable, the unvisited, even the uninviting, which he
may or must invest with his own deprivations, his own private war.
The distinctness of impulse in the language, the movement organized
in single syllables by the craving mind:

> *I dreamed this coast before Croatia*
> *was a word. Each tree stood alone.*
> *Rocks were darker but the slant of light*
> *across the bleak cliff was the same.*
> *Birds were just that black, the silence*
> *broken by the faint wash of our wake.*
> *That's right, too. The only town was walled . . .*

this credible richness is related to, even derived from, the poverty of
the places, local emanations free (or freed) to be the poet's own.

What startles, then reassures in all this canon of the inconsolable, the unsanctified, the dispossessed, is Hugo's *poetics*, the analogy of language to experience. If significance is to be discovered in a world of refusals, then the method as well as the madness must be policed by the negative, by the demands of resistance overcome, rhythm completed, meaning presumed which we call *form*. It is no accident that we must develop a *negative* in order to produce a true *image*. Neither silence nor screaming would generate this utterance, but merely—merely!—that submission to negation, sacrifice, denial and constraint which makes up the entire justice (and generosity) of prosody. One trusts the veracity of Hugo's stoic despair not because matters veer so mercilessly to the bad, but because the verse is managed, is maneuvered so much to the good. As Valéry reminds us, a man is no poet at all if the difficulties inherent in his art deprive him of what he has to say; Richard Hugo is an important poet because they provide him, rather, a means of saying it.

Poetry, 1971

DONALD JUSTICE

"As the Butterfly Longs for the Cocoon or the Looping Net"

To account for the insistent reticence of this poet, for what he himself, in a characteristic oxymoron, calls "the major resolution of the minor," we must a little recuperate the blurred meaning of elegance—a term very promiscuously accorded these days and very precariously worn—from the original sense of the term itself: a consistent choice of words and their arrangement in the exemplification of a single taste. An American impulse, as it were: from many, one. At the age of forty, Donald Justice had not produced, or at least had not ventured to publish, so *many* poems, perhaps three dozen in his first book, *The Summer Anniversaries* (which was the Lamont Poetry Selection for 1959), and a dozen more in *A Local Storm*, five years later. To pursue the patriotic figure, about as many poems as there are States in the Union. But he has written enough—as there are States enough—for us to collect from the whole sum and tenor of his discourse, as Berkeley would say, a provisional perspective, and the winnowed singleness of that perspective, the unmistakeable and unmistaken unity of an artistic identity, is proof, then, of his elegance, a reminder too that the word glamor, a cheaper sister of elegance in misuse, is merely a Scots corruption of the word grammar:

> *How shall I speak of doom, and ours in special,*
> *But as of something altogether common?*
> *No house of Atreus ours, too humble surely,*
> *The family tree a simple chinaberry*
> *Such as springs up in Georgia in a season.*

(Under it sags the farmer's broken wagon.)
Nor may I laud it much for shade or beauty,
Yet praise that tree for being prompt to flourish,
Spite of the worm and weather out of heaven.

I publish of my folk how they have prospered
With something in the eyes, perhaps inherent,
Or great-winged nose, bespeaking an acquaintance
Not casual and not recent with a monster . . .
Citing, as an example of some courage,
That aunt, long gone, who kept one in a bird-cage
Thirty-odd years in shape of a green parrot,
Nor overcame her fears, yet missed no feeding,
Thrust in the crumbs with thimbles on her fingers.

There is a glamor, certainly, about such poetry: it is there in the voice,
shifting from courtly to country, Southern and soft and just under the
tension of song, in which it is uttered so cunningly:

By seventeen I had guessed
That the "really great loneliness"
Of James's governess
Might account for the ghost
On the other side of the lake . . .

and even so complacently:

Heart, let us this once reason together . . .
An antique, balding spectacle such as thou art,
Affecting still that childish, engaging stammer
With all the seedy innocence of an over-ripe pomegranate!

a voice that has studied, has mastered the cadences of Mr. Ransom, as in
this further bit from the poem I quoted first, "Tales from a Family
Album":

There was a kinsman took up pen and paper
To write our history, whereat he perished,
Calling for water and the holy wafer,
Who had, ere that, resisted much persuasion.

But it is yet a glamor of selfhood, beyond manners, not accountable to
such indenture alone—else we should have to course after too many
masters for it, from Auden:

The danger lies, after all
In being led to suppose—
With Lear—that the wind-dragons

> *Have been let loose to settle*
> *Some private grudge of heaven's.*
> *Still, how nice for our egos!*

or from Ogden Nash, of all people:

> *Meanwhile the petty lord who must have paid*
> *For the artist's trip up from Perugia, for the horse, for the boy, for*
> *everything here, in fact, has been delayed,*
> *Kept too long by his steward, perhaps, discussing*
> *Some business concerning the estate, or fussing*
> *Over the details of his impeccable toilet*
> *With a manservant whose opinion is that any alteration at all would*
> *spoil it . . .*

to William Carlos Williams:

> *Grandeur, it seems,*
> *Comes down to this in the end:*
> *A street of shops*
> *With white shutters*
> *Open for business . . .*

It derives, this glamor of Justice's, not from a red wheelbarrow or from bells for anyone's daughter, but from a special accommodation of the poem's shape and body to its impulse or "message" until nothing remains outside the form, left over to be said in any way *except by the poem itself:* until nothing is epactal. Experience, when judged, arrested, enacted and committed to the language in this indivisible fashion, becomes difficult to discuss, difficult to distinguish apart from the very poems, whose weather and working enforce a finer rehearsal of their "sense" than any paraphrase or reduction. But of course this is generally true of all successful poetry, and if Plotinus is right that criticism is the progressive explication of the implicit, we must be nothing if not critical in precisely the cases where the success is most evident. Moreover, for all the glamor of language which seems to slide these poems off our minds, what must attract us even further into Donald Justice's poetry is that it is alien as well as assimilable to other poetry, that it is autonomous. The differentia are there, are even there in the poems' gist, but I prefer to suggest that they are not thereby essential just because we can detach them—merely detachable. It will be *more* interesting to trace this elegant idiosyncrasy in what are mostly regarded as the poem's means and machinery, its joints and surfaces, though I suppose it is interesting enough, even so, to remark that what we must put up with here is a poetry *about* the mind's circular movement, its apprehension of an imprisonment within itself, and *about* the impoverishment of the world as a consequence of this servitude. So much for the message, then, as a sop to Plotinus, let us say; to find the means of a poetry is a surer step toward finding its real message, we suspect, and cherish an ignorance of "subject," an ignorance that is likely to be as illuminating as any knowledge we have already or are likely to come by. To the means, then, the pulleys, cranks and motors that keep the message running. It is no accident, indeed it is a necessity that Donald Justice writes so many sestinas, for this is a strict form that bends the poem's motion, that binds and braids into a halter the poet's impulse to run away with himself in all directions; what satisfies and even delights about Donald Justice's sestinas is that they are invented by their "sense"; called into being by their burden, they are inevitable and necessary emanations of entrapment. Poems about circuit and constraint, whose forced conclusions can be unpeeled like a great onion of foreclosures:

> *There is no way to ease the burden.*
> *The voyage leads on from harm to harm,*
> *A land of others and of silence.*

That is the final stanza of one, with all six terminal words; another:

> *Round me they circle on the hill.*
> *But what is wrong with my friends' faces?*
> *Why have they changed that way to wood?*

But perhaps the most astonishing and original of them all is the one called "The Metamorphosis," a decorously Southern Gothic narrative of a man proceeding homeward through an emblematic landscape of mortal encroachment:

> *Past Mr. Raven's tavern*
> *Up Cemetery Hill*
> *Around by the Giant Oak*
> *And Drowning Creek gone dry*
> *Into the Hunting Woods*
> *And that was how he went . . .*

and finally thrusting his key into the lock six stanzas on, only to be held fast, confiscated by the nameless horror that he finds in his own hall:

> *Then bent he to the keyhole*
> *Nor might his eyes withdraw*
> *The while the hall unwound*
> *That thing which afterwards*
> *No man should know or its like*
> *Whether dead or living.*

But the transformation has occurred not only in the subject, as recorded or remarked by the natural terrors of this moralized landscape: "Then owls cried out from the woods," the following hound "moaned and whined / as she some fit were having"; and not only in the grave and practiced saraband of the sestina's actual structure, the last word of the first stanza's last line becoming the last word of the second stanza's first line and so on; but in the very metamorphosis of the six words themselves on which the sestina is built, so that the first stanza's "tavern" passes through "heaven," "haven," "having," and "heaving" before it becomes "living" in the last, and the other five teleutons undergo a similar process, snared yet in the pitiless rhythm of their exchanges. Everything is the same and yet is utterly different: that is the terror of "The Metamorphosis," and it is accomplished, enacted, perpetuated by the poem's formal will as by its subject or story. The nightmare is derived, in fact, from the daylight means of existence, as the transformed words are derived from the initial set: and that is Donald Justice's whole object and outrage in the rest of his poems.

For example, the rondeau "Women in Love" perfectly exemplifies the paralyzing effect of feeling it discusses—"they cannot stay or go" —by its formal necessities, the three rhyme words on two rhymes and the six recurring lines out of thirteen; so that the poem's ultimate meaning is, and is only—its actual form:

> *It always comes, and when it comes they know.*
> *To will it is enough to bring them there.*
> *The knack is this, to fasten and not let go.*
>
> *Their limbs are charmed; they cannot stay or go.*
> *Desire is limbo: they're unhappy there.*
> *It always comes, and when it comes they know.*
>
> *Their choice of hells would be the one they know.*
> *Dante describes it, the wind circling there,*
> *The knack is this, to fasten and not let go.*
>
> *The wind carries them where they want to go,*
> *Yet it seems cruel to strangers passing there.*
> *It always comes, and when it comes they know*
> *The knack is this, to fasten and not let go.*

Take a further instance, neither narrative nor analytic this time, but stating a kind of artistic credo. In the little poem called "Thus," in two stanzas, the description of a piece of music, a theme and variations, is undertaken in the first eight lines—key, character, mode and orchestration are announced; in the second eight-line strophe, the same teleutons are employed, though the meaning of the words is altered in every particular by the statements, even by the rhythms, in which they occur. So that where the first group concluded:

> . . . *As for the theme,*
> *There being but the one, with variations,*
> *Let it be spoken outright by the oboe*
> *Without apology of any string,*
> *But as a man speaks, openly, his heart*
> *Among old friends, let this be spoken.*

the second takes up the strain metamorphically:

> . . . *It would do certain violence to our theme.*
> *Therefore see to it that the variations*
> *Keep faith with the plain statement of the oboe.*
> *Entering quietly, let each chastened string*
> *Repeat the lesson she must get by heart,*
> *And without overmuch adornment.*

Abruptly, it is the final word, "adornment," that breaks the form, the sequence—of course, one almost adds. The adornment is the variation, and how else, *where* else might it occur? The congruence, then, the mutual mirroring of means and meaning in this poetry is precisely the glamor of Donald Justice's art, and if it makes, in its stern demands, for the relatively few poems in his canon, it must also be held responsible for their elegant necessity.

In an essay on Karl Shapiro's anti-poem *The Bourgeois Poet,* Donald Justice once said that he liked best those parts which were at once wildest and most formal, "surely a winning combination," as he put it then. And even more suggestively, in the preface to his edition of the poems of Weldon Kees, Justice speaks of being original "in one of the few ways that matter" as a question of a "particular tone of voice, one we have never heard before." Bearing in mind the fierce adequacy of this poet's performance to his purposes, the inextricability of formal pattern and wild theme, I should like a little more emphasis on that tone of voice in which we may hear his poems. I mentioned above the gist of these half-a-hundred poems as being, when logically arrayed, the self's apprehension of its own duress and bondage to its own instruments, and the consequent despoiling of the physical world: a void at the center which causes a curling of the edges, so to speak. There would seem to be a tradition, or at least a convention, in lyric poetry for dealing with a world thus enchanted, thus held in thrall, and it is this conventional tone which releases Donald Justice's "particular" gentle and ruinous tone of voice, "humbly aspiring" as James Dickey says, but aspiring to apocalypse out of a frenzy with mortality, aspiring to extirpate everything that might stand between the naked self and the absolute—which is not humble. We may trace the articulation of such a convention for dealing with enchantment, in this century, in poems by De La Mare, by Graves, by Yeats before 1916, by Frost and Ransom in America; the decorum of this kind of poetry admits of sharp observation, but not much experiment or originality with the tools of that observation, either words or senses. The language of this poetry is one already received by poets, not invented to satisfy new needs (which is why we must except the later Yeats from this group). There is, for instance, a direct and admirable succession—though I think no immediate influence—linking these "Bells" by De La Mare:

> *I saw a ploughman with his team*
> *Lift to the bells and fix on them*
> *His distant eyes, as if he would*
> *Drink in the utmost sound he could!*
> *While near him sat his children three,*
> *And in the green grass placidly*
> *Played undistracted on, as if*
> *What music earthly bells might give*
> *Could only faintly stir their dream,*
> *And stillness make more lovely seem.*

to these "Belles," without the period inversions, by Justice:

> *They lean upon their windows. It is late.*
> *Already it is twilight in the house;*
> *Autumn is in their eyes. Twilit, autumnal—*
> *Thus they regard themselves. What vanities!*
> *As if all nature were a looking-glass*
> *To publish the small features of their ruin!*
> *Each evening at their windows they arrive*
> *As in anticipation of farewells,*
> *Though they would be still lingering if they could,*
> *Weary, yet ever restless for the dance . . .*

The next two lines, with their allusions to the fairy-tale, clinch the resemblance to the poet of *Peacock Pie:*

> *Old Cinderellas, hearing midnight strike,*
> *The mouse-drawn coach impatient at the door.*

but it is the rhetoric of the ruined self, or at least of the self incarcerated, that is more strictly analogous to De La Mare than even the nursery-rhyme trope. The more dramatic poems in *A Local Storm* extend the range of this rhetoric:

> *Meanwhile they quarrel and make it up,*
> *Only to quarrel again. A sudden storm*
> *Pulls the last fences down. The stupid sheep*
> *Stand out all night now coughing in the garden*
> *And peering through the windows where they sleep.*

and the final one in this pamphlet makes the tone itself into a kind of *ars poetica:*

> *. . . it would be too late:*
> *The artist will have had his revenge for being made to wait,*
> *A revenge not only necessary but right and clever—*
> *Simply to leave him out of the scene forever.*

But though Donald Justice has made it reach farther than the sleeping princess and the broken tower, the rhetoric of enchantment is always the same, consonant with Stendhal's remark that "one must write with equal application at all times"—when one is always in the same fix, I should add. There is a deep, committed reverence about the way Justice celebrates his defeats: madness, love, old age, death—in all, the violence, the wildness is inside, working outwards, showing up the world in a reluctant, leave-taking light, either in the mode of the times:

> *Jane looks down at her organdy skirt*
> *As if it somehow were the thing disgraced*
> *For being there, on the floor, in the dirt . . .*

or in the mode of the timeless:

> *Weary the soldiers go, and come back weary,*
> *Up a green hill and down the withered hill,*
> *And Jack from Joan, and they shall never marry . . .*

But given such a burden altogether, and such a resonance, and such a claim on the coincidence of the will's rhetoric and the world's wreck, the wonder is not that Donald Justice had written, for his forty years and his book and a half, only fifty poems, but that we have an elegant monument of fifty such poems to testify to his doomed transactions with life:

> *The aging magician retired to his island.*
> *It was not so green as he remembered,*
> *Nor did the sea caress its headlands*
> *With the customary nuptial music.*

He did not mind . . .

. . .

If now it was all to do again,
Nothing lacked to his purpose, only

Some change in the wording of the charm,
Some slight reshuffling of negative
And verb, perhaps—that should suffice.
So, so. Meanwhile he paced the strand,

Debating, as old men will, with himself
Or the waves, though as it was the sea
Seemed only to go on washing and washing
Itself, as if to be clean of something.

In 1967 a dozen poems from the pamphlet *A Local Storm* were added to another twenty-five written since 1963; the new book, *Night Light*, is for the most part a matter of what Justice's Prospero discovers his future to be in the fragment just quoted: "some slight reshuffling of negative and verb, perhaps" to produce "some change in the wording of the charm"—the charm, one notices, remaining the same in either sense ("he did not mind if . . . it was all to do again"). The illumination of *Night Light*, insofar as it is not merely reflected from an earlier achievement, is low indeed, a blue glow which if not fitful nonetheless emits as well a kind of vexed buzz close to the fretful; as Justice says in "The Thin Man":

I indulge myself
in rich refusals.
Nothing suffices.

I hone myself to
This edge. Asleep, I
Am a horizon.

The little lines with their rhythm of carping speech seem to be all the poet can afford, and it is remarkable, in fact, how richly he can make them work for him, or at least how readily recall the splendors that once were in his grasp: "the dream . . . repeats, / and you must wake again to your own blood / and empty spaces in the throat." The book moves from the galled expectation of song, "Orpheus Opens His Morning Mail," to the complacencies of "Narcissus at Home": "Alone at last! But I am forgetting myself . . ." And surely that is the progress, from a myth of effective music to one of self-satisfied musing, which

Justice wishes us to trace. The obsessive imagery is indeed one of mirrors: in "Men at Forty"

> *. . . deep in mirrors*
> *They rediscover*
> *The face of the boy . . .*

and in "The Missing Person"

> *. . . in the mirror*
> *He sees what is missing*
>
> *It is himself*
> *He sees there emerging*
>
> *Slowly, as from the dark*
> *Of a furnished room . . .*

and in "For the Suicides of 1962"

> *. . . Even*
> *Those mirrors, to which always*
>
> *You must have turned to confide,*
> *Cannot have recognized you,*
> *Stripped, as you were, finally . . .*

and in "The Tourist from Syracuse"

> *. . . Mine is the face which blooms in*
> *The dark mirrors of washrooms*
> *As you grope for the light switch . . .*

and finally, most frankly, in "Poem for a Survivor":

> *Holding this poem*
> *Close, like a mirror,*
> *I breathe upon it . . .*

and elsewhere the pervasive narcissism is merely adulterated, not exorcized, by occasional gestures to the outside world:

> *As though the simple*
> *Death of a pet cat,*
> *Buried with flowers,*
>
> *Had brought to the porch*
> *Some rumor of storms*
> *Dying out over*
> *A dark Atlantic.*

The negatives reshuffled are indeed those of a consciousness held captive in the impounding self and which, being conscious, knows that it is a captive, *captivated* in precisely the sense or the two senses that Narcissus is subject to himself. Donald Justice perpetuates his powers, however low the wattage, by taking leave of them, and in the characteristically titled "Man Closing Up" offers at least his warrantable intentions for the enterprise:

> *He wants to keep the light going,*
> *If he can.*

After the initial statement, in all its elegant postures, of the withdrawn consciousness, of the indentured ego, writing poetry is now a continuous farewell tour of duty ("the rhythms, the meters, how they paralyze"), and as the poet himself manfully asserts, in an otherwise peevish apostrophe to his own early poems,

> *Now the long silence. Now the beginning again.*

Departures by DONALD JUSTICE

We live in the past because there is nothing else to live in; our relation to the present is asymptotic—we are forever approaching a point, a moment, a limit which we recognize as what gives us life, yet we can make nothing of it, do nothing with it, until it is out of our hands, literally out of our senses. Asymptotes are what fail to fall together (as *symptoms* do), and it is interesting, in considering Donald Justice's later poetry, to notice that the Greek verb for falling is akin to the Greek verb for flying: here is a poet who perpetuates his powers by taking leave of them, "patient," as he says, "and, if anything, somewhat reluctant to continue." Even the epigraph of the wonderfully titled *Departures* sounds the tonality—calculated, wounded, gorgeous in that it is full of gorges, lapses, holes—which we will hear in the last line of the book, consistent from the "still slowly diminishing echo" to "everything going away in the night again and again."

If everything goes away *again and again*, there must be a time when it comes back—and that is the present, the difficult Now to which Justice keeps making an asymptote, a reconnaissance. His preoccupation is, in every sense, with *tense*, as when he so characteristically observes: "the typewriter will be glad to have become the poem"—the future and the past conjugated in order to reach the Present, Justice's Muse, a goddess to be worshipped in absentia, "the

more beautiful, especially when suppressed." As we remember from
Night Light, suppression is a significant way of making room for
possibility in this poet's work, though of course it is the possibility of
farewells that is thus lodged in the language. "You have begun to
vanish . . . " and again, "our cries diminish behind us"—all of these
stabs at what Justice calls "the promised absence" are so many
"furtive illuminations" of his theme, which is given in one of his
most striking titles, "An Elegy is Preparing Itself", *i.e.*, I am alive.

Life's best means of articulating an advance upon the present is
that peculiarly native constructive, the gerundive phrase, the ultimate
asymptote: "my place in line *is evaporating*", Justice observes drily,
or again, apostrophizing stars "that fade and *are fading*, but never
entirely fading . . ." In these poems, for all their exactitude and
their exactions (Justice is not easy—he is determined about his asymp-
tote: "the address if not the destination"), nothing is either here and
now, or everything is there and then. The utterance is suffused, is
soaked with process, unable to initiate being, and unable to call a
halt ("Is that a scar, or a birthmark?", the 19th question suggests
Justice's uncertainty about beginnings and ends). These poems—odes,
by title, elegies, fragments, questions, white notes, notebooks, riddles,
variations, homages—are "shaken with premonitions of a time when
they will have begun to stop," and indeed such shaking affords them
their rhythm, their breath, their aspiration to movement. Death is
"still to be escaped from," even as one of Justice's heroines feels life
"closing about her now": here is a delicate dialectic between calligra-
phy ("most beautiful in its erasures") and cancellation ("eventual
flame, some final smoke"), where the usual signs attached to remem-
bering and forgetting are reversed; in Justice's poetry now, the posi-
tive value is not attached to what is "already falling away, already
in memory," but rather to what is not yet experience, "a poem in
hiding . . . the unfolding page": it is the "absent flowers abound-
ing" he cultivates, for the actual ones, as Mallarmé knew, are erased
by words, by recall . . . The last two poems in the book, "Ab-
sences" and "Presences" trade places with each other over and over
again, and we never know, in these "bleached mirrors," where we
stand. It is not indeed a matter of standing, of *instances*, that Donald
Justice affords us, but a manner of *ecstasy*, the lunge for the present,
the ablation of ontology, the denial of likeness, for as the master
whom he so lovingly chides, and so challengingly lionizes—as the
greatest actuary of them all remarked, "identity is the vanishing
point of resemblance." There are many deprecations in this little
book, many withdrawals and tergiversations, but what matters is
material: some of the most assured, elegant and heartbreaking—not
broken, but breaking—verse in our literature so far.

GALWAY KINNELL

"Everything That May Abide the Fire Was Made to Go Through the Fire."

W HEN WE SPEAK, as in criticism we are bound and determined
to do, of a man's *poetry*, we do a certain fond injustice to his
poems. As readers, as men ourselves, it is our duty to acknowledge the
supremacy of the poem not only over the poet *—our literary experi-
ence has taught us to suspect biography, to scorn the equation of soul
with sonnet that would enable an Albert Schweitzer to write good ones
and even *oblige* a Swinburne to have written bad ones—but over
poetry itself. For the language speaks misleadingly of *poetry in gen-
eral;* the word "poetry" refers poetic works to a form—ideal or
abstract—which transcends in order to explain them, in order to judge
them. This is not the case; the poem does not look to Poetry as to a
power which is anterior to it and from which it must await its
justification or even its existence. The poem is not the glow reflected
from a constant star, it is not even the momentary manifestation of a
power always superior to its works. To understand that the poem is the
creative instrument, the primary force of discovery, is to understand
that what is general depends on what is unique. A man's poetry, then,
comes after the fact—the fact of his poems—and there is always
something a little painful, a little patronizing in our collections of
evidence, from a man's victories over the silence (or over speech, as the
case may be, and was for Swinburne himself), toward that serene and
uncontested unity: the poetry of, say, Galway Kinnell. If a poem, as

* "Perhaps a certain contempt for poetry," Galway Kinnell remarks of Villon's
status as the prototype of the *poète maudit*, "is behind a preoccupation with a
poet's life."

Char once said, detaches itself convulsively from the world's body, then it is our task to account for the withdrawal symptoms.

Yet the reader, even the critical reader, is faced with the paradox of coming only *after* the poem that comes *before* the Poetry. He cannot help seeing chiefly its engagements with the past—the past of the poet, and the past of all poetry. Of course it is because there is the poem that, for the poet, the future is possible—the poem is that movement toward what does not yet exist and, still more, the ecstasy of what is not granted, the appropriation of a mere possibility. But it is because there is Poetry, on the other hand, that the past is available to us as readers, as critics; and if I indulge a certain guilt upon instancing what the poetry of Galway Kinnell amounts to, if I admit that I am neglecting a little the travail of his poems in order to account for the triumph of his poetry, the culpability of my admission is relieved though not excused because, as a critic, I am committed to the past, the past which accommodates the existence of all of a man's poems taken together—as his poetry—rather than to the present which accommodates the existence of one poem, the poem I am reading (the domain, too, of the teacher), and rather than to the future which is enabled by the writing of the new poem (the domain of the poet alone).

The poetry of Galway Kinnell, then, is an Ordeal by Fire. It is fire which he invokes to set forth his plight, to enact his ordeal, and to restore himself to reality. It is fire—in its constant transformations, its endless resurrection—which *is* reality, for Kinnell as for Heraclitus: "The world is an ever-living fire, with measures of it kindling and measures of it going out." As the American poet translates this, it becomes:

> *And in the sky there burns this shifty jellyfish*
> *That degenerates and flashes and re-forms.*

And just as the pre-Socratic had affirmed that "all things are an exchange for fire, and fire for all things," so Kinnell muses, in his broken, aphoristic way that has so many analogies with the Greek's:

> *The invisible life of the thing*
> *Goes up in flames that are invisible*
> *Like cellophane burning in the sunlight.*
>
> *It burns up. Its drift is to be nothing.*
>
> *In its covertness it has a way*
> *Of uttering itself in place of itself . . .*

Yet there is a terrible and tremendous inflection in Galway Kinnell's
pyromania, which we shall trace out in a moment, that altogether
transforms his impulse from the orphic pitilessness of Heraclitus.
When the Greek says "Fire in its advance will judge and convict all
things," there is awe but no tragedy in it, for there is no belief in
incarnation. But when Kinnell evokes mortality as a commitment to the
fire, there is an unappeasable grief in his "heart's hell": it is the grief of
history, the pain of things happening once and once only, irreversibly,*
that is the burden of Christianity, of the Incarnation:

> . . . *It is true*
> *That only flesh dies, and spirit flowers without stop*
> *For men, cows, dung, for all dead things; and it is good, yes—*
>
> *But an incarnation is in particular flesh*
> *And the dust that is swirled into a shape*
> *And crumbles and is swirled again had but one shape*
> *That was this man. When he is dead the grass*
> *Heals what he suffered, but he remains dead,*
> *And the few who loved him know this until they die.*

Between Heraclitus, then, and Kinnell the agonized Believer who
remarks, in *Black Light,* of his abject hero: "It was as if his virtue, his
very devotion to God, were succeeding where vice had failed, in
making an atheist out of him"—the proper mediator, the exegetical
figure that will set us coursing over Kinnell's burning landscape in
search of clues to the resurrection is, of course, Hopkins, the Hopkins
who in his sonnet "That Nature is a Heraclitean Fire and of the
comfort of the Resurrection" watched while "Million-fueled nature's
bonfire burns on" and declared that the "world's wildfire leaves but
ash / in a flash, at a trumpet's crash." ** The agony of that knowledge
—the knowledge or at least the conviction that all must be consumed in
order to be reborn, must be reduced to ash in order to be redeemed—
gives Galway Kinnell's poetry its astonishing resonance, the accents of
a conflict beyond wisdom as it is beyond piety: "I don't know what
you died of," one of the characters in his novel says, "whatever it was,
that is what will bring you alive again."

---

* Kinnell dramatizes this situation, the suffering brought about by Nature's
irreversibility, in his novel *Black Light:* "He looked at the leaves again. How
would it be, he thought, if one of them, even an unimportant one, should wither
of its own free will and creep back into the limb?"

** One of the opening poems in Kinnell's first book takes for its title the
dedication of Hopkins' "Windhover": "To Christ Our Lord," and the poem ends
with a characteristic Hopkins vision of "inscape":

> *Then the Swan spread her wings, cross of the cold north,*
> *The pattern and mirror of the acts of earth.*

Before collecting our evidences of arson, it might be well to account for the use of quotations from *all* of Kinnell's works indifferently: the three volumes of poetry, *What a Kingdom It Was* (1960), *Flower Herding on Mount Monadnock* (1964), and *Body Rags* (1968), the translation of the poems of François Villon, with an Introduction (1965), and the short novel or *récit*, *Black Light* (1966). Kinnell is one of those writers insistently present in all his forms, and therefore unlikely to discriminate powerfully among them: his poetry has, as noted, a jagged aphoristic thrust without much patience for rhythmic consecution or, after the first poems, for regularity of rhyme. The prose, on the other hand, is heavy with hypnotic cadences, and likely to be the vehicle for a more evidently "poetic" manner than Kinnell will permit himself in his verse: "that is the way with poetry," he remarks in the novel: "when it is incomprehensible it seems profound, and when you do understand it, it is only ridiculous." I take my license to look beyond any formal enclosure for the revealing utterance from Kinnell himself, then, who in presenting his plain version of Villon, without rhyme or regular meters, observes: "It may be that in our day these formal devices have become a dead hand, which it is just as well not to lay on any poetry." Upon such suspicion may be based a highly various practice, as is the case with Kinnell's work—it is not a body of work susceptible of too intent a formal scrutiny. Let us recall merely that, as in his efforts with Villon, Kinnell is concerned "to keep the poetry factual, harsh and active."

The fire opens Kinnell's first book, where it is seen benevolently enough as the vital energy of earthly things:

> *Cold wind stirs, and the last green*
> *Climbs to all the tips of the season, like*
> *The last flame brightening on a wick.*
> *Embers drop and break in sparks . . .*

The sense of the self-consuming candle as the characteristic avatar of flame is one that will remain with Kinnell to the end—as in *Black Light*, where he speaks, about to blow out the candle, of "the point of the flame, that shifting instant where the flame was turning into pure spirit." Even in this early poem, "First Communion," the fire is seen not only as vital impulse, but as the agent of transmutation, the "last flame" moving up the wick of the trees until they are burnt away to "pure spirit." Then comes the poem called "Burning," the anecdote of a man of the woods who kills the dog that has saved him from drowning, buries it, and goes back into his shack to sleep, leaving the speaker to watch:

I saw him sleepless in the pane of glass
Looking wild-eyed at sunset, then the glare
Blinded the glass—only a red square
Burning a house burning in the wilderness.

Here the notion of the universal conflagration is more subtly diffused, not only in the sunset that gives all things fire's color ("a red square burning a house burning"), but in the particulars of aberrant human conduct ("a house burning in the wilderness")—it is the man inside, his conscience and his craziness, that are given the appropriate outer emblem by the setting sun reflected on the glass. Between this poem and the next to rehearse Kinnell's fiery theme, intervene a pair of studies in primitivism, "The Wolves" and "Westport," where life's cautery is only obliquely touched on—shooting buffalo in the days of the great herds ("I fired . . . He looked, trotted off, and became dead"), and the look of the land after a storm ("a red streak in the west lit all the raindrops . . . and the shining grasses were bowed towards the west as if one craving had killed them"). It is of course the craving of fire, as murderous as any gunpowder, that Kinnell sees in the west; in a further poem, "Lilacs," he sees that craving not only in the sun's red decline, but in the day's very warmth:

. . . Down the south slope
A bitch stretched, and swaths of fierce lilacs
Opened astonishing furnaces of scent . . .

. . . The blossoms climbed
And blazed in the air . . .

The nuance of sexuality is added to the mere growth of animals and plants, and in this poem the woman subject to the "burning" lilacs, "her dry legs crackling in darkness," is drawn into the universal fire, "the hot scent of herself beating herself out of closets in the well-governed flesh." The recognition of sensual riot, "the nestfire of roses," is another emblem of destruction for Kinnell, one that will obsess him in later work. But at this point in his first book, he is concerned to come, still, to terms with his given faith: in "Easter," one of Kinnell's most successful poems in his earlier, "formal" manner, the death of a nurse, "raped, robbed, weighted, drowned," is conjugated with the Easter service, "the extensive sermon, the outcry of the inaudible prayer"; speculating on the rotting body, "trapped or working loose," and on the mystery of Christ's rising, the poet promises to crown the victim with an "Easter Fire" as the "brown water shoves [her] senselessly on past smoking cities, works of disaster"; he urges her to turn her "unwavering gaze" on "the dream you lived through":

> *It is as you thought. The living burn.*
> *In the floating days may you discover grace.*

Life is just that continuous conflagration ("the smoking cities") which it is Christianity's effort to transcend by a final "Easter Fire." The beautiful, tentative last line ("In the floating days . . .") of this carefully joined poem suggests, though, that no such glory waits for us, victims rather than victors of death this Easter. *The living burn*, and the dead, if they are lucky, merely dissolve.

That vision of burning and drowning together is extended in "Alewives Pool," which begins:

> *We lay on the grass and gazed down and heard*
> *The world burning on the pulse of April . . .*

and which ends with an eloquent vision of the possibilities of transfiguration, once the mortal flesh has been consumed away by the processes of life itself:

> *In the trees even the birds are astonished*
> *By the fierce passion of their song. The mind*
> *Can only know what love has accomplished*
> *When love has consumed it in the burning pond.*
>
> *Now on the trembling pulse let death and birth*
> *Beat in the self as in the April grass—*
> *The sudden summer that the air flames forth*
> *Makes us again into its blossomers—*
> *Stand on the pulse and love the burning earth.*

The ecstasy of knowing oneself a part of the world's *physis*, of knowing that within oneself there is the same pulse on which "the world burns," the radiant interchange between mind and love, between body and earth, between water and fire, is here registered in Kinnell's happiest key, when Being is so wrought up in its oneness of possibilities —"the air flames forth"—that a man's "days to come flood on his heart as if they were his past."

It is an easier thing, I suppose, merely to report the world in conflagration without insisting on an engagement of identity, without being rigorously *in question*. Easier or not—and in any case, the act of *seeing* the world as on fire, consuming itself away to a transfigured life, is certainly an involvement of a heroic order—some of the "nature poems" of this book have allowed Kinnell a delicacy in his art that he shrinks from when his persona is committed. "Leaping Falls," an account of a frozen cascade, reveals the diction of a poet who can, when he chooses, enact by the movement of language on the lips and in

the mind the very transaction—distinct yet expanding, icy yet intense
—he would rehearse in vision:

> *. . . A topmost icicle came loose*
> *And fell, and struck another*
> *With a bell-like sound, and*
> *Another, and the falls*
> *Leapt at their ledges, ringing*
> *Down the rocks and on each other*
>
> *Like an outbreak of bells*
> *That rings and ceases.*
> *The silence turned around*
> *And became silence again.*
> *Under the falls on the snow*
> *A twigfire of icicles burned pale blue.*

There is a wonderful play of contraries here, sound and silence, liquid
and solid, heat and freezing, ice and flame—but they are resolved in a
place beyond contraries, at a moment of vision, and at that moment the
"fire of icicles burned pale blue." It is the ecstatic moment the surreal-
ists were always trying for, when the conventional notions of opposites
no longer stood opposed, but worked toward a transcendence where
up and down, hot and cold, stillness and motion ceased to gainsay each
other, and a man's existence glowed into a kind of godhead—this is
what Kinnell means, or it is one of the things he means, by "burning."

Of course he is easier about it than that, sometimes; sometimes it is
merely a notation of intensity he wishes to record, existence not
transfigured, but merely heightened:

> *. . . the duck took off,*
> *Skimmed the swells as it ascended,*
> *Brown wings burning and flashing*
> *In the sun as the sea it rose over*
> *Burned and flashed beneath it.*

Yet if this is not a major instance of Kinnell's igneous reading of the
world, it is significant that the conjugation of water and fire is here
enlarged from the alewives pool and the frozen falls to the sea itself
that is said to burn. It is as though the poet were reaching for
Heraclitus' great truth, as he enlarged his focus like a burning glass:
"The transformations of Fire are, first of all, the sea . . ." reads one of
the Heraclitean fragments, and in Kinnell's second book, one of his
most arresting poems—a kind of nature-log, "Tilamook Journal," in
which the poet stares at "the Burn as it went out in the twilight, its
crags broken, its valleys soaked in night"—comes to its triumphant

conclusion: "It is only steps to the unburnable sea." Unburnable because it is the one thing that cannot be transformed, being already all transformation. Unburnable because it is always burning.

But to continue with *What a Kingdom It Was*, and Kinnell's fire sermon as he develops it, poem by poem: one of the most ambitious poems in the collection, "Seven Streams of Nevis," memorializes seven ruined lives the poet invokes as he climbs Ben Nevis. Speaking of one of these friends, Sir Henry, Kinnell observes that he

> *Decided fire brings out the best*
> *In things, and that anyone who*
> *Has cooked his eyes at the sunrise*
> *Of beauty, and thumbed himself blind, is wise.*

Though merely a characterization, we have had enough clues from the poet to take such wisdom to heart. Especially when, on the top of the mountain, in one of those moments where contraries are resolved,

> *Where merely to be still was temperate,*
> *Where to move was brave, where justice was a glide,*
> *Knowledge the dissolving of the head-hung eyes;*
> *There my faith lay burning, there my hope*
> *Lay burning on the water, there charity*
> *Burned like a sun.*

So even the theological virtues are seen enkindled, sun and water united in the same drastic combustion: "In the heart's hell you have it; call it God's Love." And in the last and longest poem in the book, "The Avenue Bearing the Initial of Christ into the New World," where Kinnell turns on New York's Lower East Side the incandescent scrutiny of a visionary, the religious tenor of the burning is given its most explicit, almost ritual voice. After a few decorative notes, like describing the pushcart vegetables in terms of his old antinomies: "Icicle-shaped carrots that through black soil wove away like flames in the sun"—Kinnell warms to his theme:

> *Children set fires in ashbarrels,*
> *Cats prowl the fires, scraps of fishes burn.*
>
> *A child lay in the flames.*
> *It was not the plan. Abraham*
> *Stood in terror at the duplicity.*
> *Isaac whom he loved lay in the flames . . .*
>
> *The children laugh.*
> *Isaac means he laughs.*

> *Maybe the last instant*
> *The dying itself, is easier . . .*

Only the pain of such sacrifice, here in "the living streets, where instants of transcendence drift in oceans of loathing and fear," can redeem the Fallen City,

> *Burning in the night, flames opening out like*
> *Eyelashes from the windows . . .*
>   *But this evening*
> *The neighborhood comes out again, everything*
> *That may abide the fire was made to go through the fire*
> *And it was made clean.*

From there, the poem goes on in an ecstasy of accountability, for whatever Kinnell sees—and he sees everything:

> *The garbage disposal truck*
> *Like a huge hunched animal*
> *That sucks in garbage in the place*
> *Where other animals evacuate it*
> *Whines, as the cylinder in the rear*
> *Threshes up the trash and garbage,*
> *Where two men in rubber suits*
> *(It must be raining outside)*
> *Heap it in. The groaning motor*
> *Rises in a whine as it grinds in*
> *The garbage, and between-times*
> *Groans. It whines and groans again . . .*
> *If it is raining outside*
> *You can tell only by looking*
> *In puddles, under the lifted streetlamps.*
> *It would be the spring rain.*

—has gone through that refining fire, has been *made clean.* By his ransacked, purified, literally inflamed imagination, Kinnell is able to ransom his world, having reached in his most sustained effort that place where everything which is is blessed.

It is no easy thing to write a sequel to the apocalypse, and one feels, often, about Kinnell's second book, *Flower Herding on Mount Monadnock*, something of the strain, the broken impulse that commands the versification as well as the patchy moments of pyrophany. The moments come, though; after a pair of grim poems on the port of New York, "The River That Is East" and "The Homecoming of Emma Lazarus," Kinnell turns to the Statue of Liberty itself:

> *The Lady stands by herself*
> *Her electrical hand on fire . . .*
> *. . . her hand, burning,*
> *Hair, flesh, blood, bone.*

Facing the Old World, the statue burns, an emblem of the Redeemed City, though only an emblem—"it fades, and the wounds of all we had accepted open." The theme returns, each time "the sun's swath of reality" falls "on the objects of faith, buildings, rocks, birds, oranges" —returns, for example, in Kinnell's tribute to Robert Frost, which begins with the natural world, "a farm, a countryside, a woodpile in its slow smokeless burning," as the poet of "Fire and Ice" had put it, and moves to a vision of Frost himself

> *Who dwelt in access to that which other men*
> *Have burnt all their lives to get near . . .*

acknowledging that there is a point of the flame to which we aspire, a point where all that is "vain" is refined away, and the flame "turns into pure spirit":

> *. . . And from the same doorway*
> *At which you lived, between the house and the woods,*
> *We see your old footprints going away across*
> *The great Republic, Frost, up memorized slopes,*
> *Down hills floating by heart on the bulldozed land.*

There follow, as if like Frost this poet would "set up in the wilderness of his country," a considerable number of poems of the woods, where the "junco flames up from the junkpile" and life consumes itself. As in his more violent vision of the transfigured city, Kinnell sees the natural world redeemed ("the song of the whippoorwill stops and the dimension of depth seizes everything"), and of course it is redeemed by fire, though a slower fire, not one that must be kindled in pain and sacrifice, but consented to as a natural process:

> *I wake in the night,*
> *An old ache in the shoulder blades.*
> *I lie amazed under the trees*
> *That creak a little in the dark,*
> *The giant trees of the world.*
>
> *I lie on earth the way*
> *Flames lie in the woodpile . . .*

Holding up a shell, "fan of gold light," to the sun, the poet sees "as it blazes, the lost life within, alive again in the fate-shine." These are the moments of sanctity, a kind of Godless stigmatization as the poet looks and listens:

> *Turning and craning in the vines*
> *I can make out through the leaves*
> *The old, shimmering nothingness, the sky.*

By the time he gets to the title poem at the end of this short book, Kinnell has earned for himself what he says of Villon in the introduction to his "factual, harsh, and active" version: "He writes in a passion for reality and a deep anguish at its going . . . it is a cry not only over the brevity of existence and the coming of dark, but also over this dying life, this life so horrified by death and so deeply in need of it." In the final section of "Flower Herding," a ten-part journal of natural devotions, Galway Kinnell makes his penultimate accommodation of the life that is being consumed in the fire—it is an accommodation so transfigured that it can be expressed, finally, in a few simple declarative sentences, the ecstatic constatation of the death that is in being, the being that is in death:

> *In the forest I discover a flower.*
>
> *The invisible life of the thing*
> *Goes up in flames that are invisible*
> *Like cellophane burning in the sunlight.*
>
> *It burns up. Its drift is to be nothing.*
>
> *In its covertness it has a way*
> *Of uttering itself in place of itself,*
> *Its blossoms claim to float in the Empyrian,*
>
> *A wrathful presence on the blur of the ground.*
>
> *The appeal to heaven breaks off.*
> *The petals begin to fall, in self-forgiveness.*
> *It is a flower. On this mountainside it is dying.*

After the fire, then, a still small voice. Humbled, reduced, but reduced in the sense of *intensified*, concentrated rather than diminished, life, having passed through what Arnold called "the gradual furnace of the world," life for Galway Kinnell becomes a matter of sacred vestiges, remnants, husks—as he says in his third book of poems published in 1968, *Body Rags*. Consider, from the titles alone, the emblematic leavings, survivals of the initiating arson: "Another Night in the Ruins," "Lost Loves," "The Fossils," "The Correspondence

School Instructor Says Goodbye to His Poetry Students," "Last Songs," "Testament of the Thief," "One Who Used to Beat His Way." In all of these, whether testifying as in "The Last River" to the destructive glory of human society ("the air brightens as though ashes / of lightning bolts had been scattered through it"), or observing as in "The Burn" the merest dissolving appearances of the elements ("on these beaches / the sea throws itself down, in flames"), the poet has kept faith with his own fires:

> *On ashes of old volcanoes*
> *I lie dreaming,*
> *baking*
> *the deathward flesh in the sun . . .*
>
> *And yet I can rejoice*
> *that everything changes, that*
> *we go from life*
> *into life,*
>
> *and enter ourselves*
> *quaking*
> *like the tadpole, his time come, tumbling toward the slime.*

In these poems of astonishing metamorphosis, Kinnell has been concerned to enact, by his "dance of solitude" as he calls the shaman's performance in "The Bear," to articulate the truth of Goethe's great dictum: One learns nothing, but one becomes something. Ever larger in these late poems bulks or—for bulk is not what we get, but rather a flickering ballet around the circumference of what is guessed at in the darkness—breaks in upon us the awareness that in order to achieve transformation the ritual imagination of burning must in our time be abjured for a natural process, with all its attendant waste and weariness: "our faces smudged with light from the fingertips of the ages." It is a sacred flame Kinnell tends:

> *I can hear*
> *a mountain brook*
> *and somewhere blood winding*
> *down its ancient labyrinths. And*
> *a few feet away*
> *charred stick-ends surround*
> *a bit of ashes, where burnt-out vanished flames*
> *absently*
> *waver, absently leap*

—but not, or no longer, a magical one, no longer a pure transfiguring blaze but, like his "smudged" poems, a tragic flare, "a palimpsest, streaked / with erasures, smelling / of departure and burnt stone"—as is revealed by the poet's renunciation of the myth of the phoenix:

> *How many nights must it take*
> *one such as me to learn*
> *that we aren't, after all, made*
> *of the bits of that bird*
> *which creates itself again*
> *in its ashes,*
> *that for a man*
> *as he goes up in flames, his one work*
> *is to open himself, to be the flames?*

It is interesting to see that in his final version of these last lines, Kinnell literally opens himself, breaking apart the language until it illustrates the aperient nature of all such poetry:

> *that for a man*
> *as he goes up in flames, his one work*
> *is*
> *to open himself, to* be
> *the flames?*

These further poems, then, in their licking rhythms, their ragged edges that "break in gold, frankincense and myrrh" like Kinnell's rooster that

> *thrashes in the snow*
> *for a grain. Finds*
> *it. Rips*
> *it into*
> *flames. Flaps. Crows.*
> *Flames*
> *bursting out of his brow—*

these fiery fragments "breathing the burnt odor / of old rocks" quite literally hand on the torch Kinnell has been carrying for a life redeemed:

> *the drifting sun that gives us our lives,*
> *seed dazzled over the footbattered blaze of the earth,*

and for a death transfigured:

> *that sticky infusion, that rank flavor of blood, that*
> *poetry, by which I lived.*

The formal attentions bestowed upon such utterances are by now no more than the bandages for first-degree burns. In "this poem, or chopped prose" of his, what Kinnell wants is not the emollient hands of the nurse, but the fierce dedication of the Vestal:

> *flowers brightening about you,*
> *the skills of fire, of fanning*
> *the blossoms until they die . . .*

The lines are as unique and therefore as perishable, in the strong sense, as flames: not enduring but *changing*, treating reality transitively, and expressly kindled for the fiery impulse they enact:

> *On some hill of despair*
> *the bonfire*
> *you kindle can light the great sky—*
> *though it's true, of course, to make it burn*
> *you have to throw yourself in.*

The Book of Nightmares by GALWAY KINNELL

For Galway Kinnell, in his fourth book of poems, it is not the death of others which creates or even moderates the self; Kinnell does not have much truck with others. Rather, it is the death of the self which, simply, creates. The poet puts it to us with his characteristic tone, a tone of manliness without machismo, of force without brutality, in a statement from his collected interviews *Walking Down the Stairs:* "Poetry has taken on itself the task of breaking out of the closed ego . . . The death of the self I seek, in poetry and out of poetry, is not a drying up or withering. It is a death, yes, but a death out of which one might hope to be reborn more giving, more alive, more open, more related to the natural life." One cannot take exception to these good intentions without simultaneously opposing motherhood (though Kinnell, in his exaltation of fatherhood, might be said to do just that), but I should like to note the pervasive superstition, one of the most inescapable of our times, the superstition of openness as, in itself, a Good Thing. Here Kinnell, though as concerned with the myth of metamorphosis as any of our poets, is on marshier ground, for he is all concerned with changing *to*, not changing *from*. He does not give much heed to the past, for is there not the future? To put it another way, he is forever opening up, and so what is left behind, untended, tends to assume a charred and neglected aspect as Kinnell greets the new life, the life of his children, of the earth, of his own transfigured body.

The Book of Nightmares is a single poem in ten parts ("it is right / at the last, that one / and zero / walk off together, walk off the end of these pages together, / one creature walking away side by side with the emptiness"), and it is about the consummation of the self in the one sense in order to achieve consummation in the other. It is about how "the raindrops trying / to put the fire out / fall into it and are / changed"—leaving therefore "this wet site / of old fires" which is the poet's body, which is the earth and the human mind. But not human memory. Memory and all it implies of convention, decorum, recurrence and discretion are largely flouted in the ordering of this work. It is wonderfully ordered, composed, this dream book of Kinnell's, and Denise Levertov is quite right, in her jacket comment, to remark how brilliantly the poem holds its disparate apertures together, how it coheres; it is all one text, but it is not written in verse, it is written, merely, in poetry, and there are findings of loss in the performance which founder in a waste of invention. As Wordsworth said about Goethe, it is not memorable enough, for it does not come back enough to itself. One discovers this when the poet himself, an astonishing performer indeed, recites this work— he alters it in the recital; for him it is not a piece of language with which nothing more can be done, but a text, a piece of language with which anything may be done, provided it is done by himself. What Kinnell calls "the body-Arabic of these nightmares" never allows us to cool down, to enjoy that interval between burning and burning with is implied, precisely, by the work of *lines;* instead, as the poet himself accounts for it:

> *on the absolute whiteness of pages*
> *a poem writes itself out: its title—the dream*
> *of all poems and the text*
> *of all loves—"Tenderness toward Existence."*

Exulting, then, in the general conflagration which leaves no member standing, Kinnell employs "this languished alphabet / of worms, these last words / of himself" in order to discover what is not himself. And he does discover it. The translator of Villon and Bonnefoy has a justified confidence in his own compositional energies—"the carnal / nightmare soars back to the beginning"—the power to make up a poetry out of hope, a wonder, a question:

> *Can it ever be true—all bodies, one body, one light*
> *made of everyone's darkness together?*

And he answers with the old stoic rapture, if the oxymoron will stand, the one so flagrant in *Body Rags,* his previous book:

> *Never mind.*
> *The self is the least of it.*
> *Let our scars fall in love.*

Addressing himself throughout to his totem animals, the bear and the hen, and to his daughter and son, as well as to various shadowy loves who are indeed unselved, Kinnell closes his fire sermon ("this corpse will not stop burning!") with a magnificent apostrophe to his own powers, the powers he has referred to in his interviews as "the standard of what it is to be alive—very high. It was set in our infancy" —powers which are irregular, vast and unpropped, as well as, or because, unpolicied:

> *This poem*
> *if we shall call it that,*
> *or concert of one*
> *divided among himself, this earthward gesture* . . .
> *this free floating of one*
> *opening his arms into the attitude*
> *of flight, as he obeys the necessity and falls* . . .

Partisan Review, 1972

CAROLYN KIZER

"Our Masks Keep Us
in Thrall to Ourselves..."

A TEACHER and a friend and even a subject of Miss Kizer's, as in
this pair of apochromatic *tankas*:

> *The stout poet tiptoes*
> *On the lawn. Surprisingly limber*
> *In his thick sweater*
> *Like a middle-aged burglar.*
> *Is the young robin injured?*

> *A hush is on the house,*
> *The only noise, a fern*
> *Rustling in a vase.*
> *On the porch, the fierce poet*
> *Is chanting words to himself.*

—Theodore Roethke once listed the charges most frequently levelled
against poetry written by women: lack of range in subject matter, in
emotional tone; lack of a sense of humor; spinning out; the embroider-
ing of trivial themes; a concern with the mere surfaces of life; refusing
to face up to existence; lyric or religious posturing; running between
the boudoir and the altar, stamping a tiny foot against God; lapsing
into a sententiousness that implies the author has re-invented integrity;
carrying on excessively about Fate, about Time; lamenting the lot of
the woman; caterwauling; writing the same poem about fifty times:
and so on. These are scarcely the faults of a sex, of course, unless they
are those faults of men which they *prefer* to see in women, as Simone
de Beauvoir would say, or as Miss Kizer does say:

Juvenal set us apart in denouncing our vices
Which had grown, in part, from having been set apart . . .

No, these are the faults of selfhood itself, to oppose which is very much like being dead set against sin—they are no more than the possibilities and the problems that must be faced by any writer. Miss Kizer, whom Roethke himself acknowledged as "willing to take chances with unusual material," has approached the baleful list in the bravest way, not seeking to escape the damages but rather to incur and so transcend them. She does not fear—indeed she *wants*—to do all the things Roethke says women are blamed for, and indeed I think she does do them (though if she lacks a sense of humor, it is never when the joke is on *her*), and this makes her terribly suspect, of course—no one could be *really* womanly if so womanly as all *that*. But doing them or not, being *determined* to do them makes her a different kind of poet from the one who manages to avoid the traps of his condition, and gives her a different kind of success from the one that "in circuit lies," as Emily Dickinson put it. Carolyn Kizer has succeeded otherwise, has succeeded head on, in a most difficult exertion—she has transformed her character into fate, or shown, by the most markedly contrasting and often contesting means, that aspect of her character which *is* fate. Employing or suffering—undergoing, at any rate—all the potential disqualifications Roethke asserts to be imminent in her enterprise—"the raw material of a ritual"—Miss Kizer has made the woman of her poems a Figure rather than a Character, an emblem rather than a case, so that what we discover in reading her, or what we deserve if we have heard the poems in the right voice—one that allows if it does not itself release the Grand Gynaesic Gesture—is something larger and more luminous than life, though composed, surely, of just the details we are accustomed to reckon with in accounts of selfhood smaller than life— the accounts of prose, I mean, and smaller in that their scrutiny is more intense and deliberate than our living will ordinarily bear. In her idiophany, Carolyn Kizer has been able to raise our implicit recognition of the *via naturaliter femina* into explicit distinction; from the fatal etcetera of things in a woman's life, as well as from its unique occasions, from the household bonds as well as the heroic body:

We who must act as handmaidens
To our own goddess, turn too fast,
Trip on our hems, to glimpse the muse
Gliding below her lake or sea,
Are left, long-staring after her,
Narcissists by necessity;

Or water-carriers of our young
Till waters burst, and white streams flow

> *Artesian, from the lifted breast:*
> *Cup-bearers then, to tiny gods,*
> *Imperious table pounders, who*
> *Are final arbiters of thirst.*

> *Fasten the blouse, and mount the steps*
> *From kitchen taps to Royal Barge,*
> *Assume the trident, don the crown,*
> *Command the Water Music now*
> *That men bestow on Virgin Queens;*
> *Or, goddessing above the waist,*

> *Appear as swan on Thames or Charles*
> *Where iridescent foam conceals*
> *The paddle-stroke beneath the glide:*
> *Immortal feathers preened in poems!*
> *Not our true, intimate nature, stained*
> *By labor, and the casual tide.*

—from these acknowledgments worthy of a Colette, Miss Kizer has wrought a new shape of consciousness; with the admission that the prison and the desert are not within everyone's range, that the Criminal and the Adventurer, as in, say, the work of Genet and of T. E. Lawrence, do not represent forms of activity which most appeal to her as life, she has worked out of the old Austrian precept *immer fortwurschteln*, always muddle along, a kind of bourgeois sanctity—out of these "dull and partial couplings with ourselves . . . afraid to become our neighbors," by some brilliantly contrived and often exotic distancing effects, she has created what I like to call a *Figure,*

> *. . . nailed to our domesticity*
> *Like Van Gogh to the wall, wild in his frame,*
> *Doubling in mirrors, that the sinister self*
> *Who moves along with us may own at last*
> *Her own reverses . . .*

something impersonal and unaccommodating, as Antigone and Phèdre would be Figures—of that condition which the personal only hides.

Miss Kizer was born in Spokane, spent her girlhood vacations in the San Fernando Valley north of Los Angeles, has lived in Seattle, where she edited the magazine she founded, *Poetry Northwest*, and is engaged, as she says, "in the practice of poetry." Her first book, *The Ungrateful Garden*, published when she was in her early thirties, is by its reach West, to "the Japanese Mode," and East, to Vienna and the Greek myths, an ambitious reversal of the usual directions in which we venture to possess such things. "One half the individual is locality," Frost once wrote to a friend, and it was early that Miss Kizer discovered the advantages to the other half of her situation on the stiff upper lip of the Pacific: the exile that belongs to oneself, the interior exile. The "gravely gay" book is dedicated, in its three parts, to her mother, her father and her children, in fulfillment of those ritual pieties she has taken care to repossess in her own uncomfortable way:

> . . . *in these austerities,*
> *These arbitrary disciplines of mine,*
> *Most of them trivial: like covering*
> *The children on my way to bed, and trying*
> *To live well enough alone, and not to dream*
> *Of grappling in the snow, claws plunged in fur,*
> *Or waken in a caterwaul of dying.*

Its content, in every sense, is what the author knows already—as a child knows best, first of all:

> *Thomas Love Peacock! Thomas Love Peacock!*
> *I used to croon, sitting on the pot,*
> *My sympathetic magic, at age three.*
> *These elements in balance captured me:*
> *Love in the middle, on his right hand a saint*
> *and doubter . . .*
> *On Love's left hand, the coarse essentials: . . .*
> *Thomas Love Peacock! Thomas Love Peacock!*
> *The person unsung, the person ritually sung.*
> *But that was thirty years ago; a child's loving*
> *Of God, the body, flesh of poetry . . .*

then what as a woman writer she has learned:

> *Perhaps not happiness, but still*
> *A certain comfort . . .*
> *I know, I know. I've gone before . . .*

> *A poet to whom no one cruel or imposing listens,*
> *Disdained by senates . . .*

> *Our limited salvation is the word,*
> *A bridge between our Nature and our Time.*

and what as a human being she must merely endure:

Delivered at last from my thought and my things,
My net weight, my engorged heart,
So humbled that my purposes grow grass . . .

Accepting ravage as the only tribute
That men can pay to gods . . .

The book's title and a good deal of its business—the practice of poetry which reveals perfection to be impossible—is an acknowledgment that we perform our functions—bodily, creative, official—in an alienated nature:

We live on ironed land like cemeteries,
But cemeteries are a green relief:
Used-car and drive-in movie lots alike
Enaisle and regulate the gaudy junk
That runs us, in a "Park" that is no park . . .
The seagull is our bird, who eats our loot,
Adores our garbage but can rise above it—
Clean scavenger, picks clean, gets clean away!—
Past bays and rivers of industrial waste,
Infected oysters, fish-bloat, belly up
In sloughs of sewage, to the open sea . . .

as well as in an alien one: "a whole wild, lost, betrayed and secret life." To render that life, to recover at least the sense that something has been lost, Miss Kizer learned a lot from Mr. Roethke. Take worms:

pearly and purple,
curling and opal . . .
bruised as a blueberry,
bare as a rose,
vulnerable as veins,
naked as a nose . . .

But where Roethke would rush out and fling himself upon the thorns of life, ecstatic even in natural ruin, there is a sour or at least a wry centripetal impulse in Miss Kizer's witty emblems of womanhood, as shaped in the magnificent "Columns and Caryatids":

THE WIFE: *"I am Lot's pillar, caught in turning,*
Bellowing, resistant, burning . . .

I saw Sodom bleed, Gomorrah smoke.
Empty sockets are a joke of that final vision.
Tongueless, I taste my own salt, taste
God's chastisement and derision."

> *. . . God's alliance with weather*
> *Eroding her to a spar, a general grief-shape,*
> *A cone, then an egg no bigger than a bead.*

THE MOTHER: *"I am God's pillar, caught in raising*
> *My arms like thighs to brace the wall . . .*

> *The world is a womb.*
> *Neither I nor the foetus tire of our position.*
> *My ear is near God, my temples to his temple.*
> *I lift and I listen. I eat God's peace."*

THE LOVER: *"I am your pillar that has fallen . . ."*

> *Stripped of all ornament she lies,*
> *Looted alike by conquerors and technicians;*
> *So boys will turn from sleep and search the darkness,*
> *Seeking the love their fathers have forgotten.*
> *And they will dream of her who have not known her,*
> *And ache, and ache for that lost limb forever.*

And there is a bitter acceptance in her myths of identity: Persephone pausing on the sill of her downward journey, "nerves dissolving in the gleam / of night's theatrical desire"; Hera hung from the sky, "half strangled in my hair, / I dangle, drowned in fire"; Midas cut and bruised by his ungrateful garden, who

> *Hugged his agues, loved his lust*
> *But damned to hell the out-of-doors.*

—certainly history and human disposition, as certified by myth, turn out tragically. The consolation, not the hope, is in natural process, the rhythm of nights and days, of breathing, of decay and rebirth:

> *Wreathed in our breathing,*
> *We will exceed ourselves again:*
> *Put out in storms, and pitch our wave on waves . . .*

> *Get thee to a compost heap.*
> *Renew, the self prays to decay. Renew!*
> *And buckles on its shell to meet the day.*

The shell Miss Kizer has contrived to encounter necessity with is, in her second book, *Knock upon Silence*—"for an answering music," as its Chinese epigraph advises—both more exotic and more capacious than the studied and tough-minded poems of *The Ungrateful Garden*. She has looked East and West again for personae, masks and voices that will "renew" her need, and if her wit is less explicit in reference than when she sang:

> *Come candidly, consort with me,*
> *And spill our pleasure for a day . . .*

it is more inclusive, it can afford, in a declension of the same refrain, the music of experience rather than that of convention:

> *I am monogamous as the North Star*
> *But I don't want you to know it. You'd only take advantage.*
> *While you are as fickle as spring sunlight.*
> *All right, sleep! The cat means more to you than I.*
> *I can rouse you, but then you swagger out.*
> *I glimpse you from the window, striding toward the river.*

Abandoning Marlowe and Heine and the careful rhymes of what it would be perversely modest to regard as her apprenticeship, let us call it her initiation, Miss Kizer here lights on Arthur Waley and on Juvenal—the received English version of classical Chinese and that most relaxed of Western metrics, the Roman hexameter. The book is deceptive, appearing to be given over altogether to literary ventriloquism, though as soon as we get beyond the titles of its four sections—"Chinese Imitations"; "A Month in Summer, after Issa's *The Year of My Life*," which revealed to Miss Kizer "the most satisfactory method of writing *haiku*"; "from *Pro Femina*," and "Translations of Tu Fu"—we discover that the stomach Miss Kizer is speaking from is her own, and that all the masks are necessary to keep her pangs from drowning out her perceptions. The Chinese "imitations" reveal how much more personal this poet has allowed herself to become in what Colette once called the honorable if not the lively pleasure of not speaking of love:

> *By the time we reach middle life, we've all been deserted and robbed.*
> *But flowers and grass and animals keep me warm.*
> *And I remind myself to become philosophic:*
> *We are meant to be stripped down, to prepare us for something better.*

And surely it is because of the wonderful poise-in-disaster she has learned in the twenty translations from Tu Fu (A.D. 712–770), with their resignation to exile and disgrace yet their insistence on the value of nature, "randomness, Art's impulse, true disorder" and of friendship, drinking and memory, that she has made these imitations so much her own. Like Morris Graves, whom she had already praised in her first book for his Oriental capacity to make something out of unpromising materials—

poor crockery, immortal
on twenty sheets of paper—

Carolyn Kizer has found a voice for her woman's condition, and her human one, which allows her to bring forth only the more for all she has borrowed:

> *You, my brother, are a good and violent drinker,*
> *Good at reciting short-line or long-line poems.*
> *In time we will lose all our daughters, you and I,*
> *Be temperate, venerable, content to stay in one place,*
> *Sending our messages over the mountains and waters.*

As in this message to Creeley, "Amusing Our Daughters," the poet gathers up all her tones, all her tempers into a hovering posture of control, a swaying form, so that such "Chinese imitations" are indeed what Coleridge said an imitation was: the mesothesis of likeness and difference. The difference is as essential to it as the likeness, for without the difference it would be Copy or Facsimile.

The volume further contains a curious record, in the form of a prose diary, of a broken love affair, or of its actual breaking, punctuated by *haiku*. The prose pieces keep pulling away from the agony, seeking release in the distractions of learning or of knowing:

> One of the profound consolations of reading the works of Japanese men of letters is their frank acknowledgment of neurotic sloth. Or the overwhelming impulse, when faced with hurt or conflict, to stay in bed under the covers!

but the demanding little syllables of the *haiku* are relentless in their return to the pain:

> *Alone in my house*
> *I can make gross noises*
> *Like a caught hare or stoat*
> *Or a woman in labor.*

Why these artifices appropriated from a culture that does not belong to her? Perhaps, Miss Kizer suggests, because the only way to deal with sorrow is to find a form in which to contain it.

As an equipoise to this mutilated apology for a love poem, *Knock upon Silence* also contains Miss Kizer's public voice: fragments from a Juvenalian apology *Pro Femina*, dedicated to two of our star translators from Greek and Latin, Robert Fitzgerald and Rolfe Humphries. Here the critical intelligence that in the first book focussed so sharply inward is allowed its most generous locus in the Situation Abroad. The independent woman, the woman of letters are cracked open, in these looping hexameters, like so many husks, and the satiric truth threshed:

Our masks, always in peril of smearing or cracking,
In need of continuous check in the mirror or silverware,
Keep us in thrall to ourselves, concerned with our surfaces . . .

Freed in fact, not in custom, lifted from furrow and scullery,
Not obliged, now, to be the pot for the annual chicken,
Have we begun to arrive in time? *With our well-known*
Respect for life because it hurts so much to come out with it;
Disdainful of "sovereignty," "national honor" and other abstractions;
We can say, like the ancient Chineses to successive waves of invaders,
"Relax and let us absorb you . . ." Meanwhile, observe our creative
     chaos,
Flux, efflorescence, whatever you care to call it!

I would care to call it poetry, of a fruitfully damaged, unresolved and nearly inescapable order. There is, on the jacket of this second book, a photograph of the poet, a beautiful woman looking out at us in a Japanese gown, on a Consular chair—with just that combination of the Roman Matron and the Oriental Courtesan which makes up all her authority and all her indecision—"creative chaos." It is odd to find Cornelia and the Geisha together, but Carolyn Kizer proves that such manners are no more than the means by which a poetry obtains access to reality, to the expressed values of a life otherwise merely lived out, eluded:

Now, if we struggle abnormally, we may almost seem normal;
If we submerge our self-pity in disciplined industry;
If we stand up and be hated, and swear not to sleep with editors;
If we regard ourselves formally, respecting our true limitations
Without making an unseemly show of trying to unfreeze our assets;
Keeping our heads and our pride while remaining unmarried;
And if wedded, kill guilt in its tracks when we stack up the dishes
And defect to the typewriter. And if mothers, believe in the luck of
     our children,
Whom we forbid to devour us, whom we shall not devour,
And the luck of our husbands and lovers, who keep free women.

Midnight Was My Cry by CAROLYN KIZER

It is a dangerous interval, the one somewhere between juvenilia and senilia, when poets decide they must represent their achievement (concilia?) at the retrospective pitch, the abyss of "selection": the danger is one of sclerosis, for the trouble with getting it all together, as we say now, is getting anything, afterwards, apart. Consider Carolyn Kizer's case. To thirty-five poems from *The Ungrateful Garden* (1961) and to eight (less shapely, more ambitious) from *Knock upon Silence* (1965), both books being out of print, she has added another sixteen from the last decade, two of these poems no more than newspaper leaders (or followers), one or two others no less than autovoyeurism, the remainder as fine as anything she has done, unresolved but inescapable, learned but not knowing, fluent yet anything but easy—say, then, she has reinforced her canon by some dozen first-rate poems, observant, solicitous, lithe: where does the new emphasis thereby fall, the refinement and recognition, now, of certain shared contours, of welcomed limits? An answer is brought home to me as much by what is left out as by what is committed to the leavings: an early villanelle *On a line from Julian* has given way to—or been outdistanced by—one *On a line from Sophocles*. And the new line is "Time, time, my friend, makes havoc everywhere"—a poetical *sententia* which must be earned, as it is here, by a concrescence of experience, disastrous, wide-ranging, amical. To forego the Apostate and his futile rebellion against the odds of history for the all-seeing Greek, tragic in his presentment of events but articulating so much more life in his very acknowledgment of what happens— that is the burden Miss Kizer so gracefully shoulders here. The additional poems are not fractious, merely frank in their response to hopes and horrors alike ("for women learn to be a holy show . . . but we break out of the harem of history!"), and there is no effort merely to will The Enemy out of the way by stamping a tiny foot ("You failed, I failed . . . we are true neither to life nor nature, / but perhaps to one another as we write"). Instead, the Kizer poem "wrapt in a caul of vulnerability", weds chaos and failure, welcomes pain and farce, "signalling, / self-amazed, its willingness to endure," for as the poet writes to an attempted suicide to whom she sends, with her words, white azaleas:

> . . . *we live in wonder,*
> *Blaze in a cycle of passion and apprehension*
> *Though once we lay and waited for a death.*

The effect, *en gros* and better still, in fine, of this selection is to dispel the dangers of its program. She has submitted her figure to her fate, has worked out of the exoticisms which once rather specialized and so limited Carolyn Kizer—this is to say, she has given up impersonating Mae West and Shanghai Lily and your all-purpose Women's Libertine for the sake and the success of a style we may recognize anywhere, in Holland, in Ohio; in dudgeon, in delight—as consistently Carolingian, fruitfully injured:

> *This bronze is mortal, gaping in defeat,*
> *The form that wombed it split to let it be.*

Poetry, 1972

KENNETH KOCH

"What Was the Ecstasy, and What the Stricture?"

To be interested, we are reminded by no less an authority than Martin Heidegger, means to be among and in the midst of things, to be at the center of a thing and stay with it, though today's "interest" accepts as valid only what is *interesting*—the sort of thing that can readily be regarded as indifferent *the next moment* and be replaced by another thing. The conflict between these attitudes, the contradiction between these acceptations of a word—the psychomachia, really, between the ecstatic moment-out-of-time and the movement *of* time (resolved only if we remember that the moment *is* the movement, the smallest unit of movement being a *momentum*); between what Kenneth Koch calls "the imagination in which there is no advance, in which one is always at the peaks" and what he calls, though the chronal italics are mine, "an imagination that demands to be thrilled *at every instant*"; between "a poem in which the same thing happens on every page" and "a poem which is *continually* gorgeous and exciting" —this confrontation supplies the torque, the twist of impulse which makes us stay with this poet, "tourists / in recognition as we are," which makes us stand for the patter: the combat of delight and duration, of eternity and time, of death and life even, is merely a matter of words to Kenneth Koch, as it must be, for he is a poet, the man for whom words matter, for whom they are *material*:

> . . . *a cry*
> *Of joy and sorrow both, of understanding,*
> *That pleasure, which is ever so demanding,*

> *Demanded that he follow through his plan . . .*
> *Or else with aftermath would be alloyed*
> *His perfect moments.*

He begins far and wide, he begins with an epic, though an epic in which "all's transformed into / one shimmering self!" Kenneth Koch's first book, published in 1959, is a comic epic (though in fact all epics are comic for they are recounted *at length*, they rest or come to rest in *duration*) called *Ko, or A Season on Earth.* By truncating his own name (one shimmering self indeed), the poet gets his Hero's, conveniently that of a Japanese baseball player,

> *Ko was more than a mere fan,*
> *But wished as a playing member to do a hitch*
> *with some great team—something to think about*
> *More interesting than merely Safe and Out.*

And by his subtitle, with its lovely punning message—that is, a *baseball* season embracing the globe ("Meanwhile the Dodgers . . . In Athens, Do- / ris climbs the Acropolis . . . While their big barge is moving down the Thames / let's turn to Indianapolis . . . Meanwhile Ko / is pitching, pitching, pitching . . ."), and also the obverse of Rimbaud's *saison en enfer* ("by what we love / spontaneously, we gain awareness of / our freedom and the realizeable world!")—Koch defines his genre and defends his theme: this is to be a poem of secular impulse ("no matter where he is / a man is cheered to see a naked girl") and celebratory echoes ("Oh, how great is art / that brings us on a purple-rainy day / a world of sunshine, insights"), episodic, haphazard ("it's an esthetic moment. Be content"); and by its personnel (including, besides Ko, a neurotic financier who wants to control all the dogs on earth, an English Private eye, an "Action Poet . . . as calm as any man can be / whose poems do not lie in any book / and so are dead to his posterity" and some two dozen others we may find "in an airplane, forest, soap-mine, gulch or tower") as well as by its geographical accommodation, *general.* The clue to what Koch calls "the courage of his large designs" is given out even more insistently than it can be taken in by the epigraph to the entire work, a distich from Ariosto's *Orlando Furioso* I translate here because Koch supplies it only in Italian and, with that fecklessness so typical of the erudite anti-intellectual, misplaces it in the source: "Now, no more! return another time, / you who would hear the splendid tale." *Ko*, then, is to be the "other time," yet here is also a warning that the story will not be splendid, but rather splenetic, sporadic, in every sense of the word a *sport.* We recall that Ariosto's mock-epic "completed" (or at least completed the destruction of) Boiardo's chivalric romance *Orlando Innamorato,* and in its swamping size and apparently chaotic structure reflects a world apart, a world *falling* apart. The gap between the poem's decorous surface and its riotous substance, between seeming order and sensed mutability is not a rift the poet unwittingly creates or creeps into: the split is the poem's subject, and no one is more aware of this than Ariosto, or than Koch hard upon his heels:

> *integrity*
> *Makes him, unlike most poets, actualize*
> *In everyday life the poem's unreality.*

Countless episodes of *Ko* reveal and revel in its own shortcomings, delusions, absurdities. Koch has Byron's delight in the preposterous rhyme: "oranger" / "porringer" or, my favorite, "naturally" / "catcher will he"; he has his own disconcerting sense of simile: "remorseless as a parking meter"; he has the born storyteller's sense of convincing detail: "dachshunds swinging sideways with delight"; and he has, of course, when he wants to invoke the gorgeous, a French symbolist's appanage of correspondences:

> *The city of Paris forming in the clouds*
> *And in that wrack of whitest whisperies.*

At the whim of a rhyme, at the beck of a metaphor, things in *Ko* are never what they seem, though they often become what they might be —too much is going on, impinging, underlying, to allow any one set of standards, any one apparatus of judgment the last word, the final say: there is no *final say* here, no ultimates of any sort, only the pleasure of speaking on, and on—*la bella istoria*. The poem—even more radically in Koch's five cantos and 438 stanzas and 3,504 lines than in Ariosto's immensities—is fatally, or at least fitfully (in *fits*, as the old name for stanzas of heroic action had it) examining the poem, rejecting or *showing up* its own criteria by showing them, in order to substitute other possibilities, other *interests*. The success of this enormous poem of vignettes—and it will be the success of all Koch's projects, a prowess which marks, which *is* the borderline between accident and will, between hysteria and method—amounts to the tension between the moment of ecstasy and the movement elsewhere; to the pressure built up in the reader's mind—"in nervous patience till the glory starts"—as the result of a promise to remain at the center yet a *practice* of eccentricity. Over and over, the poet twitches the text away from us with a teasing laugh: "I leave this sportive celebration / and go to England"; which capricious topography is more than the conventional advancement of the narrative on several fronts ("Meanwhile in Tampa . . ."); rather, it is the fear that ecstasy is escaping us, leaking out of duration, that we are not always likely to be on the heights if we stay, merely, where we are. In order to bind the poem to the Interesting forever, in either the sense of instant gratification or the sense of the gratification of the *next* instant, Koch is forever searching the natural world for new contingencies, now models of ordering, "new seeds of interest and a cure for care." What he wants is some disposition of the poem suggested, even instituted, by a perceived disposition of the Real World or the rational one—say, a poem that, being about the United States, had fifty versicles, mentioning one State in each. Take the scene in *Ko*, when all the girls in Kansas shuck off their clothes; their bodies become

> . . . *almanacs to teach*
> *The . . . poet how to shape his lines,*
> *The woodsman what is lacking in the pines.*

The Body Beautiful as an *ars poetica*, then. Though Koch will use, often to hilarious point ("I thought Axel's Castle was a garage"), the *données* and distractions of literary culture, about which he is wickedly informed ("the poetry / written by the men with their eyes on the myth / and the Missus and the midterms"), his own poems will not submit to the familiarities and fashions of the past except in travesty. He is, for instance, the best parodist of our time, and his Frost, Pound and Perse pieces cannot be excelled, save perhaps by his "Variations on a Theme by William Carlos Williams," which concludes:

> *Last evening we went dancing and I broke your leg.*
> *Forgive me. I was clumsy, and*
> *I wanted you here in the wards, where I am the doctor!*

Reversing the standard pedagogic point, Koch says, "we cannot know anything about the past unless we know about the present," and flings himself into today's loose, baggy garments with tremendous abandon: "Is there no one who feels like a pair of pants?" The heartening if equivocal discovery that art can be ransomed from its fitfulness, from its fretful discontent with the here and now ("Dear coolness of heaven, come swiftly and sit in my chairs!") by a subservience to the natural order, or at any rate to some other order not its own ("we are not / inside a bottle, thank goodness!"), is Kenneth Koch's special Eureka, the resonance ("the fur rhubarb did not please Daisy") we might elsewhere have recognized and rejected in the characteristic modern hero's daydream:

> Then the band would play a march, an amnesty would be declared,
> the Pope would agree to retire from Rome to Brazil; then there
> would be a ball for the whole of Italy on the shores of Lake Como
> at the Villa Borghese (the lake of Como being for that purpose

transferred to the neighborhood of Rome); there would come a scene in the bushes, and so on—

We might spot this as the idiosyncratic tonality of our poet * if it were not that the *pleasure* of his poems is lacking in it, "the recurring and instinctive joy that is tied to speech," the joy that lets us escape the hysterical aggression in *Ko*, for example, more readily than we may duck away from the anxiety of Dostoievsky's famous invalid in *Notes from Underground* which I have cited here. The point is worth emphasizing, for it determines the absence from these poems of the negative in all its labor and labefactation as well as the presence of so much gaiety and good spirits; as Koch says in his outrageous swipe from the realm of psychological novels, indeed from the realm of psychological novelty which he calls "The Departure from Hydra":

> *I can't judge vitality in any way but the way*
> *It gives me pleasure, for if I do not get*
> *Pleasure from life, of which vitality*
> *Is just the liquid form, then what am I*
> *And who cares what I say? I for one don't . . .†*

Elsewhere Koch speaks prescriptively of "the detachment of beautiful words from traditional contexts and putting them in curious new American ones," by which we must realize that he indeed *believes in* "beautiful words," in the pleasure they will bestow, once they are put in their curious American contexts. Pleasure and beauty, aesthetic moments, are discovered as "a cure for care." But it is only when the discovery is made without the imposition of the will that Kenneth Koch succeeds in these "large designs" of his; it is only when the composition is come upon rather than compelled that his long poems do more than astonish us (they astonish as a matter of course, a matter

---

* It is the parallel if not the progenitor of any random quote from Koch's "novel"—his habit, by the way, of casting a distance upon just about anything by quotation marks is as infectious as a giggle—a kind of Raymond Roussel collage of compositional procedures called *The Red Robins:*

The ennui became almost unbearable. Forests shook. Lynn took off her sweater and performed "semi-nude" imitations of all the Japanese prints of Hokusai. This time the country began to deliberate quite a lot about the hawsers . . .

† The terrible trot of these prose pentameters—what else to call them?—is the march Koch has stolen on the blank-verse deliberations of a Wordsworth, a Wallace Stevens. Whenever he speaks normatively, Koch claps on a mask, a costume he accounts for thus in his text "The Postcard Collection": "There are a great many human relationships and a great many situations inside other relationships in which there is no communication without disguise and self-mockery . . . They are rarely, except at the heights of hysteria or inspiration, recognized as such."

of taking their course, "as of course they must if they are to please").
The entire Occidental program, in poetry, of *la difficulté vaincue* is in
Kenneth Koch's enterprise given over or gainsaid in favor of *la facilité
trouvée*. That is why, henceforth—and henceforth means the work
included in two volumes of poems, *Thank You and Other Poems* (1962)
and *The Pleasures of Peace* (1969) and a volume of little plays, *Bertha
and Other Plays* (1966)—his poems will be written in a prosody attuned
to his heart's meters, the stanzas of his breathing, the paragraphs of
organs and limbs, but never in the old verse, the versions instinct with
some energy of recuperation, of return, of reference to a *given:*

> *Until tomorrow, then, scum floating on the surface of*
>   *poetry! goodbye for a moment, refuse that happens*
>   *to land in poetry's boundaries! . . .*
> *Ah, but the scum is deep! Come, let me help you! and soon*
>   *we pass into the clear blue water. Oh GOODBYE, castrati*
>   *of poetry! farewell, stale pale skunky pentameters (the*
>   *only honest English meter, gloop gloop!) until tomorrow,*
>   *horrors! oh, farewell!*
> *Hello, sea! good morning, sea! hello, clarity and excitement,*
>   *you great expanse of green—*
> *O green, beneath which all of them shall drown!* *

This outcry is from Koch's rhetorical manifesto *Fresh Air*, a screed
which explains, or at least explodes, the fallacies of all other poets
except Kenneth Koch. In it he asserts that his form must be come
upon, must be *invented* (*benedictus qui invenit in nomine Naturae*) or
risk losing interest. Hence the terrorism of many of Koch's larger,
more deliberate creations which drive themselves by recipe and will to
the end of their tether and of ours, a final triumph of method whereby
nothing can be made of them except the stunned constatation that *they*
have been made. Such poems stand or rather loom at the edges of
Koch's career like barbarous temples, brightly lighted but without a
congregation to distract us from the hard brilliance of the great
American monosyllables—blue, girl, ugh, fun, lunch, pants—festooning
every capital, every vault; and on the altar, very reverently placed, as
H. G. Wells once said of Henry James' later style, lie a dead kitten,
two egg-shells and a bit of string. The significance of a passage like the
following from "January Nineteenth":

> *The sheep tree, the lightning and thunder!*
> *Powder writes another novel to itself:*
> *Passengers, adroit pyramids, and blue triremes!*

* The ocean, beneath the scum of forms, is of course the necessary and obdurate
antagonist of the metrical norms: "nothing gives so much pleasure as the sea."

Oh how I hate to "Gogol"! Now, baby sweater!
The Green Cab Sighs have fallen in love.

is precisely that it is not a *passage*, a passing-through the lines, but rather a series of tiny—or immense—epiphanies, unavailing in their tug at one another save as the will decides. For all the "adroit pyramids" of syntactical maneuver, these teratomas of Koch's are made up only of "beautiful words," and fail to be interesting at length because of their willed insistence on the interest of the instant; again and again this poet affords us the enormous trapped *instances* of his genius, his unique posture in our gallery of *outrances:* the victory of moment over movement.

The late Frank O'Hara, who in 1952 (specifically in a text called "Day and Night in 1952") had already diagnosed the poet's situation shrewdly: "Kenneth continually goes away and by this device is able to remain intensely friendly if not actually intimate," suggested to Koch the following year that he undertake something monumental. "I had no clear intention," the poet confides in a note of 1964 on O'Hara, "of writing a 2400-line poem (which it turned out to be) before Frank said to me, on seeing the first 72 lines—which I regarded as a poem by itself—'Why don't you go on with it as long as you can?'" The astounding poem *When the Sun Tries to Go On*—truly, with some things by Roussel and George, one of the monster feats of all modern letters—was published in 1960 in Alfred Leslie's one-shot review *The Hasty Papers*, and its hundred 24-line stanzas, full of soft-drinks, patent medicines, candy bars and the frantic pullulation of overheard trivia, certainly compose a monument—a monument to what the will can accomplish, or if that is too honorific a verb, let us say can *accommodate*, when it articulates itself "as long as it can." Here are the closing lines of the third stanza, originally the conclusion of what the poet "regarded as a poem by itself" (which it certainly is, in one sense of that phrase):

> *O hat theory*
> *Of the definite babies and series of spring*
> *Fearing the cow of day admonished tears*
> *That sigh, "Blue check. The tan of free councils*
> *Cloaks the earth is hen blonde, oh want*
> *The dye-bakers' coke and hilly plaza, too*
> *Sunny, bee when halls key tuba plaza corroboration*
> *Mat nickels." O tell us the correction, bay*
> *Ex-table, my cocoa-million dollars! Next*
> *To. O dare, dare-Pullman Car! The best way*
> *You howling confetti, is "Easter tray,*
> *As moat-line, promise." How teach the larks!*

How indeed. Certainly there are principles of organization, or at least of control, in the work—the repetition of certain classes of nouns, certain expletives, the demands upon innocent syntax which may make any two words together generate some sort of comic effect ("jewelry sevenths," "simplex bumblebees")—but the "interest" in any extent of the thing, and here we are asked to extend our interest over a passage of two thousand four hundred such lines, is so excessively local that the poem becomes, is indeed intended as, a challenge to stay with it as well as a defiance to get a move on. Few who brave the defiance or take up the challenge will reach the end of it, the dying fall: "Gentle hiatus of sarabande cuckoo eep-lariat!"

A dilemma, then, in Koch's poems—"Is the basketball coach a homosexual lemon manufacturer? . . . Is he a lemon memnon?"—will be to hold the line, to draw it at least, and to draw it *in* at best, between the list and the lyric, between the rapture and the (mere) record:

> *We must figure out a way to keep our best musicians with us.*
> *The finest we have always melt into the light blue sky!*

Without the mediating tension of a form, an outline of expectation ("we're due to be dawned on, I guess"), a figure from the world of given shapes, taken signals, which is capable of modelling the poem beyond the compulsive anxieties of the poet's gift ("I love you but it's difficult to stop writing"), the poems turn in the one direction into no more than vicious catalogues:

> *Messalina gave the canned roastbeef to Horace Greeley*
> *While Robert Browning sat inside the mudpie.*
> *A tuneful tribute to attitudes rose up*
> *From the far stretches of the salt wampum.*
> *The Queen of Sheba guzzled the iced salad oil like a veteran*
> *And January visited the swings . . .*

and into catastrophes in the other, reality "profaned or talked at like a hat," cut-ups and explosions of posture momentarily fertile at the expense of any possible continuity:

> *If I boiled you father*
> *I am sorry and*
> *St. Roch. Still, sex and scary*
> *He wanders over the*
> *She abides*
> *They trade kisses in barefoot hallways*
> *The lemon-sun shines only for them*
> *It will burn their feet! watch out!*
> *But no,*
> *For them it is gentle.*

One solution for this conflict between the ecstasy and the stricture, as Koch calls them, is hinted at in the plays, which exploit a tremendous variety of traditional orders to keep the premises up and the pressure down: Elizabethan chronicles, court masques, miracle-plays, No-plays, ballet and opera. Almost anything will feed "the modern idea of fittingness, / to, always in motion, lose nothing"; but the nourishment *as play* offers at least the notion of a cartilage, the connective-tissue of attention between one conniption and the next. In addition to the triumph of *Bertha*—the kind of historical pageant which makes Beerbohm's *Savonarola Brown* seem literal and listless, for Koch conjugates his imperious command of genre with the genuine lunacy of his aggression to produce tableaux of daemonic insouciance—the most significant development, for his poems, in Koch's dramatic devices is the "improvisational play," a scenario or set-piece in which the willfulness can be elided by being described rather than endured. The effect, surprisingly, is the same (we recover, I mean, as much from being *told* that two Monks try to explain the gold standard to each other for four hours as from listening to them do it), and the effort greatly reduced; the "play" element triumphs over the neurotic defense:

> Eight or ten actors come on stage, being anyone they want. They speak for 30 minutes. The only requirement is that every sentence they utter must contain the phrase "coil supreme." They may distort the language in any way they wish in order to do this. They should try to generate as much excitement as possible by what they say and do, and the play should end on a note of unbearable suspense.

The great successes in Koch's collections of shorter poems incorporate, whether by flattering or flouting the tradition, some sort of dramatic outline, generally the contour of persecution, as in "Thank You" itself, a grand paranoiac fantasia on themes of disqualification and withdrawal ("and thank you for the pile of driftwood. / Am I wanted at the sea?") singular for its tonality of glee, its brain-splitting peacock laugh that comes just before the damages must be added up and paid for:

And thank you for the chance to run a small hotel
In an elephant stopover in Zambezi,
But I do not know how to take care of guests, certainly they would
*   all leave soon*
After seeing blue lights out the windows and rust on their iron beds—
*   I'd rather own a bird-house in Jamaica:*
Those people come in, the birds, they do not care how things are kept
*   up . . .*
It's true that Zambezi proprietorship would be exciting, with people
*   getting off elephants and coming into my hotel,*
But tempting as it is I cannot agree . . .

Tantrums, tears of extravagance, follies . . . The supreme achievement in all this is *The Artist,* a jolting, savagely funny account—this is not witty poetry, it is *funny* (as in funny-papers, funny-bone)—of a kind of expanding Gutzon Borglum-persona, pieced together from his journals, remarks, and newspaper clippings. The privilege of the text—it is eight pages long—is in its final propriety of form: high-voiced, light-headed, dangerous, abashing, the speaker faces Koch's own problem and solves it—what to do next, what to make now, where to turn. *The diary* is precisely that discourse which lies between the enumeration and the aria, it is the ledger of the will, and Koch can therefore inflect it between his ecstatic interests and his interests in being elsewhere. Offered in analogy to some of the artistic and social follies of our age, the text transcends satire and parody because in this cascade of nutty impositions we hear the poet's own dilemma, his own desperation voiced on its giddy spiral from interest to interest, from moment to moment, just one damned thing after another; here are three swatches from "The Artist"—at the start, in mid-career, and at his gasping, speculative end:

Cherrywood avalanche, my statue of you
Is still standing in Toledo, Ohio,
O places, summer, boredom, the static of an acrobatic blue!

And I made an amazing zinc airliner
It is standing to this day in the Minneapolis zoo . . .

Old times are not so long ago, plaster-of-paris haircut!

I just found these notes written many years ago.
How seriously I always take myself! Let it be a lesson to me.
To bring things up to date: I have just finished Campaign, *which is*
a tremendous piece of charcoal.
Its shape is difficult to describe; but it is extremely large and would
reach to the sixth floor of the Empire State Building. I have been
very successful in the past fourteen or fifteen years.

June 3rd. It doesn't seem possible—The Pacific Ocean! I have
ordered sixteen million tons of blue paint. Waiting anxiously
for it to arrive. How would grass be as a substitute? cement?

Having ransacked every genre, every convention, every possibility of outrage and confiscation—"never stop revealing yourself"—Koch has in "The Artist" and in several other uproarious instances ("You Were Wearing," "Locks," "Lunch," "Down at the Docks") produced poems which are entirely *his own*. That is their limitation of course, but it is their great resource too, their great and problematic *interest*, flickering between the intolerable moment and the intolerable movement, the unendurable *now* and the unendurable *next*, an oscillation which, as the poet himself remarks, can conclude only "when Kenneth is dead"—

> . . . *like the sunlight at the end of the tunnel, like my rebirth*
> *in the poems of Kenneth Koch.*

DENISE LEVERTOV

"*I Don't Want to Escape,*
Only to See the Enactment of Rites."

I T IS EASY to misunderstand her, and to miss the sense. One cannot trust even the senses, at first. After a long time crashing and stumbling up against resemblances, bruised by analogies suggested, if not spelled out, between her "fronds of wild parsley" and the thickets of our Atlantic poesy, and by the community (call it log-rolling!) exhibited, in another part of the forest, with our Big Timber out West, you come to wonder just whose woods these are, and ask with Denise Levertov:

> *What's human here? what hope is here?*
> *thumbing the dry leaves*
> *eager, eager for the fabulous*
> *poem there may be*
> *in this delight or battle*
> * day coming and the moon not gone . . .*
> *And only after the wind is quenched*
> *the tree dull*
> *a quietness come*
> *does the scraping mind perceive*
>
> > *   what is possible:*
> *there are no miracles but facts.*
> *To see! (there might be work*
> *   a challenge, a poem)*

One way out of the woods, of course, is to pull rank. Truth is a woman; psyche, we say, is declined in the feminine—hence the girlish rhapsody:

> *I'm tired*
> *of all that is not mine. Lighting*
> *two cigarettes by mistake, lying back*
> *one in each hand, surprised,*
> *Buddha of the anthill. A great day!*

and the womanly rapture:

> *Your skin*
> *tastes of the salt of Marmora,*
> *the hair of your body casts*
> *its net over me.*
>
> > *To my closed eyes*
> *appears a curved*
> *horizon where darkness*
> *dazzles in your light. Your arms*
> *hold me from falling.*

There is even the note of the shrew ("Hypocrite women, how seldom we speak / of our own doubts, while dubiously / we mother man in his doubt!") to spice up what is often all too Dryadic about the affair; surely the antidote for "A Psalm Praising the Hair of Man's Body," which incredibly enough accommodates this goofy refrain:

> My great brother
> > Lord of the Song
> Wears the ruff of
> > forest bear

(three times!), is the acidity of:

> *Something to*
> *nullify the tall women on Madison*
> *sniffing, peering at windows, sharp-eyed,*
> *the ones with*
> *little hope beyond the next hat.*

And though all this free-versified Lucy-Stonerism is no accident ("Don't lock me in wedlock," she cries, "I want marriage, an / encounter— / I would be / met / and meet you so, / in a green / airy space, not / locked in"), though the sentimentality about male narcissism is never indulged in dealing with *women*, where all Miss Levertov's shrewdness is operative, it is not by heaving her up onto the double standard of penis envy that we can see this poet plain. Beyond her monostrophic discipleship to the Boys, and the relic imagism that labels her still one of the Girls, Denise Levertov has a further —and happily, decisive—range of experience which she has committed to the language, that makes her poetry important and makes it in fact *her poetry:* for her, the poem is a sacramental transaction, permitting, even enforcing access to a released state of being, an ecstatic awareness that is so much concomitant to a religion, with its stern implications of community and service, as to a gnosis. The contradictions of her mode and her mood, the pressure of events and the price of evangelism have all worked to her harm, somewhat, upon what I take to be her authentic and native impulse, and if I am often confused by her poems—as I was in writing about her work several years ago, when I had reported her "a moralist whose manner forbids her to develop what she *knows;* yet whenever she manages to defeat the assumptions of her mindless mode, her authority convinces me utterly"—I am also convinced by them and prompted, in the course of six books, to an admiration whose nosography I shall attempt to trace here.

The gnostic impulse in Miss Levertov, if that is what it is, must from the start have been curiously inflected by the spiritual accents of her life at home, of which she gives a characteristically cheerful and illuminating account:

> My mother was descended from the Welsh tailor and mystic Angel Jones of Mold, my father from the noted Hasid, Schneour Zalman, "the Rav of Northern White Russia." My father had experienced conversion to Christianity as a student at Königsberg in the 1890s. His lifelong hope was towards the unification of Judaism and Christianity. He was a priest of the Anglican Church (having settled in England not long before I was born), author of a Life of Saint Paul in Hebrew, part translator of the *Zohar,* etc. I was born in October 1923 at Ilford, Essex. I did lessons at home, and never attended any school or college, except for some years at a ballet school. However, we had a house full of books, and everyone in the family engaged in some literary activity. Jewish booksellers, German theologians, Russian priests from Paris, and Viennese opera singers visited . . . and perhaps my earliest memory is of being dandled by the ill-fated son of Theodore Herzl, the great Zionist.

Not surprisingly, then, at 23 Miss Levertoff, as she spelled it those days, published her first book, a spineless and rather whining affair with the unexplained but Audenesque title *The Double Image* (the real or outer aspect of things and the "imagined" or inner vision; in this partition, the experiential surface receives much less than its due, and the emphasis is all on the visionary recital. The language cannot support the strain.)—30 poems divided into two persuasions, "Fears" and "Promises." The fears are mostly for her own possibilities as a poet—an untried vocation, challenged by the example of her predecessors, whose influence is mostly nefandous, as this translation from Auden suggests:

> *Rags of childhood flutter in the woods*
> *and each deserted post has sentinels;*
> *bright eyes in wells watch for the sun's assassin:*
> *the regions bereft of our desires are haunted,*
> *rags of childhood flutter in the woods . . .*

and jeopardized by the war and its persisting encroachments:

> *The wind has tales to tell of sea and city,*
> *a plague on many houses, fear knocking on the doors;*
> *how venom trickles from the open mouth of death,*
> *and trees are white with rage of alien battles.*
> *Who can be happy while the wind recounts*
> *its long sagas of sorrow? Though we are safe . . .*
> *we dare not laugh; or if we laugh, we lie.*

The deleterious degree to which these statements, with their easy personifications and slack rhythms, have been abstracted from experience is best suggested by Miss Levertov's own account of the war years: "I received partial training and lots of experience as a (civilian) nurse. A different world! I was in London during all but a few of the airraids, but it does not seem to have been such a memorable experience as one might expect." The reality of fear was to come—to her poetry, at least—much later, in her third American book, which affords the canonical account of such an experience survived; the poem is called *Terror:*

> *Face-down; odor*
> *of dusty carpet. The grip*
> *of anguished stillness.*
>
> *Then your naked voice, your*
> *head knocking the wall, sideways,*
> *the beating of trapped thoughts against iron.*
>
> *If I remember, how is it*
> *my face shows*
> *barely a line? . . .*
>
> *How did morning come, and the days*
> *that followed, and quiet nights?*

So much of life, and not only life but a judgment upon it earned by accurate presentment, by the motion of the meaning in "minute particulars," as Blake called them, charges Denise Levertov's poetry by this time (1956—ten years later) that we can but marvel at the early work, so unreal in its insistent archetypes, its loricated surface of poetical tropes. The persistent figure in both the "fears" and the "promises" sections (the watershed is not marked, by the way, in the body of the book, but is suggested, perhaps, by a tone of shrill resolve:

> *Beyond the forest black and still*
> *I shall find you, where the fire*
> *burns the wing of my desire.*)

is that of the *ascensus*, the journey or ordeal upward through experience to knowledge: "they rise and go / up the inevitable stony slope to search / untravelled valleys for the land of wonder"; "I travel on another road / climbing the long hill to a weary town"—here the resolve falters, and we glimpse "the brown hill arid in its pride"; the hill becomes "the hill of lies, high and frozen" until love thaws it, offering "promises of treasure / over the hill, among the burning worlds." The moralized landscapes, the personifications of time and terror, the archetypes of rock and water, hill and hollow, all yoke together in a proper poetic conspiracy, but seem to leave the experience of the poet altogether out of account. Not quite altogether—there is a single poem, "Christmas 1944" in which we hear Denise Levertov's idiosyncratic voice as we shall come to recognize it—fresh, hortatory, resolved to cut losses and keep on living:

> *Come in, then, poverty, and come in, death:*
> *this year too many lie cold, or die in cold*
> *for any small room's warmth to keep you out.*
> *You sit in empty chairs, gleam in unseeing eyes;*
> *having no home now, you cast your shadow*
> *over the atlas, and rest in the restlessness*
> *of our long nights as we lie, dreaming of Europe.*

Here too, of course, the mysteries are rhetorical, found *outside* the poet. As she says, with that saving insight so reflexively her own: "These are my valid symbols, but to you / I know they are the distance and a veil . . . I need," she continues in another poem, "I need a green and undulating line, / the hill's long contours in my words." How to get the effort of the ascent *inside* herself and enacted by her language, rather than by a heap of found symbols to which her language could be only applied—that was to be Denise Levertov's discovery, and one that she made coterminously with her discovery of America. The poet who had been encouraged by Herbert Read and Wrey Gardiner, who had read her "neo-romantic" effusions—

> *The air of life is music; oh, be still*
> *one moment while I listen! But the dark*
> *consumes the sounding minutes constantly—*

on the B.B.C., who celebrated Regent Street, W. 1:

> *The long street is silent under stars;*
> *red, gold, green, the formal fugue of light*
> *continues northward . . .*

was to become a different kind of poet, encouraged by different masters to a different metric, fable and quest.

Had there ever been any doubt about the identity and the autonomy of the language of American poetry after the Second World War, the work in *Here and Now*, published a decade after *The Double Image* by the City Lights Bookshop in San Francisco, would resolve it, and would prove, further, that Denise Levertov had learned, had mastered that language with all the authority of an autochthonous maker; she made herself, that is to say, not merely an agent but an origin of that language, a means by which poetry gains a purchase on reality.

Miss Levertov accounts for the change in her verse within the verse itself, of course—that is why so many of her poems are concerned with the way to find, to come upon, to invent in the true sense of the word, the poetry of her life: "the courage / of natural rhetoric . . . / a chance / poetry that gives passion to the roses" . . . "poems / leaping from shattered windows" . . . In her first of many versions of an *ars poetica*, she says:

> *I want to give you*
> *something I've made*
>
> *some words on a page—as if*
> *to say . . . "Here's a bright red leaf I found on*
> *the sidewalk" (because*
>
> *to find is to choose, and choice*
> *is made).   But it's difficult:*
>
> *so far I've found*
> *nothing but the wish to give . . . Take*
> *this instead, perhaps—a half-*
> *promise: If*
>
> *I ever write*
> *a poem of a certain temper*

(wilful, tender, evasive,
sad & rakish)

I'll give it to you.

Here and Now, a very little book which is kind of a progress report on
her affair with the American language, records the strategies by which
she sought to achieve that poem "of a certain temper." The landscapes
of Mexico and New York which alternate in all her subsequent books
are introduced here, and the imagist notation of experience by an
elegance of phrasing so compressed that we are obliged to "see" life as
an imaginative meld of disproportions:

> *What a sweet smell rises*
> *when you lay the dust—*
> *bucket after bucket of water thrown*
> *on the yellow grass.*
>   *The water*
> *flashes*
> *each time you*
> *make it leap—*
>   *arching its glittering back.*
> *The sound of*
>   *more water*
> *pouring into the pail*
> *almost quenches my thirst.*
> *Surely when flowers*
> *grow here, they'll not*
> *smell sweeter than this*
>   *wet ground, suddenly black.*

It is in such domestic bonds of life, henceforth, that Denise Levertov
will choose to hang, as it is from them that she will seek release. These
poems of epiphany grow together into a union of moments, a rhythm
of exchanges which become, ultimately, such a ritual as the sea's is,
when one sits

> *in sunlight*
> *near the bright sea, listening*
> *to the crash and sighing, crash*
> *and sighing dance of the words.*

The following year, Miss Levertov published (with Jonathan Wil-
liams, adumbrating a connection to the Black Mountain group) an-
other short book, *Overland to the Islands,* which affords a further
glimpse of her hopes for a possible poetry:

The Rav
of Northern White Russia declined
in his youth, to learn the
language of birds, because
the extraneous did not interest him; nevertheless
when he grew old it was found
he understood them anyway, having
listened well, and as it is said, "prayed
            with the bench and the floor." He used
what was at hand—as did
Angel Jones of Mold, whose meditations
were sewn into coats and britches.
            Well, I would like to make,
thinking some line still taut between me and them,
poems direct as what the birds said,
hard as a floor, sound as a bench,
mysterious as the silence when the tailor
would pause with his needle in the air.

Robert Duncan, whose work and friendship had become, she says, a large part of her life, has most astutely gauged this element of her work when he says that "in her clarification of a scene—moving traffic, Mexican girls after First Communion kicking a basketball, or the arrival of sharks off shore at sundown—we recognize that the world contains exact images of our terrors and joys." Yet the unitary perception of experience is not enough—or not enough for the poet who desires in her epiphanies "a radiance consorting with the dance." Her next collection, three years later, is largely a constatation of "the world indivisible," and a submission to the difficulties of continuity; "How much," she begins in a poem called "At the Edge" in this longer book, *With Eyes at the Back of Our Heads,*

How much I should like to begin
a poem with And—presupposing
the hardest said—
the moss cleared off the stone,
the letters plain . . .

Yet, not desiring apocrypha
but true revelation,
what use to pretend the stone discovered,
anything visible?
That poem indeed
may not be carved there, may lie
—the quick of mystery

in animal eyes gazing
from the thicket,
a creature of unknown size,
fierce, terrified, having teeth or
no defense, but whom
no And may approach suddenly.

Gently, then, Miss Levertov undertakes the approach to life as a continuum and to poetry as a rite by which its rhythms may be recorded:

The gods die every day
but sovereign poems go on breathing
in a counter-rhythm that mocks
the frenzy of weapons, their impudent power.

She begins, as most poets do, with an aporia—"no skilled hands / caress a stranger's flesh with lucid oil before / a word is spoken, / no feasting / before a tale is told . . . / nor is there an exchange of gifts, stranger / to stranger, / nor libation, / nor sacrifice to the gods, / and no house has its herm." The longing for rituals, the need to "transform into our flesh our deaths" is the subject, then, of all her later poems, though their object is generally elsewhere, out *in the world* which, as much for Miss Levertov as for a poet like Gautier, absolutely exists as it is. Her undertaking will be to convert: to connect as by a kind of magic that can be neither criticized nor institutionalized nor brought to a full expression of its own intentions, the eternal consciousness of disparities into a momentary unity of association. The literary conventions available—by conquest—to her for this transaction are not always adequate to the ultimate ambition of her task, but in two of her latest books, published in 1963 and 1965, and called *The Jacob's Ladder* and *O Taste and See*, "something sundered begins to knit. / By scene, by sentence, something is rendered / back into life, back to the gods." The titles of these two books suggest the poles from which the poet must swing—on the one side the Jacob's Ladder which is the "path between reality and the soul, a language excelling itself to be itself," and on the other the delectation in the world as *data*, as given: "The world is / not with us enough." Between transcendence and immanence. Riven often into chaos by discrepant and indeed divided allegiances, Denise Levertov has so far devised three principal tactics for reconciling herself with her own spirit, her own flesh. One is the return to an esoteric wisdom—Hasidism, Zen, and that impulse of energy-worship which runs through English and American poetry from Blake and Whitman to Lawrence and Olson—a doctrine that must stand for her as a danger as well as a lure:

Those who were sacred have remained so,
holiness does not dissolve, it is a presence
of bronze, only the sight that saw it
faltered and turned from it.
An old joy returns in holy presence.

Another is the intensification of momentary consciousness to ecstasy, a kind of *via corporis naturaliter* of which she speaks in "The Depths":

Cold of the sea is counterpart
to this great fire. Plunging
out of the burning cold of ocean
we enter an ocean of intense
noon. Sacred salt
sparkles on our bodies.
After mist has wrapped us again
in fine wool, may the taste of salt
recall to us the great depths about us.

And the third is the exploration of her own history, "something forgotten for twenty years." In one of her finest poems so far, "A Map of the Western Part of the County of Essex in England," Denise Levertov turns and addresses her past:

All the Ivans dreaming of their villages
all the Marias dreaming of their walled cities,
picking up fragments of New World slowly,
not knowing how to put them together nor how to join
image with image, now I know how it was with you, an old map
made long before I was born shows ancient
rights of way where I walked when I was ten burning with desire
for the world's great splendors, a child who traced voyages
indelibly all over the atlas, who now in a far country
remembers the first river, the first
field, bricks and lumber dumped in it ready for building,
that new smell, and remembers
the walls of the garden, the first light.

There is a loyalty to experience here that ransoms all that seems only wispy or modish in some of her work as it had been published earlier. The poem picks up the thread of "Christmas 1944" from that first little "Jungian" book, and like an Ariadne in the labyrinth of herself (of which she is also the Minotaur and the Theseus), Denise Levertov follows its scarlet lead with a kind of reverence for its mystery. The lights she once watched on Regent Street, "silent under stars," she sees again in New York:

> *The lights change: the avenue's*
> *endless nave echoes notes of*
> *liturgical red.*

And the poems of sexual fulfillment and protest which began, a decade earlier:

> *Maybe I'm a "sick part of a*
> *sick thing"*
> > *maybe something*
> > *has caught up with me*
> *certainly there is a*
> *mist between us*
> > > *I can barely*
> *see you*
> > > *but your hands*
> *are two animals that push the*
> *mist aside and touch me*

are deepened to compass great disorder as they approach what Yeats called "the mystery that touches the genitals, a blurred touch through a curtain"; indeed in this mode I think Miss Levertov has found her finest successes, in her own sense that finding is choosing and choosing is making. She has fused her initial response to what Jung calls the *mysterium coniunctionis* with an image of desire given by experience, its gratification and ensuing poverty, all transfigured by the language taken into her own hands:

> *Long after you have swung back*
> *away from me*
> *I think you are still with me:*
>
> *You come in close to the shore*
> *on the tide*
> *and nudge me awake the way*
>
> *a boat adrift nudges the pier:*
> *am I a pier*
> *half-in half-out of the water?*
>
> *and in the pleasure of that communion*
> *I lose track,*
> *the moon I watch goes down, the*
>
> *tide swings you away before*
> *I know I'm*
> *alone again long since,*

> *mud sucking at gray and black*
> *timbers of me,*
> *a light growth of green dreams drying.*

It is the handled language she trusts to, in her following book, *The Sorrow Dance*, published in 1967, with a confidence that bears out the rite-enacting energy of her entire career: Denise Levertov can rely on her control of the *shapes* of speech, now, to release her into that ecstatic awareness she has sought in the esoteric and the momentary and the autobiographical, fused in this book into a single change, or if not a change, then a *choice* of surrender, a letting-go that is the final mastery:

> *. . . Hypocrisies*
> *of seemly hope, performed to make a place*
> *for miracles to occur; and if the day*
> *is no day for miracles, then the preparations*
> *are an order one may rest in.*
>
> *But one doesn't want*
> *rest, one wants miracles. Each time that note*
> *changes (which is whenever you let it)—the kettle*
> *(already boiling) passing into enlightenment without*
> *a moment's pause, out of fury into*
> *quiet praise—desire*
> *wakes again.* Begin over . . .

The tone here, characteristically combining the domestic and the dutiful with the sacramental, is the proper measure of this poet's mature authority; as she says at the end of this same poem, "The Unknown," "the awakening is / to transformation, / word after word." In this new collection, a series of poems about her dead sister recovers for poetry, by the intensification which only poetry can afford, the narrative energies we tend to associate, weakly, with the makeshifts of prose, and in "A Lamentation," for example, from which the title phrase comes, there is a cumulative energy which derives, I think, from her present talent for combining what were once only different ways of acceding to the gnostic trance—combining, that is, the urge to *tell* with the impulse to *stand* within the moment and with the celebration of the energy that celebrates itself:

> *That robe or tunic, black gauze*
> *over black and silver my sister wore*
> *to dance* Sorrow, *hung so long*
> *in my closet. I never tried it on.*

> *And my dance*
> *was* Summer—*they rouged my cheeks*
> *and twisted roses with wire stems*
>   *into my hair . . .*
> *I was compliant . . .*
> *betraying my autumn birthright . . .*
> *Always denial. Grief in the morning,*
>   *washed away*
> *. . . crumbled to a dozen errands between*
> *busy fingers . . .* Grief,
> have I denied thee? Denied thee.
> *The emblems torn from the walls,*
> *and the black plumes.*

One of the sources of this rite-making, of course, is the capacity to see things so clearly in the world, living "each minute the last minute," that "nothing was changed, all was revealed otherwise; / not that horror was not . . . / not that I thought there was to be no more despair, / but that as if transparent all disclosed / an otherness that was blessed." The capacity to see the way things seem, to chart appearances accurately in a "world / of terror, filling up fast with / unintelligible signs" is what makes possible that other transaction, that inward acknowledgment: "her being / is a cave, there are bones at the hearth."

In fact, when this poet cries "look inward: see me!" we are tempted to obey, to follow her into "the other country / sacred to desire" largely because of her success in the *given* one, the country where things are first themselves, where a man is "the temple of himself," before they are or stand for other things. All her practiced insight—*penetration*, one might say—into erotic transactions, the realization of the smile, in "Face to Face," that

> *leaves us each at ravine's edge*
> *alone with our bodies . . .*

is gained by a surrender to surfaces, a willingness to cherish ignorance of the depths provided it is accompanied by a wisdom of exteriors:

> *Cold shine of sun on swamp water,*
> *cold caress of slant beam on bough,*
> *gray light on brown bark.*
> *Willows—last to relinquish a leaf,*
> *curious, patient, lion-headed, tense*
> *with energy . . .*

Miss Levertov, herself "curious, patient, tense with energy," calls the section of her new book from which this comes "The Crust," and the implication is that the lineaments of things, their outward circumstances, their rind and rim, provide the immanent measure of the inward ones,

> *indicate measure, that is, they present*
> *limits that confine the way to a single path.*

There is another world, Paul Éluard once exclaimed, and it is in this one! So Denise Levertov has discovered, though the other way round: in her longing for "miracles," and "otherness that was blessed," she has come upon the world, *this world*, and in it, out of it, has created the forms, the rites that grant her access to that first, divined reality which is the object of her faith: they are her poems.

JOHN LOGAN

"I Am Interested in the Unicorn Underneath the Wound."

JOHN LOGAN was born in a place called Red Oak, Iowa, in 1923, was educated in Iowa City, has taught in South Bend, Indiana and more recently at the University of New York State at Buffalo. The poetry of this landlocked life has often ransacked literature and history for its pretexts, drawing resourcefully on quotations from Augustine, Virgil, biographies of Rimbaud, Christina Rossetti, Heine, retellings of Homer and observations from Pliny, Dr. Brill and a "source-book of Animal Biology." Imitations and epigraphs, versifyings and translations stiffen these poems, which for their length are formally dependent upon few enough means to keep them erect in the reader's mind. Logan's invocation of Dante and of Botticelli, for example, is altogether inward, not a cry from the rooftops or even from the depths, but an assimilation of substance, as when the catgut stitches suturing a wound are absorbed into the tissues of the traumatized body—this poet is not concerned to derive from his apprenticeship to these creators of Christian formality any semblance of decorum as an Outward Sign. Hence his ardors of dedication, rewritings and apostrophes to *them*, not to their achievement. A further stiffener, often to the point of rigidity, is a recourse to Doctrine, the machinery of the Church which so often makes it hard for us to be sure what a poet would be if he were not part of a going concern larger than himself. The spirits said they had come to give Yeats "metaphors for poetry," and the Catholic Church has often afforded as much, though interested in doing so only, to be sure, as a by-product. One of the rewards of Logan's work is the sense that he must have struggled *against* dogma, must have appealed first to, then away from it (dogma being not the absence of thought but the end of thought), in order to *achieve* transfiguration, not yield to it. Anything else than such an engagement, such a grappling which is as much a flight from faith as a foundering within it, is indeed a succumbing, not an approach, of course, and when we read, in the dedication of Logan's third volume: "The Redemption has happened. The Holy Ghost is in Men. The art is to help men become what they really are," it is apparent, even before we expose ourselves to the poem's action upon us, that we are not in the hands of a mere pietist, that Logan is possessed by no theory but a thirst.

Tautologically enough, in the understanding of Christianity, for a man to become *what he really is* means that he does not become something else, does not undergo or initiate upon himself a metamorphosis, which is the central symbol of divine love as the understanding of Paganism conceived it. For Logan, a man initiates or undergoes a *transfiguration*, is made over only by becoming more intensely and ecstatically himself—becomes what he really is to the exclusion of accident and change. That is the lesson, for him, to be learned from the lives of the saints and the deaths of the martyrs, and to be rehearsed, dreadfully enough, in the very *realia* of his own existence, no less profound for being the more profane: "if some people find my subjects less religious now than they used to be, the reason is that I now think poetry itself more religious than I used to do . . . It's not really the skeleton in our closets that we fear, it's the god."

John Logan's most remarkable and happily most characteristic poems, then, will not be versified accounts of the torture and death of the British poet-martyr Southwell, or even Freudian *aperçus* into the overmothered life of a Heinrich Heine, individual and even indicative as the latter are:

> *But his tough old mother stayed on*
> *And he never became*
> *The husband; he took to his marriage*
> *Couch interesting women,*
> *Remaining a curious virgin.*
> *In the last years of his life*
> *He wept at the pain of lust*
> *Stirred in his tree-like limbs*
> *Already dry. And he left*
> *Framing with paralyzed lips*
> *One more note to his mother.*
> *Only the ambiguous Dumas cried*
> *At the holy rite they danced when he died.*

Logan's highest achievement, I think, the basis and perhaps the residue of all the other poems, are those—they are to be found in all of his books, more densely in the later ones—of confession, the kind of writing in which experience has not been mediated by knowledge, or at least by learning, and in which the risk, consequently, attendant on transfiguration is greatest precisely where it is run most egregiously—fastest. The autobiographical mode allows this poet to exploit to intense profit the confusion, if not the identity, of his beliefs in God and in the Oedipus Complex. Sometimes indeed I am not so sure about God, but the Western tradition of parricide and piety is certainly furthered here, whether acknowledged baldly ("Man's central difficulty is his old hell with his prick") or in the terms of violent metaphor:

> *My mother died because*
> *I lived or so*
> *I always chose to believe . . .*
> *I watched at last for her*
> *Among our sacred*
> *Stones, for I was grown*
> *Before I found her tomb.*
> *Today I point to that:*
> *It's there my heavy mother*
> *Rots. Remember!*
> *. . . She suffers there the natural turns;*
> *Her nests on nests of flesh*
> *Are spelt to that irrational end,*
> *The surd and faithful Change. And stays*
> *To gain the faultless stuff reversed*
> *From the numbers' trace at the Lasting Trump.*
> *So here my mother lies. I do not*
> *Resurrect again her restless*
> *Ghost out of my grievous memory:*
> *She waits the quiet hunt of saints.*
> *Or the ignorance of citizens of hell . . .*

This, by the way, is the poem that along with posterior attributions to Xenocrates, Richard Eberhart, T. S. Eliot and Alejandro Carrion, begins with epigraphs by Augustine and Dr. A. A. Brill's famous "Years ago I came to the conclusion that poetry too is nothing but an oral outlet." The Quest for Mom, Everyman's Children's Crusade, so to speak, is conducted and pursued in these poems through other biographies and into hagiography, as the "Cycle for Mother Cabrini" attests; yet as Freud insisted, always and only can be resolved in individual experience. Hence the apposite tone of "The Picnic," from which I quote only a glint at the center, an echo of the departure from Eden:

Afterward we walked in the small cool creek
Our shoes off, her skirt hitched, and she smiling,
My pants rolled, and then we climbed up the high
Side of Indian Gulley and looked
Where we had been, our hands together again.
It was then some bright thing came in my eyes,
Starting at the back of them and flowing
Suddenly through my head and down my arms
And stomach and my bare legs that seemed not
To stop in feet, not to feel the red earth
Of the Gulley, as though we hung in a
Touch of birds . . .

That is the articulation of a style, I think; that is a level of meaning: open, unarguable, ecstatic. I find it in the title poem of Logan's third book, *Spring of the Thief*, preeminently, and in perhaps a dozen disbosoming poems elsewhere. Not that Logan's other poems are a loss, or even a lessening, of necessity—just that they are so often something added to experience, not something made out of it, that they substitute for what they cannot enclose. By a paradox which is a commonplace of critical experience, the poems which involve the surface of recondite minds, of recorded lives, are for Logan an excuse for private (rather than personal) locution; after all, the facts we have not discovered for ourselves are those we can—indeed, those we must—use as symbols. Whereas the poems committed to the often dreary processes of an Iowa boyhood and an Indiana surround—*they* are the poems of an exemplary publicity, personal but not private, not content with or confined to a merely surface report—indeed, like J. F. Powers' fiction, not competent to offer surfaces in any consistently attractive fashion —but condemned to deal with centers, surds, insights, illuminations witnessed in chosen, obsessive, *suffered* images.

John Logan's first brief book, *Cycle for Mother Cabrini*, was published in 1955. In it the poet initiated his series of versified abstracts from the lives of the holy and the modishly hellish. This is their strategy: an oblique title establishing the poet's intimacy with an alien world of discourse, furthered by a quotation in the epigraph, generally in a foreign tongue and untranslated. Then the body or at least the skeleton of the poem itself, usually in short lines and broken—splintered, actually, since this is never a discourse cut at the joints—into several stanzas and parts. Followed by further attributions of subject matter, as "after Athanasius; and after a painting by Morris Graves." There are poems commenting on or at least reporting a pathological case in Pliny and a *pensée* by La Mettrie, the latter full of Logan's peculiar rash learning (Plato, Diogenes, Descartes, Harvey, Boyle and Bacon of Verulam all brought forth) invariably exercised in the refutation of "a chemical function":

> . . . *A few more wheels a few*
> *More springs than in*
> *Say your better animal?*
> *And with a closer heart*
> *To fill the brain with blood*
> *And start the delicate moral*
> *Hum in the anxious matter.*
>
> *Suppose I agree the soul is*
> *An engine, admit Descartes*
> *And the rest never saw*
> *Their pair of things—never,*
> *As you say, counted them;*
> *Then here's the ambiguity,*
> *And a further problem:*
>
> *You say you find an inner*
> *Force in bodies, and watch*
> *The smallest fiber turn*
> *Upon an inner rule.*
> *Now I don't see that this*
> *Is such a clear machine!*
> *In fact I think I wish it were.*

This is like listening to one end of a telephone conversation whose significant sense depends on the words inaudible at the other. Yet if we do not know precisely what the familiar words drag after them into the poem ("their pair of things" refers, I guess, to the body and the soul as separate and separable entities), still we know vaguely what the weight of it feels like and, as in all these "commentary pieces," that seems enough to make a poem at one level (or remove) of listening. Logan himself puts it this way: "these poems try to disprove materialism by coming into existence; and that is the extent of their apostolate."

In the poem on Saint Augustine's sixteenth centenary, Logan comes closer to himself, to the experience he may appropriate, not merely cite:

> . . . *The brass knobs*
> *On doors twist easily*
> *Spring back*

And I lift bread to mouth
Without trouble, at the corner

Turn right sin is like this
Why sin is natural as blue is
But drags at joints
Unnaturally
Dries membranes with sand

Is most clinging most cold most
Crabbed of all the casual
Things. And you lost your mother
Just as you learned rejoicing
And before you studied

How not to grieve: your brilliant
Bastard Adeodatus
Died too . . .

The fear of being too perfectly understood, the fear that banishes punctuation marks as it borrows puzzling material from the context of biography, is mastered a little in one astonishing poem of transfiguration in this book, "Grandfather's Railroad," which I give with punctuation adduced from a prose version Logan published three years later in the *Chicago Review,* part of an impressionist chronicle (by impressionist I mean that desperate skepticism which casts about to find, but cannot find, a floor to the universe) of boyhood called "The House that Jack Builds":

I think my grandfather knew
I'd never seen a negro
Before. I thought I saw

The shallow trough that cut
The field he showed me real
As a railroad, and reached

North for Kemling Store.
I could have seen the bright
And keen two rails where they

Grow so thin I could have
Run, vanishing where they did.
My grandfather told me

The old underground railroad
Wound through Montgomery
County; he pointed a fine

Haired finger and led
Across the dust-lit land
The believed negroes—gold,

Lithe and wild as the wind-
Burned wheatfield.
My grandfather didn't see

My pickaninny doll had three
Pigtails she shook like
Ribboned wings on wires

From the train windows. Fires
Shivered in our capturers' eyes.
Who cares! The cars of great

Black men roar past
Shadowing the field like clouds
Or giants that seem to slow

And stride as lean as trees
Against the north sky.

Here the world of the child, its unexplained terrors and inexplicable tininess are really *enacted* in the verse; "I knew my limbs sang on me sometimes," Logan acknowledges (and the humility is really an assertion), his midwest vernacular strong in another song of experience, "Pagan Saturday," and it is such singing which makes him the religious poet he seeks to be rather than the strained or anyway the strenuous devotions to the saint celebrated in the cycle for which this first book is named. Frances Xavier Cabrini, an Italian-born nun who became the first Beata from the United States, was canonized in 1950 by Pius XII, who named her the patron saint of emigrants; in her grimy, unglamorous work founding schools, orphanages and convents, hospitals and nurseries, across the continent and even in Latin America until her death in 1917, she looms for this poet as one of his company of "saints as heroes of the will." It is because "Mother Cabrini" knows "our schools / our stores our gods and business rules" that Logan says he invokes her, and finds, visiting her body that is subject to the laws of mortal decay, his peculiar comfort, rather like the solace afforded by viewing Jocasta's corpse after she has been embalmed:

I thank God Mother Cabrini's
Body is subject to laws
Of decay. To me it is
A disservice when flesh

Will not fall from bones
As God for His glory
Sometimes allows. I speak thus
For flesh is my failing:

That it shall rise again
Salvation. That it shall not
Conquer is my blind hope.
That it shall rise again

Commanding, is my fear.
That it shall rise changed
Is my faith. I think
I can love this saint

Who built highschools
And whose bones I came upon
Today . . .

This is closer to oratory, and then abruptly to natural utterance, than the rest of Logan's cycle, which depends for its music, its incantatory extension, on a single effect, that of the rhyme concealed within the arbitrary line:

But Christ what do we do
That hate pain and can't
Pray and are not able
Not to sin; that stay
Contrite, until night: did you
Not die for us too?

In fact, as James Dickey has pointed out in one of the few critical notices of Logan's work that signifies beyond the jacket blurb, this poet's technical abilities are relatively slight, and really begin and end with an uncommon capacity for coming up with a strangely necessary and urgent observation and setting it among others by means of ordinary, unemphatic but rather breathless language "which makes his lines read something like a nervous onrushing prose." That is why we find, in the same number of the *Chicago Review* that published "The House that Jack Builds," Logan reviewing Edward Dahlberg as:

Sad with the melancholy of the young who yearn for freedom from the curse of snakes—of Hippolytus turned by the thought of Phaedra from his beloved horse and bow. And sad with the other sadness of the old who have failed to save their sons, the awful agony of Laocoön seeing the ruin of his sons . . . But nowhere the tenderness of the father whose serpent is the instrument of his love, and his sons the arrows of his quiver, his daughter the apple of his eye.

And then find him in his second book, *Ghosts of the Heart,* 1960, versifying the passage into his own transfiguration of experience, in the "Lines to his Son on Reaching Adolescence":

> . . . *But for both our sakes I ask you wrestle*
> *Manfully against the ancient curse of snakes,*
> *The bitter mystery of love, and learn to bear*
> *The burden of the tenderness*
> *That is hid in us. O you cannot*
> *Spare yourself the sadness of Hippolytus*
> *Whom the thought of Phaedra*
> *Turned from his beloved horse and bow,*
> *My son, the arrow of my quiver,*
> *The apple of my eye, but you can save your father*
> *The awful agony of Laocoön,*
> *Who could not stop the ruin of his son.*
> *And as I can, I will help you with my love.*

This self-imitation, quarrying one's marble from one's own (already exhibited) bleached bones, is variously instructive, but most of all a lesson in what formal transactions and achievements we should *not* look for in Logan's verse and in his attitude toward versifying. In these long, incremental poems about the intensification of reality—the "starry pinnacle of the commonplace"—into an ephiphany of being, the rhythms do not discover themselves in lines, or even in units cut from the lines "as the poet's mask is cut out of the flesh of his face—to amplify the light gestures of his soul"; rather Logan's verse is accessible —to him, to us—as mass, not as unity, so that his most successful poems are, like "The Picnic" in the second book and like the title poem in the third, *Spring of the Thief,* published in 1963, too long to illustrate favorably by quotation. If this is prose, though, if it is difficult to see the cause of the form (the appearance on the page) in this:

> . . . *but if I look the ice is gone from the lake*
> *and the altered air*
> *no longer fills with the small*
> *terrible bodies of the snow.*

Only once these late winter weeks
the dying flakes
fell instead as manna or as wedding rice
blooming in the light
about the bronze Christ
and the thieves. There these three
still hang, more than man-
sized and heavier than life
on a hill over the lake
where I walk
this Third Sunday of Lent.

—if this is prose, it wears, and not vainly, the poem's vestments, the apparel of priesthood. As Logan himself explains: "A poet is a priest or a necromancer of the baroque who dissolves by the incantations of his cadenced human breath the surface of earth to show under it the covered terror, the warmth, the formal excitement . . ." Cadenced human breath, call it, as an instrument to get at transfiguration. The energy of spiritual substance driving through endless labyrinths, the very corridors of the lungs, which occasionally coil into form. There is a strange innocence about this voice, for all its ecclesiastical knowingness and all its bookish insistence, the innocence of a man who does not say, like Jarrell's despairing Woman at the Washington Zoo, "Change me! change me!" but rather, "Make me Myself!" Besides the centripetal mode of confession he has come upon, the one I think most effective and convincing in his repertory:

I was born on a street named Joy
of which I remember nothing
but since I was a boy
I've looked for its lost turning.
Still I seem to hear my mother's cry
echo in the street of joy.
She was sick as Ruth for home
when I was born. My birth
took away my father's wife
and left me half
my life. Christ will my remorse
be less when my father's dead?
Or more . . .

—besides this guilt-ridden litany which manages never to sound like Robert Lowell even if it does so at times merely by not being very accomplished, Logan has two other means of approaching transfiguration: one is the historical commentary I have mentioned, which in

Spring of the Thief he brings to a characteristic pitch of laceration, as in "The Experiment That Failed":

> *I have not written my poem*
> *about the Pope and the two young men*
> *the obscure muddle-headed muse*
> *first sent when I first read*
> *histories of the transfusion experiment.*
> *And I do not know why,*
> *except for the bitter fight*
> *in me—about the fact*
> *the boys died. (But so did he.)*
>
> . . . .
>
> *What can I find out?*
> *I don't even know what killed them.*
> *Or him. And I do not want*
> *to think it was the loss of the blood*
> *of manhood. There is always more of that.*
> *Besides, it is really feminine*
> *to bleed and be afraid.*
> *Well, what then?*
> *The old one and the two young*
> *men. Two fresh stones, or wells—*
> *and the powerful untried pen.*
> *What cut them down? . . .*
> *Yet my mind keeps holding back*
> *with its bloody axe of stone*
> *another idea*
> *nobody wants known:*
> *that it was the hope of a fresh, transmuted life*
> *for which the Pope*
> *and the two sons died.*

The other mode of access to transfiguration is the ecstatic identification of the poet's consciousness with objects, with landscape, with a weather intromitted into the self. Thus in his "Eight Poems on Portraits of the Foot," Logan comes right out with it:

> *It is the wish*
> *for some genuine change other than our death*
> *that lets us feel (with the fingers of mind)*
> *how much the foot desires to be a hand*
>
> . . . .
>
> *The man yearns toward his poem.*

The wish for some genuine change other than our death, the trans-
figuration of life not in immortality but in the living of it—that is
Logan's manfully shouldered burden and his quest: the body of this
man's work *cries out* to be poems, and in that exploration, which is his
own form of prayer, who can doubt he has already succeeded and will
—over his towering argument as over his tottering art—prevail.

The Anonymous Lover by JOHN LOGAN

If there has appeared among us—at Carmel or Niagara Falls, most
recently in Hawaii, youngest state "where grace gives back to sight /
what beauty is"—one poet who might be said to write for (and
reach) not merely "the" public but his public, an audience which
is truly what the French call it, an *assistance*; one poet who is indeed
among us, not off to one side, in the predictable Empyrean or the
profitable Inferno, that would be John Logan:

> *Soon,*
> > *we begin*
> > > *to say the poems again*
> *and to touch each other—*
> > > > *the older*
> *man, me,*
> *the boys and the girl read-*
> *ing over the sea's*
> *sounds*
> > > *by the candles'*
> *light and the moon bright, burgeoning*
> *shin-*
> > > *ing time to time*
> > > > > *as*
> *the clouds pass.*

From the spattered page (to which I shall return: the example just
given is fairly flagrant) onto the speaker's platform, Logan has found,
has invented, has convulsed his way to that listening body which in
viridescent America is generally identified not so much with a reader-
ship as with witnesses, people who prefer performances to books, the
young:

> *I want to open (willingly) the mouth*
> *of my youth*

> and breathe musical breath
> into it.

And so he does; he does want to, and he does breathe it—into his youth, their youth, whatever youth is around, "for our conscience views itself / in the mirror of the flesh." With a choking intensity altogether characteristic of a man so deep-throated, so large-hearted, Logan has labored to divest his poetry, as we find it now in his fifth collection, of all that is arduous, exacting, exclusive, professional, to make it efficient outside the clique of the learned. By efficient I mean *operative*, working, irresistible even, upon that kind of cursive exposure which is not at all sure it will have—or require—a second occasion. This is poetry for the first time around, when the first time is at once acknowledged to be the last as well:

> *The limbs of my poems*
> *come within your reach.*
> *Perhaps it is you whom I seek.*

And of course—as the resonance of Whitman reminds us—this is poetry at more than one remove from *verse:* the designs upon us which Logan's language will have cannot afford that larger-scale ceremonial of hovering expectations—expectations met, violated, restored—which depend upon a unit, a model constituted by at least the line, at best the paragraph or, decorously, the stanza (the *room* in which to turn back, to walk up and down). A hand-to-mouth music is to be heard here, there is no time for setting the table, for courses; the rhymes are discovered in passing, and like anything which passes, they vary in quality, but they are there, usable, functional—they serve to mark the end of something which language itself accommodates, the end of effort.

But before I lounge a little among the dissipated ardors of *The Anonymous Lover,* with its idiosyncratic landscapes, photographs, paintings, inventories and addresses, I want to look back first to its predecessor, *The Zigzag Walk,* which gathered up Logan's poems from 1963 to 1968. I want to look back because I want to show, in brief, what it is that this poet has labored to divest himself *of;* what the baggage is, or was, that Logan is now the lighter for having jettisoned. In an earlier account of Logan's first three books, I remarked upon his versions of transfiguration, achieved by fervors of dedication to dead poets and mages, to landscapes and objects, and to his own insulted and injured experience, his confessed biography. In the case of past masters, Logan's apostrophes are always to *them,* not to their achievement. That is wonderfully so in the Keats elegy from *The Zigzag Walk,* a representative (and gorgeous) achievement in itself. I shall not quote the poem entire, but let me refer to it as if it were before you, for Logan's enterprise here is indicative of all that he has decided no longer to bother about.

If not despairing, then desperate in their fluttering apostrophe, Logan's "Lines for the Twice-drowned" (once in death, again in the realization of death: "You, Keats . . . and I . . . drown again / away from home . . . as you once drowned in your own phlegm, / and I in my poem. I am afraid.") offer that typical terror of process which is this poet's signal—his signal to write poems, one might say, at any rate, at any cost, to break silence by that fond utterance of the situation, that Recognition Scene he sets over and over again. Logan's zeal of identification is of course to the *man* Keats, the Keats of the letters quoted in the epigraph and of the terrible deathbed so hallucinatorily figured in the body of the poem itself—rather than to the poet Keats, the Keats of the Odes, say. The slow, unpersuadable triumph registered by a poem like "To Autumn" is not to be collected from an exile in the sopping Roman graveyard. Logan cannot, in his own poem, keep from casting experience in its charnel terms, for so the occasion appears to demand of him ("Since my birth / I've waited for the terror of this place"), but his capacities and his task as an artist come to his rescue here, save him from being no more than the Beddoes of the affair. For the care he takes with notation, indeed the almost musical play against each other of things heard and felt and seen ("the sky moans long" . . . "Ruth's hand is cold in my cold hand" . . . "the streams that shape and change along the tender's rubber back") is warped by the end into a kind of patience: reluctantly, painfully, the revelation is given: the living poet can read the gravestone of the dead one. He can learn, by fraternal concession, that there *is* a process in that final fierce violet, as in the "furious August rain" which, if only acknowledged, if only *imagined* intensely enough, can permit the kind of ultimate acceptance which so loads "To Autumn." For all Logan's pangs, he achieves or is granted a patience, for that is what patience originally means: a *suffering*, here a sufferance of the worst in order to gain not the best but no more than being—that ongoing life which is writ in water indeed, "streams that shape and change," for we must alter in order to exist.

There are not many poems in *The Zigzag Walk* so good as the Keats elegy, nor need there be; there is throughout the book a passionate striving between language and experience to represent each other—an energy *toward* that transfiguration of experience which will relieve Logan of the process, the patience:

> *For like the lost or stolen flesh of God,*
> *the self, more alive or more dead,*
> *opens on to the truth*

> *of earth*
> *and sea and sky—*
> *and the thieves' cave yawns empty*
> *of our smuggled body.*

In Logan's new book, of course, there is no patience to be relieved; the transfiguration has always and already occurred—*elsewhere*, outside the poems, which are merely the marginalia of metamorphosis, a prolegomenon to any future ecstasy. It is foolish to speak any longer of Logan's "task" as an artist, for these poems are the discovery of a method which will obviate tasks, their mastery, and in a sense their mystery. The poems of *The Anonymous Lover* are perhaps the first in the history of the art which are set down, by an authentic artist, to take care of themselves; hence the buckshot lines, the broken words, the determination of movement by the "revealed" rhyme of language off the transfigured tongue-tip. In the representative achievement here, the final poem "Tears, Spray and Steam," Keats is indeed mentioned (there is someone around who "knows / all the Odes / by heart / as well as many / bawdy songs"), but he is merely a prop, not a passion now. Logan is past passion in these exploded notations—he is ready and willing to let the language wash over him, noticing its casual arrests and declaring, there! that will be the poem. The risk of his decision is ours, and of ours, his. Consider, if you will, this example of the recipe:

> *But in that warm spring*
> *water which we briefly left, everything*
> > *eventually heals*
> *for, by*
> > *the sea*
> *it flows out of these ancient, California hills,*
> *which are the trans-*
> > *formed*
> *giant body of a once*
> *powerful, feather, bone and turquoise-adorned*
> *Indian Prince,*
> > *and the sulphur is the changéd*
> *sharp incense*
> > *he burned daily as he chanted*
> *year and year over for the sick young princess—*
> *who took her loveliness*
> *from the many-colored, fragrant trees*
> *and the flickering sea.*

You will notice that *once*, *prince* and *incense*, for instance, terminate the lines in which they occur, or rather the word-clusters, for there

are no lines here, there is nowhere the axiological sense of enjamb-
ment whereby the beginning and end of what is set on the page
gives, as Ammons says somewhere, a certain downward rush to the
movement, something like a waterfall glancing in turn off opposite
sides of the canyon, something like the right and left turns of a river.
You will notice that the poem is organized by the words in which
it occurs, no more than that, and no less—which is true of the very
greatest writing, or it is felt to be true, and of another kind. Again,
the risk is Logan's; the rhythms here, or the intervals, at least the
passages from one damned thing to the next, are determined by no
more than the possible assonance, the color of an else-despised rhyme,
wherever it may occur. You will notice these things, and you will be
satisfied because it is John Logan who has set them before you—or
you will not. The poem submits to no further order—and hence to
no argument—of a larger cause than what the individual words drag
out of it. An artist of this stature—and Logan's audience is of course
correct: he has found them because *they have found him*—is doing
no more than taking his life in his hands. No wonder he says, or the
prose says through him:

> *I feel somewhat*
> > *panicky,*
> *weird, about my sweat-*
> > > *ing body.*
> *For where do we and our vapors end?*
> *Where does the bath begin?*

WILLIAM MEREDITH

"All of a Piece and Clever and at Some Level, True"

ART BY its very nature asserts at least two kinds of good—order and delight." So William Meredith, in his introduction to a selection from Shelley, a poet who interests this decorous American for his patience with established verse forms, being "otherwise impatient of everything established." Meredith's declension of order and delight as versions of the good, a paring susceptible of a whole range of inflections, from identity to opposition, is the generating trope of his own poetry, its idiopathy or *primary affection.*

In his four books of poems, even in his translations of Apollinaire,* a curious restraint, a self-congratulatory withholding that is partly evasive and sly, partly loving and solicitous, testify, like so many essays in emphasis, to the war between delight and order, and yet to the necessity of divising them in each other: if order is not found in delight, the world falls apart; if delight is not taken in order, the self withers. Success, for Meredith, is provisional—he does not ask more.

In 1944, Archibald MacLeish, inheriting the editorship of the Yale Series of Younger Poets from the late Stephen Vincent Benét, commended to his predecessor's exhibited taste his first choice of poems, *Love Letter from an Impossible Land* by a "William Meredith, Lieutenant (jg) U.S.N.R."—so the poet signed himself on the title page— for its "quality of reticence and yet of communication, almost unwill-

---

* "Readers may feel that the inaccuracy that remains in these translations stems from deliberate and humorless conviction rather than from good-natured ignorance."

ing communication . . . after a difficult and dangerous campaign. It has an accent of its own." Dedicated to Christian Gauss of Princeton, prefaced by MacLeish, published in the Yale series, and gravely committed to military transactions, Meredith's first book certainly stands under the sign of every kind of authority: military, educational, institutional and, as an expression of them all, the formal authority of closed verse forms: strict songs, sonnets, bookish roundels worn as so many masks. If such verse has "an accent of its own," it is the accent of a young poet (Meredith was 25 when the book was published) for whom the very notion of an accent was concrescent: his success is in mastering the accent of others, so that only at odd moments, turning abrupt corners, do we hear a voice that will be, so indisputably, the poet's own:

> *This is the old, becoming grief of shepherds,*
> *This is the way men have of letting go . . .*

or again:

> *. . . respite from passion, real change?*
> No, we shall want again later and greatly all over.

and most characteristically:

> Only the delights of the body
> Which I am convinced are godly,
> And the brave ones, do not disappoint me now.
> *The brave ones with black hair and good eyes*
> *Come round like January and are sure;*
> For these only I resolve, wearing tokens
> And putting checks on calendars not to forget,
> Not to betray, if possible.

Against the rest, the lines printed here in roman type have a resonance that will recur, one characterized by self-doubt, submission to the evidence of the senses and an eagerness to invoke the ethical generalization; here is a final sample, from a poem called "Altitude: 15,000":

> *One does not shout to end the quiet here*
> *But looks at last for a passage leading out*
> *To domesticity again and love and doubt,*
> *Where a long cloud makes a corridor to earth.*

But for the most part, these earliest poems have other echoes, or rather echo others, often with beautiful ease, but all the more evidently borrowings. Yeats is a constant aspiration:

> *Only an outward-aching soul*
> *Can hold in high disdain these ties . . .*

> *The dedicated and the dead,*
> *Themselves quite lost,*
> *Articulate at last . . .*

and Matthew Arnold a several-times invoked preceptor; the kind of phrasing Arnold developed in "Dover Beach" is splendidly engaged in the title poem here:

> *Providence occurs to me;*
> *I will salvage these parts of a loud land*
> *For symbols of war its simple wraths and duties,*
> *Against when, like . . . sailors*
> *Disbanded into chaos . . .*
> *I shall resume my several tedious parts,*
> *In an old land with people reaching backward like many curtains,*
> *Possessing a mystery beyond the mist of mountains,*
> *Ornate beyond the ritual of snow.*

Sonnets on suicide ("Empedocles came coughing through the smoke") and war cleverly assimilate the Auden chime that we hear in the well-stopped lines:

> *The maps were displaced and most of the men dispersed,*
> *And worst perhaps of all, I have lost the wanderlust.*

And in the flagrantly mimicked adjectives here:

> *He was seized with an enormous remorse:*
> *The native stone was bright, the lines untrue.*

At the end of the book, though, something happens to these brevities uttered with such a stiff upper lip, these clipped phrases which embody The Good-as-order. The experience of war, the actual displacement of the poet's person to the Aleutians, provoke a mode of discourse in which the mind's response to behavior threatens order and bids, in desperation, for delight:

> *We lie in khaki rows, no two alike,*
> *Needing to be called by name*
> *And saying women's names.*

In the long title poem, in "June: Dutch Harbor" and in the astonishing "Notes for an Elegy" (where the loss of a single airman—

> *Who had not fought one public battle,*
> *Met any Fascist with his skill, but died*
> *As it were in bed, the waste conspicuous—*

is by a tone of obedient resolution reconciled with the public war, when

Morning came up foolish with pink clouds
To say that God counts ours a cunning time,
Our losses part of an old secret, somehow no loss.)—

in these poems Meredith wrote what stand among the best poems of
service in the Second World War, odes to duty that constitute a
lamentable genre but a real distinction. Buttressed, as I have said, with
Auden and Arnold, alienated by, say, Kodiak Island from the compla-
cencies the word "Princeton" may be taken to represent, this Navy
flyer discovered an equilibrium sufficiently endangered to be poignant,
yet sufficiently realized in experience to be possessed:

But for your car, jeweled and appointed all for no delight,
But for the strips that scar the islands that you need,
But for your business, you could make a myth.
Though you are drawn by a thousand remarkable horses
On fat silver wings with a factor of safety of four,
And are sutured with steel below and behind and before,
And can know with your fingers the slightest unbalance of forces,
Your mission is smaller than Siegfried's, lighter than Tristan's,
And there is about it a certain undignified haste.
Even with flaps there is a safe minimum;
Below that the bottom is likely to drop out.

Meredith's second book, *Ships and Other Figures*, published
promptly in 1948, is a beating to quarters after the risks of such battle
pieces. Even the tactical exercises carried over—"Battlewagon,"
"Transport," "Carrier" and "Middle Flight"—from the earlier experi-
ence of war are by now tamed, as another title put it, "against excess
of sea or sun or reason." Various traditions are assayed: wedding song,
dedicatory verses (one in a copy of Yeats' poems), an *Ubi Sunt*, an
Envoi, even an "Homeric Simile" whose elaboration still affords a
glimpse of the self inside:

And each man thinks of some unlikely love,
Hitherto his; and issues drop away
Like jettisoned bombs, and all is personal fog . . .

But in most of its poems, this smug little book is a retreat to modes of
learning and convention. Meredith even provides several pages of
notes, explaining, for example, that by "Middle Flight" he "would like
to convey the negative of Milton's grandiose phrase," and synopsizing
Sophocles as a (quite supererogatory) gloss on these last lines in the
book:

We flourish now like Theban royalty
Before act one: right now Delphi seems far,
The oracle absurd. But in the wing
Is one who'll stammer later out of pity
—I know because I've seen these plays before—
To name his actions to the fatal king.

If in this collection, then, the poet has occasion to juice up his tone, to rehearse the sequestering pleasures of order perceived as a submission to the old conventions by which we cope with or understand our experience, producing such anthology-pieces as "A Boon" and "Perhaps the Best Time" with their bright and barbered lines, yet the impression given by the twenty-nine brief poems taken generally is one of constraint rather than control The excess against which the poet urges himself is not *in the poems*, and the solutions come too pat:

Everything the years do
Can be called a kindness
And what lies behind us,
Howsoever candied
By the memory,
Has for only virtue
That it lies behind.

Even so, there is a saving discontent here too, and in the "Envoi" to the book, with its Chaucerian echo, Meredith accounts for his activity as a poet by a covering confession of inadequacy:

. . . the comeliness I can't take in
Of ships and other figures of content
Compels me still until I give them names . . .

Awareness, then, that *figures of content* compel by their comeliness must disqualify mere decorum, though it is always easier for this poet to "give names" to what he discards than to specify what it is he keeps. At least by his third book, *The Open Sea*, which was published in 1958, Meredith insisted on play, on a response to selfhood as pleasure, on the morality of virtuosity. By this time, he is sure enough of his vocation to invoke it as an ethical force. Back in his first book, he had characterized a Beethoven quartet as "not tune nor harmony nor a wild sighing, but strings only . . . taught this wisdom that returns on itself with such insistence." In the second book, there had been another poem about the string quartet, dedicated to the composer Randall Thompson, in which Meredith observed that when we attribute intentions to the instruments, "these novel troubles are our own we hear." Still more determinedly, this third book insists on the autonomy of art, and with it of form. Music, for example, means only itself (the bird "holds a constant song; / He calls to what he calls") and yet is "at some level, true." Tautology is here declared a significant fiction. Everything, conversely, which does not mean only itself is, at some other level, untrue. For Meredith, all art, poetic or otherwise, is an act of self-defense against the world changing its meaning from moment to moment, against the difference, against things becoming *other*, against their loss of identity. For him, poetry is a way of asserting that things are what they are—the insight of self-reference—and that when they mean something else, order as well as delight is endangered. Hence *The Open Sea* contains many poems about works of art, amounting almost to a poetics—poems about Chartres, about the Brooklyn Bridge, about a Persian miniature, about Robert Frost's poems read aloud by him, as well as "Thoughts on One's Head (in Plaster, with a Bronze Wash)" and, in this context most important, "To a Western Bard Still a Whoop and a Holler away from English Poetry." Here as in a number of poems he would write subsequently, Meredith defends the very decorum that endows as well as endangers him—defends it desperately:

> *It is common enough to grieve*
> *And praise is all around;*
> *If any cry means to live*
> *It must be an uncommon sound.*
>
> *Cupped with the hands of skill,*
> *How loud their voices ring,*
> *Containing passion still,*
> *Who cared enough to sing.*

His meters and sentences, as Robert Lowell remarked of Meredith, "accomplish hard labors," and he will not see them jeopardized by mere exuberance, mere rebellion. Moreover, he has arrived with great certainty at his own destination now, his own tone of voice—playful, even chatty sometimes, indulgent or willful, but the movement of the lines, for all the prose syntax, is the movement of music:

> *A person is very self-conscious about his head.*
> *It makes one nervous just to know it is cast*
> *In enduring materials, and that when the real one is dead*
> *The cast one, if nobody drops it or melts it down, will last.*
>
> *We pay more attention to the front end, where the face is,*
> *Than to the interesting and involute interior:*
> *The Fissure of Rolando and such queer places*
> *Are parks for the passions and fears and mild hysteria.*

The things that go on there! Erotic movies are shown
To anyone not accompanied by an adult.
The marquee out front maintains a superior tone:
Documentaries on Sharks and The Japanese Tea Cult . . .

This particular head, to my certain knowledge
Has been taught to read and write, make love and money,
Operate cars and airplanes, teach in college,
And tell involved jokes, some few extremely funny . . .

The achievement of this tone, and it is a very inclusive one, brings Meredith to his final stance, which I mean to compliment when I say it is of a rueful maturity. Decorum is questioned but must be, he acknowledges, abided, and in the best-known poem of this third book, "The Chinese Banyan," the heroism and "dark capacity of quiet" are celebrated with a wisdom which gives every evidence of a deepening investment in life. Meredith's adherence to reality is more powerful and complete than his—or our—acquiescence in pain and despair, though he knows, and allows, that they always win "in the end." He is not, then, an eschatological poet, for he is concerned with what is *going to happen* between now and the end:

I speak of the unremarked
Forces that split the heart
And make the pavement toss—
Forces concealed in quiet
People and plants . . .

he observes in "The Chinese Banyan," and this heroism of modesty is the gravamen, too, of his latest and best book, *The Wreck of the Thresher*, which was published in 1964. Here the academic notes (which had persisted in *The Open Sea*) are dropped, nor is the book dedicated (as that volume was to Professor Stauffer) to a celebrated educator "who could write / Commonplace books"; indeed the entire collection has a freshness and an amplitude of assurance which shows the poet to be in possession not only of his own voice now, but of his own vision as well. There are still the poems "about Poetry," the ritual tributes to Frost and the redeeming one to Apollinaire; there are also more charms or spells cast against chaos and change, for by opposing mutability Meredith would say that words are not a medium in which to copy or record life; their work is to restore life to order, and in doing so to enable delight. This enterprise succeeds best, I think, in the book's longest poem, "Roots," which continues the impulse of "The Chinese Banyan" and develops the dialectic of identity and alteration, selfhood and extinction in the form of a conversation between the poet and his elderly neighbor, Mrs. Leamington, a widow wrestling with a mysterious tree-root in her garden in May, "when things tend to look allegorical." Here all of Meredith's gifts converge: the lucid, easy phrasing—easy, I mean, to read; Meredith makes no secret of the fact that "poems are hard"—the ingratiating self-deprecation, the ready sense of character:

> *Her face took on the aspect of quotation.*
> *' "The Magus Zoroaster, my dead child,"*
> *—That's Shelley, the Spirit of Earth in Shelley—*
> *"Met his own image walking in the garden*
> *That apparition, sole of men, he saw . . ."*
> *—Prometheus Unbound, a long dull poem.*
> *Please use the ashtray, not my luster saucer.'*

and the recovery of the terror which resides in the usual. The poem has the rich, seemingly random detail of a novel, yet never loses its intensity as a poem: a clear presentment of life, its preoccupation with death is made normative by wit and the self-stroking charm this poet elsewhere employs a little too consciously. The other great successes in the book are the meditation on "his Hands, on a Trip to Wisconsin" (from "Five Accounts of a Monogamous Man"), the most intimate of Meredith's poems, and the Phi Beta Kappa poem read at Columbia in 1959, "Fables about Error." A poem in four parts, this work is a masterpiece of phrasing, image and, again, reticence, in which the poet has turned all of what had been his conventional accomplishments in the earlier volumes to his striking advantage. Consider first the management of the verse mechanics, as in this report of a dead mouse found in a trap:

> *His beady expressionless eyes do not speak*
> *Of the terrible moment we sleep through.*
> *Sometimes a little blood runs from his mouth,*
> *Small and dry like his person.*
> *I throw him into the laurel bush as being too small*
> *To give the offenses that occasion burial.*

The music of that concluding couplet, with its significant retard on the last word as it takes the rhyme, preceded by the rightness of "occasion" as a verb here, and the prose sensibility of that description of the mouse's mouth, could not be equalled by any poet younger than Marianne Moore except, perhaps, Richard Wilbur. Then the felicities of image as carried by phrasing, in this figure of grackles:

> *Like a rift of acrid smoke*
> *A flock of grackles fling in from the river*

And fight for the winter sun
Or for seed, is it, in the flailed grass.
Their speech is a mean and endless quarrel
And even in their rising
They keep a sense of strife, flat across the orchard;
Viciousness and greed
Sharpen the spaces of sky between them.

Next the control of learning—for in his intellect-despising way, Meredith is learned—the mastery of reference appropriate in this context is here conjugated with a stunning awareness of what it is like to be alive now:

Many people in Massachusetts are moved by lust,
Their hearts yearn for unseemly fittings-together
Which their minds disown. Man is aflutter
for the beautiful, Diotima told Socrates,
But the flesh is no more than an instance for the mind to consider.

And finally, the old reverence for order, the mistrust of pleasure, the withdrawal into convention is given a new moralizing pitch, where art is seen as the mode of bringing delight and discipline needfully together:

The mind should be, like art, a gathering
Where the red heart that fumes in the chest
Saying kill, kill, kill, *or* love, love, love,
Gentled of the need to be possessed,
Can study a little the things that it dreams of.

The persistent modesty of this disarming poet makes an assessment of his achievement—its value, and in the old sense its virtue—something of a violation of his very temper. The arms of which he would strip us are self-importance and heedlessness, those devices we employ to get through life more cheaply. Meredith's voice now, submissive to his experience and the representation of a discipline at a higher frequency than itself, recalls us to a more expensive texture:

What little I attend, I know
And it argues order more than not.

Earth Walk: New and Selected Poems by WILLIAM MEREDITH

To a careful culling from his four books of poetry published between 1944 and 1963, this poet who aspires, by now, to praise "a benign selfhood" has added 14 new poems, "poems that are devious in ways I still like better than plainspokenness," as he says in his ingratiating foreword. It is when Meredith is most devious that he is indeed best: sermons, uplifts, sententious dallyings with mortality are not only plainspoken, they are outspoken, and they do not serve to advantage the subtle art, the resilient devices Meredith has accommodated with such determined mildness. They are here, though, the moralizing and the temperance and the terrible monosyllables—*love* and *guilt* and *time* and *heart*, sending their spondaic juices through the verse, dithering:

> *now my wish is that it [the heart] will continue to pump*
> *easily, with the pulse love has taught it.*

A poet so solicitous of natural appearance, natural process as Meredith has made himself disappoints when he abandons nature so flagrantly; is it *love*, then, that "teaches" the heart its pulse? is it Time that is "without forgiveness"? A reader shrinks from these dim personifications, especially when there is a poet at hand, in his own person, as we say, to surprise us with the real aspect of things—as *he* says, "to hold the light steady and make no comment."

Devious, then, in the most ordinary sense, Meredith's worthiest poems take the long way around, collecting their evidence gradually from the ground, grateful for the show of affability on earth, as in the title poem:

> *Now I unstrap the rented Avis car*
> *and, opening the hatch, step boldly out*
> *onto the Planet Earth. My skull is bare,*
> *thin animal hide is fitted to my feet.*
> *The autumn air is fresh, a first pepperidge tree*
> *has turned mahogany and red. This is a safe walk . . .*

Though he is anything but naive, Meredith has a great gift for innocence, for the recovery of terror and joy which reside in the usual. And it is from the usual that he rises to his moments of the genuinely, vatic, not preaching but prophecy, inviting the mediation of the ordinary in its original sense, the sense of participating in an order, so that the poem is an ordination. Meredith is a poet who would single out experience only provisionally, only to remark the more readily on its affinities with other experiences rather than on its ecstatic isolations. Not ecstasy but instance, not the standing-outside but the abiding-within:

> *A widening spiral in all elements is our way.*
> *Alone, or coupled like geese, or leather kids in a bunch,*
> *We own to swirling forces that pull us. If a man's going by*
> *Hardened the sweet air, he would leave a conch.*

The strategy of the poem "Whorls", from which this eloquent quatrain comes (consider the fine management of slant end-rhymes, and the splendid full rhyme of "alone" with "own" which gives that curious locution "own to" such ambiguous force), is characteristic of Meredith's arrival at success by so many departures from the straight and narrow. He gathers his version from the movement of oceans, the current "starting toward the poles", and from the movement of the child "issuing" from the womb even as "the planet hugely circles, and as it spins", and from the movement of young men who nightly "harness motorcycles and cars", though "sleeping elders have tied their lives in arcs"—only when he has engaged his themes from journalism to geography, from cosmic to cosmetic, is Meredith ready for "the figure everything makes that spirit pulls," the figure which will be his poem, the conch which is the hardening of air in "a man's going by". When they proceed directly to their end, Meredith's meditations are, in the alienated sense of it, unearthly; he requires, as in the wonderful poem "Last Things", to stun the homiletic impulse in himself with random profusion, indirect notations, like that of the porcupine moving "with the difficulty of relics":

> *Having crossed the road oblivious, he falls off*
> *Deliberately and without grace into the ferns.*

This is followed at once by relics of another kind quite, for the next stanza switches to a "junkyard of old cars, kept for the parts" and concludes with a wry eschatology analogous to the porcupine's: "cars the same age are parked on the road like cannibals." The instances pile up, as in another of Meredith's part-songs, "Hydraulics", they abound against the single vision, the mere knowledge of precept. "This is happening all the time," he marvels, and in such confrontations with process, with "the real aspect of things" is Meredith's true (devious) wisdom, stupent, uneasy, matte: "this is me knowing, this is what I know."

Hazard, the Painter by WILLIAM MEREDITH

Relentlessly affable, ruefully shrewd on not only the uptake but the sharp putdown as well ("the merest rag of glory / will keep ambition warm"), William Meredith and his creature of chance, apparently a painter fallen, in middle age, upon that autumnal decline which is perceived to characterize his America as well ("his unpopular conviction / that his nation has bitterly misspoken itself") swathes sixteen fashionably casual poems, no two alike and one not casual at all, inside a beautifully reproduced dust jacket, a Breughel detail ("Harvesters"—a cool fall, of course) which could overpower any poet more ambitious, less devious than this one. But it does not overpower Meredith and his Hazard ("resemblances . . . are not disclaimed"), it merely offers a gloss—heroic for all its melancholy mists, panoramic, and beyond appeal—on the lenient *aperçus* of this brief book, this little life so determined not to be convulsive, cauterizing, calcined.

So skillful in his mild modernism ("Here at the seashore they use the clouds over and over / again, like the rented animals in *Aïda*"), so various in his errant annotations is Meredith that we do not know even at the end what hit us—a caress of ground glass and very finely honed feather blades, most likely, so that hits just aren't in it. Mortality and the dimming senses are the apparent pretext of these ruminations:

> *I think dear one that one day I'll fall off*
> *this galaxy, leaving husk and canvas behind,*
> *the loneliness I'll take with me made whole,*
> *myself made whole, by what we've said*
> *in these knocking moments, oh,*
> *and keeping, as hearts keep,*
> *(husk and canvas being little abandoned houses)*
> *and going away so.*

Thus Hazard in "a note which she takes to be a valentine and on the whole well-meant" to his wife, effaced supernumerary for such purposes as this "characterization" requires—the personnel of the poems are there to reflect Hazard reflecting, to pay attention in order that we do. But the real subject is *ressentiment*, even anger, and the real object throughout is America the Imperial, these States in their warring "decline" viewed from a perspective which has only darkened since Emerson unbosomed himself to his journal, 1847 (was that year, too, a decline—were all years?):

> *Alas for America, as I must so often say, the ungirt,*
> *the diffuse, the profuse, procumbent—one wide ground-*

juniper, out of which no cedar, no oak will rear up a
mast to the clouds! It all runs to leaves, to suckers,
to tendrils, to miscellany. The air is loaded with
poppy, with imbecility, with dispersion and sloth . . .
America is formless, has no terrible and no beautiful
condensation.

It is to produce such terrible and beautiful condensation that Hazard paints, that he is stuck on the one figure, or figure in a landscape, for the duration of the poems, but I must not pursue the Emerson parallel further, for though Meredith runs in a following groove, Emerson is the greater poet, the prophet, as Meredith would be first to insist. Meredith doesn't want to be a prophet, only an artist, a messenger, an angel maybe. But the observation, the organic detail plucked out and brooded upon until it yields up its sense, its significance—that is Emersonian (the Ground-juniper), and it is Meredithian too:

> *Near the big spruce, on the path that goes*
> *to the compost heap, broken members*
> *of a blue-jay have been assembled*
> *as if to determine the cause of*
> *a crash without survivors.*
> > *Walking*
> *with Hazard, the cat does not observe*
> *them. The cat will be disassembled*
> *in his own time by underground technicians.*
> *At this point Hazard's thought turns chicken.*
> *It is the first warm May day, the rich*
> *black compost heap is full of promise.*

Promise! The decline which is the asseveration of mortality in a moribund democracy holds like a freeze in this little novel until winter sets in, the real freeze, and Hazard sets out again. And the book ends there, in a wonderful epitome of the two poets who have meant the most to Meredith's making, Frost and Auden—Frost for precisely that "beautiful condensation" not to be formed by our affluent drecky lives, Auden for the recognition of sacred sites, a commitment to Earth as transcendence:

> *Gnawed by a vision of rightness,*
> *that no one else seems to see,*
> *what can a man do*
> *but bear witness?*
> *And what has he got to tell?*
> *Only the shaped things he's seen—*
> *a few things made by men,*
> *a galaxy made well.*

Though more of each day is dark,
though he's awkward at the job,
he squeezes paint from a tube.
Hazard is back at work.

No fuss is made, the enduring is everything. I guess Hazard couldn't exist without Berryman's Henry, without Lowell's *History*, yet how much less posturing in this man—how much less is more! Maybe there *is* posturing ("devious in ways I still like better than plainspokenness," is Meredith's vaunt), but it is so attractive, so ingratiating, that it seems, merely, how meaning turns in the mind's mouth, enjambment a way of walking, figuration a dead reckoning. I would not make overweening claims for the little suite which is mostly spoken under the breath, from a procumbent posture as it were, but the life is in it, unreconciled surds of identity, and I am grateful for the record of what it has been like, existing—if not exacting—in *my* hazardous time, too.

JAMES MERRILL

"*Masked, as Who Was Not,*
in Laughter, Pain and Love"

Y OU BITCH," squealed Ezra Pound, not surprisingly to the author of
the just-completed *Wasteland* which had been submitted to his
assessment, "I am wracked by the seven jealousies and cogitating an
excuse for always exuding my deformative secretions in my own
stuff . . . I go into nacre and objets d'art. Complimenti." That—
especially the casting about for an excuse, but also the metaphor of
secretion, whether nacre or amber, to represent a part of the self which
has become precious by hardening—that is the artisan's honest resent-
ment of the artist; that is the poet who can see no more than the design
in *things* envying the poet who can also see things in a design. Pound's
version of his own limitation, with its characteristically shrewd diag-
nosis of his mode, helps us to understand better the whole sense of
Keats' beautiful remark that we hate poetry which has a palpable de-
sign upon us—poetry, that is, which would enforce the *design*, the
restrictive pattern and the decorative detail, at the expense of the
ongoing enterprise, the poem's project which is "evermore about to
be." But the jealous voice of a man capable of no more than objets
d'art addressing a man capable of an art transcending objects might
easily be the voice of the early James Merrill apostrophizing the writer
he was to become: one who managed to make what was merely his
poetry into what was necessarily his life. For such is the case of an
American writer whose several books of poetry stand upon one another
like "huge pale stones shining from within," the latest affording the
widest view of the country which had hitherto been seen only by
wisps and pebbles, never as—in the entire sense of the word—a
prospect.

In 1951, Merrill published a numbered edition of his *First Poems*, a nacreous volume indeed, which prompted Howard Nemerov in a review to the wicked but supported comment that the work was certainly very good for first poems; "probably some of them would do even for second poems." And, as we shall see, Merrill has made some of them do. But for all their exquisiteness, these early poems have a strength of their own, the strength of standing against an undecided element, initiating "valors of altitude." The things that make them precious make these poems precise as well, and the bright conjugation of his triviality, or at least his frivolity, with his truth makes Merrill's gently nurtured voice, from the first, one we listen to with more than just a concession to grace:

> . . . *Luminous in these schools*
> *Language is a glittering of flint rituals*
> *And a race of sober children learns long smiles.*

In so many poems about the perishable, though, there is a polite and almost impenetrable patina on these pretty things "that in / such curious vividness begin," a glassy lacquer evident in Merrill's vocabulary —"gracile," "chryselephantine" and "idlesse" suggest the baubles plucked from "the shallowest stratum of the past"—as in his diction. The articulation of an abstractive sensibility round an armature of minimal *given* excitations—"roulades of relinquishment," or better and worse still, "the night was a warm nubility"—is this poet's characteristic verbal gesture. The real but unrelenting wit is a matter of local color, often so incidental as to arrest or surely distract the attention that is trying to get on with it:

> . . . *Consider other birds: the murderous swan*
> *And dodo now undone* . . .

or again:

> . . . *fine red sand brought*
> *From where sun makes a stab at majesty* . . .

We do not feel that the poet's enjoyment of his devices (often invented by trusting to the language, letting the experience accumulated in words shine through, as when Merrill speaks of "hillsides *original* with joy") has ever been sacrificed to a development of his understanding. He indulges the finite, or anyway the finished. Hence a good number of emblem poems ("The Peacock," "The Parrot," "The Pelican," "The Black Swan"), in which everything is given from the start, nothing allowed to happen or become. Indeed, the problem this poet rather languidly wrestles with and does not always resolve in these *First Poems* is how to get the reader through his poem to its end (always, in such instances, something elegaic and anguished, something decorative and heartbreaking:

> *Love's monuments like tombstones on our lives*),

how, simply, to drag "the enchanted eye, the enchanting syllable" down the page and still enact upon the reader the literally arresting design which is Merrill's original talent in both senses. One hope, though often rather a wan one, is the exploitation of baroque syntax, the long sentence looped like an anaconda upon its punctuation and pronouns in such a way that we can find no release from it, once we are within its toils, but at the stanza's close:

> *Glass fragments dropped from wholeness to hodgepodge*
> > *Yet fasten to each edge*
>
> *The opal signature of imperfection*
> *Whose rays, though disarrayed, will postulate*
> *More than a network of cross-angled light*
> *When through the dusk they point unbruised directions*
> > *And chart upon the room*
>
> *Capacities of fire it must assume.*

Here the quibble on "rays . . . disarrayed" and the elaborate conceit of prismatic refraction in its paradoxical relation to broken edges ("pointing unbruised directions") can be assumed—an idiosyncratic Merrill verb, offering every possibility for agnomination—by the elaborately wrought sentence, which without letting the mind settle down accommodates a (disputed) statement, an antithesis, a relative clause of detail (also antithetically modified) and a temporal clause doubled to match "unbruised directions" and "capacities of fire" with the notions of "wholeness" and "hodgepodge" introduced in the first line. Yet Merrill's serpentine sentences are too often a motionless coil to get us past the nodes in the line: the action is already over when the poem begins and, as in the stanza quoted here, when the crystal bowl has been broken and we are asked to ruminate upon the pieces, there is nothing left to do but moralize an aesthetics of the *fait accompli*. Of the accomplishment itself, there can be no question; most of these poems are successful in affording us "astounding images of order"; and if their shellac and jewelry make them seem, like the rococo armor of the Sun King, little more than machinery brought out only for festive occasions and worse than vulnerable for being invulnerable, even so "there's keen delight in what we have"—indeed the rest of Yeats' description of modern poetry is perfectly apposite to Merrill's early work, though to it only—"the rattle of pebbles on the shore, under the receding wave":

> *. . . To drown was the perfection of technique,*
> *The word containing its own sense, like Time;*
> *And turning to the sea he entered it*
> *As one might speak of poems in a poem*
> *Or at the crisis in the sonata quote*
> *Five finger exercises: a compliment*
> *To all accomplishment.*

For there is always a tidal undulation beneath these poems, always a fascination with the sea—the movement of water, the periodic destruction and recurrence of waves, the "makeshift waterfalls" of fountains —as the one entity and element refractory to the poet's designs, and therefore beyond any willed arrest mirroring (*reflect* is another Merrill favorite: Narcissus as Neoplatonist) the treasures of a drowned identity. In water, "change is meaningless, since all is change," and the poet can bear, for all his glossy, stilled performances, to confront "disordered gleams from under the tide (analogous to his "root's long revel under the clipped lawn"). In a capital poem, "The Drowning Poet," Merrill details this enthrallment with great care: water is an element

> *Familiar as, to the musician, scales,*
> *Where to swim is a progression of long vowels,*
> *A communication never to be sought*
> *Being itself all searching: certain as pearls,*
> *Simple as rocks in sun, a happiness*
> *Bound up with happenings . . .*

Here the sea becomes the locus of a final, farthest selfhood, that place and state where history can at last be assented to, where process is indulged if not invited, and where tautologies like "a communication never to be sought / being itself all searching" find a natural, a necessary home. Such reflexive constructions—"the gaze that of all weariness / remains unwearied"—like the encapsulated notions of Time as "the word containing its own sense," of love as "a thing in itself," and most grandly, of "time and love and doom" as

> *Those great blue grottos of feeling where the rank intruder*
> *Is moved to think in rhyme—*

suggest the problem which obsesses this poet, at least at this point in his career: how to get past the local excitement ("where every paradox means wonder") and into the stream of occurrence; past the "brim of what may be" and into the element of what is. Merrill wearily thrusts from himself these "sea's accumulations shored and salted" in favor of the sea itself, complaining that, for all his cunning in the cutting of a cameo, "alone, one can but toy with imagery." He wants to get beyond or below what he merely enjoys and therefore repudiates, down to "the base of stone":

> *. . . as one descending*
> *The spiral staircase of association*
> *Around the well of substance . . .*

One way down to this lithic level is pointed to in—among other poems, but here at its most sustained articulation—the sixth variation of a series of changes rung on the phrase "The Air is Sweetest that a Thistle Guards"; it is the way of prose, of prose talk, the self soliloquizing in that reflexive, persistent babble we recognize as the bedrock of utter- ance, and a far cry—or rather no cry at all, but really a near and nestling murmur—from the lacquered plangencies, the bejewelled in- cantations of most of this volume:

> *Friday. Clear. Cool. This is your day. Stendhal*
> *At breakfast-time. The metaphors of love.*
> *Lucky perhaps, big Beyle, for whom love was*
> *So frankly the highest good, to be garlanded*
> *Accordingly, without oblivion, without cure.*
> *His heedful botany: not love, great pearl*
> *That swells around a small unlovely need;*
> *Nor love whose fingers tie the bows of birth*
> *Upon the sorry present. Love merely as the best*
> *There is, and one would make the best of that*
> *By saying how it grows and in what climates,*
> *By trying to tell the crystals from the branch,*
> *Stretching that wand then toward the sparkling wave.*
> *To say at the end, however we find it, good,*
> *Bad, or indifferent, it helps us, and the air*
> *Is sweetest there. The air is very sweet.*

What a departure—really an exodus—from the stanza of "The Broken Bowl" already quoted! How different the running, conversational blank verse, with its halts, its telegraphic notations, then its burrowing monosyllables ("love as the best there is and one would make the best of that . . .") which constitute the *Gerede* of an identity unsure of its own grounds for understanding. How startling here the dismissal of jewels and emblems in favor of happening. In "The Peacock," Merrill speaks of that figure of pride as "trailing too much of itself, like Proust"; here a different novelist is invoked, and one whose tubby "egotism" apparently represents less of a threat to continuity than the vanity of a perfect beauty. Stendhal's famous "metaphor of love," the branch dipped into the saline solution, is preferred to the "great-pearl" version—it is not the precious product which interests the poet, but the

process, "saying how it grows and in what climates . . ." Of course
Merrill still delights in what he knows he has, his quibbles:

> . . . *love, great pearl*
> *That swells around a small unlovely need . . .*

and the outright, even outrageous puns:

> . . . *the bows of birth*
> *Upon the sorry present . . .*

and certainly there is a fastidiousness in the diction, a knowing, *triste*
music of selfishness in a phrase like "to be garlanded / accordingly,
without oblivion, without cure," which reminds us that not everything
has been sacrified to the Code Napoléon. Still, the effort here—and it is
an issue, an exit—is "to tell the crystals from the branch" rather than to
appreciate "curvings of glass artifice"; the sound of sentences, as Frost
put it, utterance accountable to a limited and thereby illuminated self,
transcends, or begins to transcend

> . . . *that slight crystal lens*
> *Whose scope allows perfection to be conceived.*

In 1954, three years after *First Poems*, Merrill published semi-pri-
vately (sixty copies for sale and one hundred and fifty for "friends of
the poet and the printer") an even handsomer volume, or rather a
pamphlet of some ten poems, with the very important title *Short Stories*.
Almost all the longish poems here are blank verse recitals, someone
telling something which happens, partly in the telling, partly before-
hand, so that the event is enlarged or countered by the narrator's tone,
as in "The Cruise":

> *Poor little Agnes cried when she saw the iceberg.*
> *We smiled and went on with our talk, careless*
> *Of its brilliant fraction and, wakeful beneath,*
> *That law of which nine-tenths is a possession*
> *By powers we do not ourselves possess.*
> *Some cold tide nudged us into sunny gales*
> *With our money and our medications. No,*
> *Later in shops I thought again of the iceberg . . .*

Of course we recognize some of the old turns—"a possession by
powers we do not ourselves possess" is just that reflexive mordant
Merrill prefers, especially when it involves a pun on "powers"—but the
unaerated columns of print and the distrust of rhyme suggest the prose
impulse in these pieces, the effort to melt down the jewel-like stanzas
into a continuous discourse. As stories, the poems are not very success-

ful, far too elliptical and emblematic as they are to articulate, even yet, "a happiness bound up with happenings." But as dramatic monologues, portraits of voices limned at a crucial corner of an incident, these poems indicate a great extension of Merrill's means, a playfulness in terms of genre and tone which will serve him more and more seriously. By varying the number of syllables—sometimes eleven, sometimes nine, rarely ten—the poet gives a nice corrugation of surface to his pentameter, and he is very good at speeding up the poem by suspensions of syntactical structure and by enjambment. "Gothic Novel," for example, begins with a swift pastiche of prose manners, disposed like a surrealist colonnade in an infinite regress of archness:

> *How rich in opportunity! Part of a wall*
> *Gave back a hollow sound. Forthwith, intrigued,*
> *The Contessina knew her mind, consulted*
> *No one. A door! Annunziata darkly*
> *Swept up after the workmen and withdrew.*
> *Lost in thought, her mistress was already*
> *Rehearsing what to say in thirty years:*
> *'Only after our marriage did I begin*
> *To fear your father'—but she broke off*
> *And went with a candle down the dank stair*
> *Leading she knew not where . . .*

This is in part the poet making a mockery of his own postures in those of Wilkie Collins, but it is also his way of learning how to *recount*, a test of style which will help him on. Even when he employs rhyme in these pieces, Merrill disguises it in a device introduced, I think, by Auden in *Nones* (1950)—rhyming only the accented syllable of a feminine word with the final syllable of the next line—thereby enhancing the prose effect for the eye but keeping the ear alert to a sequestered music:

> *There are many monsters that a glassen surface*
> *Restrains. And none more sinister*
> *Than vision asleep in the eye's tight translucence.*
> *Rarely it seeks now to unloose*
> *Its diamonds. Having divined how drab a prison*
> *The purest mortal tissue is,*
> *Rarely it wakes. Unless, coaxed out by lusters*
> *Extraordinary, like the octopus*
> *From the gloom of his tank half-swimming half-drifting*
> *Toward anything fair, a handkerchief*
> *Or child's face drifting toward the glass, the writher*
> *Advances in a godlike wreath . . .*

There are still jewels here too—"glassen surface" (glassen!), vision's "diamonds," "lusters extraordinary"—and the characteristic vocabulary of a self-deprecating urbanity, as if to tell the truth one had to be very, very tired. But there is also a truth to the *telling* (it is a real octopus Merrill shows us, though one invoked only as a figure of vision) which coaxes us through the poem, beyond the "lusters" and to the end, just as vision must for this poet be coaxed out of the "prison" of even the purest mortal tissue . . .

Alongside Current Events, poems about The Phoenix, The Vampire and Midas (all crucial figures for this poet, versions as they are of the disproportionate relations between life and artifice, but the last a paradigmatic emblem, rehearsing precisely Merrill's quandary: how to grasp the world yet somehow leave it intact) approach the myths obliquely, through a gossipy genre of runs and gushes. The narrator's occasional surrogate, an elegant and perverse Young Man named Charles introduced in *First Poems* ("Charles was like that"), is the last *persona* we might expect to meet up with in the refurbishing of such august categories, but he is evidently Merrill's first choice in escaping from the kind of emblematic stasis which fetters him:

> *There followed for each a real danger of falling*
> *Into the oubliette of that bland face,*
> *Perfectly warned of how beneath it lay*
> *The bat's penchant for sleeping all day long*
> *Then flying off upon the wildest tangents*
> *With little self-preserving shrieks, also*
> *For ghastly scenes over letters and at meals,*
> *Not to speak of positive evil, those nightly*
> *Drainings of one's life, the blood, the laugh,*
> *The cries for pardon, the indifferences—*
> *It was then Charles thought to wonder . . .*

What Charles wonders is what "on earth" the Vampire means by confessing herself a symbol of the "inner adventure." And with a teasing laugh, Merrill ends his poem: "Her retort is now a classic in our particular circle." It is not the story, not even the retort, but the notation of a world in which the retort is possible that matters to him; these poems are concerned to create a climate of opinion, a variable weather of discourse, and the provoking resonance of privacy about them—"a classic in our particular circle"—is little enough to pay for the freedom they afford the poet, though it is a freedom he cannot always himself afford. The resolution of one difficulty invariably prompts another, and the decorative impulse is ever ready to capture Merrill's new beachheads:

> *. . . the dread*
> *That, civilizing into cunning shapes,*
> *Briefly appeased what it could not oppose.*

In 1957, Merrill published his first novel, *The Seraglio*, a good deal of which seems to have been written by Charles; though the first half is a narrowly observed account of life among the very rich and the very bored at what one Smith girl calls "the tippy-tippy end of Long Island," the remainder of the book turns into the glittering topography of a fantastic mythological opera, whose performance has overwhelming symbolic consequences for the novel's personnel as well as its prose. Two years earlier, Merrill's full-length play *The Immortal Husband*, a graceful Giralducian treatment of the story of Aurora and Tithonus, had been performed off-Broadway in New York and was later published. Both works indicate that the poet was concerned to explore the directions by which he might best work himself out of the lysis into which his *First Poems* had brought him: the direction of prose narrative and the direction of characterized speech. And in 1959 Merrill's new book of poems, *The Country of a Thousand Years of Peace*, was published, encompassing too all the *Short Stories* but "Gothic Novel." It is a brilliant, opalescent book and provides samples not only of all the accomplishments in form and decorum which *First Poems* had rather stiflingly insisted on, but realizations of the experiments in tone and identity initiated by *Short Stories*, now absorbed and even outstripped in some of the new pieces. In the eight years since his first book of poems, Merrill had made himself a "good European"— that is the first thing we notice about these poems, their wide but personal range of allusion to the experience of a transcontinental sightseer, shopper and sleeper (O the dreams in the "Hôtel de l'Univers et Portugal!"

> *We had begun perhaps to lack a starlit Square.*
> *But now our very poverties are dissolving,*
> *Are swallowed up, strong powders to ensure*
> *Sleep, by a strange bed in the dark of dreaming),*

and their ready understanding of Europe's history in the terms of Europe's myths: not only the Vampire and Salome, but an updated Marsyas, and Orpheus, even Europa herself in a couplet sonnet (one of the book's half a dozen jokes on the form) typical of Merrill's heightened method, whereby geography and puns, gossip and elegy are melted into the one vision:

> *The white bull chased her. Others said*
> *All interest vanished. Anyhow, she fled,*

Her mantle's flowing border torn
To islands by the Golden Horn,
Knee bared, head high, but soon to set
One salty cheek on water, let
Flesh become grass and high heart stone,
And all her radiant passage known
Lamely as Time by some she dreamt not of.
Who come to pray remain to scoff
At tattered bulls on shut church doors
In black towns numberless as pores,
The god at last indifferent
And she no longer chaste but continent.

It is a metamorphosis Ovid never dreamed of! Here the failure of classical religion ("the god at last indifferent") and the degeneration of a Christian successor (with its glancing reversal of Goldsmith's pious line and the camp on papal bulls in "Who come to pray remain to scoff / at tattered bulls on shut church doors") are wittily subsumed not only in the figure of Europa herself turning into Europe ("her mantle's flowing border torn / to islands by the Golden Horn"), but in puns inherent in her languages: "no longer chaste but continent" is almost inhumanly clever in its ultimate apprehension of the tourist's happy hunting ground. The notion of the Continent as a vast declining bazaar:

Mild faces turned aside to let us fondle
Monsters in crystal, tame and small, fawning
On lengths of ocean-green brocade.
"These were once nightmares," the Professor said,
"That set aswirl the mind of China. Now
They are belittled . . . into souvenirs."
"Well I'm still famished," said a woman in red
Whose name escapes me now . . .

follows Merrill through all his poems henceforth, even affording him a subject in his *refusing* to buy: the negative version of experience, the turning from love, the renunciation of the voyage, the impatience with possessions ("tame . . . fawning . . . belittled into souvenirs"), all such rejecting moments become increasingly momentous for this "future sleuth of the oblique," and poems about Amsterdam, Italian lessons, India and Japan, the Sculpture Museum and the Hall of Mirrors rehearse the genre of dissatisfaction. The dream narrative *suffers* this poet to memorialize his losses, to conjugate the downward history of Europe with the backward anamnesis of identity:

. . . As my eyes close, nearby
Something unwinds and breaks.
Perhaps the Discus Thrower has let fly
Or Laocoön stepped from his snakes
Like old clothes. The scene changes . . .

But a white eyeless shape
Is gesturing deep in my dream.
I turn back to you for companionship . . .

Well, I shall wake you now,
Smiling myself to hide my fear . . .

I judge it now in your slow eyes
Which meet mine, fill with things
We do not name, then fill with the sunrise
And close, because too much light stings,
All the more when shed on these
Our sleeps of stone, our wakenings.

It is in rhis metropolitan book (the title refers to Switzerland, where "they all come to die, fluent therein as in a fourth tongue"), that Merrill is able, to a degree because of the technical innovations already discussed and to a degree because of a larger confidence in his own powers as a *persona* in the poem, the latter the fruit of travel—is able and ready, then, to shift from history and myth, through dream, to an unmediated confrontation with his own life, his own voice. Even in the persistent emblem poems, the moralized centrepiece is transformed, as in "A Timepiece," from a made or found object (a broken bowl, a black-and-white cameo, a decorative bird) to a living person—here the poet's pregnant sister:

. . . It was not her life she was heavy with . . .
Let us each have some milk, my sister smiled
Meaning to muffle with the taste
Of unbuilt bone a striking in her breast,
For soon by what it tells the clock is stilled.

And if in other object lessons, like "Thistledown," there is still the static indulgence—a pleasure quite properly earned, of course; there is nothing in Merrill's airs and graces which is merely willful or willed, but rather the sense that we are watching a virtuoso who will shift into his heartbreaking Mad Scene just as soon as he gets through what are "roulades of relinquishment" indeed:

Ha! how the Scotch flower's spendthrift
Stars drifted down
Many to tarn or turf, but ever a canny one
On the stem left—

if there is still the preening of a feathery tautology: "Bewildered what to want past the extravagant notion of wanting," there is also a new responsibility to what it is that is being so spangled. Even in the ornamental "Charles" pieces, like the "Laboratory Poem" in which the queasy hero watches his mistress dissecting turtles to test their hearts on the kymograph, there is a new instance of plain-speaking:

He thought of certain human hearts, their climb
Through violence into exquisite disciplines
Of which, as it now appeared, they all expired.

Here, as in "A Timepiece," Merrill has found a way (it is mostly a prose way, a twist of the living idiom which combines the Jamesian with journalese) of adjusting his lust for the self-enclosed and the self-referring to metaphors of life far more appropriate than his old, ominous emblems of Time, Love and Doom. The patinated narcissism has been literally roughed up, and the resulting corrugation of surface corresponds, of course, to a new agitation of the depths. There is a rightness about the conceit of a heart which by its very "discipline" destroys itself, as there is in the image of the gravid woman "thrusting fullness from her, like a death"—more than a rightness, there is an *interest* in being told such things: the poet has *made over* his experience to language at a level deeper than that at which one wants merely to write poems, or to have written them, "given to grand personifications." In consequence, his poems, even when they are merely allegorized *things*, show a gain in consequence. Many succeed further in condensing the duration of larger narrative forms into their careful rhythms; for example "Mirror," in which a looking-glass that has weathered the fortunes and defeats of a family speaks:

. . . as if a fish
Had broken the perfect silver of my reflectiveness,
I have lapses. I suspect
Looks from behind, where nothing is, cool gazes
Through the blind flaws of my mind. As days,
As decades lengthen, this vision
Spreads and blackens. I do not know whose it is,
But I think it watches for my last silver
To blister, flake, float leaf by leaf, each milling-
Downward dumb conceit, to a standstill . . .

Here even Merrill's ingenious rhyme on unaccented syllables and feminine words has a new justification beyond ingenuity, as if the moribund mirror itself enforced the "faulty" correspondence of "silver" and "standstill," "gazes" and "days." It is very close, this kind of technical iconography, where the self impersonates in speech its own decaying surface, to a direct image, or rather a discourse without images but rather of process—the poet speaking, as he will often henceforth do, in his own person, assuming his own past, acknowledging in the actions and rejected actions of the present his designs upon the future. In one of the brightest poems in the book, "The Doodler," designs on the future are precisely what the poet observes as he watches his unconscious spin itself out before his eyes, reflecting as he does on an aetiology of representation:

> . . . *Far, far behind already is that aeon*
> *Of pin-heads, bodies each a ragged weevil,*
> *Slit mouthed and spider-legged, with eyes like gravel,*
> *Wavering under trees of purple crayon.*
>
> *Shapes never realized, were you dogs or chairs?*
> *That page is brittle now, if not long burned.*
> *This morning's little boy stands (I have learned*
> *To do feet) gazing down a flight of stairs.*
>
> *And when A. calls to tell me he enjoyed*
> *The evening, I begin again. Again*
> *Emerge, O sunbursts, garlands, creatures, men,*
> *Ever more lifelike out of the white void!*

That is a characteristic Merrill invocation—riddling, chatty, sincere—of his own secret powers, the energy addressed showing a development away from mere embellishment ("sunbursts, garlands," the substance of *First Poems*) toward a responsible creative life ("creatures, men, / ever more lifelike out of the white void!"). There is a humility now in his "designs" ("I have learned to do feet"). The accountability of the form tends to screen what is dangerous and abashing in these revelations (his mirror's last word is "I am amenable"—it might have been Petronius'). But the submission to such powers is not only expressed, it is welcomed, and the book's last poem, "A Dedication"—to the same Hans to whom the first and title poem was addressed—puts it with unheard-of frankness, or at least with a frankness unheard before in Merrill's poems:

> *These are the moments, if ever, an angel steps*
> *Into the mind, as kings into the dress*
> *Of a poor goatherd, for their acts of charity.*

There are moments when speech is but a mouth pressed
Lightly and humbly against the angel's hand.

The lines I distinguish by roman type are moving in every sense, for
they surely define a poetics unavailable to this writer hitherto. Hence-
forth, it will be such moments that justify, even as they jeopardize, Mer-
rill's powers.

In 1962 Merrill published a shorter but also more consistent volume
of poems named this time not for a country but for the street in Con-
necticut where he had set up house, *Water Street;* not only is there
a domestic impulse in most of these poems, and a residential resonance
to many of their names: "An Urban Convalescence," "Scenes of Child-
hood," "The Lawn Fête," "A Tenancy," "A Vision of the Garden"—
but the very division of impulse suggested in the book's title, the
opposition between that which abides and that which flows, haunts the
poet throughout this sober, disabused group of poems. Even the "tech-
nical" emblem poems, like "The Parrot Fish" and "To a Butterfly" are
concerned, as in the latter case, with getting down to the single vision:

> *Goodness, how tired one grows*
> *Just looking through a prism:*
> *Allegory, symbolism.*
> *I've tried, Lord knows,*
>
> *To keep from seeing double,*
> *Blushed for whenever I did . . .*
>
> *I am not yet*
> *Proof against rigmarole . . .*
> *The day you hover without any*
> *Tincture of soul,*
>
> *Red monarch, swallowtail,*
> *Will be the day my own*
> *Wiles gather dust. Each will have flown*
> *The other's jail.*

And the consciousness of failure—these wiles are anything but dusty
—seems not only to be ever at the poet's elbow, but to be a kind of
consolation as well. Love is attended to as loss and separation, and
wisdom is knowing it:

> *For a decade love has rained down*
> *On our two hearts, instructing them*

In a strange bareness, that of weathered stone.
Thinking how bare our hearts have grown
I do not know if I feel pride or shame.

These are no longer the poems of paste and sequins or even of genuine gems: the pressure is off which would make this coal into diamonds. The poems are consequently longer, looser, they echo to the sound of a man talking less to make himself heard than to permit what he *has* to say (the compulsion is his own) to be overheard:

. . . Wires and pipes, snapped off at the roots, quiver.
Well, that is what life does. I stare
A moment longer, so. And presently
The massive volume of the world
Closes again.
Upon that book I swear
To abide by what it teaches:
Gospels of ugliness and waste,
Of towering voids, of soiled gusts,
Of a shrieking to be faced
Full into, eyes astream with cold—
With cold?
All right then. With self-knowledge . . .

If so many of these poems are about to make a habitation out of some pretty disorderly houses, it is because the poet has confessed "the dull need to make some kind of house / out of the life lived, out of the love spent." For the soul's snowbound weather ("out of the white void!") he must find analogies in the world—hence homely poems of blizzards ("A new day. Fresh snow.") and of summer's end ("days when lover and beloved know / that love is what they are and where they go."). Love, travel and the scenes of childhood offer the occasion, learning and sympathy determine the form. The Proust of *Water Street* is no longer a conceit for the peacock "trailing too much of himself," but the sick man seen:

Your eyes grown wide and dark, eyes of a Jew,

You make for one dim room without contour
And station yourself there, beyond the pale
Of cough or of gardenia, erect, pale.
What happened is becoming literature.

Feverish in time, if you suspend the task,
An old, old woman shuffling in to draw
Curtains, will read a line or two, withdraw.
The world will have put on a thin gold mask.

In these clear stanzas ("What happened is becoming literature" is a remarkable line for a poet who, though he knew happiness was bound up with happenings, once could not permit anything in his finished pieces to "become") where the inner rhyme word is always itself, in a different acceptation—"pale" vs. "pale," reflecting the kind of transformation that time effects in Proust—the novelist is now conceived as an agent of preservation as well, not like the peacock merely showing off or showing others up, nor like Stendhal "making the best of love, the best there is," but as a man concerned to perpetuate the universe. The thin gold mask is not a defence against reality, nor a concealment from it; it is a funerary enduement which will withstand and redeem the wreckage of a life. Similarly the "Prism" in this book is understood not in the baroque diction and faceted rhythms of a broken bowl's "lucid unities," but as the standing refutation of old dreams:

> *. . . Look:*
> *You dreamed of this:*
> *To fuse in borrowed fires, to drown*
> *In depths that were not there . . . Now and then*
> *It is given to see clearly. There*
> *Is what remains of you, a body*
> *Unshaven, flung on the sofa. Stains of egg*
> *Harden about the mouth, smoke still*
> *Rises between fingers or from nostrils.*
> *The eyes deflect the stars through years of vacancy.*
> *Your agitation at such moments*
> *Is all too human . . . Yet the gem*
> *Revolves in space, the vision shuttles off.*
> *A toneless waltz glints through the pea-sized funhouse.*
> *The day is breaking someone else's heart.*

Of course the old wit is there—as in the last two lines, where the refraction of light is given as a "toneless waltz" and the explosion of the spectrum is defined, in terms of both narrator and prism, as "breaking someone else's heart." But there is nothing starched and nothing self-pitying about these poems—the note of the dandy has been dropped: they are simply very unhappy and very attractive. The opening and closing poems in this collection represent the deepest sounding, along with the "Scenes from Childhood," which Merrill has been able to make of his self-knowledge. If they are disillusioned, "the primal figures jerky and blurred," they are never dim or dull: every skill the poet has, and I think he has them all, has been turned into an instrument for coming to terms with the self:

> *. . . in this new room,*
> *Mine, with my things and thoughts, a view*

Of housetops, treetops, the walls bare.
A changing light is deepening, is changing
To a gilt ballroom chair a chair
Bound to break under someone before long.
I let the light change also me . . .

And the next step, in this progress of wisdom which seems to consist in putting off every garment, every mask but one of the thinnest gold, is to release into the world a naked identity—"leaner veteran"—that will not only endure but persist:

. . . I put the flowers where I need them most
And then, not asking why they come,
Invite the visitors to sit.
If I am host at last
It is of little more than my own past.
May others be at home in it.

In 1965, Atheneum published Merrill's second novel, *The (Diblos) Notebook*, a tenuous but extending experiment with versions of "happiness bound up with happenings" which bears the same relation to his 1966 book of poems *Nights and Days* that *The Seraglio* showed to the earlier poems. The novel takes place (and takes very little else: its characters are as uncertain of their margins as the X'd-out though legible phrases of its languorous narrator) in the ruined but still adorable Greece of the previous travel pieces:

. . . All through
The countryside were old ideas
Found lying open to the elements.
Of the gods' houses only
A minor premise here and there
Would be balancing the heaven of fixed stars
Upon a Doric capital. The rest
Lay spilled, their fluted drums half sunk in cyclamen
Or deep in water's biting clarity
Which just barely upheld me
The next week, when I sailed for home.

And *home* of course is the self-cannibalizing New York: "it is not even as though the new / buildings did very much for architecture." *The Notebook* seems to have afforded Merrill a freedom in his erotic gestures, an elation in his surrender to the physical world that not even the allotted bonds of *Water Street* insured. Witness the long and

intricate poem "From the Cupola," which takes up the romance of
Eros and Psyche where the poet had left it in his very first book:

> *So, where he slept in the dark bed, she took*
> *A candle, wooed his profile with the kiss*
> *Of all things bodiless . . .*

and inflects it through a series of verse forms and even prose passages
(some appear to be from a forgotten work called *Psyche's Sisters* by
one A. H. Clarendon, which the author disingenuously quotes in
another poem altogether), combining a modern version of the myth
rather like that of *The Immortal Husband* with a psychoanalytic tale of
Psyche and her sisters Alice and Gertrude who live in a Greek Revival
house on the Connecticut shore of Long Island Sound. Into this teasing
and iridescent farrago, the poet himself intrudes, pricking the fable and
the sisters' memories with the insistent reminder that he is making the
whole thing up:

> *Psyche, hush. This is me, James.*
> *Writing lest he think*
> *Of the reasons why he writes—*
> *Boredom, fear, mixed vanities and shames;*
> *Also love.*
> *From my phosphorescent ink*
> *Trickle faint unworldly lights*
>
> *Down your face. Come, we'll both rest.*
> *Weeping? You must not.*
> *All our pyrotechnic flights*
> *Miss the sleeper in the pitch-dark breast.*
> *He is love.*
> *He is everyone's blind spot.*
> *We see according to our lights . . .*

and after the whole story is over, or at least overt, after Psyche has
cleaned the windows of the cupola and at last seen, as Marivaux (surely
the right mentor here) would say, clear into her heart, the poet breaks
in again, reviewing all the props and personages of the story, even
Psyche's lamp:

> *The lamp I smell in every other line.*
>
> *Do you smell mine? From its rubbed brass a moth*
> *Hurtles in motes and tatters of itself*
> *—Be careful, tiny sister, drabbest sylph!—*
> *Against the hot glare, the consuming myth,*

Drops and is still. My hands move. An intense
Slow-paced, erratic dance goes on below.
I have received from whom I do not know
These letters. Show me, light, if they make sense.

the psyche moth is the last version of selfhood, battering itself against
the "consuming myth," that Merrill allows in this long, funny, self-de-
feating poem. It offers glimpses of course of the old Merrill of the
lacquer-work and decorative flourishes:

My sisters' gold sedan's
eyes have gone dim and dark   windows are sealed
For vision's sake two wipers wield
the automatic coquetry of fans . . .

but released from the servitude of making sense by letting his senses
make it. There is a new reality, or at least a new realism here, even in
this fanciful and preposterous fable, a notation of experience quite
beyond fooling; travel's spoils have effected a change of heart, and
nothing is trivial because everything is interpreted, mediated, indulged
by the five senses:

Dear ones *I say bending to kiss their faces*
Trust me   One day you'll understand   Meanwhile
suppose we think of things to raise our spirits
and leading the two easiest to beguile

into the kitchen feed them shots of Bourbon
Their brother who loves Brahms conceives a wish
for gems from L'Africana played at volumes
that make the dwarf palm shudder in its dish

The pale one with your eyes restively flashing
Takes in the dock the ashen Sound the sky
The fingers of the eldest brush my features . . .

Merrill's self-conscious suspicion of his own learning ("Do you smell
mine?") and his delight in novelistic complication (breaking up the
narrative by interpolated quotations, discrepant verse forms, conversa-
tion) are more consequentially articulated, I think, in the other very
long poem in this book, "The Thousand and Second Night." A kind of
catch-all travel journal, Merrill's narrative puts Scheherazade on as
easily as—it puts her off, say; and includes an attack of facial palsy, a
visit to Hagia Sophia:

You did not want to think of yourself for once,
But you had held your head erect

Too many years within such transcendental sculls
As this one not to feel the usual, if no
Longer flattering kinship. You'd let go
Learning and faith as well, you too had wrecked
Your precious sensibility. What else did you expect?

and to the Turkish bath; a prose memory of his grandmother's hand intervenes, whose shape was like the skyline of Istanbul, and then a terrifying bout of acidie in Athens:

. . . The day I went up to the Parthenon
Its humane splendor made me think So what? . . .

Try, I suppose, we must, as even Valéry said,
And said more grandly than I ever shall—

followed by a stern fragment of autobiography, which leads in turn to a dazzling examination of some dirty postcards that have turned up in a family legacy. Love, of course, follows logically, and is subjected to a going over, though here the speaker fails us:

And now the long adventure

Let that wait.
I'm tired, it's late at night . . .

postponing his account until his return:

Lost friends, my long ago

Voyages, I bless you for sore
Limbs and mouth kissed, face bronzed and lined,
An earth held up, a text not wholly undermined
By fluent passages of metaphor.

And the poem ends with a mocking exegesis of its own forms in a classroom parody, and a burst of feeling when the Sultan and his Scheherazade are parted—she now released and he enslaved. In a sense, the nights and days of this book's title are the dreams and experience of Merrill's life, opposed and ruefully—by lethargy, almost—united:

She and her fictions soon were one.
He slept through moonset, woke in blinding sun,
Too late to question what the tale had meant.

The rest of the book is a virtual inventory of Merrill's dazzling repertoire: another "Charles" poem, an expatriate portrait, several family studies and scenes from childhood, emblem poems and dream sequences:

Again last night I dreamed the dream called Laundry.
In it the sheets and towels of a life we were going to share
The milk-stiff bibs, the shroud, each rag to be ever
Trampled or soiled, bled on or groped for blindly,
Came swooning out of an enormous willow hamper
Onto moon-marbly boards. We had just met . . .

Poems still about the movement and measure of water, like "The Current," and poems about possessions renounced, like "A Carpet Not Bought," indicate this poet's loyalty to his own mastered impulses. But beyond the variety and the complexity of Merrill's accumulated lusters, beyond the two long poems that are obviously the set-pieces of *Nights and Days*, there is the book's final poem that I take to be the poet's finest salute to his own continuing powers, indeed his hostage to their continuation: "Days of 1964." Named for those terrible late poems of Cavafy's—"Days of 1909," "Days of 1911," portraits of debauchery and transcending love—Merrill's long envoi has the true Alexandrian tone: in its certainty of place and circumstance—

. . . Our neighborhood sun-cured if trembling still
In pools of the night's rain . . .
Across the street that led to the center of town
A steep hill kept one company part way
Or could be climbed in twenty minutes
For some literally breathtaking views,
Framed by umbrella pines, of city and sea.
Underfoot, cyclamen, autumn crocus grew
Spangled as with fine sweat among the relics
Of good times had by all. If not Olympus,
An out-of-earshot, year-round hillside revel. . . .

and its charity and grace in characterization:

. . . Her legs hurt. She wore brown, was fat, past fifty,
And looked like a Palmyra matron
Copied in lard and horsehair. How she loved
You, me, loved us all, the bird, the cat!
I think now she was love. She sighed and glistened
All day with it, or pain, or both . . .

the poem moves through a shocking encounter with this mythological factotum ("I think now she was love"), half gossip and half goddess disguised as a temple prostitute—for its subject is possession by the god:

the erotic mask
worn the world over by illusion
to weddings of itself and simple need—

and returns, as "by a commodious vicus of recirculation" to a confrontation of love in the narrator's own life:

> *I hoped it would climb when it needed to the heights*
> *Even of degradation, as I for one*
> *Seemed, those days, to be always climbing*
> *Into a world of wild*
> *Flowers, feasting, tears—or was I falling, legs*
> *Buckling, heights, depths,*
> *Into a pool of each night's rain?*
> *But you were everywhere beside me, masked*
> *As who was not, in laughter, pain and love.*

Such a poem dramatizes the astonishing truth that this poet, the most decorative and glamor-clogged America had so far produced, has made himself, by a surrender to reality and its necessary illusions, a master of his experience and of his own nature.

The Fire Screen by JAMES MERRILL

Not an end in themselves but an ongoing ("a nature / which existed to be overthrown"), not pride of place but the modesty of replacement ("tones one forgets / even as one is changed for life by them"): continuing powers! To them is made the apostrophe, to them is offered the hope of what we prosaically call, in a poet's career, his *transitional* work. The hinge (as the word *hinge* once meant a hesitation, a hanging between) holding together the familiar, the accomplished, the *done for* on one side of the door ("certain things die only with oneself"), and on the other the hankered-after, the heterogenous ("to greet the perfect stranger")—that is the function and the emblem of James Merrill's new book. A look, in fact, at the characteristically emblematic title and its provenance will serve to show what we are up against, what we are squeezed between. In a poem of Proustian recall entitled "Mornings in a New House" (continuing the series of domestic studies, nesting grounds for divorce, disorderly houses held open in all six of Merrill's books of poems, in both his novels), "a cold man" wakes at dawn and once the fire is lit and the frosted window thawed, the worst is over:

> *. . . Now between*
> *His person and that tamed uprush*
> *(which to recall alone can make him flush)*
> *Habit arranges the fire screen.*

The first acceptation, then, is the one on the wrong side of the hinge: the fire screen is that grid of decorative devices ("all framework and embroidery") which protects against the blaze or at least the glow (even the fire, here, is "that *tamed* uprush"). Evidently uneasy about so much lamplight and crewel-work, Merrill adds a curious prose footnote to the phrase "fire screen", a revisionary impulse "days later" which suggests he missed his way, took the wrong road: "Fire screen—screen *of* fire. The Valkyrie's baffle, pulsing at trance pitch, godgiven, elemental . . . some such meaning might have caught, only I settled . . . Oh well. Our white heats lead us on no less than words do. Both have been devices in their day." A second acceptation, then, of the fire screen: not the comfortable household convenience, but the flaming curtain, the destructive element. And crucially, the realization—wry, chastened, ultimately cheering—that we are "led on" alternatively and equally by our white heats and our mere words. Brunhilde's trance is as much of a convention, a device, Merrill reassures himself, as Praed's trimeter. Both will be invoked and utilized in this book—we are *led on* in both senses: the sense of infatuation and the sense of futurity.

If a poet has mastered his own nature; if he has, like the sea, in his surrender to constraint found his continuing, what becomes of his poetry—poetry which he himself has taught us to take as the record of a struggle, as the terms of that surrender? Often enough—too often, as in the case of Browning, the case of Tennyson, though less outrageously there—nothing at all *becomes* of his poetry, he goes on writing it, he opens a museum of manners, a smiling public man indeed, or even a frowning one. The task, for the poet in this dilemma, will be to discover what lies beyond himself, what extends outside the literally charmed circle of his accomplishment by which he is merely entranced, what is on the other side of the fire screen.

With all his urbanity on the ready like a revolver, Merrill will proceed into new territory then, as resolved to mistrust the trance— "godgiven, elemental"—as to transcend the merely mastered. Chief among the preoccupation in this new book, thus, will be harping upon, the harking back to pure personality: the calcined, clarified contour of identity when the accidents of period and place are consumed. "The Friend of the Fourth Decade", "Words for Maria", "Kostas Tympakianakis" are scorched portraits, attempts to reach that region of the self where, as the Friend himself writes, "individual and type are one." *L'individu seul est esclave; l'espèce est libre* is what Buffon wrote about falcons, and in the hawklike profiles of Merrill's sitters we recognize the bondage and the freedom both, recognize and salute. "Who could have imagined such a life as mine?" asks Kostas Tympakianakis at the end of his monologue. Why, no one *needs* imagine, Merrill's strict poems reply, not here, among the lineaments of reality.

For such a poet, at such a point in his making ("scene upon scene's immersion and emergence / rinsed of the word"), not only certain selves but certain sites will catch fire. Mostly Greek places for Merrill, landscapes reduced to "this or that novel mode of being together / without conjunctions." Harsh, bare, yet these "coastlines of white printless coves [are] already strewn with offbeat echolalia." Like Gide in the desert, Merrill finds in these waste places of the heart's landscape the most *inexhaustible* locus for his celebration. As he puts it at the end of "To My Greek," a poem inextricably dedicated to a language and a personality, "the barest word be what I say in you."

Corrective, deprecatory, incredibly entertaining, another half of the book is offered up to framework and embroidery—what Merrill may call "settling for the obvious," though so subtle is the crewel-work and so restless the self-consciousness ("The meter grows misleading, / given my characters . . . I have no such hero, / no fearful deeds—unless / we count their quiet performance / by Time or Tenderness") that even the most diverted reader is not likely to be unaware of the depths he has been diverted from. When the Valkyrie's baffle proves to be merely portentous, Merrill turns, indeed returns, to his "household opera":

> *The love scene (often cut). The potion. The tableau:*
> *Sleepers folded in a magic fire,*
> *Tongues flickering up from humdrum incident . . .*

In a wonderful sonnet sequence called "Matinées" from which this other fire screen comes, in the filigree indulgence of a ballad of other lives called "The Summer People", in poems of emblem and recall beyond the wildest dreams of cleverness, Merrill counterpoints and orchestrates what I have called his transition. These civilities, these reticences ballast that other impulse so searing as to be suspect: the impulse which in one poem titled after Yeats (a constantly invoked figure here, even when he is gently mocked) is called "More Enterprise"—the impulse to reduce to anonymity, which in poetry is to be reduced to riches.

Shenandoah, 1971

Braving the Elements by JAMES MERRILL

A few seasons ago, I spoke of Merrill's previous book *The Fire Screen* as "poems not an end in themselves but an ongoing." Here, in

considerable splendor, is what they went on to, the new poems which
are indeed an end in themselves, a consummation, marriage and holo-
caust both, for they seek—and extensively, patulously, find—that
point endured by the mystics and dared by the surrealists, that point
which affords access to *reality*, to Being understood as existence
without contradictions or conditions, where up and down, before
and after, are no longer to be construed as opposites, where opposi-
tion is not construed at all. These, then, are poems of ecstatic appre-
hension, in which the dialectics of an identity, a biography, are
renounced in favor and fervor of those great converging energies
which bear the utterance to a pitch, a register where there is no
longer what Shelley called the burr of self that sticks to one so, but
that transparency which *renders* the world—others, weather, land-
scape, love: this poetry is, in every sense and with all the weight the
phrase will bear, a *burning glass*.

Anything but accidental then, that the book begins with the as-
severation "Everything changes, nothing does"; sustains this version
in the center somewhere with the equivalent sense, "nothing lasts and
nothing ends"; and concludes—in one of Merrill's many instrumental-
ities, the poem-as-lens, the self-as-the-*medium*-of-others—with the
astonishing overtones of "Syrinx", in which the compass-rose be-
comes the final wisdom of transformation:

> *Nought*
> *Waste   Eased*
> *Sought*

In a recent interview, Merrill wraps it up (*it* being just this poise of
perception where the responsibility of form is not contested by the
personal, the perversity of *wanting*): "How one tries—not just in
writing—to escape from these opposites, from there being two sides
to every question." Merrill tries, Merrill succeeds, by every means
at his disposal, and he disposes of those means, dissolves them subse-
quently in the service of illumination: "centimeters deep yawns the
abyss", he observes, and is therefore entitled to observe each centi-
meter with an exactitude ordinarily reserved for distances. Of course
there are distances too—huge views, up mountains and down bank
vaults, the landscapes of Greece and New Mexico, the *paysages d'âme*
of a lover, a son, a master. And there are those explorations of the
past, of memory and hallucination, of dreams and dramas ("the temp-
est used to be my cup of tea") which in Merrill's own earlier poems
were merely memorial, merely elegiac. They have been transformed,
transmuted, under tremendous pressure, like coal into crystal, so that
it is no longer possible to say what was fantasy, what was flesh: it is
all one ecstasy now, in Merrill, one modality:

I tremble, still

A thinking reed. Who puts his mouth to me
Draws out the scale of love and dread—
O ramify, sole antidote!

And the crystals do branch out. I used to reproach this poet, or at
least to approach him warily, for being, as I called it, bejewelled.
Cloudy emeralds, star sapphires, glaucous pearls were on every page,
studding the desolations like tears. No longer: everything has been
clarified, consumed, and one looks through the brilliant poems to the
experience they render, they render *possible* by their intensity of
purpose, their diamond-hard joy; nothing is decoration or decor
now in Merrill's poetry, for the poet has discovered the link between
what is cosmetic and what is cosmic. His poems are orders of ex-
perience from which he has won the right to be the *deus absconditus*,
present everywhere in his works, and only there:

> *. . . at once*
> *Transfiguring, transfigured. A voice grunts*
> MATTER YOU MERELY DO I AM
>
> *Which lies on snow in dark ideogram*
> *—Or as a later commentary words it,*
> One-night's-meats-another-morning's-mass-
> Against-inhuman-odds-I-celebrate.

Shenandoah, 1973

W. S. MERWIN

"We Survived the Selves
That We Remembered."

IN THE AGE of the Interesting Deathbed it was customary, I understand, to inquire of the Departing, "Are your feet on the Rock?" That stony metaphor of stability—"On this Rock I will build my Church"—crumbled or at least eroded under Lyell's researches, apparently, and it is Tennyson, always the most "punctual" exponent of contemporary feeling, who laments the loss of a geological faith:

> *The hills are shadows and they flow*
> *From form . . .*

Yet we are, nowadays, quite as avid of a petrous certainty as the Victorians, quite as anxious to discern an assured consistency in our poets, even while they are still with us; and the reviews of, say, Roethke's successive books articulate a mounting bewilderment as the transformations followed one upon the other, as the responsibilities to a ripening form obliged the poet to shed—and after we had at last learned what to expect!—the mode Kenneth Burke once called "vegetal radicalism" in favor of the mode of Yeats' final manner. Yeats himself is disconcerting here (as the phrase "final manner" indicates) —for my parents' generation, Yeats was still the minstrel of the Irish Renaissance, the Celtic Twilight and the Forlorn Romance, while for my own he is altogether the Modern Poet, the post-Visionary realist, self-proclaimed exemplar of the "Rocky Voice." Both versions of the poet choose to elide what makes the partisans of each uncomfortable, a deliberate *change* from one style to another.

When so many diagnosticians assert that Poetry is on its deathbed, it is indeed difficult to refrain from asking any poet "are your feet on the Rock?" and easy to declare the metamorphoses of a man's style no more than the symptoms of a fatal disintegration. The more mastery a practitioner reveals over a variety of idioms, the more we come to mistrust his accomplishment, finding in that word itself the ambiguity which so troubles us in the poet who would prove that the unified is the opposite of the uniform. *Accomplishment* is of course the fulfilling of an impulse, but it is also an embellishing as when De Quincey says "to fold and seal a letter adroitly is not the lowest of accomplishments." Once poetry is assimilated to the arts of folding and sealing a letter adroitly it is discredited, and who would not prefer the monolithic failure—the failure of a *single stone*—to that plurality of success which, along with art-sewing and spinet-etudes, so gaudily betokens the trifling, "the rattle of pebbles under the receding wave?"

One asks such a question more readily, more tendentiously, in some cases than in others. Our suspicions of accomplishment, and of the diversity which the facile sense of the word implies, are allayed in two cases explicitly: the case of duration, the case of intensity.

If only it takes long enough, we forgive a man his transformation, and the word *becoming* is an honorific. Indeed, since Darwin, the superstition of Evolution has replaced the superstition of Inspiration, and today's Great Commoner is more interested in the age of rocks than in the Rock of Ages. Provided we can call it Development, provided we can literally *endure* it, our poet's mutation is acceptable: gradually but perceptibly Yeats fashioned himself a new style, and because it compassed the memories of three literary generations, he was pardoned the artifice.

In the second case, if only it appears hard enough, we allow the bird to moult, and the word *tormented* is a compliment. In the modern consciousness, as Susan Sontag says, the discovery of the self is equated with the discovery of the suffering self, and the truths we respect are those born of affliction. Provided we can call it Pain, provided it is literally *unendurable*, a poet's new style is admissible: the visible, audible agonies of a Roethke, a Lowell, a Berryman, reassure us for the brevity of the interval during which they have remodeled themselves.

But what if a poet affords us the spectacle of a quick-change artist *performing*—that is surely the word, practicing upon our duplicity as bewitched spectators of his "act"—performing, then, not only with ease but with enjoyment? What if an entire career is raced through (as the word career originally meant a racecourse), what if a whole chorus of voices is raised in the time we should judge miraculously abridged for the sounding of but one genuine note? What if the tonality is not the grudging one of a difficulty overcome, but the trump of a facility rediscovered, a delighted accession to means which simply transcends any question of struggle, conquest and renunciation? Are we so certain that our evolutionary co-ordinates by which we decide these matters, our Calvinist criteria of accreditation, are not likely to deprive us of a singular (because superabundant) voice, a sudden joy? Perhaps when we so righteously abjure the *unearned* increment we renounce our birthright as a poet's audience: to consider the art not as a privative function of our being, but a providing one?

No poet's work, however eagerly scanned, can afford us answers to these questions—nor would such responses, even if we deduced them from the practice of the most consensually honored figure, be more than conditional. The most, and I think the best, a poet's work can do is make us ask them of each other, make us put to ourselves the possibility that we are not sure, that the way lies open, that Others exist. It is the honor and the outrage of W. S. Merwin's poetry to raise these doubts, to make us wonder.

For in fifteen years, Merwin has published six volumes of poetry—rather, three *pairs* of volumes—and even before the sixth came out in 1967, further collections of both prose and verse were brimming, and only the seemliness of an interval during which the reader might blink and the printer catch his breath keeps the canon closed or at least throttled. The three braces of existing books represent, moreover, three entirely different masteries of style, mysteries of stance so disjunct as to exceed the usual Trinitarian specifications—we are presented not only with Three Persons in the One Substance, but with Three Substances, three utterly discrepant (and equally "accomplished") instances of how poetry works, emanating from one Person who is, incredibly, forty years of age.

Nor is this all. During his "middle" or discursive period, Merwin's "fascination with the theater . . . and a fascination with simply writing drama—with that way of writing" resulted in four plays, the first of which, *Darkling Child*, in verse, was produced in London in 1956, and another, *Favor Island*, in prose with a verse epilogue, was published in New York in 1957; the latter affords, incidentally, the most concise account of the human universe in Merwin's *oeuvre*, defining man

> *Part beast, part shadow, [who] tracks and flees*
> *Beasts and shadows round their valleys,*
> *Outdoing both their cruelties,*
> *Comes to much harm, some rightly his,*
> *And yet endures, and on the darkness*
> *Still sires his changeless miseries,*
> *His singular and painful glories.*

The spooky stoicism of these relaxed octosyllabics is stiffened somewhat by the attention, throughout the play, to marine detail; further, about half of Merwin's poems in this median aspect are concerned with the sea, its never-ending finality, its irreversible otherness "beyond reckoning" of which he remarks, in *Favor Island*, "there's only one side to the ocean, and nothing on the other . . . and always there is the noise, making a kind of silence in which nothing can be heard." Merwin's capacity to moralize his surround, to win from the not-self an appropriate emblem of what the self intends, becomes more conscious, of course, in *his* course, and by 1962, in his next maritime venture—an entire issue of *The Nation* reporting on the voyage of the *Everyman*, in which three men protested a United States nuclear explosion in the Pacific—he comes up with a statement startling for its application to his own enterprise, in the context of no more than a very able piece of journalism:

> Symbolism is never far from a man's efforts inevitably, in acts of conscience—he is reduced to consoling himself with considerations of what his project might signify rather than what it might accomplish.

I am trying to show that even in those productions falling outside the canon of his poetry, Merwin is loyal to his identifying impulses, his sustaining conflict as realized within that canon: the dynamic confrontation of an order understood as including chaos with a chaos understood as contesting order. In 1961 Merwin had been made poetry editor of *The Nation*, and in a published interview given at that time he remarked, "if a feeling of crisis goes on long enough, I suppose, one of two things happens—either a person or a society becomes numbed or they get interested in poetry." As an alternative to "numbness," then, poetry is the vehicle of an interest in life, a lesson in survival. Hence Merwin's concern with the tradition, with the way men have made their projects *signify:* "you can be taught that people have been in danger before and the way they behaved." Though scarcely a card-carrying intellectual himself (he does not teach in a university, does not regularly review, does not often lecture), Merwin has paralleled his career as a poet with a successful investigation of how people behaved in danger: he has translated their poems. Particularly their poems about danger, the two major poems which stand at the sources of French and Spanish literature, *The Song of Roland* (1963) and *The Poem of the Cid* (1959). He has devised the finest versions I know of these great works, filtering out of the latter a narrative line of great importance to his own projects, "a rough, spare, sinewy, rapid verse"; and in the former recognizing and recovering "a clarity at once simple and formal, excited and cool, a certain limpidity not only in the language and the story but in the imagination behind them, qualities I find myself trying to describe in terms of light and water." A volume of Spanish *romances* ("simple, direct, precise") and the *Satires* of Persius ("the basic conception of the *satura* is one of conversation"), both published in 1960, amplify Merwin's exploration of the past, to plunder and placate. One of his surest spoils is a metric which avoids the drumming decasyllabon, as it used to be called, of English poetry since Dryden. His disposition against "even *reading* another transposition of *Roland*, or most anything else, into a sort of blankish verse" has found, in the frequentation of these Romance poems anterior to our own "gallery of connotations," an issue, and it is evidently a strait (*i.e.,* non-iambic) way from the figured prose of Merwin's *Roland:*

> *It is said in the country from which he comes*
> *the sun does not shine, the wheat cannot grow,*
> *the rain does not fall, dew never forms, and*
> *all the stones are black. Some say that the land*
> *is inhabited by devils . . .*

to the prosaic figures of his own most recent poems:

> *In new rocks new insects are sitting*
> *with the lights off*
> *and once more I remember that the beginning*
> *is broken*
> *no wonder the addresses are torn*
> *to which I make my way eating the silence of animals*
> *offering snow to the darkness . . .*

Not only the past is laid under contribution in Merwin's pursuit of the means against numbness, the means he might labor into strength; not only the earliest and greatest French and Spanish poems are ransacked for their strategic terms in the face of danger, but the latest and greatest French and Spanish poets, Char and Guillén, whom Merwin has translated in search of "a hand I had never seen, a hand that puts an end to the fire, straightens the sun, reshapes the beloved." It is specifically in his later poems that Merwin sees a use for Char's enigmatic aphorisms, echoing the broken cadences of that pulverized Lucretius in his own, finding in destitution itself the means of power: *Rien n'annonçait une existence si forte*, or as Merwin has it, "Nothing had heralded so strong an existence." From Guillén's ecstatic praise of the natural world—"in terms of light and water" Merwin had sought to speak, or at least to conceive of speech, and that is Guillén's very achievement—a single translated scrap will show the American's indenture: "the flesh, in greater Reality, ascends thus naked unto fortune."

But the rewarding impoverishments of the great modern makers are a long way from Merwin's earliest practice, which is rather to exploit an embarrassment of riches, an impediment of gifts, under the liberating aegis of Ezra Pound. Even before we consider the poems themselves, it is well to glance at the sole critical text Merwin has published, on the French Classic Theater (Merwin himself has translated plays by Lesage and Marivaux, and speaks of the poetic drama of Racine and Corneille as "an exemplar perhaps more direct in its uses than either Greek tragedy or Shakespeare"), which came out long before his own first book and stands, therefore, as a kind of liminary discourse, a Blackmur-inspired gloss on all that glitters. He starts, crucially, with Hulme's suggestion that "man is the chaos highly organized but liable to revert to chaos at any moment," understanding Corneille "as concerning himself principally with the means and possibilities of organization and Racine with the inevitability and suddenness of reversion." Thus we might properly call Merwin's early work Cornelian, and the later books Racinian. About the confrontation of chaos and control, the poet speaks with particular relevance for his own work as a whole:

> The necessity, the provocations and concerns of disintegration are seen most clearly where the original order was most nearly complete. We cannot proceed simply to consider the organization as specious. A false order would not contain but be its own process of reversion. A judgment of any order will involve considerations of how much is contained in balance how well, of how strong the form can remain while allowing all possible variations.

The order will be judged differently as the balance is seen to shift from enclosure to imprisonment in Merwin's consideration; certainly at the outset he gives us a notable insight into the nature of his enterprise when he remarks that even so disintegrative a poet as Racine "both condemns and affirms the order he presents; the tools of condemnation in his hands assume their own summary and unimpeachable order." For in his first book, *A Mask for Janus*, published in 1952 in the Yale Series of Younger Poets, that is just what we find the order to be: "summary and unimpeachable." It is what Auden means, I think, when he says in his foreword that the young poet, employing the great myths which instill "that wonder and reverence without which no man can become wise," achieves "*an assumed authority*." For Merwin is concerned, in these intricate, prodigal verses, to institute an order, however summary, and to assume an authority that will contain, even as it is being contested by, "its own process of reversion." The violence works outward from the center, and by the time it has reached the surface it becomes "a kind diction out of the shadows" as Merwin says, a decorum that is a mask indeed, covering always one face of the god beneath—but the god is two-faced, and there is yet the unmasked countenance which survives, "saved by violence from violence."

The first thing one remarks about these 30 poems, glancing down the table of contents, is that each firmly announces its generic sympathies, insisting on an order and class felt to be not only a guise, a protection and an armor, but even—at extremes—a danger; thus if there are ballads and songs ("Blind William's Song" and "Song with the Eyes Closed" suggest already that something must be given up to attain such mastery: "all colored creation is tamed white . . ."), they are associated at the worst with "a dissolving music" as well as, at the best, with "dictions for rising, words for departure." Echoes of other writers are indulged—the book starts off with a pair of poems called *Anabasis* which in their slant rhymes and many slack endings, their deceptively neat-looking quatrains and languid rhythms, suggest a St.-John Perse rewritten by Hugh Selwyn Mauberly:

> *Still we are strange to orisons and knees.*
> *Fixed to bone only, foreign as we came,*
> *We float leeward till mind and body lose*
> *The uncertain continent of a name.*

Indeed the sestina dedicated to Robert Graves makes clear how diligent Merwin has been about his apprenticeship, how necessary he finds it to take everything ("ballad," "rime," "carol," "epitaph," "ode," "dance," "prayer," "roundel," "canción y glosa") from everyone and everywhere in order to constitute himself—

> *in every place*
> *Under different lights, evening and morning,*
> *Under many masters studied one song.*

The tutor to the children of the Princess de Braganza in Portugal and to the household of Robert Graves in Majorca (not since Laforgue served as Court-Reader to the Empress Augusta in Berlin has a poet indentured himself so meiotically!) Merwin has pursued, beyond the reach of American newspapers, American English Departments, and has overtaken, every "daze and fall" of speech, every priceless scrap of the old precisions ("disbodied," "perdury," "sembled," "euphory"), all the enigmatic figures (of which his favorite is the Shakespearean doublet, violently yoking two nouns, one abstract, one concrete, into a resonant, unresolvable matrix:

> *. . . Wonder and white sheep lying like tombs . . .*
> *. . . Through that peripety and afternoon . . .*
> *. . . Our eyes believed a garden and reserve . . .*),

all the archaic postures which might best "make new" by making us puzzle out the diction * as if Merwin were writing an inflected language, as if poetry were "the covenant we could but seize / fractionally by the ear" (and integrally only by the occular proof of the page:

> *Is mine this shade that to all hours the same*
> *Lurches and fails, marine and garrulous . . .*

> *The ear and intellect of death*
> *Direct of love the heated forms . . .)*

—all these engines of order, of artifice, of ornament, then, Merwin has set humming and whirring in his first book of poems that he might compass and keep down a chaos suffered as imminent and implacable, devouring his past ("an anomalous / speech no longer understood") and debilitating his future ("that unison we faintly, toward / our time and litany, invoke"), condoning only a present that must be defended by the most rigorous conventions and promptings.

Promptings, *stage directions*—that is the genre of what Auden calls the best poem in Merwin's book, "Dictum: for a Masque of Deluge"; an authoritative statement, a prescription for an enactment (in the most artificial of theatrical forms, the masque, at the end of which the audience joins the performers in a general revel) of the ultimate and perhaps the redeeming chaos. In eight unrhymed ten-line stanzas, the Flood is rehearsed ("the hush of portent / must be welcomed by a diffident music / lisping and dividing its renewals"—even at the start, there is the possibility of renewal, effected by music), in a language tormented by inversions and archaisms to a new order, a new directness: "the patter of speech / must lilt upon flatness." The fascinating animals are itemized as they enter "the sullen ark," a foretaste of Merwin's later concern with bestiaries, the emblematic presentment of the world's fierce energies:

> *Why is it rumored that these beasts come in pairs*
> *When the anatomies of their existence*
> *Are wrought for singularity? They walk*
> *Beside their shadows; their best motions are*
> *Figments on the drapery of the air.*
> *Their propagation is a redoubling*
> *Merely of dark against the wall, a planetary*
> *Leaning in the night unto their shadows*

* "I use the word diction," Merwin says in his piece on French classicism, "to include everything organized and everything of the organization from the sounds of the words to the patterned actions of the speakers."

> *And stiffening to the moment of eclipse;*
> *Shadows will be their lean progeny.*

So much for sexuality, for the actual life of the body, which is not so much disallowed as disbelieved; the very rhythms of the stanza have a kind of wandering faineance about them, and in the absence (unusual in Merwin's early work) of terminal assonance and of metrical whalebone, it is the high syntax alone which holds the verse paragraph together, accounting for the lovely disembodiment of the poem's surfaces. As Merwin's Palmers say in another place, and they might be speaking for his prosody:

> *Our motion is our form*
> *And our passage raiment;*
> *Between stillness and time*
> *We pass, improvident.*

Anticipating the "all-colored paper rainbow" of his charade, Merwin's man stumbles off the ark and for his very submission to submergence will be granted "an amazement of resurrection"—will find himself, in a drying vista of ruin, "solitary, impoverished, renewed."

Those three adjectives, precisely, are apposite to what Merwin will make of himself, but it is to be a long way, and one that must accommodate "tall fables of strangers, lisped visions of other men" before Merwin can reach such indigence, can reduce his style of luxuriance to that anonymity which is riches. Here, not even the catastrophe has really occurred, except in a masque, and the summoned chaos is all too complacent to impress us with the urgency of the speaker's fate; he is quite at ease with his decorous flood—

> *And time will be sufficient before that revel*
> *To teach an order and rehearse the days*
> *Till the days are accomplished—*

and the clever deluge ("continents / submerged . . . and the artful world rushing / incontinent") looms no more than an ominous decoration on the horizon:

> *So now the dove*
> *Makes assignations with the olive tree,*
> *Slurs with her voice the gestures of the time:*
> *The day foundering, the dropping sun*
> *Heavy, the wind a low portent of rain.*

The poem ends there, and beautiful as it is, with its powerful verbs and participles, its paucity of adjectives, and its weighted monosyllables, so that the elements in the last two lines are obliged into a significance neither objective nor otherwise, but pervasive—beautiful and even bountiful, it is too self-gratulatory to persuade us into the kind of naked conviction Merwin was to master a decade later in handling the same theme. In the recent poem there is an aphoristic economy, a fierce commonness in the speech of "Noah's Raven" which is altogether alarming:

> *Why should I have returned?*
> *My knowledge would not fit into theirs.*
> *I found untouched the desert of the unknown,*
> *Big enough for my feet. It is my home.*
> *It is always beyond them. The future*
> *Splits the present with the echo of my voice.*
> *Hoarse with fulfilment, I never made promises.*

That has the flat assurance, and the inward violence, which makes the earlier poem sound fussy and smug. But the art and the achievement of *A Mask for Janus* must not be scanted. At least a dozen poems here, especially the Ransomed "Ballad of John Cable and Three Gentlemen" with its triumphs of rhyme and phrasing:

> *Now Cable is carried*
> *On the dark river;*
> *Not even a shadow*
> *Followed him over.*
> *On the wide river*
> *Gray as the sea*
> *Flags of white water*
> *Are his company*

—the inceptive "anabasis" poems, with their lingering adieux to the countries of occasion ("but sentenced are the seasons that we know"), and the Carols in which "sufficient" is the permeating adjective and "bone" the most prominent noun—make this first book the most glinting, prosperous debut in all our poetry. Something of the limitations as well as the loveliness of this mineral glamor is apparent in its final set-piece, "Hermione on Simulacra," in which Paulina, Shakespeare's chthonic wardrobe mistress, draws back a curtain and discovers Hermione as a statue, in the last scene of *The Winter's Tale*. Here what Merwin has called "the necessity and the provocations of disintegration" submit a little too readily ("for comfort I became a stone"), and the hieratic cadences of the little quatrains articulate precisely the lack of a true confrontation between the order *imposed* and the chaos alluded to; when Hermione discovers her fate:

> *I had intended but to be*
> *My picture in a stone, but I*

> Took shape of death and have become
> Death, and all things come to me . . .

she realizes Merwin's prediction that "a false order would not contain but be its own process of reversion." In so many of these accomplished, finished, *done-for* poems ("The Bones of Palinurus Pray . . . ," "A Dance of Death," "Epitaph," "Over the Bier of the Worlding"—the titles gloss the mortuary dimension, the sense of an ending), we hear the brilliant, assigning poet gasp for breath, for "an air of promise, as the waking birds in the poplar trees." It is meet that the great ghost most often conjured, consciously invoked, is Villon—mentor, touchstone and despair. Yet there is no promise made to the world's body— no faith can be shared with natural process by the poet who

> Dreams fixed beasts that drowse or wonder,
> Not blinking; by the stream a few
> Poplars and white beeches where
> Exhausted leaves, suspended, through
>
> The distant autumn do not fall,
> Or, fallen, fired, are unconsumed,
> The flame perduring, the still
> Smoke eternal in the mind.

It is from the "dying generations" of Nature that we look for abundance, for the saturation of possibility by chance and unstinting surmise. Hence we are all the more astonished when an art which has declared itself to be—with characteristic reliquism—"a demeanor of distance," when a poetry which in all its lustrous finality asserts that it is merely "miming at mutability," offers itself with an opulence not only of surface but of supply, a luxuriance of volume as well as of value. *Quantities* and *numbers* have been traditional synonyms for poetry, yet when a mimesis of decorum is as emphatic as Merwin's—

> an improvisation,
> Though in an ancient mode, a paradigm
> For the unmentionable. Yet may the word
> Be celebration of a permanence,
> Make so, a presence and a permanence,
> The articulate dance, the turning festival—

when "the idiom of order" is so exalted, one attends rather to the singularity of the talent, the exclusive discriminations rather than to the promiscuous minglings. "Why should I complain," one might ask with the heroine of Merwin's retelling of "East of the Sun and West of the Moon" as a parable of metaphoric action,

What if these pheasants amble in white glass,
Ducks strut ridiculous in stone, the streams
Slither nowhere in beryl; why should I
Complain of such inflexible content,
Presume to shudder at such serenity,
Who walk in some ancestral fantasy,
Lunar extravagance, or lost pagoda
That dreams of no discipline but indolence?
What shall be rigid but gems and details
While all dimensions dance in the same air?

Merwin's princess does complain, of course, for she and the poet himself both seek more than this paralyzed perfection in eternity, seek rather to "ride a while in the mortal air before we go . . . for the love of fading"; yet such affluence of expressive means is truly beguiling, for at the very moment Merwin complains of the bondage of the Immutable, "impossible silence on the impossible air," he celebrates his release into mortality by the exuberance of his protest—copious, accomplished, gorgeous:

What shall I say,
How chiseled the tongue soever, and how schooled
In sharp diphthongs and suasive rhetorics,
To the echoless air of this sufficiency?
Where should I find the sovereign aspirate
To rouse in this world a tinkle of syllables,
Or what shall I sing to crystal ears . . . ?

More of the same is scarcely, in these overconsuming days, an encomium; yet in Merwin's case, another book of poems in the enchanted accents of the first, a second menology of magical acts, "repeated and perpetual rummage / in the lavish vestry," converts the phrase to praise, proves that what we marveled at from the outset and mistrusted a little for its very encroachment upon—substitution for—innocence was not just the frisky affectations of complacency but the control, by legend, ceremony and masquerade, of the central and welling energies of selfhood and of what lies beyond selfhood:

Finding mortality too mysterious
Naked and with no guise but its own,
—Unless one of immortal gesture come
And by a mask should show it probable . . .

Just two years after *A Mask for Janus* Merwin's new book of poems was issued. It contains the 500-line fairy tale from which I have been quoting and which more acutely urges the argument, the aporia, of a thirst for mutability in the guise, or the disguise, of perfection. "Among all dictions," Merwin seeks "that ceremony whereby you ['love,' or the imagination, or poetry] may be named / perpetual out of the anonymity / of death." It is in the rhetoric of completion that Merwin utters his longing for the partial, since

> *Mention, though*
> *It be the scholiast of memory,*
> *Makes yet its presences from emptiness . . .*

The paradox is a true one, and explains why *The Dancing Bears* of 1954 takes its title from Flaubert's bitter remark that "human speech is like a cracked kettle on which we pound out tunes fit to make bears dance, when what we want is to win over the stars." The figure of art as a cosmic failure, a grotesque second-best instead of a sympathetic magic—that is the ironical sign, affording a tremendous field to his talents for assimilation and apprenticeship, under which Merwin inscribes his elegance and his eloquence (did not even his first book borrow for its epigraph an assertion from John Wheelright "habit is evil, all habit, even speech . . ."?). The aspiration to commanding utterance ("the dicta for the only poem") is from the start renounced, decried, and the dandy's posture of supreme defiance, cast up to the indifferent stars, justifies the *made* music (as opposed to the miraculous natural harmonies) of these further poems; furthermore, there is a gaudy acknowledgment that in the decrepitude of "the only poem," that Orphic spell which might hold the world in thrall, plurality with all its chances and changes must make do, and "in defeat find such re-creation" as the world's disguises afford:

> *I walk multifarious among*
> *My baubles and horses;* unless I go in a mask
> How shall I know myself among my faces?

In the poet's repertory, then, there are to be found again among the titles "songs," "runes," a "colloquy" and three of the long, ode-like Provençal love-poems called "canso"—all thus labelled to reinforce the *wrought* (rather than the *given*) aspect of Merwin's enterprise:

> *. . . As though a man could make*
> *A mirror out of his own divinity,*
> *Wherein he might believe himself, and be.*

There is, too, an augmented or at least more explicit weight given to legend and to the legendary reading of history. In the opening poem, "Tower," the pilgrimage is like Childe Roland's (here, to "a darkling tower / hung with no flutter of birds, / puff of smoke or banner") out of the usual world into a place where "I cannot learn from mirrors": it is once more that echoless country of immutability, alluring and astounding ("I saw my body / as a smooth alien") but ultimately ruinous which the hero must escape if he would be heard:

> *. . . the shadows*
> *Turn alike about flesh*
> *About stone, about trees,*
>
> *Till dizzy would the wind be*
> *If wind there were; and yet*
> *No apple falls, nor the green*
> *Light like leaves from the trees . . .*

The quest for "neither a solar nor a lunar story / but a tale that might be human," for a more responsive (because mortal) state of being is further inflected in the gentle William Morris-like archaizings of the lover as traveller-returned, who would persuade his incredulous audience that the marvels he reports participate in the reality of everyday contour:

> *. . . Most I spoke of fine linen*
> *But did, in truth, tell something*
> *Of Jason who had come sailing*
> *And poised upon that shore*
> *His fabulous excursion . . .*
>
> *From Troy, over the water*
> *Returning, I recounted*
> *The tale of wrecked walls, but said*
> *That gray waves lap and surround*
> *That shore as any other . . .*

Submitting to the defeat, "the scandal that is time," these poems rehearse an inner contradiction (since it is, precisely, their *diction* which "is one of immortal gesture, / finding mortality too mysterious, / naked and with no guise but its own," while it is their *action* to reveal "the sense of dawn beneath pretence / of an order of darkness . . . ," to "infuse the real upon this dust"). By this divided or conflicting situation, the poet's projects are made either fictive or futile, "and love / becomes itself a sense of leave-taking."

Not that Merwin's poetry is hard to come by, for all its wars with its own mode at this point. Despite the dim nomenclature ("sleeking," "ensample," "suasive") extended from the first book's glamor into what is here a kind of Pre-Raphaelite glaze:

> *. . . That I, perfected in your love, may be*
> *Against all dissolution sovereign,*

> *Endlessly your litany and mirror,*
> *About your neck the amulet and song;*

despite the medieval catalogues (Vidal, Hercules, Samson, "Adam, our father, eating from his wife's hand"), the fabulous tapestries stitched with teasing half-rhymes and troubadour rhythms, Merwin has yet developed a more accessible idiom within this iridescent mythic discourse of his, a kind of verse paragraph which owes much to Stevens and which, as in this valorization of Homer, engrosses its object with an assurance that is positively festive:

> *The idiom of order is celebration,*
> *An elegance to redeem the graceless years;*
> *So those the nine-years-enraged for a filched doxy*
> *Who contend forever in the fanciful song*
> *Are the real, and those who with tangible*
> *Bronze fought are now the unbelievable dead,*
> *Their speech inconceivable, their voyages in vain,*
> *Their deeds inaccurate, save as they coincide*
> *With the final tale, the saving celebration.*

Perhaps the single decisive poem in this book, though, the one that best accounts, in terms of the poet's identification of his own role, for the discipline which keeps these bears dancing, the suffered discrepancy between the music of the spheres and of the side-show, is the address to Columbus, "You, Genoese Mariner." Here, in a single sentence, characteristically tormented into an ironic salute that is 31 lines long, the poet apostrophizes the resolute explorer—

> *Your face most perfectly*
> *A mask about a vision,*
> *Your eyes most clear when turned*
> *On the bewildering west—*

hails him as himself (the identification is made abruptly by no more than an anacoluthon, the dash which separates "you . . . who fancied / earth too circumscribed / to imagine . . . the unfingered world" from "I whose face has become / suddenly a frame / for astonishment"), thereby associating the Columbus who voyaged West for "gilt and spice" with his own disaster as a lover, as a poet, and closing on both "mistaken sailors" staring in sad wonderment at the world's "unknown dimension." The shared delusion was to believe that a Westerly direction, a held course

> *Must by its own token*
> *Continuing, contain*
> *A grammar of return . . .*

The line I have set in roman defines Merwin's entire project so far, for all the devices and designs of this courtly despot tend toward a cyclical theory of existence, the notion—so comforting to a poet who has the imagination of recurrence—that one can move onward only by preparing to move back: yet the vision fails, the changeless and diagrammatic universe ("an utter prey to mirrors") of the Genoese mariner as of the American jongleur dissolves in the forfeits of a lifetime, in fact of time itself. Ruefully, Merwin takes leave of his fantasy of perfection:

> I, after so long,
> Who have been wrong as you.

The navigational error discredits, for Merwin if not for us, his grammar of return (that magnificent phrase for a poetics of immutability); but as we shall see, the mistake, like Christopher Columbus', was a creative one: the result in both cases was the discovery of America.

Supposing he had found a transit, then, a passage through the shoals of mere circumstance to a metamorphosis that would make Being, in the words of "Epipsychidion," *conscious, inseparable, one*—Merwin had sought in his first pair of books to bind occasion as by a chain of analogies and emblems, a traditional determination of imagery which would fling in playful decorum—that "concupiscence of jigs" Jonson heard in Shakespeare's last comedies—a kind of *cordon sanitaire* "in fayre and formall shapes" around the accidental filth of the world. Yet the elimination—or the choking off—by order, however festive, of the unpredictable, the quotidian, the *facts*, must have outraged some still undisclosed impulse in his poetry as in his very personality, must have disgusted some taste for the actual. For when, two years later in 1956, Merwin's *Green with Beasts* was published, that quarrel with the methods and measures of immutability (which had hitherto found expression, as I have said, only in an exasperation of surface, a hypertrophy of the verse paragraph often eschewing rhyme for, instead, an archaizing involution of syntax) had utterly transmuted the poetry. His discontent with an orbific music which might charm into an imaginative unity all the disparates of experience now led Merwin into an expression so sharply disjunct from his initial achievements that we must look hard to see what bearing those earlier charged counsels of perfection could have on these long looping lines, these distended paragraphs of slackened expatiation unstarred by an incandescence of vocabulary or syntax, any rich and strange transformation of the very bones of speech.

It is another harmony these poems assert (one which fastens to the Eliot of the *Quartets* and later verse plays), just as it seems a different poet altogether from the celebrant of the Final Festival who now addresses himself to the world as a suffered presence, an endured pressure rather than an encompassed plaything; *how* different is evident not only in the gravamen but in the very grammar of the lines, no longer a "grammar of return" but of realization:

> *And I moved away because you must live*
> *Forward, which is away from whatever*
> *It was that you had, though you think when you have it*
> *That it will stay with you forever . . .*

The titles, as before, indicate the nature of the material, and that the material has altered: of the 39 new poems (set up on the page in long blocks of language, without the shapely stanzas and refrains which had given the work in the past its demurely marshalled aspect) only one, the "Mariner's Carol," makes the old generic commitment; the rest come to grips with their action without the mediation of a regular form: "Burning the Cat" or "The Eyes of the Drowned Watch Keels Going Over." The poems tend, then, to be ruminations or arguments, affording what Miss Moore calls "a gallantry of observation" rather than the exuberance of design—they are not prose, but they have some of the virtues of prose, for they are able to accommodate the ordinary sights and sounds of life without transforming them into myth, without impairing their specific quality as events:

> *And hours I fed*
> *That burning, till I was black and streaked with sweat;*
> *And poked it out then, with charred meat still clustering*
> *Thick around the bones. And buried it so*
> *As I should have done in the first place, for*
> *The earth is slow, but deep, and good for hiding;*
> *I would have used it if I had understood*
> *How nine lives can vanish in one flash of a dog's jaws,*
> *A car or a copperhead, and yet how one small*
> *Death, however reckoned, is hard to dispose of.*

What in *The Dancing Bears* had been presented as legend has consequently become dramatic monologue here, the difference consisting in the distance abolished; in "East of the Sun and West of the Moon," there is a teller of the tale, a containing narrative consciousness which is also a governor of the poem's magical decorum; in Merwin's third book we are inside the experience itself, not in a poem about the experience; "The Annunciation" is uttered by Mary herself, and the very hesitations, repetitions and overlaps of her discourse enact the growth of her knowledge, her helplessness and her hope:

> *. . . and because I was nothing*
> *It could be there. It was a word for*

The way the light and the things in the light
Were looking into the darkness, and the darkness
And the things of the darkness were looking into the light
In the fullness, and the way the silence
Was hearing, like it was hearing a great song
And the song was hearing the silence forever
And forever and ever. And I knew the name for it;
There in the place where I was nothing in
The fullness, I knew it, and held it and knew
The way of it, and the word for how it was one,
I held it, and the word for why. Or almost . . .

This dramatic awareness draws closer and closer inward in these poems, which murmur around the edges of autobiography with a confidence in the circumstantial entirely unknown—or at least unavailable—to Merwin the Preterist:

. . . I noticed
Near the bottom of the park, just below
The high-water line, an old coat hanging
Snagged on a tree-branch, and caught myself wondering
What sort of drunken creature had passed there.

That is, rather, Merwin the Prosaist speaking, for whom the reality of earth—"Low Fields and Light," "Fog," "Birds Waking" are characteristic subjects *and* titles—is poetry enough, the spell consisting in the acknowledgment of the world's alterity, its endless alien force which makes of the poet no more than a channel for its energies:

But you would think the fields were something
To me, so long I stare out, looking
For their shapes or shadows through the matted gleam, seeing
Neither what is nor what was, but the flat light rising.

The notion of somehow becoming a vehicle for vision, rather than a manipulator of it, is what informs or even commands these poems, imparting an air of submission to the lines ungirt on the page, a certain droning resonance which, for the poet of so many rimes and sestinas, is a tremendous risk, but one knowingly taken. The critical poem in this third series, I think—critical in the sense that it defines the *crisis* of the poet's project, and also in the sense that it offers a conscious reflection on what Merwin has undertaken—is "Learning a Dead Language"; the "dead language" is of course unspecified, for it is not Latin or Greek but poetry itself, with its "grammar of return" and its "governing order," that is at issue. By the spellbinding repetition of words ("remember" 9 times in 30 lines), of phrases:

What you remember is saved . . .

What you are given to remember
Has been saved . . .

What you come to remember becomes yourself . . .

What you remember saves you . . .

and the gradual mutation of sense by the transposition of words which
are discovered to contain their complements:

Learning will be to cultivate the awareness
Of that governing order, now pure of the passions
It composed, till, seeking it in itself,
You may find at last the passion that composed it . . .

—by all these means which are much more implicit in common speech
(it is for the poet to disclose them, that is all) than they were credited
to be in the earlier verse, with its emphasis on devices of the will,
Merwin articulates the achievement of poetry, learning a dead lan-
guage as a kind of spiritual exercise, an emptying out or using up of
the self ("what you are given to remember"), so that—final lesson of a
"night green with beasts as April with grass"—

. . . passion may be heard
When there is nothing for you to say.

And in the succeeding, companion volume, *The Drunk in the Fur-*
nace (which was published in 1960, in the full spate of Merwin's
translations and after the speech-experiments of the verse plays, as the
"roughed-up, clunking diction" indicates), the poet intensifies the *uses*
of autobiography, the disposability of "what you are given to remem-
ber" and the consequent discovery of what is not yet known ("because
I was nothing / it could be there"). Landscapes ("In Stony Country,"
"The Highway") and sea pieces ("Fog-Horn," "The *Portland* Going
Out") extend the impulse of *Green with Beasts* to inflect the con-
sciousness, to subdue the identity so utterly to the given scene that
some other passion beyond the merely personal speaks out of observa-
tion. There is an enlarged sense of the *menace* of nature, of some
obscure opposition to human life in the mere process of the universe,
that makes these poems less complacent than the meditations of the last
book; where once Merwin had gratefully announced that "the ground
where we find we stand is holy," he now greets the earth with a
shudder, finding its course at least as diabolic as divine:

The whole night is alive with hands,
Is aflame with palms and offerings
And racked with a soft yammer for alms
Disclosing always the same craving
Through the three seasons of leaves
And in mid-winter when the trees
Are hung with empty gloves all over:
The coin called out for is ourselves.

But the astonishment of the book is its last dozen poems (including the title piece to which I shall return): these are autobiographical American studies—the poet grew up in Union City, New Jersey, and in Scranton, Pennsylvania—of an ungainliness and an intimacy one would have thought inaccessible not only to the singer of all those carols and cansos, but even to the connoisseur of numinous landscapes and emblematic weathers. One can conceive, if high style is understood as an oppression, one can pursue the effort to escape its strictures by a movement from created—*i.e.*, conventional—reality to an external one; but having achieved, let us say, the new convention of a landscape received and responded to without acknowledging the medium, as in "Cape Dread" in the first part of this new book:

. . . But what we found
You will find for yourselves, somewhere, for
Yourselves. We have not gone there again,
Nor ventured ever so far again. In
The south corner of the cove there is
An inlet flowing with sweet water,
And there are fruits in abundance, small
But delectable, at least at that season.

—having achieved something as beautiful and unforced as that, radically different though it may be from the "curious-knotted garden" of Merwin's initial manner, it is still a far cry, in fact quite out of hearing, from the depleted scenery which litters these nagging, underprivileged genre-pictures of his pure-products-of-America-go-crazy sequence:

. . . the best
Went west long ago, got out from under,
Waved bye-bye to the steep scratched fields and scabby
Pastures: their chapped plaster of newspapers
Still chafes from the walls, and snags of string tattling
Of their rugs trail yet from stair-nails. The rest,
Never the loftiest, left to themselves,
                    Descended, descended.

This is to turn from the example of Robert Graves, whose practice has counted for so much in Merwin's exploitation of his art, to that of Robert Lowell. In this fourth volume of Merwin's, the dramatic monologues are family portraits now, the derelict fancies of marooned eccentrics, and no longer the inward dynamics of myth or metahistory. When comment on these wrecked heritages of his is offered at all, the poet makes it in his own person, speaks for his own bruised past. Invoking, for example, the "Pool Room in the Lions' Club" which "must be still the same, / year after year," Merwin finally turns away in disgust, horrified by the recent illusions in which men must participate in order to endure their existence:

> . . . *They must think*
> *The whole world is nothing more*
> *Than their gainless harmless pastime*
> *Of utter patience protectively*
> *Absorbed around one smooth table*
> *Safe in its ring of dusty light*
> *Where the real dark can never come.*

The institutions of our life in society are seen—and scorned—as so many hopeless measures against the power of death, the gaining outer darkness. *What is remembered*, these poems assert in their cold-hearted attentiveness (they are the poems of a deathbed nurse, in fact: detailed, watchful, withdrawn), *what is connected is what draws the self down;* as Merwin apostrophizes one of his relatives, "Uncle Hess":

> . . . *Canny and neat, whatever*
> *You were was unmistakable, but never*
> *Could be explained. And I wonder whether*
> *Even now you would tell me anything more*
> *Of every kinship than its madness . . .*

The poet sloughs off *family ties* just as utterly as he discards the *festival order* of his early work: ecstasy and extinction, giant energy and giant annihilation are the poles of Being that concern him—the rest is merely process, the hateful regress from organization to chaos Merwin spoke of, at the first, in terms of Corneille and Racine. The culminating poems of this series advance an almost rapturous apprehension of loathing, the rhetoric no longer neutral but tense with negativity; there is a convulsive music of disgrace here, though it is still mortised into a narrative frame:

> . . . *spooled snakes sleeping under*
> *The stone dairy-floor stir with the turned year,*
> *Waken, and sliding loose in their winter skins*

Like air rising through thin ice, feed themselves forth
To inherit the earth.

One of the firmest achievements, and one of the least editorialized in this infernal mode of Merwin's (one is reminded, in fact, of Rossetti's remark about *Wuthering Heights:* the action is laid in hell, only it seems places and people have English names there) is "Burning Mountain," in which a half-worked coal mine is perpetually on fire; the combustion, as Merwin apprehends it, spreads in the earth with its own hellish life, countered and quenched ultimately by a greater, more ominous cosmic exhaustion:

> *They have sealed off all the veins they could find,*
> *Thus at least setting limits to it, we trust.*
> *It consumes itself, but so slowly it will outlast*
> *Our time and our grandchildren's, curious*
> *But not unique: there was always one of these*
> *Nearby, wherever we moved, when I was a child.*
>
> *Under it, not far, the molten core*
> *Of the earth recedes from its thin crust*
> *Which all the fires we light cannot prevent*
> *From cooling. Not a good day's walk above it*
> *The meteors burn out in the air to fall*
> *Harmless in empty fields, if at all . . .*

It is interesting to note contemporary reactions to this book, the comment being neatly divided between regret for the surrendered "techniques of one of the master prosodists of our time" and, as James Dickey (whose qualification of Merwin's new diction as "roughed-up, clunking" I have already cited) put it, "an impression that this poet, though he may now seem to be stalled after a prodigal beginning, is gathering force." Observing with characteristic asperity that Merwin was now past "the intricacies of what is so easy for him to say concerning almost anything," Dickey predicted—and he was the only critic at this stage who saw his way so far into Merwin's intentions, so violently realized in the subsequent volumes—that "he should soar like a phoenix out of the neat ashes of his early work." The image of the phoenix, a creature which repeatedly consumes itself in order to reappear altogether different though still . . . the phoenix, jibes precisely with the disquieting but authentic succession of accomplishments we confront in Merwin today.

The fourth book closes, significantly, with its title poem, "The Drunk in the Furnace," which we must consider as a fulfillment of the epigraph to *The Dancing Bears,* to wit, Flaubert's bitter observation that our speech is as the hammmering on a cracked kettle to make bears dance, when we would seduce the stars—in order to record Merwin's advance—or is it a retreat?—to his own chaos from a borrowed or inherited order. The poem sets one of his typically graceless scenes: the deprived community ("in their tar-paper church . . . they nod and hate trespassers") and, in the naked gully out back, a huge scrapped furnace:

> No more to them than a hulking black fossil
> To erode unnoticed with the rest of the junk-hill
> By the poisonous creek, and rapidly to be added
>   To their ignorance

An unaccountable drunk ("where he gets his spirits / it's a mystery") takes up residence inside, to the scandal of these bigots, and there performs his preposterous rites:

> Hammer-and-anvilling with poker and bottle
> To his jugged bellowings, till the last groaning clang
> As he collapses . . .

But though the booze-ridden minstrel is deplored in "his bad castle," the smoke is said to stagger out of its "chewed hole like a pale resurrection," and when the furnace-music wakes,

>   . . . all afternoon
> Their witless offspring flock like piped rats to its siren
> Crescendo, and agape on the crumbling ridge
>   Stand in a row and learn.

This is the apotheosis of Merwin's emblem of the poet, his progress-report, this comic horror which for all its obloquy and abuse is yet redeemed by the consistency and energy, by the reality of the treatment. It is one quality of an important writer that the exigencies of his form—whether they be the celebrations of an order or the "jugged bellowings" of a chaos—become not the flaws of his work but its strength, and in each phase of Merwin's accomplishment, we can observe the same extremity of commitment and the same phoenix-like consummation. Here, certainly, the ashes are not the least bit neat, but rather the desperate calcination of a man in a death-struggle (what else could it be?) with his own *realization*, in all the senses that word will bear, of mortality.

In 1963, Merwin published his fifth book, *The Moving Target*, whose very title suggests, and whose contents enforce, another avatar of the phoenix, a paroxysmal shift in the order of discourse lest the poet "not contain but be his own process of reversion." Not the anecdotal and smoky *realia* of Robert Lowell, now, but the orphic notations, the cryptic aphorisms of René Char stand behind these poems which appear to be not so much a new apparition of the phoenix as an attempt—perplexing but finally persuasive—to register its incremation, that ecstasy of identity on the brink of ash:

> *Tell me what you see vanishing and I*
> *Will tell you who you are . . .*

The long book opens with a couple of dramatic monologues, a "Letter from Gussie" which rehearses further the kind of maiden-aunt derangement already broached in those family portraits at the end of *The Drunk in the Furnace*, and a more suggestive piece, "Home for Thanksgiving," which is a gloat of spiritual sanctity recounted by one of those bums who seem to be borrowed from Beckett's personnel, the extremity of whose destitution allows him the kind of abrupt but homely imagery Merwin will accommodate even more drastically on his own:

> *I bring myself back avoiding in silence*
> *Like a ship in a bottle.*
> *I bring my bottle . . . my fingers sifting*
> *The dark would have turned up other*
> *Poverties, I bring myself*
> *Back like a mother cat transferring her only kitten . . .*
> *Oh misery, misery, misery,*
> *You fit me from head to foot like a good grade suit of longies*
> *Which I have worn for years and never want to take off.*
> *I did the right thing after all.*

Though the postures of renunciation and impoverishment are a suitable prologue to Merwin's new undertaking, as we shall see, there is still, here, an accountability of phrasing, a metrical propriety ("I bring myself / back": such enjambments are almost ideograms; and the feminine endings of the irregular lines keep the sense moving right down to the close, where it can, rightly, rest; though transformed, this is yet the practice of a caretaker) which keep the poem from breaking loose. No, there is a fiercer alienation than that of the disinherited which Merwin covets, and a far more convulsive diction than these gentle displacements warrant. Merwin places next in his book the decisive poem over which the reader must pass as through those barred doors in the asylum which lead into the violent ward: "Lemuel's Blessing," whose epigraph from the mad Christopher Smart establishes the tone: "Let Lemuel bless with the wolf, which is a dog without a master, but the Lord hears his cries and feeds him in the desert." In the last book, Merwin had a

poem about a "caught fox" in which he spoke of the "captive, twist-
ing / the raw song of its debasement . . . In your delicate nests tast-
ing / nothing but its own decay / (as at first hand I have learned) / Oh
kill it at once or let it go." Here the same savagery which the poet,
speaking now as Smart's Lemuel, resolves to salvage is worked into a
litany of unconstraint, a kind of lupine credo:

Deliver me
From the ruth of the lair, which clings to me in the morning,
Painful when I move, like a trap;
Even debris has its favorite positions but they are not yours;
From the ruth of prepared comforts, with its
Habitual dishes sporting my name and its collars and leashes of vanity;
From the ruth of approval, with its nets, kennels and taxidermists;
It would use my guts for its own rackets and instruments . . .
Teach me to recognize its platforms, which are constructed like
*   scaffolds;*
From the ruth of known paths, which would use my feet, tail and ears
*   as curios,*
My head as a nest for tame ants,
My fate as a warning.

The merciless effects of a successful literary career are here outdis-
tanced by a brutal program of neglect and non-participation; the recipi-
ent of a fair share of the shared fare, the lagniappe our Establishment
showers on the decorous practitioner, Merwin has had the desperation
("I have been brought to bay . . . preserve my tongue and I will bless
you again and again") to strike out for the woods, snarling at "those
who would track me for their own twisted ends" yet wanting, with a
kind of fierce probity, to be heard, even so:

But let me leave my cry stretched out behind me like a road
On which I have followed you.
There when I crouch to drink let me catch a glimpse of your image
Before it is obscured with my own.
And sustain me for my time in the desert
On what is essential to me.

These are the wild articles of faith by which Merwin will henceforth
abide, apart from the community of believers ("Goodbye iron Bible
containing my name in rust"), apart from any inherited lore ("Good-
bye what you learned for me I have to learn anyway"). On the page,
the generally unpunctuated poems look as though they had been
exploded, not written down, the images arranged so that the lines never
enclose but instead *expose* them:

> Here I am once again with my dry mouth
> At the fountain of thistles
> Preparing to sing

There is, further, a great deal of white space among the words, between the lines, within the phrases, for Merwin now invites the participation of silence as he once warded it off with all the words in his armory. There are six or seven generating nouns here, around which experience gathers in figures of force like filings in a magnetic field; once we perceive the web constituted by *lock* and *key*, *knife* and *mirror*, *clock* and *stone*, as well as the basic movements of *opening* and *closing*, we can track Merwin like a *moving target*, indeed—like the dangerous quarry he has become in his flight from the menagerie of mannerliness; if we read this book through not as a set of discrete poems but rather as a sequence of *sentences* in the full meaning of the word—not only a judgment and a "musical idea," but a discernment by the *senses*—as a notation of the central man who has cut away almost all the connective tissue of rationalization that made, once, his circulatory system so easy to trace, then there is no obscurity here, though the outrage, the brilliant abruptness is certainly stunning. Merwin himself is not beyond, or above, a certain rueful coquetry in the matter of his new poetics:

> Maybe I thought
> I could go on and on flying the same rag,
> Like the fire,
> But it's faded white and I'm
> Not the fire, I'll have to find
> Something bright and simple to signify
> Me, what an order.

The whole burden of Merwin's discovery that "I'm not the fire" is the shift from a posture of mastery to one of submission or of resistance to submission ("to just sit down and let the horizon ride over me"); the corollary is that if I am not the fire, I am what the fire feeds on, and consequently there is a certain grandeur about the victimization:

> This must be what I wanted to be doing
> Walking at night between the two deserts,
> Singing.

It is a grammar of departure, now, that Merwin employs, without any of the comforting associations that had kept the world familiar; here *things*, natural objects, are seen or somehow acknowledged with such clarity that for the moment nothing else exists except the space around them. From the first terrible desolation:

438   (W. S. Merwin)

> *All shores but the first have been foreign*
> *And the first was not home until left behind*

to the ultimate and exultant indigence—the nakedness of the anchorite
in his Thebaid beset by gaudy temptations—of Merwin's triumph in
the desert places:

> *On plates upside down in token of mourning*
> *I eat to your vanishing*
>
> *I bearing messages*
> *With all my words my silence being one*
>
> *From childhood to childhood the*
> *Message Goodbye from the shoulders of victory*
> *To the followers*
> *From the sea to the nearest of kin*
>
> *From the lightning to*
> *Its nest from myself to my name*
> *Goodbye*
>
> *I begin with what was always gone*

—we follow a shocking spoor, the fewmets of what Yeats rightly
called a dying animal. When *The Moving Target* was published, it was
naturally James Dickey, the one critic aware, in the preceding book, of
the wild creature gathering for its spring, who called these new poems
"incomparably the author's best . . . there is a sense of going beyond,
of linguistic adventurousness." And given the already imposing record
of achievements in "going-beyond" that Merwin had sown or strewn so
prodigally behind himself, this was little enough to say, except that
Dickey added, with more pertinence: "poems that have upon them
the handprint of necessity." In the obsessive network of these images,
these sudden, stark phrases which ring with the resonance of some
proverb or adage we have heard since childhood—

> *I am still begging the same question*
> *By the same light,*
> *Eating the same stone,*
>
> *And the hands of the clock still knock without entering—*

the necessity Dickey refers to as imprinting its sign on Merwin is the
mortal necessity, the instance which has driven him through all his
handsome and then his hellish avatars in order to avoid and, finally, to
embrace in an ecstasy of certitude this killing knowledge:

I have seen the spider's triumph
In the palm of my hand. Above
My grave, that thoroughfare,
There are words now that can bring
My eyes to my feet, tamed.
Beyond the trees wearing names that are not their own
The paths are growing like smoke.

The promises have gone,
Gone, gone, and they were here just now.
There is the sky where they laid their fish.
Soon it will be evening.

Without an adjective, almost without an image save for that curious trope of mackerel clouds,* there is nothing the least bit out of the way about any part of this, from a poem called "October," except that the stanzas *entire* have a wild anonymity, a familiar strangeness, so to speak, that is the sign of the objective "achieved at the blessed expense of the personal" (in the phrase of R. P. Blackmur, to whom this book is dedicated). The poems are intimate, of course—but they are not private, for they have worked their way down into the very hinges of the language, and by an interlocking system of "directorates," like some chthonic cartel, they have managed to control a tremendous range of experience by a very few figures. I shall glance at just one of these through the book, and then look at a single poem in which it is pervasive, for though there are many splendid individual works here— "Standards," "The Way to the River," "The Next," "For Now" are the greatest singular triumphs, I think—in general Merwin's present personation of the phoenix requires a general conflagration, the fire running in all his members, if we are to see the figure transfigured at its heart. Let the one figure, then, be knives, though locks and mirrors are just as tempting . . . They appear almost at once, in the versicles of "Lost Month":

> . . . *One fine day the first knives come through the mirrors,*
> *like fins of sharks. The images heal, but imperfectly*

This sense of the cutting edge of mortality, the knife as *memento mori,* is indeed often conjugated with the mirror: where Merwin pleads, on the one hand, "I know I've no excuse to be stuck here turning / like a

---

* The poet writes: "mackerel sky was the origin of that image: the marks of fish and everything they evoke, to me at least, imply rapid fading, from the drying of sand or springing up again of grass where they have been lying, to the actual markings themselves that start to change within minutes of death; . . . a phenomenon implying a particular kind of meteorological instability, more or less predictable . . ."

mirror on a string," he portends, on the other: "The old hunger, left in
the old darkness, / turned like a hanged knife." The aimless dangling of
both emblems, mirror and knife, signify the helpless identity under the
sign of its life and death, though it is those sharp limits of selfhood the
blade suggests which Merwin mostly invokes:

> *I will lay it beside us, the old knife,*
> *While we reach our conclusions.*

Not always disruptive, the knowledge of death can also be a resolving
influence, constitutive and buttressing: "I would say, 'I will gather these
pieces together, / any minute now I will make / a knife out of a
cloud.' " Indeed, the knife is not only a weapon but an instrument—like
the mirror, a source of vision:

> *As the bats flower in the crevices*
> *You and your brothers*
> *Raise your knives to see by . . .*
> *As for us, we enter your country*
> *With our eyes closed.*

It is the means, then, by which the self is measured against existence,
against the energies which transcend it: "the light flowing over a knife."
And against non-existence, against the void which cancels it: "my
love / outlined in knives." But the purest, because the most implicit, use
of the image, after all these inflections, occurs in the most directly
moving poem in the book, an address to the poet's brother who was
born and who died on the same day, a year before the poet's own birth
("My elder, born into death like a message into a bottle"). Here, in
accents alternately pathetic and clownish, Merwin manages not only in
his tone but in his reconciliation of images to hit the moving target:

> *If I address you . . . it is in hope of no*
> *Answer, but as so often, merely*
> *For want of another, for*
> *I have seen catastrophe taking root in the mirror,*
> *And why waste my words there? . . .*
>
> *But I do what I can. I am patient*
> *With the woes of the cupboards, and God knows—*
> *I keep the good word close to hand like a ticket.*
> *I feed the wounded lights in their cages.*
> *I wake up at night on the penultimate stroke, and with*
> *My eyes still shut I remember to turn the thorn*
> *In the breast of the bird of darkness.*
> *I listen to the painful song*
> *Dropping away into sleep . . . I*

Got away this time for a while. I've come
Again to the whetted edge of myself *where I*
Can hear the hollow waves breaking like
Bottles in the dark . . .

It is as if Narcissus had become Achilles: Merwin has abandoned the mirror and, in that extraordinary figure which I give in roman, has *become* the knife, has become his own death which he thereby defeats. The exorbitant book ends with a little song of thanksgiving, "Daybreak":

> *The future woke me with its silence*
> *I join the procession*
> *An open doorway*
> *Speaks for me*
> *Again*

In 1967, four years after *The Moving Target*, Merwin brought out his sixth book, *The Lice*. The odd title is taken from Heraclitus' fragment about Homer and the boys' riddle: "what we have caught and killed we left behind but what has escaped we bring with us"— their lice. Homer's failure to guess the riddle proves, Heraclitus says, that all men are deceived by the appearances of things. Merwin is content to abide by this knowledge, or this ignorance: he will present the appearances of things and welcome the deceptions in an effort to defeat them by suggesting their thinness and incompletion; for these are all poems of a visionary reality, hallucinatory in their clarity of outline, their distinctness of detail:

> *It is cold here*
> *In the steel grass*
> *At the foot of the invisible statue*
> *Made by the incurables and called*
> *Justice*

The poems are entirely unpunctuated, and the virtuosity of their accessibility is great, for the continuities are extended beyond those of the last book, the voice sustained for longer units of expression; but (in keeping with Merwin's habit of articulating each of his modes in pairs of books) the work, whether wisps of a couple of lines and a single image, or deliberations of several pages and almost novelistic detail, are of the same inner coherence, the same outer necessity as those in *The Moving Target* ("May I bow to Necessity," he prays in "Wish," in the new book, "not / to her hirelings"). All the poems appear to be written from one and the same place where the poet has holed up, observant but withdrawn, compassionate but hopeless, isolated yet the more concerned, at least in quantity of reference, by the events of a public world. "The Asians Dying," "For a Coming Extinction," "When the War Is Over" are some of the titles, and one poem ends:

> *On the door it says what to do to survive*
> *But we were not born to survive*
> *Only to live*

It is as though the poet had decided, or determined, his own fate, which is one of dispossession and the *aigre* wisdom to be derived from it: "Now all my teachers are dead except silence / I am trying to read what the five poplars are writing / on the void." And once these interior distances have been explored:

> *I think all this is somewhere in myself*
> *The cold room unlit before dawn*
> *Containing a stillness such as attends death*
> *And from a corner the sounds of a small bird trying*
> *From time to time to fly a few beats in the dark*
> *You would say it was dying it is immortal*

—Merwin is free ("I know I'm free / this is how I live / up here") to attend to his visionary task, his responsibility to others:

> *I take no pride in circumstances but there are*
> *Occupations*
> *My blind neighbor has required of me*
> *A description of darkness*
> *And I begin I begin . . .*

There is a cool radiance in these poems, as Merwin himself had put it: "a clarity at once simple and formal, excited and cool, a limpidity"

> *Of frost stirring among its*
> *Stars like an animal asleep*
> *In the winter night*

—a detachment from the glamor of language as the canonical order had wielded it, from the glare of reality as the discursive impulse had submitted to it, and even from the gleam of vision as the latest web of fragmentary correspondences had invoked it. Part of the weird effect is simply the result of loneliness ("I am strange here and often I am still trying / to finish something as the light is going") and of the fantasies to which the self in isolation, unmoderated by social tact, is subject:

> *At times night occurs to me so that I think I have been*
> *Struck from behind I remain perfectly*

Still feigning death listening for the
Assailant perhaps at last
I even sleep a little for later I have moved . . .

If I could be consistent even in destitution
The world would be revealed . . .

But even when Merwin speaks as a prophet out of his solitude into that opposing solitude which is Other People, as in "A Scale in May":

To succeed consider what is as though it were past
Deem yourself inevitable and take credit for it
If you find you no longer believe enlarge the temple

—even when he acknowledges Other Poets ("you who were haunted all your life by the best of you / hiding in your death"), there is a chill, almost a silence that lines his speech, and a difference about his notation of the world which I take as the final achievement of his vast mutations; it is the welcoming of his destitution among men in this book (as in the last it was the encompassing of his death in a private history) that sounds the special note of *The Lice:*

All morning with dry instruments
The field repeats the sound
Of rain
From memory . . .
It is August
The flocks are beginning to form
I will take with me the emptiness of my hands
What you do not have you find everywhere

These lines are from a poem called "Provision," and if we recall that the word means, precisely, a looking ahead, a vision of the future, we can see that the poetry of this man has moved from preterition to presence to prophecy, and that it is, in its latest, mastered avatar, *provisional* in the proudest as well as the humblest sense, foreseeing and providing for its own metamorphosis; perhaps what I have called coolness and detachment is merely the effect of a poetry which has altogether committed itself to that encounter with identity we call, at our best, reality; for no poetry, where it is good, transcends anything or is about anything: it is itself, discovering its own purpose and naming its own meaning—its own provision, as Merwin provides it in "For the Anniversary of My Death":

Every year without knowing it I have passed the day
When the last fires will wave to me

(*W. S. Merwin*)

And the silence will set out
Tireless traveller
Like the beam of a lightless star
Then I will no longer
Find myself in life as in a strange garment
Surprised at the earth
And the love of one woman
And the shamelessness of men
As today writing after three days of rain
Hearing the wren sing and the falling cease
And bowing not knowing to what

The Carrier of Ladders: Poems by W. S. MERWIN
The Miner's Pale Children: Prose by W. S. MERWIN

Merwin's seventh book of poems is of course his best—of course, because he has made his career what the word means: a course, a passage out, with just those overtones of self-overcoming which bring this book, so rewardingly, into the homestretch.

The new poems are the progress report and the prognosis of a development which has been under way, in terms of prosody, in Merwin's last two books of verse; in terms of imagery, in the last four. They are intimate poems, but not in the least personal. For Merwin, for the poet who is the one voice raised in Merwin's book, anyone or anything can be the "key"—"key / unlocking the presence / of the unlighted river / under the mountains"—another person, his own body, an event, a landscape: the key to darkness, to unconditional life. That is the real goal of these poems, what they are developing toward: a quality of life which used to be called visionary, and which must be characterized by its negatives, by what it is not, for what it is cannot be spoken.

A phenomenology of darkness, then, of loss, absence and removal, will govern the imagery here—as Merwin says in the poem actually called "The Removal": "the soles of our feet are   black stars / but ours is the theme / of the light." And a prosody of pauses, of halts and silences which will let the language thicken to unwonted suspensions, enjambments which reveal, chiefly, *weight* to the ear hasty for conclusions, as they show *disparity* to the eye seeking recurrence.

And if the source and subject of the poems is a vision of integrity, of a life entire, unmediated by any expectation but that of death, their enemy is division. "What I live for I can seldom believe in /

what I hope is always divided," Merwin says in "Plane", the determinative first poem:

> *my mind infinitely divided and hopeless*
> *like a stockyard seen from above*
> *my will like a withered body muffled*
> *in qualifications*
> *until it has no shape*
> *I bleed in my place*
> *where is no*
> *vision of the essential nakedness of the gods . . .*

Undivided life, which means unqualified life: many of these poems will be concerned, therefore, to put off the past—the social past ("my father has voted for me / I say no I will vote in my own name") and the cultural past ("It is true that in / our language deaths are to be heard / at any moment through the talk"); indeed the very gesture of poetry as we have it from the past is questioned in all these poems:

> *. . . the ends and the beginnings*
> *are still guarded*
> *by lines of doors*
> *hand in hand*
> *the dead guarding the invisible*
> *each presenting its message*
> I know nothing
> learn of me

Yet these poems also make it their concern to resist expectations of the future, hopes, assurances ("if I can say yes / I must say it to this / and now / trying to remember what the present / can bless me with / which I know"). The exultation must be *now*, it must not depend on what we have had, it must not count on what we may have; and *now*, as we all know, is *never*—untenable, untenantable. The exultation, then, will be an ecstasy of loss, the sense of what Wordsworth called fallings from us, vanishings, yet experienced as a revelation of ourselves, a birth:

> *the birth of speech*
> *that must grow*
> *in pain . . .*
> *oh objects come and talk with us while you can . . .*

The present can be realized, Merwin psalmodizes, only by reversing the signs, in proportion as one cancels out the data of an irreversible course: "I am the son of thanksgiving but its language is strange in my mouth / I am the son of the future but she shows me only her mourning veil / I am the son of the future but my own father . . ." Forever beginning again, emptying his hands, the poet assumes—in deprivation, loss, absence—that emblematic accountability which was his ancient privilege when he possessed those powers of which he has been stripped, the conviction that his separated, perishable fate may yet be of use to us, a talisman to the City; the sense that precisely because his heart is "beating by itself" he may understand, may nourish our impulse.

An irreversible course "which prizes less / as it receives than as it loses" is what Merwin would versify, hence what he must oppose, for the entire justice of verse is precisely that return, that reversion, that recovery of constants in experience which can be varied or departed from because acknowledged to be there. And Merwin acknowledges nothing to be there ("silence the messenger runs through the vast lands"): his verse is verse only because he declares it to *have been:* "a country he thinks is there because / he thinks he left it." Whence a saving tension in these poems, a continuing struggle between the cry and the crater, the hymn and the silence. In the last poem, "In the Time of the Blossoms," Merwin ends his long unpunctuated litany of dispossessions with an imploring look at (what else?) an ash tree:

> *on white heaven*
> *staves of one*
> *unbreathed music*
> *Sing to me*

That capital letter tells us: we are overhearing an invocation to the deciduous life, source of all this song.

There is no such agon in Merwin's copious prose, no such relentless twist of idiom in the systematic destructions which constitute *The Miner's Pale Children.* For prose is the proper medium for removals, separations, "the blandishments of decay", and with remarkable ease Merwin parades his mastery of half a dozen tonalities—fussy aridities and rich mythologizing, emblems, tales, memories, riddles. The book is arranged with a distinct presentiment of a design upon us, from the first piece "The Dwelling", in which Merwin announces that "disappearance could be considered a kind of beginning", to the last, "Dawn Comes to its Mountain in the Brain", in which he celebrates "a darkness like the darkness in wires through which a message is flowing . . . and a silence like that around a wire through which a message is passing." Between the disappearance at the outset and the silence at the end occurs a great deal of undoing, dissolving, erasing. Indeed, in one of his characteristically named fragments, "Forgetting", Merwin interrogatively defines and describes the nature of his prose: "Was its disappearance what it was? . . . It has to pass through us in order to reach us. It has to go through us without pausing in order to be clear to us: will we be able to receive it? Will we not be in our way?"

And certainly all these texts are so many efforts, whether parodic, lyrical, emphatic, even critical, to get out of his own way, to become transparent. "I am an abyss that I am trying to cross," Merwin announces, "an absence waiting for what belongs to it." The hope here is to rid the self of the self, to be born to the world, to be silent—and that is the supreme aspiration of prose. As Merwin says in "Knives", speaking too of the cutting edge of his fine-honed utterances, "We see only the service we ask of them—separation, separation and pain. Without which, as we say, we would be nothing."

The imaginative largesse of this book of prose is astonishing. Clearly, the negative offers Merwin a mode of getting on with his undoing which is as prodigal as all our pieties about "creativity", about "affirmation": "he could hear the pain of disappearance itself," he says of one of his creatures, "of which night is one form and day another." King Lear was wrong—everything comes of nothing, or out of nothing. And by the agency of prose it goes on, leaving behind only history—which Merwin calls the form of despair reserved for the living—and darkness ahead. How well Merwin has listened to Beckett: "The voice must have come. Because it has gone." And how hard he has looked at Magritte: "An occasional glimpse through an open window of a fly on an empty table, or a plate standing on edge." Fragmentation and forgetting are the method this writer employs to use himself up, to exhaust himself in "a travail which in itself of course is a delivery from confinement." Forgetting, because we are fallen creatures, because, as he puts it, "there is no returning to the ungrieved world. Now that it no longer exists, it never existed." And fragmentation, because the process is linear, persistent, unending; as he says in "The Fragments," a perfectly named morsel: "parts of it keep appearing. I have begun to have glimpses of all that I am doing, crossing the place where they have all been satisfied, and still finding fragment after fragment."

In one of the great "Psalms" from *The Carrier of Ladders*, Merwin makes a discovery: "in front of me it is written / This is the end of the past / Be happy." And in one of his fragments from *The Miner's Pale Children*, he glosses that discovery: "most of what we call our virtues have been made of necessities by processes we later tried to forget." Poetry then is the felicity of a redeemed world, ungrieved, regenerate. And prose? A *fabula rasa*.

I have not attached the usual tags of praise and blame to these enterprises which are so complementary, so instinct with one another's energies. Merwin long ago reached what I should call his majority as a poet, and when a man travels this far—or craves so to travel: "if only we could set out now just as we are, and leave ourselves"—it is

impertinent to assign grades, to hand out marks. The interesting thing
is not to say that Merwin is a wonderful poet, or a wonderful prose
writer, for "how many things," as he says, "come to one name /
hoping to be fed!" *One reaches for definitions and touches darkness.*
Pertinent, I hope, is the application to Merwin of what he says of
his man "In a Dark Square": "that though no one is listening, he re-
peats aloud to the darkness that he will continue to put all his faith in
himself."

The Nation, 1970

Writings to an Unfinished Accompaniment by W.S. MERWIN

A world of which we are, by living in it, dispossessed: that is W.S.
Merwin's world—"the world is made of less and less", *unless* we can
bring ourselves to forget. So there is an exercise in forgetting among
these new "writings", a calisthenics of oblivion, a workout extending
from mere numbers, counting,

> *going on to the alphabet*
> *until everything is continuous again*
>
> *go on to forgetting elements*
> *starting with water*
> *proceeding to earth*
> *rising in fire*
>
> *forget fire*

—a characteristic process in this poetry of deprivals and erasures. In
this eighth volume, published concurrently with his translations called
Asian Figures (Merwin ransacks world literature for absences, for un-
doings even more exotic than the local product, and there are plenty
here, Mongol, Arab, Sioux, *Märchen,* and Egyptian Figures, though
they are not translations, merely "someone touching / a silence / an
opening"), Merwin sustains and a little attenuates the magnificent
obliterations of *The Carrier of Ladders,* led on by what vanishes:

> *before me stones begin to go out like candles*
> *guiding me*

Without punctuation, without prosody, without companions, "speak-
ing another language / as the earth does", he pursues his asymptotic
phenomenology of thresholds, doors, passages, "the gates about to
close / that never do." For the first time, I think, there is the after-
taste of method, an intimation of formula—as Merwin says, "you say
nothing / once." The book's title gives us a cue to the difficulties

of a raised voice in the fallen world; it is Merwin's first *self-conscious* title (by which I mean, non-metaphorical) in the teeming procession of his works, the first title which acknowledges that he knows, when he confesses himself haunted by "something not done," that he must add "its story to my regrets / and its silence to my compass." The unfinished accompaniment is of course life itself, and these writings aspire to that condition of voiceless verse which would be the true ob-bligato: "on each journey there is / a silence that goes with it."

Naturally—or preternaturally, in the nature of the case—there are astonishing successes, poems which illustrate because they make il-lustrious the canon of "remembered darkness" that Merwin has made so incomparably his own: incomparably because, as I began by inti-mating and as Merwin spells out, "while we sign our names / more of us / lets go / and will never answer."

But there is a languor now in the elementals, a sense, in the stillness, of a lounging energy. When Merwin covers his tracks—"my memory / the flame far from the candles"—we are made to wonder if he doesn't really want to be followed, after all, into those wildernesses of white ease. Not that it is easy to *do*—this is a poetry of ground-down collaborations between what is given out and what is held back or even taken in, a kind of fence-sitting on "the gate where the nameless / cries out." For all his imitators, only this poet among us sounds the true *lacrimae nihilis* note. But there is—if I hear him right—a pathos acknowledged at the end of this book, this *acknowledged text*. It is the pathos of a man who discerns that it is life which is the accom-paniment to a finished writing.

Or so I read the invocation at the close, the heartbreakingly lovely poem "Gift" which ends or signs off on this blank hope, its very majuscules reminiscent of Shelley:

> *I call to it Nameless One O Invisible*
> *Untouchable Free*
> *I am nameless I am divided*
> *I am invisible I am untouchable*
> *and empty*
> *nomad live with me*
> *be my eyes*
> *my tongue and my hands*
> *my sleep and my rising*
> *out of chaos*
> *come and be given*

HOWARD MOSS

"Beginnings Spin a Web
Where Endings Spawn."

I N 1960, Howard Moss selected an appropriate showing of poems
from his first three volumes—the restrictive, jaunty titles suggest
the intonaton and thence the intention of those fifteen preceding years:
The Wound and the Weather (1946), *The Toy Fair* (1954) and *A
Swimmer in the Air* (1957); to these accomplished trophies he joined—
"I add their substance to subtract my sum"—two dozen new pieces,
including the ten-poem set about King Midas and his family, and stood
forth revealed, though hardly proclaimed, as our consummate melic
poet, a kind of Manhattan Campion who had in his cautious practice
renewed the art, or at least the artifice, of small forms. Though most of
his poetry first appeared in *The New Yorker*, of which he was—
and still is—poetry editor, Moss has done a great deal, if not always
enough, to ransom the notion of "magazine verse" from the decorous
doldrums of trinominate ladies, suburban complaints and the kind of
"light verse" *Time Magazine* is always approving, provided it is writ-
ten by happily married housewives not too far from the distaff or the
Disposall at any moment. The title of Moss' big collection affords a
clue to what is his saving grace among so many others that are merely
suave or serviceable (for example, he uses a rare word only when its
music is irresistible and self-articulating, as in "the skyline's hyaline
transparencies, emptying its architecture by degrees"); for *A Winter
Come, A Summer Gone* describes, in an odor of urban mortality this
poet insists on, like Schiller with his rotting apples, the cosmic proces-
sion, the docile ecliptic of the seasons, the heavenly bodies and the
earthly embodiments of their rhythms ("a renaissance of rings") that

stand over and against the individual consciousness, the shrieking plasm
of the self. Even at his tightest—and Moss can be relentless in working
out a conceit:

> . . . *the baited poles of light*
> *Angling through the way the sun today*
> *Fishes among the clouds*

—this poet suggests always some connection between the human order
of apprehension and the universal order, or what we may perceive in
the universe as order, for lack of the terms to come to with chaos. And
in 1965 was published a further book of poems—by now Moss had
written a book about Proust as well, and edited selections from Lear
and Keats—with an even more suggestive and despondent title, exhibit-
ing the poet's characteristic turn, one based partly on some experience
already acquired by the language, and partly on a sense of diminution
and loss, "fallings from us, vanishings" . . . *Finding Them Lost.*

Reading any number of these always short, always sheared and
clean-shaven lyrics together benumbs; one feels like the old Faust
marvelling at the Sign of the Macrocosm in his shadowy study, seeking
in its flickering lights and mysterious alterations the signal for that
Great Change which would transform all things and make him young
again:

> *I turn away from those black speakers. More*
> *Leaves fall, and falling, comment on the time*
> *And Time—the thin clock faces winding down*
> *In spinning parachutes suggest that autumn*
> *When I will rend the watches of the night*
> *In someone else's sleep—someone who will*
>
> *Fall also. The sleep that takes it all!*
> *The slowly rusting graduates of spring*
> *Schooled in one history to which they cling,*
> *Divest themselves of knowledge, and begin*
> *To flake away, to file into the ground . . .*

The latest work—of which this is an exemplary evidence, with its
insistent puns on *fall* and *watch*, its brilliant pursuit of the figure of
leaves as students, and its cumulus of meanings, earned by a confidence
in the words to drag the sense out of the form, in that last verb, *to file
into the ground*, dazing the mind with at least three acceptations—and
the earliest are not to be divided into such categories of biographical
convenience, cannot be discriminated except where the poet has told us
so, as in a note ascribing this passage to the first book:

> *Cicadas cried bitterly*
> *The language of their briefness.*
> *Then, in the wet eye,*
> *A hopeful desert shook*
> *Its windward, dear oasis,*
> *But I with a backward look,*
> *Ran from the dread seducers*

—another fall, this could be *any other* fall. In fact, the poems from each of Moss' books are all of a piece. This poet's work shows no commitment to that piety of development, the biological simile of juvenilia, maturity, and final fooling which we cry up these days as a literary necessity, after the example of Shakespeare and Yeats or even Verdi. The poems of Howard Moss are determined once and for all by a sensibility that appears *given* from the start; they are a macrocosmic sign indeed, and refuse all the identifications with organic life a man's career is supposed to imply, in our literary handbooks. The shellac of logical figuration, the reliance on a literate following, the rhythms of a conventional mope in treating even the apocalypse, give this poet a startling assurance in his "early work":

> *Plants cannot travel,*
> *Water cannot speak;*
> *The green leaf is rooted,*
> *The blue lake is mute.*
> *(O dark in the dark.)*
> *But if love is a miracle*
> *And I may marvel,*
> *Last night, when I woke,*
> *Plants knew distance*
> *And the water spoke.*

The registered tone or more exactly the *note* of the clipped and the clever, perpetually piping up, is never to leave this poet, no matter how anguished his theme, nor how agonized his pursuit of it; not because he is frivolous or obsessed, as most men who pun all the time seem to be, but because he relies on the wisdom that is innate in language itself to enforce his moment, on the wit of words as they work together or against each other. "Somewhere a slow piano scales the summits of the air" Moss says of music overheard on a city night, and by the pun the language is, or becomes, his memory, a memory he can partially master, of approximate intrusions of the real into the actual. "The portents of this night," he says about Christmas Eve,

> *The portents of this night ascend to mourn*
> *Our deaths in theirs; on two crossed sticks, on stone,*
> *By thorn or beak, in anguish, Gods are born.*

The pun on mourn, the music demonstrate a relevant sense of what language can do, of its inherent—its natural—resources. Moss has found the homophone to be a figure of order, and in his dependence on the experience immanent in our speech, has reached to the bottom of things. For the long survival of such basic and homely homonymies as *sun-son, mourn-morn, light-light, still-still,* and the ecclesiastical *fall-Fall* (operative only in America, it would seem, since in Britain autumn is the sole term for the season between summer and winter) testifies to the fact that there is nothing repugnant in the ideas thus linked or distinguished, and even that there is some harmony in the linkage. The philologists tell us that *light* as applied to colors and *light* meaning not heavy are sometimes felt, by a kind of synesthesia, to be merely different meanings of *the same word.* For Howard Moss, certainly, the occurrence of *light-light* in the language makes a poetic situation, and in the use of *mourn* as an aural pun above (musically reinforced by the word *thorn* in the body of the verse as well as by *born* as the rhyme word, an effect Moss practices to the borderline, as in

> *Here the fountain's question marks of haze*
> *No longer glaze the marble. Winter's spare*
> *Bone monuments of stone and glass appraise*
> *Themselves across the plaza, the evening air*
> *Holds up the starlight . . .*

where *glaze* would be intolerable if it chimed one more time; fortunately *glass* and *plaza* arrive as witty and reassuring variants: there is nothing superficial or slight about the qualities of a well-managed verbal surface), the puns endorse in the deepest sense, indeed *become* the subjects of his poetry. In few poets can it be so true that to find the means of poetry is a step toward finding the matter, for the poetry will be in its actual form. For Moss, the doubleness of existence, in fact the duplicity of Being, as when he says, in the last quotation, "the evening air holds up the starlight" and means both *supports by its cold weight* and *retards by its cold obstruction,* as in a hold-up, is an enunciation of his theme, the cyclical nature of reality. Everywhere, but majorly in words—which for Moss are no mere signalling system but the instrument of all our distinctively human development, of everything in which we go beyond the other animals—Moss finds the cosmic round-robin rehearsed. Puns, chimes, quotations, parodies ("Shun the pain of others, or in contemplating theirs the fear you bare will be your own") and allusions are all means of bringing home to himself a man's imagination of the universe as order, as cycle, as a spiralling potentiality of death and rebirth, departure and return:

> *. . . my wound has been my healing,*
> *And I am made more beautiful by losses.*

It is true that leaves do leave, and that even the verb *to leave* can be made to mean both *to depart* and *to form leaves*, but it becomes a truth of experience, which is a different thing from a truth of knowledge, only when rehearsed in our consciousness by a special sense of life, that realm of natural recurrences in which the impression of the unique is elided:

> *When frost moves fast and gardens lose their ground*
> *And gold goes downward in the trees, no sound*
> *Accompanies departures of the leaves,*
> *Except when the wind hurtles into air*
> *Dead shapes the coming winter will inter;*
> *Then the thinnest music starts to stir*
> *A faint, crisp scraping in the startled ear:*
> *The leaves that feed the new leaves of next year.*

It is the natural *bonds* that quicken this poet, not the events of nature—relations, not occurrences. Hence his poetry has a highly abstractive tendency—it is any tree, any leaf ("the green leaf, the blue lake"), not the blighted elm on the corner, the maple in the hedgerow. It is the experience language encloses that Moss is after, not the language that encloses experience: it is with a shock as of recognition that in the fifth line of the foregoing quotation, we find that *winter* encloses *inter* even as the action of the season dictates. What is *known* in the way science knows nature can serve the turn as well as what the poet sees. To refer, as above once more, to gardens "losing . . . ground" is to employ, again, an expression *in the language* as a version of natural process: in winter, the earth freezes and gardens do "lose ground" in both senses. In the poem "A Winter Come," from which I have quoted the first stanza—and the title, characteristically is only half the whole truth; for Moss, any statement is always only half the truth, to be completed, contradicted or advanced by the next turn of the screw—there are any number of references to circular forms:

> *Look up! The scimitar of the moon*
> *Is but a remnant of the round it was,*
> *Is but a ringlet of the ring to be,*
> *As, riding forth, the breath that marked your birth*
> *Will have its heir, before it comes to death.*

Here, aside from the cyclical *statements* about breathing and the moon's phases—two of the ultimate sources, by the way, of our intuition of rhythm—the aural pun on *heir-air* has even, I suspect, a further trace in the visual pun on *heir-hair* carried on from ringlet. And all this exuberance of theme, the hypertrophy of linkage, serves the poet's sense of the anti-apocalyptical. Apocalypse is the One Event, casting out Nature, and confronting the naked self with God, extirpating process and the cyclic order. Howard Moss is interested in doings that are never single but forever repetitions and rehearsals of the process of being—what in rhetoric is called *the turn*, the trope, the snake biting its own tail:

> *The racing waterfall that slowed in fall*
> *Has thinned to a trickle or an icicle*
> *And stands as quiet as the rocks it willed*
> *To move. As though expecting it to fall,*
> *A listener stands upon a rim of silence,*
> *Seeing a changed world prepared to change,*
> *The waterfall silent on its breakneck shelf,*
> *And silence a spectacle in itself.*

Even the apparent rigors of that frozen fall are jolted into life by "a changed world prepared to change." "We make of love a stillness, though the world can turn on its moment, and be still. Or turn and turn"—this is what Moss, like his Hermit, "writes, in a circle, on his shield."

It is only to be expected that this poet would find himself, by every affinity, invited to translate Valéry, and that the final section of *Finding Them Lost* would be a vitreous English version of *Le Cimetière marin:*

> *. . . Great sea endowed with deliriums,*
> *Panther hide and Grecian mantle slashed*
> *By a thousand, thousand idols of the sun,*
> *Absolute hydra, drunk on your own blue flesh,*
> *Circling to bite your sparkling tail again,*
> *Forever, your tumults are your silences.*

That sense of process sustaining life, breaking "this form that is all thought," sends Moss not only to Valéry but to the sea itself—past the graveyard and into the water. The jetty speaks:

> *Each has its element, but I am bound,*
> *A bit in earth, in water, and in sky,*
> *To know three elements the seasons round;*
> *I ran aground by putting out to sea.*
> *I am a silent witness of the whirl*
> *The winds map out upon the monstrous deep.*
> *My back is turned upon a stretch of beach.*
> *The sea's horizon I shall never reach.*

> *This paradox is all my garden plot,*
> *Whether the waves come over, or not.*

The sea, as grand dissolution of all apocalypse, as eternal rhythm of
tides, recurrence and rebirth, the respiration of life itself, is of course
Moss' great figure, friend and temptation, and generally he is worthy
of it, as in poems like "Painting a Wave," "Sea Change," "Water
Island" and "Mariner's Song"; often, though, as he moves by high-
speed conveyance from one watering-place to the next, from Venice to
Fire Island, wherever there is an appropriate decor of littoral detritus
to juice up his "grave and testamentary reverence," as Howard Neme-
rov calls it, Howard Moss seems mechanical. It is too easy to see the
cycle in the sea, we long for some single thing to happen that will not
always bypass the self, the person, in a cosmic undulation. When Moss
concludes his brilliant metaphysical emblem "A Swimmer in the Air,"
with its echoes of Yeats ("Caught in a cellular ecstasy") and its
Darwinian figures:

> *In the same vein, all flesh conceals*
> *Articulation's fishnet, whose thread-bones*
> *(A metaphysic harp from sky to heel)*
> *Hang in the flesh that dangles from the creel*
> *Depending from the weedy Hand that owns*
> *All fishnets and all fishing reels*

—when Moss undertakes to moralize the sea with his patented ship-to-
shore Abercrombie-and-Fitch scavenger's kit that will surely sweep all
the beach before it:

> *. . . Mummers of the ocean's Word*
> *Our dry translations, tidied from the deep,*
> *Bespeak its ancient languages. The salt*
> *Our tears and blood must harbor from its vault*
> *Is shed on every beach-head where we creep,*
> *Part man, dry fish, and wingless bird*

—we identify him too easily with the awful Sebastian in Tennessee
Williams' shocker, the deliquescent hedonist who visited a new and
sunbaked shore each year, and there, wreaking immense destruction on
the treasures of himself as reflected in the sea, produced, each year too,
one Very Beautiful Poem.

Of course the poet who makes "our dry translations, tidied from the
deep" is much too cunning, most of the time, to be hooked on such
solemnities. He wields all the forms of counterlogical verbal meaning

—pun, rhyme, agnomination, alliteration and the trope—to dramatize his sense of comic proportions. Even at his most agonized, as at his most bejewelled, Howard Moss can always rouse the stunned mind to action:

> . . . *as if two curtains fell*
> *On each side of another, and when each rose,*
>
> *One by one, revealed a triple world:*
> *The seen, the recollected, and the scene*
> *To come, all lit at once, whose figures stain*
> *Each meaning with another meaning, whose*
> *Cruelties outdo past cruelties,*
> *The lightning of their blood now branched in mine.*

The wittiness capable of "the seen, the recollected, and the scene / to come" would betray any other poet into "humorous verse," but is for this one a stay against the mechanical sublime, and as such, characteristic of him as a poet of New York City, that estate of the "expensively provisional" as Henry James called it. For if Moss often writes about the shore, the country and the natural emblems of suburbia, he has reached them and will return from them on the terrible expressways that let Americans get away from their purposes even more quickly than they want to get to them. The city—source, only naturally, of Moss' urbanity—is the site he would escape from and escape to, in precisely that cycle of withdrawal and recurrence his poems suffer into existence. The metropolis is the only place where he can feel private, without the restraints of community so paradoxically binding in the open air, on the blank coast as in the blooming tree—thus all the poems on roof-gardens, balconies, library steps, parks. Thus the poem in the office, where the "much too delicate hands still tapping the Underwood seem now . . . five or ten young Balinese children hopping up and down in a clearing . . ."

> *Inside that drawer, among the blotters, folders,*
> *Memos, carbons, pencils, papers,*
> *. . . the youngest animal of all is awaking*
> *In that coarse nest where he's been sleeping . . .*
> *If I should reach into that dangerous drawer,*
> *What singular teeth might pierce my skin?*
> *Or if he should leap, should I then kill him,*
> *And watch . . .*
> *The marvelous animal blood go thin?*

Equally, on the beach when it "looks like dirty travertine," then in "the passing headlights of a jeep . . ."

> *The jetties, triple-spaced, the lifeguard stand*
> *Make carbons and go out.*

This reversibility of image—Bali in the Underwood, carbon copies on
Fire Island—is the product of urban preoccupations, the sensibilia of
environing lives of license, tears and debt, none of which exist in
nature, hours ticking in men's faces as they move through the terrible
fluorescence of the working day in a place where the engineers have
defeated the architects: when the tree surgeon speaks in New York, it
is to say:

> *What should I prune where you have fastened brick*
> *To brick, and all the rest is white, electric*
> *Dazzle that no flower can endure?*
> *You praise the plane and gingko, but I swear*
> *You are tree worshippers without a tree,*
> *And I am a prophet in the wrong country.*
>
> *You mimic me. From your geranium*
> *You flick a dead leaf. But my green thumb*
> *Does more for you than even nature does,*
> *Think of me, high up in your offices—*
> *You are a branch of all the medicines*
> *I practice in the sky among sparse limbs.*

The crowning example of this kind of poise, the nervous mastery
momentarily granted Industrial Man as he fights for his place in the
dormitory, for his love in the lab, choked by products and the terrible
man-made weather, is Moss' apostrophe to one of the most revealing
sources of myth in our society, "Horror Movie," in which the very
monsters of urban life are hugged close as the fount of our strength:

> *We thank you for the moral and the mood,*
> *Dear Dr. Cliché, Nurse Platitude.*
> *When we meet again by the Overturned Grave,*
> *Near the Sunken City of the Twisted Mind,*
> (*In* The Son of the Son of Frankenstein),
> *Make the blood flow, make the motive muddy:*
> *There's a little death in every body.*

The apostrophe to Cliché and Platitude is intimate and right, here, and
the last line proves this poet's point to perfection: only Moss could
have made that meaning move out of mere language and into our
minds. He shelters in his wit, even when he is drawing character, as in a
remarkable series of portraits called *Lifelines* which remind us that, as
V. S. Pritchett said, New York is the capital of group therapy; the
intestines are public:

She took to doing inappropriate things,
A bland and ludicrous tragedy,
Like fainting at Altman's, bleeding at Schrafft's—
She could think of no other scenery
(The Greeks eluding her and pleasure being
All that there was to Italy).
Soon everything grew very tiny,
Her primness and her sensuality
Locked in a battle of rubber bands . . .
After electric shock therapy,
Her memory came back. And with it came
Nothing to remember:
The sea was a toilet for the gulls,
The draperies a possible noose . . .

Here the detached pieces of scientific self-observation, or observation of others so eager that it becomes a research of the self, would have petrified most poets, as it petrified the early readers of Freud. But Moss eludes the solemnities of the clinical by his trust in the word—as in this description of a man suffering from *ejaculatio praecox:*

He saw the fireworks hit the sky
In fistfuls of ejaculations—
It was his daily 4th of July,
The celebration occurring nightly,
While he, in a sweat, lit the fuse . . .

If the city has hardened the human shell, it has also forged the instruments for penetrating that shell. Certainly a kind of sympathy or ease or warmth has been given up, but only to gain something else:

. . . Any vision must mean that something
Is being omitted; being discrete
By making the possible seem like one thing
Means lopping the head off or the feet,

Or leaving a leaf out or one wave
Of that merciless connoisseur, the sea,
Or pretending the body exists for love,
Or forgetting the pictures of misery

That are found in the news each day, that spell
Out fortunes each night across the sky:
The terrible kingdoms of the small,
The crystal ball of every eye.

The enthralled acceptance of such limitations, in fact the insistence upon them, is what makes Howard Moss the poet he is: funny, unhappy, deprecating, intense, centripetal, urban. And if we grow restless time and again beneath the unrelenting grid of his rhymes, his neat and tuneful meters that seem to imprison experience as often as they release it, it must be remembered that no poet has been more conscious of what he surrendered to get what he achieved. A man writes as he can, those who receive his writing have the further responsibility of accommodating its scope. The chaos relinquished for the control gained—that surely is the ominous burden of Moss' Parnassian cycle *King Midas*. Once we invite this poet's gifts and explore what they can do for us, transforming the world into a rhythm of sad observances, we must hear the personal poignance in Howard Moss' voice when his Midas pleads:

> *Before gold kills me as it kills all men,*
> *Dear Dionysus, give me back again*
> *Ten fingertips that leave the world alone.*

In the years which followed *Finding Them Lost*, Howard Moss wrote several plays—drawing-room farces, melodramas of manners, tragic charades sufficiently discrepant in motive to sustain a title like *The Oedipus Mah-Jongg Scandal*—and plucked together out of the periodicals his careful, uncomplaining literary criticism for a volume published in 1969; the results, the resonances of these urbane undertakings are clear, are more than clear, are *clarified* (as we say butter is clarified by melting until the impurities sink to the bottom of the pan) in his sixth collection of poems which was published in 1968 and which carries (to its conclusion or at least to its consummation in an emergent platitude, a banal exception) that model Moss title *Second Nature:* it is death, of course ("the first dead leaf in the hall / is surprised, taking on its second nature"), and it is the City ("a dirty city / that prowls the sky and is my shade"), and chiefly it is art ("grammar becoming poetry is what / you're after") which is this poet's second nature; which this poet, rather, sees as *our* second nature, the work in which play is acknowledged, and allowed, to produce that release of impulse almost but not quite within arm's reach. Unlike his Midas, Moss has learned to let the universe alone, and at the end of a canonical poem like "Piano Practice" his fingers have shed their golden touch: "now your hands / are on the mysteries of the commonplace," and that is quite mysterious enough, as his Lady of Situations in another poem, "Drinks with X" remarks in one of Moss' transfigured commonplaces:

> *I would have preferred so much more to be*
> *At home, engrossed in a mystery—*
> *And aren't we all engrossed in one?*

What the plays contribute or what has been dearly bought from them, the impulse to characterize, to lodge the poem under someone else's tongue like a recording lozenge and let the alien words melt it down to its irreduceable, idiosyncratic shape, had been broached before in Moss' work, but a great deal more about otherness has been learned than the cool or even cruel observation of "Lifelines" in the preceding volume had enabled the poet to register. And the impulse of prose, the self-cancelling impulse to move onward (as *prose* itself is but the past participle of the verb *provertere*, so one might say its impulse is *to have moved on*) conjugates the quirk of idiom in many of these poems into something more than rich and strange—better, into something rich and familiar, as when Moss' arsenic-taker writes his third letter:

> *Now I am going back to the house*
> *For a drink. From the upper porch, I see*
> *A gull go by on the steadiest wings*
> *You ever saw. If a scavenger's*
> *That gorgeous, what will they say of me?*
> *There's something to be said for everything.*
> *For garbage, for instance, in this case.*

"Another Life" the poet calls one of his finest poems here, and the name is emblematic of a final impulse which Moss had not encouraged or suffered from before, the effort of masks, of allowing the self its ardors by transforming them. "A poet writes always of his personal life, in his finest work out of its tragedy, whatever it be, remorse, lost love, or mere loneliness; he never speaks to someone at the breakfast table, there is always a phantasmagoria . . . he is never the bundle of accident and incoherence that sits down to breakfast; he has been reborn as an idea, something intended, complete." Yeats has exactly described the victory of these latest poems of Howard Moss; it is because we feel the phantasmagoria—in "A Dead Leaf," "Front Street," "The Love Songs of Horatio Alger, Jr." and other dramatic monologues which often encapsulate prose forms: the confession, the secret journal, the mash-note, the expiring memo—because we hear an ideal completion in these confidences, that they are so much more than testimony. "Rinsing the world once more with self," yes, but dramatizing the tears until they are no longer a "waste of water" but "a fire at the bottom of the sea."

To this new wrinkle in his seamless art, Moss has added, in *Second Nature*, the requisite complement of sea-pieces ("The Bay Stone," "Beach Glass," "The Dune Wig") and city-studies ("The Building," "Going Dutch," "The Persistence of Song"), and it is in these latter that he has found a further torque for his reversionary theme, a way of

braiding the poem into its own undoing which all the more perfectly
articulates his endless recoveries, reclamations, circular turns: *verses.*
Moss starts, in "The Building," with a characteristic split-line lament:

> *Removed by half a city, not the world,*
> *I see the building you are working in.*
> *It is a winter day. The branches clash*
> *On the few trees that mark the avenue . . .*

which he works up, or works out, by taking the part of each line on
each side of the caesura and recombining it with another line until,
three stanzas and 24 lines later, the poem mirrors itself in a kind of
fugato despair, the form *performing* just that inversion of identity by
structural series which makes the title of the poem so adequate an
account of Moss' *poesis:*

> *On the few trees that mark the avenue*
> *The branches clash. It is a winter day.*
> *I see the building you are working in*
> *Removed by half a city, and the world.*

In the analogously titled "Persistence of Song," the cityscape runs
through its first 18 lines to the center fold, the Rohrschach crease at the
midpoint of personality:

> *What is the weather doing?*
> *And who arrived on a scallop shell*
> *With the smell of the sea this morning?*
> *—Creating a small upheaval*
> *High above the scaffolding*
> *By saying, "All will be well.*
> *There is a kind of rejoicing."*

And then simply—simply! with that delicate adjustment of conjunc-
tions and pointing only a dentist could properly appreciate, with its
dosage of filigree and pains—runs backward line by line:

> *Is there a kind of rejoicing*
> *In saying, "All will be well?"*
> *High above the scaffolding,*
> *Creating a small upheaval,*
> *The smell of the sea this morning*
> *Arrived on a scallop shell . . .*

to end with its beginning (and with the arrival of Aphrodite, after all,
of that Eros Plato called the child of penury and resource) as it had
begun, we now see, with its ending:

> *And though it is not yet evening,*
> *There is the persistence of song.*

Not only the persistence but the recurrence, the recuperation of song from the maze of self, otherwise recognized as an imprisonment but here discerned as more than durance, as duration, and thus endured, and celebrated, "so that each footstep, taking time, made time."

Buried City by HOWARD MOSS

Some ten years ago I had occasion, writing about earlier writing of Howard Moss, to remark that according to philologists, *light* as applied to colors and *light* meaning not heavy are sometimes felt, by a kind of synesthesia, to be merely different meanings of the same word. It is true, I went on, that leaves do leave, and that even the verb *to leave* can be made to mean both *to depart* and *to form leaves*, but it becomes a truth of experience, which is a different thing from a truth of knowledge, only when rehearsed in our consciousness by a special sense of life, that realm of natural recurrences in which the impression of the unique is elided. How heartening, now, for the critic of a decade ago to find in the new book an emblematic account of "The Old Poet"—well, none of us is getting any younger—which offers these confirming subversions:

> *The word for leaves gave birth to more than leaves,*
> *The word for light made possible more light*
> *Before sleep took the very word for word*
> *And drowned it back into a pool so wide*
> *Its underground of nerves lay everywhere.*

We take what we know and bury it, drown it, *down it* until it turns into ourselves, an endless and eternal body whose "undergound of nerves lay everywhere." Apocalyptic for such a polite poet? The special sense of life on which I animadverted so long since has been ever and again rehearsed by Howard Moss, gathering to its fulness in the *Selected Poems* which won him the National Book Award in 1972, and now further. What is so special about his sense of life is that it has death in it—not beyond, or beneath, but within. Immanent death so drags these lines, these images down that they have a new range, a new plumb, even for Moss, beyond the imminence of the ominous, for they reach to the eminence of the undone, what he calls "the lapsed thing."

Though of living poets he resembles, as in "At the Masseur's,"
James Merrill in comparable dedication to involuntary memory as his
Muse, and of the great dead often, as in "Shorelines", "Saratoga",
and "Tattoo", Auden in like submission to disciplines below the ten-
sions of the lyre, Moss has become, has made himself, authentically
idiomorphic ("a potion of petals. They're thorns by evening"—such
is wisdom). This is the more wondrous and strange in that he has not
surrendered for a moment, for a meter, his charmed civility, the wit
that can "wake to see the curtains blow their cool" and the worldli-
ness that dismisses even as it entertains "our three false languages: /
government, medicine and law." Moss remains and renews himself by
keeping up precisely that "keeping", in the old sense of the word,
which has shown him all along to be, in the hustle of so much pro-
vincialism, our most metropolitan poet.

And of course it is only the poet of the polis who can have such a
rendering response, in both senses, to the pastoral—the shore, the
mountains, the places where we nurse our wounds and sometimes
worsen them: "the clearest of all sleeps, then nothing clear." Such
alienations, as we stare across the estranging bay, sharpen the eye:

> *A particle of sail*
> *Hurrying to meet its particle of sun,*
> *Shakes the whole slack surface into speed.*

But Moss has always been waterproof, and like a proper scholar of the
sea, can sever what is ripe from rottenness. In his new book there are
the much-frequented littorals, the beach gets its going-over, whence
Moss can discern all the settings, declines, *goings-down:*

> *The moon puts down its gangplank in the sea*
> *As if pure light could disembark.*

And indeed all the characteristic gestures in these careful, exactly ad-
ministered yet desperately deranged poems are downward ones. Moss
knows that "the darkness takes the longest time to darken," and he
bears with his losses as they leave him, going under. The truth of his
condition, of ours, is a very stark truth: "We were. We are. We will
not be." His exceptional gift is to work a visible, audible justice upon
all three conditions, for it is only by making certain horizontal,
continuing gestures that it is possible to plummet to the bottom,
which as Eliot once observed is a great way down, and to return.
"How deeply the wounds stay on the surface!" Moss exclaims, whose
surface is intimate with his depths, as again Eliot said of another poet;
it is a circumstance which has enabled Moss to produce, along with
much fine work, what I take to be his finest, a long poem called
"Buried City", appropriately given title status and referring to the
palimpsests of our bodies, our human history as city-dwellers, and

most of all to that archeology of ignorance and doubt which has become *the* science of our incomparable modernity:

> *Now we know that what we do not know*
> *Stamps its print upon the brain in shadow.*

It is this beautiful poem which is developed, as the photographers say, from a negative ("the darkroom is waiting"), from a situation of untoward deperition ("The fire's out. The animals are gone"), that affords Moss his upward and outward movement, his surfacing, after all his descents and declines:

> *Slowly this buried city came to light*
> *Up from the ruins, all its riddles blank*
> *(Its verses, too), with no one to look out*
> *While all of us looked in.*

The wilderness, the *wildness* now in Moss's grasp just because, I think, of his decorum, of his patience with negativity, makes "B.C." (for that is one of its references) a poem not only worthy of the Valéry whom Moss has translated and whom the poem itself invokes, but in its tough simplicities, its tense expectations, makes it one of the masterpieces of our poetry, one of the definitions of the canon—this is how Prospero renders the real:

> *Exiled from Exile, you will always bear*
> *Two sacred marks of the interior:*
> *Memory and art. How early it grows dark!*
> *They say the snow will bury us this year.*

Georgia Review, 1976

FRANK O'HARA

"Since Once We Are We Always Will Be in This Life Come What May"

A MAN, in particular that emblematic man a poet, who by his surro-
gate office must stand, in particulars, for the generality—a man
who dies at forty is at every moment of his life, we say, a-man-who-
has-died-at-forty. It is our fashion of sparing ourselves the offence of
the arbitrary, the scandal of the fortuitous. The disaster occurs, the
poet dies, and we are appalled by the event, the outcome, the *occur-*
rence, precisely, which in its first sense means a collision, a clash "as of
two bodies"; every happening is an outrage to duration, a violation of
existence—God is the impulse of things to persist in their Being ("I
want you to be," *volo ut sis*, is Love's supreme affirmation, not "I want
you to happen"), and it is only Satan, the Prince of this World, who is
responsible for *events*. Hence we are shocked by the "accidental,"
which Freud alone of our moralists has confronted in all its tyranny,
including it within the vocabulary of intention when we had sought to
escape responsibility for our actions, and insisting on its meaningless
sway where we seek still to declare its purpose: the final pages of
Freud's study of Leonardo offer what must be the ultimate apologetics
of accident, a terrible necessity for all who would account for the
"occurrence" of genius among men. But we have not Freud's courage
so often, and retrospectively we glean, in the course of a broken-off
existence, the seeds of a destiny which, planted perhaps only by
ourselves and cultivated however arbitrarily by our hunger for the
inevitable, will bestow upon the blasted biography this flowering: a
more grateful contour, an acceptable outline. We say, he was death-
ridden, doom-haunted, and that he belonged to the race—as Thomas

Mann said of Cocteau—which dies in the emergency ward.

Nothing is more open to question than this notion. But only for one reason: we use the wrong tense. What we mean is that for those who will remember him—and the poet is, precisely and intentionally, *the man who will be remembered*—the man who dies at forty will appear, at whatever period of his life we wish to evoke him and whatever products of his career we find characteristic, as the man who was to die at forty. On the level of life, real life, the formula has no meaning; in the order of memory, there can be no escaping it. It defines better than any other what is, in its essence, the character of the work of art, of a career, the myth of the personality. Indeed, only death reveals the meaning of the personality's life.

Frank O'Hara, who died at forty-two in an accident, run down on the beach at night in the summer of 1966, had a constant apprehension of what death must reveal in the life of his personality—or rather, a constant conviction that it was death itself which would reveal that life:

> Our art [he said, in his essay on Jackson Pollock] should at last speak with unimpeded force and unveiled honesty to a future which well may be non-existent, in a last effort of recognition which is the justification of being.

Without death, the opacities of a selfhood would mean nothing to him, would deprive him of eternity: "doom has held off / perhaps it is waiting like a smile in the sky." Mere life, more and more living, would strip the poet of that senseless creature inhabiting him, that self to whom he owed the best of his illusions and his conflicts. Only his flaws, properly nursed, could "save" him, allow him to *keep* for the rest of us. From his earliest poems:

> *Yet I am racing toward the fear that kills*
> *them off, friends and lovers, hastening through tears*
> *like alcohol . . . I run! closer always move,*
> *crying my name in fields of dead I love.*

to one of his last inspissated lines:

> *I historically belong to the enormous bliss of American death—*

O'Hara urged himself—with a loyalty astonishing in a poet who prayed for "grace to be born and live as variously as possible—the conception of the mask barely suggests the sordid identifications," even *obliged* himself to see life as an ensemble of impulses not for resisting but for bearing us toward death: "I don't think I want to win anything I think I want to die unadorned." It is appropriate that O'Hara should invoke the mask here, even while proclaiming its inadequacy to represent so protean an enterprise as the central effort of his poetry, which is to delineate without distortion or timidity the telling gestures of personality, the lusts and refusals of an identity anxiously scrutinized for the signs of *difference:* "all that you have made your own, / the kingdom of yourself sailing." Indeed personality itself is a mask, through which the idiosyncratic sound is made, sounding through . . . *per sonans,* and its constant transformations are the very substance of O'Hara's poems; here is how he put it, in a "statement" for Donald Allen's *New American Poetry* in 1959:

> What is happening to me, allowing for lies and exaggerations which I try to avoid, goes into my poems . . . My formal "stance" is found at the crossroads where what I know and can't get, meets what is left of what I know and can bear without hatred.

There will be many occasions, we discover, when O'Hara's ambivalence toward his "captured" personality is similarly stated, when "the black bitch of my nature" is exposed and, for therapeutic purposes, indulged:

> *. . . Now I am quietly waiting for*
> *the catastrophe of my personality*
> *to seem beautiful again,*
> *and interesting, and modern.*

The undertaking—something in the nature of a heroic quest, a crusade to rescue personality from "literature" even while arresting it *in* poetry —leads the hero to mistrust any completion, any statement which does not allow for or even insist on its opposite. "Romantic in nature, voluble in speech and passionate in discourse," as he said of Gorky, Frank O'Hara rehearses a fidelity to the worst in himself because it is alive and must die with the best: "an ounce of prevention's enough to poison the heart." Thus the fractious voice that asks itself, testily, "do you think everything can remain the same, like a photograph? What for?" will answer, quite as testily from another vantage:

> *Leaf! . . . How can you change your*
> *color, then just fall! As if there were no*
> *such thing as integrity!*

We must not look, then, for the consistency of a doctrine or the formal dispositions corresponding to some body of beliefs that can be codified. "Everything is in the poems," O'Hara insists, and the implication is that it is nowhere else, that in a life shadowed, "chased" by a murderous consciousness, or at least by a consciousness of murder, the poems are the one haven he can apostrophize with any confidence as the sure lodging of personality, as in "Personism: 1959," that wild, unflinching manifesto:

> Everything is in the poems . . . I don't believe in god, so I don't have to make elaborately sounded structures. I don't even like rhythm, assonance, all that stuff. You just go on your nerve. If someone's chasing you down the street with a knife you just run, you don't turn around and shout, "Give it up! I was a track star for Mineola Prep."

It is obvious that for the artist obsessed with his expressive vocation—and I take an obsession with personality to *be* an expressive vocation, the need to *manifest* that personality, to invite for our amusement and even instruction its distinctive postures—anything and everything is doomed to become occasion, including the pursuit of occasion:

> *How I hate subject matter! melancholy,*
> *intruding on the vigorous heart, the soul telling itself*
> *you haven't suffered enough . . .*

Yet no occasion is ever adequate to the impulse that wants to make it an occasion—all poetry is in this sense the acknowledgment of failure, the aporia of poetry's impossibility ("if you don't eat me I'll have to eat myself"), and what is required of the poet is to make this submission, this admission, this fidelity to failure as Beckett calls it, into a new occasion, a new term of relation between the poet and his poem, a new expressive act. This requirement O'Hara fulfilled from the first:

> *Let's take a walk . . .*
> *and be washed down a*
> *gigantic scenic gutter*
> > *that will be*
> *exciting! . . . then*
> > *maybe blood*
> *will get meaning . . .*
> *and the landscape will do*
> *us some strange favor when*
> *we look back at each other*
> > *anxiously*

—and indeed *from* the first carried over into all his later work the preoccupations with glamor, modernity and deliquescence that he makes so seductive, confiding with a sob or a chuckle "what is happening" to him, the "daily dragon." As he says of Pollock, his method was inclusive: he did not debar, from one period to another, elements in which he had found a previous meaning of a different nature. His myth of a monumental self, or at least of a self monumentally recorded in all its erratic silliness:

> *the longing to be modern and sheltered and different*
> *and insane and decorative as a Mayan idol . . .*

its erotic despair:

> *My hands beneath your skirt don't find weathers,*
> *charts. Should my penis through dangerous air*
> *move up, would you accept it like a torch?*

and ecstatic perception:

> *How am I to become a legend, my dear? I've tried*
> *love, but that hides you in the bosom of another and*
> *I am always springing forth from it like the lotus—*
> *the ecstasy of always bursting forth! . . . I will my*
> *will, though I may become famous for a mysterious*
> *vacancy in that department, that greenhouse . . .*

enforces O'Hara's abandonment ("I want listeners to be distracted") of the poetical machinery, "the lump and crush of archness" he had pretty carefully sounded (and found wanting: "there's no art to free me, blinded so"; or in another mode: "as for measure and other technical apparatus, that's just common sense—if you're going to buy a pair of pants you want them to be tight enough so everyone will want to go to bed with you—there's nothing metaphysical about it"), and in the fifteen years that his work had occasion to develop—if as I suggest we take development to mean not a linear progression but an unfolding from a given center outward, like the revelation of a rose from the bud, an efflorescence—we note a growing scorn of any artifice, any device of consistency beyond the responsibility of sheer syntax to register the poet's sense of voluble election:

> *The center of myself is never silent*
> > *I have been selected*
> *to bear the gift of fire.*
> > > *I am really*
> *an Indian at heart, knowing it is all*
> *over but my own ceaseless going.*

Artifice, though, is what O'Hara entertains to begin with, if only to overturn it for the fun of watching the conventions expire, feet in the air, wiggling to their death in a series of feeble convulsions. I use the coleopteran figure because the proprieties of form, even in the early performances as well as in the ultimate non-stop poems, evidently loom for O'Hara as something hard, glassy, shell-like, the scarab's wing-cases evident only when the creature is *not flying;* before abandoning the decorum of his legacy outright, O'Hara will therefore traduce it with all the beguiling ardor he can muster: "he steps into / the mirror, refusing to be anyone else."

In 1952 the Tibor de Nagy Gallery published Frank O'Hara's first collection, a plangent, Frenchy pamphlet of a dozen poems plus five sonnets, the latter sequence giving its name to the entire group, *A City Winter.* The liberties taken with imagery here are mostly an indication of an understanding reached, a marriage arranged, with surrealism, particularly the surrealism of the marches (Lorca, Mayakovsky), always a more virulent affair than the metropolitan variety. In thematic organization and provenance, a great many respects are paid ("I suffer accelerations that are vicarious and serene"), though more in the fashion of settling scores, perhaps, with a certain French heritage now regarded as burdensome:

Yet Another Fan

It's a great shame
Madame Mallarmé
that to sad us your
hands seem swans
on tortoises drifting
elegant in the sea . . .

The favored conjugation of poetry with art-criticism appears at once, though perhaps *criticism* is never the proper term for O'Hara's transactions with painters; rather there is an attempt to find, in his own vocabulary and rhythms, a means of appropriating what he responds to (the often-cited poem "Why I Am Not A Painter" demonstrates the mechanism) in the work before him—for O'Hara a critical statement is always an *appropriation,* which is why I feel justified in quoting so much of his criticism in application to his own poetry.* In "Early Mondrian," the concision and understanding of the Dutch master are entirely assimilated into something desired from the poet's own sensibility:

Love makes it poetic though blue . . .
and before us from the foam appears
the clear architecture
of the nerves . . .

* As he said of the painter Alex Katz, O'Hara has "the ability to understand, or better, interpret an enthusiasm so it will work for his individual interests."

Perhaps the only truck with tradition O'Hara will have, from the start, is a certain yearning—also shared with the French poets he has "mastered"—for the body and beauty of Classical myth:

> *Ah!*
> *To be at vespers with Mediterranean*
> *heroes!*

he exclaims in "The Argonauts," and after musing over his own inadequacies in love and war ("so near the blood and still so far from harm"), apostrophizes the longed-for ideal in "Jove"—

> *His thighs*
> *how easily in love pressed being*
> *from mere mythical praise.*

These intuitions of a world of shared fable disappear from the later work, for O'Hara took to heart Rimbaud's command and Apollinaire's campaign to be "absolutely modern." There are beautiful traces, though, of the impossibility of the old wisdom—for example, an uncollected poem of 1952, "Day and Night," whose intense prose accounts, precisely, for the *unusability* of the classical, if not the heroic, mode:

> The ancient world knew these things (Be not obedient of the excellent, do not prize the silly) and I am unable to convey as well as those poets the simplicity of things, the bland and amused stare of garages and banks, the hysterical bark of a dying dog . . . I do not want to be the victim of the ability to enthuse myself . . . Most of my thoughts are blue with miles of figures and chariots and nudes on paths of primrose, going down the drain of modern times like a rhymed heroic tragedienne.

Four years later, in one of the first of his over-all poems, where the energy is distributed in a pattern of looping enunciations, without linear impulse or accumulated tension, but rather with the obsessive ubiquity of a Pollock drip-painting—precisely in the valedictory poem "In Memory of My Feelings," dedicated to the painter Grace Hartigan, O'Hara speaks for the last time in his poetry of the Classical past, and his final sentence is a withering rebuke to his own nostalgia:

> *And the mountainous-minded Greeks could speak*
> *of time as a river and step across it into Persia, leaving*
> *the pain at home to be converted into statuary.*
>   *I adore*
> *the Roman copies.*

I do not suggest, though, that O'Hara had lost sight of such possibilities for others; indeed, in the last year of his life, discussing the "classical" themes of the sculptor Nakian, the poet offers a transcendent vision of the meaning of Greek art, which if it remained outside his poetry stood out clearly in his mind:

It is philistine to decry as childish the content of pop and junk art, as Nakian is apt to do in conversation, unless you, like Nakian, have achieved a relation with physical truth that is both stoic and sybaritic, wherein the dead live and the living wait in a kind of despairing sensual delight.

Such a relation—and the expression of it is the finest account of the Mediterranean Canon I know—is utterly alien to the poet of *A City Winter,* who is reproachful ("you have left me to the sewer's meanwhile") or whimsical ("Had not all beautiful things become real on Wednesday?"), but never possessed of that visionary authority we hear even in O'Hara's prose at the end. Too troubled by "the fierce inventories of desire" to keep his voice from breaking and too tantrum-prone to suffer "the fabulous alarms of the mute," O'Hara's first book acknowledges his salient sulkiness most characteristically in "The Lovers," fretting over the failure of inherited genres to accommodate his enormous and narcissistic appetites (they will never, of course, be assuaged):

> *The mean moon is like a nasty*
> *little lemon above the ubiquitous*
> *snivelling fir trees, and if there's*
>
> *a swan within a radius of 12 miles, let's*
> *throttle it. We, too, are worried.*
> . . .
> *If no one is racing towards him* [*the lover*]
> *down intriguingly hung stairways*
> *towards the firm lamp of his thighs,*
>
> *we are indeed in trouble, sprawling*
> *feet upwards to the sun, our faces*
> *growing smaller in the colossal dark.*

The following year O'Hara wrote his "long poem"—*Second Avenue,* 520 lines "in memory of Mayakovsky." There are two illuminating, though perhaps inadvertent, observations offered about this seemingly endless *olla podrida* of melodramatic diction and associations of imagery so compulsive they can scarcely be called free: a poem, let us say, of promiscuous agglomerations, a virtuoso *performance* in discourse without composition. Both these insights come from the poet's friend the poet Kenneth Koch (whose own long poem *When the Sun Tries to Go On* compels the acknowledgment that *Second Avenue* merely *seems* endless; Koch's enterprise is really interminable), in a note on "Frank O'Hara in the Early Fifties":

> I had no clear intention of writing a 2400-line poem (which it turned out to be) before Frank said to me, on seeing the first 72 lines—which I regarded as a poem by itself—"Why don't you go on with it as long as you can?" Frank at this time decided to write a long poem too . . . While we were writing our long poems, we would read each other the results daily over the telephone. This seemed to inspire us a good deal.

During an earlier collaboration with O'Hara, Koch remarked that he was impressed by "Frank's feeling that the silliest idea actually in his head was better than the most profound idea actually in somebody else's head . . ." Combining these two notions—of form limited (or extended) by "going on with it as long as you can" and of content coincident with what the poet feels to be exclusively, even privately, his own—we arrive at this astonishing lode of a poem; each time I read *Second Avenue* I bear off a handful of glittering lines, gold flakes that have quite literally panned out of the sand, but they are never the same lines and never suggest anything converging, opposing or even subordinating in the kind of tension that makes for a unity: "as in a rainbow the end keeps leaping toward the middle," and perhaps the iridescence is enough. As O'Hara said of Jackson Pollock, "the artist absorbed or assimilated very few things. They were left intact and given back." Nonetheless there are a few notations we should rescue from the mountainous matrix of *Second Avenue*, that "sea of asphalt abuse which is precisely life in these provinces"; they stand, once detached, as a set of maxims which will orient us in the consideration of O'Hara's subsequent work, and with a little prodding afford, I think, their own justification for being thus disengaged from an all too baffling context:

Your lamp will never light without dirt

*Shall I ever be able to avail myself of the service called
"Same Day Cleaning"?*

> *. . . I yield up
my lover to the reveries, completely, until he is taken away
by the demons who then deliver me their bolts from afar*

*To be able to throw something away without yawning
and thus make good our promise to destroy something but not us*

Farce is germane to lust

The sense, here, of the infinite preciousness of the real world, perpet-
ually threatened by fantasy, self-loathing and conformism, is what will
galvanize O'Hara's energies throughout his career, will goad him to
recognitions and recollections of "whatever is the case" that he can
trust. *Second Avenue*, at least in these fragmentary crystallizations I
can chip off it, is the product of what O'Hara, in it, calls "love when the
head is turned off." It is directed toward the perception, more availably
realized in later work, of the world as *there*, as other, as real:

> . . . *the mere presence*
> *changes everything like a chemical dropped on a paper*
> *and all thoughts disappear on a strange quiet excitement*
> *I am sure of nothing but this, intensified by breathing.*

It will henceforth be confession all the way, acknowledgment of what
is happening, of "fallings from us, vanishings" occasioned by the lover
when he yields up the beloved to his "reveries"; and of fulfillment,
"light and clarity," when he realizes instead, as by sexual action, the
presence of an alternative to himself. The imagery is not "privately
sensual," as O'Hara remarks of Pollock's "Male and Female," but "cate-
gorically sexual, forensically expounded. The obscurity of the relation-
ship is made utterly clear ['you're gorgeous and I'm coming']. The
occasion is important and public . . . in the state of spiritual clarity
there are no secrets."

The submission to facts, to what is already there, is neatly exempli-
fied in O'Hara's note on his successful one-act comedy *Try! Try!*, a
versified extravaganza on the usual soap-opera triangle:

> This is the second play of this title and with these characters . . .
> not a second version but an almost completely new play written
> for the New York cast and for the decor of Larry Rivers.

The poetry, then, is to serve, to *observe* some existing combination of
admired structures, as we say a player observes the rules of the game.
Not only painters and sculptors, not only writers and composers, but
movie-stars, public idols and simply fellows O'Hara finds attractive
will be invoked as part of a poetic mythology, providing occasion to
"inscribe a sexual bliss upon the page of whatever energy I burn for
art."

Four years after *Second Avenue* was written and *Try! Try!* per-
formed, Frank O'Hara's first full book of poems *Meditations in an
Emergency* was published in 1957. It was reprinted unaugmented ten
years later, a commemorative effort so set about with ironies and
disputes (the body of O'Hara's *work* is as disjunct as the limbs of
Orpheus after the visitation of the Thracian women; until some com-

plete assemblage is made available by the Estate, we are unable to pay effective heed to the poet's plea: "and do not watch over my life, but read and read through . . .") that it is difficult to recollect the atmosphere of casual joy O'Hara generated around his enterprise, "an equation in which attention equals life, or is its only evidence," as he said of Edwin Denby's criticism. The very title suggests the poet's idiosyncratic balance of the drastic and the giddy, an appetite for legendary status ("an eagerness for the historical look of the mirror") conjugated with an almost comically withdrawn consciousness ("once you are helpless, you are free"); if O'Hara's raptures occasionally thicken to sentimentality, there is nothing solemn about his debacles, and it is his victory to exemplify, with a noun no one else would have supplied, "the endless *originality* of human loss." Appropriately, the collection, which includes three poems from *A City Winter*, opens with O'Hara's most beautiful poem, a kind of "rejected address" as precise and moving as anything written since Keats on the fate of the poet committed to the world and dissolved by his experience of it. "To the Harbormaster" is a liminary apostrophe, setting forth that fidelity to defeat under which the entire book glistens as if loricated with tears, and it is also a testament—how much of one we did not suspect until we stood in the little Long Island cemetery and listened to it being read over O'Hara's new grave by his old friend the poet John Ashbery —of faith in vacillation, of trust in failure, of confidence in chaos; a testament, above all, of an existence "which defies all epithets, demanding self-destruction," as O'Hara wrote, quoting Pasternak, in a review of *Dr. Zhivago* written in 1959, "and passing into myth":

> *I wanted to be sure to reach you;*
> *though my ship was on the way it got caught*
> *in some moorings. I am always tying up*
> *and then deciding to depart . . .*
> > > > *. . . I am unable*
> *to understand the forms of my vanity . . . To*
> *you I offer my hull and the tattered cordage*
> *of my will . . .*
> > > *I trust the sanity of my vessel;*
> *and if it sinks, it may well be an answer*
> *to the reasoning of the eternal voices,*
> *the waves which have kept me from reaching you.*

Not in the harbor, then, not within the rim of any consoling structure, but in the Sargasso Sea of personality—intermittent, unpredictable, impure, O'Hara will choose to founder (but not fail); where others discern no more, sometimes, than the gestures of a man drowning ("je suis un homme qui se noie" O'Hara had said in his exceptional collabo-

ration with the French language, "*Choses Passagères*"), no more than
"muddy instants," there occur nonetheless those fabulous illuminations
which are the utter excuse of this wracked poetry, as in "River":

> . . . *My very life*
> *became the inhalation of its weedy ponderings*
> *and sometimes in the sunlight my eyes,*
> *walled in water, would glimpse the pathway*
> *to the great sea. For it was there I was being borne.*
> *Then for a moment my strengthening arms*
> *would cry out upon the leafy crest of the air*
> *like whitecaps . . .*
> *and I'd sink back upon that brutal tenderness*
> *that bore me on, that held me like a slave*
> *in its liquid distances of eyes, and one day,*
> *though weeping for my caresses, would abandon me,*
> *moment of infinitely salty air! sun fluttering*
> *like a signal! upon the open flesh of the world.*

O'Hara addresses himself (as one might address a parcel, a time-bomb
in this instance, for he is convinced of his election to fatality:

> *You may not be allowed*
> *to die as I have died,*
> *you may only be allowed to drift downstream*)

to whatever terminations he cannot encompass, to whatever inconceiv-
able finality exceeds his curriculum, and of the jubilation—as of the
catastrophe—the size, as he once said of Alex Katz, "the size is intimate,
but the scale is vast."

Of all the glamorous figures from the public world whom O'Hara
marked out as psychopomps for his Passage through the Dead Sea,
none was more touchingly appropriate, in his long catalogue of desira-
bles (detailed in the brilliant "To the Film Industry in Crisis," which
opens with the characteristic determination that "in times of crisis, we
must all decide again and again / whom we love / and give credit
where it's due"), none was more *inevitable* than James Dean. Around
this exemplar of mortality, whose disappearance from the world was
(rightly) understood as a harbinger of his own, O'Hara crystallizes his
polar impulses: one is the accommodation of sentiment, a triumph in
the poetry of a certain compromise between the diction of *Silver
Screen* and the indulgence of self-pity beyond the limits ordinarily set
by mere autobiography:

> *Miss Lombard, this is a young*
> *movie actor who just died*
> *in his Porsche Spyder sportscar*

near Paso Robles on his way
to Salinas for a race. This is
James Dean, Carole Lombard. I hope
you will be good to him up there.
He was not ill at all. He died
as suddenly as you did. He was
twenty-four . . . If
there's love up there, I thought that you
would be the one to love him. He's
survived by all of us, and so are you.

This is adorable but, for all its pop-Lycidas charm, it is no more than
vers de circonstance—without transcendance. The other pole is
O'Hara's version of the egotistical sublime, in which the poet's voice is
disengaged from *kitsch*-worship and from the occasions of anamnesis
(it seems to me this happens when *the will* intervenes, though O'Hara
doubtless mistrusted a voluntary poetics; the quotations in support of
my contention all lead to this one: "You know that I am not here to
fool around, that I must win or die . . ." Frank O'Hara fooled around
nevertheless, *and* he won, *and* he died) to strike the true *lacrimae*
rerum note, achieving an intensity of significance we recognize as
prophetic. When O'Hara addresses James Dean as

A spirit eager for punishment
which is your only recognition,

he lifts that sybilline voice by which we know his vocation, a voice
detached, outrageous and sure, for poetry, as this poet once said, "does
not collaborate with society but with life"; the collaboration with life
and with the death life *intends* (tends toward, is attentive to) is the
scandalous choice of O'Hara's work in this truest tonality, an elegance
as every choice is an elegance, an election which involves—as he said of
the new Spanish painters—a man's defiance of his logical limitations:

Men cry from the grave while they still live
and now I am this dead man's voice,
stammering, a little, in the earth.
I take up
the nourishment of his pale green eyes
out of which I shall prevent
flowers from growing, your flowers.

In the last ten years of his life after *Meditations in an Emergency*,
O'Hara published three more books, a great many poems uncollected
in these, and a good deal of prose on the artists of his time; and in 1967
the Museum of Modern Art published a memorial collection of

O'Hara's poems, some for the first time, with decorations by the American artists who were his friends. There is a pervasive discontent in most of this work (it is what permits O'Hara to cherish all the more those realizations in the art of others which he despairs of or despises in his own), an impatience with mere "poems" that exceeds, even, his own *façon* and attaches to the very process of "making": "I seem to be defying fate, or am I avoiding it?" In the cult of personality, as the Supreme Soviet hinted a few years back, there is an inherent desolation, an ultimate *acedie* that aureoles every moment which is not the distinctive gesture, the defining act, what Thomas Hardy called the moment of vision. And so much of life—even so much of literature, O'Hara intimates, so much of art: "what good does all the research of the Impressionists do them / when they never got the right person to stand near the tree when the sun sank"—is quotidian, belongs to *other people*, not oneself! Most of the poems that are not fragments of an apotheosis, in O'Hara's later work, are interim reports, then, notes on getting through the pleasures and palliations of a much-befriended existence, newsy, fretful and of course *entertaining:*

> *. . . It is most modern to affirm some one*
> *(we don't really love ideas, do we?) . . .*
> *let's advance and change everything, but leave these little*
> *   oases in case the heart gets thirsty en route . . .*
> *If Kenneth were writing this he would point out how art has*
> *   changed women and women have changed art and men, but*
> *   men haven't changed women much*
> *but ideas are obscure and nothing should be obscure tonight . . .*
> *we peer into the future and see you happy and hope it is a sign*
> *   that we will be happy too, something to cling to, happiness*
> *the least and best of human attainments.*

Both *Lunch Poems*, which was published in 1964, and *Love Poems* (*Tentative Title*), which appeared in 1965 as one of a series of poetry pamphlets published by the Tibor de Nagy Gallery, suggest even in their titles how generously they participate in this interim production of O'Hara's; the poems are *information*, accounts of Frank O'Hara's activities insofar as he belongs to a collectivity; they are suspicious of themselves—

> *I see my vices*
> *lying like abandoned works of art*
> *which I created so eagerly*
> *to be worldly and modern*

—insofar as they are not independent of a generalized communications system; they are poems of discomfort because they fail to accommodate that crisis of the personality inherent in its extinction: like every individual experience, death can be confronted only by knowledge *without* information. Among the laments for Billie Holliday, Lana Turner and Rachmaninoff, the celebrations of his friends' movements ("Janice is helping Kenneth appeal to the Ford Foundation in / her manner oft described as the Sweet Succinct and Ned is glad / not to be up too late for the sake of his music"), we overhear the restless whimpers of a self desperately aware that time is being snatched out from under—

> *I make*
> *myself a bourbon and commence*
> *to write one of my "I do this I do that"*
> *poems in a sketch pad*
> > *it is tomorrow*
> *though only six hours have gone by*
> *each day's light has more significance these days*

—and the longing for those moments of excruciation which will rescue personality from mere experience ("now the past is something else the past is like a future that came through"), which will redeem duration or, in Maritain's phrase, *ransom the time*. There is evidence that O'Hara saw himself as the Byronic personality of our day, a role which accounts for his eagerness to get the uncertainties of our daily skirmishes ("what you don't know will hurt somebody else") over and done with:

> *I want, too, to go to Missolonghi*
> *pouring out the whenever part*
> *of my life . . .*
> > *a long story*
> *ending in the shallows.*

What is to be left after telling the story—not a long one, after all, but a biography charged with trivial incident, shallows indeed, "the whenever part" that makes

> *noises, heaving or clearing*
> *in the crowded abyss of the west . . .*
> *as we must go on*
> *out into the mesmerized world*
> *of inanimate voices like traffic—*

is enacted in *Odes*, the ontological book of O'Hara's career, published in 1960 by the Tiber Press (with silk screens by Michael Goldberg), a disparate collection, if I may employ the oxymoron, plaiting the incivility of over-all and open-end form—

> *I first recognized art*
> *as wildness, and it seemed right*
> *I mean rite, to me . . .*

—with the prophetic recognition of death:

> *It's amusing, like dying after a party*
> *"click" and you're dead from fall-out,*
> *hang-over or something hyphenated . . .* *

into the crucial twist of idiom. Here, in the "Ode to Willem de Kooning," the "Ode on Lust," the "Ode to Mike Goldberg's Birth and Other Births" and most cruelly in the "Ode on Casualty" with its preposterously apt title, O'Hara exhausts his possibilities, satisfying for once his hunger for extremity ("not to fall at all, but disappear or burn!") and still retaining, after scalpeling out all connective tissue that is not a part of his personality perceived as ecstasy, a discourse which hangs together: "there is a sense of neurotic coherence," he says in the "Ode on Casualty," announcing that "it's nobler to refuse to be added up or divided, / finality of kings." Two of the odes initiate political postures, both rebukes to the kind of activism likely to elide personality; in the "Salute to the French Negro Poets," O'Hara justifies his intimism at its highest pitch, projecting an emphasis on function rather than on result:

> *the only truth is face to face,*
> > *the poem whose words become your mouth*
> *and dying in black & white we fight for what we love, not are;*

and in the "Two Russian Exiles" he offers the rueful comfort which is all that the dispossessed can give their own:

> *to be an exile in your homeland*
> *is far worse than the concert emigration of a thousand sounds . . .*

Nonetheless, O'Hara never flinched from the marginal or problematic nature of his calling; in the same year as *Odes* he published his Firbank-haunted historical drama "Awake in Spain," in which the Duke replies tartly to the messenger asking "which way to his Majesty?", "Better to be an exile than to be exiled." The willed aspect of

---

* Indeed. The term, in the event, was *beach-buggy*. One stares at the lines: "we are sick of living and afraid / that death will not be by water, O sea," then turns in equal incredulity and assent to these, from an uncollected poem:

> *I stand here . . .*
> *a figure of scorn to myself to others a memory*
> *the pain of my faulty joinings doesn't subside . . .*
> *I think I will not be rebuilt*
> *I think I have started to fall and will end in the sea*
> *I think half-thoughts I do not reach the other shore*

defeat and loss must never be lost sight of in O'Hara's work—he is not a victim but a scapegoat of his visions; the ideal, as he phrases it in the "Ode to De Kooning," is

> to be standing clearly
> alone in the orange wind
> *while our days tumble and rant through Gotham . . .*
> *for now a long history slinks over the sill, of patent absurdities*
> *and the fathomless miseries of a small person upset by personality . . .*

Thus the entire effort of these truly pulverized poems consists in O'Hara's *fulfilling* his vanquishment, in extending his understanding of perdition ("I have not the courage to convict myself of cowardice or care"), until the lineaments of personality are no longer "upsetting" but, simply, obvious forever. This insight was stopped by accident—that accident, as O'Hara wrote of Pollock, which had so often been his strength and companion in the past, was fatal. *Passing into myth,* Pasternak had said, and surely O'Hara would have recognized his death on that beach, the onslaught of a monster sent against him by the very powers of meaninglessness he opposed—would have recognized his death as the death of Hippolytus (his true Phaedra was New York), and that death does deny accident, leaving behind the hero's name and his poetry which is the nomination of what he was:

> *the momentary smile and underneath, a small irresponsible glory*
> *that fits.*

SYLVIA PLATH

"And I Have No Face, I Have Wanted to Efface Myself . . ."

THE FIRST review I ever wrote of a book of poems was of *her* first book of poems, that breviary of estrangement (the rhymes are all slant, the end-stop avoided like a reproach), *The Colossus* (1961; all the poems in it were completed by 1959), and in my account—

> her eye is sharp and her wits responsive to what she sees. She prefers, though, to make you *hear* what she sees, the texture of her language affording a kind of analogue for the experience she presents . . . Event is reproduced in the aural imagery: "a racket of echoes tacking in crooks from the black town . . . gave way to fields and the incessant seethe of grasses." Once in a while this concern for texture as the dramatization of experience blurs the poem's movement, but in most cases what catches in the ear is governed, checked, and we grasp what it is she wishes us to know because of the way we hear it—

my *audition*, then, of these well-behaved,* shapely poems by a *summa cum laude* graduate of Smith who had worked as a guest editor of Mademoiselle and won a Fulbright to Newnham, the wife of Ted Hughes and the mother of two children, I missed a lot—I had no premonition of what was coming. Perhaps I glimpsed, though, what was *going*, what was being discarded, or stepped over, or fended off; for once I had identified the girl who speaks in "The Manor Garden":

* The quality of their good conduct is fixed by her later account of her vocation: "I feel like a very efficient tool or weapon, used and in demand from moment to moment . . ."

> *The fountains are dry and the roses over.*
> *Incense of death. Your day approaches . . .*
> *Hours of blankness. Some hard stars*
> *Already yellow the heavens . . .*
> *The small birds converge, converge . . .*

as an Oracle at the world's funneling center, as the Lady of Situations who acknowledged herself the victorious victim of paralysis, the world round about locked in a process of corresponding necrosis ("the crow *settles* her garments"):

Sylvia Plath's burden is, throughout, the disaster inscribed within the surface of landscape (if she is a "nature poet" it is not because she runs ahead down the path and holds out her hand: she makes us push through the weeds with her every step of the way, and occasionally snaps a bramble back in the most unladylike manner:

> *Grub-white mulberries redden among leaves.*
> *I'll go out and sit in white like they do,*
> *Doing nothing. July's juice rounds their nubs . . .*
> *Berries redden. A body of whiteness*
> *Rots, and smells of rot under its headstone*
> *Though the body walk out in clean linen);*

her poems, though there are no people in them, are instinct with Presences, which best arrive of themselves through the accurate evocation of their site. She has a genius for the *genius loci* . . .

once I saw that much, once I saw that the spirit of place, for her, was *her* spirit in *that* place: "mist-shrouded sun focussing all the white and silent distances that poured from every point of the compass, hill after pale hill, to stall at my feet," why then I could see more—my notice ended so:

The last poem in *The Colossus*, "The Stones," is what I take to be a new departure. Here there is more than the Pythoness' expectancy as she broods over a broken landscape: here is a vividly human voice, speaking from "the city of spare parts, the city where men are mended." I look forward to hearing more about that.

And indeed I was—we all were—to hear a great deal more about that, more in her novel or narrative of renewal *The Bell Jar* (1963), where the same note is struck that *I* had been so struck by in "Stones":

> *There ought, I thought, to be a ritual for being born*
> *twice—patched, retreaded and approved for the road,**

---

* There is more to it than surviving another suicide attempt. "We are all," said Wordsworth, the least suicidal of poets, "we are all children of a second birth."

and more in her second, posthumous book of poems *Ariel* (1965—Sylvia Plath took her life, or rather left us her death, in 1963) as well as in the uncollected poems to be found, along with some valuable studies of her work, in the "Womanly Issue" of *Tri-Quarterly* (#7, Fall 1966).

Of course when I spoke of "The Stones" as a departure, I did not intend the word in all the drastic sense it has come to have in Sylvia Plath's case. Still, the valedictory was there, and the words certainly drastic:

> . . . *I entered*
> *The stomach of indifference, the wordless cupboard.*
> *The mother of pestles diminished me.*
> *I became a still pebble.*

The conflict, or at least the confrontation between what I should designate the lithic impulse—the desire, the need to reduce the demands of life to the unquestioning acceptance of a stone, "taciturn and separate . . . in a quarry of silences"—and the impulse to live on, accommodating the rewards as well as the wrecks of existence so that "the vase, reconstructed, houses / the elusive rose": such was the dilemma I glimpsed as a departure at the end of *The Colossus*, and whatever it was I missed then of the true bent, or actually the breach, of Sylvia Plath, what I *did* make out is interestingly ratified by Ted Hughes' notes on the order of her poems:

> "The Stones" was the last poem she wrote in America. The immediate source of it was a series of poems she began as a deliberate exercise in experimental improvisation on set themes. She had never in her life improvised. The powers that compelled her to write so slowly had always been stronger than she was. But quite suddenly she found herself free to let herself drop, rather than inch over bridges of concepts.

Yet now that we have the whole thing together, the two books of poems and the novel—their interdisciplinary relevance, by the way, is suggested by conferring, as the old books used to say, such a quotation as this from the novel:

> Wherever I sat . . . I would be sitting under the same glass bell jar, stewing in my own sour air and listening to the old brag of my heart. I am, I am, I am . . .

with these lines from "Suicide off Egg Rock":

> *Sun struck the water like a damnation.*
> *No pit of shadow to crawl into,*
> *And his blood beating the old tattoo*
> *I am, I am, I am . . .*

—now that we can see Sylvia Plath's life, as she kept meaning us to, from the vantage of her death, we must not make too great a disjunction between the "conceptual" and the "immanent," the bridged and the engulfed in her utterance. It was all one effort—as Hughes says perfectly: "she faced a task in herself, and her poetry is the record of her progress in the task . . . The poems are chapters in a mythology" —and it was all one quest, as Sylvia Plath says imperfectly (that is, with the abiding awareness of imperfection), in an uncollected poem:

> *. . . With luck I shall*
> *Patch together a content*
> *Of sorts. Miracles occur,*
> *If you care to call these spasmodic*
> *Tricks of radiance miracles.*

Her entire body of work can be understood best as a transaction—out of silence, into the dark—with otherness: call it death, or The Stone, or as she came to call it, "stasis in darkness" ("Ariel"), "great Stasis" ("Years"), in the first book such negotiations taking the form of a dialogue ("your voices lay siege . . . promising sure harborage"), which is to say *taking a form;* while in the later poems she is speaking from a point of identification with stasis which is complete, resolved, irreversible ("the cold dead center / where spilt lives congeal and stiffen to history")—she is on the other side, within the Deathly Paradise, so that it is the triumph of her final style to make expression and extinction indivisible ("I like black statements"). Which is why A. L. Alvarez says that her poems read as if they were written posthumously, for the very source of Sylvia Plath's creative energy was her self-destructiveness.

We say that a particularized self is original—not in the paltry sense of being new, but in the deeper sense of being old: original in the sense which deals with origins—when that self acknowledges it begins somewhere and lives its own life and, being as we also say individual, lives no other life, which is to say, dies:

> *. . . It is Adam's side,*
> *this earth I rise from, and I in agony.*
> *I cannot undo myself . . .*
>
> *It is so small*
> *The place I am getting to, why are there these obstacles—*
> *The body of this woman . . .*
> *An animal*
> *Insane for the destination . . .*

In the experience of the original individual self, then, it is true as Freud says that the aim of all life is death; the effort of the mortal self is to reduce stimuli to an equilibrium, to cancel out tension, to return to the inanimate condition. The urge to restore an earlier state of things:

> *What I want back is what I was*
> *Before the bed, before the knife,*
> *Before the brooch-pin and the salve*
> *Fixed me in this parenthesis; . . .*
> *A place, a time gone out of mind . . .*

to impose, indeed, a *statics*, is indeed an expression of the *conservative* nature of organic life, of the inertia inherent in it ("my bones hold a stillness"). These urges toward homeostasis, these impulses to cancel out, to level off ("how she longed for winter then! / scrupulously austere in its order / of white and black / ice and rock"), to "stall"— *stalling* indeed is one of Sylvia Plath's favorite words: "distances that poured from every point of the compass to *stall* at my feet"; "desolation, *stalled* in paint, spares the little country in the corner"; "hammers hoisted, wheels *stalled*"; another favorite is *stilled*, as in "these *stilled* suburbs," "air *stilled*, silvered," "I became a *still* pebble"; both words being derived, like the series clustering round the Latin *stolidus*, from an earlier root meaning "to be rigid"—all these yearnings toward deadlock, then, are indeed beyond the pleasure principle; they tend rather to that great kingdom of alienation, of *otherness* we call ecstasy (standing outside oneself) which is not a matter of moving around but of being encircled, of being the center of an orbit, of being transfigured, *standing still:*

> *. . . till there you stood,*
> *Fixed vortex on the far*
> *Tip, riveting stones, air,*
> *All of it, together.*

Not movement but ecstasy, then; not pleasure but—joy. We shall best realize the goal and the gain of Sylvia Plath's poetry if we reckon with Joy as Nietzsche accounts for it:

> . . . All that suffers wants to live, longing for what is farther, higher, brighter. "I want heirs"—thus speaks all that suffers; "I want children, I do not want *myself*."
> Joy it is that wants *itself*—the ring's will strives in it . . .
> Joy, however, does not want heirs, or children—joy wants itself, wants eternity, wants everything eternally the same.

And we shall best recognize the vestal responsibilities of the woman occupied by such joy if we invoke the demonstrated responsibilities of

other women—such heroic initiates as Pauline Réage and Doris Less-
ing; it is in the cause of a sacramental joy that *Histoire d'O* and *To
Room Nineteen* survey the entire sweep of a spiritual evolution, an
ascesis whose inevitable conclusion—after everything else has been
endured—is the body's destruction. With a like submission, a like
dedication:

> *My heart under your foot, sister of a stone . . .*
> *Father, bridegroom, in this Easter egg*
> *Under the coronal of sugar roses*
> *The queen bee marries the winter of your year—*

Sylvia Plath enters upon her apprenticeship to otherness, to ecstasy;
more ceremonious than Lessing, more ingenuous than Réage, but like
them prepared to obey a tragic ontogeny ("I am ready for enormity"),
she sloughs off—we see her divest herself of—mere personality like the
cloud

> *. . . that distils a mirror to reflect its own slow*
> *Effacement at the wind's hand,*

in order to achieve the ecstatic identity conferred by Joy. Throughout
her first book, there are recorded many impediments to this nuptial
occasion. Often the very instances which are meant to provide the
means, the measures of acceding to stillness refuse to enter into a
dialogue with the postulant. Though she submits herself to the ordeal,
the process refuses to *take*, and the would-be victim is left with only
the impenetrable surface of existence:

> *Sun's brass, the moon's steely patinas,*
> *The leaden slag of the world.*

On other more fortunate occasions, the initiation proceeds, through
trials by trituration, drowning, petrifaction, calcination, all manner of
murderous espousals:

> *Stars grinding, crumb by crumb,*
> *Our own grist down to its bony face.*

But even when the universal processes are willing to do their part, some
unready revulsion in the bride-apparent spoils everything, and as so
often in *The Colossus*, the spell breaks:

> *. . . The whole landscape*
> *Loomed absolute as the antique world was*
> *Once, in its earliest sway . . .*
> *Enough to snuff the quick*
> *Of her small heat out, but before the weight*

Of stones and hills of stones coud break
Her down to mere quartz grit in that stony light
She turned back.

There is darkness ("my hours are married to shadow"), there is silence ("I saw their mouths going up and down without a sound, as if they were sitting on the deck of a departing ship, stranding me in the middle of a huge silence"),* there is stupefaction ("the no-color void . . . in some secret part of her, that long, blind, doorless and windowless corridor of pain was waiting to open up and shut her in again")—all the conditions, one might assume, for the wedding between the self— "the profane grail, the dreaming skull"—and the system, between the victim and the vortex. But no—joy cannot be willed, it can only be surrendered to, gained when it has been given over:

> *I tire, imagining white Niagaras*
> *Build up from a rock root, as fountains build*
> *Against the weighty image of their fall.*

That is why the poems in this first book, as the quotations from the novel, are all confessions of failure, records of estrangement, even boasts of betrayal: "in this province of the stuck record," Sylvia Plath laments, she is excluded from that true stillness which is at the center ("it seemed / a sly world's hinges had swung / shut against me. All held still"—all, that is, except her own awareness, circling even yet in the stream of mere animal perpetuation,

> *The stream that hustles us*
> *Neither nourishes nor heals).*

The exhaustion before its term of the lithic impulse, as I have called it, the impoverishment of the effort to escape effort ("the stars are no nearer . . . and all things sink / into a soft caul of forgetfulness . . . This is not death, it is something safer") is the worry of *The Colossus*, and we may take the aporia of the title poem as the correct centerpiece of these poems that implore the broken earth for rest:

> *I shall never get you put together entirely,*
> *Pieced, glued, and properly jointed . . .*
> *Thirty years now I have labored*
> *To dredge the silt from your throat.*
> *I am none the wiser.*

* The kinetic image of withdrawal is reworked so strikingly in *The Bell Jar* that it is worth noting here: "it's like watching Paris from an express caboose heading in the opposite direction—every second the city gets smaller & smaller, only you feel it's really you getting smaller and smaller and lonelier and lonelier, rushing away at about a million miles an hour . . ."

Landscape and weather have failed her, have refused to take her into their stony certainty ("clearly the genius of plenitude," she observes wryly, "houses himself elsewhere"), and in two poems of supplication, the most poignant in this first book, Sylvia Plath apostrophizes the Rock Maidens—the Mothers, the Sisters, the Fates, the Muses, the Lorelei: her names are many for the Medusa-figures that will release her from the bonds of life ("my mendings itch") into the barrow of death ("by day, only the topsoil heaves. / Down there one is alone"). In the first of these, "The Disquieting Muses," she acknowledges the gradual take-over of her being by these "muses unhired by you, dear mother . . . these three ladies nodding by night around my bed, / Mouthless, eyeless, with stitched bald head." The changeable earth is stanza by stanza renounced, the mortal mother is occulted, "and I faced my travelling companions." A little guilty still, as the last two lines suggest, her loyalties to life dividing her a little from the nodal peace she seeks, Sylvia Plath accounts for her situation, says plainly enough (though I for one failed to hear her) where she is, fixed fast:

> *Day now, night now, at head, side, feet,*
> *They stand their vigil in gowns of stone,*
> *Faces blank as the day I was born,*
> *Their shadows long in the setting sun*
> *That never brightens or goes down.*
> *And this is the kingdom you bore me to,*
> *Mother, mother. But no frown of mine*
> *Will betray the company I keep.*

And in the second poem of petition, "The Lorelei" (which in my first review I took for mere stage properties, though now I see—she has helped me, made me see—the *auto sacramental* which employed such devices, ritual objects in the passion of achieved death), the prayer goes up to the overpowering yet elusive forces for which she is not, palpably, ready—"it is no night to drown in." Except for John Ashbery's early poem "Illustration," I know of nothing that echoes farther into that undiscovered country of suicide felt to be as yet unearned, unmerited. Deterred, recalled, Sylvia Plath pleads to make the journey for which she is unready ("all the gods know is destinations"), though so eager:

> *Your voices lay siege. You lodge*
> *On the pitched reefs of nightmare,*
>
> *Promising sure harborage;*
> *By day, descant from borders*
> *Of hebetude, from the ledge*

> *Also of high windows. Worse*
> *Even than your maddening*
> *Song, your silence. At the source*
>
> *Of your ice-hearted calling—*
> *Drunkenness of the great depths.*
> *O river, I see drifting*
>
> *Deep in your flux of silver*
> *Those great goddesses of peace.*
> *Stone, stone, ferry me down there.*

So much has been said about *Ariel*, and its success—or at least its cessation—has been so vividly acknowledged, that it would be politic to agree with Sylvia Plath, or with Ted Hughes' account of her, in dismissing everything prior to "The Stones" as juvenilia, produced in the days before she became herself. But as I hope I have shown, it was not herself she became, but totally Other, so that she (or the poems—it is all one now) looked back on "herself" as not yet having become anything at all. The poems we know were written first in *Ariel* still admit an uncertainty:

> *I am exhausted, I am exhausted—*
> *Pillar of white in a blackout of knives*

—but one soon to be resolved. "Your first gift," she says to death in "The Rival," "is making stone out of everything." And in most of these poems, we have the sense that the fierce calm sisters apostrophized in "The Lorelei" have done their work for her, and that she has come to that place to which she asked to be ferried: the last poem in the book, "Words," is that poem of Nietzschean Joy which dispenses with heirs, with children, which wants itself, wants eternity, wants everything eternally the same:

> *Words dry and riderless,*
> *The indefatigable hoof-taps.*
> *While*
> *From the bottom of the pool, fixed stars*
> *Govern a life.*

No longer a postulant, she has been accepted in that "country far away as health," and we may take all these terrible *statements* as the spousal-verses of the marriage arranged so long ago: "the soul is a bride / in a still place." There is no pathos in the accents of these final poems, only a certain pride, the pride of an utter and ultimate surrender (like the pride of O, naked and chained in her owl mask, as she asks Sir Stephen for death); "Tulips," for example, is a poem of total purification—not even the rhythms any longer resist the run of utterance from what Sylvia Plath called her "silent center":

> *My body is a pebble . . . they tend it as water*
> *Tends to the pebbles it must run over, smoothing them gently . . .*
> *I am a nun now, I've never been so pure.*
> *I didn't want any flowers, I only wanted*
> *To lie with my hands turned up and be utterly empty.*
> *How free it is, you have no idea how free—*
> *The peacefulness is so big it dazes you,*
> *And it asks nothing . . .*
> *It is what the dead close on, finally.*

Deliver me from the body of this death! is the great sacramental cry of our culture, and in these unquestioning last poems of Sylvia Plath's, it is to death that the words are addressed, and what she is delivered of, as of a child, is the world itself, to which, in her mystical marriage, she has given birth:

> *Let it not come by the mail, finger by finger.*
> *Let it not come by word of mouth, I should be sixty*
> *By the time the whole of it was delivered, and too numb to use it.*
> *Only let down the veil, the veil, the veil . . .*
> *There would be a nobility then, there would be a birthday.*
> *And the knife not carve, but enter*
> *Pure and clean as the cry of a baby,*
> *And the universe slide from my side.*

ADRIENNE RICH

"*What Lends Us Anchor*
But the Mutable?"

T HE POET must be entranced," Robert Frost once wrote, "to the
exact premonition." Then, in that disquieting, secular way of his, as
if to renounce whatever smacked of the hierophant's complacency, he
added at once: "No mystery is meant." It is hard, I think, to keep
mystery out of the business, even in the case of a poet so often praised
for her reticence, her transparency, as Adrienne Rich. For if we take
"exact premonition" to mean no more (and no less) than the work
which *form* does for the poem, it is still by *entrancement*, some energy
beyond mere activity, that the poet must come to it, must commit
himself to it (and I construe Frost's "must" as a real imperative here).
Perhaps it is no more than the everyday mystery we spend so much of
our lives overlooking: "When familiar friends approach each other in
the street, both are apt to have this experience in feeling before
knowing the pleasantry they will inflict on each other in passing."
That was Frost's way of getting rid of the problem, and it can be ours
as well, if we fiddle with the emphasis and say, with him, that no
mystery is *meant;* it is, just, there. At different times in her career, Miss
Rich has come to terms with this strange necessity, indeed her poetry
constitutes those terms—for her first two books are all about *exact
premonition*, while her last three lay the emphasis on the *entrance-
ment*. What seems, initially, domestic and even a little prim is to be
harried and harrowed until it yields, often from "neighborhoods
usually zoned for prose," as Miss Rich herself remarks, a singular
wildness. So for all the reserve she is habitually—and too easily—com-
plimented on, this poet's *oeuvre* reveals and revels in a paradigm, an

emblematic trajectory of the course of American poetry since the
Second World War, and indeed of the course of any poetry conscious
of its nature as Second Growth: from constraint to variety, from ritual
to romance, from will to experience. And should my choice of Frost as
the source of Adrienne Rich's poetic appear prejudiced in favor of
exactitude against entrancement, I think that is only because we have
not enough considered the lonely incivility of our great precursor. At
his frequent best, Frost is the one American poet who compresses the
whole range of order and savagery, identity and chaos, into a figure of
possibility, and it is from his example, as well as from his esthetic as I
have quoted or quarried it, that Adrienne Cecile Rich, shrewdly,
begins.

In 1951, when she was twenty-one and still a senior at Radcliffe,
W. H. Auden selected Adrienne Rich's first manuscript as volume 48
of the Yale Series of Younger Poets, remarking on her "confessed rela-
tion" to Frost, to Yeats as well (though it is merely the Georgian aspect
of Yeats she echoes, one easy to catch in its decorative archaism:

> *All images once separate and alone*
> *Become the creatures of a tapestry*
> *Miraculously stirred and made our own*),

and on her good manners: "the poems a reader will encounter in this
book are neatly and modestly dressed, speak quietly but do not mum-
ble, respect their elders but are not cowed by them, and do not tell
fibs." The assurance of being properly turned out and the presence of
certain elders—both Robinson and Dickinson seem to me pervasive; the
former in the long post-Browning dramatic monologues with their
smooth pentameter, the easy iambics stretched out for metrical glut:
"Life and Letters," "Mathilde in Normandy" and, in the next book,
"Autumn Equinox" and "The Perennial Answer," though this is a
Robinson interpreted by Frost as the poet whose "guarded pathos
made him merciless"; the latter in an aphoristic, polysyllabic intensity
("I have inhaled impossibility, and walk at such an angle . . . ," so
suggestive of "Inebriate of Air am I . . . the little Tippler / leaning
against the sun") and a sharp metaphysical assertion:

> *There's enormity in a hair*
> *Enough to lead men not to share*
> *Narrow confines of a sphere . . .*

—do not deprive this little book, even when the poems are sometimes
merely pretty, merely demure, of the rudimentary predictive pattern
of *plot;* if they are occasionally no more than the rehearsals of a

formula, there is always, still, the implication that these clipped lyrics are enclosed by, that these orderly accents emerge from, some encompassing drama, whose nature it is Miss Rich's exact premonition, indeed, to specify. From the first poem of *A Change of World* ("the changes coming are due to last"—mutability is seized upon at once as this poet's prop and stay), the drama is seen as the pathos of the unaccommodated self, helpless between "instruments" on the one hand and "bad weather" on the other, a self both Stoic and recording: "knowing better than the instrument . . . I draw the curtains . . . against the insistent whine of weather":

> . . . *Weather abroad*
> *And weather in the heart alike come on*
> *Regardless of prediction.*
>
> *Between foreseeing and arresting change*
> *Lies all the mastery of elements*
> *Which clocks and weatherglasses cannot alter.*
> *Time in the hand is not control of time,*
> *Nor scattered pieces of an instrument*
> *A proof against the wind; the wind will rise,*
> *We can only close the shutters . . .*
>
> *This is our sole defense against the season;*
> *These are the things that we have learned to do*
> *Who live in troubled regions.*

The very bravery of this attitude, the assent to seeing "the bed invaded, and the game / played till the roof comes tumbling down / and win or lose are all the same," is embodied in the form's Stoical exactitude; "form," Miss Rich remarks in "At a Bach Concert," being

> . . . *the ultimate gift that love can offer—*
> *The vital union of necessity*
> *With all that we desire, all that we suffer.*

Haunted, in her vulnerability ("what if the terror stays without the meaning?"), by instruments, by unavailing measurement, as in the *ur*-Frost lyric "A Clock in the Square," she presents always the image of an ego defenceless and unhoused—waiting it out:

> *Time may be silenced but will not be stilled,*
> *Nor we absolved by anyone's withdrawing*
> *From all the restless ways we must be going*
> *And all the rings in which we're spun and swirled,*
> *Whether around a clockface or a world.*

Even the most intimate, most domestic scenes, the most familiar land-scapes—as in "Eastport to Block Island," where "along the coastal waters, signals run / in waves of caution and anxiety"—are pregnant with this anxious attention which is Adrienne Rich's overmastering sentiment:

> *News of a local violence pricks the air,*
> *And we who have seen the kitchen blow away,*
> *Or Harper's children washed from sight, prepare*
> *As usual in these parts for foul, not fair.*

Nature as well seems to be in something of the same case as ourselves, Miss Rich observes, and in "Purely Local" cites the analogy of a "January tree" that fecklessly puts out green shoots in a few days' unseasonable warmth; the same defiance of instruments and of history results, for us as for the precocious tree, in the same damages:

> *No matter how the almanacs have said*
> *Hold back, distrust a purely local May,*
> *When did we ever learn to be afraid?*
> *Why are we scarred with winter's thrust today?*

Identity without structure, being without belonging, is further ex-plored in these spruce poems of exile and estrangement, and since the orders of religion and myth are inaccessible ("we eat this body and remain ourselves"), Miss Rich hankers vainly for the "sense of bondage to some place"—her sightseeing poems, for instance, always turn sour as she realizes what it is to be

> *By no means native, yet somewhat in love*
> *With things a native is enamored of.*

We shall see in her next book how history and strange places can be used to articulate the terrors of the withdrawn consciousness; here, she uses Dickinson's accents to organize her despair:

> *Mariner unpracticed,*
> *In this chartless zone*
> *Every navigator*
> *Fares unwarned, alone . . .*
> *These are latitudes revealed*
> *Separate to each.*

To the isolated mind, absolutes are anathema, and perfection, whole-ness, unity are unspeakably alien. The surest version, therefore, of Miss Rich's partial vision and of her thirst for mutability, unmediated by any scale of measurement, is necessarily her most intimate occasion in this book: "Stepping Backward," a poem about saying a provisional goodbye to someone she sees every day. The almost suburban circumstances here:

> . . . *when we come into each other's rooms*
> *Once in a while, encumbered and self-conscious,*
> *We hover awkwardly about the threshold*
> *And usually regret the visit later.*
> *Perhaps the harshest fact is, only lovers—*
> *And once in a while two with the grace of lovers—*
> *Unlearn that clumsiness of rare intrusion*
> *And let each other freely come and go . . .*
> *The door may open, but the room is altered;*
> *Not the same room we look from night and day . . .*

are potent because the poem, as Miss Rich remarks in one of her rare critical essays, "is created as experience, not as a reaction or defence against experience." The poet steps backward for another glance at her beloved as she says her quotidian farewell ("because we live by inches"), and offers, in the finest lines of *A Change of World*, her guage of morale—lonely, tart, gallant, and with an almost desperate stiffening in the lines' insistence on "ceremony" in order to master solitude:

> *No longer wandering after Plato's ghost,*
> *Seeking the garden where all fruit is flawless,*
> *We must at last renounce that ultimate blue*
> *And take a walk in other kinds of weather.*
> *The sourest apple makes its wry announcement*
> *That imperfection has a certain tang.*
> *Maybe we shouldn't turn our pockets out*
> *To the last crumb or lingering bit of fluff,*
> *But all we can confess of what we are*
> *Has in it the defeat of isolation—*
> *If not our own, then someone's anyway.*

In 1955, Adrienne Rich—now married, a mother, a much-travelled Guggenheim Fellow and far less tentative about her conclusions, which for all that are mostly initiations—published her second, and much more generous, book *The Diamond Cutters*, whose title suggests the precision and deliberation we find everywhere in these magazine-tooled pieces, though as we shall see the title poem at the book's end promises something further, something not to be discovered in the poems written, as I have said, under the aegis of *exact premonition*. This new book, however, brought the poet a great deal of praise, enough to make it wonderful that she did not, merely, stick with it; when Randall Jarrell exulted over her talents—"her scansion is easy and limpid, close to water, close to air; she lives nearer to perfection than ordinary poets do"—Miss Rich simply moved farther away from perfection. But we shall measure that impulse of entrancement and unravelling later—first we have the pleasure of these lapidary and incisive pieces to account for, the crystallization of an energy which runs not underneath but throughout the body of this poetry. It is an emphatically mortal body, as collected first in a group of twenty poems under the rubric "Letter from the Land of Sinners"—fickle, feverish, and perfectly content to err, to wander relishing "the incompleteness of a natural thing." Europe—the landscapes of England,

> *. . . so personal that every leaf*
> *Unfolds as if to witness human life,*
> *And every aging milestone seems to know*
> *That human hands inscribed it, long ago;*

the "vanished whims" of Versailles, commemorating a "leisure that no human will can hasten"; the luxuriance of Italy, even crumbling to mere "frescoes of appetite"—Europe affords a consoling surround for the psyche haunted by inacceptable absolutes; the Old World utters a "patois of the Earth, obscure and local" which Miss Rich snuggles into, adding history to the list of alien and alienating forces that, like weather, are just too much for the lorn self and its untrustworthy instruments. Yet for all the outward justice she does to the scenery—

> *. . . the Rathaus fountain,*
> *The skaters in the sunset on the lake*
> *At Salzburg, or, emerging after snow,*
> *The singular clear stars at Castellane . . .*

—Miss Rich knows she does not own these things, is—as she remarked in her first book—"by no means native"; indeed she is more interested, in her voyaging, to consider the *mechanism* of the traveller than any particular "obligatory climate" in which he finds himself. What is the structure whereby the self is made at home, afforded the *chez soi* that, anything so absolute as the Great Good Place being forever denied, is not at least merely an Estrangement? Her answer is given in "The Tourist and the Town," a representative achievement in this group; walking around San Miniato al Monte, she finds that she can neither own nor belong to the place: "the light has changed / before we can make it ours. We have no choice . . ." For we must always, as tourists, choose happiness, or at least pleasure, "reading the posters on the station wall," so that nothing in this focussing climate brings us home to ourselves::

There is a mystery that floats between
The tourist and the town. Imagination
Estranges it from him. He need not suffer
Or die here . . .
His bargains with disaster have been sealed
In another country. Here he goes untouched
And this is alienation.

Belonging, as my emphasis suggests, means being mastered by more than satisfaction—it compels a responsibility to a continuing inward discontent: the tourist must be *touched* by all that has sent him, in the first place, into this land of sinners and made him feel even partially at home there:

. . . Only sometimes
In certain towns he opens certain letters
Forwarded on from bitter origins,
That send him walking, sick and haunted, through
Mysterious and ordinary streets
That are no more than streets to walk and walk—
And then the tourist and the town are one.

To work and suffer is to be at home.
All else is scenery . . .
To work and suffer is to come to know
The angles of a room, light in a square,
As convalescents know the face of one
Who has watched beside them. Yours now, every street,
The avenue of chestnut-trees, the road
To the post-office. Once upon a time
All these for you were fiction. Now, made free,
You live among them. Your breath is on this air,
And you are theirs and of their mystery.

Liberated precisely by her bondage to life, Adrienne Rich celebrates the paradox of all journeys: that only when we cease to see what is around us is it really there, a part of us as we are a part of its mystery. It is to "Lucifer in the Train," as the first great tripper, that the poet addresses herself for help, riding "out of worlds we shall not see again" and watching "from windows of a smoking train / the ashen prairies of the absolute":

O foundered angel, first and loneliest
To turn this bitter sand beneath your hoe,
Teach us, the newly-landed, what you know;
After our weary transit, find us rest.

Having discovered, then, in the land of sinners, in Europe, the indulgent continent, that for the mere onlooker "there's a division nothing can make sweet," having registered, in all its facile exuberance, not revelry but only "a replica of days we've married / with still the same old penances to do," Adrienne Rich returns to those New England landscapes and losses of hers which once seemed to insist on an impossible dedication but which now ("within a world my soul could recognize") stretch before her "mutable in detail yet always one"—returns fortified, since the very collapse she had feared from an outer weather, an alien history, appears in the perspective of her European sojourn the sign of a possible life, promises survival:

> *. . . we have made another kind of peace,*
> *And walk where boughs are green,*
> *Forgiven by the selves that we have been,*
> *And learning to forgive . . .*

Those are the last words of the poem "Letter from a Land of Sinners," and they are followed, suitably, by a series of character studies called "Persons in Time"; the native strain is comfortably lodged in these long narrative poems, particularly "Concord River" and the dramatic monologues I have said were under the sign of Frost and Robinson; the poet is concerned here—in time, as she says, and in place, with all the allowances for a local region, a specific weather—to acclimatize the very identities she had once declared to be sequestered from any local influence; her preoccupation is to turn "mere" decor into a duty:

> *. . . all entranced*
> *By such concerns in their perfected hour*
> *That in their lives the river and the tree*
> *Are absolutes, no longer scenery.*

A final group of lyrics celebrate, then, this poet's course which has brought her to the acknowledged zenith of her careful art: starting from a shrinking apprehension of the severed consciousness, Adrienne Rich has found what seems to be a pardon for life's injustices in their very acceptance, and like Shakespeare's Parolles has determined in foreign engagements that "simply the thing I am shall make me live." Her ultimate purpose is

> *To do what men have always done—*
> *To live in time, to act in space*
> *Yet find a ritual to embrace*
> *Raw towns of man, the pockmarked sun . . .*

Yet her experience of fallibility is such that a different style of determination seems requisite. "The thing I am" is not so easily arrived at, though by the end of *The Diamond Cutters* it is so much closer. "Provincials on the grand express / that whirls us into dark and loneliness," we require at least another scansion, a metric not so close to perfection to account for our nature. An *exact premonition* will no longer do, once we have come to some sort of terms with the fallen world; that is why so many of these poems close with the sense that the clear form achieved is insufficient now, that more is needed: "The stream ran on, and all that walking was to do again," one finishes, and another—the title poem itself—advises the diamond cutter, that "careful arriviste" who stands, surely, for the artist, to love only "what you do, and not what you have done":

> *The stone is still a stone,*
> *Though it had once resisted*
> *The weight of Africa . . .*
>
> *Nothing's left this day*
> *Except to see the sun*
> *Shine on the false and the true,*
> *And know that Africa*
> *Will yield you more to do.*

With the awareness that life exceeds the form, the poet was faced with the alternative of devising a new form, or dealing only in partial terms with life. She makes her choice, having not the exact but the obscure premonition that the trope or forward stress of life must be accounted for less neatly, more provisionally than any such "incisions in the ice" have heretofore allowed. Our gifts, Adrienne Rich resolves, are probably more surprising than the style of the will provides for—very well then,

> *Our gifts shall bring us home: not to beginnings*
> *Nor always to the destination named*
> *Upon our setting-forth. Our gifts compel,*
> *Master our ways, and lead us in the end*
> *Where we are most ourselves . . .*

Seven years after *The Diamond Cutters*, Miss Rich published her third book of poems, whose very title, *Snapshots of a Daughter-in-Law*, and caption, "Poems 1954–1962," already indicate a more casual, hence a readier rejoinder to life, a day-to-day, literally a *journalistic* accommodation of what had earlier been such a lapidary necessity. The poems are each dated, as though by this bondage to the here and now, instead of any "more exact and starry consolation," the poet could look back and say "we have been truthful . . . in a random universe." Even

the earliest poems here, written still within the formal prescriptions
that had once seemed the only stay against wilderness ("inhuman
nature says: inhuman patience is the true success"), take up the defence
of movement, or at least acknowledge that there is no holding out
against such flux as living enforces upon experience:

> *Facts could be kept separate*
> *by a convention; that was what*
> *made childhood possible. Now knowledge finds me out;*
> *in all its risible untidiness*
> *it traces me to each address,*
> *dragging in things I never thought about.*
> *I don't invite what facts can be*
> *held at arm's length; a family*
> *of jeering irresponsibles always*
> *comes along gypsy-style*
> *and there you have them all*
> *forever on your hands . . .*

The daughter-in-law of the title poem is actually an evolving version
of Everywoman, tracing the grappling irons and ironies of the female
estate through ten irregular pieces, full of personal gripes against "the
argument *ad feminam;* all the old knives / that have rusted in my back,
I drive in yours, / *ma semblable, ma soeur!*" and a kind of natural
history of women writers: "Our blight has been our sinecure: / mere
talent was enough for us— / glitter in fragments and rough drafts."
Dickinson, Wollstonecraft, Burney and De Beauvoir are laid under
contribution, though the desperate conclusion belies whatever accom-
plishments are registered:

> *A thinking woman sleeps with monsters.*
> *The beak that grips her, she becomes. And Nature,*
> *that sprung-lidded, still commodious*
> *steamer-trunk of* tempora *and* mores
> *gets stuffed with it all . . .*

The rhythms, as Miss Rich herself has said of Karl Shapiro, though it is
far more characteristic of her own later practice, are "at one with the
language most of the time." She no longer cuts across her own speech
by a *made-up* verse, but entrusts what she has to say—

> *Is this* fertilisante douleur? *Pinned down*
> *by love, for you the only natural action,*
> *are you edged more keen*
> *To prise the secrets of the vault? has Nature shown*
> *her household books to you, daughter-in-law,*
> *that her sons never saw?*

—to the vessel that is her impulse to raise her voice in the first place.
The hand-to-mouth rhyming picked up from Lowell, and the imagist
phrasing

> (*Her mind full to the wind, I see her plunge*
> *breasted and glancing through the currents,*
> *taking the light upon her*
> *at least as beautiful as any boy*
> *or helicopter,*
> > *poised, still coming*
> *her fine blades making the air wince*)

adapted from Levertov, the *means* of this poetry which is not so much
reduced from the traditional panoply as *restored* to the resources of
speech and wit as they are gleaned from the mind's despite ("I'm
sulking, clearly, in the great tradition / of human waste")—none of
Adrienne Rich's transformations suggest that she has surrendered a
particle of her demands on the poem to harbor her against an impossi-
ble void; rather she has sought a lodging, quite literally a stay, in the
very element that is sweeping by her, as she echoes the famous line
from *Fleurs du Mal* ("*Andromaque, je pense à toi! . . . Paris*
change"):

> Baudelaire, I think of you! Nothing changes,
> *rude and self-absorbed the current*
> *dashes past, asking nothing, poetry*
> *extends its unsought amnesty,*
> *autumn saws the great grove down.*
> *Some voices, though, shake in the air like heat . . .*
> *Certain old woods are sawdust,*
> *from now on have to be described?*
> *Nothing changes. The bones of the mammoths*
> *are still in the earth.*

The confidence the poet exhibits, now, in her own unpropped diction
("much will blind you, / much will evade you . . . The door
itself / makes no promises. It is only a door") allows her to extend her
imagination much farther into the world; in the most ambitious work
thus far, a six-part register of mortality called "Readings of History,"
Adrienne Rich ranges through most of our ways of remembering,
dismissing all standard versions of the past, even revised ones, as "se-
duction fantasies of the public mind." She is after a reading of history
that will include herself, a perspective that will contain not only what
she knows herself to be *now*, the present woman who is an anthology
of all her wounds and wanderings, not only the *summa* of her past:

> *Split at the root, neither Gentile nor Jew,*
> *Yankee nor Rebel, born*
> *in the face of two ancient cults,*
> *I'm a good reader of histories . . .*

but also "my dotage and my total absence"—she wants to be able to say (as she *does* say, once she has accepted the equation of life and vulnerability, the notion that not only is to err human, but that error *alone* constitutes our humanity): "I, too, have lived in history."

It is the throes of life that award a consciousness of belonging to it; the terrible sad poems about marriage in this book, which have nothing of the sensational about them, for nothing is *exposed*, everything, merely, acknowledged:

> *The world breathes underneath our bed.*
> *Don't look. We're at each other's mercy too . . .*

and the accepted blights of family intercourse, the *scenes*, the internecine assaults that constitute, as Giraudoux once said apropos of the Atrides, those weekly conflagrations that break out in families where feelings run high:

> *The children quarrel in the attic.*
> *She has no blood left in her heart.*
> *The man comes back to a dark house.*
> *The only light is in the attic.*
> *He has forgotten his key.*
> *He rings at his own door*
> *and hears sobbing on the stairs.*
> *The lights go on in the house.*
> *The door closes behind him.*
> *Outside, separate as minds,*
> *the stars too come alight . . .*

the exhaustion of pure biology, the illusion that history must be running down because, evidently, *we* are:

> *dying a little every day*
> *from the inside out*
> *almost imperceptibly*
>
> *till the late decades when*
> *women go hysterical*
> *and men are dumbly frightened . . .*

—such disasters acknowledged, even embraced, afford by the book's end a perspective of a life seen entire, from a childhood dismay at the coming wreck to a cherishing look back to "the daily warfare that takes its toll of tenderness"; there is even a sense of comfort offered, with a knowledge of its futility which makes such womanly ministering all the more affecting:

> *Here's water. Sleep. No more is asked of you.*
> *I take your life into my living head.*

A submission to the destructive elements which the earlier poems had so prudently avoided or resisted brings Miss Rich—now that she has dramatized her psyche, soma, and strong intellect, has rehearsed the very scenes which her earlier poems had relegated to the wings, *offstage*—to the situation where she hopes to see her eventual Everywoman: naked, ignorant,

> *but her cargo*
> *no promise then:*
> *delivered*
> *palpable*
> *ours.*

So entranced, then, has this poet become by a vision of life as fallible, as a fractured medium whose very cracks let in the light, that she no longer dares approach the mystery (there is one, then, even if none is *meant*—perhaps there can be one *only* if none is meant, as Frost would say) from an "exact premonition"; rather she has reversed the terms, for it is now her commitment to the rhythms of entrancement—a "swaying form" if ever there was one, tentative, repetitious, prehensile rather than the diligent topiary of her first two books—that will lead her, if she trusts herself "blind to the triumphant sea," to new premonitions, these exacting perhaps rather than exact, but no less an achieved style for that.

In 1966, Adrienne Rich's fourth book of poems was published; it includes a group of translations from the Dutch commissioned by the Bollingen Foundation; the rest, twenty-five carefully dated poems of her own, are prefixed with a quotation from Montaigne, explaining the inextricability of death in any trope of life; "you flee yourself," Montaigne says, if you attempt to evade *"cette belle contexture des choses,"* and in these centripetal pieces Miss Rich carries still further her attempt to define or at least demonstrate what are, as the book is called, *Necessities of Life.*

Death is certainly one of them, and alienation another; whether watching her child in the throes of a nightmare:

Your eyelids work. I see
your dream, cloudy as a negative,

swimming underneath.
You blurt a cry. Your eyes

spring open, still filmed in dream.
Wider, they fix me—

—death's head, sphinx, medusa?
You scream.

Tears lick my cheeks, my knees
droop at your fear.

Mother I no more am,
but woman, and nightmare . . .

or sitting with her old father, who is falling asleep while his reconciled daughter keeps the doomed vigil of consanguinity ("blood is a sacred poison"):

I'll sit with you there and tease you
for wisdom, if you like
waiting till the blunt barge
bumps along the shore.

Marriage too, and sex, are penetrated for their inevitable burden of mortality, union as the glyph of separateness:

They're tearing down the houses
we met and lived in. Only
a fact could be so dreamlike.
Soon our two bodies will be all
left standing from that era . . .

That "old last act"!
And yet sometimes
all seems post coitum triste
and I a mere bystander . . .
I make it—
we lie fainting together
at a crater-edge
till he speaks—
in a different language

> *yet one I've picked up*
> *through cultural exchanges . . .*

In all these engagements with life, as in those "fierce attentions" to her own memory ("The mind's passion is all for singling out. Obscurity has another tale to tell"), the poetry devises its own form, its own emphasis, "making a jar of pencils, a typewriter keyboard / more than they were." Entrancement is where Adrienne Rich begins:

> *Whole biographies swam up and*
> *swallowed me like Jonah.*
> *Jonah! I was Wittgenstein,*
> *Mary Wollstonecraft, the soul*
> *of Louis Jouvet, dead*
> *in a blown-up photograph.*
> *Till, wolfed almost to shreds,*
> *I learned to make myself . . .*
> *What life there was was mine,*
> *now and again to name*
> *over the bare necessities.*
> *So much for those days. Soon*
> *practice may make me middling-perfect, I'll*
> *dare inhabit the world*
> *trenchant in motion as an eel, solid*
> *as a cabbage head. I have invitations . . .*

and an exact premonition is where she ends. A loyalty to her own insights lets her keep the figure of a helicopter she had pounced on in De Beauvoir for the last book, and the vehicle carries her far:

> *. . . this morning*
> *lying on a dusty blanket*
> *among the burnt-out Indian pipes*
> *and bursting-open lady's-slippers.*
> *My soul, my helicopter, whirred*
> *distantly, by habit, over*
> *the old pond with the half-drowned boat*
> *toward which it always veers*
> *for consolation: ego's Arcady:*
> *leaving the body stuck*
> *like a leaf against a screen.*
> *Happiness . . . found! ready or not.*
> *If I move now, the sun*
> *naked between the trees*
> *will melt me as I lie.*

Except that her entrancement, her ardor, and as quoted here her *ecstasy* have brought her to a diction, a natural run and roll of the lines that is entirely right for the unarmored self that utters them, there is nothing to be said about these poems: one can only say *them*. Miss Rich, in an art that reckons more with waste and destruction than her old economies, has made out of experience a self that is like the Emily Dickinson she returns to, once again, in these poems, a woman who "chose to have it out at last / on her own premises":

> *for whom the word was more*
> *than a symptom—*
> *a condition of being.*

"Our gifts lead us," Adrienne Rich had promised or rather admonished in that stern self-scrutiny of hers which reminds us that *stern* is no more than a kind of past participle of *stare*, a matter of having been looked at *hard*—"our gifts lead us," she had *prophesied*, let us say, "in the end / where we are most ourselves." In the end . . . a region disclosed by her fifth book of poems *Leaflets* (published in 1969) as a waste of urban wants and losses, desolations ("children are dying my death / and eating crumbs of my life") of the public and the private life, of family, school and voting-booth in which "everything we stood against has conquered / and now we're part / of it all"; a wilderness, too, beyond the city and the shut-in self, which for all the once-relished country pleasures institutes no more than another abandon in the lonely landscape:

> *The old masters, the old sources*
> *haven't a clue what we're about,*
> *shivering here in the half-dark 'sixties.*

> *The wall of the house is bleeding. Firethorn!*
> *The moon, cracked every which-way,*
> *pushes steadily on . . .*

and wherever we may look about us, a general sense of the general senselessness ("a man reaches behind my eyes / and finds them empty / a woman's head turns away / from my head in the mirror"), the perishability not merely of the self in its surround, but of what we have hardened and sharpened against ourselves and our situation, of our *art*—"the clear statement of something missing," the poet calls it, *tidings of the immaculate present* brought by a harbinger less of doom than of daemonic irrelevance, tragic disinterest:

Do we have to feel jealous of our creations any longer?
Once they might have outlived us; in this world we'll die together . . .

and entrusted to anyone listening, anyone likely to be around in the
hope or the humility of *use*, of *helping:*

> *I want this to be yours*
> *in the sense that if you find and read it*
> *it will be there in you already*
> *and the leaflet merely something*
> *to leave behind, a little leaf*
> *in the drawer of a sublet room.*
> *What else does it come down to*
> *but handing on scraps of paper . . .*
> *because the imagination crouches in them . . .*
> *I am thinking how we can use what we have*
> *to invent what we need.*

In this scenery of bewilderment, the new poems of Adrienne Rich
create a trajectory of solicitude, or critical concern for other people
which initiates its parabola in the impulse to withdraw with the be-
loved to some snowbound fastness, the hut in the woods, as in one of
the first poems, "Holding Out":

> *Late in the afternoons the ice*
> *squeaks underfoot like mica*
> *and when the sun drops red and moon-*
> *faced back of the gun-colored firs,*
> *The best intentions are none too good.*
> *Then we have to make a go of it*
> *in the smoke with the dark outside*
> *and our love in our boots at first—*
> *no matter.*

And the book ends with the forsaking of that hope, the downward
curve of love's aspiration, in the terrible question which closes the final
group of *ghazals*, a form borrowed from the nineteenth-century Urdu
poet Ghalib:

> *How did we get caught up fighting this forest fire,*
> *We, who were only looking for a still place in the woods?*

Between the withdrawal and the bewilderment, between the retreat
and the return, Adrienne Rich speaks no longer, now, merely for
herself, as in her earliest books; she speaks *to* herself, certainly, in her
recension of a woman's lot—"posterity trembles like a leaf / and we go
on making heirs and heirlooms"—but most of all she speaks *to* others,
addressing her music (for it is still, in the clutch of circumstance, a
music, a sweet paramour's tune like Barbara's remembered in extremity
by Desdemona, the "living fall" of notes sustaining yet the patient
humor:

Only where there is language is there world.
In the harp of my hair, compose me
a song. Death's in the air,
we all know that . . . Still, for an hour,
I'd like to be gay. How could a gay song go?
Why that's your secret, and it shall be mine.
We are our words, and black and bruised and blue.
Under our skins, we're laughing—

no constants in prosody can be endured here, no consonances echoed more than irregularly, but the lines are *lines*, still, and lead the poem back into itself, forming however surreptitiously a *verse*, an energy of recuperation and refrain) to her beloved with the gallant conviction of transience, of merely momentary solace:

> *. . . my love is just a breath*
> *blown on the pane and dissolved.*
> *Everything, even you*
> *cries silently for help, the web*
> *of the spider is rippled with rain,*
> *the geese fly on into the black cloud.*
> *What can I do for you?*
> *what can I do for you?*

That is the great question these poems ask, repeatedly: Adrienne Rich has been able, by the savoring of a "precious loss" which includes all the old certainties of composition and commonwealth, to inflect the roles in which women are cast by men—the coloratura of disregard, the contralto of matriarchy, the screech of penis-envy, and the role she herself has finally chosen, the *lyrico spinto* of caring—to her reft apocalyptic purpose, which is to order and commend the whole of the natural world as the content of an infinite and eternal—however outraged—human body, her own, as in "Nightbreak":

> *. . . I don't*
> *collect what I can't use   I need*
> *what can be broken.*
>
> *In the bed the pieces fly together*
> *and the rifts fill   or else*
> *my body is a list   of wounds*
> *symmetrically placed . . .*
> *The enemy has   withdrawn*
> *between raids   become invisible*
> *there are*
> >   *no agencies*
> > >   *of relief*

> *the darkness becomes utter*
> *Sleep   cracked and flaking*
> *sifts over the shaken   target*
>
> *What breaks is night*
> *not day   The white*
> *scar   splitting*
> *over the east*
> *The crack weeping*
> *Time for the pieces*
>   *to move*
> *dumbly back*
>   *toward each other.*

Here she creates a voice as exact and premonitory as that of any nurse, as entranced as that of any virgin, as erotic as that of any temple prostitute, all of whom she resumes and restores when she says, at that end where she is most herself:

> *For us the work undoes itself over and over;*
> *The grass grows back, the dust collects, the scar breaks open.*

The Will to Change: Poems 1968–1970 by ADRIENNE RICH

Like other cultivated poets of her generation—like Merwin, Snodgrass and James Wright—Adrienne Rich is haunted into significance as much by what she has changed *from* as by changing at all or by what she is changing to. Recurrence, memory, any presentiment of the old order, of the poem as contraption, is what this poet obsessively, creatively combats. In her sixth book, then, there will be a constant imagery of inconstancy, of breaking free, of fracturing, of shedding and molting:

> *how you broke open, what sheathed you*
> *until this moment*
> *I know nothing about it*
> *my ignorance of you amazes me*
> *now that I watch you*
> *starting to give yourself away*
> *to the wind*

The governing (or anarchic) emblems in this taut, overturning book are more likely to be drawn from almost anywhere than from poetry, from anything but verse in its decorous, accorded sense, the ritual of a departure and return, a refrain which is indeed a refraining as well, a reluctance to violate repetition. Rather the figures will be derived from dreams and dedications, letters, elegies, photographs, movies: "I am an instrument in the shape / of a woman trying to translate pulsations / into images / for the relief of the body and the reconstruction of the mind," she says in one place, and in another: "I pledged myself to try any instrument that came my way. Never to refuse one from conviction of incompetence." Ridding the self, then, of what it had been, of what it had done ("language is the map of our failures") in order to get on with it, to make room, to make way: these poems are that way, a trail blazed, a transformation wrought chiefly by burning. The implication throughout is that you do not know what you are, all you know is the ashes of what you have been; death creates you:

> to float free
> up through the smoke of brushfires
> and incinerators.

The movies (how right that word is for a poet who says "seeing is changing", or again, "I thought of my words as changing minds, / hadn't my mind also to suffer changes?") are the major representative form here, and the major piece in this book is an extended series of writings called, focally, "Shooting Script"—what Adrienne Rich herself calls a conversation of sounds melting constantly into rhythms, "a cycle whose rhythm begins to change the meanings of words." Preoccupied by the wreckage of urban and amatory experiment and tradition alike, this poet abandons what she calls the rhythms "of choice, the lost methods" for the sake, the favor of something much more likely, an explosion of possibilities:

> once the last absolutes were torn to pieces
> you could begin . . .
> every impulse of light exploding
> from the core
> as life flies out of us.

That concern of her earlier books which is indeed a myth of concern, a critique of solicitude, of caring, nursing and tending, is pretty much done away with here, except in one tender instance:

> I have sucked the wound in your hand to sleep
> but my lips were trembling.
> Tell me how to bear myself,
> how it's done, the light kiss falling

accurately
on the cracked palm.

And even here, the familiar—familiar, I mean, to Adrienne Rich's other poems—taking of pains is turned into body English, the somatic discharge of disaster ("I am bombarded yet / I stand") which will allow her to expose, and even exult in, "external" events in terms of self-sufficiency as well as of first-aid to others:

> *the sole of the foot is a map, the palm of the hand a letter*
> *learned by heart and worn close to the body*

As is apparent in these quotations, pieces of language broken open, dated but unpunctuated, with their axiological rather than external use of enjambment—the line as notation rather than as unit, as tessera rather than as structural member—*The Will to Change* is not made up of discreet poems, in any sense, nor is it made up at all. It is a text, a graph ("the surface is always lucid, / my shadows are under the skin") which must be read through to the end, yielded to, held fast, for these are notes toward a supreme somatic fiction:

> *The notes for the poem are the only poem*
> *the mind collecting, devouring*
> *all these destructibles . . .*
> *the mind of the poet is changing*
> *the moment of change is the only poem*

What is striking, what is even stricken about Adrienne Rich's poetry is her probity and resource in the face of fracture, "the fracture of order / the repair of speech / to overcome this suffering." For she is, like her radical affiliates, determined to overcome. She is Sylvia Plath in reverse, not eager or even willing to be still, to be stone, to be dead; but rather letting the stillness be broken within and around her, letting herself be lapidated (can we say stoned, any more?), letting herself discover what the death of others does to the self—Adrienne Rich lets herself discover that, for one thing, the death of others creates the self, as the renunciation of illusion creates identity:

> *Now to give up the temptations of the projector; to see instead*
> *the web of cracks filtering across the plaster.*
> *To read there the map of the future, the roads radiating from*
> *the initial split, the filaments thrown out from that impasse.*
> *To reread the instructions on your palm; to find there how*
> *the lifeline, broken, keeps its direction.*

Diving Into the Wreck: Poems 1971–1972 by ADRIENNE RICH

When a poet, for her seventh book, offers, as what she calls "many names for pieces of one whole," the twenty-five scrupulously dated poems of some eighteen months, then we are obliged to assume that something is meant by the delimitation of dates, something more than spiritual journalism:

> *Every act of becoming conscious*
> *(it says here in this book)*
> *is an unnatural act*

—something more than a mere record of that determination of the private life by "a wider public life" which George Eliot is here invoked to remind us of; something more than the intention of focused clarity in the account of our damages, political, urban, marital, sexual. What is meant by the composition of such a book may be something unknown to the poet: so disposed, the poems effect a discovery otherwise off the record, beyond the mere sufficiency of writing enough to "make up" another book.

A signal is afforded by the frame, a clue to the tonality in which we should read these severe fragments:

> *these scars bear witness*
> *but whether to repair*
> *or to destruction*
> *I no longer know—*

For the book is framed by two French statements concerned, as Adrienne Rich is, with the values of the irrational. In both instances, the speaker is not identified with the "irrational" principle itself, but rather is a man confronted by the problem of coming to terms with it. Cited at the outset, André Breton, prefacing his transactions with the psychotic waif he calls Nadja, says: "perhaps I am doomed to retrace my steps under the illusion that I am exploring"; and at the end J.-M. Itard, attempting to educate the wild boy of Aveyron, notes with characteristic Enlightenment pessimism: "He would certainly have escaped into the forest had not the most rigid precautions been taken." Between these famous French caveats, between the mad girl and the wild boy, emblems of something valuable in human life that society legislates out of existence or out of recognition, stand the poems of *Diving into the Wreck;* they are the terms, then, of passionate address, in which a tremendous discovery is being made—it is a discovery the poet cannot yet say she *has made:* she is making it.

> *. . . there is no one*
> *to tell me when the ocean will begin . . .*

> *the sea is another story*
> *the sea is not a question of power*
> *I have to learn alone*
> *to turn my body without force*
> *in the deep element . . .*

In her preceding book there had been a constant imagery of inconstancy, of breaking free, of fracturing, of shedding and molting. Here, in poem after gerundively titled poem—"Trying to Talk with a Man", "Waking in the Dark", "Diving into the Wreck", "Living in the Cave", "Burning Oneself Out"—the effort is to pierce, to lift stone from stone until the self that speaks penetrates a region mistakenly held to be unspoken, even unspeakable:

> *an underground river*
> *forcing its way between deformed cliffs.*

She finds this buried stream, the course of true possibilities in her life, as often in the blasted city ("shudder of the caves beneath the asphalt," or, again, "looking straight down the heart / of the street to the river") as in the blistering desert ("that valley traced by the thread / of the cold quick river Merced"). She finds the "risks of the portage, risks of the glacier" in her own body, in the body of the lover, of the friend, of what the French call the other:

> *drawing me*
> *into the grotto of your skull*
> *the landscape of bone;*

And she performs her odd underwater archeology in order to discover "what on earth it all might have become." The gesture of diving into the wreck, the immersion in the alien element, occurs in many poems, many places, as she says:

> *I dive back to discover you . . .*
> *we go on*
> *streaming through the slow*
> *citylight*
> *forest ocean . . .*

so that as we read through the book we realize that Adrienne Rich is a kind of Lot's wife who refuses rigidity. She has been "composing the thread / inside the spider's body" which will lead her on, lead us all on, "guiding each other / over the scarred volcanic rock." The preparation is as much for failure as for finding; the poet accepts, as poets always do, the admonition of dreams:

> *. . . out of the blurred conjectures*
> *your face clears, a sunken marble*

> *slowly cranked up from underwater.*
> *I feel the ropes straining under their load of despair* . . .

But mainly the poems are a testimony to the task, to the digging and diving and mining. What keeps Adrienne Rich from becoming a pillar of salt as she surveys the territory behind her, the wreck that is our history and our body politic, is work, the poem as labor—shared, assumed, chosen:

> . . . *working like me to pick apart*
> *working with me to remake*
> *this trailing knitted thing, this cloth of darkness,*
> *this woman's garment, trying to save the skein.*

When I call her poems testimony, I do not mean to suggest that Adrienne Rich is a poet to be offered in evidence, merely. She is not a reporter, for all her concentration upon the truth. The poet is telling of something now standing before her eyes of which her heart is full. She is not collecting reports, she is not remembering events. If she overhears the words of others, it is by telepathy; if she sees scenes, it is in a vision; if she knows truths, it is by faith. These poems are not loose facts, they are parts of a revelation:

> *I came to see the damage that was done*
> *and the treasures that prevail.*

Harper's Magazine, 1973

ANNE SEXTON

"*Some Tribal Female Who Is Known But Forbidden*"

THERE ARE some areas of experience in modern life, Theodore Roethke has said, that simply cannot be rendered by either the formal lyric or straight prose. We must realize—and who could have enforced the realization upon us better than Roethke—that the writer in "freer forms" must have an even greater fidelity to his subject matter or his substance than the poet who has the support of form—of received form. He must be imaginatively "right," his rhythm must move as the mind moves, or he is lost. "On the simplest level, something must happen in this kind of poem." By which Roethke meant, I am certain, that it is not enough to report something happening in your life merely—it must be made to happen in your poem. You must begin somewhere, though, generally with your life, above all with your life when it seems to you to welter in a particular exemplary status. Such is Anne Sexton's case, and she has begun indeed with the report of her case:

> *Oh! Honor and relish the facts!*
> *Do not think of the intense sensation*
> *I have as I tell you this*
> *but think only . . .*

In fact, she has reported more than anyone else—anyone else who has set out to write poems—has ever cared or dared, and thereby she has gained, perhaps at the expense of her poetry, a kind of sacerdotal stature, the elevation of a priestess celebrating mysteries which are no less mysterious for having been conducted in all the hard glare of the marketplace and with all the explicitness mere print can afford.

Anne Sexton is the true Massachussetts heiress of little Pearl, who as the procession of Worthies passes by asks Hester Prynne if one man in it is the same minister who kissed her by the brook. "Hold thy peace, dear little Pearl," whispers her mother. "We must not always talk in the marketplace of what happens to us in the forest." Like the sibylline, often insufferable Pearl, Anne Sexton *does* speak of such things, and in such places, and it makes her, again like Pearl, both more and less than a mere "person," something beyond a "character"; it makes her, rather, what we call a *figure*, the form of a tragic function. If you are wearing not only your heart on your sleeve, your liver on your lapel and the other organs affixed to various articles of your attire, but also a whole alphabet in scarlet on your breast, then your poetry must bear with losing the notion of *private parts* altogether and with gaining a certain publicity that has nothing to do with the personal. Further, if you regard, as Anne Sexton does, the poem as "a lie that tells the truth" (it was Cocteau who first spoke of himself this way), then you face the corresponding peril that the truth you tell will become a lie: "there is no translating that ocean," as Miss Sexton says. And it will become a lie because you have not taken enough care to "make something happen" —in short, to lie in the way poems must lie, by devising that imaginative rightness which Roethke located primarily in rhythm, but which has everything to do as well with the consecution of images, the shape language makes as it is deposited in the reader's mind, the transactions between beginnings and endings, the *devices*—no less—of art.

"Even one alone verse sometimes makes a perfect poem," Ben Jonson declared, and so much praise (it is the kind of praise that leaves out of the reckoning a great deal of waste, a great deal of botched work) it will be easy, and what is more it will be necessary, to give Anne Sexton; like the preposterous sprite whose "demon-offspring" impulses she resumes, this poet is likely, *at any moment*, to say those oracular, outrageous things we least can bear but most require:

> *Fee-fi-fo-fum*
> *Now I'm borrowed*
> *Now I'm numb*

It is when she speaks beyond the moment, speaks as it were consecutively that Anne Sexton finds herself in difficulties; if we are concerned with the poem as it grows from one verse to the next, enlarging itself by means of itself, like a growing pearl, the real one (Hawthorne's, for all he tells us, never grew up), then we must discover an Anne Sexton dead set, by her third book of poems, against any such process. Hers is the truth that cancels poetry, and her career as an artist an excruciating trajectory of self-destruction, so that it is by her failures in her own enterprise that she succeeds, and by her successes as an artist that she fails herself.

In 1960 Miss Sexton's first collection of poems, *To Bedlam and Part Way Back* was published with an epigraph from a letter of Schopenhauer to Goethe echoing Hester Prynne's reproof: "Most of us carry in our heart the Jocasta who begs Oedipus for God's sake not to inquire further . . ." The poems begin right there in Bedlam, unacclimated, unexplained, and take shape, apparently, as a therapeutic project —the very ingenuity of their shape, indeed, has something of the basket-weaver's patience about it, it is the work of a *patient*. The very first, addressed to the doctor "who walks from breakfast to madness," refers to the speaker and the other inmates as "magic talking to itself, / noisy and alone." Only gradually are we given a hint of the circumstances that brought her there, circumstances it will be Sexton's life work to adumbrate until the shadows fall indeed over her entire existence as a poet—here we simply start out in the asylum, where "my night mind / saw such strange happenings." The poet is in her own dark forest:

> . . . *I am afraid of course*
> *to look—this inward look that society scorns—*
> *Still, I search these woods and find nothing worse*
> *than myself, caught between the grapes and the thorns.*

She is even, like Daphne, her own tree:

> *I live in my wooden legs and O*
> *my green green hands . . .*
> *I am a fist of my unease*
> *as I spill toward the stars in the empty years.*
> *I build the air with the crown of honor; it keys*
> *my out of time and luckless appetite.*
> *You gave me honor too soon, Apollo.*
> *There is no one left who understands*
> *how I wait*
> *here in my wooden legs and O*
> *my green green hands.*

That strikes the proper note of the priestess: it is the voice of a woman defiled by the very life she would expose, and whose knowledge has been granted by her defilement and is thereby partial, momentary and changing: "caught between a shape and a shape and then returned to me."

In these first poems, Anne Sexton has already mastered not only an idiosyncratic stanza, but a verse paragraph whose characteristic diction has, in Robert Lowell's choppy wake, restored to our poetry not only the lyric of self-dramatization which had hidden out in the novel for so long, but an unmistakable notation of events—not witty but always *grinçant,* and without more music than mere accuracy affords:

> *It is a summer evening.*
> *The yellow moths sag*
> *against the locked screens*
> *and the faded curtains*
> *suck over the window sills*
> *and from another building*
> *a goat calls in his dreams.*
> *This is the TV parlor*
> *in the best ward at Bedlam.*
> *The night nurse is passing*
> *out the evening pills.*
> *She walks on two erasers,*
> *padding by us one by one.*

The line break at "passing," the intermittent rhyme and the rhythmic subtlety, particularly in the last two lines, suggest the gifts employed here (Flaubert himself would have been pleased with that second sentence), even or especially when the matter is "given" so unbearably that no further gifts can, in short, matter:

> *. . . because we mind by instinct,*
> *like bees caught in the wrong hive,*
> *we are the circle of the crazy ladies*
> *who sit in the lounge of the mental house*
> *and smile . . .*

There is, demonstrably, a care in these first poems for the poem's *making;* invariably it is Sexton's practice to use rhyme to bind the poem, irregularly invoked, abandoned when inconvenient, psychologically convincing. It is the rhyme introduced into English verse by Arnold, refined by Eliot, and roughed up here by Miss Sexton, who seeks to recover for poetry the expressive resources of chaos and is not to be coerced, "in that narrow diary of her mind," to any spurious regularity:

> *Today is made of yesterday, each time I steal*
> *toward rites I do not know, waiting for the lost*
> *ingredient, as if salt or money or even lust*
> *would keep us calm and prove us whole at last.*

She conducts her funneling and furious tour of the wards, in this collection, so that the final third of the book is focussed on the purely private horrors: on the separation from individual impulse that leaves us

> *. . . too alien to know*
> *our sameness and how our sameness survives;*

and on the terrible demands, nonetheless, of the ego imprisoned in the woman's wanting body:

> *My dear, it was a time,*
> *butchered from time,*
> *that we must tell of quickly*
> *before we lose the sound of our own*
> *mouths calling mine, mine, mine.*

The last three poems, "For John, Who Begs Me Not to Enquire Further," "The Double Image" and "The Division of Parts" are specifically concerned with a disengagement from the sacred world of madness and a weary return to sanity, or at least to a version of secular (bourgeois) life which must seem sane for being so bleak. The painful poems to the estranged daughter, to the mother dying of cancer, and about the two suicide attempts (Sexton is more than half in love with easeful death; as her envying poem to Sylvia Plath insists, she is altogether enamored of a difficult one) are an exorcism, a caveat and a mustering of forces; to the daughter is assigned the disabused confession:

> *I, who was never quite sure*
> *about being a girl, needed another*
> *life, another image to remind me.*
> *And this was my worst guilt; you could not cure*
> *nor soothe it. I made you to find me.*

And to the mother, an outraged voice with whom Sexton is to wrestle in almost every poem, a deferred reconciliation:

> *You come, a brave ghost, to fix*
> *in my mind without praise*
> *or paradise*
> *to make me your inheritor.*

While to herself the entire book stands as a valorization of the present, a way of facing up to a perishable existence, all transgressions acknowledged and even embraced—were they not the source of ecstasy?—and of recognizing the daily extinctions that make suicide not undesirable but unnecessary:

> *Today the yellow leaves*
> *go queer. You ask me where they go. I say today believed*
> *in itself, or else it fell.*

"Her first book, especially the best poems, spills into the second and somehow adds to it," Robert Lowell said when *All My Pretty Ones* was published in 1962: the title comes, of course, from the "one fell swoop" passage in *Macbeth*, in which the operative phrase, for Miss Sexton's retrospective purposes, quite defines the volume's enterprise:

> *I cannot but remember such things were,*
> *That were most precious to me.*

There is also an inner epigraph, parallel to the remark from Schopenhauer in the first collection, this time from a letter of Kafka's, to the effect that "a book should serve as the ax for the frozen sea within us." Thus the therapeutic requirement is still served, along with the memorial function, by these poems which, as Lowell remarked, pursue what Anne Sexton has always had in view, "the tongue's wrangle, the world's pottage, the rat's star," the minimal furniture, too, of a life confined but also privileged by madness, disease, death and violence to "spells and fetishes":

> *I cannot promise very much.*
> *I give you the images I know.*

Such knowledge has afforded the poet a certain abundance, and if the harshness of her concern makes us wonder with her "how anything fragile survives," there is in *All My Pretty Ones* an intimation of survival that is the more powerful, not the less, for its obsessive mortality. "Nothing is sure. No one. I wait in doubt," Anne Sexton confesses after surgery, "my stomach laced up like a football / for the game." Attending to herself between the periods when those other attendants must take over, she continues to catalogue the ills not only the flesh is heir to, but the mind and the body politic as well, always convulsively yet with a vividness generally aassociated with a more sanguine view:

> *Outside the bittersweet turns orange.*
> *Before she died my mother and I picked these fat*
> *branches, finding orange nipples*
> *on the gray wire strands.*
> *We weeded the forest, curing trees like cripples.*

It is strong stuff and invariably brought to a devastating close—by postponed rhymes, or by pruning down the stanza to the simplest terminal phrase, standing alone as a line: "my son," or "I wish I were dead"—the cadences of agony, loss and division. What a relief when the design works against the poet's distemper, as in "The Abortion" and "The Operation," instead of surrendering—condescending, really —to the awfulness of it all. Such titles suggest Sexton's preoccupations, but not the lucid obstruction to sentimentality which her firm control, at her best, of the stanza and her fine colloquial diction set up. I cannot guess what another generation—before or after our own—might make of such incisions as this, from "Housewife":

Men enter by force, drawn back like Jonah
into their fleshy mothers.
A woman is her mother.
That's the main thing.

But abjuring incantation of any obvious kind for statement, choosing truth and taking the always discreditable consequences does not, for all that, mean that Anne Sexton has given over the oracular role, the Pythian occasion. Once she is on the tripod, it does not matter that images are extinguished, metaphors dissipated, words harrowed. What is left is a poem which utter necessity seems to have reduced to absence and which, nonetheless, is acknowledged in such absence as the image —the final image—of an absolute plenitude. Though nothing is smooth or caressing here—it is a rough magic indeed that Sexton, unlike Prospero, refuses to abjure—it is still "The Black Art" she practices, as in the poem of that name:

> *A woman who writes feels too much,*
> *those trances and portents!*
> *As if cycles and children and islands*
> *weren't enough; as if mourners and gossips*
> *and vegetables were never enough.*
> *She thinks she can warn the stars . . .*

By 1966, Miss Sexton had completed another book of poems, with the almost expected, certainly self-parodying title *Live or Die*—from Bellow's *Herzog*, and the quote goes on, in what I take to be an exacerbated self-adjuration: "But don't poison everything"—and also written a full-length, theater-of-the-mind play called *Tell Me Your Answer True*. It is not surprising, after the tremendous series of intimacies to which she has made us a party, to find now in any one poem not only a case-history versified into its most painful crises, the analects of continuing dissolution ("life enlarges, life takes aim"), but also accounts of drug addiction, the bloody accidents of children, the death by cancer of at least one parent, and certainly the disappearance of God ("need is not belief").* A lessening of attention to what

---

* Typical titles: "Menstruation at Forty," "Wanting to Die," "Pain for a Daughter," "Suicide Note." The accommodation of violence, always a matter of diminishing returns, becomes, with its characteristic dependence on cruel verbs, the *raison d'être* of whatever consecutive discourse is to be found in these poems:

> *The thoroughbred has stood on her foot . . .*
> *The marks of the horseshoe printed*
> *into her flesh, the tips of her toes*
> *ripped off like pieces of leather,*
> *three toenails swirled like shells*
> *and left to float in blood in her riding boot.*

happens in the poem, as Roethke prophesied, has obliged Sexton to move into it every kind of event that can compel *our* shocked attention, if not our assent, to that other world, the world where "I am the target." The poet's attitude toward her art is defined, I think, by the fact that many of the speeches in her garishly articulated psychodrama are the word-for-word texts of poems from the third collection, written out as prose and simply *uttered*, always by Daisy, the self-exploring heroine who is "tired of the gender of things":

> *Dreams came into the ring*
> *like third-string fighters . . .*
> *each one a bad bet*
> *who might win*
> *because there was no other.*
>
> *I stared at them*
> *concentrating on the abyss,*
> *the way one looks down into a rock quarry . . .*
>
> *You taught me*
> *to believe in dreams,*
> *thus I was the dredger.*
>
> *I have come back*
> *but disorder is not what it was.*
> *I have lost the trick of it!*
>
> *I stand at this old window*
> *complaining . . .*
> *allowing myself the wasted life.*
>
> *This is madness*
> *but a kind of hunger . . .*

However effective, and ultimately reductive, such utterance may sound within the play, the mere fact that it is set down there as merely spoken prose suggests what Sexton's entire career—"submerged in my own past / and my own madness"—has imposed upon her talent: the priestess' commitment to survival at the expense of artifice or appearance:

> *To be occupied or conquered is nothing—*
> *to remain is all! . . .*

and again, from the final "affirmative" poem, "Live":

Even so,
I kept right on going on,
a sort of human statement,
lugging myself as if
I were a sawed-off body
in the trunk . . .

a hostage to the perpetuation of the self, even if it is in "the domain of silence, / the kingdom of the crazy and the sleeper." So assured, in these poems which won her a Pulitzer Prize, and in the ones to come after, is Anne Sexton of her hieratic position ("Everyone has left me / except my muse *that good nurse*") that she can afford, literally, to say anything and know that for all the dross it will be, in some way, a poem. "I am an identical being," she proclaims, and it might indeed be the sibyl talking, confident that what is said has its virulent, its vatic status because *she says it*, out of the welter of love, "that red disease," and of death, "an old belonging"—

I am your daughter, your sweetmeat,
your priest, your mouth and your bird
and I will tell you all stories
until I am laid away forever,
a thin gray banner.

LOUIS SIMPSON

"The Hunger in My Vitals Is for Some Credible Extravaganza"

ALEGENDARY predecessor of mine, this poet, I can remember, was the object, almost the victim of my envious wonder as I regarded him, obliquely, in the halls of Columbia University, where his three years of wartime service had caused Simpson's classroom education to overlap with my own. I knew he had been raised in Jamaica—not the suburbs but the South, that West Indian island where "the sun was drawn bleeding across the hills," as he said of it in a poem written when he was nineteen, that Caribbean paradise where

> *Death, a delightful life-long disease,*
> *Sighs in sideways languor of twisted trees . . .*

—and that he had renounced this tropical nurture in some dissatisfaction, anyway some ambiguity of response. In his novel *Riverside Drive*, as a confirmed if adoptive New Yorker, he was to define the situation this way, with a characteristic insertion of self into surround, seeking a dozen years later the widest possible locus for perception:

> Only in the north is history made. In the north man has contended with nature and earned his right to a roof, a hearth and a book. But in the tropics how can you achieve anything? You can't even tell good from bad. There are no seasons; the sun shines equally on good and evil; there are neither punishments nor rewards . . .

As I saw him, then, Louis Simpson was resuming an academic career interrupted by the war—though as he was often to put it later in his poems, he was also resuming a war, a war that *was* inward, according to Miss Moore's famous prescription, a war with these United States that had been merely intermitted by an overseas engagement, from Normandy through Holland and Bastogne to Berchtesgaden, which was surely the last of its kind: "to every man," Simpson remarks in one of his terrible aphorisms, "his war seems final, for *that* was the war in which he had exhausted himself." After winning the bronze star and the purple heart in all that fighting,* Simpson was back in the arena of his own true hostilities, the national conflict having given him, like Yeats' spirits, metaphors for poetry; if in fact we consider Simpson's war poetry as a version of pastoral, and his poems about America and his life there as a collection of military tattoos, we shall come closer to the exasperated spirit of the man, who like any modern Odysseus returns from his wanderings to find the real battle on his own doorstep, in his own hall, at his own bedside. But I saw none of this as I spied on Simpson between classes. I had heard that he was finishing up his degree—weren't we all?—before leaving New York for the Sorbonne, and neither the exoticism nor the heroism of the poet's career inspired my envy: what made him legendary for me and for my friends was that in 1949, *while still in school,* Louis Simpson had published a collection of his poems, "more or less in the order of composition, the poems his friends like best," as Theodore Hoffman said in his preface to *The Arrivistes,* a privately printed book in very plain wrappers, dedicated to Mark Van Doren, and including work from the author's seventeenth to twenty-sixth years.

If Simpson's military career and the sense of his displaced biography afforded the nourishing terms for his poetic progress, which has steadily, even relentlessly, attached itself to the condition of his country, his academic career has fed upon itself, and as we look *back* on the honors list, it is difficult to discern the breach at all, so perfectly healed is the tissue of achievements and distinctions: corresponding to those military medals, a Ph.D. from Columbia and a Prix de Rome; a doctoral dissertation on James Hogg, the author of the *Memoirs of a Justified Sinner;* a clutch of fellowships even as the poet, along with two others, produced a first selection of the most effective anthology of the period, *New Poets of England and America,* a compilation which required Simpson to read the work of some three hundred poets by his own count. The ineluctable current bore Simpson onward—a Pulitzer Prize for Poetry in 1964 and Professorships in English at various universities, a wife and children. Simpson's own commentary on this trajectory can be, perhaps unfairly, elicited from the titles of his first four books in the order of their writing:

---

* And receiving his American citizenship at Berchtesgaden.

> *The Arrivistes* (1949)
> *Good News of Death* (1955)
> *A Dream of Governors* (1959)
> *At the End of the Open Road* (1963)

It is a sad, successful story.

What I think spurred my envy along with my admiration of *The Arrivistes* as it came to my hands in 1949 was that it seemed not so much different from what the rest of us wanted to do, even in school, but that it seemed, simply, better: wittier, more intelligent, and crowded with a sense of a various and complex experience unavailable to undergraduates whose careers were altogether unexposed to the illuminations that led Simpson to say, as a soldier on leave in Paris:

> *. . . We, on the other side,*
> *Are still intruders to our atmosphere.*
> *Concrete and cactus are the real*
> *American tragedy.*
> *We should collect our souvenirs and leave.*

What we lacked, and what we felt or rather heard in Simpson, was "syllables of other people's time," the sense that having seen something else, however awful or elegant, he could return to what we were seeing and see it more clearly than we. Of course, reading the book today, it is easy to discover and to smile—though surely more in appreciation of the successful apprenticeship than in any spirit of dismissal—at the variations on traditional themes:

> *Love's funeral requires*
> *A lyrical instrument.*
> *A hollow heart with wires*
> *Will make the wind lament.*
> *The wreath I've sent*
> *Is roses wrapped with briars.*

This conjugation of the wry with the sweet, the savage with the neat, is articulated further by the poet into a typical learned imagery, a trope of experience *via* erudition in his long poem "Laertes in Paris." Here the control of the quatrain-and-couplet stanzas sets off the illuminating action of the poet's intelligence, which has moved beyond imitation to metaphor, beyond assimilation to invention:

> *Each man has his Hamlet, that dark other*
> *Self who is the conscience left behind,*
> *Who should be cherished clearly as a brother*

But is a sort of madness of the mind:
A serious dark-dressed entire shape
From which no slightest duty can escape.

And every man his Denmark, that dark country,
Familiar, incestuous, to which
He must return, in his turn to stand sentry
Until his blood has filled the Castle ditch,
And clear his father's honor with his life,
And take a perfect ignorance to wife.

From this point, Simpson is able to look in several directions at once—back to his easy exploits as a university wit, the archaizing elegist who has read everything and rearranged everything:

Who sails into the seagirls' teeth
A lifebuoy it shall be his wreath;
Who stands admirant of such views
His bones shall little boys amuse . . .

—and inward to a kind of Oedipal *acedie*, as disenchanted with promiscuity ("I think we have ruined our fathers") as he is with the domestic relations which leave "you and her nothing much to say / except the children," the muddle of middle-class marriage:

O marriage, the one sail to catch a wind!
Man comes from forests and from furnished rooms,
Out of the Egypt Land of Eat-Your-Spinach.
Love leads him like a river over booms
Into a woman like an open beach . . .

—and ahead to the dominant, sullen vision of America, or of what America, that *given dream*, has come to, when "the earth, so often saturated by colors false as blood, takes on your American gray." The secret, Simpson determines,

. . . is to overhear the world,
Seeing at once all phases of the moon.

An ambitious project, even for the disabused poet who has shelved the suburban sanctities in a heartless couplet:

So shall we manage, till the day
Death takes the furniture away.

But even in this first book, that to me had seemed the epitome of what one could aspire to as court jester to the College Outline Series, the tonality in which Simpson is to deal with his ambiguous citizenship is established, perhaps so precociously because of the European confrontations. "The West," Simpson said with an early arrogance he was later to dispute with himself, to question as he had questioned the provincial pieties which generated it, "the West was never an original, but one of many copies." Having discovered what the copies were of:

> *Back to Paris for a kindly refuge*
> *You come, demoralized and drenched again*
> *With your poetic soul like a black dog . . .*

or again, in prose: "In Italy, where everything had already happened, and every kind of man had already existed, I could pick up the life that someone else a few years or centuries ago had discarded. There I could sink into oblivion or happiness"—having determined that "the sadness of the provinces is the thought of life vanishing without a mark," the poet sets out to anatomize the prospect before him, determined to spare himself nothing, and to spare the landscape and its attendant blank history nothing of himself:

> *A night-sky like the passion of a saint*
> *That clears to let the sudden moon look through.*
> *It seems the very gods come here to paint*
> *And hang their pictures up for public view.*
> *Not like that sullen city in the West*
> *Blazing in a romantic solitude*
> *Where each American's a self-made artist*
> *Who knows his masterpiece will not be viewed.*

The wit of Simpson's rhymes keep whatever is apocalyptic in his emblems of a national *manteia* from toppling into the sententious, and of course he also wields a kind of wild humor, a post-dada wackiness which is exploited (read, diluted) in his later work but here has a kind of inspired ease to it, without strain or evasion:

> *The sun is reversible and may be used*
> *As a moon when necessary.*
> *The poodles of spring*
> *are on winter's traces.*

The book closes with something of all these notes mustered for two eclogues, very much influenced by the pastoral—in both senses—Auden (*For the Time Being* was published in 1944, and *The Age of Anxiety: A Baroque Eclogue* in 1948) and, at least in the title poem, suggesting the torment of the young poet still within my view: "In their confused state, Peter and Athridat cannot separate words from meaning." The *façon* of these poems was to be pursued by Simpson (to

pursue him?) into his second book, but in their gleeful unpleasantries
and elegiac wrenches—

> *The barge Espoir*
> *Thumps upstream with wet laundry*
> *On her gay lines.*
> *Lend me your camera—*

they suggest not so much concerted works as the advice Pound gave
the old Yeats, to write plays for the sake of the songs that would occur
in them, lyrical pieces, fragments and even figments which would
retain something of the intensity of their dramatic function even when
the matrix had fallen away. But these questions take Simpson into his
second book, and out of my envying purview at Columbia.

When a poet has initially presented himself, revealed his intentions
with all the stunning insolence of talent which Simpson displayed and
even commanded in his first book, affording a variety of tone along
with a persistence of temperament, it is surprising to come upon not so
much a development in his production, with that word's implication of
wraps being removed, the cerements trailing away like fussy clouds
from the transfigured body inside the sarcophagus, not so much a
growth as a gap, a silence just when, indeed, we had expected the
echoes so featly raised to ring still louder. But the echoes, as Simpson
says, increased the silences, and it was to be six years before the poet
published his second book (1955). "My mind," as he accounted for it
later, "was a negative on which colors and sensations were being
photographed"—a registering process which, in its necessary elisions of
the actual ("it is one thing to know, another to exist," the poet adds),
permitted Simpson to articulate his themes: the erosion of selfhood as
an analogue of the land's breakdown; the brutality of history which
affords a tenderness only in combat, in warfare and in erotic engage-
ments ("I never met a man who regretted making love"); the assump-
tion of a position outside the battle but not above it, the poet as a kind
of Lord of Misrule, the clown whose buffoon's mask suddenly falls off
and we look straight into the face, as Northrop Frye says about certain
Shakespearean comedies, of a beaten and ridiculed slave:

> *The city tilts and founders in a turbulence of gulls . . .*
> *Enough of these images—they set the teeth on edge!*
> *Life, if you like, is a metaphor of death—*
> *The difference is you, a place for the passing of breath.*
> *That is what man is. He is the time between,*
> *The palpable glass through which all things are seen.*

> *Nothing. Silence. A syllable. A word.*
> *Everything.*
> > *After your death this poem occurred.*
> > *You were the honored fragments from the Greek.*
> > *After your death these stones would move and speak.*

And not merely his themes but his music, the characteristic cadence of his sense-making, set down with a sharper relevance, the succinctness which is the illumination of a focussed method. Apposite here is Simpson's own brash note at the start of the collection:

> I do not apologize in these poems for my own experience, nor do I feel these things have been said before . . . I once thought of calling them Lyric and Dramatic Poems. They are lyric in manner, the sound is the form—the sound gives a dimension of feeling. Dramatic, because the poems deal more or less with a Dramatic or human situation, as opposed to metaphysics, literature or a transitory mood.

Songs from plays, in other words, as I suggested in other words about the eclogues which close *The Arrivistes,* a genre which applies *a fortiori* to the title poem of *Good News of Death.* Simpson is less successful, however, in enclosing the lyric impulse within his varsity-show pastoral than he is in letting the whole dramatic contour break through the order of lyric itself. In this sense, he is an apocalyptic or revelatory poet, rather than a dramatic or satiric one, and that is why the occasional poems, as one must see them to be, in *Good News of Death,* do so much more for Simpson than the affected structures which contain, and prop, and ultimately impede them:

> > > *. . . The Furies, vexed,*
> > *From Hades in their endless coils arise,*
> > *I see them at the corners of my eyes,*
> > *I run into the dark . . . And from this day*
> > *I run, I run, and can no longer stay*
> > *Than sleep, but that's another kind of pain,*
> > *And when I sleep I cry to wake again.*

The neat reversal of Caliban in the last line reminds us of the exploitive gift of this cultivated man, and if we consider Simpson a moment from this point of view, what is as surprising as the intervening silence is the increased mastery he shows in the deployment of the purely lyric instance upon a derived or conventional theme. Take the new poem "Early in the Morning," a highly condensed, three-stanza witticism about Antony, Cleopatra and Caesar, which in the first book would have run—indeed, *did* run—to the Higher Sententiousness in the form of symbolic glamor. Here, the form itself does the judging, and Simpson is free to concentrate the "story" and its referents into just a few tart words, as in this final stanza:

> *Caesar Augustus*
> *Cleared his phlegm.*
> *"Corpses disgust us.*
> *Cover them."*
> *Caesar Augustus*
> *In his time lay*
> *Dying, and just as*
> *Cold as they.*

There are a number of other poems still dedicated to the *conceded* mythologies in this second book, though Simpson is evidently less patient with the old stories than he was in his days of arrival, and more concerned to get on to the themes which will, from now on, seem unquestionably his if only because to no one else have they seemed even to be themes: the unpossessed yet ruined country whose promise was celebrated before its possibility. The briskness with which the poet deals with "The Man Who Married Magdalen" or gets on, in his poem "John the Baptist," with "the matter of the platter and the sword" has something dismissive about it. Even as the emptiness of "Aegean" has a certain relief in its gaiety:

> *There's no one any more*
> *But Echo on the shore,*
> *And Echo only laughs and runs away . . .*

so Simpson's old favorite, the theme of war's disasters, is considerably distanced by its formal precision and witty touristic allusions, as in "Memories of a Lost War":

> *The scene jags like a strip of celluloid,*
> *A mortar fires,*
> *Cinzano falls, Michelin is destroyed,*
> *The man of tires . . .*

Significantly, the one mythological subject lingered over is "Ulysses and the Sirens," for what concerns Simpson now is not the time away at the wars, but getting back to the home place. And in the first important poem of the book, "The Return," he transforms the Odyssean restoration into something very personal and strange—the characteristic discovery of this poet that in growing older we do not necessarily grow in any other way, but rather are *outgrown* by what we thought we had been and owned:

The entrance of the liner to the city
Was pure confusion, as if whales should neigh,
And you have lost your sea simplicity . . . *

As we grow older everything comes true . . .
We are the giants and we are the elves,
And soon we are the only mystery
And we must make the voyages ourselves,

And learn a parlor trick, wear one false nose,
And act as uncles, and do not disclose
What is not there at all,
Until we turn into the scenery
And children swing upon us like a tree.

It is the sense of being possessed by his landscape, and dispossessed by the terrible American emptiness which he sees so clearly, that gives Simpson his extraordinary poise and presence of mind—literally that allows his mind to be present in scenes ordinarily qualified by the absence of imagination: "the river glittered in moonlight. The dark Palisades loomed against the sky and the moon paced through heaven." That is the unmediated locus, upon which the poems, the consequential poems in *Good News of Death,* get to work, for as Simpson says in perhaps the darkest and deepest of all his exergues to the American experience, "whatever we imagine is real. The life we have not lived can never be finished."

Hence the studies in post-Columbian anecdote, beginning with the group called "American Preludes" which flashes before us the entire sweep of continental chaos, from the Elizabethans' view of us as Setebos:

This isle hath many goodly woods and deer,
Conies and fowl in incredible abundance;
The woods, not such as you find in Bohemia,
Barren and fruitless . . .

to the decline of the Wild West:

Vaquero, I have seen your ending days,
Looped in a lariat, dragged at the heels
Of the black horses . . .

and sets the scene for the drama of waste and spoliation which follows in the wake of the invasions to come; it is a *mise-en-scène* without allegory, and in its initial terms almost without affect:

* "The sea reminds us of our early loves," Simpson says in another poem in this book.

Maple and berry dogwood, oak, are kings.
The axe is lively and your pale palm stings
While Echo claps her hands on the bare hill.
The scene is clear. The air is chill.

The swish of the scythes of judgment, though, is audible in a poem like "Mississippi," where the kind of neat lament Simpson had reserved for fallen myths and wars lost abroad is now brought to bear—quite coolly, with more facts than fuss—on the home truths, the outrage of the War Between the States and inevitability of regional decay:

When we went down the river on a raft
So smooth it was and easy it would seem
Land moved but never we. Clouds faded aft
In castles. Trees would hurry in the dream
Of water, where we gazed, with this log craft
America suspended on a gleam . . .

And Brady photographs the men like flags
Still tilted in the charges where they died . . .

The river is too strong for bank or bar,
The landmarks change, and nothing would remain
But for the man who travels by a star,
Whose careful eye adjusts the course again . . .
Still shadowed at the wheel, his rich cigar
Glowed like a point of rectitude—Mark Twain.

If ever there were Mississippi nights,
If ever there was Dixie, as they sing,
Cry, you may cry, for all your true delights
Lost with the banjo and the Chicken Wing
Where old St. Joe slid on the water lights
And on into the dark, diminishing.

The wonder of it is that in this first apprehension of the native strain, Simpson's movement inward (in all literary structures, surely, the final direction of movement is inward) from Jamaica, that offshore island, to the other island, Manhattan, and penetrating ever deeper to that final dead center which is the end of the open road indeed, Simpson's grasp of the American transit is distributed with such equanimity that he can accommodate, in his vision, the buildings of New York, "dull pyramids, too large to be destroyed, / that even ruined could not be enjoyed," as well as the eroded pastoral of the redwoods "that held the eagles in their state / when Rome was still a rumor in the boughs." In the climactic poem in this book, a poem in which Simpson assigns himself his mission like a doom, it is the City which is hypostatized when "her father asks her where she's going—'Out!' And that means America. She may go far . . ." That mission is the burden of civilization itself, the enterprise of making a total human form out of a despised nature, and in "Islanders" the poet accepts in the person of his compatriots his tragic perspective:

> *. . . Beyond the daily wage*
> *They're caught in their own lives, the outer cage,*
> *And cry for exits, hoping to be shown*
> *A way by others, who have lost their own.*
> *And yet, seen from a distance and a height,*
> *How haunting are the islands of the night,*
> *The shores on which we dream with the deep tide*
> *Of darkness rushing in on every side . . .*

Four years later, in 1959, Simpson's third book was published, *A Dream of Governors*, which included four pieces from *The Arrivistes* of a decade before though none from *Good News of Death*, and borrowed its title from an Orphic line by Mark Van Doren (who has never shied out of the harness that pairs poetry and politics): "The deepest dream is of mad governors." And it is America from which, as from a sign of the apocalypse, Simpson will henceforth speak, whatever his enterprise and however despairing his undertaking:

> *It was my generation*
> *That put the Devil down*
> *With great enthusiasm.*
> *But now our occupation*
> *Is gone. Our education*
> *Is wasted on the town.*

The reminiscence of Othello in the topiary, the vainglorious black mercenary ("our occupation is gone") peering through the carefully clipped verses, is a typical effect of Simpson's at this point. The book, in fact, is chambered like a heart, its five parts patiently receiving their energies as the poet chooses to administer his sentence, never communicating or overlapping, so that the metahistorical group of lyrics which opens the book is curiously—though deliberately—irrelevant to the war poems in the section called and containing "The Runner" or to the love poems, and so forth. The partitioning is a way the poet has of knowing what he is talking about, and the voice in which he addresses himself to his task—"an easy and natural lyric charm," as Randall

Jarrell called it, veraciously if we take "charm" in its old sense as a magic, an incantation, a song—is certainly appropriate to the thirst for discretion, the kind of intellectual *apartheid* from which this poet draws his surest effects, being something of a mad governor himself, as I mean to show.

The indifference to History of personal history, the enclave-nature of the private life which particularly in its erotic and ecstatic course, as the word implies, is linear in form, irreversible in temper, accumulating a one-way anthology of significant episodes—the severance of individual happiness from the endless round of the cosmic comedy which is the history of nations, constitutes the doom of these first five poems, along with a certain redeeming satisfaction that human life persists at all, for as Simpson has said, "the will of things is for man not to exist; whatever we are, we are in spite of things." In any case, the drama of selfhood has nothing to do with the pageant of the Eternal Return:

> *Now Portugal is fading, and the state*
> *Of Castile rising purple on Peru;*
> *Now England, now America grows great—*
> *With which these lovers have nothing to do.*
>
> *What do they care if time, uncompassed, drift*
> *To China and the crew is a baboon?*
> *But let him whisper, always, and her lift*
> *The oceans in her eyelids to the moon . . .*

"These lovers" are the green shepherds—green in fecundity, green in lack of experience—whom Simpson has apostrophized in all his books, people who are concerned to endure the pains of their largely unconscious existence in order to enjoy the pleasures:

> *The groaning pole had gone more than a mile;*
> *These shepherds did not feel it where they loved,*
> *For time was sympathetic all the while*
> *And on the magic mountain nothing moved.*

Appropriate to this acceptation of selfhood *against* history and the promptings of mere reason is an imagery of fairy-tales, hieratic and rich in tropes of dismissal. So in the title poem, which is found in this section too, that double-barrelled notion—always associated, never assimilated—of life as a dream and the world as a stage, is inevitably invoked, *Märchen*-style:

> *The chorus in a play*
> *Declaimed: "The soul does well*
> *Keeping the middle way."*
> *He thought, That city fell;*

> *Man's life is founded on*
> *Folly at the extreme;*
> *When all is said and done*
> *The City is a dream.*

There is a towering irresponsibility, always, in metahistory, a refusal to commit the self to more than a handful of cyclical myths which for all their inclusive appeal ("everything is perfect, calm and clear") cannot save the poet, speaking in his own person, from his anguish:

> *In conversation, silence, sitting still,*
> *The demon of decorum and despair.*

We start over in the section called "My America," which offers an easy survey of the betrayed Cytherea, Simpson's beautifully "civilized" verses running counter to the awful wilderness that was here first and then so immediately converted into an awful subculture without ever passing through a metropolitan phase; consider these two pictures, the poet urges, on the one hand:

> *The treasures of Cathay were never found*
> *In this America, this wilderness*
> *Where the axe echoes with a lonely sound,*
> *The generations labor to possess*
> *And grave by grave we civilize the ground.*

and on the other,

> *Some day, when this uncertain continent*
> *Is marble, and men ask what was the good*
> *We lived by, dust may whisper "Hollywood."*

I have spoken of these poems as apocalyptic in their enterprise of converting the fallen nature which is the object of their vision into a total human form; the apocalyptic poet sees all of experience as part of his poem, assigning it a place in his vision, rather than (stoically) accepting his vision as one more fact in nature. There is an interesting parallel in the very construction of Simpson's verses to this terrorism of vision; it seems to me that his great lines, for instance the famous one I quoted earlier about the redwoods or the terrible "and grave by grave we civilize the ground," devour the poems in which they occur in precisely the way apocalyptic works devour nature; that is, refusing to occur *within* another structure, they attempt to *contain* everything they approach or touch—accounting in a sense for the exasperated or shrill or even frantic overtones in this poet's later work, "while beauty loses all her evidence." That is what I mean by Simpson as a mad governor—the intuition that he is always swallowing his substance by a judgment which *must* contain all the evidence, rather than letting the evidence reveal the judgment. Certainly, as Simpson says about women, "their selfishness will always entertain," and in the American poems he has been able to compass his prophetic rage within a language so physical, so *fitting* to the "country Columbus thought he found" that we *do* listen, we *are* entertained, understanding selfishness finally to be a conviction of identity, gained by governance:

> *The country that Columbus thought he found*
> *Is called America. It looks unreal,*
> *Unreal in winter and unreal in summer.*
> *When movies spread their giants on the air*
> *The boys drive to the next town, drunk on nothing.*
> *Youth has the secret. Only death looks real.*
>
> *We never die. When we are old we vanish*
> *Into the basement where we have our hobbies . . .*
> *And life is always borrowing and lending*
> *Like a good neighbor. How can we refuse?*

It is no surprise that this poet announces, in another place in this section, "the melancholy of the possible / unmeasures me"—for it is precisely the impossible that calls forth measure from him, permitting him and probably forcing him to assign the kind of coherent "government" to his oracles that makes the unreal so actual here. Simpson skips from his epiphanic America to "The Old World" for five poems to remind himself that this is not his matter; as before, he resents the metaphysical tourism which would allow his countrymen the comforts of self-acceptance:

> *Humankind, says the poet, cannot bear*
> *Too much reality.*
>   *Nor pleasure.*
> *And nothing is more melancholy*
> *Than to watch people enjoying themselves*
> *As much as they can.*

The war and love poems which end the book, including the long battle narrative "The Runner," which indeed Simpson rewrites in his novel *Riverside Drive*—though I prefer the earlier verse rendition for its speed and exhibited confidence in the medium—are far less interesting —less interested—achievements, and the sections are impatiently filled out by repeats from earlier work. Having come down from the hills, the dark fanatic delivers his alarums in the marketplace and withdraws, mission accomplished, the warning spoken. *A Dream of Governors* ends, then, on a characteristic note of removal. I have already spoken of Simpson as a Lord of Misrule whose mask, when the revels get beyond him, suddenly falls off—and that is what happens here. The fist is shaken one last time, in "Against the Age":

> *. . . our lives*
> *Are lives of State, the slogans for today.*
> *That wind is carrying the world away . . .*

and then abruptly, in "The Goodnight," a poem of astonishing tenderness when one notices how much it owes to those fierce old men Yeats and Frost, Simpson turns into his own green shepherd, saying good night to his sleeping daughter and dismissing the inevitable Armageddon he has just announced, abiding by his own humanity:

> *Who said that tenderness*
> *Will turn the heart to stone?*
> *May I endure her weakness*
> *As I endure my own.*
> *Better to say goodnight*
> *To breathing flesh and blood*
> *Each night as though the night*
> *Were always only good.*

Another pause of four years, and in 1963 appeared a book of Simpson's poems, his fourth, which won the Pulitzer Prize and brought him a certain wondering fame from the Quarterlies, whose critics (I was one of them) marvelled that a poet could speak so harshly of these States and still be prized by them. Further, *At the End of the Open Road* appeared to jettison all the scrimshaw-work which had been such a typical and such a reassuring aspect of Simpson's verse: as if, surely, anyone who had troubled to accommodate his vision so elegantly, so arbitrarily to the modes of convention could not be seriously troubled, or worse still, *troubling*. But the new book urged two conclusions upon us: first, that Simpson, determined as he was "to live in the tragic world forever," was a dangerous, a monitory presence among us:

> *There's no way out.*
> *You were born to waste your life.*
> *You were born to this middleclass life*
>
> *As others before you*
> *Were born to walk in procession*
> *To the temple, singing.*

and second, that the poet, acknowledging the presence of "that same old city-planner death" as he went about his duties in California, deploying "among the realtors and tennis-players his dark preoccupation," had achieved a cadence when he merely *spoke*, barely raising his voice above the unquestioned prose of the quotidian:

> *In the morning light a line*
> *Stretches forever. There my unlived life*
> *Rises, and I resist,*
> *Clinging to the steps of the throne . . .*
> *And my life, pitilessly demanding*
> *Rises forever in the morning light . . .*

had found a measure which fell as strictly within the compass of his requirements:

> *Love, my machine,*
> *We rise by this escape.*
> *We travel by the shocks we make.*
> *I am going into the night to find a world of my own . . .*

as any of his old lilt, yet with a new freedom that had the whole autonomy of the man's body under it; Simpson's lyric had become one with his speaking voice, a congruence which for any poet is the moment of release into himself, the moment when, no matter what is said, "the waves bring Eros in," as the Western Sea confirmed:

> *When men wanted the golden fleece*
> *It was not wool they wanted.*
> *They were the trophies that they sailed toward.*
>
> *They were the sea and the wind*
> *That hurled them over*
> *Into the sea. They were the fishes*
> *That stripped their thin bones. And they rose*
> *In the night in new constellations.*

Here, even when Simpson is not admonishing his country, his apocalyptic impulse to enclose the natural within the human until the elements themselves are encysted in man's form, to turn the heroic quest into an exploratory operation, is patent. Also, I think the poet relies more on *personality*, his own awareness of his voice ("I seek the word. The word is not forthcoming, O syllables of light . . . O dark cathedral!"), as a mortar to hold his lines together, dispensing him from certain evidences, certain cartilages in his text. There are still the devouring, oracular lines, of course—"The Open Road goes to the used-car lot," or again,

> *Then all the realtors,*
> *Pickpockets, salesmen and the actors performing*

> *Official scenarios,*
> *Turned a deaf ear, for they had contracted*
> *American dreams*

—but they no longer blow up the rest of the poem in Simpson's new rhythmical dispensation, but rather dig where they stand, as Browning said of the lyric necessity. I believe Simpson has said things just as devastating before, but in their new accommodation the damages are apparent, are not to be avoided:

> *We cannot turn or stay*
> *For though we sleep, and let the reins fall slack,*
> *The great cloud-wagons move*
> *Outward still, dreaming of a Pacific.*

Now that he has engorged his America, from the Atlantic cities where "when darkness falls on the enormous street the air is filled with Eros, whispering" and there are whole blocks "where no one lives," to that Hesperidean verge he cannot forgive himself for despising ("surely there is a secret which, if I knew it, would change everything"), Simpson speaks with the true might of apocalypse, finding everything within his own vision, nothing *outside* himself. That is what gives him the right to his ferocity: his refusal to dismiss anything that is not already encompassed by his own life. When he apostrophizes "the future in ruins!" and addresses himself to the rest of us:

> *O businessmen like ruins,*
> *bankers who are Bastilles,*
> *widows sadder than the shores of lakes,*
> *then you were happy, when you still could tremble!*

his own fate is also in question, and his version of our future, the terrible prophecy of "The Inner Part," cannot be muffled or missed as we would miss the imprecations of someone who separates himself from our condition:

> *When they had won the war*
> *And for the first time in history*
> *Americans were the most important people . . .*

> *When their daughters seemed as sensitive*
> *As the tip of a fly rod,*
> *And their sons were as smooth as a V-8 engine . . .*

> *Priests, examining the entrails of birds,*
> *Found the heart misplaced, and seeds*
> *As black as death, emitting a strange odor.*

Simpson ends this brief, brilliant book with his finest poem so far, "Lines Written Near San Francisco," an achievement that reaches so far outward largely because it reaches so far in, though the talent for the apocalyptic image, the oracular rhythm must not be discounted in the total effect, the gift for seeing the *telling* detail in a landscape otherwise determined to give away nothing, to repress its self-loathing even as it boasts of its prosperity:

> *Every night, at the end of America*
> *We taste our wine, looking at the Pacific.*
> *How sad it is, the end of America!*
>
> *While we were waiting for the land*
> *They'd finished it—with gas drums*
> *On the hilltops, cheap housing in the valleys*
>
> *Where lives are mean and wretched.*
> *But the banks thrive and the realtors*
> *Rejoice—they have their America.*
>
> *Still there is something unsettled in the air.*
> *Out there on the Pacific*
> *There's no America but the Marines . . .*

Discovering the whole of his country to be held in an everlasting and endless body, as Blake does, Simpson offers his revelations with a strange detachment at the end—or now, not strange but simply necessary in a poet who no longer finds the enemy outside or over the water, but in the vitals of a titanic self, that "credible extravaganza":

> *Whitman was wrong about the People,*
> *But right about himself. The land is within.*
> *At the end of the open road we come to ourselves.*

In 1965 was published that sober recognition of a poet's presence on the scene, a *Selected Poems of Louis Simpson*, who chose to include only the three love lyrics from his first book which he had reprinted in his third, a fair sampling from the second and third books, and a very full series from *At the End of the Open Road*, suggesting the perspective in which he wished to consider his own work, and the direction he intended to take. This direction was confirmed, even rather insistently sign-posted by a dozen new poems which continue, like Simpson's old classmate at Columbia Allen Ginsberg, "to cry out against the cities," and which initiate a more personal note in the loosened stanzas. From the first, Simpson has known how to entertain, how to underscore his effects with a shrewd application of clown white, and doubtless the terrible shopping centers of California feed his theatrics with a profound and deserving futility:

> *. . . I have suspected*
> *The Mixmaster knows more than I do,*
> *The air conditioner is the better poet.*
> *My right front tire is as bald as Odysseus—*
> *How much it must have suffered!*

The tonality is different, but it is still the old paranoiac articulation of the adversity of *things.* The city, of course, is the largest thing of all, and though Simpson declares himself resigned to the likelihood that Salvation will be granted by some kind of electric pencil-sharpener—

> *I must be patient with shapes*
> *Of automobile fenders and ketchup bottles.*
> *These things are the beginning*
> *Of things not visible to the naked eye—*

he sees the urban matrix as a failure, a force *counter* to our lives: "the streets lead on in burning lines / and giants tremble in electric chains . . . It seems that a man exists / only to say, Here I am in person." Of course the city is inside the self in Simpson's apocalyptic view, a sort of cancer to which the "young man" who is the poet's surrogate appeals:

> *Yet, over the roofs of the city*
> *The moon hangs, faithful to the last,*
> *Revealing her amorous craters.*
>
> *Muse of the city, hope of the insane,*
> *What would he do without you?*

And as the poet explores this transformed landscape ("a country that cannot fail," his Columbus reports, "for there's no finding it") by the moonlight which is his hope, he finds that in the cellar of his habitation, "shattering roots had broken through the wall, as though there was something in my rubbish that life would have at last." It appears, then, that even the city can be forgiven, can be given life, at least, and that nature, now inside the mind and body of an infinite man, can be given the "lineaments of gratified desire." It is not reality, Simpson says at the end, but it is, in terms like Dante's, conceivable:

> *. . . a vision*
> *Of mankind, like grass and flowers,*

The same over all the earth.
We forgave each other; we gave ourselves
Wholly over to words.
And straightway I was released
And sprang through an open gate.

Adventures of the Letter I by LOUIS SIMPSON

A poet will cast himself out by casting himself in other roles, voices overheard, vices overtaken, victories undermined until Louis Simpson's *Adventures* come to remind us that poetry is a lie that tells the truth, not a mere confession (so often forged) or even a proclamation (so often forced). He has enough confidence in himself to speak not only for but *as* others, now, and a good deal of this vigorous new investment of Louis Simpson's gifts takes stock in *behavior*, what other people do. It is the same confidence which has shed, in recent years, so many of the formal responsibilities which once made Simpson so recognizeable: the poet trusts in his unpropped utterance, and the poems therefore do not lean on, so much as they take loans from, the energy ordinarily associated with fiction—prose narrative, affabulation, talking about people. Idiosyncratic, and triumphant, is the poem "Simplicity", from the section called *Individuals*, in which the "letter I" pays a visit to a failed vampire from his past. What matters more than tone, mode, or even genre—what matters most in Simpson's evocation here is the capacity to typify and characterize *period perdition*, the style-of-loss of the times. Sparing us nothing, though he promises to, Simpson—or "I"—sketches his "portrait of a lady", and her horror is our own, for the failure of a woman is always the failure of a society, the collapse of a projected hope. When "a voice / from a high, barred window cries / 'write me a poem!' " the adventurer does his creature's bidding—he writes her a poem, but the poem he writes is an exorcism, for she is a condemned witch ("they want to remove my personality"), this modern lady with her bored solution ("when you're tired of something / you just throw it away"), her desperate self-cancellation ("someday, I suppose I'll be cured"). By its refusal to fall in with itself in matters of versification, the poem, like most of the others in this book, sustains the interest we take in stories, in *story-telling*, though the clarified emblems, the shaped experience remind us that for Simpson, in all his later work, a *poem* and a *fiction* are "as good as done", for they mean the same thing: what is made, like prayers.

He moves, in this book, from the imagined Russia where his mother was born to the imagined Indian Country he has so frequently apostrophized as our American Cytherea, then to the "individuals" whose fatuities and fates he is at a loss to discriminate (and happy to be there), and thence to that old "matter of the twentieth century" so close to his heart:

> *I am taking part in a great experiment—*
> *whether writers can live peacefully in the suburbs*
> *and not be bored to death.*
>
> *As Whitman said, an American muse*
> *installed amid the kitchen ware.*
> *And we have wonderful household appliances . . .*
> *now tell me about the poets.*

The finale of these adventures, and I think the finest poem in the book—a collection constantly tugging itself in the direction of *interest* quite literally, in the direction, that is, of being *in the middle of things* —the poem which suggests where Simpson will turn up next, and certainly what he will turn down, is the one which gives its title to the last section, "The Foggy Lanes." Here, where "the houses seem to be floating / in the fog, like lights at sea," Simpson's "I" visits a kind of litmus-paper locality with various allegorical figures—"a man who spoke of the ancient Scottish poets", and then "a radical who said that everything is corrupt", and even "a man from an insurance company / who said I needed 'more protection'." Dismissing these *others* whom he has so tellingly invoked throughout the book, "I" concludes:

> *Walking in the foggy lane*
> *I try to keep my attention fixed*
> *on the uneven, muddy surface . . .*
> *the pools made by the rain,*
> *and wheel-ruts, and wet leaves,*
> *and the rustling of small animals.*

It is only by casting out, as I have intimated, that Simpson has come upon his identity, that aspiring openness to experience, neither imposing nor opposing, but ready: "I try to keep my attention fixed / on the uneven, muddy surface." It is a good program for poetry, and likely to afford, in the future, the same rewards we have come to enjoy at present, as in the past, from this poet:

> *And now we talk of 'the inner life'*
> *and I ask myself, where is it?*
> *Not here, in these streets and houses,*
> *so I think it must be found*

in indolence, pure indolence,
an ocean of darkness,
in silence, an arm of the moon,
a hand that enters slowly.

American Poetry Review, 1972

W. D. SNODGRASS

"There's Something Beats the Same in Opposed Hearts."

T HE TIMES divide us against ourselves, so that we propitiate what
we would save of personality by savaging what falls from us,
what vanishes; there is a dialectical impulse we all endure, I think, a
vexed energy forever urging the meaning of our loves by means of our
hates, the justification of gardens, say, by the weeds we guard them
from, the hope of selfhood to be found by expelling the foreign self
rather than frequenting it. As if we remembered that *divorce* and
diversion share the one root, we project upon the world the forking
members of our will, casting about for dualities, oppositions, enemies
—indeed *casting* (in both the thrusting and the immobilizing sense)
into dichotomous roles men who would be astonished to find them-
selves so encamped in controversion. And women too; think, as this
poet has thought, of the dissociation of the Naughty Mommy, the
witch, the vampire ("Why so drawn, so worn, my dearest," Snodgrass'
vampire asks, in the cadence of Sir John Suckling—of course—"When
I do need looking after / and there's so much to be done, / Dear, it
surely isn't fair / so to hang on everyone. / Or don't you care?"), from
that aspect of our mothers which ranges quite as delusively from
Miss America to the Madonna. "She stands in the dead center," the
poet has written in a poem called "The Mother," and he glosses the
line by this remark in an essay: "woman and death are one; [it is]
our common tendency to see death as a mother, the grave as a
womb." And there is the other, equally common tendency which the
poet accounts for in a late, rich poem (wittily titled "Leaving Ithaca":
it is Ulysses setting out from Cornell, leaving "the old house rough-

hewn as we found it . . . / no doubt it would have spoiled us to remain"), the tendency to see life itself as a loved woman, invagination as voyaging. The poem is dedicated "to my plaster replica of the Aphrodite of Melos" and thus liminally, thus intimately, the characteristic Snodgrass note is struck, the goddess invoked, the Real Presence affirmed—but in plaster; and rightly enough, Love's Lady in this poem comes, like death, from the poet's mother, "who mailed you, packed in towels, when I first married." The complications of Snodgrass' response to Eros are articulated by the transient households, the odyssey of faculty decorums, made evident in the neat facture of the encapsulating quatrains, the exasperated diction of all English teachers who must make do, and in this case make don't, with replica love-goddesses:

> . . . *Oh everloving Lady,*
> *You had been ruined quite enough already;*
> *Now the children have chipped off half your nose.*
>
> *My first wife tried to keep you in the attic;*
> *Some thought your breasts just so-so and your waist,*
> *Thick with childbearing, not for modern taste.*
> *My father thought you lewd and flicked your buttocks.*
>
> *One giddy night, blonde Susan tipped your stand—*
> *You, true to your best style, lost your head.*
> *You just won't learn how much smart girls will shed*
> *This year. Well, we must both look secondhand.*
>
> *Lady, we've cost each other . . .*

Expenses of the flesh, though, can be accounted for with a certain grim and grainy efficiency which keeps the early poetry of Snodgrass cool. The first pieces in his first book, *Heart's Needle* (published in 1959, awarded the 1960 Pulitzer Prize), are poems of homecoming, the squalor and spookiness of repatriation (as a soldier, a son, a citizen, a lover . . .) bringing home indeed a fatal division from the self:

> . . . *you never*
> *Escape the sense in everything you do,*
> *"We've done this all once. Have I been here, ever?"*

And it is precisely by this dividing, this sundering of self from the data which generally reassure, and by peering for a significant glimpse of "the shore of our first life," that Snodgrass, with what Robert Lowell calls "a shrill authoritative eloquence" in this first book, pairs himself off in order to arrive at identity, "to kneel by my old face and know my name."

This goal, the destination of all divided passages, is announced at

once, in the next group of poems, which are an inspection of childhood
(*Heart's Needle*, it should be said, is arranged in clumps of poems
along the choked watercourse of the poet's biography: return from
war, stock-taking of self and surround which includes the body and
the body's history, then teaching, and marriage, fatherhood and di-
vorce), and though such completion is not here to be achieved in terms
of what Macbeth calls "understood relations" that bring forth the
"secretest man of blood," the goal is nevertheless sighted, sensed as a
poet will sense such things, in terms of the senses. For in—or out
of—the welter of our experience, we look for the *sign* of that experi-
ence, the emblem to mediate it, as T. S. Eliot distinguishes between the
experience and its meaning when he says that a man may have the one
and yet miss the other. It is in the earlier poetry of Snodgrass that we
have the experience presented, but divided somehow from its meaning,
and in his later poetry that we have the meaning too, the sign not
merely stated, named, but enacted. Here in *Heart's Needle*, then, sen-
sory images will be the *materia melica*, even in compositional stresses,
so that the four little strophes ("Now I can earn a living," Snodgrass
crows in his second book, "by turning out elegant strophes") of "At
the Park Dance" have the gritty concreteness of stones, conglomerates,
made things, poems:

> As the melting park
> darkens, the firefly winks
> to signal loving strangers
> from their pavilion
> lined with Easter colored
> lights, fading out together
>
> until they merge with
> weathered huge trees and join
> the small frogs, those warm singers;
> and they have achieved
> love's vanishing point
> where all perspectives mingle,
>
> where even the most
> close things are indistinct
> or lost, where bright worlds shrink,
> they will grope to find
> blind eyes make all one world;
> their unseen arms, horizons.
>
> Beyond, jagged stars
> are glinting like jacks hurled

farther than eyes can gather;
on the dancefloor, girls
turn, vague as milkweed floats
bobbing from childish fingers.

The formal organization of this bleak lyric, along with the imagery and the action of it, deserves inspection, for it is cunning in the rehearsal and incarnation of its theme ("William Empson was my first love," says Snodgrass, who has loved many times since), that elusive and perhaps illusory fusion of separates achieved at "love's vanishing point where all perspectives mingle." Though the poem, glanced at on the page, appears not to rhyme, when it is read aloud certain harmonies inhere, inhabit the reading voice, and enhance the effect of a fugitive unison which is the poem's burden: we notice almost simultaneously that the first syllable of each second and fifth line rhymes or assonates with the final syllable of each first and fourth line; and that the stanzas are in fact constructed in paired crescendos of five, six and seven syllables thus bonded by the edge-rhymes, the five- and six-syllable lines ending in an accented syllable, the longer seven-syllable lines ending in an unaccented one, with a single exception (the third line of the third stanza, where the final accented syllable *shrink* seems to withdraw from the missing seventh syllable). Yes, and then we see that there are terminal rhymes too, but separated by apparently irregular groups of lines: *strangers* in the third line of the first stophe, *singers* and *mingle* in the third and sixth lines of the second strophe, *fingers* in the sixth line of the last strophe; then are the intervals at which these terminal rhymes occur so irregular after all? They come always in the third or the sixth lines in each strophe—and if we consider the remaining third and sixth lines in the other strophes, we find further congruities—*together* in the sixth line of the first strophe, rhymes with *gather* in the third line of the last; there is a rhyme series related to the *singers / fingers / strangers / mingle* group in *winks, indistinct* and *shrink*, and further rhymes in *join* and *point* in the second strophe and in *world* and *hurled* in the third and fourth. In fact, then, after a little unravelling, *all* the teleutons but one (which is, appropriately, *floats* in the penultimate line) are bound into the system of sound-relationships which articulate, which *are* the poem's meaning: "all one world." But it is, in Snodgrass' early work, a world made one in part by blindness, by abjuring the clear vision and the firm grasp—hence the evanescence, the unreality of the things in the poem, the phenomena of toying: the amusement park, the fireflies, the pavilion with Easter-colored lights, the small frogs that are "warm singers," I believe, because of the mating season, the stars glinting like jacks in a reduction of the cosmos to a child's game, and the final, crucial likeness of girls drifting across the dancefloor "vague as milkweed floats / bobbing from childish fingers." Before we conflate a certain prepubertal insistence, which is carried through the poem to this clinching figure, with the *action* of the poem, the locus of its verbs, let us loiter about the image of those milkweed floats, for they will recur, a few poems on in this book, again accorded a curious ambiguity of intent, a sexuality both gathered and dispersed, won and lost in the consciousness of the speaker. In the poem "Winter Bouquet" Snodgrass speaks of the "dry vaginal pods of milkweed" and of the war years when "many a wife / wandered the fields after such pods to fill life / preservers so another man might not be lost." And ends the poem, another of his returning-soldier, peace-is-war emblems, with the scattering of the bouquet, "white bursts of quilly weedseed for the wide arms / and eyes of the children squealing where they drift /. . . like an airlift / of satyrs or a conservative, warm snow." In this poem, as in "At the Park Dance," the outright sexual, generative function of the milkweed is scanted, flouted actually, for the elusive, fantastic ("like an airlift of satyrs") and even asexual ("a conservative, warm snow") aspect: "vague as milkweed floats / bobbing from childish fingers." If the pods are vaginal, they are also dry; and if they are seeds, suggesting the same regeneration as the Easter lights earlier in the poem, they escape our grasp, as the lights fade out. And that is the other significant organization of the poem— the image of fading, impressed upon us throughout by the verbs which indicate the transient in their very convergence: the *melting* park *darkens,* the firefly *winks* (suggesting the dark rather than the luminous intervals of his cycle), the colored lights *fade out* until they *merge* with the *weathered* (blurred? in any case no longer untouched) trees, and *join* the singing frogs to *achieve love's vanishing point* (the expression is a study in itself, being both that location toward which all impulses tend and one where all are cancelled out), where all perspectives *mingle;* the *lost* and the *unseen* contribute to this intensity of the void, and *beyond,* out of eyesight, the stars, *hurled* there, are *glinting;* finally, the girls *turn* like the milkweed *floats,* and elude childish fingers, *bobbing* on the dancefloor.

Every effect, then, every device and technique and principle of organization in this little poem supports its cause in the same way: a unison, a sounding-as-one, but fugitive, costly, and not to be trusted. The experience of convergence, more hinted at than held onto, is less significant to Snodgrass than the separations to be overcome, the divisions registered.

Dissociation—the breakup of personality into what Melville called *isolatos,* "not acknowledging the common continent of men," a place that *contains* the human condition, nor even trusting that we are members of ourselves as well as of one another—dissociation has no further range, no finer ruse than the one Snodgrass, a man ruefully assenting to masks:

> Poets of our generation—those of us who have gone so far in criticism and analysis that we cannot ever turn back and be innocent . . . have such extensive resources for disguising ourselves from ourselves . . .

was to employ at about this period, when his poems were being published in those Ghibelline reviews and anthologies which, among the blood-feuds of our postwar poetry, stood for the kempt and the cooked against the Guelph party which did not stand at all but rather coasted downstream. For if we look Snodgrass up in the "biographies and bibliography" section of the anthology *A Controversy of Poets* (which attempted to muster forces from both factions), we find the following laconic entry:

> Born in Wilkinsburg, Pennsylvania, in 1926 . . . Teaches at Wayne State University in Detroit. Deeply influenced by the Texas poet S. S. Gardons.

And if, concerned to get to the bottom of that *deep influence* and undistracted by something odd in the sound of the name, we should look up S. S. Gardons (who does not appear to have published a volume of verse) in, say, the second selection of the *New Poets of England and America* anthology (almost entirely a Ghibelline affair), we find two poems and the following preposterous entry in the biographical notes:

> Born in Red Creek, Texas, 1929. Works as a gas station attendant in Fort Worth . . .

Now when a man spells his name backward and concocts another biography for his reversed self (slicing three years off his age and adding, with that gas-station attendant's job, a touch of Noble Savagery to a *universitaire* career felt to be perhaps too unremittingly tame), it is evident that he is crucially conscious of the divided nature of his aims, of the separatist impulses which lead him to come down so much harder on the divorce than on the marriage of true minds.

Indeed, I think Snodgrass abandoned the supposititious self because it was insufficiently opposing. The poems by S. S. Gardons are not different *enough* from the poems by W. D. Snodgrass to warrant the labor of sustaining a pseudonym; both of those in the *New Poets of England and America* anthology (others appeared in the *Hudson Review*) fit too neatly into the anfractuosities of *Heart's Needle*—indeed, "To a Child" actually belongs among the torments of the title poem, that excruciating cycle of apostrophes to the seed and symbol of division, the poet's daughter ("an only daughter is the needle of the heart"), the child addressed as the identity lost in divorce proceedings, so that when S. S. Gardons, a highly psychoanalytical type for a pump attendant, reports:

> *We have seen the dodder*
> *That parasitic pale love-vine that thrives*
> *Coiling the zinnias in the ardor*
> *　Of its close embrace.*
> *　We have seen men abase*
> *Themselves to their embittered wives;*
>
> *And I have let you see my mother,*
> *　That old sow in her sty*
> *　Who would devour her farrow;*
> *We have seen my sister in her narrow*
> *Grave. Without love we die;*
> *　With love we kill each other . . .*

we know he is saying no more, and no less, than W. D. Snodgrass who says, in the third poem of "Heart's Needle," to "the child between them":

> *Love's wishbone, child, although I've gone*
> *As men must and let you be drawn*
> *　Off to appease another,*
> *It may help that a Chinese play*
> *Or Solomon himself might say*
> *　I am your real mother*

—too neatly and too needfully to fit anywhere else. With one terrible delineation of "The Mother," generating precisely that opposing self which Gardons invokes in order to ward off (which is what, after all, *gardons* means): "She hallucinates in their right places / their after-images, reversed and faint," the *alter ego* is offered up, one may say, on the altar of egoism, and Snodgrass returns to Snodgrass, to that triumphant or at least intrepid assertion of his own old wretchedness:

> *Your name's safe conduct into love or verse;*
> *Snodgrass is walking through the universe.*
>
> *Your name's absurd, miraculous as sperm*
> *And as decisive. If you can't coerce*
> *One thing outside yourself, why you're the poet! . . .*
> *If all this world runs battlefield or worse,*
> *Come, let us wipe our glasses on our shirts:*
> *Snodgrass is walking through the universe.*

And the universe, since Snodgrass is but the one poet, unable to pair off his responses, his responsibility, into that second, separate self—the universe will not be one but rather, in the body of this man's poetry, divided against itself, disparate in his despair. *Oppositions* will contrive all of Snodgrass' poetry, in both *Heart's Needle* and in the book that followed it in 1968, *After Experience;* will control what I have called its body, since a living body must have two parents, must branch its passions in two directions until, as Snodgrass says, they may be neither humane nor loyal; will contribute that tone of characteristic *aigreur* we hear in his Orpheus' address to the Powers of the Underworld, "who are all bright worlds' negative":

> *. . . And I went on*
> *Rich in the loss of all I sing*
> *To the threshold of waking light,*
> *To larksong and the live, gray dawn.*
> *So night by night, my life has gone.*

Not only the confrontation, the combat of self and others, mothers against fathers, fathers against sons, mothers against daughters, brothers against sisters—Snodgrass articulates every member of the family romance, the family rebellion under the terrible rubric:

> *Whom equal weakness binds together*
> *none shall separate . . .*

—but the conflict of self against its accommodating yet refractory body engages this poet's art. Among the most striking of Snodgrass' poems are those that deal with sickness, with dying, with the recalcitrant soma doing battle against the raging psyche. "I was drifting," he says in "The Operation," and all the identity which that enormous pronoun wields is set against that other, that unknown non-person on the hospital card:

> *The body with its tributary poisons borne. . . .*
> *To the arena, humming, vast with lights;* blank hero,
> Shackled and spellbound, to enact my deed.

The sense that our body is not ourselves, yet does our deed, is a cruel one, and made crueller still by any afternoon in the woods. The cardinal sings, and his message, to the victimized poet, hankering after reconciliation, "outspeaks a vital claim" unavailable to opposing human selves "that only in circumference embrace / and by divorce." Here is what the cardinal says, and it is not until the end of *After Experience* that Snodgrass, some fifteen years later, can come up with a comparable song, an equivalent assertion of undivided selfhood:

> *The world's not done to me;*
> *it is what I do;*
> *whom I speak shall be;*
> *I music out my name*
> *and what I tell is who*
> *in all the world I am.*

For the rest of *Heart's Needle,* and for the ten parts of the title poem in particular, there will be a lyric necessity, a formal requirement to stand over and against singleness of experience, unity of identity. The poet who reminds us—in his accomplished verse-making, his *turning,* that is, upon himself—of Verlaine, as we see by setting "Autumn Scene" beside "Colloque Sentimental":

> *In the public gardens they are walking.*
> *The skies appear correct and glum.*
> *Their heels click drily; they are talking.*
> *Behind their backs, the elms repeat some shocking*
> *News of what's to come . . .*

> Dans le vieux parc solitaire et glacé,
> Deux formes ont tout à l'heure passé.

> Leurs yeux sont morts et leurs lèvres sont molles,
> Et l'on entend à peine leurs paroles.

> Dans le vieux parc solitaire et glacé,
> Deux spectres ont evoqué le passé . . .

And who reminds us—in his bitter mistrust of precisely the accomplishments he is prized (and paid) for—of Heine, as the next double exhibit proves:

> *I memorize you, bit by bit,*
> *And must restore you in my verses*
> *To sell to magazines.*
> *We keep what our times allow*
> *And turn our grief into play . . .*

> Sie [die Kastraten] sangen von Liebessehnen,
> Von Liebe und Liebeserguss;
> Die Damen schwammen in Tränen
> Bei solchem Kunstgenuss.

And who reminds us, most of all—not only in his bereft landscapes, the scenery of a disquieted soul, but in his agonized inquest of motives—of

Tennyson, the parallel indicated if we set some of "The Examination" beside a little of Tennyson's "The Dead Prophet":

. . . *"We shall continue, please." Now, once again, he bends*
To the skull, and its clamped tissues. Into the cran-
ial cavity, he plunges both of his hands
Like obstetric forceps and lifts out the great brain,

Holds it aloft, then gives it to the next who stands
Beside him. Each, in turn, accepts it, although loath,
Turns it this way, that way, feels it between his hands
Like a wasp's nest or some sickening outsized growth.

They must decide what thoughts each part of it must think;
They tap at, then listen beside, each suspect lobe;
Next with a crow's quill dipped into India ink,
Mark on its surface, as if on a map or globe,

Those dangerous areas which need to be excised . . .

. . . She tumbled his helpless corpse about.
'Small blemish upon the skin!
But I think we know what is fair without
Is often as foul within.'

She crouched, she tore him part from part,
And out of his body she drew
The red 'blood-eagle' of liver and heart;
She held them up to the view;

She gabbled, as she groped in the dead,
And all the people were pleased;
'See what a little heart,' she said,
'And the liver is half-diseased!' . . .

The poet who suggests and sustains these associations—and Snodgrass has translated, we recall, from many German and French poets as well as taught widely in the standard English and American repertory—reaches, in *After Experience*, to a new richness of dialectic energy in the declaration of hostilities, in the choosing up of sides. There are, indeed, two poems here which are the masterpieces of Snodgrass' sundered song, the title poem and another, "A Visitation," which initiate—by their very accommodation in formal terms of the division, the opposition, the partition of voices—that ultimate and utter state-ment which becomes a closing of gaps, a filling of the rift within the lute. "A Visitation" is a dialogue in terza rima (so that the two voices are joined by their braided rhymes, even when the alternating indented stanzas pursue entirely discrepant lines of statement) between the ex-soldier poet and Eichmann's ghost. It is a dialogue, not a quarrel, in which the offended self realizes (when reminded by the obsequious spirit, "there's something beats the same in opposed hearts") that by the very attempt to fend off, to avert the monster *other* (as by Gardons, explicitly), it will creep upon us:

> . . . *All the more cause I should keep you there—*
> *How subtle all that chokes us with disgust*
> *Moves in implacably to rule us, unaware.*

And the ghost, ending the visitation, replies with a final pun ("you can look through me") which indicates how clearly Snodgrass has seen that the despised *other* can be exorcised only by acknowledgment, by acceptance, by assimilation, as in the rhyming central line of the ghost's last tercet (*somewhere* referring back to the poet's *there* and *unaware*), which indicates that the Eichmann in all of us is a recognized participant:

> *My own love, you're all I could wish to be.*
> *Close your eyes—I'll just wander off somewhere*
> *Or watch the way your world moves—you can look through me.*

The other supreme poem in Snodgrass's canon of Great Divorces is the one from which the second book draws its title, "After Experience Taught Me . . ." and it too is devised as a pairing off: it too consists of two voices, in alternating and indented pairs of lines, the rhymes again imbricating the whole thing together, though the voices are not, this time, in dialogue. "It seemed to me," Snodgrass remarks in an essay about the composition of one of the parts of "Heart's Needle," "and I have often found this to be so, that my poem could develop a structure adequate to my experience only if, like the old sonata form, it carried two separate thematic areas at the same time." Precisely, and for one area, in "After Experience Taught Me," he has taken the opening of Spinoza's essay "On the Improvement of the Understanding" in John Wild's translation:

> After experience has taught me that all the usual surroundings of social life are vain and futile; seeing that none of the objects of my fears contained in themselves anything either good or bad, except in so far as the mind is affected by them, I finally resolved to inquire whether there might be some real good having power to communicate itself, which would affect the mind singly, to the exclusion of all else; whether, in fact, there might be anything of

which the discovery and attainment would enable me to enjoy continuous, supreme, and unending happiness.

Casting this into rough pentameters, and with a little significant editing (such as the very modern substitution of "something" for "some real good having power to communicate itself"), Snodgrass achieves some eight lines of his poem, its "first area."

And for his second area, Snodgrass has recreated a lecture he says he heard in the Navy on the most effective way to kill a man in hand-to-hand combat. Unlike the cool, abstract and deliberative discourse of Snodgrass-as-lens-grinder, this second voice is brutal, colloquial and without modulation—it is Gardons-the-commando, and by an inspired piece of carpentry, the military lecture on jiffy-killing is bonded by rhyme with the inquiry into supreme and unending happiness to produce the disconcerting and critical music of this poem ("like the old sonata form") by which the poet had sought to enact his suffered oppositions from the start:

> *After experience taught me that all the ordinary*
> *Surroundings of social life are futile and vain;*
>
> *I'm going to show you something very*
> *Ugly: someday, it might save your life.*
>
> *Seeing that none of the things I feared contain*
> *In themselves anything either good or bad*
>
> *What if you get caught without a knife;*
> *Nothing—even a loop of piano wire;*
>
> *Excepting only in the effect they had*
> *Upon my mind, I resolved to inquire*
>
> *Take the first two fingers of this hand;*
> *Fork them out—kind of a "V for Victory"—*
>
> *Whether there might be something whose discovery*
> *Would grant me supreme, unending happiness.*
>
> *And jam them into the eyes of your enemy.*
> *You have to do this hard. Very hard. Then press . . .*

and so forth, to the last, unendurable opposition—

> *You must call up every strength you own*
> *And you can rip off the whole facial mask.*

> *Wishing to be, to act, to live. He must ask*
> *First, in other words, to actually exist.*

Snodgrass, however, is more than a mere intellectual terrorist, and he is not content merely to offer these versions of death-in-life, apparently exclusive and only related by their very unlikelihood together. The poem ends with a further-indented quatrain in yet a third voice, the poet's own, in which the other two speakers transcend their subjects, or are transcended—for the first time in all this poet's work—by a subject which includes them both, and the significances become one, united in an unanswerable but enduring question of the poet to himself:

> *And you, whiner, who wastes your time*
> *Dawdling over the remorseless earth,*
> *What evil, what unspeakable crime*
> *Have you made your life worth?*

In this final quatrain, where the Spinoza-poem and the commando-poem unite, death has taken the role of a continually regenerative process. The enemy in the commando-poem is also what stands between the speaker of the Spinoza-poem and his happiness: the external, superficial self. It is exactly the "facial mask" which the *philosopher* must rip off; and it is the *soldier*, executing a murder, who is asking to actually exist. Only such a violent, assertive response to life as the "unspeakable crime" of self-murder can justify living, and thereby lead to happiness. For it is a self-murder the poem presents, two times over. And this terrifying act of killing a self, even a false self, is the definitive act which runs death at last irrevocably into life, thought into action, all elements into their apparent opposites.

After this poem, Snodgrass no longer needs to divide in order to conquer, no longer needs to double himself—once he had said:

> *We shout along our bank to hear*
> *our voices returning from the hills to meet us.*
> We need the landscape to repeat us—

in order to create himself. He ends his second book with half a dozen poems of the unified self, the undistracted voice, speech of Shakespeare's "great creating nature" in whose accents death is heard unsevered from life, in whose rhythms the antagonism of the sexes, of self and body, parents and children, is absorbed, dissolved, fused. A clue to the subject of these poems, their necessary cause, is given by the best of the translations Snodgrass has included, fine English versions of Rilke's "Tapestry of the Lady with the Unicorn" and his "Archaic Torso of Apollo." Yes, the poems are about *art*, about works of art, about—with the exception of "Planting a Magnolia," which is the answer in this volume to the cardinal's overheard assertion in the first—five modern paintings, a Matisse, a Vuillard, a Manet, a Monet and a Van Gogh. All are written with a release, an expressive leisure, though never a looseness, from the old clinching forms which indicate that Snodgrass has come to terms with his own form, and the terms to which he has come *are* that form,

> *That will excite us, without hope,*
> *Returning in the rumors of*
> *Obscene blunt beauty that surrounds*
> *And will survive us.*
> *Before it dies.*

Only art can afford occasion for such transcendence, and Snodgrass has seized it with an authority which his embrace of otherness, his resolution of opposites, his death, if you like, alone warrants. "In nature," he says in an essay, "man alone has the choice to withdraw from the reality in which he lives, and so has the power to die, either metaphorically or literally." Snodgrass has, in these magnificent and explicit poems, died into the work, the created reality, of those other men, and of course made out of just that otherness something altogether his own —someone, as he says in "Manet: 'The Execution of the Emperor Maximilian,' " though I have twisted the tenses in his favor—

> *. . . someone has come,*
> *Declared significance, solved how these things relate*
> *To freedom, to our life's course, to eternity.*

GARY SNYDER

"To Hold Both History and Wilderness in Mind"

Pertinently, on the title-page of his first publication, appearing in 1959, when he was not yet thirty, this poet defined the name assigned to the work gathered together there: *Riprap*—"a cobble of stone laid on steep slick rock to make a trail for horses in the mountains." Advisedly, I take the term "work" in its strong sense, for Snyder has provided a gloss on these substantial poems which deserves to stand as a determinative frame for any account of his undertaking: "The rhythms of my poems follow the rhythm of the physical work I'm doing at any given time . . . *Riprap* is really a class of poems I wrote under the influence of the geology of the Sierra Nevada and the daily trail-crew work of picking up and placing granite stones in tight cobble patterns on hard slab. Walking, climbing, placing with the hands." And in his second collection, *Myths and Texts*, completed by 1956 but published only in 1960, Snyder intensifies the notion until it becomes an emblem of the art in general: "Poetry a riprap on the slick rock of metaphysics."

The poems that follow this defensive recipe:

> *ants and pebbles*
> *In the thin loam, each rock a word*
> *a creek-washed stone . . .*
> *all change, in thoughts,*
> *As well as things . . .*

constitute a mill of process: autonomous voices seem to speak through the poet, grinding together the conflicting perceptions of reality that permit the poet, in a state of rapt self-communion, to utter rather than merely address:

> Pressure of sun on the rockslide
> Whirled me in dizzy hop-and-step descent,
> Pool of pebbles buzzed in a Juniper shadow,
> Tiny tongue of a this-year rattlesnake flicked,
> I leaped, laughing for little boulder-color coil—
> Pounded by heat raced down the slabs to the creek
> Deep tumbling under arching walls and stuck
> Whole head and shoulders in the water:
> Stretched full on cobble—ears roaring
> Eyes open aching from the cold and faced a trout.

The point of riprap is to enable the traveller to ascend—to ascend on earth, not to slide back, nor to fly. The stone laid down has already been dressed by Pound, and by the famous formula of Dr. Williams: "no ideas but in things," yet it is his own work that Snyder is doing with it. Evidently he is as much in mortal fear as in mortal danger of vanishing with a screech into the Whitman Wind Tunnel, that celebrated American patent, and consequently clings to whatever will prop and counterweight his spirit, as by the work of hands:

> Lay down these words
> Before your mind like rocks.
> 　Placed solid, by hands
> In choice of place, set
> Before the body of the mind
> 　in space and time:
> Solidity of bark, leaf, or wall
> 　riprap of things

For all their oracular stance, then, turned away from the listener toward some inward audience, something in the self that may be convinced by all this substantiation, these poems are tough, sharp-edged, concentrated on the thing shown, "this moment one time true." Without Snyder's lifting a metrical foot, the plain facts are allowed, are obliged to comment on each other, and except for the reminder that it was the poet to whom they "happened," the facts are made to speak for themselves, as if they were their own occasion:

> We finished clearing the last
> Section of trail by noon,
> High on the ridge-side
> Two thousand feet above the creek—
> Reached the pass, went on

Beyond the white pine groves,
Granite shoulders, to a small
Green meadow watered by the snow,
Edged with Aspen . . .
                              I spied
A glitter, and found a flake
Black volcanic glass—obsidian—
By a flower. Hands and knees
Pushing the Bear grass, thousands
Of arrowhead leavings over a
Hundred yards. Not one good
Head, just razor flakes
On a hill snowed all but summer,
A land of fat summer deer,
They came to camp. On their
Own trails. I followed my own
Trail here. Picked up the cold-drill,
Pick, singlejack, and sack
Of dynamite.
Ten thousand years.

The tremendous impact of that last line, a concussion against the "things," the obsidian arrow-flakes which precede it, is a characteristic example of this poet's *ideas*. Once he has announced his occupational skills as logging, forestry, carpentry and seamanship, it is not surprising that Gary Snyder, who says that as a poet he holds "the most archaic values on earth," should have left this country where the forests have been stripped or burned off, where "the crews have departed," for the interior exile of Japanese monasteries and the rapturous life of a cosmic bum: "There is not much wilderness left to destroy, and the nature in the mind is being logged and burned off. The soil and human sensibilities may erode away forever, even without a great war." Thus this first little book can be read through as a circumstantial journal of alienation, a progressive engrossment by otherness:

                . . . a week and I go back
Down 99, through towns, to San Francisco and Japan.
All America south and east,
Twenty-five years in it brought to a trip-stop
Mind-point, where I turn
Caught more on this land—rock tree and man,
Awake, than ever before, yet ready to leave.

It is a departure from a world of fragments. The literature of process, as Northrop Frye has pointed out, being based on an irregular and unpredictable coincidence of patterns in experience, tends to seek the brief or even the partial utterance—to center itself in the lyrical:

> *Raven*
> *on a roost of furs*
> *No bird in a bird-book*
> *black as the sun.*

Lapidary as they are—and there is a visionary clarity about these twenty or so poems, "all the junk that goes with being human / drops away" and we are left with remarkable objects, revenant landscapes:

> *One granite ridge*
> *A tree, would be enough*
> *Or even a rock, a small creek,*
> *A bark shred in a pool . . .*

and lovely too—for this poet has the capacity for both planetary scope ("I will not cry Inhuman & think that makes us small and nature great . . .") and microscopic focus ("Granite: ingrained with torment of fire and weight, crystal and sediment linked hot") that satisfies Nabokov's famous requirement: "there is a point, arrived at by diminishing large things and enlarging small ones, that is intrinsically artistic"—and even heartbreaking:

> *I cannot remember things I once read*
> *A few friends, but they are in cities.*
> *Drinking cold snow-water from a tin cup*
> *Looking down for miles*
> *Through high still air.*

Yet these poems do not connect, they are discrete and for all their entanglement with *realia*, they are partial: that is the quality by which they are limited and compromised and finally determined. We remember that riprap, by a definition the poet does not provide, is also a kind of firework that when lighted makes a succession of sharp explosions and jumps.

Modesty, though, is its own reward as well as its own restriction. The imagery of a poetry is positive insofar as it names things that have a visible, tangible existence. *Riprap*, then, is a positive step taken in the mind's myth of itself. The dialectical step, cutting nature at the joints, as Plato said, is afforded and in part taken by *Myths and Texts*, a longer book, in which the texts are the world itself, the myths what the mind, that hearth of provisional faiths, puts together out of them. The work is divided into three long sections of some sixteen numbered parts each: "Logging," "Hunting" and "Burning." The decor of these poems is partly the American Northwest, partly Japan, and the rhythms are not so much those of work, of labor, as of contemplation—"long days of quiet in lookout cabins":

> *Sourdough mountain called a fire in:*
> *Up Thunder Creek, high on a ridge.*
> *Hiked eighteen hours, finally found*
> *A snag and a hundred feet around on fire:*
> *All afternoon and into night*
> *Digging the fire line . . .*
> *Toward morning it rained.*
> *We slept in mud and ashes,*
> *Woke at dawn, the fire was out,*
> *The sky was clear, we saw*
> *The last glimmer of the morning star.*

—and the songs and dances of Great Basin Indian tribes:

> *Deer don't want to die for me.*
> *I'll drink sea-water*
> *Sleep on beach pebbles in the rain*
> *Until the deer come down to die*
> *in pity for my pain.*

The very title of the book, again, is the clue to Snyder's conjugation of the possibilities—it refers to "the two sources of human knowledge, symbols and sense-impressions. I tried to make my life as a hobo and worker, the questions of history and philosophy in my head, and the glimpses of the roots of religion I'd seen through meditation, peyote, and 'secret frantic rituals' into one whole thing." The example of Pound, even more closely than before, is embraced and exalted, and into the narratives are woven a lot of quotations—from anthropological handbooks by Boas, Sapir and others, from John Muir (an extraordinary account, versified by Snyder, of nearly falling off Mount Ritter, of which the conclusion is relevant to the ethical impulse and the *ars poetica* Snyder has been urging:

> *Life blazed*
> *Forth again with preternatural clearness.*
> *I seemed suddenly to become possessed*
> *Of a new sense. My trembling muscles*
> *Became firm again, every rift and flaw in*
> *The rock was seen as through a microscope.*
> *My limbs moved with a positiveness and precision*
> *With which I seemed to have*
> *Nothing at all to do.*),

from the Buddhist texts (which for me are about as opaque, as purely
decorative, as the Pound ideograms; they seem to be used as insurance
for the poems, rather than to be taking the risk), even from the titles of
paintings by Morris Graves, whose venue is very much a part of this
poet's vocabulary (I am thinking of Graves' painting of a fish in the
beak of a fierce bird of prey, eagle or osprey, between two streams
represented in a highly symbolical manner, called "Each Time You
Carry Me This Way." Snyder has a totemic boar emerging from the
sea-depths, bearing "his treasure," the sacred being Prajapati on his
tusks: "skewered body of the earth / Each time I carry you this
way.").

The first section of the book, for all its syncretic references to St.
Paul, Cybele, Buddha and the prophets of Israel, is the most secular. It
is in part a complaint against "the ancient, meaningless / abstractions of
the educated mind" which fails to perceive, to *sense* the very world it
is destroying:

> *Sea-foam washing the limpets and barnacles*
> *Rattling the gravel beach*
> *Salmon up creek, bear on the bank,*
> *Wild ducks over the mountains weaving*
> *In a long south flight, the land of*
> *Sea and fir tree with the pine-dry*
> *Sage-flat country to the east.*

Laboring among "the rise and fall of rock and water," deploring as he
wanders the "sense of journey in space that modern people have lost,"
the poet loops his steel cables around logs and watches the lumber
industry die:

> *The groves are down*
> > *cut down*
> *Groves of Ahab, of Cybele*
> *Pine trees, knobbed twigs*
> > *thick cone and seed*
> > *Cybele's tree this, sacred in groves*
> *Pine of Seami, cedar of Haida*
> *Cut down by the prophets of Israel*
> > *the fairies of Athens*
> > *the thugs of Rome*
> > > *both ancient and modern;*
> *Cut down to make room for the suburbs*
> *Bulldozed by Luther and Weyerhaeuser*
> *Crosscut and chainsaw*
> > *squareheads and finns*

> *high-lead and cat-skidding*
> *Trees down*
> *Creeks choked, trout killed, roads . . .*

That is the outrage and the lyric measure of Pound, entirely possessed and transformed to new purposes. As James Dickey has said, "the music, drifting series of terse, observant statements, does fix Snyder's experiences and beliefs in such a fashion that they become available for us to live among and learn from." The "Logging" section concludes with an impassioned reproach to his kind by a poet who knows he must be ransomed by the messages of his senses:

> *Men who hire men to cut groves*
> *Kill snakes, build cities, pave fields,*
> *Believe in god, but can't*
> *Believe their own senses*
> *Let alone Gautama. Let them lie.*

"Logging" has been part of the physical world, laborious, repetitive, and grounded in an apprehension of nature. The ritual of labor seems to be something of a voluntary effort to regain a vanished relation to the natural cycle. From it, the next sections take a great, a dialectical step—for the imagination works dialectically, separating what is desired from what is not, by higher organization determining what is wanted and what is not. In fact, the entire book has rather the structure suggested by Hanna Arendt in her division of the human condition into labor, work and action: "Logging" represents the first, with its repetitive, ritual motions in a physical world:

> *Each dawn is clear*
> *Cold air bites the throat.*
> *Thick frost on the pine bough*
> *Leaps from the tree*
> *　　snapped by the diesel*
> *Drifts and glitters in the*
> *　　horizontal sun.*
> *In the frozen grass*
> *　　smoking boulders*
> *　　ground by steel tracks.*
> *In the frozen grass*
> *　　wild horses stand*
> *　　beyond a row of pines.*
> *The D8 tears through piss-fir,*
> *Scrapes the seed-pine . . .*

while "Hunting" suggests what Miss Arendt means by *work*—the making or doing which dramatizes the instrumental, symbolic qualities of life: irreversible, unique, meaningful. Hence the "shaman songs," the poems "for birds," "for bear," "for deer," and most significant, "the making of the horn spoon":

> *The head of the mountain goat is in the corner*
> *for the making of the horn spoon.*
> *The black spoon. When fire's heat strikes it*
> *turn the head*
> *Four days and hair pulls loose*
> *horn twists free.*
> *Hand-adze, straightknife, notch the horn-base;*
> *rub with rough sandstone*
> *Shave down smooth. Split two cedar sticks*
> *when water boils plunge the horn,*
> *Tie mouth between sticks in the spoon shape*
> *rub with dried dogfish skin.*
> *It will be black and smooth,*
> *a spoon.*

And "Burning" is of course an adumbration of that stage of human action—the religious—by which life is illuminated for men individually and together, as the word religion itself suggests, beyond the laborer's ritual for survival and the craftsman's solitary joy—"Burning" has to do with the Buddha's fire sermon and with the burning of the great forests, "the hot seeds steaming underground, still alive." Here the sections are more nearly abstract:

> *The thin edge of nature rising fragile*
> *And helpless with its love and sentient stone*
> *And flesh, above dark drug-death dreams.*
> *Clouds I cannot lose, we cannot leave.*
> *We learn to love, horror accepted.*

But here, as in the "Hunting" poems, there is a continual, resuscitating summons to the natural world, to its essentially foreign being:

> *One moves continually with the consciousness*
> *Of that other, totally alien, non-human:*
> *Humming inside like a taut drum,*
> *Carefully avoiding any direct thought of it,*
> *Attentive to the real-world flesh and stone.*

At the end of "Burning" ("It's all falling or burning—rattle of boulders / steady dribbling of rocks down cliffs"), we leave the poet, still talking to himself, uncertain of everything but his upward movement, advancing through "a night of the long poem and the mined guitar" on the riprap of a reality perceived:

Walked all day through live oak and manzanita,
Scrabbling through dust dust down Tamalpais—
Thought of high mountains;
Looked out on a sea of fog.
Two of us, carrying packs.

I do not mean to suggest, of course, that it is such an easy thing to achieve the stage of action, of religious reality—especially within the gestures of the quotidian, the demands of the insignificant untranscended, or that the poet has found his way to this sanctified state—"we fled and stumbled on the bright lit plain"—without let or hindrance. In the ten years since *Myths and Texts* was written, the poet has been living, mostly in Japan, in various stages of spiritual and economic vagrancy:

In the dark   white lanterns
*   sending out rowboats, swinging*
a thousand foot net
*   five times down the length of the beach.*
we help haul . . .
*   a full-thighed young woman*
*   her dress tucked up in her pants*
*   tugs and curses*
*   an old man calling*
*   across the dark water sculling . . .*
they beach their boats
full of nets
their lamps bob over the dunes

we sleep in the sand
and our salt.

It is perhaps his very aspiration to an illuminated existence *within* what other men call reality that makes Snyder so poignantly aware of the waste, the devouring slough of human life, and in his later work there ceases to be anything so neat as a division between a poem of detritus and a poem of ecstasy, for merely the litany of constatation provides the poet with his ascent:

*   . . . unfixed junk downstair—*
All emblems of the past—too close—
*   heaped up in chilly dust and bare bulb glare*
of tables, wheelchairs, battered trunks and wheels
& poets that boiled up coffee nineteen ten, things

Swimming on their own and finally freed
              from human need. Or?
     waiting a final flicker of desire
To tote them out once more . . .

This is from a long poem Snyder has been promising for years, "a long poem I'm calling 'Mountains and Rivers Without End' after a sidewise Chinese scroll painting. It threatens to be like its title." In 1965 a pamphlet was published in San Francisco by the Four Seasons Foundation containing six sections from "Mountains and Rivers Without End," and there is every reason to expect more of this spiritual journalism in the future, for in these notations of "lost things—a universe of junk, all left alone" nothing begins or ends, all is an unremitting effort to rise through the compunctions of a rootless life to that heightened sense of Being where everything is divine. The six sections of the poem that have been published and the marginal poems attendent on its production suggest, within the dialectic of spiritual tug and material weight, a return to the necessary riprap or ballast to weight down the overwhelming Pursuits, all the more slippery as they are for being voiced, now, in the catechisms of Zen ("What is the way of non-activity? It is activity"). Thus in the fifth section, "The Market," there is a long, characteristic descant in the best Pound style on the worth of some change in the poet's pocket:

     to market, the
                   changes, how much
              is our change:

     Seventy-five feet hoed rows equals
     one hour explaining power steering
     equals two big crayfish =
              all the buttermilk you can drink
     = twelve pounds cauliflower
     = five cartons greek olives =
     hitch-hiking
              from Ogden Utah to Burns Oregon
     = aspirin, iodine, and bandages
     = a lay in Naples = beef
     = lamp ribs =
              long grain rice, eight pounds
     equals two kilogram soybeans . . .

The indications of equivalence are more than the articulation of a commercial undertaking that must, in these out-of-the-way places, do without common coin; here the equal signs are a token of spiritual

indifference, or rather of spiritual equality, precisely: all things are
worthy, Snyder is saying, and all things are blessed. Such lists (there
was another great one in "Hunting" of "what food we lived on then":
some forty-eight items from yucca flowers to turtles) are really a kind
of religious mnemonics, an exercise recalling the self to the world that
is its home, when its impulse—as classically in the American experience
—is to transcend. We are reminded that Snyder is the true heir of that
Thoreau who retired to Walden in order to discover the meaning of
the word "property" and found it meant only what was proper or
essential to unbound human life. This self-exiled poet, like the one who
withdrew from Concord, ballasts with what his senses tell him—as in
another late poem, "Eight Sandbars on the Takano River," from which
I quote but two beautifully phrased "bars":

> *gone wild*
> *strawberry vine*
> *each year more small*
> *sour*
> *mulched by pine*

> *white peeled logs*
> *toppled in sap*
> *scalped branch*
> > *spring*
> > > *woods*

—the radical assumptions of the soul, as in the greater, syncretic
statement of "This Tokyo," in which the Buddhist mistrust of matter is
earned, is justified by a milling, personal transaction with spirit; such
statements require the strongest and most pervasive recuperation of the
physical world, without which, as we know, existence is the "greatest
impoverishment":

> *. . . We live*
> *On the meeting of sun and earth.*
> *We live—we live—and all our lives*
> *Have led to this, this city,*
> *Which is soon the world, this*
> *Hopelessness where love of man*
> *Or hate of man could matter*
> *None, love if you will or*
> *Contemplate or write or teach*
> *But know in your human marrow you*
> *Who read, that all you tread*
> *Is earthquake rot and matter mental*

> *Trembling freedom is a void,*
> *Peace war religion revolution*
> *Will not help.*

No wonder the phenomenology of Snyder's landscape is so difficult to pin down! He is forever exchanging the trough of the wave for the crest, the mountain-top for the abyss, the world of cars and haircuts for the rocky desolation in which we are accustomed to find, reading the scroll inch by inch, a tiny, radiant sage under some tremendous crag—and that will be this odd American poet, our post-Hiroshima Lafcadio Hearn, who ends his latest excerpt from the endless poem-scroll of his life with this classic bit of spiritual geography, a human universal from Dante to Hiroshige:

> *. . . We were at the bottom of the gorge.*
> *We started drifting up the canyon. "This is the*
> *way to the back country."*

In 1966, the Fulcrum Press of London published, in a handsome and virtually inaccessible edition, Snyder's *Collected Poems* which reprint not only *Riprap* and *Myths and Texts* entire, but add the poet's two groups of translations, from Miyazawa Kenji (1896–1933) and, more impressively to my sense, from the T'ang master Han-Shan or "Cold Mountain." Snyder says the poems are "colloquial: rough and fresh," and he has had great success bringing them over into English, for indeed they echo and occasionally initiate his own project—as he says, Han-Shan became an Immortal "and you sometimes run on to him today in the skidrows, orchards, hobo jungles and logging camps of America":

> *In my first thirty years of life*
> *I roamed hundreds and thousands of miles.*
> *Walked by rivers through deep green grass*
> *Entered cities of boiling red dust.*
> *Tried drugs, but couldn't make Immortal;*
> *Read books and wrote poems on history.*
> *Today I'm back at Cold Mountain:*
> *I'll sleep by the creek and purify my ears.*

The translator has so evidently confounded his voice with the possibilities of his text that we cannot know whose impulse is being borrowed, whose lent; but the progress is certainly a logical one to the final section of the new book, the new poems gathered under the rubric already defined for us in the last quotation given from "Mountains and Rivers Without End," the unemphatic but suggestive label for all that is not here and now: *The Back Country.*

Thus Snyder has collected into four "books" of some dozen poems each all the "incidental" poems he has written outside the series. Explicitly, he says, "it is not necessary to think of a series," and indeed the word incidental goes far toward determining the category of these lyrics. All are under the sign of a quotation from Basho: "I, drawn like blown cloud, couldn't stop dreaming of roaming, roving the coast up and down . . . ," and the diffuse, rambling lines recount the incidents of a wondering vagrancy as

> *a hawk sails over the roof*
> *a snake went under the floor*

> *how can hawks hunt in the rain?*

> *I walk through the hallway:*
> *the soul of a great-bellied cloud.*

There is a different poignancy, an odd, rueful glance at an alternative convention in the several love poems here:

> *I might have gone to you*
> *Hoping to win your love back.*
> *You are still single.*

> *I didn't.*
> *I thought I must make it alone. I*
> *Have done that . . .*

as if it were impossible for the poet to admit the existence of Others in his rhapsody of concrete universals, though at least he knows *why* it is impossible and acknowledges the likelihood of failure, for he "may never now know / if I am a fool / or have done what my / karma demands." As for men in general, "all these crazed, hooked nations," Snyder claims to be merely an observer, exempt as he sinks into the detail of things ("spider gleams in his / new web / dew on the shingles, on the car, / on the mailbox—the mole, the onion, and the beetle / cease their wars") from the miniscule preoccupations of the humankind below:

> *I sit in the open window*
> *& roll a smoke . . .*

> *a soft continuous roar*
> *comes out of the far valley*
> *of the six-lane highway—thousands*
> *and thousands of cars*
> *driving men to work.*

Watching the vapor-trails of two jets, the poet renounces all concern for the linear, the ongoing impulse of Being, for he is not only content but capsized by the perception of immediate pattern, the recurrent process that has swung him, rapt, in its endless commencements, "new rain / as we begin our life"; the terrible planes streak off toward "the day of criss-cross rockets / and white blossoming smoke of bomb" and Snyder, very much on the ground, aspires only—it is the supreme purpose—to sentience:

> *I stumble on the cobble rockpath,*
> *Passing through temples,*
> *Watching for two-leaf pine*
> *—spotting that design.*

It is all there, the stumbling, the riprap, the sacred places and the participation in their significant pattern by "watching," "spotting." In fact, the entire venture is labelled and limited and then released by the over-all title Snyder gives his book of collected poems: "A Range of Poems." The mountainous suggestion of movement up and away, back of beyond, must not keep us from noting that there are *other* ranges, other registers and arrays of possibility which this poet has refused. Making it alone, he watches "the land drift north" and accounts for all that he sees while

> *plain men go into the ground . . .*
> *plain men come out of the ground.*

Turtle Island by Gary Snyder

To a large group of devotional poems which date back twenty years in some cases, in others which refer to attitudes and events of the most intimate proximity, Gary Snyder has added five prose texts, essays in solicitude and advocacy which afford a conscientious prospect of where we are and where he wants us to be, though the discrepancy registered between the two locales is so vast that the largely good-humored resonance of the poems attests to Snyder's forbearance, his enforced detachment. When the poet tells us, in his prose, "I wish to bring a voice from the wilderness, my constituency," he is not preaching to etiolate city-dwellers as a voice *in* the wilderness; there is, refreshingly, very little of the Jeremiad in Snyder's tone, very little of the howl in his timbre. In his poems, rather, the world becomes largely a matter of contours and traces to be guessed at, marveled over, left alone. And in prose Snyder seeks to recommend ways by which this listening life, this identity of observation merely, may be made easier—not only for himself (he does not particularly look for easy ways *there:* it is why we trust him), but for the rest of us, in suburb pent.

"At the root of where our civilization goes wrong," Snyder writes, in literally radical fashion, "is the mistaken belief that nature is something less than authentic, that nature is not as alive as man is, or as intelligent, that in a sense it is dead." One of the fashions, the senses in which nature is alive, poetically alive, for Snyder is its opacity, its resistance to being more than the signifier in what Hegel calls the prose of the world. That is why he can say "the poem was born elsewhere, and need not stay. Like the wild geese of the Arctic it heads home, far above the borders, where most things cannot cross." And the principal charm of *his* poems—transitory, elliptical, extraterritorial—will be, again and again, in the most unexpected contexts, that precipitate of experience without interpretation, the *salts* of an evaporated life, not raw (because not even conflated with the cooked, the processed) but rapt, "an offer", as he says, quite unconcerned with the taking, with our response:

> *the smell of bats.*
> *the flavor of sandstone*
> *grit on the tongue.*

There will be nothing transcendent about such realia, vivid but never evoked, present because (merely!) perceived: there are no symbols in Snyder's poetry, no metaphors even, nothing ever stands for anything else: "There is no other life," he remarks with characteristic laconicism, though he is never wry, never sour. In fact, he is the master of a peculiar sweetness—peculiar in that it is not sentimental, not even consistent. A considerable poem like *The Bath* can celebrate with an exact exuberance the pleasures of bathing his two children and his wife as well, yet the "action" Snyder urges in a later (or earlier, for all I know) prose text is that we "try to correct traditional cultural attitudes that tend to force women into childbearing". Well, of course there is no forcing in the home-life thus exhibited, where it is not exposed, and perhaps that is the chill which these poems communicate—or what causes the chill. So accustomed are we, in the thirty centuries of our literature, to the notion that at *some* level, in *some* way, the poem is the product or the presumption of constraint, of conflict (even as the family is subject to social, to ritual pressures), that it is with a tighter breathing indeed, and zero at the bone, that we meet these narrow fellows:

> *Muddly slipping trail*
> *wobbly twin pole bridges*
> > *gully throat*
> *forks in*

somebody clearing brush & growing tea
& out, turn here for home
along the Kamo River.

hold it close
give it all away.

The very punctuation—periods but no capitals, more often than not—
(though when not, why not? one wonders, idly) is wonderfully in
accord with Snyder's recuperation of a world not manhandled but
merely, for once, inhabited by a humanity intended "to draw out
strength from the realization that at the heart of things is some kind of
serene and ecstatic process which is beyond qualities and beyond
birth-and-death." The poems, then, being beyond qualities too in their
endeavor to realize that process, to receive it, will not articulate an
emotional shape we can recognize, they will not have a drama, they
will be intransitive, and though we may thirst for more of a conclu-
sion, more of an integral close than is afforded by Snyder's birds
which

. . . arc and loop & then
their flight is done.
they settle down.
end of poem.

our thirst is to remain our thirst. We must be told that the poem ends.
Such makings are neither found nor transformed things, neither in-
ventions nor fictions—they are doings, actions, but not *to* anything
else, not *for* or *from* or *upon;* without prepositions in their perform-
ance, such poems are evidences of what the poet calls "true affluence
—not needing anything," and that is their sensational (though low-
keyed) departure from most poems, from poetry: they do not need us.

Poetry, 1975

WILLIAM STAFFORD

" 'Tell Us What You Deserve,' the Whole World Said."

A POET—the Greeks had precisely that word for it, for the calling to which the poet William Stafford apprentices himself, which he masters and thereby chooses *over* himself (as anything which is mastered is a transcendence of the mastering power too, a submission of self for the sake of the song) in this terrible descrial:

> *Remembering the wild places, bitter,*
> *where pale fields meet winter,*
> *he searches for some right song*
> *that could catch and then shake the world*

—a poet is a maker, a *makar* our old Scots word too for the man who sings "some right song," who fashions language into a contrivance that may not come apart but rather comprehend such disintegration:

> *For all we have taken into our keeping*
> *and polished with our hands belongs to a truth*
> *greater than ours,*

as Stafford says again, his emphasis rightly on the manual finish, the *handling* of utterance ("we open the book with care and hold our breath: begin—translating the vast versions of the wind"); congruently, a *scop*, the Anglo-Saxon poet, is a shaper, imparting form or *scape* to what he finds shapeless, whether it be the land:

> *calling for human help in the wide land, calling*
> *into all that silence and* the judgment of the sky,*

---

* Emphasis mine. The notion of a judgment passed by what is not included in some human assessment, of a sentencing by the missing parts of the contexts from which we draw our delegated efficiency, is crucial to Stafford, and I shall return to it, though its appearance, so immediately, in a quotation is characteristic.

or the imperatives of life upon it:

> *Right has a long and intricate name.*
> *And the saying of it is a lonely thing,*

performing some gesture or ceremony of containment by means of the word-hoard bequeathed to him. As it is said of the *scop* in "Widsith," the oldest poem in English, or in Old English:

> *. . . his wierd [fate] is to be a wanderer:*
> *the poets of mankind go through many countries,*
> *speak their needs, say their thanks . . .*

an errantry echoed by William Stafford, our Widsith of the Great West, in his own effort to speak his needs, say his thanks, thirsting for some act or emblem of ritual which might give *scape* to the endless prospect, as in "Watching the Jet Planes Dive":

> *We must go back and find a trail on the ground*
> *back of the forest and mountain on the slow land;*
> *we must begin to circle on the intricate sod.*
> *By such wild beginnings without help we may find*
> *the small trail on through the buffalo-bean vines.*
>
> *We must go back with noses and the palms of our hands,*
> *and climb over the map in far places, everywhere,*
> *and lie down whenever there is doubt and sleep there.*
> *If roads are unconnected we must make a path,*
> *no matter how far it is, or how lowly we arrive.*
>
> *We must find something forgotten by everyone alive,*
> *and make some fabulous gesture when the sun goes down*
> *as they do by custom in little Mexico towns*
> *where they crawl for some ritual up a rocky steep.*
> *The jet planes dive; we must travel on our knees.*

If there are the shamanistic gestures here which precede, even, a poetry of the land—"we must begin to circle on the intricate sod. . . . With noses and the palms of our hands, climb over the map . . . and lie down where there is doubt and sleep there . . . We must make some fabulous gesture . . . as they do by custom . . . where they crawl for some ritual up a rocky steep"—there are also the movements of making and shaping, the powers of the *scop* mustered and mastered, for all his disinherited status—". . . we must make a path, no matter . . . how lowly we arrive . . . we must make some fabulous gesture"; and there is also in this easily phrased, evasively rhymed meditation the other action of the poet, the function of discovering the past, of recovering, which reminds us that the poet is, as well as a *makar* and a *scop*, a *trobatore*, a *trouvère*, a *trovatore*—all Mediterranean words for the enterprise: presumably in the south it is more frequent to find than to fashion—the poet is a *finder*, then, who comes upon (literally, who *invents*) his matter, his treasure-*trove:* "Your job is to find what the world is trying to be," Stafford adjures himself, though in his case, the case of the alienated *scop*—alienated from the community, the *kin* which might elect him to celebrate itself and which, in the wrecked wilderness of the American West, has departed from the land ("the jet planes dive; we must travel on our knees")—it is distinctly a matter of *finders, weepers.* And of *losers, keepers,* for Stafford continually rehearses the maker's fortunate fall, his desolation which, like Cleopatra's, does begin to make a better life:

> *It is too late now for earlier ways;*
> *now there are only some other ways,*
> *and only one way to find them—fail.*

Again and again, Stafford asserts his paradox: "reality demands abjection . . . you prove you're real by failing," he remarks in a note on Richard Eberhart; and in his poems, acknowledging that, sacerdotally, "we are somehow vowed to poverty," Stafford exults: "a perfect flower blooms from all failure."

It is pleasing and profound, this identity or rather this convergence of the poet's vocation, which in each instance, Attic, Romance, and Germanic, suggests that a man accountable to other men for the way life is or has been framed—

> *our molten bodies remembering some easier form,*
> *we feel the bones assert the rites of yesterday*
> *and the flow of angular events becoming destiny—*

engages by definition in an undertaking ("meanings in search of a world") which concerns something more than himself, rather a transaction with something *out there,* whether landscape, love or war, which can in part be learned, mastered, come into, as by apprenticeship or indenture, "some little trap to manage events, / some kind of edge against the expected act." But what is truly unified can never be uniform, and the *nuances* of the calling, too, the partings of the poet's ways as the various cultures distinguish them—"maintaining the worth of local things," Stafford calls it—are precious; such distinctions may help us out, may help us on to the recognition by their variance, by their chosen emphasis, of one poet or another—which is all we may ask of general terms, that they may aid us in the recognition of specific cases. There are, we notice, different kinds of poets, nor shall we

expect the same performance, the same obligations of an open man, a
man isolated in space, as of a closed one, a man isolated in society:

> *It is all right to be simply the way you have to be,*
> *among contradictory ridges in some crescendo of knowing—*

that is Stafford giving himself permission to exist in his *paysage moral-
isé*, and it is so particular a voice, with such particular claims upon the
soil, that we do well to remember Hawthorne's warning: "We must
not always talk in the marketplace of what happens to us in the forest";
for from the start of American experience there have been discrepant
dialects for the seacoast and the plain, the woods and the mountains,
not always understood to each other.

Thus I find it a matter of expedience, when I cannot make it a matter
of ecstasy, to identify, to exalt one of our poets, the William Stafford
who calls it his *duty* (just as he calls his duty a certain "high kind of
waiting—the art of not knowing" and confesses "our need reaches for
duty"):

> *. . . to find a place*
> *that grows from his part of the world—*
> *. . . an imagined place*
> *where finally the way the world feels*
> *really means how things are,*

as a *scop*. In a society of the great Inlands, where Stafford's poetry has
since 1960 been launched:

> West of your city * *outside your lives*
> *in the ultimate wind, the whole land's wave,*

and sometimes lodged (his second book, *Traveling Through the Dark*,
was given a National Book Award in 1962) and sometimes merely left
around (so that the poet gathered up the leavings, some fifteen pieces
from that first book, and included them in his third, *The Rescued Year*,
in 1966, without any sense, either reported by the poet or registered by
his public, that there might be some division, some cleavage between
his early utterance and his late), the *scop* discovers his function—to
bring together, to bridge, to braid into the one strand the double
vision:

> *Love is of the earth only,*
> *the surface . . .*

---

* The title of his first book: the lines in which it occurs suggest something of the
arrogant otherness of Stafford's persona, the separateness, the exclusion in which
his voice is raised, and yet the assurance—almost, the complacency—that he has
got hold of an eschatological argument—"the *ultimate* wind," "the *whole* land."

Not so the legend under,
fixed, inexorable . . .

So, the world happens twice—
once what we see it as;
second it legends itself
deep, the way it is.

By a fidelity to failure, a submission to his own exile, he will "lease a place to live with my white breath," and ultimately, a favorite word of Stafford's, by an attention so urgently bestowed as to become *intention,*

by listening with the same bowed head that sings,
draw all into one song . . .
the rage without met by the wings
within that guide you anywhere the wind blows.

By means of a one-man anabasis from Liberal, Kansas and environs to Portland, Oregon, with intervals of teaching and degree-taking in Indiana and California and Iowa—

I found so misty a trail
that all not-you cried, "You!"
like a wedding bell—

the poet discovers himself, as the quotation affirms, identified by precisely what he is not, by what I have called *the missing parts of the contexts*, and the identification is a nuptial occasion: by his alienation from the land, the *scop* becomes one with it. "The Hero Learning to Leave Home" is the title of one Stafford poem, and "Truth is the Only Way Home" of another; and both leaving and returning are accommodated by the union longed for and finally attained:

My self will be the plain,
wise as winter is gray,
pure as cold posts go
pacing toward what I know.

I spoke just now of the society of the great Inlands, the space so cruelly open to interpretation ("beyond this place is many another place / called *Everywhere*"); barely a society ("where I come from withdrawal / is easy to forgive") and barely indeed a landscape ("a continent without much on it"), the West of Stafford's poetry is nonetheless, or all the more, a focus of judgment ("I'd speak for all the converging days . . ."); the *scop* is the sentenced keeper of the traditions, guardian of the word-hoard, celebrant of the rites—meager, harsh, necessary:

We weren't left religion exactly . . .
but a certain tall element,
a pulse beat still in the stilled rock
and in the buried sound along the buried mouth of the creek—

which hold the *kin* or tribe together, just as the ruler of the kin, the *king,* is the keeper of that other hoard of gold which is the kin's only possession and defence. The older a sword, the older a word, the more it is valued by the *kin.* In such a society, such a landscape, *because* of their very minimal realizations, all language has a religious, literally a *binding* significance. That is why the language of the *scops* is so profoundly conservative, conventional, *given,* and that is why William Stafford's words and verses, why his *art* accommodates so many simplicities of repetition and so many echoes, so many correspondances between early and late, between poem and poem—the diction is unchanging because the task is unchanging, it is all one poem by which the labor of recuperation is performed:

> *. . . I plow and belong, send breath*
> *to be part of the day, and where it arrives*
> *I spend on and on, fainter and fainter*
> *toward ultimate identification, joining the air*
> *a few breaths at a time.*

But suppose the king dies or withdraws his favor—then the kin is dissolved, the *scop* is alienated, as we should say, literally exiled, "travelling through the dark," as our own *scop* calls it. Born in 1914, Stafford was drafted in 1940, and served as a conscientious objector throughout the war (forestry, soil conservation in Arkansas and California); in 1948, Stafford published his Master's Thesis, a book about conscientious objectors, *Down in My Heart* (whose title collides meaningfully with that of his first book, *West of Your City*), and it was not until he was 46 that that first book of poems was ready. For the king *had* died, the kin *was* dissolved, and justice, judgment, sentence could be sought, could come only from the severed land ("we were judged; our shadows knew our height") or from the severe weather of the place:

> *the final strategy of right, the snow*
> *like justice over stones . . .*

The *scop* cannot look to his community or even to his communication with himself ("to sigh is a stern act—we are judged by this air") for the sanctions of conduct, the meting-out of verdicts in the actual sense of the word, *truth-tellings:*

> *Where are the wrongs men have done?*
> *He holds out calloused hands*
> *toward that landscape of justice.*

And he wanders through the empty, forbidding land, past the kind of trees "that act out whatever has happened to them," in mountains where every rock "denied all the rest of the world," apart, dry, but not dumb, "catching at things left here that are ours," seeking a vindication, a judgment, a rank:

> *And so I appeal to a voice, to something shadowy,*
> *a remote important region in all who talk.*

For if it is the *scop* who assigns meaning, value, significances to the world of his disgraced kin ("we live in an occupied country, misunderstood; / justice will take us millions of intricate moves"), it is just that world which in turn justifies his own being, allows his existence to work out the salvation for which Stafford craves; when he says, in his third book, "our lives are an amnesty given us," we are reminded of Aquinas' proposition that the Creation was an act of generosity, not of justice, and when the poet, in a poem to Willa Cather in his first book, says that the "land required some gesture: conciliation," we recognize that longing for sacrifice, for submission which will bring this *scop* home to himself by identifying him with "one tree, one well, a landscape / that proclaims a universe." Accusing himself of holding the land away with "gracious gestures," Stafford seeks the kind of wound, the infliction of pain which will, as in the poem "Ceremony," wed him to the source of judgment, even by a muskrat bite:

> *The mangled hand made the water red.*
> *That was something the ocean would remember:*
> *I saw me in the current flowing through the land,*
> *rolling, touching roots, the world incarnadined,*
> *and the river richer by a kind of marriage . . .*
> *Under the bank a muskrat was trembling*
> *with meaning my hand would wear forever.*
>
> *In that river my blood flowed on.*

Only by such submission to earth ("the little clods come to judge us again"), by an imploration of the "promise of the land," as in this little prayer:

> *Yew tree, make me steadfast in my*
> *weakness: teach me the sacred blur*

can the disinherited *scop* regain his authority, his hope of authorship. No longer from the center of a society, Stafford speaks from the verge, the brink, the margin where his desolation is informed by an alien knowledge:

> *It is people at the edge who say*
> *things at the edge: winter is toward knowing.*

No longer imparting shape, no longer daring to impart it, to the land ("if we purify the pond, the lilies die"), the *scop*, by a radical reversal, by choosing other, outer claims over his own, allows the land to shape *him*, and from that submission, that surrender of privilege, "while earth whirled on its forgotten center," as well as from that mastery, that rehearsal of celebration ("while meager justice applauds up through the grass"), achieves, earns his heroism. There is a poem, central to Stafford's central book, in which the poet I have preferred to see as an outcast *scop* is able, by this very vision where the land prevails and speaks *through* him—

> *. . . there is a reward*
> *here: maybe the mountains, maybe only the sense*
> *that after what is must come something else, always—*

to recognize his *authority*, to *find* himself for once with the great Mediterranean, the great Classical figures (also fugitive, also disinherited) he had seemed to be forever sequestered from; at the end of "In Medias Res," having seen on the Main Street of his own bleak town, "one night when they sounded the chimes," his father walking ahead of him in shadow, his son behind coming into the streetlight, and on each side a brother and sister, and his wife "following into the shades calling back," Stafford realizes in a great explosion of identity who he is, who he might be ("not able to know / anything but a kind of Now"), for all the black hills and blocked heavens:

> *as overhead*
> *the chimes went arching for the perfect sound,*
> *I had not thought to know the hero quite so well.*
> *"Aeneas!" I cried, "just man, defender!"*
> *And our town burned and burned.*

Someday, Maybe by WILLIAM STAFFORD

In 1970, on the jacket of *Allegiances,* probably the best of his five books written from and about 'the hard country / no one can misjudge, where we survive / out indulgences and mean just the earth again," a book given over to "weaving the dark and the cold" into a texture of losses, till the poet had "woven a parachute out of everything broken; my scars my shield," William Stafford, in one of his rare critical pronouncements, remarked that he was interested in what he called "incremental progression in single works . . . a level delivery of non-rhetorical poems." *Single works,* I believe, because, as Stafford also moralized, in one of the poems, "we are led *one thing at a time* through gain / to that pure gain—all that we lose." (Italics mine).

There is, certainly, a relation of consequence between the rejection of "rhetoric" and the refusal of cumulative structure. The poems in all Stafford's work come at us in the register of winter, "the great repeated lesson," and as he says of the creatures of earth, "everything cold can teach, they learn." Cold can teach everything except one thing—how to structure. There is no articulation, no development in this determinedly erasing voice; determined, I mean, to abide by the provisional and the negative:

our work is to forget in time what if remembered might block
that great requirement which waits on its wide wings: the wilderness.

So the poems accumulate but they do not *grow;* they drift like snowflakes into a great and beautiful body of canceling work ("You wake / from dreams and hear the end of things: No One, No One, No One", or again, "At the end we sense / here none of you, one of us—no one"), for Stafford is, in all of his determinations, minor. A reader confronted by two poems of his of equal merit—and there are a great many poems of equal and enormous merit—but written at different times cannot immediately say which was written first, cannot settle their chronology on the basis of the poems themselves. That is the world of minor poetry, but it is, as Stafford says, "a good world to be lost in," and if it is predictable ("we follow by going ahead of what we know is coming"), it is never assertive or greedy ("I beg of the wind: *Read my lips, forget my name*"), and over and over, instance after instance, or ecstasy after ecstasy, as we do what he says, as we "let that—the nothing, the no one, the calm night—often recur," we feel that "in what he says a giant is trying to get out."

The giant does not get out very far in Stafford's new book, *Some-day, Maybe*, partly because of the minority determinations I speak of, the insistence on no more than one damned thing after another—"the authentic is a line from one thing / along to the next"—and partly because in order to achieve his remarkable effect, the effect of discursive purity untempered by social compromise, Stafford relies upon and requires the mediate, the entrapped, the contingent language: "we study how to deserve / what has already been given us . . ." All society, in Stafford, is in the past, remembered, elegized; in the present is solitude, "a calm face against the opening world"; and in the future, only death. The allegiances are unwavering—

> . . . *I will reach*
> *carefully, eagerly through the rain, at the end—*
> *toward whatever is there with this loyal hand.*

The hand is loyal to water, to sources, to the perishable clay and the imperishable changes. These poems are brief, they do not take more than a page to make their stoic observances (hence they have appeared in 47 periodicals), and in the wars between movement and stillness they constitute little more than a brief joust, "a sound like some rider saying / the ritual for help, a chant or a song." They do not concern themselves much with the world of culture, which is the world of memory, except to cross it out. A wonderful poem, "Ozymandias's Brother", is a rare instance, the canyon tomb making "about the right degree of assertion, holding forth / what there is, no despair": Shelley's overthrown idol summoned up and dismissed to a superior negation. These are poems of chthonic release, their weather is storm, their season winter, their time of day darkness, and Stafford reaches for no more of what he calls "his grabbed heritage" than, in a rustling, subversive breviary of estrangements, these "close reliable friends / in the earth, in the air, in the rock."

It is mistaken, then, as I have been mistaken, to call *Allegiances* a "better" book than *Someday, Maybe;* to credit one way of putting it:

> *we live in that cold range now*
> *where the temporary earth tries*
> *for something greater, with the keen air's aid,*
> *and more, where the world perishes*
> *day by day in the tall winter beyond any range.*

as superior, as in any way higher in aspiration or reach than any other way of putting it:

> *. . . we come, we*
> *celebrate with our breath, we join on the curve*
> *of our street, never lost, the surge of the land*
> *all around us that always is ours,*
> *the beginning of the world and the end.*

For William Stafford, the important thing, the ineluctable thing, is that one poem be written in that *level delivery* of his, and then that another poem be written, that the poems keep coming, replacing each other, like leaves released from the tree at the start of winter—is the leaf that will come *better* than the life discarded? more nearly the *right leaf?* The point is all in the process, the seasonable realization until, as Stafford says in his extraordinary diction of some three hundred words, the voice never raised above the sound of one man talking to one other man at nightfall outdoors, no one word given more energy or pitched higher than any other word, no one poem enhanced by the glamors of compositional stress beyond any other poem—until

> *. . . unbound by our past we sing*
> *wherever we go, ready or not,*
> *stillness above and below, the slowed*
> *evening carried in prayer toward the end.*

Parnassus, 1974

MARK STRAND

"The Mirror Was Nothing Without You."

T HE SIGNIFICANCES of the verb *apprehend*—by learning, we learn to fear, and as in Shakespeare "apprehend a world of figures here"—open out, one from another, like the sections of a paranoiac spy-glass—first to take hold of, then to take possession of, hence to seize by criminal process; by extension from the first sense, to become aware of through the senses, hence to recognize the meaning of; ultimately to anticipate, especially with dread or alarm—and when articulated to its full power, erect, such an instrument, the lens of anxiety, affords an encompassing view of the double shore of this poet's initial work, the workings of a divided self, strand opposite and opposing (even as it mirrors) strand: on the one verge an apprenticeship to reality, on the other an imprisonment *in* reality; *apprentice*—

> *The windy sum of my own motion,*
> *I marvelled at myself*
> *In passing. I kept in step*
> *With what I was. Oh, I was dashing,*
>
> *Or thought I was, until I saw*
> *The distance I had to go . . .*

and *prisoner*—

> *We sit behind*
> *Closed windows, bolted doors,*
> *Unsure and ill at ease . . .*
> *We cannot take ourselves or what belongs*

> *To us for granted . . .*
> *We do not feel protected*
> *By the walls, nor can we hide*
> *Before the duplicating presence*
> *Of their mirrors . . .*

personifying not merely the same man but the same word, rooted both in *apprehension*. And between these strands, separating bewilderment from bogeys, "enhanced by atmospheres / of pure decorum," flows the stream of utterance,

> *The certain voice telling us over and over*
> *That nothing would change,*

a discourse of absence, a lament for the missing contexts ("I am / not capable of force, / feeling myself at stake") to which the thirty-year-old poet entrusts his experience, confident that the language itself will not only find him out ("a sense of our remoteness / closes in") but save him up ("my fears were groundless"), ransoming by its traditional structures ("a world of familiar views / and fixed conditions") what in himself he has discovered to be doomed, marked, precisely, for *destruction:*

> *My role is forced on me,*
> *It keeps my nerves on edge . . .*
> *I take things as they come*
> *And let them go. I have*
> *No final say in the matter*
>
> *And I don't get anywhere:*
> *My mind does not support*
> *My pastime well . . .*

The puns (as on *pastime,* here) and the quibbles on current speech ("I marvelled at myself / *in passing*," the enjambment thrusting the statement into a life of its own) are strong semblances of a jeopardized propriety in Strand's early work, and they are the catechumen's means —endemic to *all* poetry discovering itself in the course of . . . discourse—the means of hedging his bets, playing both sides, keeping things whole:

> *. . . no more than one*
> *In a series whose end*
> *Only the nervous or the morbid consider.*

Strand is both nervous and morbid, and a consideration of finality is his constant project, sustained here by shifting the responsibility for the imminent wreck from "the reaches of ourselves" to the ambiguity instinct in *language*. Thus, referring to "summer at its most august" or calling trees "nothing after all but the heart / of their own matter" is a blazon of what used to be called *keeping*, a literal propriety Strand will later let go. In his first book, he is holding on for dear life.

He takes its title from John Fletcher's distich, "Let one Eye his watches keep / While the other Eye doth sleep," thereby instancing an author we inveterately double with a collaborator missing here, and insisting too on the duplicity of our very bodies, the symmetry which allows our eyes their double vigil in daylight and darkness together. *Sleeping with One Eye Open*, published in 1964, is a book of forebodings and apprehensions, of mirrorings and divisions, the very titles of the poems articulating menace: "When the Vacation is Over for Good," "Something Is in the Air," "A Kind of Weakness," "A Reason for Moving," and of course the title poem, with its twitching echo-rhymes, its broken rhythms:

> *Unmoved by what the wind does,*
> *The windows*
> *Are not rattled, nor do the various*
> *Areas*
> *Of the house make their usual racket—*
> *Creak at*
> *The joints, trusses and studs . . . The shivers*
> *Wash over*
> *Me, shaking my bones, my loose ends*
> *Loosen,*
> *And I lie sleeping with one eye open,*
> *Hoping*
> *That nothing, nothing will happen.*

By writing an existing language as if it were his own invention, by confiding his endurance of dissolution to traditional discourse, Strand achieves, in these first poems of his, the spooky sense that he is being written by someone else, by some*thing* else, an energy his own only in that it moves *through* him, for it does not proceed from him—

> *The dim allegory of ourselves*
>   *Unfolds, and we*
> *Feel dreamed by someone else,*
> *A sleeping counterpart*
>   *Who gathers in*
> *The darkness of his person*
> *Shades of the real world.*

So perfectly achieved is the sense of being life's dummy, the ventriloquism of diction merely (as he puts it in "In the Privacy of the

Home," one of a group of prose poems which are an effort to break the spell, "at a loss you examine the mirror. There you are, you are not there"), that these poems, with all the decisive delicacy Strand has leached from Richard Wilbur, from Elizabeth Bishop, are something of a foreclosure; though they register a collapse, a defeat, a disintegration of the identity they are concerned to disclose, they do so with the tenantless decorum of alienation, of *otherness;* and the poet registers, in "The Map," his discontent with his early making by just the accents of scruple and certitude he is protesting:

> *The map draws*
> *Only on itself, outlines its own*
> *Dimensions, and waits,*
> *As only a thing completed can,*
> *To be replaced*
> *By a later version of itself . . .*
> *Because nothing*
> *Happens where definition is*
> *Its own excuse*
> *For being, the map is as it was:*
> *A diagram*
> *Of how the world might look could we*
> *Maintain a lasting*
> *Perfect distance from what is.*

It is not, after all, a false sense of security Strand seeks to give himself and the reader, but a true sense of jeopardy, recalling that the word means not only danger, hazard, but originally a divided game, a *jeu parti* in which the chances are even because they are exposed. For such an enterprise, the larger scene, the more licentious action of *occurrences* are required—a grotesque *gestus* in the place of all this finicking topiary—and the direction is shown, even here in this first book, by one poem, "The Tunnel," which Strand will reprint in his next and in which the implicit condemnations of our speech—the buried metaphors which haunt all language but which hobble poetry to a traduction of wit—are discarded in favor of the explicit ones of narrative, of anecdote, as we shall see; a farewell to that dilemma which *lies* in human discourse is best made, then, in one of Strand's beautiful transparencies, "In the Mountains," where the entire rhetorical system appears to break down under the weight of its own duplicity, the burden of presented absence:

> *. . . the dark has made us*
> *Wonder where we are, and where*
> *We were, and who we are*

Thinking of where we were
And, even, if.

In 1968, after sojourns in Italy and Brazil, having translated Alberti and trained himself upon the dislocations of Magritte, Mark Strand published his second book, *Reasons for Moving*, two dozen poems in which he not only raises his voice but rouses his vision with it, so that we do not again forget what we have seen, what we have heard. This time the undertaking is placed under the sign of Borges' observation—still within the thematics of waking and sleeping, still committed to a doubleness of existence—that "while we sleep here, we are awake elsewhere, and that in this way every man is two men." Even in the epigraph, so carefully paired with Fletcher's, the articulation of duplicity is extroverted, theatricalized, and the book itself begins with a triumphant aggression against the old decorum, a victorious stamping upon the buried implications of mere verse—Strand's fears will no longer be *groundless*, as he exults, to the dismay of librarians, in "Eating Poetry," the opening poem:

> *Ink runs down from the corners of my mouth.*
> *There is no happiness like mine.*
> *I have been eating poetry!* . . .
> *I am a new man.*
> *I romp with joy in the bookish dark.*

New man, new methods. Though he keeps his axiological way with an enjambment, Strand now lower-cases his run-ons, and most lines in this book are coincident with the simplest declarative statements, a litany of *incidents* in the ulterior sense the word has, the sense of *chances*, a double game, a hazard. The poems Strand is eating are those of his first book, and the diet affords him a distinct playfulness, a grotesquerie unthinkable in the old forebodings. The generally short lines, moving into memory by a chain of *statements*, construct a simple report of things seen with all the odd exactitude of a documentary film:

> *Closer, closer.*
> *They embrace.*
>
> *She is making a bed.*
> *He is pulling off his pants.*
>
> *They marry*
> *and have a child.*

> *The wind carries them off*
> *in different directions.*
>
> *The wind is strong, he thinks*
> *as he straightens his tie.*
>
> *I like this wind, she says*
> *as she puts on her dress.*
>
> *The wind unfolds.*
> *The wind is everything to them.*

Such poems comfort our suspicions ("Why did I want so badly'/to get through to you?") precisely when what is being recounted is most dangerous or grotesque. "Things are not only themselves in this light," Strand concedes—and what they are *as well* is most often funny or frightening. It is good to remember, reading poems like "The Man in the Tree," "The Man in Black," "The Suicide," and the most extended achievement in the genre, "The Man in the Mirror," that the root of *experience* and the root of *peril* is the same, and that *grotesque* means, merely, out of a cave—the cave where lovers, say, take shelter from a storm.

The poems tell one story and one story only: they narrate the moment when Strand makes Rimbaud's discovery, that *je est un autre*, that the self is someone else, even something else; "The Mailman," "The Accident," "The Door," "The Tunnel," even "The Last Bus" with its exotic Brazilian stage-properties, all recount the worst, realizing every *apprehension*, relishing the things possible only in one's wildest fantasies of victimization, and then with a shriek as much of delight as of despair, fall upon *the fact*—

> *It will always be this way.*
> *I stand here scared*
> *that you will disappear,*
> *scared that you will stay*—

that the victimizer is, precisely, the self, and that the victim is the other, is others. It is what Hegel meant when he said that "hell is other people." Our poet discovers, time and again, that the nightmare of normal life is simply the narcissist's wet dream, the spasm of ego, the convulsion of identity. When the mailman brings a new letter containing "terrible personal news," the obliging hero of these poems welcomes his oppressor inside, where

> *he curls up like a ball*
> *and sleeps while I compose*

> *more letters to myself*
> *in the same vein:*
>
> *"You shall live*
> *by inflicting pain.*
> *You shall forgive."*

And when "I" dig a tunnel to avoid the implacable visitor lounging in front of "my" house, the result is identical with that of Kafka's celebrated narrative "The Burrow":

> *I come out in front of a house*
> *and stand there too tired to*
> *move or even speak, hoping*
> *someone will help me.*
> *I feel I'm being watched*
> *and sometimes I hear*
> *a man's voice,*
> *but nothing is done*
> *and I have been waiting for days.*

"I" have become the visitor, the victimizer, though I know not what I do. Even the act of recording my terrors makes them, in a sense, no longer mine: "The poem that has stolen these words from my mouth / may not be this poem," Strand boasts, for by dramatizing these goofy horrors in scenes, in stories, he is enabled to step out of them, saying as he says in the poem which gives the title to this second book *that is not it, that is not me—I am someone else, somewhere else:*

> *In a field*
> *I am the absence*
> *of field.*
> *This is always the case.*
> *Wherever I am*
> *I am what is missing . . .*
>
> *We all have reasons*
> *for moving.*
> *I move*
> *to keep things whole.*

A new and particular pleasure of these poems, a fringe benefit which the calculations and measurements of Strand's earlier work had made impossible, is an observation of occurrence, a communication of the *quality* of an occasion incidental in every sense to the scenario, the relation; Strand's spell is not broken by the intrusion of "particulars," rather it is sustained and indeed woven by the kind of generous awareness this new genre of allotropic poem vouchsafes the poet: "the carnation in my buttonhole / precedes me like a small / continuous explosion," he will say as he walks down the hall to his fated encounter with "The Man in the Mirror"; or again, turning the simplest meteorological phenomenon to his advantage, "in the white air of winter . . . a field of ferns covers my glasses; I wipe them away / in order to see you." It is justice to the visible world which Strand renders, though he walks "in the morning sun / invisible / as anyone," and the wonderful thing about these startling *fits* in the old sense, about these paragraphs of hallucination whose everyday emblems and conversational phrasing are lifted to sudden lyric intensity by syntax, by "the sound of sentences," is that in the richest possible acceptation they are *visionary poems.*

Strand's work since *Reasons for Moving* widens his scope, even as it sharpens his focus; just as he had divided his body against itself in order to discover an identity, he now identifies the body politic with his own in order to recover a division; in a series of political prospects, "Our Death," "From a Litany," "General," and finest of all, "The Way It Is," the poet conjugates the nightmares of Fortress America with his own stunned mortality to produce an apocalypse of disordered devotion:

> *Everyone who has sold himself wants to buy himself back.*
> *Nothing is done. The night*
> *eats into their limbs*
> *like a blight.*
> *Everything dims.*
> *The future is not what it used to be.*
> *The graves are ready. The dead*
> *shall inherit the dead.*

But what gives these public accents of Strand's their apprehensive relevance is not just a shrewd selection of details ("My neighbor marches in his room, / wearing the sleek / mask of a hawk with a large beak . . . His helmet in a shopping bag, / he sits in the park, waving a small American flag"), nor any cosy contrast of the poet's *intimeries* against a gaining outer darkness ("Slowly I dance out of the burning house of my head. / And who isn't borne again and again into heaven?"). Rather it is the sense that public and private degradation, outer and inner weather, tropic and glacial decors (Saint Thomas and Prince Edward Islands, in fact) are all versions and visions of what Coleridge called the One Life, and that the whole of nature and society are no more than the churning content of a single and limitless human body—the poet's own. Such a sense—and in Strand it occupies all the senses ("the flesh of clouds burns / in the long corridors of sunlight. / I have changed. No one's death surprises me")—enables the poet to include much more life in these later poems of his; to invoke the wars of filiation, marriage and paternity; to explore the ennui of mere survival:

> *Must we settle for a routine happiness?*
> *Tell me something rotten about yourself.*
> *Tell me you've been to the doctor and he says*
> *I am going to die. Save me!*

and to endure the depredations of the past, the claims of merely *having been:*

> *Time tells me what I am. I change and am the same.*
> *I empty myself of my life and my life remains.*

But not merely "I" and "me"—all the pronouns are here now; the personnel of these poems multiplies precisely as the self unifies. In a series of related elegies which constitute the most astonishing meditation of the period on the death our bodies create and court as the cost and the consequence of identity, as its reward, Strand forges lines whose music has nothing to do with verse, stanzas whose coherence has nothing to do with decorum, visions whose necessity has nothing to do with dreams. "My Life" he calls the first of the sequence, which ends:

> *I grow into my death.*
> *My life is small*
> *and getting smaller. The world is green.*
> *Nothing is all.*

And in the second, an apostrophe to the redeeming yet resisting Poem, Strand resumes all his old themes of the alienated spirit, the sundered self, so that it is with a giddy, near-hysterical compression that "My Life by Somebody Else" ends:

> *Why do you never come? Must I have you by being*
> *somebody else? Must I write* My Life *by somebody else?*
> My Death *by somebody else? Are you listening?*
> *Somebody else has arrived. Somebody else is writing.*

Others are called, of course, "My Death," "Our Death" and (the climactic piece in the series) "Not Dying," which gains its triumph by conceding loss ("these wrinkles are nothing. These gray hairs . . . these bruised / and swollen ankles, / my darkening brain, / they are nothing") and gainsays that same loss by rehearsing the thing within us which says "I"—for to *it* we never die. Our identity is there when we think of ourselves as dead, when we think of the earth falling into the sun, the sun disappearing into space, the whole universe wiped out. We cannot reach further than that into annihilation, but if we could "we" would survive:

> *I shall not die.*
> *The grave result*
> *and token of birth, my body*
> *remembers and holds fast.*

That is the close of "Not Dying," and it shows that confidence in mortality which enables Strand, at his most generous reach, to address himself at last to otherness *apprehended* not merely as a version of the self misplaced, fallen, but as a genuine act of love, a transaction which admits the possibility and the value of the second person, of what the Gospels call the Neighbor and what Strand himself calls the Stranger; in twelve lines ending, inevitably, with a comma (*i.e.*, not ending), Strand offers himself to, and thereby receives the world that is within, his dying body; he gives the world away and thereby creates himself; the poem is called "Letter":

> *Men are running across a field,*
> *pens fall from their pockets.*
> *People out walking will pick them up.*
> *It is one of the ways letters are written.*
>
> *How things fall to others!*
> *The self no longer belonging to me, but asleep*
> *in a stranger's shadow, now clothing*
> *the stranger, now leading him off.*
>
> *It is noon as I write to you.*
> *Someone's life has come into my hands.*
> *The sun whitens the buildings.*
> *It is all I have. I give it all to you. Yours,*

The Story of Our Lives by Mark Strand

His fourth and finest book—finest because the focus is so clear, the resonance of an already "placed" voice so unmixed and yet so unforced—begins with a sustained lament for the poet's father, for his father's life rather than for his death. Death is not to be mourned in Strand's thematics, of course, it is only to be identified:

> to lose
> again and again is to have more
> and more to lose, and losing is having . . .

One more celebration of an empty place, this elegy is an emblematic trajectory, a six-poem acknowledgment of the necessity to put off knowledge, to deny, to refuse, to gainsay: "There were no secrets. There was nothing to say." Strand insists, or broods, which is his brand of insistence, on the importance, for individual survival ("they cannot reach your dreams"), of rejecting that extremity of consciousness which process, which historical existence, cannot endure or transcend. Sometimes—later on in the book—he is wistful about such ecstatic apprehensions ("If only there were a perfect moment . . . if only we could live in that moment"), but he is quite certain that they are not available to him, that they are not within life, as indeed the sense of the word *ecstasy* makes evident they are not. So Strand divides to conquer, divides the self to conquer the self ("you are the neighbor of nothing"), for the price of experience, experience which Blake has told us cannot be bought for a song, is negation.

Which is why Strand writes his lament not in verse but in the very dialect of negation, in prose, the one linguistic medium out to eliminate itself, to use itself up in the irrecoverable rhythms of speech rather than in the angelic (or ecstatic) measures of repetition and return. No recurrence, no refrain here, but the horror of knowing too much, of suffering more than is to be borne: "I have carried it with me too long, I give it back," Strand says to his father's "shadow", that Blakean spector of the mortal body which is life without time, or death within eternity where "there is silence instead of a name." For once we accept, once we put on the consciousness of others, Strand implies, we are lost. Such an assumption is a "rejoicing among ruins," a "crystal among the tombs"; to say No to consciousness—

> . . . to stand in a space
> is to forget time, to forget time
> is to forget death . . .

is the one way of evincing and yet evading the horror: negation is a mask which points to itself (*as* a mask), advancing. The prose sentences of "Elegy for My Father" are for life in their refusal to recuperate a rhythm, to reverse. They insist upon process, upon the rudiments of narrative ("The beginning is about to occur. The end is in sight") which will get past those nodal points when it all becomes so saturated with Being that life has nowhere to go and so cannot go on. Strand's poem is a way of outdistancing the mind in its submission to consciousness—it is a discarding in order to pick up the blank card, the next . . . "that silence is the extra page."

And yet the next goup of poems in the book shows that what I have called prose is not entirely that, for all the abjuration of repetition, of predictable (and therefore violable) interval which must constitute verse. "What are the blessings born of enclosure?" Strand asks, and proceeds to count them. He counts the way a child does, sliding beads across the abacus until the line is empty. Emptying, in fact, is the creative performance of these poems: "sorrow leads to achievement which leads to emptiness." For it is only when you and the world are empty that you taste what Strand calls "the honey of absence". Only when enclosure is voided does it become space—allow for event, possibility, the dynamics of annihilation:

> *this is the celebration, the only celebration:*
> *by giving yourself over to nothing*
> *you shall be healed.*

The comparatively short poems grouped in the appropriately titled second part of the book "The Room" are a discovery, then, of a new prosody for Strand, for the poet who "could not choose / between sleep and wakefulness," between ecstasy and process. Whereas most of us, poets or not, begin with the story of our lives and must find those ecstatic apices which afford it a value, a meaning; Strand begins with the ecstasy, the astonishment, the stupor, and seeks to empty it out, to put it behind him, to silence it in order that the story may occur—for him the story has not yet happened, or has already happened but has never been lived ("there was no more to our lives / than the story of our lives"). The only way for the poet who seeks an issue out of Being into Becoming is by negation. It is a perpetual nay-saying in the face of what is given, what is too much with us:

> *He would have preferred*
> *the lake without a story,*
> *or no story and no lake.*
> *His pursuit was a form of evasion:*
> *the more he tried to uncover*
> *the more there was to conceal . . .*

The presented cacuminations of life—this woman, this room, this bed, this weather—are too full, too loud, too much there *already:*

> *The silence was in him*
> *and it rose like joy,*
> *like the beginning.*

As is apparent from these quotations, Strand has discovered a scansion for his dilemma, a style for his despair: "He would follow / his words to learn where he was. / He would begin . . . and in the sound of his own voice beginning / he would hear" the words which would allow him to be *forthcoming,* rather than merely, ecstatically, here:

> *What he had written told him nothing.*
> *He put it away and began again.*

What the book ends with, then, is that beginning: three long poems about utterance as enema, "The Story of our Lives", "Inside the Story" and—crucially—"The Untelling." Evident in the titles alone is that concern with process, movement and trajectory which in even the most fragmentary lyric is felt to underly the impulse to speak at all; even the wildest cry has a cause, even the weirdest lament has an effect. The story begins in raw feeling, or cooked form ("the sun dragging the moon like an echo"), and it is what will save the speaker, it is the end of the beginning, "knowing that what I feel is often the crude / and unsuccessful form of a story / that may never be told." How to tell the story if it rejoins, once spoken, what is merely there, suffocating in its presence, meaningless in its existence? Strand has found out: he must *untell* the story so that he does not accumulate his experience but rather, by words, so that he *rids* himself of experience, empties himself out of memory and foreboding, lays waste to the past and the future so that there is that space about him in which the story—the life, the poem—may occur.

There is a famous cartoon by Saul Steinberg in which a drawing hand draws a drawing hand which draws it. We have, as Gombrich has remarked about this little diagram, no clue as to which is meant to be the real and which the image; each interpretation is equally probable, but neither, as such, is consistent. The drawing illustrates the limit to the information that language can convey without introducing devices—they are, precisely, the devices of poetry—which differentiate between language and "metalanguage." Strand's final poem in this book is such an achievement, for in it "he" is writing a poem which, as it is produced on the page, becomes the unacceptable production of the poet himself. By successive rejections Strand brings the poem round to its end, the story-as-Ourabouros, the serpent devouring its own tail, for the last lines are:

> *He went to the room*
> *that looked out on the lawn.*
> *He sat and began to write:*
> ## THE UNTELLING

which is of course the title of the poem, so that we do not know where to take "him," here at the end which is his beginning, or at his beginning which it now appears is his end. Indeed we do not take him at all, we are taken by him: we are moved. By untelling the story, Strand has recovered, then, the old circular or cyclical wisdom of poetry, indeed of verse, which is always a turning, a returning. He has made the room in which he can move . . . around.

Such a commentary does no justice whatever to the great beauty of visualization in these poems—"The Untelling" is as vivid and unforgettable as a Bergman film, a Hopper landscape, with all the despairing notification those great names imply—but that is not what is new in Strand's book. What is new is his recovery of what might have seemed, to the merely finger-tapping critic, a lost art: the prosody of erasure. These astonishing poems remind us that originally the word *verse* and the word *prose* come from the same old Latin word, *pro-vertere,* which in its prose past-participle means *to have moved on,* but which in its poetic infinitive means *to roll around again.*

Ohio Review, 1974

MAY SWENSON

"Turned Back to the Wild by Love"

Whenn May Swenson, speaking in her thaumaturgical fashion of poetry, says that "attention to the silence in between is the amulet that makes it work," we are reminded, while on other occasions in her work we are reassured, that there is a kind of poetry, as there used to be a kind of love, which dares not speak its name. Indeed, it was in the latter's heyday (1891, when Mallarmé thanked Oscar Wilde for *The Picture of Dorian Gray*, "one of the only books that can move me, for its commotion proceeds from an essential reverie, and from the strangest silences of the soul"), that the former's program was devised, by the thanker: "to *name* an object is to suppress three-quarters of our pleasure in the poem, a pleasure which consists in gradually divining . . . ; to *suggest*, that is the ideal. That is making perfect use of the kind of mystery which constitutes the symbol." Of course, there is a complementary impulse to *identify* in this reluctance to call a spade a spade; it is an impulse implicit in the very paradox supported by the word *identification*, which we use both to select an object in all its singularity, and to dissolve that "identical" object into its likeness with another. The refusal, or the reluctance, to *name* in order that she may the more truly *identify* is what we notice first about May Swenson's poetry—though she does not proceed so strictly with the enterprise as Mallarmé, for whom the designation of a flower enforced its *absence* from any bouquet. When Miss Swenson says:

> *beautiful each Shape*
> *to see*
> *wonderful each Thing*
> *to name*

she means the kind of ascertaining of Existence Hölderlin meant when he said that poetry was a naming of the Gods—and for such an appeal (such an appellation), the ordinary labels do not suffice. Miss Swenson would not be so extreme about her magic as the symbolists, but she is plainly aware of the numbing power of proper names; as the story of Rumpelstiltskin demonstrates, there is an awful mastery in knowing what a being is called, and in so calling him—indeed such mastery suggests, to May Swenson at least, a corresponding lack of attention to the quality of being itself, a failure, by the wielding of nomination's "mace petrific," to encounter, to espouse form as it *becomes* what it is.

It is an old kind of poetry, then, that this poet resumes in her quest for "my face in the rock, my name on the wildest tree," a poetry that goes back to Orpheus, probably, and moves forward through Blake and Emily Dickinson, whom May Swenson specifically echoes, I think, in her eagerness to see Being wherever she looks:

> *Any Object before the Eye*
> *can fill the space can occupy*
> *the supple frame of eternity*
>
> *my Hand before me such*
> *tangents reaches into Much*
> *root and twig extremes can touch*
>
> *any Hour can be the all*
> *expanding like a cunning Ball*
> *to a Vast from very small*
>
> *any Single becomes the More*
> *multiples sprout from alpha's core*
> *from Vase of legend vessels of lore . . .*

It is the poetry which comes into existence whenever the need is felt (as by Valéry most recently, most magisterially) to *charm*, to *enchant*, to *bind by spells* an existence otherwise apprehended as inaccessibly other. For as Valéry says of Orpheus, it was only by his songs that trees knew the full horror of dancing. Similarly, in May Swenson's kennings, their method "a parliament of overlappings" and their goal "an assuaging singleness," we find that the hand in her lap, the cat on the sill, the cloud in the sky become, before we have a chance to adjust our sights and to enslave our other senses as well to what we *know*, fables of unlabelled Being:

> *For each path leads both out and in*
> *I come while going   No to and from*

There is only here   And here
is as well as there   Wherever
I am led I move within the care
of the season
hidden in the creases of her skirts
of green or brown or beaded red
And when they are white
I am not lost   I am not lost then
only covered for the night

Evidently, Miss Swenson's effort has been to discover runes, the conjurations by which she can not only apostrophize the hand, the cat and the cloud in their innominate otherness, but by which she can, in some essential and relieving way, *become them*, leave her own impinging selfhood in the paralyzed region where names are assigned, and assume instead the energies of natural process.

From the first—in 1954 came *her* first collection, the significantly titled *Another Animal*—May Swenson has practiced, in riddles, chants, hex-signs and a whole panoply of invented *sortilege* unwonted in Western poetry since the Witch of Endor brought up Samuel, the ways not only of summoning Being into her grasp, but of getting herself out of that grasp and into alien shapes, into those emblems of power most often identified with the sexual:

. . . on this ball   *oh to Endure*
half dark   *like the stone*
half light   *sufficient*
i walk Upright   *to itself alone*
i lie Prone
within the night   *or Reincarnate*
                     like the tree
the longing   *be born each spring*
that i know   *to greenery*
is in the Stone also
it must be   *or like the lion*
the same that rises *without law*
in the Tree   *to roam the Wild*
the longing   *on velvet paw . . .*
in the Lion's call
speaks for all

Consider the array of instruments in this fragment of the first poem from that first book, "Evolution": the incantatory use of rhyme; the rhythms of the spell; the typography that lines up the first column to stand not only pat but put, as it were, against the outer verticality of the second column, so that the poem on the page articulates, by the space it leaves as by the form it takes, a regular *passage* through which the forces can move to their completion; the lower-casing of the first-person pronoun, and the capitalization of the three Entities addressed, then their relegation to lower-case too, and the assumption of capital status by the two crucial verbs, "Reincarnate" and "Endure," and by the hypostatized adjective "Wild"; the irregular little stanzas content to exhibit, in loving complacency, a single word as an entire line; the rejection of punctuation as an unnecessary artifice in this organum of being. Evidently, this poet is engaged, and more than engaged, is elated, by the responsibilities of form. In subsequent poems in *Another Animal,* as in her other books, Miss Swenson exhibits a very determined attitude toward *contrivance;* aware, I suppose, of the danger inherent in her own siren-songs, with their obsessive reliance on the devices of incantation, she is more than eager to cast off the blasphemies of "Satanic Form":

> *Things metallic or glass*
> *frozen twisted flattened*
> *stretched to agonized bubbles*
> *bricks beams receptacles vehicles*
> *forced through fire hatched to unwilling form*

—and to assume in their place the "blessed" and organic avatars it is her art to invoke, not so much to counterfeit as to conjure:

> *flower and stone not cursed with symmetry*
> *cloud and shadow not doomed to shape and fixity*
> *the intricate body of man without rivet or nail*
> *O love the juice in the green stem growing . . .*

Contraption, like naming, is seen as the wrong version of experience. The paradox of the riddling poet is that she must identify without naming, make without artifice, "a model of time, a map of space." Miss Swenson is engaged in the Higher Fabrication, that *poesis* which is the true baptism; when she fails to devise charms that capture Being in their toils, she becomes, like Dickinson, again, merely charming; the appeal is no more, at times, than appealing, when it needed to be a summons:

> *I lived by magic*
> *A little bag in my chest held a whirling stone*
> *so hot it was past burning*
> *so radiant it was blinding*
>
> *When the moon rose worn and broken*
> *her face like a coin endlessly exchanged*

in the hands of the sea
her ray fell upon the doors which opened
and I walked in the living wood . . .

Throughout this book, as the title itself suggests, and in the course of the collections to come, May Swenson has found a figure which allows her to escape the difficulties of both nomination and mechanism; it is the figure of the centaur, which cannot be merely named for it is imaginary, and which cannot be merely artificial for it is alive. She begins, in the title poem:

Another animal imagine moving
in his rippling hide
down the track of the centaur . . .

the shaped verses undulate down the page in a first presentment of "dappled animals with hooves and human knees"; in "To Confirm a Thing," the figure is moralized a little:

In the equal Night where oracular beasts
                         the planets depose
and our Selves assume their orbits . . .
My thighs made marble-hard
                         uncouple only to the Archer
with his diametrical bow
                         who prances in the South
himself a part of his horse . . .
Then let me by these signs
                         maintain my magnitude
as the candid Centaur his dynasty upholds
                         And in the Ecliptic Year
our sweet rebellions
                         shall not be occulted but remain
coronals in heaven's Wheel.

And finally, in "Question," the same figure, which has become perhaps too cosmic, too "mechanical" in its astronomic implications, is returned to its erotic energies, the self addressed in that animal form where, by a certain incantation, Miss Swenson best finds her being in its highest range:

Body my house
my horse my hound
what will I do
when you are fallen

Where will I sleep
How will I ride

> *What will I hunt*
> *Where can I go*
> *without my mount*
> *all eager and quick . . .*
>
> *With cloud for shift*
> *how will I hide?*

May Swenson's second book was published in 1958; *A Cage of Spines,* garlanded with praise by Elizabeth Bishop, Richard Wilbur and Robert Lowell, among others; of these, only Howard Moss seems taken with the notion that in Swenson's "world," Being is illuminated so that "whatever she describes is not only more itself but more than itself." The strategies and devices, the shamanism and sorcery this poet deploys have become, in this larger, luminous collection, more elaborate, more convinced, and deserve further attention; their accommodation of the mystery that only when a thing is apprehended as something else can it be known as itself is fierce and full in *A Cage of Spines.* But we must note, first, an interesting development, from implication to statement, of the Centaur theme, the projection of energies and erotics into animal form, so that the poet may ask, "to what beast's intent / are we the fodder and nourishment?" The new note sounded occurs at the very start of the book, in a poem explicit enough to be called "The Centaur." For the first time, Swenson evokes life—her life—in the chatty, novelistic mode previously judged "too effusive in design for our analyses":

> *The summer that I was ten—*
> *Can it be there was only one*
> *summer that I was ten? It must*
>
> *have been a long one then—*

Looking down the prospect of her imagination, the poet reports how she would ride her willow branch all morning:

> *I was the horse and the rider,*
> *and the leather I slapped to his rump*
> *spanked my own behind . . .*

and come inside, after an exhausting morning's riding (and being ridden):

> Where have you been? *said my mother.*
> Been riding, *I said from the sink,*
> *and filled me a glass of water . . .*

Go tie back your hair, *said my mother,*
and Why is your mouth all green?
Rob Roy, he pulled some clover
as we crossed the field, *I told her.*

Here not by incantation but by exactitude in narrative, Miss Swenson
gets across the doubleness in being she strives for throughout. It is a
method she will resume in the book after this one, but the rest of *A
Cage of Spines* is dedicated to the means of witchcraft. By riddles and
charms, the poet aspires to a more resonant being than the life grudg-
ingly acknowledged in her own body:

> . . . *I would be inheritor*
> *of the lamb's way and the deer's,*
> *my thrust take from the ground*
> *I tread or lie on. In thighs of trees,*
> *in recumbent stones, in the loins*
> *of beasts is found*
> *that line my own nakedness carried.*
> *Here, in an Eden of the mind,*
> *I would remain among my kind,*
> *to lake and hill, to tree and beast married.*

Not only the shaped poems, the compulsive rhymes and puns ("what
seams is only art"), the riddles and agnominations ("the shape of this
box keels me oval / Heels feel its bottom / Nape knocks its top"—from
the conundrum about eggs), but the discovery of the secret messages
hidden within ordinary speech, as Being is concealed by Labels, excite
Miss Swenson to poems of an almost frantic hermeticism: in two
homages to writers, she extends her method to a kind of esoteric
dalliance. First in "Frontispiece," which appears to describe a picture
of Virginia Woolf in terms of the circumstances that led her to suicide,
we realize from an odd, ominous resonance the lines have, that not only
the names of the writer herself ("your chaste-fierce name") but the
titles of all her books have been braided into the verse; thus the
"frontispiece" is a compendium of names indeed, only disguised,
worked back into the texture of Being and used not as nominations but
proof:

> *The waves carve your hearse and tomb*
> *and toll your voyage out again again.*

The second poem of dedication is even more curious, for in it not
merely names but all words are susceptible of disintegration into their
secret content; what we are offered is ostensibly a description of Frost
("R. F., His Hand Against a Tree") but the account is continually

breaking down as Miss Swenson discovers, like Nabokov (whose English is so often a matter of perpetual inside jokes), that she can say more about her subject by letting the language speak for itself, merely doing a little pruning and spacing to let the sense in:

> *Lots of trees in the fo*
> *rest but this one's an O*
> *a K that's plan*
> *ted hims elf and nob*
> *oddy has k nots of that hand*
> *some polish or the knarl*
> *edge of ear th or the obs*
> *tiny ate servation his blueyes*
> *make or the tr easures his sent*
> *ient t humb les find.*

These are, as she calls them, "glyphs of a daring alphabet" indeed, and "hide what they depend on." There are other diableries in this book likely to exasperate as well as to exalt; chiefly a poem called "Parade of Painters" in which 36 painters are "assigned" first a characteristic color, then a texture ("Manet porcelain, Matisse thistles," etc.), then a shape. Then the whole thing is assembled in a litany of 36 lines which reads something like a dada catalogue, save that Swenson has shown us her method and its underlying logic: we cannot fault it, but we may fail to be *charmed* by the procession, as it passes, of painter, shape, texture and color:

> *. . . Delacroix mouth viscera iris*
> *Degas witchmoth birch clay*
> *Pissaro dhow privet marble*
> *Seurat hourglass linen popular*
> *Dufy glove pearl azure*
> *Rouault mummy serge blood . . .*

Much more characteristic of Swenson's excellence, I think, is "News from the Cabin," in which all her impulses congregate joyously around a less arbitrary theme: visits from four creatures, none named but all identified by the characteristic textures, rhythms, and vocabulary we should associate with a woodpecker, a squirrel, a jay and a snake, if we were to *become* them by the power of our *recital* (rather like the interludes young Arthur experiences, in T. H. White's books, as he serves his apprenticeship to fish, hawks, even hedgehogs in order to learn how to be a man). Consider the sound of this from "Hairy":

> *Cried peek! Beaked it—chiselled the drupe.*
> *His nostril I saw, slit in a slate whistle,*
> *White-black dominoes clicked in his wings.*

> *Bunched beneath the dangle he heckled with holes,*
> *bellysack soft, eye a brad, a red-flecked*
> *mallet his ball-peen head, his neck its haft.*

and the movement of the end of "Scurry":

> *Sat put, pert, neat, in his suit and his seat, for a minute,*
> *a frown between snub ears, bulb-eyed head*
> *toward me sideways, chewed.*
> *Rocked, squeaked. Stored the stone in his cheek.*
> *Finished, fell to all fours, a little roan couch;*
> *flurried paws loped him off, prone-bodied,*
> *tail turned torch, sail, scarf.*

In these extraordinary poems, animal life is invoked, is actually *acquired* for the conjurer's purposes (extended energy, a generalized erotic awareness) by the haptic qualities of language itself, even more than by the riddling process so programmatically set up in the other pieces. The generosity, the abundance of Swenson's means may allow her, on the one hand, to speak somewhat sentimentally in "East River" of Brooklyn seen across the water as "a shelf of old shoes, needing repair, but clean knots of smoke are being tied and untied," and thereby we see, though both are patronized, Brooklyn *and* the shoes; but in "News from the Cabin," on the other, she also commands, as in the last section, "Supple," an utterance whose imagery is assimilated without condescension to its very movement, a diction so wedded to appearances that the speaker "leaves the spot" enriched with an access of being, an increment which comes only when life has been enchanted to its own understanding:

> *I followed that elastic: loose*
> *unicolored knot, a noose he made as if unconscious.*
> *Until my shadow touched him; half his curd*
> *shuddered, the rest lay chill.*
> *I stirred: the ribbon raised a loop;*
> *its end stretched, then cringed like an udder;*
> *a bifid tongue, his only rapid, whirred*
> *in the vent; vertical pupils lit his hood.*
> *That part, a groping finger, hinged, stayed upright.*
> *Indicated what? That I stood*
> *in his light? I left the spot.*

In 1963, a large group of poems from Miss Swenson's first two volumes, with some fifty new poems, was published under the general title *To Mix with Time,* a phrase which in its own context reiterates her⸺

project: "One must work a magic to mix with time / in order to become old." Here the very compression, the proliferation *inward* of the new abracadabras seem to have enabled the poet to be elsewhere quite explicit about her undertaking:

> . . . *There unraveled*
> *from a file in my mind a magic motion*
> *I, too, used to play with: from chosen words a potion*
> *could be wrung; pickings of them, eaten, could make*
> *you fly, walk*
> *on water, be somebody else, do or undo anything, go back*
> *or forward on belts of time* . . .

It is good to have it spelled out, for there are here many poems of a specifically esoteric quality, whose organization on the page, as in the ear, suggests the location of a mystery in Being which the poet would attain to only by a ritual, a litany of participles and lattices of space:

. . . There is a	*Swaddled Thing*
There is a	Swaddled Thing
There is a	*Rocking Box*
There is a	Covered Box
The	*Unwrapping*
the	*Ripening*
Then the	*Loosening*
the	*Spoiling*
The	*Stiffening*
then the	*Wrapping*
The	*Softening*
but the long long	*Drying*
The	*Wrapping*
the	*Wrapping*
the	*Straightening*
and	*Wrapping*
The rigid	*Rolling*
the gilded	*Scrolling*
The	*Wrapping*
and	*Wrapping*
and careful	*Rewrapping*
The	*Thinning*
and	*Drying*
but the	*Wrapping*
and	*Fattening*

There is the worm	Coiled
and the straw	Straightened
There is the	Plank
and the glaucous	Bundle
the paper	Skull
and the charred	Hair
the linen	Lip
and the leather	Eyelid
There is a	Person
of flesh that is a rocking	Box
There is a	Box
of wood that is a painted	Person

To which the poet, her own exegete, adds this "Note from a diary: I remembered Giotto's fresco, 'Birth of the Virgin' in a cloister in Florence: the 'Mother of God' was a swaddled infant held upright, like a board or plaque, by her nurse . . . and I remembered a mummy in the Vatican Museum in Rome: in her sarcophagus shaped and painted like herself, an Egyptian girl 2000 years old lay unwrapped to the waist." The notation, in the poem, of identities between the infant and the mummy, and the enactment of vital, or mortal, differences that reaches the climax of the last four lines, with their paradoxical reversals, dramatizes the kind of formal extremes May Swenson is ready to risk. "The idea," she says in "Out of my Head," the first poem in this book, "is to make a vehicle out of it." To employ, that is, the spell in order to be taken somewhere; or as she says in another place, and in her most orphic cadences:

> *we weave asleep*
> *a body*
> *and awake unravel*
> *the same veins*
> *we travel*

The unravelling of those travelled veins is undertaken, of course, in other ways besides such necromantic ones. There is a group of poems, in *To Mix with Time*, written in France, Italy and Spain and concerned with the reporting of surfaces, not the casting of spells. As in the earlier "Centaur," the poet appears sufficiently possessed of her identity to feel no need of commanding her surround by voodoo. She can trust her sensibility, in these new old places, to do its work, and oblige the *genius loci* to give up its own ghost:

> *Gondola-slim*
> *above the bridge, a new moon held a dim*

> *circle of charcoal between its points.*
> *Bats played in the greenish air,*
> *their wing-joints*
> *soft as moths' against the bone-gray palazzi where*
> *not a window was alight . . .*

These are secular poems, then, rarely moralized or magicked, but left to speak for themselves, in the descriptive mode of Elizabeth Bishop, though there are exceptions, occurring (as we might expect) in the case of the "Fountains of Aix," where the word "water" is disjoined fifteen times from the lines and made to slide down the side of a stanza:

> *. . . A goddess is driving a chariot through   water.*
> *Her reins and whips are tight white   water.*
> *Bronze hooves of horses wrangle with   water.*
> *Faces with mossy lips unlocked*
>   *always uttering   water*
>   *Water*
>
>   *wearing their features blank,*
>   *their ears deaf, their eyes mad*
>   *or patient or blind or astonished at   water*
>   *always uttered out of their mouths . . .*

and again in a poem about death, "The Alyscamps at Arles," in which the words "bodies," "bones," "died," "stones" and "flesh" are isolated in a central column, set off like tombs in each line, and recurring some two dozen times. Europe, we take it, is sacred ground, and the mere fact of treading it is enough, almost, for Miss Swenson's genius to speak low to her. The conjugation, in this book, of a temporal response to earth and a runic riddling of it is indeed "to mix with time;" there is a relaxation of need, somehow, as if the poet had come to find things enthralling enough in themselves:

> *In any random, sprawling, decomposing thing*
> *is the charming string*
> *of its history—and what it will be next . . .*

Like "Evolution," her first poem in her first book, her last one here, "The Exchange," recapitulates her enterprise—to get out of herself and into those larger, warmer energies of earth, and to do so by liturgical means ("Words? Let their / mutations work / toward the escape / of object into the nearest next / shape, motion, assembly, temporal context"):

> *Populous and mixed is mind.*
> *Earth take thought,*
> *my mouth be moss . . .*

Wind be motion,
birds be passion,
water invite me to your bed.

Things Taking Place was the working title May Swenson had origi-
nally given *To Mix with Time,* and its suggestion of a larger interest
in a secular world where events occur, where life "happens," and a
lessening concern with the cosmic energies of "mere" Being, is even
more applicable to the poet's latest work, published in 1967 in a long
book called *Half Sun Half Sleep.* Not that Miss Swenson is any less
interested in the energies, the powers that drive the stars in their
courses, or in the measurements and movements responsible for that
formal echo of dune and wave, beach and tide—rather, the largest
impulses which often she could *handle,* precisely, as abstractions only,
are now accommodated into the observed intercourse of her body and
its environment, her life and its limits. There are charms here too, but
they are *secular* charms, and the fact that so many of the rhyme words
are tucked away in the "wrong" parts of the line suggests the profane
intentions of these cunning incantations—if Miss Swenson has designs
on life, they are subordinated to a surface she prefers unruly:

> *Well, do they sing? If so, I* expect *their*
> *note is extreme. Not something one* hears,
> *but must watch the cat's* ears *to detect . . . [emphasis mine]*

she furthers, too, her old mistrust, even her outright distaste for the
exemplars of "Satanic Form," which she finds in most of our modern
enclosures, elevator cages, Pullman cars and airplane bellies, and spe-
cifically in our satellites and space missiles. One of the most brilliant
pieces in the new book is "August 19, Pad 19," a jeering, nerve-end
journal of an astronaut "positioned for either breach birth / or urn
burial." Reminiscent of her other entrapped forms—the mummy and
the swaddled infant—the astronaut is prepared:

> *. . . Never so helpless, so choked with power.*
> *Never so impotent, so important.*
> *So naked, wrapped, equipped, and immobile,*
> *cared for by 5000 nurses.*
> *Let them siphon my urine to the nearest star.*
> *Let it flare and spin like a Catherine.*
>
> *. . . T minus 10 . . . The click of countdown stops.*
> *My pram and mummy case, this trap's*
> *tumescent tube's still locked to wet,*
> *magnetic, unpredictable earth.*

> *All my system's go, but oh,*
> *an anger of the air won't let me go.*
> *On the screen the blip is* MISSION SCRUBBED . . .

and the poem's ultimate irony is to oblige this sequestered conscious-ness, furious in its failure, to feel "out on the dome some innocent drops of rain." The titles suggest the poet's preferences: "On Handling Some Small Shells from the Windward Islands," "A Basin of Eggs," "Drawing the Cat," "On Seeing Rocks Cropping out of a Hill in Central Park" and—quintessentially—"Things in Common." There is of course a certain trust in her old ways of working, call them weapons even, the sharp-edged, riddling means of tricking us into the poem; the book itself is arranged with the titles in alphabetical order, and there are a number of shaped poems, of spells and counting-rhymes, for as she says in "The Truth," a poem about a snake that is snake-shaped,

> *Speculations about shape amount to a counting*
> *of the coils.*

But there is a moving away from the kind of hermetic indication that cannot show loss as well as gain. There is the sense, recorded in a poem about two trees leaning together, "All That Time," that our interpreta-tions of phenomena may be cruelly aberrant:

> *And where their tops tangled*
> *it looked like he was crying*
> *on her shoulder.*
> *On the other hand, maybe he*
>
> *had been trying to weaken her,*
> *break her, or at least*
> *make her bend*
> *over backwards for him . . .*

and that we must devise a form that will account for "strange abrasions / zodiacal wounds." The important thing, she says, is

> *To be the instrument*
> *and the wound of feeling.*

As the book's title suggests, the balance between sacred and profane, ritual and report, with its implication of the balance between seeing and dreaming, speech and somnambulism, is carefully tended:

> *The tug of the void*
> *the will of the world*
> *together . . .*

These poems are exuberant in their hocus-pocus, surely, but they are also a little rueful about the facility to which one can trust in the hope of getting out of the self ("One must be a cloud to occupy a house of cloud . . . refusing the fixture of a solid soul"); also they are not so explicit in exploring "the suck of the sea's dark mind": if Swenson still asks, in a poem called "The Lightning" through which a diagonal gutter of space jabs through her twenty lines to the word "entrails," "When will I grope my way clear of the entrails of intellect?" she is nonetheless prepared to use the mementoes of that gutted intellect to deal with the sea's dark mind, referring to the "ancient diary the waves are murmuring" and accounting in terms of gains as well as losses for her existence as a rational animal:

> *. . . When I was a sea worm*
> *I never saw the sun,*
>
> *but flowed, a salty germ,*
> *in the bloodstream of the sea.*
> *There I left an alphabet*
>
> *but it grew dim to me.*
> *Something caught me in its net,*
> *took me from the deep*
>
> *book of the ocean, weaned me,*
> *put fin and wing to sleep,*
> *made me stand and made me*
>
> *face the sun's dry eye.*
> *On the shore of intellect*
> *I forgot how to fly . . .*
>
> *In brightness I lost track*
> *of my underworld*
> *of ultraviolet wisdom.*
>
> *My fiery head furled*
> *up its cool kingdom*
> *and put night away.*

These are no longer nor even want to be the poems of a small furry animal ("the page my acre") nor of a selfless demiurge ("They founded the sun. / When the sun found them / it undertook its path and aim . . . / The air first heard itself / called glory in their lungs"); they are the witty resigned poems of a woman "hunting clarities of Being," asking

> *Have I arrived from*
> *left or*
> *right to hover here*
> *in the clear permission of my*
> *temperature? Is my*
> *flow a fading*
> *up or*
> *down—my glow*
> *going? Or is my flush*
> *rushing to a rose of ripe*
> *explosion?*

a woman eager still to manipulate the phenomenal world by magic, but so possessed, now, of the means of her identity that the ritual, spellbinding, litaneutical elements of her art have grown consistent, even coincident, with her temporal, conditioned, suffering experience and seem—to pay her the highest compliment May Swenson could care to receive —no more than natural.

DAVID WAGONER

"It Dawns on Us That We Must Come Apart."

DAVID WAGONER, in his forties and a professor of English, is as well the only writer his age I can think of in America today who is, by the difficult criteria which hold the noun together with the adjective in solution, *en gelée* even, both a successful poet and a successful novelist. What I mean, of course, is that he is not entirely—not merely—a Success, not a success like Allen Ginsberg, say, or Norman Mailer. If you manage to be a success like *that*—and in America today, management appears, surely, to be the best way to do it—you don't need to be a successful *anything;* in fact there isn't time to be a successful anything, you're too busy just being a Success. Indeed, ever since the curious example of Cocteau, that expert manager,* there has been a noticeable uncertainty as to *genre* in the productions of our certified successes, and the mass media have intensified the hesitation into a compulsion neurosis: Ginsberg's texts, his platform performances and his diaries become interchangeable and, I suspect, indistinguishable to himself; Mailer turns his fictions into Chautauquas or *drame-à-thèse*, offers whatever happens to interest him in straggling bundles, "advertisements for myself" quite properly ticketed. As these gentlemen have discovered, we are interested not in the poems of Allen Ginsberg or the

* In accounting for the works which constitute, in his case, only some episodes of his career, Cocteau assigns them to a series of variations on the notion of *poetry:* *poésie de roman, poésie critique, poésie de théâtre, poésie graphique,* etc. We are to assume that once a Cocteau produces novels, criticism, plays, drawings, they cease being these things and become part of *poetry,* which like electricity is not so much a thing as the way things behave. Of course, this is not the same as saying they become merely Jean Cocteau, but that is clearly the next step.

novels of Norman Mailer, but in Allen Ginsberg and Norman Mailer. We are interested in the Success, that protean phenomenon whose perpetuation depends, most likely, on an evasion of the responsibility of form; we are less interested in the successful poet or the successful novelist—less still in the successful poem or the successful novel, which of course can dispense with the Success-figure altogether, just as that figure is actually threatened by the pre-eminence (if we grant it) of the *work of art*.

Which accounts, I contend, for the relative occultation of David Wagoner in the current literary firmament. Though his eight books, as I mean to show, have nourished and renewed one another, the poems gaining precisely the humanity and texture of reality we look for in the novel, and the novels acquiring that "abandon, wild calculation and seriousness" which James Dickey locates in Wagoner's poetry; though the four volumes of poetry alternating with four novels since 1953 have garnered a lot of cross-pollinating praise,* it is surely because they insist so securely on being poems and novels that most of us have still to discover this writer's contribution to our literature. That is just it: Wagoner will not come out from behind his literature, and thereby protects himself from becoming another casualty of Success. The last word on the subject is Malcolm Lowry's, in a scrap of verse called "After Publication of *Under the Volcano*":

> Sucess like a drunkard consumes the house of the soul
> Exposing that you have worked only for this—
> Ah, that I had never suffered this treacherous kiss
> And had been left in darkness forever to founder and fail.

The first of Wagoner's books of poetry, *Dry Sun, Dry Wind*, was published in 1953 and dedicated to Roethke, who remains a pervasive force in all this poet's work—even the novels. What Wagoner gets from Roethke is a preoccupation with the movement from external to created reality, the sense that we awaken in a world possessed and informed by something in our dream, so characteristic of the older poet. It is not so much the verbal echoes that suggest Roethke's influence here, though Wagoner has an ear cocked for the cadence which he can turn to his own advantage, the question which will afford an answer to itself by the rhythm of its very interrogation: "Why shall

---

* Roethke declared that Wagoner had "an eye as well as an ear, and what is often rare in the lyrical poet, a real awareness and knowledge of people"—in other words, the gifts of the novelist too; while the novelist Robert Phelps calls Wagoner's novels "useful" because "apart from a keenly exacting eye for the outside world, he has that quality of inside feeling, growing and questioning, which is still more important"—in other words, the gifts of the poet too.

I curl? How may I touch? Who echoes me to death?" Rather than the Roethkean overtones, it is the underlying conviction that a morality abides—tragic, chthonic, buried in "the hollow of self, where no vibrations come"—in the act of vision which is the Northwest poet's gift, and one consequence of it is a focus on the arena of immediate sense-perception. There is, then, a kind of deliberate anonymity at first about the arena, for in the poems of *Dry Sun, Dry Wind* there is no way of knowing just where we are, save on the lip of some pond, upstairs in some house on a windy day, stranded in some desiccated marsh—"the rest is dreams, symmetrically absurd." The locus is Everywhere, like Pascal's definition of God, without the human consolation of the locally indentifiable; the material under close scrutiny is either too minuscule, as in "Marsh Leaf":

> But the shape of a russet leaf
> Reechoes the dry wind's cries:
> One leaf, lying underfoot,
> Speaks, though dead and fallen and deaf . . .

or too ordinary to be assigned a habitation and a name. How the poet has cherished, in all but the last of his books, the unidentifiable industrial suburb of Chicago—Whiting, Indiana—that is his "curious-knotted garden"! Even in his later poems, Way Out West as they appear to be, there persists a middling blank, a refusal of social comfort —we are concerned invariably with what Wagoner later calls "unharmonious earth, the stricken center."

The title itself of this first book is a refusal—or at least an insistence on those aspects of Being which, ordinarily fertilizing, are here to be considered in their anti-human acceptation, without that encouraging moisture which allows for new growth; in a poem called "Sudden Frost," Wagoner speaks of "all who threaten to live," and the admonitory verb is characteristic of these poems, which are about what happens to nature, and even to our human structures within nature, when no one is there to see what happens:

> Down from the culvert and the shaded spring
> The air will topple, and no lips will sing.

Even the figures of human beings, a nurse, a nun, an old man at the beach, are treated as moralized landscapes, without an autonomous principle but rather the universal imagery of natural process, as in "The Nun":

> Now quietly she lies down to sleep, but O
> What water is this, grown warm
> And red within her dream, when into the empty
> Pool the long fish glide?

It is not that Wagoner is uninterested in the separate human life, and in all that makes it separate; but in this first book, at least, it does not lie within his powers to anatomize "great creating nature"—and her destroying avatar—within the limits of selfhood. As he says of one of his figures dissolved in a landscape, "Old Man at the Beach":

> . . . The outer
> Edges of his body have begun to burn,
> Are curling inward to the nose and knees
> To render the inner man of humours.

Such combustion of outer edges, in Wagoner's early work, is a different process from the "gradual furnace of the world" as Arnold called it, and in his first book, the method of dealing with both which the poet has devised is a two-chambered structure, the first part consisting of twenty-two rigorously inhuman lyrics, and the second part of eight dramatic monologues delivered from beyond the grave by a group of landlocked men and women, addressing—as the high-wire artist Bellado, "the great Bellado," puts it—the safe others:

> Those who scurry far from a taut line,
> Turn hills, climb corners, or step back,
> Are deaf to the insides of an earth
> That calls them.

The tree-surgeon, the balloonist, the printer give us the facts from within, and though there is, in what they say of their lives, a consciousness beyond what they can, as mere individuals, lay claim to—as there always is in the successful dramatic monologue—it is nonetheless their limitation that allows Wagoner to get around them. The most convincing moments occur, in these proddings of "normal" lives, when the meaning is in disequilibrium with what the speaker reveals and understands, as when Luke of Sippo Heights (1884–1942), whose wife has already died and who is himself to die the next year, speaks to his son on the subject of noisemaking:

> O Tommy,
> Make noise. Remember how I put
> My cane one day into the bog-slime,
> Then pressed the dank-end on your shirt
> And said, "This is the bedlam of things
> Upon you." Think: living is loud;
> And when the whispering biddies soothe you,
> Cry them down; give them the thunder
> That will kill or bless.

The yearning sympathy for "the bedlam of things" that is in the very slime, the consciousness that something in nature, antipathetic to identity, *wants* us nonetheless ("O what is wrong with water that it tugs us so?" asks Edmond of New Hope: "I have stayed, drying above the loss . . ."), suggests the profounder sympathies of this poet with the Roethke who said:

> *Is my body speaking? I breathe what I am:*
> *The first and last of all things.*
> *Near the graves of the great dead,*
> *Even the stones speak.*

But in his first book, with its stern segregation of the human ("Farewell, farewell, love sleeps beside the chamberpot") from the humus ("the hot earth where lichen clings to the spoils of time"), Wagoner cannot yet command those accents of a selfhood which may reach to the speech of stones. His landscape cannot quite bear the proximity of his knowledge, and must—here again, Roethke helps—be presented in a series of line-by-line sentences, observations which, by the full stop, become aphorisms and sink into experience with a terrible weight, as in "Warning":

> *Wind rocks the pier and the green rowboat.*
> *Clusters of old fishline*
> *Bob from the logs against the water.*
> *All the ducks have gone alee.*
> *Fish scales flip across the jagged hulls.*
> *Today, only the wind sails.*
> *Sinkers float at the ends of the blown lines.*
> *Moss points all one way on the stones.*

The slant rhymes and assorted rhythms keep us from collecting the material presented into a charm, an incantation. There is no self here to "breathe what I am"—just as, in the poems about selves, there is so little breakthrough to vision ("the eye turns feebler, year by year"); the partitioning of the beautiful lyrics from the bruised lives brings Wagoner to a strange alienation, a sense that Being itself, even while he watches, is being withheld from him, or rather, not from him, but that he is not yet himself entirely *there*, in the sense of selfhood that Keats intended when he wrote, "that which is creative must create itself"— for by the end of *Dry Sun, Dry Wind*, Wagoner has not yet created himself, but only the estranged world of "familiars" in which he will henceforth operate by an alienation-effect whose apparent suspension of energy, of process, turns every known thing Other:

> *Now the lull melts all the houses*
> *And the vague yard*
> *Is full of strangers, things.*

The poet's strategy, in his dilemma—his duplicity, which he registers in his second book of poems: "This body and this thought / are strangers saying, 'What has filled us now?' "—is to carry further still the separation of goods which has resulted in such an inconvenient marriage of self and circumstance in his first collection. Recognizing that the murmurous dramatic monologues articulated a different, even a contrary intention from the lyrics of ontological certitude ("beyond this gate, there lies the land of the different mind"), Wagoner divorced his pursuits even more sternly, following in effect Cocteau's famous advice: "what other people reproach you for—cultivate *that!* it is yourself." The year after *Dry Sun, Dry Wind*, therefore, Wagoner published his first novel, *The Man in the Middle* and in 1955 his second, *Money Money Money;* and it was not until 1958, five years after *Dry Sun, Dry Wind*, that he had sufficiently released himself from the indenture to plausible surfaces, to accident and "the ravelled edge of everything" which we think of as the impulse of fiction, or at least its expedient, to produce his second collection of poems, *A Place to Stand.*

The intuition of futility in most biography, the awareness that we are impotent in the clutch of what *happens* to us, finds, in Wagoner's first three novels, a more appropriate rehearsal than in his early poems, which are committed—it is, of course, the lyric responsibility—to an order of knowledge and a hierarchy of Being. *The Man in the Middle* takes for its exergue a sentence from Donne which may stand over all of Wagoner's prose enterprises: "This minute I was well, and am ill, this minute. I am surprised with a sodaine change, and alteration to worse, and can impute it to no cause, nor call it by any name." Wagoner's hero in each instance is a creature from outside the community life—invalid, obsessed, even idiotic—who knows what he takes for his own mind and wants to be left alone with that knowledge, not to enjoy it perhaps ("it was harder to invent life by yourself") but to nurse it along, to "favor" it, in the sense of something felt to be vulnerable; but chance puts him in the world's way, and the ensuing adventures must lead to disaster along with a surrender of the separateness cherished by "the man in the middle," crushed by the social and erotic forces he is called upon to mediate even as he unleashes them: "when there were no people around, you didn't even have to think of yourself if you didn't want to." All four novels are set—embedded, really—in the outlying wastelands of Chicago (where Wagoner himself, as he says on the jacket of the second book of poems, has "worked at times as a railroad section-hand, a concentrated-soup scooper in a steel mill, a park policeman, and a restaurant grillman"),* and though

---

* The author's note to *Money Money Money* says: "Most of the places are real, some of the judgments aren't, none of the people are."

they are rich in tough-guy talk and the kind of detail usually described as action-packed, their real achievement is the conversion of a spoiled nature—exhausted earth, polluted water, befouled air—to an autonomous poetry, a beauty recognized because it generates the consciousness that inhabits it:

> They went down the road bank into the sand and started for the vague outline of the boat. He looked left at the distant glitter of the South Chicago breakwater, then right at the red smudges of Indiana Harbor. Over his shoulder he could see the squat silhouette of the pumping station, made tall only by the smokestack that came out of its middle. Beside them were the shapes of three twisted cottonwood trees, surrounded by sections of sewer pipe, chest-high and broken; and fragments of bricks, worn smooth by the waves, lay embedded in the sand.

It is customary to attach the label "poet's novel" in a rather dismissive way to novels like these, in which every object, every landscape, every episode and every observation is a centripetal expression of the book's total feeling, its emotional marrow. Of course we could say the same thing about *Anna Karenina* or *Madame Bovary:* poet's novels indeed! In fact, it is the great realists who have taught us to read a novel in this way, so that every detail becomes an incarnation of the reality invoked. Wagoner's success with the fallen life is, perhaps, only a partial one precisely because of the partitioning he insists upon, but by the time he had published his second novel, the following year, it was clear that he had enabled, for his poetry, a clearer impulse than his earlier work had afforded, a more definite commitment to the rigors of the medium. In fact, it is in *Money Money Money* (whose title comes from an odd, suggestive fragment by Roethke:

> *Goody-by, good-by, old stones, the time-order is going,*
> *I have married my hands to perpetual agitation,*
> *I run, I run to the whistle of money.*
> *Money money money*
> *Water water water)*

that Wagoner, through one of his characters who quotes Wyatt and goes on to explain what poetry is, defends and even defines his own double enterprise:

> 'They flee from me that sometimes did me seek, With naked foot, stalking in my chamber.' Poetry is almost as good as money, but it isn't. Unlike those bills, my dear, it hits you where you're looking, and that hurts because you have a right to expect to be surprised when you're defeated. Understand?

It is for the world in which poetry is not quite as good as money that Wagoner writes his novels, with their scrupulous prose and their scary plots; in the second one occurs the intimation of his second book of poems—and its title as well—to appear three years later:

> He wouldn't allow any of them inside his life any more, not if they begged. They could come holding out their bodies to be kissed or kept warm, and he wouldn't do it. And he would change all their curious, insistent words into silence . . . And there would be a place to stand till it was entirely daylight everywhere and luck and sense were given away with no strings on them.

For just as the writing of novels liberated Wagoner to do something in his poetry which could not be done with all those Other Lives weighing on his tongue, so the writing of poetry ("that lofted my tongue / and cried blue language at the enemy") afforded those necessary, utopian possibilities which the novel could not reach, but only reach toward—"a place to stand till it was entirely daylight everywhere and luck and sense were given away with no strings on them." In 1958, then, Wagoner published *A Place to Stand*, a book of poems which, in its vision of a transfigured existence, adumbrates a titanic self on the other side of appearances, a self that can be realized by an appropriate submission to organic process in which all antagonisms— the heart's immediate fire and the mind's impossible flare, as he calls them—are resolved in an ultimate conflagration of identity:

> *I wait to be consumed where my life began,*
> *My hands behind me, eyes on either blaze:*
> *The heart's immediate fire against the bone,*
> *The mind's impossible flare through paradise.*

It is a book about heroism, shaped in the imagery of monarchs ("O beautiful king of flaws," the poet cries as he asks himself, in "Part Song," the questions the world's body will be enlisted to answer: "what am I now? . . . what was I once. . . . O what will I be?"), employing in its regular stanzas and slant rhymes a tremendous diction, as if no claims upon recognition could be too drastic:

> *And the royal couple lie in a chronicle—*
> *Strewn through each other like their images:*
> *The orb, the scepter, and the whirling crown.*

And the energy that keeps one reading from poem to finished poem, not merely spotting influences (Dickey, in this case), is the energy of an enormous quest, a search into darkness ("my mind, that widower of light") and failure ("O God in Thy blur, Who is it stuffs this murdering dust in my breath?") for the lineaments of perpetuation in a universe beyond semblance:

What called me? Why? When will the flame and foam make sense?
How shall I quicken? Who are these animals? Where am I?

The journey to discover the answer to these questions is made outward, to the confines of the elements, as inward, through the body's spoils, tracking the life that went before, tracing a vitality in the world sensed as anterior and therefore transcendent—

> *We'll follow water down,*
> *Drink it and be it, grow*
> *Lengthy, till we reach*
> *Exhaustion in the dark*
> *Where the dismembered beasts*
> *Before us melted and fell.*
> *This, this is the trail . . .*

—to love, pursued amid the chaos of battles to that bright consummation or its loss. Yet for all the universals in his poetic mode, Wagoner has now found a way to introduce himself into his language, has found, that is, a way to identify *his own life* with the preposterous energies he addresses himself to. It is the destructive element he summons to his aid, once he is dispensed—by his novels, as I have suggested—from having to account for mere chance, a lower-case Chaos which rules the minor life. Rather there is, he discovers in his poems, a residual, substantive negation in the world, in himself, in the very means he has of knowing one from the other (language), which gives its particular pathos to his work. First of all, as he asks in the title poem, surely it is not in the cosmic fantasmagoria that a man will find his place to stand?

> *The whirling continents,*
> *The sky seen through a hole,*
> *The stars flashing apart—*
> *What master calls them real?*

They are not real because the master has made them up—as Wagoner says in his "Anthem for Man": ". . . and he, almighty, makes worlds with his tongue." And the made-up, the imagined world of words *cannot* be a matter wholly of exaltation, of "angelic wisdom," for words, as Wagoner declares in one of his most famous poems, "To My Friend Whose Parachute Did Not Open," *words can harbor betrayal:*

> *I know angelic wisdom leaped from your mouth,*
> *But not in words, for words can be afraid.*

It is, then, a matter of patience, of giving over, if the self is to realize its existence in the only medium it commands; the very assumptions of language are deceptive ("In my list of choices, death had not appeared . . ."), and so much must be surrendered to what Hegel called the immense labor of the Negative before there can be "a place to stand":

> *Now you must sacrifice—first to the dark,*
> *Next to the crippled underhalf of the mind—*
> *Your faces, hearts, whatever does good work,*
> *Before you come to the burrows at wit's end.*

Not only the end of wit but the end of the body too: when "the pond of flesh lay still," as Wagoner's beautiful Frostbitten phrase has it, in a masterful poem called "The Fallen,"

> *O daylight was our own,*
> *But these are the states of night:*
> *From ease, to the crying down,*
> *Then vacancy outright.*

At the end of his second book, then, or rather at the end of his fourth —the two books of verse, with their powerful assumptions of heroic futility ("Our hands, drawn up and down, / shape nothing but ourselves: / we touch all that we own") ballasted by the two novels, with their equally powerful record of accidental beauty—David Wagoner has found a means of speaking in his own, new voice by letting the two modes correct each other. At this point in the biography of his work, the novels are most purely novels, the poems only poems, with their journeying figures of discovery and rule; though as Wagoner signs off at the close of the longest poem in the book, "The Hero with One Face," it is apparent we are at the turn, and that the forces which have held his prose and verse apart will now drive them together again:

> *Now, like Ulysses, master of*
> *The world under, world above,*
> *The world between—and one beyond*
> *Which was not near enough to find—*
> *I wait, and wonder what to learn:*
> *O here, twice blind at being born.*

A few months after *A Place to Stand*, Wagoner published his third novel, *Rock;* again the story of a disaffected outsider pitted against the group, there is a significant difference to be noted: the hero is not destroyed by the confrontation, but manages to enforce his claims upon society—sexual, professional, expressive claims, in a world of the adolescent sub-group where violence seems to annul any sought discriminations of feeling and mind—rather than permitting the society to drag him under. So that the poet who, five years later in *The Nesting Ground* (1963), addresses himself to the world he can bear to consider is, in effect, "like Ulysses, master of the world under, world above, the world between" . . . It appears much easier for Wagoner to accept the world as it is, without forcing the consequences of his sad knowledge or origins and ends; further, the abstraction felt as necessary still ("the manifold continuous forms and the luminous products") can be hypostatized from the welter of observed life, and the spoils of time delighted in, even with a cognizance taken of their coming rot or wreck:

> *I shopped for the world . . .*
> *Bargained for corners and pedestrians*
> *And when I'd marketed the elms away,*
> *Swiped from the water, stole down to the stones . . .*
>
> *I lay on the week with money, lust, and vapor,*
> *Megalomania, fear, the tearing-off,*
> *And love in a coil. On Sunday, I wrote this.*

With a place to stand, the poet can afford to inventory the world around him, to list the categories that interest him ("After Consulting My Yellow Pages") before letting loose with the ultimate questions: "And where were you? What did you do today?" We are reminded that the word category itself comes from an old Greek verb *agoreuein*, to harangue or assert in the marketplace, and after some of the wild collections of bargains accumulated in Wagoner's lists—

> *From docks to lavender palaces,*
> *O what comings and goings, my rattan May basket!*
> *Adored as we fall through tissue-paper, through balconies,*
> *fountains and trellises,*
> *We shall be borne up like desserts in cream, stuffed like*
> *a brisket,*
> *And spun in the air like platters.*
> *O my snifter, my tumble-rick, sweet crank of the stars,*
> *My banjo-bottomed, fretful girl,*
> *Tear off those swatches of silk, your hems and haws, and*
> *coil them up like streamers,*
> *Get set to toss them over the bounding rail . . .*

—it is evident that this critic of capitalism has, as well, the character of the Greek *kategoros* or accuser. The poet, indeed, emerges as what Wagoner, in one poem, calls "The Emergency Maker"—someone who "needs to stir what we love." The master of categories, in *The Nesting*

Ground, produces many poems which are catalogues and manuals, handbooks to existence: "The Breathing Lesson," "After Consulting My Yellow Pages," "A Guide to Dungeness Spit," "Filling Out a Blank" and "Advice to the Orchestra." The last is a kind of internalized *ars poetica*, of course, and suggests the discerning effort this lyrical poet has made to focus his medium beyond itself:

> *Your music must consume its instruments*
> *Or die lost in the elbow-joints and valves, in snaggle and crook,*
> *ratchet and pinchbeck, in the folded winds.*

Indeed, in the overflowing poems of this third book, Wagoner has found a modulation, a cadence grateful to the range of his own voice. He has also learned to exploit the determinations already encysted in our speech (as when he refers to "drivers driven by themselves . . . The far-afield, the breakers of new ground / who cartwheel out of sight, end over end": here the condensation which makes death an exploration as well as an impasse in "breakers of new ground" and the doom of "end over end" have a rightness beyond mere invention, a finality due to something discovered in the idiom itself). Further, he shows a flickering grace with slant rhymes, as if to remind the discourse—so relaxed at times as to be beneath the tension of the lyre— that he is still touching the strings:

> *Around the compass, soap-flakes and burnt corn,*
> *A swamp, the acid cracked from boiling oil,*
> *Sulfur dioxide, plumage of soft coal,*
> *The yellow wreckage of Lake Michigan—*

in all this, it is only justice to say that Wagoner's music *has* consumed its instruments. His mastery of his own means liberates him for a kind of observation, an acknowledgment of the given world, as in the last example quoted, which he had previously been obliged, as by some lack in himself, some failure of nerve, to siphon off into the novels. In one of the two most generous (because most intimate) poems in the book, "A Guide to Dungeness Spit," there is a new adequacy of scene to agent and of agent to action; exploring the Northwest landscape which he has come to inhabit as a professor at the University of Washington (where the association with Richard Hugo is apparent in poems of a new regional dedication), the inventory of nature ends— after some brilliant puns ("between us," he says to his beloved, "we have come all the way") and one outrageous one ("the ocean, the spit and image of our guided travels")—with a kind of purified nomination, a constatation of Being such as only Orpheus could undertake, yet it has passed through the circumstantial ordeal of any novelist ("if we cross to the inner shore, the grebes and goldeneyes / rear themselves and plunge through the still surface, / fishing below the dunes / and rising alarmed, higher than waves"), so that we feel that what the poet is directing us to is, beyond the proper naming of it, simply the truth:

> *. . . Those are tears. Those are called houses, and those are people.*
> *Here is a stairway past the whites of our eyes.*
> *All our distance*
> *Has ended in the light. We climb to the light in spirals,*
> *And look, between us we have come all the way,*
> *And it never ends*
> *In the ocean, the spit and image of our guided travels.*
> *Those are called ships. We are called lovers.*
> *There lie the mountains.*

The very thing one felt to be absent in Wagoner's early poems, or to be partitioned off without much mercy for the terrain thus distributed, has now—by a curious apprehension of opposites or at least oppositions, in his own and in an outer nature—been resolved into a *presence*, and what is more, a presence within a *scene*. Addressing the owner of a ruined boat in one of his characteristic seascapes, "To the Master of *Sea Bird* of Friday Harbor," Wagoner diagrams his relation—one of exposure, of an intimacy necessary to his intent—to what had before been merely "happening," the substance of fiction, the accidents of a lifetime:

> *And if you drowned*
> *In the heaving, heavy slopes, the grey rags of the Strait,*
> *Remember the rules. No passage is endless.*
> *Over rocks, even islands,*
> *The boat came pounding thirty miles to Dungeness Spit*
> *Without your help, throwing away the compass,*
> *Dowsing its lights in the wind,*
> *And tossing its name to pieces. Between the sea and its flights*
> *Against the shore, like fish or men out of water,*
> *Birds on the ground*
> *Will be picked clean for a time. By ancient salvage rights,*
> *I claim this poem from Sea Bird of Friday Harbor,*
> *Someday to be returned.*

And at the end of this third book, in what I take to be his other most "giving" poem so far, "On Seeing an X-Ray of my Head," even the death that Wagoner had not dared consider as his own case becomes part of the converging energies of the poem. And humor—what Melanie Klein calls the effect of a benevolent super-ego—is the pervading companion of this quest for an existence beyond the self's survival, the alternating, mostly five-syllable, slant-rhyming lines affording a kind of virtuoso obbligato on the "grim" theme that is, as virtuosity always is, transcendently comic:

> ... *Oh my brainpan,*
> *When we start our separate ways*
> *With the opaque, immortal fillings clenched in our teeth*
> *Like a bunch of keys,*
> *And when your dome goes rolling into a ditch*
> *And, slack in the jaws,*
> *Stops at a hazard, some unplayable lie,*
> *Accept at your ease*
> *Directly what was yours at one remove:*
> *Light through your eyes,*
> *Air, dust, and water as themselves at last. Keep smiling.*
> *Consider the source.*
> *Go back to the start, old lime-pit, remembering flesh and skin,*
> *Your bloody forebears.*

Except for Reed Whittemore, I can think of no other American poet who could manage, with the witty relevance that is the consequence of a focussed intelligence (as in speaking of light through the eyes of a skull as direct, no longer "at one remove"), to say so much about himself and about what he considers above himself ("Consider the source. Go back to the start . . .": in a sense, it is the poet's responsibility to speak above himself, beyond his means), and still invent that image of his own skull rolling until it "stops at a hazard, some unplayable lie," a figure in which every word contains its own joke (the caddy-master as Minos) and, beyond the joke, its own judgment on the experience of living, of dying. Though he is often held up, in these poems, by a case of professional jitters:

> *I face what I don't know,*
> *Can't follow or wait for,*
> *The private enterprise*
> *For which there's no demand . . .*

he is held up in both senses: embarrassed and sustained, appalled and empowered, for the poet's enterprise is private—compared with, say, the politician's—only in an honorific sense, and Wagoner's career as a *public speaker* is confirmed by *The Nesting Ground* as "useful" indeed. In the subsequent work, both prose and verse, he will test his achievement as a man out in the open, and determine ways to persist in an "enterprise for which there's no demand"—in other words, will devote what James Wright calls his "superb technical resourcefulness" not only to the evidence of his senses, but to the sense of his evidence, the existence of that successful poet and successful novelist David

Wagoner, who two years after *The Nesting Ground,* in 1965, published his fourth and finest novel, *The Escape Artist.*

It is, in the sense of the word Hawthorne has accustomed us to, a *romance,* the genre which, as the poems and the prose have developed in this author's career, it was inevitable that the novel should approach, for the romance is a fiction (which we should remember is simply another form of the word *poem,* something made by man) whose surfaces have been more evidently tampered with, whose edges have been, in a word, *manhandled* until we are certain of abounding in the author's sense by every means at his command. As in the first three novels, the hero of *The Escape Artist* is a preposterous outsider who is accidentally stuck with a situation which involves him in other people's lives; but for the first time in Wagoner's fictions the hero triumphs by skill, luck and what one can only call love over the counterfeit world he is brutally thrust into (to demonstrate his skill, the escape artist lifts a wallet that happens to contain $7000 in "hot" or counterfeit money). The direction of the fable and its title suggest quite literally that the poet can be not only the "emergency maker" but the magical entertainer who by delighting us all saves his own neck and ours as well. The sixteen-year-old rogue whose picaresque ascent through the underside of Chicago politics and show-biz corruption to the liberation only art can afford is, in fact, an emblem of the poet, and when he performs his hocus-pocus with all the "technical resourcefulness" that is so wonderfully his, Wagoner is describing the work—or the working—of art itself:

> He wasn't thinking. Sometimes it was like talking, just a waste of attention, but when you could get your whole body doing it—the hands by themselves, feet aimed, everything doing work that hadn't been wrapped up in a thought—there was no name for it, the feeling of being led yet knowing it was your own choice: maybe yourself tomorrow, who didn't exist yet, decided for you today. It was what could always save you, always set you free: yourself going ahead of yourself and knowing what to do.

As in all romances—as Henry James said of *The Scarlet Letter,* for instance—"there is an abuse of the fanciful element, of a certain superficial symbolism. The people strike us not as characters, but as representatives, very picturesquely arranged, of a single state of mind; and the interest of the story lies, not in them, but in the situation, which is insistently kept before us with little progression, though with a great deal of a certain stable variation . . . it is admirable, extraordinary, and it has an indefinable purity and lightness of conception, for the author is perpetually looking for images which shall place themselves in picturesque correspondence with the spiritual facts with which he is concerned, and of course the search is the very essence of poetry." Lightness of conception may not be a phrase to which we cotton in describing *The Scarlet Letter*, but it is precisely the tone Wagoner desiderates for *his* romance, which for its double epigraph uses a line by that great illusionist Harry Blackstone ("Blackstone the Magician") and—in accord with the inventorying tendency I remarked in *The Nesting Ground*—the entire entry for "escape" from Roget's *Thesaurus*. In Roget's long list, the key words are "liberation," "gateway," and "weather the storm." And just as this novel has finally come to terms with "the essence of poetry"—and the terms are, in fact, *freedom, metamorphosis* and *survival*—so in Wagoner's next book of verse, the poetry comes to terms with the world of accident, appearance and disintegration which had been fiction's province hitherto.

In 1966, a year after *The Escape Artist*, Wagoner published *Staying Alive*, his fourth book of poems and, in the nature of things—a phrase, by the way, which bears a particular application to this pre-eminently Big Woods series, a *preserve* where the poet "sets loose, like birds / in a landscape, the old words"—his finest achievement to date. The long title poem is a subtly phrased and inclusive account of survival in the wilds, alternating the long and short lines that Wagoner has made so characteristic of his lyric impulse and his comic correction, and though it begins "naturally" enough:

> *By far the safer choice*
> *Is to settle down where you are and try to make a living*
> *Off the land, camping near water, away from shadows . . .*
> *But if you decide, at last, you must break through*
> *In spite of all danger,*
> *Think of yourself by time and not by distance, counting*
> *Wherever you're going by how long it takes you;*
> *No other measure*
> *Will bring you safe to nightfall . . .*

it is soon apparent ("seeing is believing / in the wilderness," Wagoner adds in the kind of aside that is his secret, a lullaby out of one side of the mouth, as he calls an earlier poem, and a laugh out of the other) that "staying alive" in the woods is his synonym for life itself, the account of experience which must accommodate its obverse, the disintegrative and negative energies as well:

> *. . . There may even come, on some uncanny evening*
> *A time when you're warm and dry, well fed, not thirsty,*
> *Uninjured, without fear.*
> *When nothing, either good or bad, is happening.*
> *This is called staying alive. It's temporary.*

What occurs after
Is doubtful . . .

The quest for some retrieved wholeness which will venture into that country of "love's divisions" is the burden of this book, and its motley wisdom can be summed up—though Wagoner resists the summary process; he likes the separate effort, the unparaphrasable enterprise: "springing again, as the birds will, to climb through wilder country before falling"—in the wry phrase "Staying Alive By Going to Pieces," with its suggestion of Osiris beneath the colloquial profanity. The very history of his art becomes something to oppose, and by opposing to extend, as in Wagoner's beautiful epithalamion, "Water Music for the Progress of Love in a Life-Raft Down the Sammamish Slough," the true Northwest Passage this explorer has been looking for so long:

> *. . . I offer these strands,*
> *These unromantic strains, unable to give*
> *Such royal accompaniment*
> *As horns on the Thames or bronze bells on the Nile*
> *Or the pipes of goatmen,*
> *But here, the goats themselves in the dying reeds,*
> *The ringing cows*
> *And bullocks on the banks, pausing to stare*
> *At our confluence*
> *Along the awkward passage to the bridge*
> *Over love's divisions.*
> *Landing at nightfall, letting the air run out*
> *Of what constrained us,*
> *We fold it together, crossing stem to stern,*
> *Search for our eyes,*
> *And reach ourselves, in time, to wake again*
> *This music from silence.*

For though this is the book in which the poet accepts himself *as* a poet, that supreme escape artist, there is a lot of self-doubt in the process—the very calling into question that keeps Wagoner from being, merely, a Success, that keeps him instead a successful poet. In one of his most personal poems—though they are *all* personal in enterprise now, Wagoner speaking through his experience with precisely the kind of self-acknowledgment he could never accept in his early poems of cosmic order and uninhabited wastes—Wagoner accepts the lineage of his "circuit-riding great-grandfather [who] rode off on horseback through the hickory woods each week" to galvanize five Methodist churches:

> *Like you, I'm doing time in the hard woods,*
> *Tracking myself in circles, a lost preacher.*

And though he mistrusts his impulse toward the transcendent, though he worries about the grandiose enterprises fostered in him by his Pacific Fastness (*vide* "A Room with a View":

> *A man in a room with a view draws back—*
> *As though on a cliff—from the edge of the operatic,*
> *Tempted to own it, to get above himself.*
> *Poets and* helden *tenors, straining for height,*
> *Mistake the roaring in their ears for the ocean . . .*)

quite as much as he prods himself to find a compromise with ordinary lives, the unexamined commercial existences he seeks to ransom from their isolation (*vide* "For the Warming of an Artist's Studio":

> *. . . Here goes an artist after a businessman*
> *Not as a panhandler*
> *But, following him through rundown neighborhoods*
> *And making over*
> *The empty premises at the end of his line,*
> *As a silent partner . . .*),

though he finds only a partial gratification in the desperate love scenes he desperately evokes, for all their comic intensities:

> *Making our hollow, diabolical noises*
> *Like Dracula and his spouse, avoiding mirrors,*
> *Clutching each other fiendishly for life*
> *To stop the gaps in ourselves, like better halves . . .*

there is, finally, an acceptance in David Wagoner's poetry, an assenting invocation to the very fractured and fragmented existence he had once most feared as a kind of death; indeed, there is a sense in which death itself is reckoned the "missing all," as Emily Dickinson called it, in the totality of experience which this poet, at the end of his book, puts together in a kind of mad song, a Christopher Smart rhapsody called "Come Before His Countenance with a Joyful Leaping"; the summons is issued to every order of life—"come coasting in circles, rearing, running aground, and flickering up the air, peeling and flaking away like handbills over the sloping daylight . . . come at a loss out of manholes and sandtraps, assaulted and blinking on dislocated ankles, come jerking free at the heart, swollen with song from the twisted wreckage, dying and rigorous after the second wind"—all possibilities, then, fused in a typical inventory by this master of categories, and for once by this categorical master, in h's ultimate hymn to the negative in us that must prevail, but not before it has shown us what we are:

Come . . . dying and rigorous after the second wind,
For He is falling apart in His unstrung parbuckles, His beard
blown loose by harmonious unction, His countenance
breaking, His fragments flopping up and around
without us to the stretches of morning.

Sleeping in the Woods by DAVID WAGONER

Sleeping in the Woods is the second book of poems since David Wagoner gathered himself into a Selection in 1969; *Riverbed*, published in 1973, included—as though to shuffle off the solemnity of the preceding occasion—a number of brilliant jokes, one of this poet's many strengths. That Victorian idyll about the husband's always falling behind his wife as they enter a drawing-room has become a sort of American classic, as good as some Praed, some Betjeman; in this new book there is only one joke (an easy one about a ladies' literary society in Ohio, as good as some Edith Wharton), but there is a quantity of careful, conscientiously serious verse, content with a kind of eloquence neither solemn nor sententious—what I should call, if obliged to account for the diction by a comparison, Northwest Georgian. David Wagoner has been a long time working out—if not elaborating—his manner of speaking, and he is by now so accomplished—the speech is simple—that we are never in any doubt that he is doing just that: speaking to us in his manner. The resonance is that of a voice mildly expostulating, gently instructing, lightly dismissing:

> *Not having found your way out of the woods, begin*
> *Looking for somewhere to bed down at nightfall*
> *Though you have nothing*
> *But parts of yourself to lie on, nothing but skin and backbone*
> *And the bare ungiving ground to reconcile.*

This is from the title poem, with its characteristic gerund (one recalls *Staying Alive, Talking Back,* a whole procession of processes) and even more characteristic didacticism. What is remarkable about Wagoner's ongoing lessons (and there are two poems explicitly called "lessons" in this book) is that they do not pretend or presume to teach us what we could learn—they never want to be of much help in the profit-column of the ledger. They want to teach us about what we could only leave behind—about the great negations, about the submissions and inadequacies and failures which will ransom our "real lives" from their "years of barely touching the surface."

In early books, one recalls poems like *Instruction to the Orchestra* and *The Breathing Lesson*, which are here rehandled in *The Singing Lesson* with the same rather dire burden:

> *For your full resonance*
> *You must keep your inspiring and expiring moments*
> *Divided but equal . . .*

But I think that as Wagoner has grown older—and have we not grown older with him? have we not discovered an analogous need?— the expiring moments, the intervals and occasions when the necessity is to give way to what exceeds and extinguishes us, prevail—and are welcomed as prevalent—in the emotional economy of our lives. That is why, in this book, there is something beyond the usual commemorative appeal to earth, there is a kind of humility which is new to this poet's tone, a tone so easily identified, earlier, as a dialect of the Higher Smartass. For instance, the strong poem *The Lost Street* ends with the usual ritual instructions (all of Wagoner's work is to take its place in a vast manual of forgetting, a handbook to helplessness, the *bricoleur's* breviary of how to leave it alone), yet the adjective now is so startling, so significant:

> *. . . you must get out*
> *Of the car and stand on the ground,*
> *Then kneel on it like a penitent gardener,*
> *Touching it with your hands, crawling again to know it.*

In another poem, *Talking to Barr Creek*, the lines bestowed on water, the lesson begged "to hold me together," are again cast in this submissive, effacing resonance which we recognize as that casting-out of self which is the preliminary to prayer:

> *Teach me your spirit, going yet staying, being*
> *Born, vanishing, enduring.*

It is surprising, but it is right, of course, that the energies of a brilliantly continued career, and of a continuing one, should seek their buttress and ballast in defeat, in erasure, in precisely the recognition of negations, of fallings from us, vanishings . . . Yet that is just what Wagoner's talking has brought him to, the garrulous stoicism of his "First People," aborigines from whom he claims, indeed, quite as much as he promises, admitting to so much of what is undone, unmade, unhelped, at the very end of his book:

> *Close all my mouths. I will sleep inside of sleep,*
> *Honoring the gift of darkness till it breaks.*
> *I sing for a cold beginning.*

THEODORE WEISS

"No Shore Beyond Our Own"

IN A PROUD snippety time I am concerned with the sustained poem, one that is more than merely personal and lyrical and happily fragmented. It is easy to go with the time or to cry out against it; but to do something with it, to take it by surprise, to make more of it than it can do itself . . ." That has been Theodore Weiss' pertinacious program, and from it he has neither backed nor filled, refusing, as Horace Gregory has said, "to compromise his gifts by writing 'magazine verse' " and perhaps satisfying his cravings for compromise by editing one of the best American magazines to print verse, *The Quarterly Review of Literature*. Weiss has also travelled widely, far afield ("the Great Migration teeming through our dreams") and merely abroad—

> *More shambling about*
> *in abandoned, clammy churches*
> *and I abjure all religion,*
> *even my own!*

—has made recordings for Yale and the Library of Congress, has broadcast for the Voice of America, has lectured on Shakespeare at the New York YMHA, has made selections from Hopkins' notebooks for New Directions, has won prizes and fellowships even as he has professed literature at Bard College and Princeton, and if not beneath (like Graves) or above (like Perse) the offices of a lifetime, then through them has published five volumes acknowledged, if at all, by the "proudly snippety time" to be among the most difficult poetry it can ignore.

Now learned, witty, musical, copious and intense writing,

> *taking any air as able to endure,*
> *a passion equal to all hope,*

is not necessarily unpopular; but Weiss has so juiced up each of these qualities at the expense, in most of his work, of a fable, a narrative or even a ritual in whose thrall the mind could submissively revel, that he has not "once or ever become the household word of the air." The direct or directive procedure is sacrificed to a complication of surface, an iridescence of the audible, to the point where any unity that is to be achieved, Weiss insists, will be the unity won—wrung—from a conflicting multitude: "all the colors drain / into one conflagration," or again, "to compose the shattered world / into one field of love."

His imagery, like Theodore Weiss' themes and his grammatical surface, is treated accordingly: the units of his verbal structure are intended and received as parts of a whole ("more than merely lyrical and happily fragmented"), redeemed from the despised fragmentary by pattern, oracular in origin and deriving from the moment of vision, the epiphanic flash of comprehension; everywhere apparent in the arrangement on the page (even when not highly ventilated, Weiss' lines are always *designed*) and in the effect on the ear, the method or better the madness inherent in Weiss' method—a rage for subsumption—is explicit in a middle-range poem, "Barracks Apt. 14," which offers a roomful of miscellanea—some pears in a basket, two houseplants, a faculty wife reading Aristotle "with difficulty" and a baby in the next room—under the imperative rubric "all must be used":

> *all are parts hopeful, possible,*
> *expecting their place in the song;*
> *more appealing because parts*
> *that must harmonize into something*
> *that rewards them for being, rewards*
> *with what they are.*
> *Do this and do,*
> *till suddenly the scampering field*
> *you would catch, the shiny crows*
> *just out of reach, the pears*
> *through which a brown tide breaks,*
> *and the cactus you cannot cling to*
> *long like that thorny Aristotle*
> suddenly, turning, turn on you
>
> as meaning, the ultimate greenness
> they have all the time been seeking
> in the very flight they held
> before you. No matter what you do,

at last you will be overwhelmed,
the distance will be broken,

the music will confound you.*

Though invariably, even relentlessly witty ("the cactus you cannot
cling to / long like that thorny Aristotle" is exemplary, with its func-
tional enjambment and its displaced epithet: Weiss putters and fusses
with his lines like an upstate Bonnard, until every figure has its own
worked-up opalescence), Weiss is not out to entertain, unless it is to
entertain the universe, and however inwardly revelatory ("more than
merely personal," he insists), however daring with his intimacies, he
does not fortify his domestic drama with pornography—it is the poetry
of marriage as an inclusive state he is after; indeed, the poetry that
comes after, in the richest sense of the phrase.

Though he is entirely certain of his borrowed effects, his derived
devices, his imitated sonorities—the stanza and what Lovejoy calls the
"metaphysical pathos" of Hopkins:

> *But who does us:*
> *Who flexes like fingers, strains*
> *in our sinews that they sing,*
> *one felicitous agony?*
> *These thoughts, these thoughts*
> *thieving through night that things—*
> *even hope and lust everlastingly*
> *raucous—heckling locals*
> *trying to distract us,*
> *fall dumb.*

—and even Hopkins' vocabulary, as in this rearrangement from "The
Windhover": "an ember / blue-lit, sudden, bleak, slashing out into the
dark"; the metric if not the aeration of William Carlos Williams:

> *in each season,*
> *gone over and over, still grief*
> *strikes, a new-forged arrow, finds*
> *out fresh wounds, its resource,*
> *surprising, relevant,*
> *of pain;*

and the phraseology of Wallace Stevens (here the opening and the
pigeons of "Sunday Morning"):

> *The amities of morning*
> *and the buxom habits of birds*

* Emphasis mine.

> *that sing a bell-bright city*
> *in their intelligent wings*

—Theodore Weiss will not indulge his reader with the complacencies of an easy iambic line, the pleasures of recognition, the privileges of condescension. His means invariably mirror a meaning which is scrolled, complicated, demanding:

> *the outrageousness of growth*
> *one of earth's original conclusions.*

It is the case: *his music will confound you,* and the sense his senses make of it often eludes. As I trace it, the central course of that meaning is the shape or structure of selfhood when it is without the armor of consciousness, when identity is invaded by a momentary and instantaneous recognition of being, a disastrous revelation—

> *each tree achieves*
> *its height the moment when it crashes*

—that comes often to this poet from nature, but also—and more damagingly—from a confrontation with the past, from the endurance of love, and from the Stoic's old problem of living, as Gilbert Murray put it, without despair and without grave, or at least without gross, illusion. And always the recognition comes, once the defences are down, from an invading consciousness of multiplicity:

> *As the sycamore makes one thing*
> *of the wind, and the birch another . . .*
> *as these roses, four kinds of roses,*
> *related in scent, yet as different*
> *as their colors, make in the vase*
> *out of their difference one fragrance . . .*
>
> *so in your moods by the gamut*
> *of glances, the narrow yet infinitely*
> *many diapason of breath, you make*
> *one sundry thing of the air.*

Theodore Weiss' first book of poems was published in 1951; a group of seventeen "shorter" pieces (though all are at least a page-and-a-half long), and the twenty-one-page monody on imperial themes, "Shades of Caesar," the latter certainly a "sustained" achievement and one of the most idiosyncratic in the poet's canon. Weiss was thirty-five when this book appeared, and the terms he had reached with his art were pretty much given, or taken; though he was to develop his apprehension of subjects in the direction, I think, of availability to the reader, and though he was to dramatize his *tone*—

> *a pomp that holds*
> *the world together worm to star,*

in subsequent books, Weiss has never written better, or with more resource, than in "The Catch," whose title refers to the artist as fisherman:

> *the woman who at last—*
> *"I do not use live models"—sculptured fish—*
> *"I remember long lonely holidays at shores*
> *when the spray alone defined green shapes*
> *approaching"—has just seen (her eyes*
> *still gleam with the gleam of it,*
> *blink like the making of many*
> *a take) a great catch.*
>
> *April, we say, is the time*
> *for fish, for reaching in the sea-*
> *like air and the outrageousness of growth*
> *one of earth's original conclusions . . .*
> *we are in the middle of a great catch,*
> *there collected . . .*
>   *the thrashing clean-*
> *scaled, clear-lit shad in the net.*

The quotation exhibits a chief distinction of Weiss' verse—the careful, self-regarding but insistent use of parenthetical stage direction, incremental turns between dashes or brackets, a kind of preening and pruning that by stroking rather than wrestling lets no angel go until it has first blessed the utterance. This kind of verbal warp was to be developed, in Weiss' masterpiece of sustentation, *Gunsight*, into a highly deliberate muddle of meanings—

> *they find their parts*
> *at the moment of burning:*
> *the appropriate pain, the fitting*
> *grief*

—functioning still in the reader's mind by a powerful sense of relevant pattern on the poet's part: only the articulate, of course, can be inarticulately expressed.

In the shorter poems, "fretful musics" in which there simply isn't time for the speaker to spread his nets very wide or warily, the governing pattern or *set* of the images,

> *shallow as the night-*
> *life of a looking-*
>
> *glass that needs*
> *celebration, the candor*
> *of bodies in the hands*
> *of dance, to be . . .*

does not operate profitably (the catch, that is, is less than the effort of seining), and a stronger narrative hook is needed than these jerky lyrics ("we strain forward / as to some fabulous story") afford—a basis in ritual or sequence, even in strong feeling made manifest within a convention—to keep us from swimming through the meshes. Most successful in this regard, in *The Catch*, is the poem to a dead friend, "The Dance Called David"—called him right out of life—in which the poet endeavors to speak to his friend again:

> *Words from me,*
> *pointing to bits of color*
> *or surprise longing*
> *urged upon me,*
> *recalled him*
> *as those that burned in hell*
> *steadied their flames to answer*
> *one earthbound.*
> *Like something*
> *mattered out of air, a smile . . .*
> *would flicker, then go out.*

The beautiful allusion to Dante here and the pun on the word *mattered* enforce the effect of the broken rhythms, a gasping and intermittent measure which not so much illustrates as establishes the justice of the final metaphor, "a smile / would flicker, then go out." Puns are always a strong semblance of propriety, of course (an indication that the balance, however shaky, is being maintained: that is why we laugh, that is why we groan), and in the speaker's uncertainty in this poem, the duplicity of what is *material* and what is *important* is central to his necromancy. But in many of these shorter pieces, there is not enough such aid, and despite many readings, the poem too successfully resists one's intelligence: the state of consciousness, for all its unguarded ardors—perhaps because of them—appears incommunicable, cut off from the narrative it would construct. Like certain drawings of Michaux, of Giacometti, the very means which call form into being are *as well* the means which impede form, and the dilemma appears a particularly contemporary one, though to be mastered in Weiss' ulterior performances.

"Shades of Caesar," in this same first volume, is not an easy or habitual poem, certainly, but it stretches out at length enough, with returns and recurrences of theme and reference—Weiss can say, with Borges, that here he sought expression but discovered that his gods granted him no more than allusion or mention—to offer the mind some purchase, some preferential roost among its riches. The poem begins at an academic ceremony above the Hudson, combining in the speaker's hyper-associative mind, outside "the vine-veined chapel," images of "disreputable old Rip Van Winkle" who abandoned the effort to confront his life, with "memories in this clearing of the Greeks / and the Romans, mixed with the Christian, / muttering dry prayer." Alexander and Caesar are invoked as exemplars of action, and Shelley and Milton as heroic voices to praise that action. Then, in the second section of the poem, Caesar's career is rehearsed, and the episode with Cleopatra is coupled with that of Calypso and Odysseus, even as the Nile with the Hudson ("the sly stream flows on"), in a dazzling Shakespearean resonance that as always when Weiss has mustered his forces masters them as well, creating out of "a tumult of mouths" that other, original sense of tumult, a rise or eminence, as of a tomb, from which the surround is dominated:

> (Her beauty, her dark
> brow bright with long-rooted eyes,
> caparisoned rivers and trees . . .
>
> winter it was, winter within the walls
> of a well-provided sly enemy,
> and only a handful of men by me:
> I trusted to the report of my exploits:
> was I expected to anticipate this? . . .
>
> Death itself to our solemn
> employment, the roaring engines
> of our siege, yielded its passion,
> a pure torrent I, confounded, could
> only submit to)
>
> *seven years Calypso*
> *kept Odysseus by her, seven years*
> *coiled in the golden loom*
> *of her hair and her spell-weaving*
> *body:*
> *despite his unbroken lament*
> *by the sea, moments, cogent beauty,*
> *must have held him—*
> *as the Nile*

> *winding—the sly stream flows on—*
> *its mysterious and redolent*
> *source, headlong over his triumphs.*

The deliquescent self, its armor literally dissolved by the river of time, evaporated into process, is magnificently Weiss' enactment here, and he carries it up "the lordly Hudson, / steeped in a purple cloud, a sail / like a drop of sleep aerial on it," to the point overlooking the American river where the long poem began, when "by strangeness taken in . . . reason made commodious, only then peace"

> *like stone . . .*
> *a rising chapel of stone, is reached*
> *again: around it, desolate earth its pit,*
> *by the roseate window of sun-up, the flesh*
> *of apple and peach, of burgeoning limbs.*

That is the end of this sad (yet witty, even to the last words, the "roseate window" and the "burgeoning limbs" which are equally of flesh and fruit-tree) meditation on the failures of the heroic imagination, a descant on the very evasion which would assert such failure as inevitable. Haunted by Homer, by Shakespeare and by Dante, yet helped only by modern hopes, by Pound, Stevens, Williams and Hopkins, Weiss has in his first book created a triumph of the ritual and rehearsing imagination, a remarkable success of literary accommodation (mention and allusion *becoming* expression)—the self engrossed by the past even as style is engrossed by historic performance.

Ten years later, "love likewise enduring . . . its own lulls and forgettings," Weiss published his second book, *Outlanders.* Here even more than in *The Catch,* though extending the same impulse which that title suggests, the singles, the disparates, the borderers of experience are caught up together, worked like the tesserae of some soft mosaic into the giant view; the effort is always to see, seized as in the talons of illumination, the various and the diverse in some inclusive over-view, or rather some enclosing verb, outspoken:

> *And I thought of sitting on a polar star*
> *a million miles away, looking down at this earth*
> *surrounded by its tiny nimbus of a day.*
> *And I saw the days—each hour a speck, twelve*
> *motes combined—like waves like sparks like bushes*
> *burning, lined up one by one, for its intricate*
> *strokes each a kind of word.*

With various assurances behind or beneath him—the existence of a first book, a Ford Fellowship (1953), and the 1956 Wallace Stevens Award (for "House of Fire," another consummately administered meditation on self-helplessness within the divine unity of being—"His much-loved creatures, / numberless as leaves, yet loved / for individual, self-willed features"—this time propped on the imagery of the Book of Job; just consider with what grace of allusion and what gravity of mention Weiss transforms to his plangent purposes "man is born unto trouble, as the sparks fly upward," at his own poem's close:

> *And so the sea*
> *is fed, and so the fire, the rampant waves*
> *and flames flared up in stubborn homage*
> *to their fathering first desire.*)

—Weiss plucked up his courage, signed his whole name to the book instead of the mere and modest initial that had appeared on *The Catch*, and in poems from the title group, decidedly, offered evidence of his willingness to *speak out* dramatically and with a less evanescent sense of the self doing the speaking: utterance is no longer in and of itself a dissolving agent—

> *I am*
> *flooded to that realm the lightnings*
> *coil, I inmost far out in the world—*

life, mere life can be relied upon to be sufficiently corrosive, as in the splendid vision of Nietzsche just over the edge of madness:

> *In that third-floor room,*
> *still going about in your academic jacket*
> *and down at heel, all the heavens rejoicing,*
> *laughing, lifting up your legs,*
> *into the middle of the rout you leaped,*
> *a satyr's dance, as always, the conclusion*
> *of the tragic truth . . .*

Or the rumination of a mad old woman working in her garden, a kind of Calvinist fanatic who must hack, pull and weed her questionable plot with the very fury which has driven her sons from her—the theme of the old woman cultivating her garden is one that is dear to Weiss, and will recur, less sensationally, more soberly; here the imminence of madness ("at night, the body laid away, / once again the mind is free and upright") releases speculation into a kind of inhuman luminosity:

> *But when the rains*
> *fall so fast, so full, wilderness alone*

prevails? Must we feel our way back all
the way of thorn and rot to glimpse the anger
of the flaming angel, else we push
God out of us, God altogether?
                    This separateness.
It stretches through words, chores, my mocking steps.
Clutch as I may, will nothing bend to me?

And most successful, I think, of these dramatic personations of the vulnerable self, "An Egyptian Passage"; here the poet, speaking in his own person—which means, affording a wide-aperture lens to mind, and employing a corrugation of syntax reminiscent of Browning in its risk of opacity:

Like the little crate—
white houses across the river, quiet enough,
but indoors, I knew, no bush for its morning
birds busier—

takes the train from New York City up the Hudson, riding beside that "icy lid" and sitting next to an immediately emblematic woman, "hand hooked and hover / ing [Weiss will often in this manner illustrate by breaking the line in the body of a word the very action of such breaking: "sky- / high change," "the lean- / to of noon," "black bed- / rooms," and of course the even more ideogrammatic "hover / ing" here], nose sharp under black-lacquered hair, / and body, skinny, curving over a brownish big / thick book" which turns out to be a German-Egyptian lexicon.

The torso of the poem develops a beautiful and bravely administered counterpoint between the detritus of the city's ragged edges which they are riding through, the limbo zone observed with the same oneiric precision as a kind of infernal Innisfree:

. . . the dumps, one burning in three spots,
lurid like old passion among heavy piled-
up boxes and black banged-in pots, and birds
floating above like ashes . . .

and the world "that fluttered under her fingers" of the glanced-at hieroglyphs, magic signs whose accurate decipherment is known to control the life of the dead as well as to account for the mortality of the living in the strictest sense, without accident or mutability:

. . . strange symbols,
curious hawk-beaked little birds at attention,
gawky beasts, stiff plants, some more than strange,

played off against the lower Hudson landscape, until the speaker is literally unseated, no longer sure of the right surround for his reflections—always the Good Moment for an enterprise of risk:

> *Along the shore a shaggy red-brown brush,*
> *so thick partridges must be crouching in it,*
> *as in the Hudson, under an icy lid,*
> *a brood of clouds. And heavy-headed, long,*
> *thin, flaggy things like the stuff we think of*
> *growing beside the Nile . . .*

All this serves as so much ballast, or the heaving of ballast—both are required: the observed detail and the transcended observation—for the leap of faith the poet then takes, from voyeur to visionary as it were, "looking down at this earth / surrounded by its tiny nimbus of a day." Vision then becomes more than an act of sense, it establishes rather the *identity* of the seer with the seen, in another word, his divinity:

> *And I saw the days—each hour a speck, twelve*
> *motes combined—like waves like sparks like bushes*
> *burning, lined up one by one, for its intricate*
> *strokes . . .*

—everything warps together here even as it frays apart to afford the poet the kind of epiphany he can get across best. The lyrical, secretive poem finds its imaginative unity in a clutch of disproportions—of style, structure, theme, tone, even figures of speech: nothing *matches*, each one pushing another back into the shape which they all make—and make only—together. There are, in *Outlanders*, other kinds of poems, of course—there is even a sonnet to Yeats at Rapallo (the sharing of a saint's statue there with the previous poet, who must also have discovered in "the steep slate path to him [the saint]" the figures which became his characteristic modes of thought, "the course / a stone takes after a bird or a runaway horse")—and any number of the terribly disabused love poems this poet affects, so often in the *persona* of Odysseus making his way back ("ears open to homespun hunger") to an equally weatherbeaten Penelope:

> *love likewise enduring*
> *(twenty years not able to take its measure,*
> *not chimerae, not orgies, able to make it*
> *forget) its own lulls and forgettings,*
> *surges of hunger the sea shrinks away in . . .*
>
> *the gods, looking down, dumbfounded,*
> *at our strangeness with vast unblinking*

incredulous eyes,
                                    envy us that we forever
change and, by our changing, settle
in this whirling place.

The poem ends with a very beautiful reply to Yeats' "once out of nature," a refusal to be lifted or erased from the natural process which is a splendid defense *pro domo* and *pro* domesticity, a circumstance relatively uncelebrated (except by relatives, as Weiss would say); Weiss' beat-up Odysseus abjures the eternal summer of the gods:

> *Better driftwood*
> *swirling in the sea, an olive's litterings*
> *over a battered body, than the ample warp*
> *of boughs that snag us—thrushes in a net—*
> *out of the complicated, mortal text.*

But for all the concerned texture of antagonisms between divinity and desuetude in these poems, for all their eager, easy acceptance of hard experience ("buffeted as he was, / clutching the last shreds of his wits / [he] saw still this was his native element"), I have the sense—perhaps too reassured by knowing, merely, what is coming next—of a summoning of powers, an exploding of some modes and an exploring (in its true sense, the opposite of imploring, the sense of the mind *crying out* upon what it finds) of others. The poet makes his farewell (it is, of course, the Diva's Adieu, and may—must?—be repeated in almost every performance) to the literature which has been, so peculiarly, his stay against chaos, in the one poem in his canon that might be called "charming" and that is so in any case, "The Fire at Alexandria," of which I join the first and last stanzas, striking unsuspected parts of them into . . . words:

> *Imagine it, a Sophocles complete,*
> *the lost epic of Homer, including no doubt*
> *his notes, his journals, and his observations*
> *on blindness. But what occupies me most,*
> *with the greatest hurt of grandeur, are those*
> *magnificent authors, kept in scholarly rows,*
> *whose names we have no passing record of:*
> *scrolls unrolling Aphrodite like Cleopatra*
> *bundled in a rug, the spoils of love.*
>
> *Now whenever I look into a flame,*
> *I try to catch a single countenance:*
> *Cleopatra, winking out from every joint;*
> *Tiresias eye to eye; a magnitude, long lost,*

> *restored to the sky and the stars he once*
> *struck unsuspected parts of into words.*
> *Fire, and I see them resurrected,*
> *madly crackling perfect birds, the world*
> *lit up as by a golden school, the flashings*
> *of the fathoms of set eyes.*

In 1962, then, Weiss produced the major work toward which I had sensed his predictive and even his predatory energies fusing—unpropped by myth, naked of literature if not of rhetoric, *Gunsight* is a long poem which records, or rather dramatizes, enacts, even *endures* the sensations and memories of a wounded soldier undergoing surgery. In the narrator's framing speech, Weiss offers an explicit version of the Stoicism he has been rowing toward in so many Ulyssean pieces, the philosophy which eschews illusion and despair in the face of the problem of living and dying, and of illusion itself, with which this poem is chiefly concerned:

> *Some things—the crag, the granite sea, the slug,*
> *this mouth that grinds incessantly in you—*
> *cannot be turned into the human. All*
> *that we can do is try, while we are men,*
> *to meet them humanly . . .*

The result is a long, beautifully joined narrative (a *linear movement*, at once ongoing and terminal, hovering yet heaving ahead, utilizing all of Weiss' arts of enjambment to keep the language moving down the page as well as the lines marching across it), in which every phrase corresponds to some other utterance in an altered mode, each color so economically related to its object that what on an early page is:

> *screams, smeared on their mouths, in time crop*
> *forth, grape- and lilac-fleshed*

becomes, in the poem's more classical exordium:

> *Remember me and these,*
> *but locally, like lilac, bunched-out grapes,*
> *and in conspirings of wind and sea.*

In *Gunsight*, war—rather than literature—is taken as man's normative activity, not only as the subject but the sum of all experience, of nature itself, gathering within its violence the central figure's childhood agonies of school and sport, hunting and whoring, and climaxing in the boredom and brutality of soldiering itself. This material is presented in Canto-like phrases, scraps sorted out from the incremental redundancy

this poet had devised as characteristic speech in his earlier books, the
different persons or presences being suggested by different typogra-
phies. Except for a remarkable speech delivered by the soldier's dead
mother, there are no set-pieces, no arias in the fifty-five page poem; the
reader's mind is continually stretched, phrase by phrase, between the
painful poles of past and present, from the operating table to the
execution of prisoners of war, but all offered metaphorically, emblem-
atically, with a certain resonance, each event transformed by the
ether-blurred mind to its nightmare analogue in past experience. The
sequence of images coincides, finally, and concentrates into one intense
impression of ultimate outrage and ultimate endurance. Weiss is not to
be distracted from his unvarying variable, his central eccentricity, the
structure, I mean, of an identity without the protection of conscious-
ness; he is not to be dismayed or dismounted by jokes, by local color,
nor by incidental music (as in earlier work); his lines are often harsh
now, certainly not sweetened by the pleasures of allusion, of Classical
mention or even modern instancing, and they yield few comfortable
pleasures along the way. But their massed effect is one of high emotion
and great exactitude; the work resists quotation from the web, but here
is one strand picked out from the meshing others, the resolving state-
ment:

> *The night*
> *involved, the Hunter on his knees, with terror*
> *and catastrophe, see the great flocks*
> *nestling in that song . . .*
> *By such gear morning*
> *comes. Back now into the motion, complex*
> *music of the Pleiades, one with*
> *Orion rounding up his stately game,*
> *the flock flooding down sky's terraces,*
> *moonlit spoils he once pursued and fled,*
> *herded like bees into the hiving dawn.*

To accommodate such diction (and I see I was mistaken—there is
indeed a Classical reference, though one so absorbed into the texture of
our experience, our way of talking about the sky at night that it has
almost ceased to be Antique or alien) in a poem which includes much
of the substance of a war novel, infinitely condensed into its harrowing
worst and best, has been Weiss' achievement, and surely one of his
means to it is, in fact, a refusal to let any single persona, even any single
voice within the central figure's experience, take over too long. The
passage just quoted is, in the text, interrupted or conjugated by others,
the apprehending mind never allowed relief from apprehension, until
the unbearable story is all told:

> *Soon, the window thawed, its frost*
> *like mountain flowers strewn upon these day-*
> *heaped sheets, the world, barefoot in my eyes,*
> *as walking to and from my bed, once more*
> *begins.*

Like his first book of fifteen years before, Weiss' next volume of poems, *The Medium* (1965) is dedicated to his wife; like his second it contains a number of those grim, bantering love poems which seem to be the body politic of the married state:

> *I never*
> *thought I'd prefer a dressed girl to one*
> *undressed. Even for me, I see, it's later*
> *than I guessed.*
> > *So let's go home to bed,*
> *Renée, and dress and dress and dress.*

As his wife's name reminds, the connubial is a condition of perpetual rebirth, continuous surfacings after plunges to the bottom, and the bottom ("I charge the center via every doubt") is a great way down. *The Medium* furnishes forth as well a number of fine literary valentines—to William Carlos Williams ("no yokel you / to luten notes"); to Hopkins ("Still, as in your words . . . this world endures . . . the earth a sweet brown study . . . you have shown what worthy thing it is / to furnish grief with all the rage and nettles / of this life"); and best of all to D. H. Lawrence ("life must be / let out to mine its basic cadence finally / in our pondering of it, free of any / obligation save the pleasure that we take / in it . . .")—and some lesser pieces that had better be magazine verse after all. But as in Weiss' second book, there is a prevailing loyalty to the self's difficult, unplated structure, to its old concerns as to its new conceits which enact a crucial truth Weiss had noted in *Outlanders* and nourished ever since:

> *. . . what unities*
> *have we but circumstance*
> *must grant them?*

The confidence that circumstance *will grant* unity, or at least The Unities, is strong in this new book of Weiss', and without the shoring-up of myth in his shorter efforts, indeed with "no shore beyond own," the poet returns, for example, to that dead friend who had been first celebrated—not mourned—in *The Catch;* he must deal with his accommodation of loss until it too is "something caught like love and war in this golden mesh," and does so this way:

And then
I said, Is only loss, its strength
ransacking all, one steady dun,

the thing I have to learn, and there
that image, feeling, thought embraces
me with grave and finished air?

Though pansies, lionhearted scholars,
ponder sorrow, in his words,
they utter gaiety and splendor.

Of blooms a girl the mignonette
engrossing me, I have him, am him,
and most of all, as I forget.

There is, as well, an extension, in *The Medium*, of all Weiss' mythical or literary fantasias, "the language passing / speakers, too imperious for words"—this time a double meditation on Socrates, "A Satyr's Hide" and "The Wine-Skin Foot," but cleverly transformed or transposed into the experience if not the person of the celebrated educator Heinrich Blücher, a colleague of the poet's at Bard College:

Cast on this shore, the language of his youth
much like the rubble of the world he fled
and foreign phrases, stubborn on the tongue
as new terrains to aging sinews, futile
also, once again he tries through speech
the market-place and the arena use
to reach the latest young.
                    The magic works.

Another in Weiss' long series of studies in exile, expatriation and the laborious colonizing which is culture's work, "Two for Heinrich Blücher" initiates what Weiss' subsequent collection is to confirm, a sense of having it both ways, an insistence that the inception of experience and its final winnowing are within the one grasp, that wisdom and madness are if not the same, then parts of the same circumstantial unity:

Risk it was no doubt, a star
standing out in the open and confidently
twirling about itself, risk or that real thing
sometimes called folly, notes laureling his head;
yet earthiness and the mystery therefrom
never left him a moment:
                    divine matters.

By this same grasp of contraries, of obscurities set forth with a luxu-
riant "directness daylight always must obscure, / cluttered as we are
with long dead habits / and with failures," Weiss embraces the dissolv-
ing self in the prophetically named last section of his book, "Airs for
Caliban," in which the outermost utterance—by which I mean the
poem closest to the surface as well as cleaving hardest to the depths, the
poem which does the highest justice to a changing world of circum-
stance as well as to an immutable realm of self-knowledge—is "The
Visit," a long journeying poem which switches from "Paris, Winter"
to "Cambridge, Mass., Summer," to "New York, Spring" and home to
"Annandale-on-Hudson, Autumn," the poet pursuing his art in the
image of another (as he had done in the very first poem of *The Catch*
("I do not use live models"). Here, two of the four sections begin:

> *To paint without a model,*
> *shun all visits so that what one wants*
> *to do cannot be interrupted or distracted . . .*

and pass into the discussion, much corrugated by the painter's circum-
stance, of what it is to *render* reality; the poet's desire for his poem, the
painter's for his model, the soul for the body—the parts that seek to
make up the whole are subject, in Weiss' supreme fiction as in Stevens',
to the imperative of change:

> *That woman*
> *may be you, you the more she changes, changing,*
> *always more the same, much like the face*
> *one finally comes to,*

he answers his old interlocutor, his better half and bitter one when she
inquires what happened to an earlier version of the woman on the
canvas, or in the poem. Joining myth and circumstance, skin and
skeleton, the poet, by the long discipline of facing himself and thereby,
the mirror becoming a window, fronting the world, would be

> *. . . open so*
> *that in these lines what, taunting, passes*
> *daily haunts and shapes, exultant*
> *through the cast-off nimbus of a name,*

would "nakedly appear." Such is the meaning of the book's title at the
last; with a *becoming* ardor, in every sense of the participle, the poet
casts off his apprehensions of failure, his fears of specious success, or
rather embraces them as the possibilities of his saying anything at all
("Perhaps / speech's primary function is to speak"); he becomes his
own "medium":

cleansed of words,
my fears and doubts cast off, the fears
that words invent, I see each thing, free
at last to its own nature, see it free
to say exactly what it is.

In 1968, three years after this scrupulous, "richly scored" utterance, Weiss' fifth volume of poetry was published, titled for its liminal piece, *The Last Day and the First;* routing a pair of Jehovah's Witnesses who have asked if he ever thinks "these may be the last days of the world" by frankly assenting to the notion, Weiss puts his long, intricate new book under the sign, then, or the double sign, of apocalypse and creation; of the casting-out of nature which brings a man's imagination directly to the god, and of the invocation of nature which submits our senses to process, to recurrence and restoration. In the second half of the twentieth century, Weiss allows, all a man need do is look around to see the apocalypse, the extirpation of the Round, yet it is his special province, his endless task as a poet to find it

hard not to believe that we are
teetering on creation's brink all over
again.

And it is when Weiss feels his selfhood invaded by a momentary but mounting recognition of both principles, where there is an identity of oracular seer with deciduous seen, when identity, in short, becomes identification, that he breaks out into poems, so that for this most elaborately fashioned of all his books the poet asks no further blessing:

so may it be, ever the last
day of this world about to burst
and ever for blossoming the first.

The book which follows is suspended (or arched: there is no sagging in these late performances of Weiss', only a tension which sets up nodal points on the vibrating string) between two long poems, "Caliban Remembers" and "Wunsch-zettel," which rehearse or resume the poet's long indentures on the one hand to literature and on the other to character, each a dramatic recital, an impersonation in which the visited self is exhibited, even exposed, delightedly snared in its "complicated mortal text." Moving in on the center are, following "Caliban . . . ," a dozen poems focussed, with that characteristic faceting of the lens which makes Weiss' diction so demanding, upon the wholeness to be derived or drained from a reticulation of partials, as in "The Eighth Day,"

> *the one in whom the rest*
> *would congregate, who, gisted of them,*
> *would at once be able to salute*
> *the thoroughfare*
> > *with names that,*
> *murmuring, afford them room to mine*
> *and bruit their teeming, secret wealth*

—and, preceding "Wunsch-zettel," a "Suite for Boris Pasternak," poems which are actually transcriptions, divisions, grand chromatic fantasias on translations from the Russian poet ("who'd have thought," Weiss asks himself incredulously, "I was meant— / and eagerly chose —to be the un- / paid Sorceror's apprentice!"), or if not on translations, then on themes and images which awaken in his American admirer an answering illumination:

> > *the light*
> *things cast out of themselves*
> *glowing in your words . . .*

And in the book's center, the enormous poem, the baffling eminence in all Weiss' history and hope of bafflement, "Mount Washington,"

> > *the poet stalking*
> *via pen onto the slippery hillock*
> *of his creased and tracked-up manuscript,*
> *then out into the air where eagles loiter,*
> *stars in undress, much at home—*
> > > > *looks down,*
> *a summer's aperçu.*

But that is from the end of the climb, the beginning of which disarmingly instructs: "Insert 942 of the poet who views / and reviews his work from summer's aperçu." It all ranges, rather than arranges, itself, this preposterous ocellation of poems, around a notation from Emerson's "Thoreau": "At Mount Washington, in Tuckerman's Ravine, Thoreau had a bad fall . . . As he was . . . getting up . . . , he saw for the first time . . . the *Arnica mollis*." Heights and depths, then, abysses and trifles and their arcane correspondences constitute the pretext, while the text itself will *range* through all of Weiss' mountainous experience, cracking over and over again his joke about the little flower, "one cocky edel / weiss, these snows its fathomings" and trusting to the apparently endless capacities of his fault-jarred strata, his quotation-rifted, allusion-roped verses, to bring his spiring imagination home to himself:

> *the earth's sweet, diverse plenitude of June,*
> *itself exactly mirrored in that multiple*
> *response . . .*

But no mere outcropping from these alps (the word, in its initial sense, means any huge mass or lump) affords a fair sense of Weiss' high spirits, the constant local-beauty and alpenstock-taking to which he subjects his discourse; here is a fair-sized peak of self-consciousness, directly won from the Sage of Concord's blank mount:

> *a flower, basking in itself as in sunlight,*
> *let its perch be pinnacle or ditch,*
> *plucked, can instantly unlock the pit,*
> *sprung up, impassioned, slavering, of Dis,*
> *sky plummeting as by that tiny ledge*
> *the body is.*
> > *And so, his pages crawling*
> *with revisions, queries to himself,*
> *and with his doodles, intricate waystations,*
> *he tries to find a certainty inside*
> *against such dreadful falls.*
> > *Nor, as he views*
> *his work, is he averse to plying tales*
> *of other travelers who climbed this way.*
> *Kindred especially as they had spent*
> *their lives striving to map part of the course,*
> *map often nothing more than accurate*
> *report of perils, loss, and being lost,*
> *scale map in color of catastrophe,*
> *and yet because they had been here a light,*
> *provisions cached in sudden crevices*
> *along the slope . . .*

Never has Weiss spoken, gloated almost, so gleefully about his pre-emption of his forbears. As for his contemporaries, that is the work of the final poem, a bodying forth of one of this poet's beloved witch-women, saner than the fanatic gardener of *Outlanders* though this lady too is a gardener, more benevolent than the beaked crone with the hieroglyphs, though this lady too is an initiatrix into the mysteries of growth and renunciation; "Wunsch-zettel" (the title means a Christmas wishing-list, the itemization of dream desires) is the monologue of a Good German who, in the great tradition of Pestalozzi and Froebel, has in her New Hampshire exile—

> *Over the mountains*
> *the woods have crept, and like the dusk they sweep*

to cover scars. And let them sweep. No, no
I'll not go back lest scars, discovering
new strength, like hungry mouths ask more of me
than I can bear—

withdrawn to muse upon the dissolution of her life as a teacher of life, the rewards and the searing reversals of an existence spent educating the displaced children of Europe how to grow a plant, a garden, a spirit proof against crop-failure. Rising to an eloquence, often, so intense that Weiss forgets his carefully created accent and the peculiarities of the recital (the lady is showing us around her mountain redoubt—near Mount Washington!—at sundown) for the generalized and generously bestowed truths which have meant so much to him, the poem is a superb vindication of the Stoicism of earlier makings like *Gunsight* in which Weiss had sadly observed: "some things cannot be turned into the human. All that we can do is try, while we are men, to meet them humanly." Here, then, is the clear wisdom of the speaker of "Wunsch-zettel," a kind of Mitteleuropa Atropos, with the same apprehended skill, displayed in *The Medium*, in letting things alone:

But how can I release, as out of books
this sprig of edelweiss, the loved ones spelled
in leaf and reed and flower? say how much
can one preserve or smuggle through in leaves,
stamped with all one's love and grief, cuttings
kept against the cold?
                    Never to come
again, not though I plant and nurse ten thousand,
thousand hyacinths, spill all my care
upon small growing things.
                    Why one could slash
through all of them and still not reach the dear ones
they are living on.
                    You may be right.
By being themselves and nothing but themselves,
to our outlandish deeds impervious,
things make, and cleanly, our lives possible.

Shapelier, I think, than the fascinating "Mount Washington" and more of a piece—ricocheting less between Weiss himself and his created reciter—than the autumnal "Wunsch-zettel" is the obvious show-piece of this latest volume, "Caliban Remembers" with its borrowings from Shakespeare and Auden, and its permanent dispossessions from Browning—the Browning whose Caliban reported

> *. . . while he kicks both feet in the cool slush*
> *And feels about his spine small eft-things course,*
> *Run in and out each arm, and make him laugh,*

which gets translated by Weiss into something much richer and stranger, at least to the innocent ear:

> *. . . shapes they do in the dark, giddily*
> *torching me that I slubber in bogs,*
> *on mad bushes burr me, furzes clawing.*

In many passages of the Browning poem and throughout the long Weiss one (about ten times as long, by the way), alliteration and internal rhyme and a certain imitative consonance appear to be struggling to become the master-principle of the meter, of the movement of the language itself, as it was in our ancient poetry; one feels that the spirit and manner of a long-obscured past have mysteriously revived, stirring in the mid-Victorian and stirred altogether to an extraordinary chthonic life in the modern:

> *Winds blow over me, the crooning*
> *night air, free now, full of nothing*
> *but its own breath, serenades*
> *the locusts chirr, scents of the sea*
> *and this my island, twining with*
> *what stars are pouring . . .*

Of course in the intermediary set of poems Weiss had spoken, to his own Prospero-figure, of that quickening, containing sense of nature within himself, the sense that Everyman is the animal kingdom and all of earth:

> *I know by feelings*
> *craning, preening deep inside*
> *the ark's still riding, riding high . . .*

But nowhere so explicitly as in "Caliban Remembers" has he been able to round upon the charge of his central theme, the identity unarmed and invaded by a momentary recognition of Being which comes to the poet from natural process. And what better representative for the unguarded consciousness, what better symbol for the unmediated self, than *Caliban?* In all his ransacking of literatures, searching out the enormous repertoires vouchsafed by his wit and his learning, Weiss has never come across a finer voice to raise, or to allow to sink, to ground itself in becoming:

> *Damned be*
> *such book when world in lark enough,*

in filbert and in plum, cries out
that I become a winged hearing,
lapping tongue, and those the ground-
work eyes and hands abound them in,
my feelings, ripened as they ripe.

And though Caliban, alone now with the drowned book and the reminiscences of his peculiar symbolic history scorns the powers which have abandoned him:

Too high
he rose, high handed reached past earth
into the clouds he sacked, while I
slumped, an earth, below—

he longs too for the other oracular possibility, the very thing he is not which would indeed make him die, but which ("the days between the spells grew longer") is the sensed *otherness* which makes for a whole humanity; so the poem ends, never having broken its terrestrial faith with itself, on a note of characteristic yearning, rich, sentient, preposterous, profound:

As I finally learned,
little though he knew it, learned
to love him, going. And do.
                    No matter
how I burrow in shadows on shadows,
leaves thick and dark mixing, dark
from inside owl wings, bat's screechy
darting, my cave sealed off, I stick out,
prickly, listening.
                    How I long
to hear once more those me-completing
voices. Come back, would cast me
at their feet. And yet . . . alone, alone
as he must be, loathing, pitying, loving.

Out of another experienc of chaos, as Stevens says, has grown another form. In the poetry of Theodore Weiss, there is then a regard for the reality that will not be reduced, the reality which is a human imagination of the inhuman; reading these anatomies of identity, "touching words, to push me out of me," as Caliban crucially says for Weiss, we understand Bacon's beautiful conditional sentence in a declarative mode: poetry could indeed give some show of satisfaction to the mind, wherein the nature of things doth seem to deny it.

JAMES WRIGHT

"The Body Wakes to Burial."

N OT MARGINS but centers, not edges but spaces, not contiguities
but distances: the thematic insistence of this poet—who by
forty had written four volumes of poetry, two in verse and two (it is
tempting to say) inversely—is plain, indeed is plane: from Martins
Ferry, Ohio to Stateline, Nevada, with significant stopovers in Minne-
apolis and in Fargo, North Dakota, it is a landlocked, borderless life
whose terms are *spread out*, articulated by James Wright in a dialect of
dispossession and deprival, "a vowel of longing" unique among his
contemporaries for its final bleakness, singular in its ultimate solitude:

> *To speak in a flat voice*
> *Is all that I can do . . .*
> *I have gone forward with*
> *Some, a few lonely some.*
> *They have fallen to death.*
> *I die with them . . .*

The wonder, though, and in this case the reward, is that when a poet's
diction, his controlled utterance, has come—or has over immense por-
tages been brought—to a true accommodation of his desire (*his* desire,
not the desire of the poem, which is for completion, for repetition, for
return; and not the desire of the culture, which is for comfort, for
confirmation, for repose), it should thereupon be adequate as well to
fulfillment, to realization, to the ecstasy which is beyond desire because
it is unknown to desire; at these moments—they are only moments, of
course, and they are few enough in any man's poetry, readily singled
out in James Wright's—poverty and riches change place, altitude and

expanse are transformed into each other, and the very immensity of space is concentrated into incandescence:

> *Miles off, a whole grove silently*
> *Flies up into the darkness.*
> *One lamp comes on in the sky,*
> *One lamp on the prairie.*

The point is to reach a point, literally, of no return, a true event which would be one that cannot recur—as Wallace Stevens calls it, "an escape from repetition, a happening in space and the self that touched them both at once and alike." For this escape, for this event the instruments of a *convention* are felt to be thereby not instruments but obstacles. Traditional versification, rhyme, the discourse which submits itself to an asymptotic norm sensed to govern *the line* however great the departures from it—these are, for James Wright's ultimate art, no means at all. Yet it is an *art*, not merely a compliance, not merely a rapture, which we are entitled to see as Wright's achievement. An art constituting itself out of what it gives away, and out of the very process of giving itself away. It is René Char's dictum that Wright quotes (Char, of whom he writes: "one passes inevitably from a perception of the form to a sense of the man," a passage we must make in Wright's own case) in his effort to constitute an *ars poetica: "to escape the shameful constraint of choosing between obedience and madness."* And the wisdom which sees a shameful constraint not only in obedience—in a subservience to the instruments—and not only in madness—in eschewing the instruments—but in the obligation to choose between them, the wisdom which would avoid that alternative and fashion out of its very abjuring what James Wright calls his "just devotions," conscious that "the spirit thrives / out of its own defeat"—that chastened wisdom is what we may most admire, I think, and what we must in any case admit in this poet's ecstatic apprehension, his final solution.

But I am getting ahead of myself, or ahead of him, for that exact calling of the turn, or of the unreturning, was not to be within James Wright's reach, not even within his range, for a long time; the true vocation of this poet, "a meagre Art / acquired by Reverse," in Dickinson's phrase, follows after not a false calling but an impertinent one, as Wright himself has insisted ("whatever I write from now on will be entirely different . . . I am finished with what I was doing"). Though it is the "art acquired by reverse" that we must enter upon and, in the wrestler's sense, close with, we must not ignore what the poet reversed *from*. We must not succumb to the temptation of despising a poet's created world just because he has desisted from it; indeed it is rather our obligation, when a conversion has been effected and another covenant vouchsafed, to trace connections, to show the Old Adam lurking about the confines of the New Jerusalem:

> *A man ought to hide sometimes on the banks*
> *Of the sky,*
> *And some human beings*
> *Have need of lingering back in the fastidious half light*
> *Even at dawn.*

What counts, then, and what is to be accounted for, when a man divides himself into a Before and an After, is the evidence throughout the change, at every stage of the transformation scene, of a great constancy, of a loyalty to the altering self which informs equally these six lines of longing for a lost *pietas* ("we have coddled the gods away"), addressed to a singer of the old religion in the first book, *The Green Wall* (1957), lines indulging, a little, the alternative of "obedience" in their rhythmic docility:

> *The sounds go on, and on,*
> *In spite of what the morning*
> *Or evening dark has done.*
> *We have no holy voices*
> *Like yours to lift above us,*
> *Yet we cannot be still . . .*

and these six lines, or rather loops, of the *dénouement,* the unknotting of links from the latest book, *Shall We Gather at the River* (1968), lines running, in their slack caprice, the other risk, the risk (by a like aspiration to ascent and to release from earth) that only the grave can afford:

> *I want to be lifted up*
> *By some great white bird unknown to the police*
> *And soar for a thousand miles and be carefully hidden*
> *Modest and golden as one last corn grain,*
> *Stored with the secrets of the wheat and the mysterious lives*
> *Of the unnamed poor.**

What makes common ground, though, between Wright's early and outward *vision of landscape* and his ultimate and endogenous *landscape of vision;* what is partaken of equally by the luxuriant account of

> *. . . things that lured me to decay:*
> *The ground's deliberate riches, fallen pears,*
> *Bewildered apples blown to mounds of shade . . .†*

---

* Not only the reference to the poor, but the explicit echoes of John, xii, 24 ("Except a corn of wheat fall into the ground and die, it abideth alone, but if it die, it bringeth forth much fruit") indicate the eschatological vestiges of Gospel rhetoric which James Wright cherishes still.

† The resonance of "bewildered" here is characteristic of Wright's elaborated practice in the first two books—the word is used not only as a personification of the apples "fallen" like the pears, but in the rarer sense of "returning to the wild";

and by the harsher, internalized accents, a decade and three books beyond, or rather inside of

> *. . . shattered hillsides of yellow trees*
> *In the autumn of my blood where the apples*
> *Purse their wild lips and smirk knowingly*
> *That my love is dead;*

what binds the outer version of natural process ("things that lured me") to the inner one ("trees in the autumn of my blood") is, precisely, *common ground*, the earth which "knows how to handle the great dead," the earth which is "this only place / we ever dared believe, for all its scars." That is why so many of these poems, early and late, require the hard ground ("the living need not seek / for love but underfoot"), require what Wright calls "the perpetual savagery of graves" to ballast and sustain his enormous spiritual yearning:

> *Walking here lonely and strange now, I must find*
> *A grave to prod my wrath*
> *Back to its just devotions . . .*

It is not until the poet is able to see the entire earth and all its processes of fruition and decay *inside* himself, contained by the arena of his own body just as "earth contains . . . a remembrancer of wild arenas we avoid," that he can stop separating, can stop alienating himself from "our gathering of the cheated and the weak," the ghosts and criminals and lunatics and perverts, the dispossessed who haunt him from the start ("My Grandmother's Ghost," "She Hid in the Trees from the Nurses," "A Poem About George Doty in the Death House," "To a Fugitive," "Sappho," "At the Executed Murderer's Grave," "The Poor Washed Up by Chicago Winter"—this is only a partial list). It is not until Wright has made himself over, from *The Branch Will Not Break* (1963) onward, converted himself from an elegiast into an apocalypst,

Wright's poetry of earth is one in which every impulse is suggested by its "normal" opposite, from being "lured" to decay by riches that are "fallen", *i.e.*, mortal and corrupt, to being "blown to mounds of shade", *i.e.*, to graves and ghostliness. In the preface to his translations from Theodore Storm, Wright speaks of the pursuit of *Stimmung*, that elusive quality which he calls "a certain luminosity of descriptive language intended to express the author's emotional attachment to the objects and persons described," and in these lovely lines on "the fruits of summer in the fields of love" Wright illustrates—that is, makes illustrious—the significance of *Stimmung* operative in all his poems, though not always by the means noted here; in the last two books, Wright avoids learned (or at least, knowing) ambiguity, preferring the more abrasive values of contradiction and ellipsis:

> *I slept a few minutes ago,*
> *Even though the stove has been out for hours.*
> *I am growing old.*
> *A bird cries in bare elder trees.*

discovering the whole of nature not as a rhythmical series of sad events but as the singular content of a ceaseless human soma:

> *How many scrawny children*
> *Lie dead and half hidden among frozen ruts*
> *In my body, along my dark roads?*

—that he can mount to that ecstasy so marvellously his own, momentarily given and not repeated but possibly followed by yet another, which is the achievement of his later poems.

Few poets, one may say, enable us to take the expression *ground form* so literally as James Wright enforces, implants the acceptation: the easy sorrows, the more difficult splendors of earth engender his utterance; the wrecked landscapes of the Ohio strip-mines and the ruined lives scattered upon them compel a recognition, once the enemy is discovered within rather than projected upon the surrounding sordor, that mortality is its own recompense, that "bodiless yearnings make no music fall" and that

> *Only the living body calls up love,*
> *That shadow risen casually from stone*
> *To clothe the nakedness of bare desire.*

The moment of discovery, of acknowledgment that the arena is the self and not the sociology of Midwestern erosion, is recorded pointedly in *Saint Judas* (1959), in the final couplet of a poem called "A Prayer in My Sickness":

> *I have lain alien in myself so long,*
> *How can I understand love's angry tongue?*

The recognition that one must be a naturalized inhabitant of the self in order to converse with love is crucial to Wright's persistence as a poet —"the main thing is not to get on in the world but to get home," Wright says of Theodore Storm, and of himself in that somatic landscape of his own discovery:

> *Close by a big river, I am alive in my own country*
> *I am home again . . .*

When what you have always thought was outside yourself and therefore against you is found to be within and therefore with you, you can deal with its mortal as with its ecstatic consequences. For the creating mind, Wright has remarked of Char, there is no such thing as irrelevancy—the corporeal and the chthonic are collected into "a single human word for love of air." "The hero," as Wright says of Gabriel Oak in Hardy's *Far from the Madding Crowd*, "is always surrounded by things that fill him with inexorable affection and with which, at last, he becomes miraculously identified." We are reminded, too, that Hardy is one of those few poets of the "voiceless earth" who has helped Wright on to his "secret he learned from the ground," as he says in his early poem "At Thomas Hardy's Birthplace, 1953." Few poets, then, except the Hardy whom Wright so beautifully apostrophizes in a characteristically self-accusing poetics have had the revelatory sense ("earth is a door") of significant soil:

> We may turn for nourishment to authors who humbly take walks in the evening over fields and under trees, hold out their words and stand patiently until the night fills them. But our usual impatience is our blindness, our abstraction is our coarseness, and our sloth is our starvation. We fail in the grace to stand still. We want devoutness: the grace to see.

Impatience, abstraction and sloth are the adversaries here, and as well as the Hardy buried at Stinsford who knew, Wright says, "the hidden joy, the secret hurt," we might deduce from this remarkable little passage other masters, native practitioners of the opposing virtues which afford "the grace to see": endurance, exactitude and labor. "Authors who humbly take walks in the evening over fields and under trees"—it is easy enough to divine that the author of

> *A sense of ocean and old trees*
> *Envelops and allures him;*
> *Tradition touching all he sees,*
> *Beguiles and reassures him . . .*

would beguilingly and reassuringly rehearse for James Wright the stoicism he required to sustain his suffering; and that the author of "Acquainted with the Night" is precisely the man—

> *When far away an interrupted cry*
> *Came over houses from another street,*
> *But not to call me back or say good-by*

—to hold out his words and stand patiently until the night fills them. We have divined the more easily, of course, because Wright names his nourishing authors: "I have tried very hard to write in the mode of Edward Arlington Robinson and Robert Frost," he says about his first two books—it is after *Saint Judas* that whatever he writes is intended to be "entirely different." And when we read a poem like "The Alarm" in the latter book, a poem as scrupulously patient with suffering, a suffering without hope of anything better, as anything in Robinson, as carefully decasyllabic, concrete and deliberate as anything in Frost, then we must recognize the success of the effort ("I have tried very hard . . ."), the adequacy of the means to the meaning, and the voice entangled, as Frost puts it, in the words and fastened to the page for the imagination's ear:

> *When I came back from my last dream, when I*
> *Whirled in the morning snowfall up the lawn,*
> *I looked behind me where my wings were gone,*
> *Rusting above the snow, for lack of care,*
> *A pile of rakes and shovels rotted away.*
> *Tools of the world were crumbling into air,*
> *And I, neither the living nor the dead,*
> *Paused in the dusk of dawn to wonder why*
> *Any man clambers-upward out of shade*
> *To rake and shovel all his dust away.*

Yet what if a poet discovered, in the very comforts of a recurrent natural order,*

> *Where the sea moves the word moves, where the sea*
> *Subsides, the slow word fades with lunar tides*

—what if a poet discovered that he was after not adequacy (". . . and things were as they were") but ecstasy (". . . you wake in a book that is shining"), not the lament of encirclement (what else is such verse as the stanza from "The Alarm" I have quoted here?) but the luminosity of a breakthrough ("the moon suddenly stands up in the darkness / and I see that it is impossible to die")?

Shakespeare, of course, accounts best for what we might call the consolation-theory of a poetry by natural analogy. "Praising what is lost / makes the remembrance dear . . . We are reconciled," says the King in *All's Well that Ends Well*—yet what if it is precisely the impulse to end well, to praise what is lost and to cherish memory, the impulse to be *reconciled* that a poet wants to be rid of? The poetry of recurrence (which most of us think of as poetry itself, for we all prefer, most of the time, expedience to ecstasy), the traditional pattern which alone can accommodate an experience of the negative, can transform what is a known loss into at least the comfort of elegy— Wright rejects these things as a betrayal of the life he knows to be within him; he does not want *his* poetry to be a consolation any more, an anesthesia, as it is shown to be at the end, say, of "The Alarm":

> *And I was home now, bowing into my dust,*
> *To quicken into stupor one more time,*
> *One of the living buried like the dead.*

---

* In his preface to *The Green Wall*, Auden says Wright sees nature as a temptation to escape human responsibility—*I* should say possibility—by imitating her ways; in Wright's poems, Auden remarks, the present is "not unhappy but unreal," and may be made real, realized, by imitating the natural cycle of seasons, tides, days.

He wants his poetry to be a *finding*, an *invention* in the literal sense of the word, not a loss comforted by rite but a discovery, however brutal, made bearable by art. It is of course other men's art which helps him to his own performance. I have already mentioned Storm as one of Wright's mediating figures, but it is important to see that Storm—like Hardy, and like Frost and Robinson, though more intensely, more nakedly—points backward to the negative experience, the endured suffering, the alienation of self in a *tragicall* nature ("the autumn landscape where we lay and suffered"). Still, in Storm there is an ellipsis, a rejection of comfort that suggests, in Wright's translation, for example, of the *Frauen-Ritornelle*, the preliminary to release, the prelude by comfortless acedie to the real illumination:

> . . . . *Nutmeg herb,*
> *You blossomed once in my great-grandmother's garden;*
> *That was a place a long way from the world, over there.*
>
> *Dark cypresses—*
> *The world is too interested in gaiety;*
> *It will all be forgotten.*

The fragmentary poems in *The Branch Will Not Break* afford many analogies to this kind of poem, in which the energy of constatation is not allowed to run out into verse, into some kind of normative, reboant movement, but is instead checked, baffled, splintered:

> *The unwashed shadows*
> *Of blast furnaces from Moundsville, West Virginia*
> *Are sneaking across the pits of strip mines*
> *To steal grapes*
> *In heaven.*
> *Nobody else knows I am here.*
> *All right.*
> *Come out, come out, I am dying.*
> *I am growing old.*
> *An owl rises*
> *From the cutter bar*
> *Of a hayrake.*

That is not ecstasy, but it is without resignation, and in its silences (the spaces the voice must leave, particularly in the last five lines) affords the likelihood, I think, for a new apprehension, generates a kind of comfortless grief, even an unknown eros. Compare, for example, the first lines of this same poem ("A Message Hidden in an Empty Wine Bottle that I Threw into a Gully of Maple Trees One Night at an Indecent Hour"—the title is certainly a jolt from the frosty pieties, "the cold divinities of death and change" to be met with in the first two books), lines of an insistent cruelty:

> *Women are dancing around a fire*
> *By a pond of creosote and waste water from the river*
> *In the dank fog of Ohio.*
> *They are dead.*
> *I am alone here,*
> *And I reach for the moon that dangles*
> *Cold on a dark vine . . .*

with these lines from "On the Skeleton of a Hound" from the first book, lines of the same visionary dedication, but self-pitying, plangent, over-determined in their adjustment of lilt to longing:

> *Then, suddenly, the hare leaped beyond pain*
> *Out of the open meadow, and the hound*
> *Followed the voiceless dancer to the moon,*
> *To dark, to death, to other meadows where*
> *Singing young women dance around a fire,*
> *Where love reveres the living.*
> > *I alone*
> *Scatter this hulk about the dampened ground;*
> *And while the moon rises beyond me, throw*
> *The ribs and spine out of their perfect shape . . .*

In the phrasing, the fractured but still bleeding bones of *statement* in the later version ("They are dead. I am alone here . . .") we are not permitted to dissolve, as the earlier iambics insist we dissolve, into a cloud, a nimbus of gorgeous condolences, "handy resurrections." Nothing so attractive (and so unreal) as "meadows where singing young women dance around a fire where love reveres the living" is now vouchsafed, but instead "a pond of creosote and waste water from the river in the dank fog of Ohio": the gain in precision, in purpose, is a gainsaying, too, of consolation. The ground is cleared.

In the third and fourth books, *The Branch Will Not Break* and *Shall We Gather at the River*, James Wright reaches occasionally—but it is the occasions which justify the effort, which ransom the expense—beyond even such rectitude of desolation which is the self's first calisthenic in the achievement of recognition, or identity made ecstatic. And the guide to this final or at least fulfilling mode of his poetry is an elusive Virgil indeed, the "silence-haunted" Georg Trakl, whose poems Wright calls—and the relevance to his own enterprise is patent—"attempts to enter and to recognize one's very self." With Robert Bly, James Wright has translated twenty of Trakl's poems "from which all shrillness and clutter have been banished," and the still raptures of these interior landscapes, with their abrupt drops and ascents into the "merely personal" and beyond it, certainly qualify and prepare all that Wright creates in his own broken but incandescent later poems, generated from moments of beatitude like the one recorded in "Today I Was So Happy I Made This Poem" and concluding—it is the *summum bonum* of Wright's whole undertaking—with these lines:

> *Each moment of time is a mountain.*
> *An eagle rejoices in the oak trees of heaven,*
> *Crying*
> That is what I wanted.

The aphoristic resonance of this ("aphorisms, representing a knowledge broken," Bacon says), the elliptical *sentences* of some seraphic wanderer, suggest what Wright found in Trakl's mysterious verses, his statements of stillness:

> *I am a shadow far from darkening villages.*
> *I drank the silence of God*
> *Out of the stream in the trees.*

> *Cold metal walks on my forehead.*
> *Spiders search for my heart.*
> *It is a light that goes on in my mouth.*

> *At night I found myself on a pasture,*
> *Covered with rubbish and the dust of stars.*
> *In a hazel thicket*
> *Angels of crystal rang out once more.*

In "Milkweed," for example, the apocalypse is not only invoked, it is *experienced*, reminding us of Éluard's great discovery: "there is another world, but it is in this one." Wright's ecstasy is earned by a tremendous renunciation, the abjuring of ritual—and in consequence his poems are not lovely, are not conveyed in a language of polished facets; rather they are splinters, jagged cleavages on which the sun, momentarily, explodes:

> *While I stood here, in the open, lost in myself,*
> *I must have looked a long time*
> *Down the corn rows, beyond grass,*
> *The small house,*
> *White walls, animals lumbering toward the barn.*
> *I look down now, It is all changed.*
> *Whatever it was I lost, whatever I wept for,*
> *Was a wild, gentle thing, the small dark eyes*
> *Loving me in secret.*

It is here. At a touch of my hand,
The air fills with delicate creatures
From the other world.

In the same book, Wright stands just off the highway to Rochester, Minnesota (a guarantee these epiphanies are real, Wright always locates them in the home counties) watching two Indian ponies; he joins them, plays with them in the pasture at twilight, and suddenly—

Suddenly I realize
That if I stepped out of my body I would break
Into blossom.

By a sensitive enjambment, Wright indicates both the breaking *and* the blossoming here, the surrender of perfection necessary to achieve . . . identity. And in the fourth book, following upon many utterances of despair and deadly terror—

I ride the great stones,
I hide under stars and maples
And yet I cannot find my own face.
In the mountains of blast furnaces,
The trees turn their backs on me . . .

—and upon a discouragement with these United States which is all the more powerful for its regional particulars:

For the river at Wheeling, W. Va.,
Has only two shores:
The one in hell, the other
In Bridgeport, Ohio.

And nobody would commit suicide, only
To find beyond death
Bridgeport, Ohio

—comes one of Wright's finest poems, "Northern Pike," a wonderful conjugation of the spoiled and the splendid which *underwrites*, in every sense, the crippling illumination of the everyday:

We paused among the dark cat-tails and prayed
For the muskrats,
For the ripples below their tails,
For the little movements that we knew the crawdads were making
    under water,
For the right-hand wrist of my cousin who is a policeman.
We prayed for the game warden's blindness.
We prayed for the road home.

We ate the fish.
There must be something very beautiful in my body,
I am so happy.

Less rapturous only because it is more inclusive, in its final vision not only of the possibilities of gratification but of depletion too, is Wright's ultimate anthem to his body, apostrophized as metonymy and synechdoche at once, product and arena of his ground form, container and thing contained: "A Late Autumn Daybreak," in which the poet sets himself free not only from the fear of death but from the craving for life, not only from the ritual but from the random, reinventing the very conventions—even rhyme!—he had had to expunge, and assuming once again the toys as well as the toils of his art:

> *I sat upright and saw the moon*
> *Blurred in the agony of cold.*
> *I knew it would be daylight soon.*
> *Agony, agony, I grew old*
> *When I dared force my gaze outside*
> *To the great bough bleeding on dead grass*
> *To death. My God, I thought, and died.*
> *That was my branch that broke, alas.*
>
> *Suddenly I left my body*
> *And flew straight up into the dawn,*
> *Crying out holy, holy, holy*
> *Be the next death I light upon.*
> *If there be trees, oh waft me down*
> *Into a body lovingkind;*
> *Leave me aloft, if there be none*
> *To bear me but a leafless wind.*

Two Citizens by JAMES WRIGHT

At the end of his *Collected Poems* (1971), whose motto might well be a retrospective phrase from *Two Citizens:* "I love myself the ground," James Wright added some thirty uncollected poems, raucous and even rakish, for they included a blank page dedicated to his horse which had eaten that particular poem, and they described with an apposite leer what they were doing:

> *not a poem*
> *not an apology to the Muse*
> *but the cold-blooded plea of a homesick Vampire.*

The satisfaction of having in one volume most of the best poems of one of our best poets made me overlook the nature—fragmentary, inchoate, the vibrato out of control—of those "new poems" at the time, though now I see they were an alluvial deposit on which *Two Citizens* draws heavily, manifesting "a deep identity / with something under / the bare stones."

All these poems are of course written in "the one tongue I can write in . . . my Ohioan," and they are concerned, as Wright has always been, with that mythology of the insulted and injured to be located alike in southern Ohio and the poet's body ("helpless and miserable / dreaming itself / into an apparition of loneliness"). And they exploit that mythology with the insolence of utter conviction:

> *The cracked song*
> *Of my own body limps into the body*
> *Of this living place. I have nobody*
> *To go in with*
> *But my love who is a woman,*
> *And my crude dead, my sea,*
> *My sea, my sepulcher, the crude*
> *Rhythms of my time. . . .*

But so deeply is the poet identified with something which has happened to him outside the poem that he cannot be bothered to make it into a coherence within the poem; the divine event is a *déjà vu;* it is as he says, "a secret of blossoms we had no business / to understand, only to remember." As no more than a reader of poems, we remember, certainly—we remember that particular *stimmung* of James Wright's past,

> *That lonely thing*
> *That fears him, yet comes out*
> *To look through him and sing;*

and we note certain clues toward what is dimly apprehended as a sort of Ohio Osiris Complex here, the sense of disintegration in dark waters, the embrace of a tree, and a resurrection ("I rose out of my body so high into / that sycamore tree that it became / the only tree that ever loved me"). But my suspicion of Wright's legend of himself as the Torn God is confirmed by no more than scattered limbs, perhaps appropriately—"wound after wound, I look for / the tree by the waters"—and in the arrogance of these disjunct, choking poems, there are but glimpses, for me, of what I divine to be gathering on the far shore, the other side of "that water I rose from." In *Two Citizens* (Tammuz and Astarte, they are) and the thirty poems which precede them, I can discern only the night journey, the *sparagmos*, except for sacred moments like this one:

> There used to be a sycamore just
> Outside Martins Ferry,
> Where I used to go.
> I had no friends there.
> Maybe the tree was no woman,
> But when I sat there, I gathered
> That branch into my arms.
> It was the first time I ever rose.

Years ago, writing about Wright's early work, I spoke of his approach to "the ecstasy which is beyond desire because it is unknown to desire"; that is the ecstasy made up to here, but it is not *made* in the poems, it stands outside them, as of course ecstasy does.

North American Review, 1973

To a Blossoming Pear Tree by JAMES WRIGHT

It has been four years since James Wright's last book, and I had better loiter a little, I think, over the situation of this most rapt, even stupent of our lyrists, halting first to say what I mean by calling Wright—whose poems are so unconcerned with repetition, refrain, or regularity that they are often, now, in prose—a lyrist at all. Lyric cancels out time, confirms and sustains a "now" which is invested with significance as long as the lyric structure (the voice itself, raised, looming and looped about the broken sentences, a narrow rivulet of print between ample meadows of margin) endures, releasing us from the pressure of ulterior things. It is a significance of the divine event, a secret, as Wright says, "of blossoms we had no business / to understand, only to remember." (One figure, here, is the source of Wright's new apostrophe, the object of his attentions, and the subject of his *askesis*: blossoming.) Out of time, the poems are so many clues toward what I have called a sort of Ohio Osiris Complex: the sense of disintegration in dark waters, the embrace of a tree, and a resurrection. But the ecstatic apprehensions of *Two Citizens* (Tammuz and Astarte, they are, though Wright always disguises his theophany as himself and his wife, even giving her a voice, a poem of her own, in this new book) are dimmed now; chastened and cautious ("Saguaro, you are not one of the gods"), a little darkened from—perhaps *by*—his old exaltations, his peerless apocalypse (in which of course the entire

earth found its death and rebirth inside the poet's own body, con-
ceived as infinite and eternal), Wright addresses himself, loyal still
to his plain chant, his ground bass, to those energies and impulses in
nature which are effervescent, fecund and even prodigal. Fifteen
years ago, this was his identification:

> Suddenly I realize
> That if I stepped out of my body I would break
> Into blossom.

By a characteristically sensitive enjambment, Wright thus indicated
both the breaking *and* the blossoming. But now, in the tormented title
poem which confronts, which invokes these same energies and im-
pulses, a discrepancy, an alienation is powerfully mourned; there is no
release into ecstasy, merely its notation as otherness, and the human
humiliation:

> Young tree, unburdened
> By anything but your beautiful natural blossoms
> And dew, the dark
> Blood in my body drags me
> Down with my brother.

The pear tree is still there, splendid but separate, and the man, in his
brotherhood with the wrecked and ruined of his kind, is here:

> How I envy you.
> For if you could only listen
> I would tell you something,
> Something human.

The poems in Wright's lovely new book are all such attestations—
diffident yet explicit, careful yet fervent, defeated yet proud—of dis-
junction, of negation, of (we must say it) failure in his vast project.
If he were to succeed, after all, we should not have the poems—we
should have silence. But he has failed, and the confession of his failure
("a half-witted angel drawling Ohioan / in the warm Italian rain")
constitutes his new book, its resonance greatly enlarged by the poems
about Italy, the region around Verona in particular: "It is all right
with me to know that my life is only one life. I feel like the light of
the river Adige. By this time, we are both an open secret." The poet
must still locate the landscape in his own soma, and the fact that Dante
has been there before him somehow makes his task if not easier, surely
then more alluring:

> In the middle of my own life
> I woke up and found myself
> dying, fair enough, still
> alive in the friendly city

> *of my body, my secret Verona,*
> *milky and green,*
> *my moving jewel, the last*
> *pure vein left to me . . .*

By discovering (and perhaps that is why so many of the pieces must be prose here: they are *on the way*, they are not realizations, they are aspirations: lyrical prose) the impossibility of his project (I am not Osiris, after all), Wright has discovered as well the possibility of his poetry ("I know what we call it / most of the time / but I have my own song for it / and sometimes, even today, I call it beauty"). No American poet is so consistent as Wright, so consigned to his peculiar, beautiful doom. The further nuance here is of course the exchange of the ruined American midlands (and the repugnant American public mentality):

> *A black crust, America is*
> *A shallow hell where evil*
> *Is an easy joke, forgotten*
> *In a week . . .*

for the Italian locus, the places and objects of Verona which afford the poet, which furnish him, his apocalyptic transformations not more easily or more readily, but more ripely; it is here in Italy that the asseveration is most richly to be made:

> *. . . it was hard to name*
> *Which vine, which insect, which wing,*
> *Which of you, which of me . . .*

Something in his own country has the more painfully cast James Wright out of his own body, and the moments when he finds himself, when he *comes to*, as we say, are more likely to be elsewhere, abroad:

> *I am sitting contented and alone in a little park near the Palazzo Scaligeri in Verona, glimpsing the mists of early autumn as they shift and fade among the pines and city battlements on the hills above the river Adige. The river has recovered from this morning's rainfall. It is now restoring to its shapely body its own secret light, a color of faintly cloudy green and pearl.*

Now surely such perceptions can be made back home, but there is some function of the self which is available to Wright *over there* and only so: the function is one of transformation, which he has gainsaid among the strip-mines, and the scrap-iron, or which has gainsaid him. "What can I do to join him?" Wright asks about the garter snake basking on a rail, and it is his very question, the interrogation proposed to a condition where being can be shared or participated in more broadly, more fully. The blossoming pear tree is no longer to be found in Wright's own veins and vesicles. The wonder of the book named for this tree is that he has put away any bitterness, any *ressentiment* about the collapse of the eager transaction as it was reported in so many other poems, so many earlier books. There is nothing to do but sit still and look very closely, very carefully at what is in front of your eyes, his eyes; the acknowledgment of the separate life, the contours which are not shared but merely shards, fragments of a unity, a totality inaccessible even to wishing—this acknowledgment makes for a poetry which, by immense repudiations, has come to accept itself, has resigned itself (what else is prose but the resignation of poetry, the submission to an element which makes no stay against that ebbing tide?) to a constatation of being which he cannot become, or rather a becoming which he cannot be; call it an acceptance of mortality rather than a god's estate, of death rather than eternal life. As James Wright asks (in prose): "What color is a hungry shadow?"

New York Arts Journal, 1978

BIBLIOGRAPHY

Listings are books of poetry unless otherwise indicated.

A. R. AMMONS

Ommateum. Philadelphia: Dorrance & Co.; 1955.
Expressions of Sea Level. Athens: Ohio State University Press; 1964.
Tape for the Turn of the Year. Ithaca: Cornell University Press; 1965.
Corson's Inlet. Ithaca: Cornell University Press; 1965.
Northfield Poems. Ithaca: Cornell University Press; 1966.
Uplands: New Poems. New York: W. W. Norton & Co.; 1970.
Collected Poems 1951–1971. New York: W. W. Norton & Co.; 1971.
Briefings: Poems Small and Easy. New York: W. W. Norton & Co.;
    1971.

JOHN ASHBERY

Turandot and Other Poems. New York: Tibor de Nagy; 1953.
Some Trees. New Haven: Yale University Press; 1956.
The Tennis Court Oath. Middletown: Wesleyan University Press;
    1962.
The Heroes (play) in "Artist's Theatre." New York: Grove Press;
    1960.
The Compromise (play) in "The Hasty Papers." New York: Alfred
    Leslie; 1960.
Rivers and Mountains. New York: Holt, Rinehart & Winston; 1966.
The Double Dream of Spring. New York: E. P. Dutton & Co.; 1970.
Three Poems. New York: The Viking Press; 1972.
Self Portrait in a Convex Mirror. New York: The Viking Press; 1975.
Houseboat Days. New York: The Viking Press; 1977.

ROBERT BLY

Silence in the Snowy Fields. Middletown: Wesleyan University Press;
    1962.
The Light Around the Body. New York: Harper & Row; 1967.

EDGAR BOWERS

The Form of Loss. Denver: Allen Swallow; 1956.
The Astronomers. Denver: Allen Swallow; 1965.

GREGORY CORSO

The Vestal Lady on Brattle. Cambridge: Audience; 1955.
Gasoline. San Francisco: City Lights Books; 1958.
The Happy Birthday of Death. New York: New Directions Pub. Co.;
1960.
Long Live Man. New York: New Directions Pub. Co.; 1962.

ROBERT CREELEY

For Love. New York: Charles Scribner's Sons; 1962.
The Island (novel). New York: Charles Scribner's Sons; 1963.
The Gold Diggers (stories). New York: Charles Scribner's Sons; 1965.
Words. New York: Charles Scribner's Sons; 1967.

JAMES DICKEY

Into the Stone. New York: Charles Scribner's Sons; 1960.
Drowning with Others. Middletown: Wesleyan University Press;
1962.
Helmets. Middletown: Wesleyan University Press; 1964.
The Suspect in Poetry (criticism). Madison, Minn.: The Sixties Press;
1964.
Buckdancer's Choice. Middletown: Wesleyan University Press; 1965.
Poems 1957–1967. Middletown: Wesleyan University Press; 1967.
The Eye-Beaters, Blood, Victory, Madness, Buckhead and Mercy.
New York: Doubleday & Co.; 1970.

ALAN DUGAN

Poems. New Haven: Yale University Press; 1961.
Poems 2. New Haven: Yale University Press; 1963.
Poems 3. New Haven: Yale University Press; 1967.
Poems 4. Boston: The Atlantic Monthly Press; 1974.

IRVING FELDMAN

Works and Days. Boston: The Atlantic Monthly Press; 1961.
The Pripet Marshes. New York: The Viking Press; 1965.
Magic Papers. New York: Harper & Row Publishers; 1970.
Lost Originals. New York: Holt, Rinehart & Winston; 1972.

EDWARD FIELD

Stand Up, Friend, with Me. New York: Grove Press; 1963.
Variety Photoplays. New York: Grove Press; 1967.

DONALD FINKEL

The Clothing's New Emperor. New York: Charles Scribner's Sons; 1959.
Simeon. New York: Atheneum; 1964.
A Joyful Noise. New York: Atheneum; 1966.
Answer Back. New York: Atheneum; 1968.
The Garbage Wars. New York: Atheneum; 1970.
Adequate Earth. New York: Atheneum; 1972.
A Mote in Heaven's Eye. New York: Atheneum; 1975.

ALLEN GINSBERG

Howl and Other Poems. San Francisco: City Lights Books; 1956.
Kaddish and Other Poems. San Francisco: City Lights Books; 1961.
Empty Mirror. New York: Totem Press / Corinth Books; 1961.
Reality Sandwiches. San Francisco: City Lights Books; 1963.
Airplane Dreams. Canada: Anansi; 1968.
Planet News. San Francisco: City Lights Books; 1968.

PAUL GOODMAN

The Lordly Hudson (collected poems). New York: The Macmillan Co.; 1962.

ANTHONY HECHT

A Summoning of Stones. New York: The Macmillan Co.; 1954.
The Hard Hours. New York: Atheneum; 1967.
Millions of Strange Shadows. New York: Atheneum; 1977.

DARYL HINE

Five Poems. Canada: Emblem Books; 1954.
The Carnal and the Crane. Montreal: McGill University Press; 1957.
The Devil's Picture-Book. New York: Abelard-Schuman; 1960.
The Prince of Darkness & Co. (novel). New York: Abelard-Schuman; 1961.
Polish Subtitles (travel). New York: Abelard-Schuman; 1962.
The Wooden Horse. New York: Atheneum; 1965.
Minutes. New York: Atheneum; 1968.

DANIEL HOFFMAN

An Armada of 30 Whales. New Haven: Yale University Press; 1954.
A Little Geste. New York: Oxford University Press; 1960.

American Poetry and Poetics (editor). New York: Anchor Books; 1962.
The City of Satisfactions. New York: Oxford University Press; 1963.
Striking the Stones. New York: Oxford University Press; 1968.
Broken Laws. New York: Oxford University Press, 1970.
The Center of Attention. New York: Random House, 1974.

JOHN HOLLANDER

A Crackling of Thorns. New Haven: Yale University Press; 1958.
The Untuning of the Sky (criticism). Princeton: Princeton University Press; 1961.
The Wind and the Rain (editor). New York: Doubleday & Co.; 1961.
The Laurel Ben Jonson (editor). New York: Dell Publishing Co.; 1961.
Moviegoing and Other Poems. New York: Atheneum; 1962.
Visions from the Ramble. New York: Atheneum; 1965.
The Quest of the Gole. New York: Atheneum; 1966.
The Night Mirror. New York: Atheneum; 1971.
Tales Told of the Fathers. New York: Atheneum; 1975.

RICHARD HUGO

A Run of Jacks. Minneapolis: University of Minnesota Press; 1961.
Death of the Kapowsin Tavern. New York: Harcourt, Brace & World; 1965.
Good Luck in Cracked Italian. New York: New American Library, Inc.; 1969.

DONALD JUSTICE

The Summer Anniversaries. Middletown: Wesleyan University Press; 1960.
A Local Storm. Iowa City: The Stone Wall Press; 1963.
Night Light. Middletown: Wesleyan University Press; 1967.
Departures. New York: Atheneum; 1973.

GALWAY KINNELL

What a Kingdom It Was. Boston: Houghton Mifflin Co.; 1960.
Flower Herding on Mount Monadnock. Boston: Houghton Mifflin Co.; 1964.
The Poems of François Villon. New York: New American Library, Inc.; 1965.

Black Light (novel). Boston: Houghton Mifflin Co.; 1966.
Body Rags. Boston: Houghton Mifflin Co.; 1968.
The Book of Nightmares. Boston: Houghton Mifflin Co.; 1971.

CAROLYN KIZER

The Ungrateful Garden. Bloomington: Indiana University Press; 1961.
Knock upon Silence. New York: Doubleday & Co.; 1965.
Midnight Was My Cry. New York: Doubleday & Co.; 1971.

KENNETH KOCH

Ko, or A Season on Earth. New York: Grove Press; 1959.
When the Sun Tries to Go On in The Hasty Papers. New York: Alfred Leslie; 1960.
Thank You and Other Poems. New York: Grove Press; 1962.
Bertha and Other Plays. New York: Grove Press; 1966.
The Pleasures of Peace. New York: Grove Press; 1969.

DENISE LEVERTOV

The Double Image. London: Cresset Press Ltd.; 1946.
Here and Now. San Francisco: City Lights Books; 1957.
Overland to the Islands. Highlands, North Carolina: Jargon; 1958.
With Eyes at the Back of Our Heads. New York: New Directions Pub. Co.; 1959.
The Jacob's Ladder. New York: New Directions Pub. Co.; 1959.
O Taste and See. New York: New Directions Pub. Co.; 1964.
The Sorrow Dance. New York: New Directions Pub. Co.; 1967.

JOHN LOGAN

Cycle for Mother Cabrini. New York: Grove Press; 1955.
Ghosts of the Heart. Chicago: The University of Chicago Press; 1960.
Spring of the Thief. New York: Alfred A. Knopf, Inc.; 1963.
The Anonymous Lover. New York: Liveright; 1973.

WILLIAM MEREDITH

Love Letter from an Impossible Land. New Haven: Yale University Press; 1944.
Ships and Other Figures. Princeton: Princeton University Press; 1948.
The Open Sea. New York: Alfred A. Knopf Inc.; 1958.
The Wreck of the Thresher. New York: Alfred A. Knopf Inc.; 1964.
Earth Walk: New and Selected Poems. New York: Alfred A. Knopf; 1970.
Hazard, The Painter. New York: Alfred A. Knopf; 1975.

JAMES MERRILL

First Poems. New York: Alfred A. Knopf Inc.; 1951.

Short Stories. Pawlet, Vermont: Banyan Press; 1954.

The Immortal Husband (play) in *Playbook.* New York: New Directions Pub. Co.; 1956.

The Seraglio (novel). New York: Alfred Knopf Inc.; 1957.

The Country of a Thousand Years of Peace. New York: Alfred A. Knopf Inc.; 1959.

The Bait (play) in "Artist's Theatre." New York: Grove Press; 1960.

Water Street. New York: Atheneum; 1962.

The (Diblos) Notebook (novel). New York: Atheneum; 1965.

Nights and Days. New York: Atheneum; 1966.

The Fire Screen. New York: Atheneum; 1969.

Braving the Elements. New York: Atheneum; 1973.

W. S. MERWIN

A Mask for Janus. New Haven: Yale University Press; 1952.

The Dancing Bears. New Haven: Yale University Press; 1954.

Green with Beasts. New York: Alfred A. Knopf Inc.; 1956.

Favor Island (play) in *New World Writing.* New York: New American Library, Inc.; 1957.

The Poem of the Cid (translation). New York: New American Library, Inc.; 1959.

The Drunk in the Furnace. New York: The Macmillan Co.; 1960.

Spanish Ballads (translation). New York: Anchor Books; 1960.

The Moving Target. New York: Atheneum; 1963.

The Song of Roland (translation). New York: Random House, Inc.; 1963.

The Lice. New York: Atheneum; 1967.

Selected Translations 1948–1968. New York: Atheneum; 1968.

The Carrier of Ladders. New York: Atheneum; 1970.

The Miner's Pale Children (prose). New York: Atheneum; 1970.

Writings to an Unfinished Accompaniment. New York: Atheneum; 1973.

HOWARD MOSS

The Wound and the Weather. New York: Reynal & Hitchcock; 1946.

The Toy Fair. New York: Charles Scribner's Sons; 1954.

A Swimmer in the Air. New York: Charles Scribner's Sons; 1957.

The Poems of Keats (editor). New York: Dell Publishing Co.; 1959.

A Winter Come, a Summer Gone. New York: Charles Scribner's Sons; 1960.

The Magic Lantern of Marcel Proust (criticism). New York: The Macmillan Co.; 1962.

Finding Them Lost. New York: Charles Scribner's Sons; 1965.

Second Nature. New York: Atheneum; 1968.

Buried City. New York: Atheneum; 1975.

FRANK O'HARA

A City Winter and Other Poems. New York: Tibor de Nagy; 1954.

Meditations in an Emergency. New York: Grove Press; 1957.

Second Avenue. New York: Totem Press / Corinth Books; 1960.

Odes. New York: Tiber Press; 1960.

Lunch Poems. San Francisco: City Lights Books; 1964.

Jackson Pollock (art criticism). New York: George Braziller, Inc.; 1959.

Awake in Spain (play), in The Hasty Papers. New York: Alfred Leslie; 1960.

Try, Try (play), in *Artist's Theatre.* New York: Grove Press; 1960.

Love Poems (Tentative Title). New York: Tibor de Nagy; 1965.

In Memory of My Feelings. New York: The Museum of Modern Art; 1967.

SYLVIA PLATH

The Colossus and Other Poems. New York: Alfred A. Knopf Inc.; 1962.

The Bell Jar (novel). London: William Heinemann Ltd.; 1963.

Ariel. New York: Harper & Row, Publishers; 1966.

ADRIENNE RICH

A Change of World. New Haven: Yale University Press; 1951.

The Diamond Cutters. New York: Harper & Row, Publishers; 1955.

Snapshots of a Daughter-in-Law. New York: Harper & Row, Publishers; 1963.

Necessities of Life. New York: W. W. Norton & Co.; 1966.

Leaflets. New York: W. W. Norton & Co.; 1969.

The Will to Change: Poems 1968–1970. New York: W. W. Norton & Co.; 1971.

Diving into the Wreck: Poems 1971–1972. New York: W. W. Norton & Co.; 1973.

ANNE SEXTON

To Bedlam and Part Way Back. Boston: Houghton Mifflin Co.; 1960.
All My Pretty Ones. Boston: Houghton Mifflin Co.; 1961.
Live or Die. Boston: Houghton Mifflin Co.; 1967.

LOUIS SIMPSON

The Arrivistes. New York: The Fine Editions Press; 1950.
Good News of Death. New York: Charles Scribner's Sons; 1955.
A Dream of Governors. Middletown: Wesleyan University Press;
  1959.
Riverside Drive (novel). New York: Atheneum; 1962.
At the End of the Open Road. Middletown: Wesleyan University
  Press; 1963.
Selected Poems. New York: Harcourt, Brace & World, Inc.; 1965.
Adventures of the Letter I. New York: Harper & Row Publishers;
  1971.

W. D. SNODGRASS

Heart's Needle. New York: Alfred A. Knopf Inc.; 1959.
After Experience. New York: Harper & Row, Publishers; 1968.

GARY SNYDER

Riprap. New York: Origin Press; 1959.
Myths and Texts. New York: Totem Press / Corinth Books; 1960.
A Range of Poems. London, England: Fulcrum; 1966.
Turtle Island. New York: New Directions Pub. Co.; 1974.

WILLIAM STAFFORD

West of Your City. Georgetown, California: The Talisman Press;
  1960.
Traveling Through the Dark. New York: Harper & Row, Publishers;
  1962.
The Rescued Year. New York: Harper & Row, Publishers; 1966.
Someday, Maybe. New York: Harper & Row, Publishers; 1973.

MARK STRAND

Sleeping with One Eye Open. Iowa City: The Stone Wall Press; 1964.
Reasons for Moving. New York: Atheneum; 1968.
The Story of Our Lives. New York: Atheneum; 1974.

MAY SWENSON

Another Animal. New York: Charles Scribner's Sons; 1954.
A Cage of Spines. New York: Rinehart and Company; 1958.
To Mix with Time. New York: Charles Scribner's Sons; 1963.
Half Sun Half Sleep. New York: Charles Scribner's Sons; 1967.

DAVID WAGONER

Dry Sun, Dry Wind. Bloomington: Indiana University Press; 1953.
The Man in the Middle (novel). New York: The Macmillan Co.; 1954.
Money Money Money (novel). New York: Harcourt, Brace & World, Inc.; 1955.
A Place to Stand. Bloomington: Indiana University Press; 1958.
Rock (novel). New York: The Viking Press; 1958.
The Nesting Ground. Bloomington: Indiana University Press; 1963.
The Escape Artist (novel). New York: Farrar, Straus & Giroux, Inc.; 1965.
Staying Alive. Bloomington: Indiana University Press; 1966.
Sleeping in the Woods. Bloomington: Indiana University Press; 1974.

THEODORE WEISS

The Catch. New York: Twayne Publishers; 1951.
Outlanders. New York: The Macmillan Co.; 1960.
Gunsight. New York: New York University Press; 1962.
The Medium. New York: The Macmillan Co.; 1965.
The Last Day and The First. New York: The Macmillan Co.; 1968.

JAMES WRIGHT

The Green Wall. New Haven: Yale University Press; 1957.
Saint Judas. Middletown: Wesleyan University Press; 1959.
The Branch Will Not Break. Middletown: Wesleyan University Press; 1963.
Shall We Gather at the River. Middletown: Wesleyan University Press; 1968.
Two Citizens. New York: Farrar, Straus & Giroux; 1973.
To a Blossoming Pear Tree. New York: Farrar, Straus & Giroux; 1977.

22568
41

RICHARD HOWARD

*Richard Howard was born in 1929 in Cleveland,
Ohio, and studied at Columbia University and the
Sorbonne. He is a distinguished translator from the
French and a poet of great versatility. His seven books
of poems are* QUANTITIES (*1962*), THE DAMAGES
(*1967*), UNTITLED SUBJECTS (*1969*), FINDINGS (*1971*),
TWO-PART INVENTIONS (*1974*), FELLOW FEELINGS
(*1976*) *and* MISGIVINGS (*1979*). *He is the author of
the commentary in* PREFERENCES, *a critical anthology
of the relations between fifty-one contemporary
poets and the poetry of the past.*